VENEZUELA VINOTINTO BÉISBOL

Edited by Leonte Landino and Bill Nowlin

Associate editors Len Levin and Carl Riechers

Society for American Baseball Research, Inc.
Phoenix, AZ

Vinotinto – Venezuela Béisbol, 1939 – 2024
85 Years of Venezuelans in the Major Leagues

Foreword by Ozzie Guillén
Edited by Leonte Landino and Bill Nowlin
Associate editors Len Levin and Carl Riechers

Cover art: Leonte Landino
Interior design: Gilly Rosenthol

Unless otherwise noted, all photographs are from SABR/The Rucker Archive.

978-1-960819-51-2 (paperback)
978-1-960819-50-5 (ebook)
Library of Congress Control Number: 2025915911

Cronkite School at ASU
555 N. Central Ave. #406C
Phoenix, AZ 85004
Phone: (602) 496-1460
Web: www.sabr.org
Facebook: Society for American Baseball Research
Twitter/X: @SABR

CONTENTS

FOREWORD

BY OZZIE GUILLÉN

Venezuelans have always believed our country is blessed with three great treasures: oil, beautiful women, and world-class baseball players.

While soccer has grown in popularity and basketball has brought us memorable victories, baseball is still baseball.

You don't need a regulation-sized diamond to play. Any sandlot will do. That's why, in every corner, every neighborhood, and every town—no matter how small—you'll find kids playing ball with whatever they can: rubber balls, rags, tape, even cardboard. And if there's no ball at all, bottle caps—our beloved *chapitas*—do the trick.

I grew up in Ocumare del Tuy, a town in the state of Miranda. I played basketball and volleyball and proudly represented my state in national competitions. But it was baseball that gave me a career, a purpose, and the ability to provide for my family.

Like most Venezuelan kids, I started with street baseball—scrappy games against children from neighboring barrios, using rubber balls and broomsticks that, in our eyes, were top-of-the-line Louisville Sluggers.

Everything changed when I met Ernesto Aparicio—my beloved *viejo Aparicio*. With him, baseball became more than a pastime; it became a path toward a profession and a better future.

He helped me take my first real steps in the game. As a teenager, I began to develop skills that caught the attention of Luis Rosas, a Puerto Rican scout for the San Diego Padres. He saw my potential and offered me a professional contract. Around the same time in Venezuela, Pedro Padrón Panza, owner of the Tiburones de La Guaira, signed me to play for his team in the Venezuelan Professional Baseball League.

Signing with the Padres brought great joy to my family, but the deal with the Tiburones was the realization of a childhood dream.

You see, the Pampero rum distillery—original owner of a team called the Licoreros—was located in my hometown. That team eventually became the Tiburones, and from that moment on, we were die-hard fans. Their players were our heroes.

Back then, we followed the games on the radio. The broadcasters, with their vivid storytelling, made us feel like we were right there on the field. We'd reenact the plays in the streets, proudly taking on the names of our idols:

"I'm Luis Aparicio... I'm Remigio Hermoso... I'm José Herrera... I'm Pipo Correa..."

Luis Aparicio—shortstop for the Tiburones—is still the only Venezuelan inducted into the National Baseball Hall of Fame in Cooperstown. But many others who wore the Tiburones uniform also made their mark in Major League Baseball. Our winter league hosted not only Venezuelan stars but legends from across the Caribbean and the Americas: Cuba, Puerto Rico, the Dominican Republic, Nicaragua, and Curaçao.

Players like Pete Rose, Steve Sax, Luis Tiant, Porfirio Altamirano, Odell Jones, Darryl Strawberry, Davey Johnson, Derrel Thomas, and many more—some whose names I may have forgotten but whose impact lives on—played in our league and became fan favorites.

They competed alongside the best Venezuelan talent, many of whom are featured in the stories ahead.

It's a true honor to introduce this book, which celebrates the lives and legacies of the Venezuelan players who have left their mark on Major League Baseball.

When I was invited to write this foreword for SABR, I immediately thought of the pioneers who paved the way, long before I ever dreamed of becoming a pro ballplayer. Then I thought of the hundreds who followed, proudly carrying our flag into the big leagues.

From Alejandro "Patón" Carrasquel, the first Venezuelan to play in MLB with the Washington Senators... to his nephew Chico Carrasquel, the first Latin American All-Star... to Luis Aparicio, Rookie of the Year... to Andrés Galarraga, batting champion—an achievement later matched by Magglio Ordóñez, Miguel Cabrera, and José Altuve.

We've witnessed no-hitters from Johan Santana, Félix Hernández, Carlos Zambrano, and Aníbal Sánchez. We celebrated King Félix's perfect game, Miguel Cabrera's Triple Crown, and countless other milestones that fill our country with pride.

All of them are role models for future generations. When I made my MLB debut with the Chicago White Sox in 1985, Venezuelan players in the majors could be counted on one hand. Today, at every level, you'll find hundreds of our countrymen across the rosters of all 30 MLB organizations.

Each one is chasing the same dream we once chased.

Each one is sacrificing—leaving home, adapting to a new culture and language, competing against the world's best—to create a better future for their families.

In 1981, at just 17 years old, I stepped onto the field at Estadio Universitario to play my first professional game, wearing the uniform of the team I idolized as a child. That moment began a journey filled with highs and lows, lessons learned, failures overcome, and goals reached through relentless effort and unwavering belief.

My story will likely sound familiar as you turn the pages of this book.

Each chapter is a testament to resilience. Each life inspires the kids who wake up every day, hop on a bus or walk dusty roads to get to a field, field grounders, swing the bat, and warm up their arms—all with the same dream in their hearts.

I hope you enjoy every word and feel proud of the legacy these players continue to build.

Because when you truly believe and give everything you have... no dream is impossible.

— Ozzie Guillén

Three generations of White Sox shortstops — Chico Carrasquel, Luis Aparicio, and Ozzie Guillén — pose together. Together, they shaped the legacy of Venezuelan infielders in major-league baseball. (Getty Images)

INTRODUCTION

BY LEONTE LANDINO

Baseball, known as America's pastime, has become a global phenomenon that unites people from diverse backgrounds. While the sport's roots lie in the United States, its influence has transcended borders, captivating the hearts of fans worldwide. One nation that has made an indelible mark on the major-league stage is Venezuela. For over 80 years, Venezuelan players have graced the fields of the major leagues, leaving an undeniable impact on the game and etching their names in baseball history.

This book is a celebration of their journey, their achievements, and the lasting legacy they have created.

As Venezuelans, living in a baseball-obsessed nation, their accomplishments on the field fill Venezuelans with immense national pride. We embrace every major-league team as if they are part of our own country, playing in our local communities. Saying Yankees, Orioles, or Reds is just part of the local sports jargon.

While the industry in the United States makes efforts to promote the product internationally, that groundwork was laid in Venezuela well over 80 years ago.

People still ask ... Why the burgundy color or "vinotinto"? Sports teams representing Venezuela started using this color as a national identity. One version explaining its origin is that the military training clothing was burgundy, and so this color was translated into national team uniforms. Another theory is that the flag colors – yellow, blue, and red – blend to create burgundy.

The fact is that during the early 2000s, the national soccer team started being identified as La Vinotinto as Venezuelan soccer progressed on the international stage. Then finally, the World Baseball Classic took place in 2006, and the entire country was excited about seeing a true national powerhouse team on the field.

This was the real Vinotinto. The one that once again geared up for the 2023 World Baseball Classic and stopped the heartbeats of Venezuelans in the country and around the world.

Today, Venezuela is vinotinto, and vinotinto is synonymous with Venezuelan sports around the globe.

To understand the significance of Venezuelan players in the major leagues, we must delve into the beginnings of baseball in Venezuela. As the game grew in popularity, it quickly became ingrained in Venezuelan culture, with local leagues sprouting up across the country. Baseball soon became an integral part of the national identity, providing an avenue for aspiring young players to dream of reaching the pinnacle of the sport.

But the journey of Venezuelan players in major-league baseball began in 1939 when Alejandro "Patón" Carrasquel became the first Venezuelan-born player to don a major-league uniform.

Carrasquel paved the way for future generations, showcasing the talent and potential within Venezuelan baseball. Throughout the 1940s and 1950s, a few more Venezuelan players made their way into the league. But it wasn't until the 1960s that a wave of exceptional talent emerged.

The 1960s marked a turning point for Venezuelan players in major-league baseball. A group of immensely talented players burst onto the scene, leaving an immediate impact. One such player was Luis Aparicio, a dynamic shortstop who became the first Venezuelan to become a true star of the game, shaping the sport in his era and eventually finding his place in the National Baseball Hall of Fame. Aparicio's success opened the floodgates, inspiring a generation of young Venezuelans to pursue their dreams of playing in the big leagues.

Then the 1990s and 2000s witnessed an unprecedented surge in the number of Venezuelan players in the majors, with a host of superstars emerging from the country. Names like Omar Vizquel, Andrés Galarraga, and Bobby Abreu became synonymous with excellence, showcasing their skills on both sides of the field. These players not only achieved personal milestones but also helped their teams reach new heights, contributing to memorable playoff runs and World Series championships.

As Venezuela became a powerhouse in talent production in both quality and quantity, more players dominated the major-league landscape. The likes of Miguel Cabrera, José Altuve, and Ronald Acuña Jr. have captured the hearts of fans with their exceptional talents and charismatic personalities. These players have shattered records, claimed batting titles, and earned numerous accolades, solidifying their place among the game's elite. Their success has further cemented Venezuela's reputation as a hotbed of baseball talent.

But as a nation of contrast, Venezuela is a country that has struggled politically and socially in the last couple of decades. With a population that once enjoyed major-league action and fervently supported the Professional Winter League, it is estimated that more than 7 million Venezuelans have massively migrated around the world, looking for better opportunities and social freedom. The social convolution has affected how baseball is consumed and even how Venezuelan players reach professional baseball.

Back home, established MLB players have contributed to charity efforts and helped social causes, from building sports academies to supporting education and healthcare initiatives in their homeland. These players have become beacons of hope and inspiration for their fellow countrymen.

As we celebrate over 80 years of Venezuelan players in major-league baseball, it is evident that their impact on the game extends far beyond statistics and records. These players have become ambassadors for their country, showcasing the rich baseball heritage that Venezuela possesses. Their dedication, perseverance, and love for the game have inspired future generations of players, instilling a sense of national pride and unity. Venezuela's baseball achievements are a testament to the talent and determination that reside within the hearts of Venezuelan athletes and the immeasurable contributions they have made to the world of baseball.

This book is a tribute to these remarkable individuals and to their extraordinary journey, and a celebration of their lasting legacy: from humble and remote beginnings, raw talent, and dreams of playing a children's game to achieving success in a foreign country, surpassing social and cultural barriers.

It aims to honor their achievements, chronicle their triumphs and tribulations, and provide an intimate look into their lives both on and off the field. Join us as we embark on this captivating exploration of the impact of Venezuelan players in major-league baseball and discover the stories that have captivated fans around the globe.

This book, published by the Society for American Baseball Research, represents the collaborative effort of 35 SABR members and provides an appreciation of some 50 Venezuelans who have starred in baseball's major leagues. It is a true teamwork project that overcame the effects of a world pandemic that stopped many projects around the world. It was only possible because of the perseverance and incredible spirit of my lead co-editor, Mr. Bill Nowlin, who understands the transcendence of international baseball with the highest spirit of leaving a mark for future generations.

My dear fat abuelo, Roberto Valbuena, would have been so proud, but mostly interested as a reader and researcher. He was the first baseball-book lover I ever met and the one who gave me his entire library when I was 11 years old. That moment set my path. The result is in your hands.

¡Que viva Venezuela!

Leonte Landino
Co-Editor
Member of the Baseball Writers Association of America (BBWAA)

PROLOGUE

VENEZUELA IS THE ONLY BASEBALL-DRIVEN COUNTRY IN SOUTH AMERICA FOR THREE HISTORICAL REASONS

BY JUAN VENÉ

Venezuela might have become a soccer-focused country, like the rest of South America, if not for three pivotal historical events:

1) Venezuelan dictator Juan Vicente Gómez and his son, Gonzalo, developed a profound love for baseball. They sponsored teams and paid the players' salaries, even when baseball was supposed to be an amateur sport. Their influence lasted from 1908 until Juan Vicente died in 1935.

2) The legendary victory at the Baseball World Cup in Cuba in October 1941. Since then, this Venezuelan team has been known as "The Heroes of 1941."

3) The arrival of U.S.-based oil companies, Creole and Shell, to Venezuela's eastern and western regions. These companies embraced the country's enthusiasm for baseball. By 1944, every oil field had its baseball diamond, promoting the growth and love of the game.

Many talented players emerged from these regions, including Luis Aparicio from Maracaibo and Luis "Camaleón" García from Carúpano.

As historian Eleazar Díaz Rangel noted in his 1967 masterpiece *El Béisbol en Caracas*, baseball had already been played in Caracas for nearly five decades.[1]

It all began in January 1895, when a group of young men who had studied in New York returned to Venezuela. They showed up one day at the Stand del Este, near the central railway station, with bats and balls. They had no gloves.

There was a group of boys nearby preparing to play "stone battle," a popular pastime among children and young adults at that time. One of these boys was Rómulo Gallegos (acclaimed writer and former President of Venezuela), then 11 years old. The wealthy boys invited the rock-throwing kids to play the fashionable sport from the United States. They left their stones and started to learn the game.

This marked the first time baseball was played in Venezuela!

In addition to "stone battles," Venezuelans also entertained themselves by playing soccer (led by European priests), practicing archery, or attending bullfights, horse races, cinemas, boxing matches, zarzuelas, operas, and plays.

Baseball quickly captivated the attention of boys and young adults in Caracas and spread throughout the country, particularly in inner cities like La Guaira, La Victoria, Maracay, Valencia, Barquisimeto, Maracaibo, and Barlovento.

Cubans in many fields: workers, businessmen, students, travelers, and entertainers were already well-versed in the game and continually came to Venezuela for various reasons. Their presence was crucial in helping Venezuelan players improve their skills and in increasing the game's popularity among spectators.

Two of the most notable Cuban players from those years were Lázaro Quesada, a catcher, and Emerito Agudín, a second baseman and shortstop who was highly educated and fluent in English. Agudín was the first to translate and publish the rules of baseball in Venezuela.

The first organized team was Caracas B.B.C. Organized by the Franklin brothers— Amenodoro, Emilio, Gustavo, and Augusto Franklin. It consisted of almost everyone who practiced at the Stand del Este—except for Gallegos, whose parents forbade him to play by saying, "That sport is a thing for young criminals."[2]

The first registered game was Caracas against Caracas, as there were no other teams. They had to divide the roster into two "novenas" or teams: *Los Rojos* and *Los Azules*. The game, which featured three Cuban players, took place on May 23, 1895, as reported by the newspaper *El Tiempo*.

Los Azules (The Blues) won, 28-19.

The final times of the nineteenth century and the early twentieth century were pivotal for the development of baseball in Venezuela. The sport evolved into a national pastime, captivating millions of people, becoming a popular activity for all ages, and developing into a significant industry that provided jobs for tens of thousands while offering national entertainment.

In 1931, Gonzalo Gómez decided to establish his team, Águilas del Concordia, by bringing in talented foreign players and hiring the best local players for the highest salaries. He paid some imported players $2,000 a month, which was equivalent to the salary of Lou Gehrig, the star first baseman for the Yankees at that time.

While the Gómez family and the oil companies played a critical role in the development of baseball in Venezuela, it was "The Heroes of 1941" who ignited the country's passion for the sport.

On October 22, 1941, the Venezuelan team won the IV Baseball World Cup in Havana. This victory convinced Venezuelans of something they had never believed before, the fact that a Venezuelan team could compete at the same level as the Cubans.

The formation of this team and its journey were seen as a national endeavor. Every Venezuelan felt they were a part of this team.

The Amateur Baseball World Series was born in 1938. The first tournament, held in London, featured only two teams, with England defeating the United States. In 1939, the tournament took place in Havana, featuring three countries—Cuba, the United States, and Nicaragua. The Cubans won, and the event was such a financial success that the 1940 tournament was again held at the Tropical Stadium in Havana.

In 1940, Venezuela participated for the first time, finishing in a modest fourth place. Abelardo Raidi, a young sports journalist from *El Universal*, took the lead in organizing the team's trip and logistics, acting as a General Manager or "Delegado," a term used to describe the person in charge of the team.

Raidi was determined to win the competition, and his efforts were wholeheartedly supported by both players and fans around the country.

From building the roster to overseeing training in Caracas and managing the logistics of the long boat trip, Raidi was in charge of every detail. He worked closely with the Cuban organizing committee to prepare the game schedule and every aspect of the tournament.

The Cuban authorities covered the costs of the return trip, while the Venezuelan government was supposed to fund the journey to Havana. However, the government funds never materialized.

Raidi then launched a public fundraising campaign under the slogan: "*A bolívar... for the Love of God!*" (The bolívar was and still is the currency of Venezuela.)

The team needed 11,000 bolívares to cover their travel expenses. Fans came together to contribute, ultimately raising 15,000 bolívares.

The team and its mission had captured the hearts of all Venezuelans.

To defeat Cuba in baseball at that time was akin to reaching Mars today. At the end of the tournament, Cuba and Venezuela were tied with seven wins each.

The tiebreaker set the stage for the now-famous pitching duel between Cuba's Conrado Marrero and Venezuela's Daniel "El Chino" Canónico, who had already recorded four victories in the tournament.

The game began with an unexpected twist. In the first inning, Marrero, typically known for his precise control, struggled to find the strike zone. The Venezuelan team capitalized on this rare opportunity, scoring three quick runs before Marrero could regain his composure. This shaky start would ultimately prove decisive.

After the difficult first inning, Marrero settled down and began dominating the Venezuelan hitters, showing the skill and command he was famous for, and effectively shutting down the

Venezuelan offense for the remainder of the game. The early damage was already done, and the three runs scored in the first inning proved critical.

Meanwhile, Canónico was in peak form. He confounded the Cuban batters with a masterful mix of pitches, keeping them off balance throughout the game. The powerful Cuban lineup, known for its heavy hitters, was held scoreless until the ninth inning. In a last-ditch effort, Cuba managed to score a lone run when Segundo "Guajiro" Rodríguez hit a double, followed by a single from Rafael Villa Cabrera. But it was not enough.

As Canónico recorded the final out, the scoreboard read 3-1 in favor of Venezuela. The Cuban crowd, a mix of disappointment and admiration, rushed onto the field to celebrate Canónico's remarkable performance. In a show of respect and sportsmanship, they lifted Canónico and his South American teammates onto their shoulders, honoring their incredible achievement.

This historic victory not only secured Venezuela's first-ever Baseball World Cup title but also solidified its status as a baseball powerhouse. The passion and skill displayed by both teams, particularly in this intense pitching duel, left an indelible mark on everyone who witnessed it.

This win was more than just a triumph on the field; it was a moment that united the Venezuelan people in their love for baseball, turning the sport from a pastime into a national obsession.

The nine teams finished thus:

Venezuela	8-1
Cuba	7-2
Mexico	6-2
Panama	5-3
Dominican Rep.	5-3
USA	2-6
Nicaragua	2-6
Puerto Rico	1-7
El Salvador	1-7

The entire Venezuelan team played their best, sensationally enough, but "El Chino" Canónico was extraordinary, recording five wins without a loss.

Here are the two rosters of that transcendental and historic game:

Cuba:

- **Pitchers**: Conrado "Connie" Marrero, Julio "Jiquí" Moreno, Pedro "Natilla" Jiménez, Ramón Roger, Tomás Hecheverría, Raúl Ávalos, Daniel Parra, PA Fernandez.
- **Catchers**: Andrés Fleitas, Rouget Avalos.
  Infielders: Bernardo Cuervo, Clemente González, Napoleón Reyes, Domingo Gálvez, Antonio "Mosquito" Ordeñana.

- **Outfielders**: Rafael Villa-Cabrera, Rogelio "Limonar" Martínez, Charles Pérez, Segundo "Guajiro" Rodríguez.
- **Manager**: Joaquín Viego.
- **Coaches**: Narciso Picazo, Bernardo Rodríguez.

Venezuela:

- **Pitchers**: Daniel "Chino" Canónico, Pedro "Diver" Nelson, Benjamín Chirinos, Juan Francisco "El Gatico" Hernández, Domingo Barboza, Julio "El Brujo" Bracho, Ramón "Dumbo" Fernández, Felipe González.
- **Catchers**: Guillermo "Aquilino" Vento, Enrique Fonseca.
- **Infielders**: Luis Romero Petit, José Antonio Casanova, Dalmiro Finol, José Pérez Colmenares, Atilano Malpica.
  Outfielders: Jesús "Chucho" Ramos, Héctor "Redondo" Benítez, Francisco "Tarzán" Contreras.
- **Manager**: Manuel "El Pollo" Malpica.
- **Coaches**: Carlos Maal, Jesús Corao.
- **Kinesiologist**: Jesús Rodil.
- **Delegate**: Abelardo Raidi.

Less than five years later, Venezuelan baseball had become fully professional. The Venezuelan Professional League championship began on January 12, 1946, with all games played in Caracas and featuring the teams Magallanes, Venezuela, Cervecería de Caracas, and Vargas.

At that time, Caracas, the capital, had a population of 561,415, in a country with a total of 3,934,429 people. With just one bolívar, a person could buy a full meal in many restaurants across the country.

As baseball became more organized, it opened the door to more international competitions and player exchanges with both the minor and major leagues in the United States. In 1949, Venezuela began participating in the Caribbean Series.

Without the Gómez family, "The Heroes of '41," or the support of the oil companies, it would have been impossible to present the 50 vibrant biographies contained in this publication.

Venezuela might not be the country it is today, producing some of the world's best baseball players who now shine in the multibillion-dollar industry of Major League Baseball and around the world.

NOTES

1   Eleazar Díaz Rangel & Guillermo Becerra Mijares, *El Béisbol en Caracas: 1895-1967* (Caracas: Ediciones del Círculo de Periodistas Deportivos, 1967).

2   Juan Vené, *5 Mil Años de Béisbol* (Caracas: Ediciones B., 2007).

BASEBALL IN VENEZUELA: A UNIFYING FORCE AND NATIONAL IDENTITY

BY LEONTE LANDINO

In the heart of Venezuela, where passion runs as deep as the Orinoco River, baseball is more than just a sport; it's a cultural phenomenon that unites a diverse nation. With a history dating back over a century, baseball has transcended its status as a game, becoming a powerful force that bridges divides and reinforces the collective identity of Venezuelans.

From the bustling streets of Caracas to the rural villages in the Andes, from the heating sandlots in Maracaibo to the remote communities in the Amazon rainforest, the diamond's allure is universal, fostering a sense of belonging and pride.

Baseball in Venezuela serves as a unifying thread in the rich tapestry of the nation's identity.

The beginnings

In the late nineteenth century, a new form of mass entertainment emerged in Venezuela, gradually transforming into a powerful symbol of national identity.

The origins of baseball in Venezuela remain a subject of ongoing debate among historians. As a researcher and historian, I support the version that attributes its introduction to wealthy Venezuelan students who studied at universities in the United States. This narrative aligns with early written accounts and has been passed down through oral tradition by some of our earliest chroniclers and writers.

While abroad, these students were introduced to the emerging sport, learning and playing it during their academic years. Upon returning to Venezuela in the early 1890s, they began sharing the game with friends and peers within the upper social circles of Caracas, planting the seeds of what would eventually become a national passion.

One well-supported and widely accepted account – documented in early Venezuelan newspapers – indicates that by May 1895, Amenodoro Franklin and his brothers Emilio, Gustavo, and Augusto founded the first organized baseball club in the country: the Caracas Base Ball Club.

According to accounts from Eleazar Díaz Rángel and Guillermo Becerra Mijares, this historic moment began on a pleasant afternoon when the Franklin brothers and a group of their friends arrived at a popular open field in the eastern area of Caracas. They came equipped with baseball gear, including bats, gloves, and balls, transported in four horse-drawn carriages.[1]

This open field, located in front of the Central Railroad Station in Quebrada Honda, had previously been used by British railway workers and local enthusiasts for a game known as "Rounders." Over time, it evolved into a game referred to as "Rondada." The field served as a space for open sports activities, distinct from the nearby tennis courts.

These areas were regarded as recreational spaces for the affluent residents of Caracas, and to this day, they stand as some of the city's finest and most picturesque locales. The lovely Parque Los Caobos, which continues to serve as a public space, is a direct descendant of those peaceful and open areas.

The Franklin brothers were enthusiastic about spreading the game they learned in the United States. Although similar to rounders, baseball held a special excitement for them. They began practicing tirelessly until Sundays became a regular day for learning and playing the new sport. As their dedication to baseball continued to grow, the Caracas Baseball Club was officially formed, and the field was later christened the Campo de Ejercicios del Caracas Base Ball Club.

The Caracas B.B.C. decided to organize the "First Official Baseball Game in Venezuela," intending it to be a grand event to generate publicity. On May 22, 1895, they sent out open invitations and published an announcement in *El Tiempo*, a local newspaper. The game was so novel and unfamiliar to the public that the reporter described it as "a new type of chess game, Base Bale [*sic*]."[2]

The following day at 3:30 P.M., the two teams of the Caracas B.B.C., Los Rojos and Los Azules, took to the field. The latter, managed by Amenodoro Franklin, won, 28-19. Some of the players were the Franklin brothers, Emilio, Gustavo, and Augusto, Adolfo Inchausti, Alfredo Mosquera, the Todd brothers – Jaime and Roberto – and Mariano Becerra.

All of them, who had studied in the United States, are considered the pioneers of the game in Venezuela. Among the other participating players were the Gonzalez brothers – Manuel and Joaquín – as well as Emilio Gramer, who were Cubans living in Caracas.

El Tiempo did not know much about baseball after the first game, and many people thought they were going to witness a "chess game" due to the reporter's mistake. A note appeared the next day describing more of the atmosphere than the game itself:

"It looked like a Sunday carnival, but without costumes, flowers, sweets, or red things. The delight of the people was such that not a single complaint about the country's poverty was heard all afternoon. And, as on other occasions, the people had fun, at least those who have more means to do so."[3]

Venezuela, filled with internal revolutions throughout the country, was led by rural or military leaders who were trying to take control of the government. By 1895, General Joaquín Crespo was the president, and the country was impoverished after many years of civil war.

El Pregonero, another newspaper, also covered the game and, in its report, mocked *El Tiempo*'s advertisement about the "chess game":

"See! 'El Tiempo'? The game was Ball, not Bale. 'El Tiempo' always gets it wrong."[4]

But it also added:

"But this game of baseball provides health and strength to the body, as well as happiness to the spirit."

Three months later, on August 15, a magazine, *El Cojo Ilustrado*, published the first photographs of baseball in the country, sent by Mariano Becerra.

Days later, everyone in the city was talking about the "new sport," and Alfredo Mosquera's father, the owner of Cervecería Caracas, built the first official stadium in the country with stands and regulation measurements. It was the Stand del Este, near the Petare train station, a suburb of Caracas.

The boys finally had a real ballpark. For its maintenance, they formed a company to manage the ballpark and even sold stock to local enthusiasts. This company, Compañía Anónima de Las Glorietas, managed the Stand del Este, aiming to improve the facility. In return, every Sunday, an entry fee was charged for adults to watch games. Children's admission was free.

Teams and players began to emerge across the baseball scene in Caracas, boosted by growing coverage in the local press. Squads such as Venezuela, Miranda, and Sucre joined the already established Caracas team to compete in the city's first organized tournament. Caracas quickly established itself as the dominant force, capturing the inaugural championship title. At the heart of their success was shortstop Emérito Argudín, who stood out as the tournament's first true star. His skill and leadership on the field earned him widespread recognition in the newspapers of the time, cementing his place in history as Venezuela's first celebrated baseball figure.

Argudín was a Cuban-born college student who arrived in Venezuela amid the turbulence of the Spanish-American War in 1898, fleeing his homeland during the American invasion to pursue studies at the Universidad Central de Venezuela (UCV). However, his academic aspirations were soon disrupted by the rise of General Cipriano Castro, who seized power in 1899 and imposed authoritarian control over the nation, including its educational institutions. In 1901, the Castro regime temporarily shut down UCV following waves of student protests, leaving Argudín – and many other upper-class students – without access to formal academic life.

The closure sparked significant public backlash, eventually forcing the government to reopen the university, albeit under tight restrictions. But the damage was done: the regime's efforts to centralize and suppress higher education – including the permanent closure of the universities of Zulia and Valencia in 1904 – transformed Venezuela's universities into epicenters of political dissent. Students and professors became active participants in resistance movements, prompting further crackdowns and intermittent closures across the academic landscape.

With his studies stalled and political tensions rising, Argudín, like many of his contemporaries, turned to baseball—not just as a pastime, but as a new intellectual and athletic pursuit.

He quickly emerged as a *maestro* of the game, introducing tactical elements that were novel in Venezuela at the time. Among these were the bunt, strategic baserunning, and the use of curveballs – concepts he had likely learned from American-influenced play styles. His contributions helped raise the technical standards of Venezuelan baseball during its formative years, laying the groundwork for what would become a deeply rooted national passion.

An established game

In the annals of Venezuelan history, October 19 and 26, 1902, hold a remarkable place. On these dates, the *USS Marietta*, a U.S. Navy gunboat, was docked at the port of La Guaira. What made these moments special was the presence of *Marietta*'s crew, who had brought along their own baseball team.

Two games were scheduled against the Caracas team, and what unfolded left an indelible mark on the country's sporting history, as it was the first time local talent faced off against experienced baseball players from the United States.

In the first game, the *Marietta* claimed victory, though not without a quirky twist. A covert player substitution took place, going unnoticed because the American players all looked alike, making identification difficult. The substitute stepped up to the plate and hit a game-changing three-run home run, sealing the contest with a win. In the rematch, Caracas bounced back with a

The *USS Marietta* baseball team from 1902. (Courtesy of historian Javier Gonzalez.)

win of their own, and notably, Emérito Argudín played in both games, showcasing his skill and power by hitting, according to those reports, "several home runs", further cementing his status as Venezuela's first great baseball star

But aboard the *USS Marietta* was a standout player – virtually unknown at the time – second baseman Frank Martin, a former major-league third baseman who had retired in 1899 and later enlisted in the U.S. Navy. Martin had played parts of three seasons in the National League, suiting up for the Louisville Colonels, the Chicago Orphans, and the New York Giants. His presence added a level of professional polish to the American squad that local fans had never seen before.

The 1902 games against the *Marietta* marked a pivotal moment in the history of Venezuelan baseball. They represented the country's first international competition – and its first victory against foreign opposition.

Caracas's triumph over a team that included a former major leaguer ignited a wave of national enthusiasm and sparked a new era of development for the sport.

In the years that followed, baseball in Venezuela experienced rapid and organic growth. New teams began to form across cities and towns, and dedicated baseball fields were built to meet the growing enthusiasm for the sport. What had begun as a curiosity imported from abroad quickly transformed into a national passion—one that would come to define generations and embed itself in the cultural fabric of the country.

In 1903, the prominent Vollmer family took a significant step in formalizing organized sports by dedicating part of their San Bernardino estate in Caracas to a variety of athletic activities. Their grounds hosted baseball, football, cricket, tennis, polo, basketball, track and field, and even target shooting. From this fertile athletic environment emerged the "San Bernardino" baseball team, which went on to defeat the established "Caracas" club and quickly asserted itself as the dominant force in the capital's baseball scene during that era.

These formative moments laid the groundwork for Venezuela's enduring love affair with baseball. What started with students and sailors evolved into a deeply rooted national identity, where diamonds became sacred ground and players became symbols of pride. More than a century later, the spirit of those early games, including the landmark contests against the USS *Marietta*, still echoes in every pitch, swing, and cheer.

Baseball in Venezuela is not just a sport; it's a legacy.

A Humble Beginning to a Legendary Legacy: The Birth of Magallanes

On October 26, 1917, in a modest gathering at the Back Stop bar – an unassuming hangout for local baseball aficionados – a few friends unknowingly laid the foundation for what would become one of Venezuela's most iconic and enduring baseball franchises: Magallanes.

Antonio Benítez, the owner of the bar and a passionate supporter of the sport, proposed the name Magallanes for their newly conceived team. The name paid tribute to the legendary Portuguese explorer Ferdinand Magellan, who had once charted the coastal waters near Venezuela. A vote was held among the bar's regulars, and though it passed by the slimmest of margins – just one vote – the name Magallanes was chosen, sealing the first chapter in the club's storied history.

The team's early days were humble. Its headquarters were established in the neighborhood of Catia. In early 1918, they held tryouts to select the first players to wear the Magallanes jersey. That same January, the club officially registered to compete in the national championship. Their debut, however, was far from glorious – a crushing 20-6 defeat at the hands of Flor del Ávila. Although they bounced back with a win in their next outing, a string of losses eventually forced the team to withdraw from the tournament.

But those initial struggles did not mark the end. On the contrary, they became the spark that fueled the team's determination to persevere.

Rather than fading into obscurity, Magallanes grew in stature, its spirit shaped by adversity. The foundation had been laid, not just for a team, but for a legacy.

A decade later, Antonio Benítez revived the Magallanes name and entered the team into Caracas's second division, part of a tiered amateur system based on playing level. Once he managed to recruit a stronger roster with more seasoned talent, Magallanes was promoted to the prestigious first category for the historic 1930 season.

That same year marked the start of an intense rivalry with Royal Criollos, a powerhouse team founded in 1927 under the sponsorship of the Royal typewriter company. With financial backing and a mission to field exclusively Venezuelan players, Royal Criollos quickly became a dominant force. The emergence of Magallanes as a worthy challenger set the stage for one of Venezuelan baseball's earliest and most passionate rivalries – an enduring battle that captured the imagination of fans and helped elevate the sport to new heights across the country.

From the bar room to the ballpark, Magallanes transformed from a casual dream into a symbol of pride, resilience, and tradition – a legacy that still endures over a century later.

1930s: The Decade of Growth and Identity

The 1930s marked a pivotal era of growth, structure, and national awakening for baseball in Venezuela. Referred to by renowned baseball historian Javier González as the country's "Period of Consolidation," this decade witnessed the transformation of the sport from an elite urban pastime into a nationwide cultural force.

As Venezuela moved from the iron grip of General Juan Vicente Gómez's dictatorship toward a slow and uncertain path to democracy, baseball emerged not just as a game but as a unifying element in the reshaping of national identity. In a country marked by political tension and social upheaval, baseball offered common ground, a shared language that transcended class and region.

The year 1930 was especially significant. It saw the creation of the Asociación Venezolana de Béisbol, the governing body that organized the first official national championship for first division teams. This milestone represented the birth of semi-professional, structured baseball in Venezuela. For the first time, clubs competed under unified rules, with clear standings and national recognition – an essential leap forward from the informal city tournaments of earlier decades.

This new championship didn't just raise the level of competition. It sparked a cultural phenomenon. Baseball became more than a weekend activity; it was now a national obsession, broadcast on the radio, debated in cafés, and chronicled in newspapers with growing enthusiasm. The players became folk heroes, the rivalries turned into neighborhood passions, and the sport began weaving itself into the social fabric of the country.

The 1930s laid the foundation for what was to come – a Venezuela where baseball wouldn't just be the most popular sport, but a defining feature of national pride, cultural expression, and international aspiration.

Just a year later, in March 1931, another milestone was achieved: the first live radio broadcast of a baseball game in Venezuela. This technological leap allowed thousands of fans to experience games in real time, regardless of physical distance. Baseball became accessible to all, not just the privileged few, in stadiums. The advent of live broadcasting fueled nationwide rivalries, deepened fan engagement, and solidified the sport's growing presence in everyday Venezuelan life.

While the Liga Nacional de Béisbol (National Baseball League) had been created in 1927 to regulate the many amateur tournaments emerging across the country, its leadership revealed a strong political tie. Its first president and vice president were Gonzalo Gómez and José Vicente Gómez, sons of Venezuela's dictator, General Juan Vicente Gómez. These brothers didn't just oversee the league—they also owned teams that doubled as political propaganda.

For instance, the club Paz y Unión bore the exact slogan of the regime: "Unión, Paz y Trabajo." Another team, Independencia, was similarly named to align with the government's messaging. However, the club that truly catalyzed baseball's competitive evolution was *Águilas del Concordia* from La Victoria, in the state of Aragua.

Backed financially by Gonzalo Gómez, Concordia was not just a political tool but a powerhouse that elevated the standard of play and brought international attention to Venezuelan baseball.

This was the era in which local heroes began to gain global traction. Legends such as Luis Aparicio Ortega and Alejandro "Patón" Carrasquel began making names for themselves beyond Venezuelan borders. Concordia served as a launching pad, becoming a traveling super-team that represented Venezuela abroad – part athletic showcase, part political soft power. The club featured elite talent from across the Caribbean, including Hall of Famer Martín Dihígo of Cuba and Dominican speedster Tetelo Vargas, further legitimizing Venezuelan baseball on the international stage.

Meanwhile, in western Venezuela, the city of Maracaibo – buoyed by the oil boom – was nurturing its own baseball culture. Local rivalries, especially between Gavilanes and Pastora, galvanized the region's passion for the game. Scouts from Caracas began recruiting heavily in cities like Maracaibo, Barquisimeto, and Cumaná, triggering a steady influx of players to the capital in search of better pay and playing conditions.

By the mid-1930s, Venezuelan baseball was no longer just a game. It was a national phenomenon – politicized, professionalized, and popularized – set on a trajectory that would eventually produce some of the greatest players in the history of the sport.

As a direct result of Concordia's success as a traveling team throughout the Caribbean, Venezuelan players began to garner international attention and opportunities. Luis Aparicio Ortega became the country's first baseball export in 1934 when he signed with Tigres del Licey in the Dominican Republic, opening the door for future generations to follow.

Acuña Jr. became one of MLB's brightest stars, winning the 2023 NL MVP after a 40–70 season. His blend of power and speed has redefined the modern leadoff hitter. (Getty Images)

Just a few years another trailblazer emerged. In 1938, Alejandro "Patón" Carrasquel received an invitation from Cuban legend Martín Dihigo to join the Cuban Winter League, playing for the modest *Club Cuba* under the leadership of Joseíto Rodríguez. Carrasquel quickly made a name for himself, dominating hitters and ultimately earning the league's Most Valuable Player honors. Rodríguez, a former infielder for the New York Giants in 1916, connected his star pitcher with renowned scout "Papa" Joe Cambria, the longtime talent spotter for the Washington Senators.

Unlike today's prospects, who often sign with MLB organizations at the age of 16, Carrasquel was already 27 when he broke through. He had spent years establishing himself as a formidable pitcher in Venezuela and Cuba, playing with clubs like Valdés, where Cambria first saw him in action. Impressed by his poise and command, Cambria recommended him to Senators owner Clark Griffith.

In February 1939, Carrasquel made his first trip from Cuba to the United States, landing at the port of Tampa. However, due to immigration laws in effect since 1917, which barred illiterate foreigners from entering the country, Carrasquel was initially denied entry and sent back to the port of origin.

Several tense days passed before Griffith intervened, paying a $400 fee and formally assuming responsibility for the pitcher. With the paperwork cleared, Carrasquel finally arrived at the Senators' spring training facility in Orlando, Florida, ready to make history.

The news of Carrasquel's imminent major-league debut reverberated back home. For a nation still new to the idea of exporting athletic talent, it was a moment of immense pride.

"News from a Cuban outlet informs us that recently our paisano and magnificent player Alejandro Carrasquel was signed to play with the Washington Senators," wrote *El Universal*, one of Venezuela's leading dailies, on January 24, 1939.

That historic milestone arrived on April 23, 1939, when Carrasquel took the mound at Griffith Stadium in Washington, D.C., facing off against the powerhouse New York Yankees.

With that first pitch, he became the first Venezuelan to play in the major leagues. The rest, as they say, is history.

The Impact of 1941 and the LVBP

However, it was in 1941 that baseball truly became ingrained as an expression of Venezuelan national identity. That year, Venezuela's amateur national team achieved a stunning victory in the World Amateur Baseball Championship held in Havana, Cuba.

The win was more than a sporting triumph – it was a cultural and emotional milestone that brought the entire country to a standstill. As the final game was aired on the radio, Venezuelans across all walks of life paused their daily routines to listen, united by a sense of pride and anticipation.

The reaction was unprecedented. President Isaías Medina Angarita declared an immediate national holiday, and celebrations erupted across cities and small towns alike. The victory stirred a powerful sense of unity and patriotic emotion, forever linking baseball with the Venezuelan soul.

In recognition of the achievement, October 22 was officially declared National Sports Day, a symbolic tribute to the moment when baseball became more than just a game – it became part of the nation's character.

This overwhelming public enthusiasm laid the foundation for the creation of a professional league, one that would affiliate with the U.S.-based National Association of Professional Baseball Leagues (NAPBL). Just five years later, in 1946, the dream took shape as the Liga Venezolana de Béisbol Profesional (LVBP) was officially born.

The inaugural LVBP season began on December 27, 1946, with four pioneering teams: Cervecería Caracas, Navegantes del Magallanes, Patriotas del Venezuela, and Sabios del Vargas. These early clubs set the tone for a league that would become a cornerstone of Venezuelan sports culture.

The league's growth in the following decades was nothing short of extraordinary. Fans filled stadiums in droves, creating an electric and passionate atmosphere that rivaled the best baseball environments in the world. As the league expanded, iconic franchises such as Leones del Caracas, Tiburones de La Guaira, Tigres de Aragua, and Cardenales de Lara emerged, intensifying rivalries and strengthening regional pride. The historic rivalry between Caracas and Magallanes – which eventually relocated to Valencia as their permanent home – became the heart of Venezuelan baseball tradition.

Meanwhile, in the western state of Zulia, the game flourished as a regional powerhouse, largely inspired by the legendary Luis Aparicio Ortega. From 1954 to 1963, Zulia hosted its own professional circuit, the Western Professional League, which showcased local talent and drew massive support in a baseball-obsessed region.

But it wasn't until 1969 that Maracaibo, capital city of Zulia state, officially joined the LVBP. That year marked the debut of Águilas del Zulia, a franchise that would grow to become one of the most beloved and successful in the country. With six championship titles to its name, Águilas has helped complete and solidify the LVBP as a truly national institution, uniting fans across all corners of Venezuela.

The league underwent a second expansion in 1992, welcoming two new franchises: Petroleros de Cabimas and Caribes de Oriente. Cabimas eventually relocated – first to Acarigua, and later to its current home on Margarita Island, rebranded as Bravos de Margarita. Caribes, on the other hand, found a stable and passionate home in Puerto La Cruz, rebranding as Caribes de Anzoátegui to better reflect the local identity.

Today, the LVBP stands as one of Latin America's premier winter leagues, deeply interwoven with the cultural, social, and emotional fabric of Venezuela.

It all began with a spark in Havana, and from that historic 1941 triumph, a nation's love affair with baseball was forever sealed.

Baseball as a Cultural Force in Venezuela

The evolution of baseball in Venezuela is more than a story of athletic development – it is a powerful cultural and national narrative. Adopting a constructionist approach, baseball in Venezuela has been consciously shaped and elevated as a symbol of national identity, developing in tandem with the nation's modern history and serving as both a mirror and an engine of social progress.

Far beyond its recognition as Venezuela's official national sport, baseball has functioned as a unifying force, transcending class, political ideologies, and geographic divides. It has brought people together through joy, competition, and shared pride, especially during moments of hardship and uncertainty. No other sport – or leisure activity – has matched baseball's penetration into the country's social fabric, educational systems, and collective imagination.

Baseball's reach extends across every layer of society. From organized school leagues and youth development programs to semi-professional circuits and the crown jewel of the sport – the Liga Venezolana de Béisbol Profesional (LVBP) – baseball in Venezuela is not merely played; it is lived. The Winter League, held annually from October to February, holds a sacred place in the hearts of Venezuelans.

It is during this season that hometown heroes, many of whom play in the U.S. major leagues, return to suit up for their national clubs, reuniting with fans and reigniting regional rivalries in sold-out stadiums.

As Venezuelan players continued to make waves internationally, the nation began to follow their journeys with intense passion. The emergence of Luis Aparicio, Venezuela's first Hall of Famer, and stars like Dave Concepción, Andrés Galarraga, Omar Vizquel, Miguel Cabrera, and José Altuve, among others, elevated the country's global baseball standing. These players not only excelled in Major League Baseball (MLB) but also carried with them the spirit of Venezuelan baseball wherever they played, becoming symbols of aspiration for generations of young players.

The success hasn't been limited to individuals. Venezuela's national team has proudly represented the country on the international stage, earning accolades in prestigious tournaments such as the Caribbean Series and the World Baseball Classic. These performances have united the nation in celebration and reminded the world of the depth and passion that define Venezuelan baseball.

Moreover, baseball has acted as a catalyst for social change. Across the country, grassroots programs and baseball academies have created vital opportunities for youth, particularly in underserved communities.

These initiatives offer not only athletic training but also education, structure, and a path to a better life. Many of today's MLB stars began their journeys in such programs, demonstrating how baseball serves not just as a sport but as a mechanism of empowerment, mobility, and national pride.

In Venezuela, baseball is more than a pastime. It is a cultural institution, a symbol of identity, a source of pride, and a unifying voice in a nation that has endured both triumph and turmoil. The sport's continued expansion, its impact on youth development, and its international acclaim underscore its profound role in the country's past, present, and future.

An Impactful Social Shift: Baseball Amid Crisis and Migration in Venezuela

The journey of baseball in Venezuela has been as dynamic as the nation itself, rich with triumphs but not without formidable challenges. Over the past two decades, economic collapse, political instability, and national security concerns have deeply impacted the sport's development at every level. Since the rise of the socialist revolution under Hugo Chávez in 1998, the professional baseball industry—once a thriving ecosystem of private sponsors, media partners, and packed stadiums—has faced immense pressure and decline.

And yet, despite this unraveling of the country's traditional structures, baseball has endured, driven by the unbreakable resilience and passion of the Venezuelan people.

The Liga Venezolana de Béisbol Profesional (LVBP) has managed to survive under increasingly adverse conditions. With corporate sponsorships and television deals evaporating, the league and its teams became increasingly dependent on financial backing from the government, a controversial pivot. Crowds once common during the golden eras of the sport are now rare, with stadiums filling only during a few key rivalry games, finals, or special appearances.

Still, baseball persists as a centerpiece of national pride. In 2023, Venezuela hosted the Caribbean Series and leveraged the event to inaugurate the Estadio Monumental Simón Bolívar, a 40,000-seat state-of-the-art stadium in Caracas, reminiscent of San Diego's Petco Park. It now serves as the new home of Leones del Caracas. That same year, the government also opened Estadio Fórum La Guaira, a modern, visually striking ballpark overlooking the Caribbean Sea. Despite its smaller capacity, the stadium features lavish fan amenities such as hot tubs, wet bars, and field-view pools, hallmarks of a world-class experience.

These grand investments, however, sparked backlash. Critics called them tone-deaf, pointing to Venezuela's crippling humanitarian crisis, record-high inflation, and the displacement of nearly 8 million citizens in search of safety and opportunity, according to the United Nations High Commissioner for Refugees [5]. Opponents questioned how a country struggling with basic needs could justify funding high-end stadiums. Furthermore, the government of Nicolás Maduro, which was only legitimately recognized by eight nations in the world[6] and widely recognized as a dictatorship[7], continues to face allegations of human rights violations, election fraud, and corruption, adding layers of controversy to any major state-sponsored project.

Meanwhile, baseball has transformed into one of Venezuela's most powerful cultural exports. As millions of citizens settle across Latin America, North America, and Europe, they carry with them not only their identity but also their passion for the game.

In corners of the world where baseball was once unknown or dormant, Venezuelan migrants are reviving the sport, introducing it in schoolyards, public parks, and local leagues. From remote towns in Chile and Spain to the streets of Miami and Toronto, baseball has become a tool of cultural connection, and Venezuelan children are growing up as global ambassadors of the game.

Back home, MLB stars rarely return to participate in the winter league, due to concerns over security, contractual restrictions, and insurance limitations. Only a few players appear for brief stints – typically as part of injury rehabs, off-season conditioning, or deeply personal tributes to family and community.

One notable exception in the 2023–2024 season was Atlanta Braves superstar Ronald Acuña Jr., fresh off winning the 2023 National League MVP award. Acuña stunned fans by playing for Tiburones de La Guaira, where he hit a staggering .441 in 10 games. He helped lead the team –fmanaged by World Series champion Ozzie Guillén – to its first title in 37 years.

Guillén made history, becoming the first Latino manager to win a World Series, a Winter League championship, and a Caribbean Series title. That crowning moment came in loanDepot Park –home of the Miami Marlins – where the Caribbean Series was hosted in an MLB stadium for the first time.

The stands were packed with expatriate Venezuelans, turning the game into a celebration of identity, pride, and resilience.

And while Venezuela continues to be a vital contributor to MLB's international talent pool, a new generation of players is rising—the children of migrants. These athletes are entering amateur draft pipelines in the U.S., Canada, and beyond, receiving development through school systems and travel ball circuits instead of traditional Latin academies.

Some, like Jesús Luzardo, a strong MLB starting pitcher born in Peru to Venezuelan parents, are redefining what it means to be a "Venezuelan" player. Others, like Abraham Toro, a versatile infielder born in Quebec and listed as "Canadian" on his baseball card, are Venezuelan to the core.

"More Venezuelan than an *arepa con carne mechada*," as fans like to say.

In the face of economic ruin and mass migration, baseball remains woven into the Venezuelan fiber. It is not just a sport—it is an identity, a bridge to the past, and a hope for the future. No matter where they are in the world, Venezuelans continue to be the game's most passionate ambassadors, spreading its joy, values, and rhythm to places that never knew it before.

The global impact of Venezuelan baseball is no longer measured only in wins and championships. It is seen in classrooms, community fields, and family traditions far from home. The game has survived war, scarcity, exile, and silence—because it lives in the heart of its people.

For Venezuelans, baseball it´s not a game, it´s not a passion. It´s a religion.

SOURCES

In addition to the sources cited in the Notes, the author consulted:

Javier González y Carlos Figueroa Ruiz, *Campos de Gloria: El Béisbol en Venezuela, 127 años de historia. 1895-2022* (Caracas: Biblioteca Digital Banesco, 2022).

Javier González, *El Béisbol en Venezuela* (Caracas: Fundación Bigott, 2003).

José Luis Salcedo-Bastardo, *Historia Fundamental de Venezuela* (Caracas: Universidad Central de Venezuela, 1996).

Juan Vené, *Cinco mil años de Beisbol* (Caracas: Ediciones B., 2006).

Juan Vené, *Las Mejores Anécdotas del Beisbol* (Caracas: Ediciones B., 2008).

NOTES

1   Eleazar Díaz Rangel and Guillermo Becerra Mijares, *El Béisbol en Caracas 1895-1966* (Caracas: Círculo de Periodistas Deportivos, 1967).

2   Díaz Rangel and Becerra Mijares.

3   Díaz Rangel and Becerra Mijares.

4   Adolfo Navas, *Mi Taller de Baseball* 2020. https://baseballtaller.wordpress.com/2020/12/14/historia-del-baseball-en-venezuela-i/.

5   UN Refugee Agency. Accessed on June 24, 2025. https://www.unrefugees.org/news/venezuela-crisis-explained

6   "Venezuela Elections: Map Shows Countries That Have Recognized Maduro's Win," *Newsweek*, July 31, 2024. Accessed on June 24, 2025. https://www.newsweek.com/venezuela-elections-map-shows-countries-that-have-recognized-maduros-win-1931498

7   "Venezuela tumbles deeper into dictatorship with Nicolás Maduro set to extend 12-year rule," *Guardian*, January 9, 2025. Accessed on June 24, 2025. https://www.theguardian.com/world/2025/jan/09/venezuela-dictatorship-nicolas-maduro-democratic-leaders-boycott

BOBBY ABREU

BY AUGUSTO CÁRDENAS

On August 3, 2019, the Philadelphia Phillies included on their Wall of Fame a Venezuelan who in the United States was known as Bobby, but in his native country called by many "El Comedulce."[1]

Bob Kelly Abreu Vásquez was born in Maracay, Aragua state, on March 11, 1974, the second of six children in the family raised with great effort by Nelson Abreu, a worker at the Kraft Heinz food company, and his wife, Águeda Vásquez de Abreu.

Living in a neighborhood called Sorocaima, Bobby began to show his affinity for sports, playing volleyball, soccer, basketball, foosball, and, of course, baseball.

His love for the sport that brought him fame and fortune was born thanks to his father. "He played baseball too. He was left-handed. And he was the one who took us together with my mother, but we followed my dad a lot, because he was good. My mom says that he didn't want to sign (to professional baseball)," Abreu said. "The people of Maracay know my dad. He was a well-known man in Maracay and in San Carlos de Cojedes, where he was born. He was our idol and he was the person we followed to play baseball."[2]

Bobby, along with his older brother Nelson, and younger brother Dennis, were the ones who applied themselves the most in that sport, all of them later signing to play professional baseball. But before they learned how to play the game, they learned a very good education, along with their other siblings, Nielsen, Anaís (who died in 2018), and Amarily.

"We grew up with the fundamentals and foundations of the home, and when I was about 10 or 11 years old, my father suffered an accident," Abreu recalled. "My older brother was 15, and that's the age when we're all rebellious, and my mom had to deal with the six children alone, because my dad was in bed."[3] Despite experiencing very hard times in their adolescence, the Abreu family managed to prevent their children from taking a bad path on the streets of Sorocaima.

"Sometimes there was not enough to eat and we wanted to make enough food for everybody, making arepas.[4] Today we laugh at that very beautiful remembrance, because with a little can of deviled ham we filled five arepas," Abreu said. "My mother is the fundamental pillar in my life, in my career, because she has been there since we had nothing. My dad was my hero, even though he didn't see me play in the major leagues, and my mom taught us to respect the values of the home, but it was a pretty hard stage, because we lived in a neighborhood where you could take any path, but we always we stood right there."[5]

Bobby began to stand out in baseball from a very young age and represented the state of Aragua in several tournaments, before joining the Houston Astros academy, which was led by Andrés Reiner, who years later became a special assistant to the general manager of the organization.

"I got there at the age of 15. Andrés Reiner for me, and for many of my colleagues, was like our father, who guided you, gave you the best advice, 'dedicate yourself, you have to work hard, you're never tired, you have to work twice as hard as others to be able to improve,'" Abreu said. "Andrés Reiner, really, was the best thing that has happened to me as a counselor, because apart from signing me as a scout, he was watching you, how your things were going, if you were doing things well or badly. He knew how to talk to you and we really always carry him with us, because he has been an exemplary person for all of us." Abreu signed with the Astros on August 21, 1990, and traveled to his first spring training, in the United States, in 1991.

"Before I got to the training camps I was scared. The farthest I (had gone) from my house was to San Carlos de Cojedes, two hours from my house, and always with the family. On that occasion (spring training), I had to be alone, without my father or my mother," Abreu recalled. "I had to go traveling with Roberto Petagine, Raúl Chávez, Henry Centeno, my compadre, may he rest in peace, Argenis Conde, (Jesús) Aristimuño, who was our coach, and I was behind them, because I had never been even in an airplane, nor in an airport. When I (got) to Miami, at immigration, you have to be alone and when the guy started to speak English to me, I wanted to cry. I wanted to go home."

Despite the fear, Abreu arrived at his first spring training remembering Reiner's advice.

"I come to spring training, at 17 years old, and you are rubbing shoulders with older people, and you come to see that the baseball that you played as an amateur was not the same as the one that you played as a professional," he said. "When they start talking to us about fundamentals, I already came with Andrés Reiner's class, who had to do everything running, jostling, you're never tired here. They would say that Venezuelans never get tired," he stressed. "At that time I was supposedly playing shortstop. I would stand there, but I didn't have those good hands. That's why they sent me to the outfield."

One of his early mentors was legendary Dominican outfielder César Cedeño, a four-time All-Star, five-time Gold Glove winner, and a Houston Astros Hall of Famer.

"At that time I was a switch-hitter. I stood right-handed, and César Cedeño saw that I always took BP from the left side. He asked me, 'How come you hit with both hands and the BP is always left-handed? From now on you are only going to hit left-handed.'… And I ended up hitting left-handed."

"César Cedeño helped me a lot in hitting. I was taking his advice and I had a good season."

Abreu played right field throughout his career and was listed as 6 feet tall and 220 pounds.

Abreu debuted with a .301 average in the Gulf Coast League in 1991, and continued to climb the circuit each year, from Class A to Triple A in 1996, also trying to apply what he saw on television from his idols.

"When I began to watch baseball games, I liked Ozzie Guillén a lot, because of the way he played, because he was a great leader and knew how to use his skills. He was not looking to do more than he could do," he said.

"Also Roberto Alomar. I saw Roberto Alomar a lot, when he went to the World Series with Toronto, also when he was in Baltimore. When I was in the minor leagues, the Baltimore games were on TV a lot and I watched him hit, how he stole the bases, how he played the ball with ease and elegance, with confidence and intelligence, he was always ahead of the plays, and Roberto Alomar was one of the people I admired. The other was Ken Griffey Jr. So I saw those patterns and I wanted to get details from them to continue growing on the game and be like them."

In 1993, when Abreu was 19, he received one of the hardest blows in his life, the death of his father, Nelson, to whom he wanted to pay a lifetime tribute.

A five-tool threat, Bobby Abreu combined power, speed, and plate discipline across 18 major-league seasons. He finished with over 2,400 hits, 400 stolen bases, and nearly 1,500 walks. (Jerry Coli / Dreamstime)

"My dad was called 'El Comedulce.' When he passed away, in 1993, I asked the media to call me 'El Comedulce' in his honor," he said.

Abreu not only honored his father with his nickname, but with greater determination in his goal of reaching the major leagues. In 1994 he hit .303 in Double-A and developed more power by hitting 16 home runs and driving in 73 runs.

Little by little he earned his place among the best prospects in the organization and as a more complete player, stealing 24 bases in Triple A in 1996.

"I was looking for my opportunity to reach the major leagues," he said during spring training. "I think as you go through the minor leagues and start watching the big-league games, you say, 'Hey, I want to be there.' More when you go to spring training."

"The Astros had all four fields and the major-league field next to it. That's where I want to be," he recalled. "You have to work hard and you tried harder every day to get to the major leagues."

The reward for that effort came in the last month of the 1996 season, after Abreu batted .283 with 86 runs scored, 14 doubles, 16 triples, 13 home runs, and 68 RBIs in 132 games in Triple A.

"(Manager) Tim Tolman calls me to his office, and as a baseball player, you don't want to go to the office. What did I do wrong? Are they going to scold me or are they going to kick me out?" he recalled. "He tells me, 'Congratulations, because you are going to Pittsburgh.'"

The Astros were finishing a series against the Pirates. "I didn't believe it. The first thing I did was cry, give (Tolman) a hug and call my mom to say, 'Mom, you have a major-league son.'"

His big-league debut came at Three Rivers Stadium, where he couldn't hide his nerves during batting practice.

"I remember that in my first BP I didn't hit the ball out of the cage. It was pure fly and fly. The nerve hits you," he said. "In my first at-bat, I was shaking. My legs were shaking. (Manager) Terry Collins tells me, 'Abreu, you're going to hit.' I was so nervous."

Abreu was called to pinch-hit for reliever Chris Holt in the top of the ninth inning, but he didn't get to have his first at-bat.

"That first at-bat they had a left-handed pitcher in the bullpen and Mike Simms was the right-handed pinch-hitter. They brought in the lefty (Dan Plesac) and they brought in Simms (as a pinch-hitter). It took me like 13 at-bats to get that first hit."[6]

His first hit came in his 11th major-league game, on September 24, 1996, at the Astrodome against the New York Mets. His first victim was Bobby Jones; pinch-hitting in the eighth, Abreu sent a line drive to right field. Afterward, he started three games, getting a hit in each, with his first double and his first RBI coming September 28 against the Florida Marlins.

The next season, 1997, Abreu became the starting right fielder for the Astros and after a slow start in the first two months, in which he averaged .245, an injury took him out of action and he underwent surgery in Houston to remove the hook of the hamate bone in his right wrist.

He returned to the field on July 3, but in a substitute role, so in the middle of the month he went to the minor leagues to get more playing time, returning to the majors in September.

Despite Abreu's being well regarded within the organization, the Astros did not protect him and he was taken in the November 18, 1998, expansion draft to stock the Tampa Bay Devil Rays and Arizona Diamondbacks.

"I was playing in Venezuela. My agent, Peter Greenberg, called me and he tells me, 'Tampa picked you in the draft.' I was happy, because I was going to have the opportunity to play," Abreu said. "Two hours later he calls me again. 'Peter, what happened? Bob, I have other news for you: They traded you to Philly, they traded you for Kevin Stocker, it's a good trade for you.'"

In a matter of minutes he had moved through three organizations, ultimately ending up with the Phillies, whom he joined in the spring of 1998.

"I went to spring training in Clearwater, in '98, and I had a good season my first year," recalled Abreu, who was the undisputed starter and hit .312 with 17 home runs, 74 RBIs, and 19 stolen bases, showing signs of a potential that was about to explode.

In Venezuela, in the Winter League, he also displayed that superstar potential and won the batting title with a record .419 average while playing for Leones del Caracas.

"It was very important, because I remember that that year I went to work against lefties, because I was hitting well against righties, but I needed to hit lefties better and use the right midfield and hit home runs toward the opposite field," he recalled. "In Venezuela, I faced many left-handed pitchers and that allowed me to work on that. Winter ball helped me a lot to work on what I was failing."

The following season, 2000, Abreu established himself as an undisputed figure for the Phillies by finishing with the third-best batting average in the National League (.335), setting career highs in all offensive categories by finishing with 118 runs scored, 183 hits, 35 doubles, 11 triples (NL leader), 20 home runs, 93 RBIs, and 109 walks, in what was the first of his eight consecutive seasons with 100 or more walks.

"That was a great season. I was fighting for the batting title with Larry Walker and Luis González. I went 20-20 (homers and steals), drove in 93 runs," Abreu said. "It was a very good year. I was hitting well all year."

In 2001 Abreu became the first Venezuelan to join the 30-30 club, after finishing with 31 home runs and 36 stolen bases, an achievement he repeated in 2004, when he hit 30 homers and stole 40 bases, the year in which he participated in his first All-Star Game and won the Silver Slugger Award, repaying in a big way the contract the organization gave him in 2002 for five seasons and $64 million.

"That season you wanted to show more of yourself. You had been doing seasons of 40 doubles, you stole 20 to 30 bases, you hit 20 homers, but you wanted more, you wanted to teach more about your game and show all your tools. Hitting, stealing bases, playing defense, taking bases on balls, I tried to get better in all my numbers and be an all-around player."

Already one of the most complete players in the major leagues, Abreu experienced one of the most exciting moments of his career when he was chosen for his second All-Star Game, in Detroit, where he participated in a memorable Home Run Derby.

"I didn't expect it, but when they told me, 'You're in the Home Run Derby. You are going to represent Venezuela. It was the only one that was made representing countries. You have to understand what it means to represent your country and the weight you have to do things well.'"[7]

Abreu reached the All-Star Game with 18 home runs, but he had no expectations other than putting on a good show for his country.

"They tell me, 'Bob, you're the first to hit.'... My legs were shaking, I was nervous, and I was just asking to hit a little home run in Detroit, in a huge stadium, completely packed, and I knew that all of Venezuela was watching me on television."

"When I took out the first ball I felt a relief. I was already calm. Then, with the pitcher I had, Ramón Henderson, I started hitting home runs and that was crazy."

Abreu stole the show and hit 24 homers in the first round, breaking the record of 15 set by Miguel Tejada.

"Venezuela was paralyzed watching the Home Run Derby. I was just asking God and my dad to help me hit at least a home run. One came out and I began to break some of Miguel Tejada's records," he said.

Abreu hit six home runs in the second round to advance to the final with catcher Iván Rodríguez, whom he dispatched with 11 homers, also a record at that time, surpassing the Puerto Rican's five, and ended up hoisting the championship trophy with a total of 41 home runs, a record for the event at the time.

"It was a very beautiful moment that I lived, a very special moment," he commented. "I was living a dream. I woke up from that dream when I got to the hotel. When I turned on the television, ESPN was showing what I did, and I was crying alone in the room."

In 2006, Abreu entered the next to last year of his contract with Philadelphia, making him one of the most coveted pieces on the trade market that season.

On July 30, 2006, he waived his no-trade clause and accepted a trade to the New York Yankees, where he would have a chance to play in the postseason, something he hadn't done since 1997 with the Astros.

"I thought I was going to spend my entire career with Philadelphia. That opportunity was given to go to the Yankees, to the Big Apple, Yankee Stadium. ... "I had the no-trade clause in my contract and I agreed to go to New York."

Abreu went to the Yankees along with Cory Lidle in a trade for C.J. Henry, Matt Smith, Jesus Sanchez, and Carlos Monasterios.

He made the most of that big stage and he began to perform. He came from Philadelphia hitting .277 and in 58 games with his new club he hit .330 to help the Yankees capture the AL East championship with a 97-65 record.

In the Division Series, Abreu hit .333 with four RBIs, but he couldn't stop New York from being eliminated by the Detroit Tigers in four games.

In 2007 he hit .283 with 40 doubles and 101 RBIs to help the Yankees return to the postseason, but again they lost in the Division Series, also in four games, to the Cleveland Indians.

New York took the option of his 2008 contract for $16 million and the Venezuelan responded with a .296 average, 100 runs scored, 39 doubles, 20 home runs, and 100 RBIs, but they did not offer him a new deal and he became a free agent.

"It was a very nice experience playing for the Yankees, because of the city, the organization, that name weighs heavily," said Abreu. "It was nice to play with 'The Captain' (Derek Jeter), with Alex Rodríguez, and I met two people who were my buddies, like Robinson Canó and Melky Cabrera."

"I thought I was going to re-sign with the Yankees, because I was a free agent. It didn't happen and I signed with Anaheim," said Abreu, who reached a deal for one season and $5 million.

Abreu didn't slow down and for the seventh straight season he finished with at least 100 RBIs (103) and hit .293, helping the Angels win the AL West title.

In 2009 he played in the postseason for the last time and in the Division Series he was 5-for-9 with four runs scored, two doubles and an RBI to be key in the three-game sweep against the Boston Red Sox.

In the American League Championship Series, Abreu had to face his former Yankees teammates, who ended up winning the ALCS and the World Series, both in six games.

"We went to the playoffs, to the league finals to play against the Yankees. We lost that year, when they were champions, and I didn't have that luck to win a World Series," Abreu said. "I have been blessed to play alongside great players. Playing with Vladimir (Guerrero) was excellent. There was Maicer Izturis, (Mike) Napoli. I was one of the oldest and we enjoyed a lot."

After the 2009 season, Abreu signed a two-year, $19 million deal with the Angels, with a $9 million option for 2012 if he had 550 plate appearances in 2011 or a combined 1,200 in 2010-11.

In 2010 he hit 41 doubles and 20 home runs, but for the first time since 1998 he fell short of 100 RBIs, and for the first time since 1997 his batting average dipped below .280; he hit just .253.

In 2011 his performance dipped further as he hit .253 with just 30 doubles, 8 home runs, and 60 RBIs, but he reached 585 plate appearances to exercise the option on his contract.

In 2012 Abreu's place in the lineup was no longer guaranteed. With Albert Pujols as designated hitter and with Torii Hunter and Vernon Wells covering the outfield corners, Abreu didn't have a day-to-day game in manager Mike Scioscia's lineup.

On April 27, after Abreu hit just .208 (5-for-24), with three doubles and five RBIs in eight games, the Angels released him to call up their best prospect, Mike Trout.

"I arrived in 2009 and he started in the major leagues in 2011. I saw him in spring training and he was with us playing up front. He was a very mature person in the game, respectful in the game and respectful as a person. Excellent person," Abreu said of Trout. "He is a very humble person, who respects everyone, and when I saw him in spring training I knew that when they gave him the opportunity to play he was going to lose sight of them."

So it was. Trout's impact was immediate and at the age of 20 he batted .326 and hit 30 home runs, leading the majors in runs scored (129) and stolen bases (49), unanimously taking the AL Rookie of the Year Award, and being second in the voting for the Most Valuable Player Award, removing the unanimity of the winner of the first Triple Crown since 1967, Miguel Cabrera.

Abreu didn't last long without a job, nor did he have to make a lengthy move, after signing as a free agent with the Los Angeles Dodgers on May 4, 2012.

With the Dodgers he also didn't see regular action and in 92 games he hit .246.

Unable to get a satisfactory contract, Abreu did not play in the majors in 2013; he played winter ball in 2013-2014 with Leones del Caracas, showing that he still had one more cartridge to burn.

In Venezuela, he batted .322/.416/.461, with 10 doubles, 3 triples, 3 home runs, and 28 RBIs in 50 games. In the postseason he batted .441/.533/.932, with 22 runs scored, 5 doubles, 8 home runs, 26 RBIs, and 13 walks in 16 games.

On his way to turning 40, the Philadelphia Phillies granted Abreu a minor-league deal on January 21, 2014, with an invitation to spring training. Abreu was released on March 27 after hitting .244/.404/.366 in 17 games.

On March 31, the New York Mets gave Abreu a minor-league contract. At Triple-A Las Vegas, he hit .360/.473/.507, with 8 doubles, 1 home run and 18 RBIs in 26 games, and the Mets brought him up.

In 78 games with the Mets, Abreu batted .248. He played his last major-league game on September 28, the last day of the regular season, against the Astros, the team that signed him and the one he made his major-league debut in 1996.

"Something curious. … Fate is fate. When I get to the big leagues, I got my first hit against the Mets and my manager was Terry Collins. And I gave my last hit with the Mets, my manager was Terry Collins and I gave it against the Houston Astros," said Abreu, who played right field that day.

In his first at-bat he grounded out to second base. In the third inning he took a walk, the 1,476th of his career, while in the fifth inning, against Nick Tropeano, he singled to left field, his 2,470th hit to end his career, leaving Citi Field to a standing ovation.

"In baseball the first at-bat and the last at-bat are the most nervous at-bats you have. In that last at-bat I was very anxious and excited, I had to control myself," Abreu recalled. "After I hit that hit to left field, Terry Collins gives me the sign, 'What do you want to do?' I told him, 'I'm done. I retire here.' I retired through the big door, with the hit I needed to say goodbye."

Collins, Abreu's first and last major-league manager, smiled and replaced him with a pinch-runner. Another Venezuelan born in Maracay, José Altuve, the Houston Astros second baseman, went to say goodbye to one of the best baseball players that Venezuela has produced.

"Altuve went to first and gave me a congratulatory hug. I couldn't control myself. At that moment there was an ovation in the New York stadium," he recalled. "It gave me chills. I didn't know whether to cry or laugh, but it was very nice to say goodbye that way, with a very pleasant ovation, because they appreciated the way I played ball and I enjoyed it to the fullest."

Despite not winning numerous individual awards, only a Gold Glove and a Silver Slugger, and participating in only two All-Star Games, Abreu retired as one of the most consistent players of his generation, with extraordinary hitting ability and an outstanding discipline that allowed him to play eight consecutive seasons with 100 or more bases on balls, and finish with a lifetime average of .291/.395/.475, with 1,453 runs scored, 574 doubles, 288 home runs, 1,363 RBIs, and 400 stolen bases.

Abreu is one of only four players in history with at least 200 home runs, 1,200 walks, and 400 stolen bases, joining Hall of Famers Joe Morgan and Rickey Henderson, as well as Barry Bonds.

Abreu also joined Bonds in the exclusive group of five players in major-league history with at least 1,000 runs scored, 1,000 RBIs, 2,000 hits, 1,000 walks, 250 home runs, and 400 stolen bases.[8]

Abreu first appeared on the Hall of Fame ballot in 2020, obtaining 22 votes for 5.5 percent, enough to stay on the ballot.

In 2021 his vote rose to 8.7 percent and in 2022 it fell to 8.6 percent. It climbed to 15.4 percent in 2023, fell again with 14.8 percent in 2024 and rising to his best voting in 2025, 19.5 percent.

His consistency has slowly earned Abreu some support for his Cooperstown candidacy.

"I think we have to keep thinking positive. I very respectfully say that there are numbers. I'm placed with select groups, with Craig Biggio, Roberto Alomar, Rickey Henderson. Barry Bonds, Bobby Bonds. ... So you see that you do have numbers, because there are people who are in the Hall of Fame and you are with them, so you see that you have numbers to be there," he said. "There is a group with Willie Mays and myself, with 150 games and more played for 13 consecutive seasons. ... You have to stay positive and ask God to make it happen."

Although he still doesn't have enough support to enter Cooperstown, Abreu has already achieved immortality in Philadelphia, where he was inducted into the Phillies Wall of Fame in 2019.

"When they called me to tell me that I was going to the Wall of Fame, I said, 'I did it. So many stars that have played for that team and your mind takes you back to your childhood, to that young man who grew up and wanted to play ball, wanted to play major-league baseball and then it takes you to put a plaque where you are immortal, because your immortality is reflected there with that team, and you just say, 'Thank you, Lord, for all of this. It is a blessing from God to give me that gift.'"

And while he waits for sufficient support to join the only Venezuelan in the Cooperstown Hall of Fame, Luis Aparicio, Abreu dedicates himself to his business as an entrepreneur, as owner of two professional teams in Venezuela, Panteras de Miranda (basketball) and Mineros de Guayana (soccer), without abandoning the sport he loves, baseball, helping to train new talents in his own academy, the Bob Abreu Baseball Academy 53.

"The academy is a dream I've always had. I always wanted to have a facility where I can provide the kids with the knowledge I've gained throughout my career, as well as teach them all the techniques they need to help them achieve their dream of signing and going far," Abreu said of his academy, located in San Diego, Carabobo state, which is part of the MLB Trainer Partnership Program.

"I want to prepare them, educate them in every aspect. At the academy, we give them English classes, because that's important for their entrepreneurship, and they also have school classes. It's something different from what we see in Venezuela at the academy level, with a complete facility to provide the kids with comprehensive development so they can achieve their dreams."[9]

SOURCES

In addition to the sources cited in the Notes, the author consulted baseballreference.com, MLB.com, espn.com, and latimes.com.

NOTES

1   A nickname meaning a person that eats a lot of candy.

2   Carlos Baerga: entrevista con el ex Grandes Ligas Bobby Abreu. June 28, 2020. https://www.youtube.com/watch?v=RoVjv2mVSeg. Unless otherwise indicated, all quotations attributed to Bobby Abreu come from this interview.

3   La Estrella Invitada en IG: Bob Abreu. August 5, 2020. https://www.youtube.com/watch?v=nN7PqmPh99Y.

4   Arepas is a type of flatbread made of ground maize dough stuffed with a filling like cheese, meat, chicken, etc., and is a very popular meal in Venezuela.

5   La Estrella Invitada en IG: Bob Abreu.

6   Abreu had 11 plate appearances before his first base hit.

7   La Estrella Invitada en IG: Bob Abreu. All quotations related to the Home Run Derby are from this interview.

8   The other four are Barry Bonds, Rickey Henderson, Craig Biggio, and Joe Morgan.

9   Author interview with Bobby Abreu, August 7, 2023.

EDGARDO ALFONZO

BY RORY COSTELLO

The New York Mets were strong contenders in 1999 and 2000, and one of their core members in those years was Venezuelan infielder Edgardo Alfonzo. "Fonzie" had his two best seasons with the bat and was steady in the field. At his peak, the *New York Times* described him as "a versatile and dependable player whose combination of a robust batting average, solid power and flawless defense could make him the premier second baseman in the major leagues."[1]

Alfonzo was mentioned alongside Derek Jeter in 2000: "Cooperstown could be their final stops."[2] He was just 27 going into the 2001 season, and it was reasonable to expect several more prime years. Yet he never produced at the same level again, owing in part to a string of injuries. His big-league career ended in 2006, but he played on in the minors, independent ball, Mexico, Japan, and his homeland as late as 2013. Alfonzo then returned to the Mets' minor-league organization, becoming a coach and manager.

Edgardo Antonio Alfonzo Pino was born on November 8, 1973 in Santa Teresa del Tuy, in the state of Miranda, southeast of Venezuela's capital, Caracas. His parents were Edgar Alfonzo, a truck driver for a medical supply company, and Mercedes Pino, a preschool teacher. Edgardo was the youngest of four children, three of whom were sons.

Baseball runs in the Alfonzo family. The oldest brother, Edgar Jr., played in the minors from 1985 through 1996, also becoming a minor-league coach and manager. Middle brother Robert (born in 1972), a Mets farmhand for 70 games in 1993 and 1994, became a scout.[3] Three of Alfonzo's nephews – Edgar Alfonzo III, Giovanny Alfonzo, and Javier Betancourt – also played in the minors and the Venezuelan winter league. A second cousin, Eliézer Alfonzo, was a big-league catcher for parts of six seasons from 2006 through 2011.

Alfonzo grew up in Soapire, a tiny town of perhaps 500 people just north of Santa Teresa del Tuy.[4] He described his youth simply in 1998: "Go to school, play ball, nothing else." He credited brother Edgar, six years his senior, with teaching him the game.[5] By that time Edgar Sr., who did not play baseball himself, had changed his mind about letting his sons do so. Previously, Edgar Jr. had been able to play only when work took his father out of town.[6]

Around the time Edgardo turned 11 years old, Edgar became a professional ballplayer, joining the winter league's Caracas Leones for the 1984-85 season. Edgardo therefore saw his first pro ballgame.[7] That Leones club included various local heroes: Andrés Galarraga, Tony Armas, and Omar Vizquel (like Edgar Alfonzo, then a 17-year-old rookie). Their veteran leader was Gonzalo Márquez, who died in a tragic car accident in December 1984.

Vizquel, one of the finest shortstops ever, was a role model for young Edgardo (who also pitched as a youth). So was another first-rate Venezuelan shortstop, Dave Concepción. Vizquel, Alfonzo, and Ozzie Guillén all chose to wear uniform #13 in Concepción's honor.[8]

At the age of 16 in 1990, Edgardo got his first big-league tryout, courtesy of Edgar. It was with the Los Angeles Dodgers, in front of scout and former star Twins pitcher Camilo Pascual at Estadio Universitario de Caracas, home field of the Leones. By the end of the workout, Alfonzo had developed swelling in his knee, making Pascual leery about signing him.[9]

Later that year, Edgar helped his brother again by talking to Gregorio Machado, a Mets scout in Venezuela. Edgardo went to the city of Valencia in November 1990 and tried out before another Mets scout, Julio Román. He made a good impression, and Román wanted to see him again. After the second tryout, Román signed Alfonzo in February 1991 for $10,000.[10]

It took Alfonzo four seasons to reach the top level. He hit .331 in rookie ball in the Gulf Coast League, earning team MVP honors.[11] He followed by batting .350 in 78 games in Class A in 1992. As he rose through the Mets system, his primary position was shortstop, although he also played the other infield spots. As it developed, third base became his primary position in the majors, followed by second. At Double-A Binghamton in 1994, skipper John Tamargo called Alfonzo "a manager's dream" in view of his all-around skills, approach to the game, and how he dealt with other people.[12]

Meanwhile, starting in the 1992-93 season, Alfonzo was also playing winter ball in Venezuela. His first team was Navegantes de Magallanes. At his brother's suggestion, he went with Magallanes, archrival of Caracas, because it would have been harder to win a spot on the Leones roster.[13] Alfonzo had a rough time in the field early on, once committing (by his count) 12 errors at shortstop in one week. Yet the atmosphere at home continued "a hardening process that made him unflappable." John Tamargo, who also managed Magallanes in the 1990s, said, "It makes New York City look like Romper Room."[14]

Going home also gave Alfonzo time with his sweetheart, Delia Campos, who had grown up down the street from him in Soapire.[15] They were married the day after the 1994-95 Venezuelan winter season ended. Alfonzo had pondered for three straight winters, wondering whether the time was right and asking his agent, Peter Greenberg, for advice. He decided to wait until he had gained more stability in baseball. When the Mets placed him on their 40-man roster in November 1994, he felt he really had a future.[16]

At that time, however, Major League Baseball was in the midst of its most crippling strike. There was a side effect on players who weren't U.S. citizens. When the Labor Department certified the strike, it authorized the Immigration and Naturalization Service to block any foreigner from getting the type of visa (typically the P-1 classification) needed to play in the majors. This kept the owners from importing strikebreakers, but Alfonzo and others couldn't return to the United States until the strike was settled.[17]

The strike officially ended on April 2, 1995, and Alfonzo jumped from Binghamton to the majors (he didn't play in Triple-A until an injury rehab assignment in 2001). Opening Day for the Mets that year, April 26, was in Colorado against the Rockies. Alfonzo's most vivid memory of that day was the cold. It snowed before the game, and the groundskeepers had to shovel out the field.[18]

Alfonzo had begun to play second base in 1994 after flashy shortstop Rey Ordóñez was promoted, so he backed up Jeff Kent there. He had also been asked to play third base that winter so Bobby Bonilla could spend more time in left field. Bonilla was traded in late July, opening up more time for the rookie. However, Alfonzo missed most of August with a herniated disc in his back. He returned in early September and finished the year hitting .278 with 4 homers and 41 RBIs in 101 games.

Alfonzo posted very similar numbers (.261-4-40 in 123 games) in 1996. The Mets moved Jeff Kent to third that year and made José Vizcaíno the regular second baseman, Alfonzo backing up both of them. On July 29, however, the Mets sent both Kent and Vizcaíno to Cleveland in the deal that brought Carlos Baerga to New York. Baerga was a second baseman, but the Mets put him at first base and made Alfonzo the starter at second.

Edgardo and Delia also welcomed their first child, Eduardo Luis, that year. The second Alfonzo son, Daniel Antonio, arrived during the 1999 season.

Alfonzo began to emerge with the bat in 1997. He hit .315 in 518 at-bats, with 10 homers and 72 RBIs. Baerga was back at second base, and Alfonzo shifted to third. Back home in Venezuela that winter, he had become a celebrity, and longtime observers of the game there were already ranking him among the best third basemen in the nation's history. Magallanes shortstop Álvaro Espinoza (a Mets teammate in 1996) said, "Hitting-wise, defense-wise. He's the best player in this league right now." His increased confidence was also visible in a greater role in the clubhouse.[19]

Alfonzo remained at the hot corner for New York in 1998, and though his average slipped to .278, his home run production climbed to 17. He also came in second in the NL Gold Glove voting for the second straight year.[20] The Mets viewed him as a key part of their team and signed him to a four-year contract worth $18.4 million.[21]

Previously, the team had signed veteran star Robin Ventura to be their new third baseman. They'd also let the disappoint-

ing Baerga become a free agent, and Alfonzo moved back to second base. Rey Ordóñez was a Gold Glover at short, and first baseman John Olerud was also a superb fielder. The four of them in total committed just 31 errors in 1999. Tom Verducci of *Sports Illustrated* called it "an infield that makes up in agility and surehandedness what it lacks in speed."[22] The quartet was pictured on the magazine's cover that September 6, with the caption, "The Best Infield Ever?"

Not long before, the *New York Times* had compared Alfonzo to the other premier second basemen of the day. "Roberto Alomar is slicker, Craig Biggio is grittier. Jeff Kent possesses more power and Jay Bell is having a special season. However, Alfonzo might be the most complete player at his position this year."[23]

Indeed, Alfonzo's batting had also stepped up markedly. He set career highs in homers (27) and RBIs (108) while batting .304 and slugging .502. He won the NL's Silver Slugger award for second basemen that year. On August 30 at the Houston Astrodome, he had the finest single game of his career, going 6-for-6 with three homers. He added a double and two singles for 16 total bases; he also scored six times.

Alfonzo had earned recognition as a clutch hitter, too. His average with runners on base was significantly higher than with the bases empty. Manager Bobby Valentine said, "He gets in an RBI situation and doesn't worry about it, he just hits."[24] Looking back, Alfonzo cited his patience and selectivity at the plate. "My mentality was, try to go the other way…let the ball come to me and explode to it."[25]

The Mets and Cincinnati Reds finished the 1999 regular season with identical records of 96-66, second in their respective divisions. There was only one wild-card playoff spot at that time, so the teams faced each other in a tiebreaker. Rickey Henderson led off the game at Cinergy Field with a single, and Alfonzo homered off Steve Parris. That was all Mets starter Al Leiter needed, as he threw a two-hit shutout.

New York advanced to the NL Division Series. Alfonzo was the hitting star of Game One with two homers: a first-inning solo shot off Arizona ace Randy Johnson and the game-winning grand slam in the top of the ninth off Bobby Chouinard. He also homered in the decisive Game Four, which sent New York into the NL Championship Series against Atlanta. Alfonzo went 6-for-27 with four doubles as the Mets lost to the Braves in six games.

Alfonzo made his only appearance in the All-Star game in 2000. Although his homer and RBI totals dipped slightly (25 and 94), he hit .324 and set career highs in slugging (.542) and on-base percentage (.425). That June, the *New York Post* quoted teammate Matt Franco on Alfonzo: "He's just a model of consistency. He is a great teammate. He is on an even keel. He plays immaculate defense [though he never did win a Gold Glove]. He is a tremendous, tremendous hitter. He's just the best player we have."[26]

During the 2000 playoffs, a *New York Times* article said that Alfonzo, by clubhouse consensus, was the team's leader in October. He burnished his reputation for clutch hitting that postseason, especially in Game Three of the NL Division Series against San Francisco. The Giants were four outs away from going ahead, two games to one. They brought in closer Robb Nen, who had not blown a save in four months. Alfonzo stroked a game-tying double, and the Mets won five innings later. Teammate Darryl Hamilton said, "When we get in a situation where we need a hit...everybody on this team wants Fonzie at the plate."[27]

When the Mets defeated the St. Louis Cardinals to win the NL pennant in 2000, Alfonzo insisted that his brother Edgar be in the clubhouse to join in the celebration. They shared a bottle of champagne, hugging and crying joyfully together.[28] The New York Yankees beat the Mets in five games in the World Series, though, and Alfonzo managed just 3 hits in 21 at-bats.

Coming off a career year, Alfonzo was shedding his "unheralded" and "underrated" labels. Alas, his batting fell off markedly in 2001. He hit just .243, with 17 homers and 49 RBIs. An injured back landed him on the disabled list from mid-June to early July but troubled him much of the season.[29]

Despite the down year, in spring 2002 the Mets offered Alfonzo a three-year contract extension worth $18 million, which he turned down.[30] His average rebounded (.308), but his homer and RBI totals (16 and 56) were still well below his peak. His left hand bothered him for much of the early season after he dove for a ball.[31] He also spent time on the disabled list again, this time with a strained oblique muscle in August. The 2002 season also featured a return to third base, since the Mets had traded Robin Ventura and acquired Roberto Alomar to play second.

Alfonzo became a free agent that fall. He very much wanted to stay in New York, which had become home, and would have for a two-year contract worth $17 million. However, their best

offer was two years for $11 million. As it turned out, he got a longer contract with bigger money from the San Francisco Giants: a four-year, $26 million deal, topping offers from the A's and Padres.[32] Meanwhile, the Mets unsuccessfully wooed Japanese third baseman Norihiro Nakamura (who flopped after signing with the Dodgers in 2005).

Alfonzo showed his appreciation of Mets fans by buying ad space on top of 30 New York City cabs for 30 days. The message read, "Fonzie ♥ NY / Edgardo Thanks You!" The ads hit the street on Valentine's Day 2003.[33]

Alfonzo replaced departed free agent David Bell at third base in San Francisco.[34] His first year there was solid but unspectacular: .259 with 13 homers and 81 RBIs in 142 games. He struggled in the first half but picked up as the season progressed. The Giants won the NL West that year but got knocked out in the Division Series by the eventual World Series champs, the Florida Marlins. Alfonzo, however, had an excellent NLDS: 9-for-17 with four doubles.

The 2004 season was fairly similar for Alfonzo, with a .289 average, 11 homers and 77 RBIs. Again he got off to a slow start, this time because of a hamstring pull in spring training.[35] He warmed up in May, though, and hit more consistently throughout the year.

Alfonzo started well in his third year with San Francisco. He was hitting .306 when he strained his quadriceps in June. He returned a month later, but by then Pedro Feliz was getting most of the time at third base. Alfonzo hit .240 the rest of the season. He asked to be traded "somewhere where they can trust me, believe in me and have faith in me."[36]

That December, the Giants granted the wish, trading Alfonzo to the Los Angeles Angels of Anaheim for 40-year-old Steve Finley. In retrospect, both were labeled high-priced disappointments. San Francisco GM Brian Sabean speculated that among other factors, Alfonzo had some "culture shock" after leaving the Mets. He added, "He gave the effort, it's just the performance didn't turn out the way it could have."[37]

In March 2006, Alfonzo represented his homeland in the World Baseball Classic. He hit 5-for-16 with a homer and two RBIs in five games, but Venezuela was eliminated in the second round.

After Alfonzo joined the Angels in camp, manager Mike Scioscia sought to maximize his playing time, saying, "This guy is a professional hitter when he's right."[38] But when the regular season started, Alfonzo went ice-cold, going 5-for-50. He found his reserve role frustrating. Angels GM Bill Stoneman tried to trade Alfonzo but found no takers, even when he offered to absorb the veteran's salary. Thus, the club released Fonzie on May 21. He was thankful, saying, "I didn't want to be stuck here for the whole year."[39]

Four days later, the Toronto Blue Jays signed Alfonzo to a minor-league contract and assigned him to New Hampshire in the Eastern League (Class AA). Jays manager John Gibbons knew him from his time as an instructor in the Mets farm system and recommended the signing to GM J.P. Ricciardi.[40]

A fan favorite in Queens, Edgardo Alfonzo anchored the Mets' infield during their late-'90s playoff runs. An All-Star in 2000, he was known for clutch hitting and steady defense. (Jerry Coli / Dreamstime)

Alfonzo got just six hits in 37 at-bats for Toronto, though, and was released on June 12. "The guys loved him," said Gibbons, "But he's slowed down a little bit. No question. It's a business."[41]

Alfonzo's next stop was independent ball. He signed with the Bridgeport Bluefish of the Atlantic League. After just four games with the Bluefish, the Mets gave him another chance, assigning him to their top farm club, Norfolk in the International League. Mets special assistant Tony Bernazard said that Fonzie would play all over the infield and that bringing him back to New York was "part of the equation."[42] However, Alfonzo hit just .241 with 3 homers and 19 RBIs in 42 games and was not called up. He was granted free agency that October.

At this juncture in Alfonzo's career, the Venezuelan league gained renewed importance for him. For much of his big-league prime, his action at home was minimal, first because the Mets were concerned about injury risk and later because he stayed in the U.S. for off-season training.[43] He appeared in just eight games for Magallanes in the six seasons from 1998-99 through 2003-04, and 33 in the two winters after that. In 2006-07, though, he got into 32 games.

Alfonzo returned to the Atlantic League in the summer of 2007, joining the Long Island Ducks. That June, he noted that "a lot of factors" had led to his decline, even though in his own mind, he was still the player he used to be with the Mets. He added, "Last year, I…began developing some bad habits. I still need to get my timing and confidence back. But I think it's coming around." Ducks manager Dave LaPoint and co-owner/first base coach Bud Harrelson believed that Fonzie would get another shot in the majors. "He's just too good," said LaPoint. "He can help a lot of teams."[44]

It didn't work out that way, though, since Alfonzo's play was reasonably solid but not eye-catching. He returned to his original position, playing 62 games at shortstop, as well as 25 at third. In 105 games overall, he hit .266 with 5 homers and 56 RBIs.

During the winter of 2007-08, Alfonzo played 54 games for Magallanes. He showed that he could still be productive, hitting .335 with 5 homers and 32 RBIs. That earned him a minor-league contract and an invitation to spring training from the Texas Rangers. However, the Rangers released him in late March. Alfonzo signed with Tigres de Quintana Roo in the Mexican League and played 55 games in that circuit. He returned to the Long Island Ducks in June and hit well (.329 with 8 homers and 27 RBIs in 59 games).

The 2008-09 season was Alfonzo's best at home. He hit .320, and his 8 homers and 42 RBIs were both winter-career highs. As a result, Japan's most prominent franchise, the Yomiuri Giants, gave him a tryout at their spring training camp. It went well enough that he signed a one-year contract for $380,000. Alfonzo called it an honor to be with the Giants and said he'd play his hardest to contribute.[45] He remembered playing Opening Day 2000 with the Mets in Tokyo and was happy to return. Although he got into just 21 games for Yomiuri, with merely 6 hits in 41 at-bats, his experience was positive. He said

Yomiuri treated him very well and politely, recognizing his work with the Mets.[46] The Giants won the Japan Series in 2009, but if Alfonzo made it to the postseason roster, he did not appear in any games.

Alfonzo still thought he had two or three years of baseball left in him, and went back to Venezuela in hopes of getting another invitation to a big-league camp. His strong preference was for another chance with the Mets, since he still felt loyal toward the team and its fans.[47] After 18 games with Magallanes in 2009-10, Alfonzo gave it a last shot in the Atlantic League in 2010. The Newark Bears, managed by Tim Raines, signed Alfonzo and his old Mets teammate Armando Benitez that March.[48] In 26 games with the Bears, he went 12-for-78.

Following that stint, Alfonzo's remaining playing days came at home. In the winter of 2011-12, after 15 seasons with Magallanes, he moved to a new club, Tigres de Aragua. He played his last 15 games for Aragua in the 2012-13 season. All told, he hit .293 in 594 regular-season games in his homeland, with 28 homers and 244 RBIs. He appeared 13 times in the Venezuelan postseason and was a member of five championship teams. Three of those were with Magallanes (1993-94, 1995-96, and 1996-97). The other two came with Aragua (2007-08, as a playoff reinforcement, and 2011-12).

Alfonzo rejoined the Mets as a club ambassador in 2013. He managed the World team in the All-Star Futures Game at Citi Field in New York on July 14. The following year, he was named to the coaching staff of the Brooklyn Cyclones, a Mets farm team in the NY-Penn League (short season Class A). As bench coach, he learned from manager Tom Gamboa. He was also a minor-league special instructor. In addition, he worked closely with countryman Wilmer Flores (whom his brother Robert had helped sign) in spring training 2014. After Gamboa retired at the end of the 2016 season, Alfonzo became Cyclones skipper in January 2017.[49]

Not long before the Cyclones' 2017 season began, the Mets selected Daniel Alfonzo with their 38th-round pick in the amateur draft. Daniel had played for Bayside High School in Queens, not far from where his father had starred. The young man went to college at Adelphi rather than turn pro.[50]

The Cyclones struggled to a 24-52 mark in 2017, the worst in franchise history since its inception in 2001 (when Edgar Alfonzo managed the team).[51] That August, Alfonzo talked about learning how to develop young pitchers, especially with limited workloads. He also spoke about mental preparation; he emphasized teaching prospects to learn as much as possible about baseball.[52]

A few weeks earlier, Alfonzo was asked about becoming a big-league manager someday. He replied that he too was still in the process of learning and getting to know the game more.[53] He reiterated in March 2018 that he didn't have the mindset yet and that he needed more experience; coaching in the big leagues was an attractive prospect.[54] In his second year, Brooklyn posted a much-improved record of 40-35.

Edgardo Alfonzo was still just 44 at the 2018 season's end, so he should have many years in baseball to come. As for his future roles, he said it best himself: "Who knows? Time will tell."[55]

ACKNOWLEDGMENTS

This biography was reviewed by Jan Finkel and fact-checked by Alan Cohen.

SOURCES

Online

www.pelotabinaria.com.ve (Venezuelan statistics)

http://npb.jp/eng/ (Nippon Professional Baseball site)

NOTES

1   Jack Curry, "The Anonymous Alfonzo," *New York Times*, August 27, 1999: D3.

2   Andrew Marchand, "Amazin' Alfonzo a Pro's Pro," *New York Post*, June 8, 2000 (https://nypost.com/2000/06/08/amazin-alfonzo-a-pros-pro/).

3   Buster Olney, "Lessons of a Sibling Rivalry," *New York Times*, January 14, 1998: C1. The mother's name was shown as "Mercedes Porfiria" in Thomas Hill, "Serious Biz for Fonz," *New York Daily News*, January 18, 1998 (http://www.nydailynews.com/archives/sports/serious-biz-fonz-mets-alfonzo-homeland-hero-venezuela-article-1.794431). Porfiria is most likely her middle name. The fourth Alfonzo sibling is confirmed to be a sister in Alexander Mendoza, "Javier Betancourt Valora la Experiencia con Leones," LVBP.com, January 12, 2015 (https://www.lvbp.com/2062_javier-betancourt-valora-la-experiencia-con-leones). Research has not yet uncovered her name.

4   Henry Schulman, "Bond of brothers," SFGate.com, March 2, 2003 (https://www.sfgate.com/sports/article/Bond-of-brothers-Giants-Alfonzo-shares-success-2666571.php).

5   Hill, "Serious Biz for Fonz."

6   Olney, "Lessons of a Sibling Rivalry."

7   Hill, "Serious Biz for Fonz."

8   Jon Springer and Matthew Silverman, *Mets by the Numbers*, New York: Sports Publishing (2008).

9   Matthew Brownstein, "MMO Exclusive: Mets Great, Edgardo Alfonzo," MetsMerizedOnline.com, April 20, 2018 (https://metsmerizedonline.com/2018/04/mmo-exclusive-mets-great-edgardo-alfonzo.html/).

10   Brownstein, "MMO Exclusive: Mets Great, Edgardo Alfonzo."

11   Schulman, "Bond of brothers."

12   Olney, "Lessons of a Sibling Rivalry."

13   Olney, "Lessons of a Sibling Rivalry."

14   Hill, "Serious Biz for Fonz."

15   Hill, "Serious Biz for Fonz."

16   Jennifer Frey, "Mets Prospect Stuck on Long Honeymoon," *New York Times*, February 22, 1995: B11.

17   Frey, "Mets Prospect Stuck on Long Honeymoon."

18   Brownstein, "MMO Exclusive: Mets Great, Edgardo Alfonzo."

19   Hill, "Serious Biz for Fonz."

20   Marty Noble, "Fonzie: Voters Made Gold Glove Error," *Newsday* (Melville, New York), November 10, 1999 (https://www.newsday.com/sports/fonzie-voters-made-gold-glove-error-1.314426). Ken Caminiti won the NL Gold Glove at third base in 1997 and Scott Rolen in 1998.

21   "Alfonzo Signs 4-Yrs with Mets," CBSNews.com, February 5, 1999 (https://www.cbsnews.com/news/alfonzo-signs-4-yrs-with-mets/).

22   Tom Verducci, "Glove Affair," *Sports Illustrated*, September 6, 1999 (https://www.si.com/vault/1999/09/06/8110328/glove-affair-a-new-man-at-third-has-dressed-up-the-mets-infield-turning-a-good-defense-into-a-great-oneand-new-york-into-a-playoff-contender). The Mets gave up just 20 unearned runs overall in 1999.

23   Curry, "The Anonymous Alfonzo."

24   David Waldstein, "Alfonzo Earning Title of 'Mr. Clutch,'" *New York Post*, July 5, 1999 (https://nypost.com/1999/07/05/alfonzo-earning-title-of-mr-clutch/).

25   Brownstein, "MMO Exclusive: Mets Great, Edgardo Alfonzo."

26   Marchand, "Amazin' Alfonzo a Pro's Pro." Cincinnati's Pokey Reese won the NL Gold Glove at second base in both 1999 and 2000.

27   Tyler Kepner, "When It Matters Most, Alfonzo Is the Mightiest Met," *New York Times*, October 14, 2000: D1.

28   Schulman, "Bond of brothers."

29   Tom Keegan, "Fonzie: I'll Be a Star Again," *New York Post*, August 22, 2001 (https://nypost.com/2001/08/22/fonzie-ill-be-a-star-again/).

30   John Harper, "The Art of the Deal," *New York Daily News*, December 22, 2002 (http://www.nydailynews.com/archives/sports/art-deal-edgardo-alfonzo-new-home-turns-giant-drama-article-1.504215).

31   Michael Morrissey, "Healthy Alfonzo Starting to Find Power," *New York Post*, June 9, 2002 (https://nypost.com/2002/06/09/healthy-alfonzo-starting-to-find-power/).

32   Murray Chass, "With Sigh of Relief, Mets Trade Ordóñez," *New York Times*, December 16, 2002: D7. Harper, "The Art of the Deal."

33   "Fonzie's Swan Song," *Adweek*, February 20, 2003 (https://www.adweek.com/brand-marketing/fonzies-swan-song-61976/).

34   Jeff Kent, San Francisco's star second baseman for the previous six years, had also left as a free agent. But the Giants signed Ray Durham to fill that hole, precluding another position switch for Alfonzo.

35   Glenn Reeves, "Alfonzo's slump is a cause for concern," *East Bay Times*, April 21, 2004 (https://www.eastbaytimes.com/2004/04/21/alfonzos-slump-is-a-cause-for-concern/).

36   Bill Shaikin, "Alfonzo Wants Regular Playing Time," *Los Angeles Times*, March 20, 2006 (http://articles.latimes.com/2006/mar/20/sports/sp-angrep20).

37   Susan Slusser, "Giants Get Finley – Alfonzo to Angels," SFGate.com, December 22, 2005 (https://www.sfgate.com/sports/article/Giants-get-Finley-Alfonzo-to-Angels-2556092.php).

38   Shaikin, "Alfonzo Wants Regular Playing Time."

39   Bill Shaikin, "Alfonzo Is Released; [Jason] Bulger Is Called Up," *Los Angeles Times*, May 21, 2006 (http://articles.latimes.com/2006/may/21/sports/sp-angrep21).

40 "Blue Jays recall Alfonzo, place [John] McDonald on DL," ESPN. com, May 29, 2006 (http://www.espn.com.au/mlb/news/story?id=2462481)

41 "Blue Jays activate McDonald, recall [Russ] Adams, release Alfonzo and outright [Luis] Figueroa," ESPN. com, June 12, 2006 (http://webcache.googleusercontent.com/search?q=cache:LvaPnyiIE84J:www.espn.com/espn/wire%3Fsection%3Dmlb%26id%3D2481108+&cd=4&hl=en&ct=clnk&gl=us).

42 Mark Hale, "Happy Days: Mets Welcome Back Fonzie," *New York Post*, July 16, 2006 (https://nypost.com/2006/07/16/pedro-in-hospital-happy-days-mets-welcome-back-fonzie/).

43 Keegan, "Fonzie: I'll Be a Star Again."

44 Jeff Pearlman, "These Ducks are waiting for 'the call,'" ESPN.com, June 22, 2007 (http://www.espn.com/espn/page2/story?page=pearlman/070621).

45 "Yomiuri Giants give Alfonzo 1-year deal," ESPN.com, February 9, 2009 (http://www.espn.com.au/mlb/news/story?id=3894804).

46 Kevin Kernan, "Alfonzo yearns for one more Amazin' shot," *New York Post*, November 14, 2009 (https://nypost.com/2009/11/14/alfonzo-yearns-for-one-more-amazin-shot/).

47 Kernan, "Alfonzo yearns for one more Amazin' shot."

48 Josh Levitt, "Armando Benitez and Edgardo Alfonzo Back Together Again," BleacherReport.com, March 26, 2010 (https://bleacherreport.com/articles/369265-armando-benitez-and-edgardo-alfonzo-back-together-again).

49 Anthony DiComo, "Franchise favorite Alfonzo to manage Brooklyn," MLB.com, January 5, 2017 (https://www.mlb.com/news/edgardo-alfonzo-to-manage-brooklyn-cyclones/c-212914644).

50 Laura Amato, "Commodores standout opting for college route," *TimesLedger* (Queens, New York), June 23, 2017 (https://www.timesledger.com/stories/2017/24/alfonzobase_2017_06_23_q.html).

51 Edgar Alfonzo also managed the Cyclones in 2007 and 2008.

52 Matthew John, "Edgardo Alfonzo making most of first season as Cyclones skipper," *TimesLedger*, August 19, 2017 (https://www.timesledger.com/stories/2017/33/edgardoalfonzo_2017_08_18_q.html).

53 Jordan Lauterbach, "Ex-Met Edgardo Alfonzo managing Brooklyn Cyclones," *Newsday*, July 21, 2017 (https://www.newsday.com/sports/baseball/mets/ex-met-edgardo-alfonzo-managing-brooklyn-cyclones-1.13813081).

54 Brownstein, "MMO Exclusive: Mets Great, Edgardo Alfonzo."

55 Brownstein, "MMO Exclusive: Mets Great, Edgardo Alfonzo."

HENDERSON ÁLVAREZ

BY RAFAEL DUARTE OLIVEIRA VENANCIO

Henderson Álvarez III wasn't a World Series champion pitcher, but he forged a notable baseball career. Many faithful Miami Marlins fans remember him best from his no-hitter on September 29, 2013, against the Detroit Tigers.

Born in the city of Valencia, in Venezuela's Carabobo State, on April 18, 1990, Álvarez started his professional baseball career in 2007 at the age of 17 after signing on October 17, 2006, with the Toronto Blue Jays as an international undrafted free agent.

The rookie right-handed pitcher made his debut with the Blue Jays in the Dominican Summer League. He started his career with a 1-2 won-lost record and a 5.61 ERA, pitching 25⅔ innings. He is listed at an even 6-feet tall and 205 pounds.

In 2008 Álvarez moved to the rookie-level Gulf Coast League Blue Jays. He almost doubled his innings pitched (46⅓) but with a similar ERA (5.63) and again a negative won-lost record (1-4).

The Blue Jays saw potential and promoted Álvarez to the Lansing Lugnuts in the Class-A Midwest League in 2009. Before that, he pitched in one game in the Venezuelan Winter League for Los Tiburones (Sharks) de La Guaira in the 2008-09 season.

The 2009 season marked another step in Álvarez's climb toward major-league baseball. He was an all-star with Lansing,[1] with a 9-6 won-lost record (his nine wins led the team) and a 3.47 ERA in 124⅓ innings pitched. He struck out 92 and walked 19.

This earned him a promotion to the Dunedin Blue Jays of the advanced Class A-Advanced Florida State League for the 2010 season. He was again an all-star and was selected to appear in the All-Star Futures Game. In 2010 his stats were a bit below those of the year before: an 8-7 won-lost record, 4.33 ERA in 112⅓ innings pitched.

Álvarez returned to his country and played for Los Tiburones in the 2010-11 Venezuelan Winter League as a relief pitcher in 10 games with a 2.13 ERA in 42⅓ innings pitched.

In the United States, 2011 was a key year for Álvarez. He started the season with the Dunedin Blue Jays, throwing 8⅓ innings in two games, then was promoted to the New Hampshire Fisher Cats of the Double-A Eastern League. For a third time he was named an all-star and made a second appearance in the All-Star Futures Game. His stats with the Fisher Cats showed a distinct improvement: an 8-4 won-lost record and and a 2.86 ERA over 88 innings. He struck out 66 and walked 17.

On August 9, 2011, after right-hander Carlos Villanueva was placed on the disabled list with a forearm strain, Álvarez was promoted to the Blue Jays.[2] His first game under manager John Farrell was a start against the Oakland Athletics the next day. He worked 5⅔ innings and gave up three runs on eight hits. The Blue Jays came from behind and won the game, 8-4, the win going to reliever Casey Janssen.

Álvarez lost two August starts when his teammates scored only one run in each. His first major-league win came in Baltimore on August 31, 2011: a 13-0 victory over the Baltimore Orioles. He worked eight innings, allowing only three base hits and walking no one. This was a major landmark for Álvarez: at 21 years and 135 days, he became not only the youngest Blue Jays pitcher to win a game since 1997, but also the youngest starting pitcher to record a win for the Blue Jays since 1979. He finished the season 1-3 but with a solid 3.53 ERA over 63⅔ innings of work.

It was a successful start, even though the team placed only fourth in the American League East Division with an 81-81 record.

In 2012, again with the Blue Jays, Álvarez played in 31 games, a season of ups and downs. He recorded his first complete game and first shutout, 4-0 against the Los Angeles Angels of Anaheim on May 4, 2012. Brandon Morrow had pitched a shutout the day before, so the duo became the first to throw back-to-back shutouts for the Blue Jays since 1993.

Álvarez, however, had the lowest strikeout rate in the league (3.80) and also was ejected by umpire Marty Foster for throwing at a Texas Rangers batter on May 26, 2012. The team (73-89) finished fourth. Álvarez had a 9-14 won-lost record and a 4.85 ERA in 187⅓ innings pitched.

On November 19, 2012, the Venezuelan pitcher was traded to the Miami Marlins in a massive 12-player deal. The Blue Jays traded Álvarez along with Yunel Escobar, Adeiny Hechavarria, Jeff Mathis, Jake Marisnick, Justin Nicolino, and Anthony DeSclafani to the Marlins in exchange for Josh Johnson, Mark Buehrle, José Reyes, John Buck, and Emilio Bonifacio, and financial compensation.

In the 2013 season, Álvarez earned national headlines. The season had started poorly for him, however. In the preseason 2013 World Baseball Classic, he pitched for the Venezuelan national team, but was the losing pitcher against Puerto Rico as Venezuela was eliminated in the group phase.

The day before Opening Day, Álvarez was placed on the Marlins' disabled list with shoulder inflammation. "He is going to be down, he's taking a break" said Marlins manager Mike Redmond. (The severity of his injury was unknown at the time.[3]) In fact, Álvarez was out for the first half of the season. He pitched in some minor-league games for two Marlins affiliates, the Jacksonville Suns and the Jupiter Hammerheads, before returning to the majors, making his Marlins debut on July 4 against the Atlanta Braves and holding the Braves to three runs over five innings. His first Marlins win came on July 26 against the Pittsburgh Pirates, a 2-0 victory with Álvarez throwing six scoreless innings of two-hit ball.

Even though Álvarez had missed nearly half the season, 2013 was a better season for him than for the Blue Jays. He had a 5-6 won-lost record and a 3.59 ERA in 102⅔ innings pitched in 17 games. The Marlins' team ERA was 3.71 and they finished in last place, with a record of 62-100. One notable game for Álvarez was played on September 2 against the Chicago Cubs at Wrigley Field. In the top of the third inning, with the Marlins down 3-1, he came to bat and hit a three-run homer down the left-field line off Travis Wood – the only home run of his major-league career – providing what turned out to be the runs that won the 4-3 game.

All told, Álvarez hit .220 in 115 major-league plate appearances, with 9 RBIs.

It was in the very last game of the 2013 season that Álvarez truly made the headlines. Against the Detroit Tigers, he threw a no-hitter, the 284th in regular-season major-league history and the first ever at Marlins Park. He just allowed three baserunners, on an error, a walk, and a hit batter. The Marlins won 1-0 – a walkoff win on a bases-loaded wild pitch in the ninth inning. The last time major-league baseball had seen a no-hitter in the final game of the season had been in 1984. It was a huge moment for Álvarez, and many anticipated a great 2014 season.

Before the 2014 season, Álvarez pitched in five games (2-0 won-lost record, 2.74 ERA in 23 innings pitched) for the Tiburones de La Guaira in the 2013-14 Venezuelan Winter League.

It was just the beginning. With the 2014 Marlins, the Venezuelan pitcher started strongly, with a two-hit, 2-0 shutout of Seattle on April 19. Two other shutouts followed. On May 6 he held the Mets to six hits in a 3-0 win and on June 3 he shut out Tampa Bay, 1-0, on eight hits.

All told, Álvarez in 2014 recorded the strongest stats of his major-league years. He started 30 games and had a 12-7 won-lost record and a 2.65 ERA in 187 innings pitched. He struck out 111 and walked 33. He was selected for the National League All-Star team and his three shutouts led the major leagues. He had to deal with a minor shoulder injury[4] but he finished a Marlins losing season (77-85) as the winningest pitcher on the team. He received one vote in the 2014 NL Cy Young Award balloting.

After his strong 2014 season, Álvarez was rightfully chosen as the 2015 Opening Day starting pitcher. Though he gave up only two runs in six innings, the game was a 2-1 loss to the Atlanta Braves.[5] With a major shoulder injury in April and a fruitless attempt to come back in the second half of May, Álvarez lost every one of his four starts that season. He had to undergo shoulder surgery on July 28.[6] The 2015 major-league season was the first major-league season in which he didn't record a win: 0-4, 6.45 ERA, just 22⅓ innings pitched.

Álvarez was granted free agency by the Marlins on December 2, 2015, and signed with the Oakland Athletics on December 28.

His 2016 season in the Athletics' organization didn't earn Álvarez a return to the majors.[7] Dealing with his injuries required additional shoulder surgery,[8] after he had played briefly with two minor-league affiliates, the Nashville Sounds (5 games, 1-0, 18⅔ innings, 3.86 ERA) and the Stockton Ports (5 games, 13⅓ innings, 0-1, 4.73 ERA), and a sole game in the fall league with the AZL Athletics.

Álvarez became a free agent on October 7, 2016, pitched for the Long Island Ducks in the independent Atlantic League of Professional Baseball (2-1 in seven starts), then signed with the Philadelphia Phillies on August 22, 2017.

He made three starts (2-0 won-lost record, 2.84 ERA, 19 innings pitched) with the Phillies' Triple-A affiliate, the Lehigh Valley IronPigs, then on September 11 was promoted to the major-league club, starting three games (0-1, 4.30 ERA, 14⅔ innings pitched). The Phillies had a 66-96 record that season.

In 2018 and 2019 Álvarez pitched for Los Tigres de Quintana Roo in the Triple-A-level Mexican League. He was 6-1 in the Spring league and 3-4 in the Autumn league.

Álvarez was signed by the Washington Nationals on November 16, 2018, but failed to be promoted, playing in for the Fresno Grizzlies of the Pacific Coast League (24 starts, 1-4 won-lost record, 5.94 , 53 innings pitched). He was released by the Nationals on July 1, 2019.

In the 2018-19 Venezuelan Winter League, Álvarez played for his hometown squad, Los Navegantes del Magallanes. With the baseball team from Valencia, he pitched in 10 games and went 3-6 with a 6.64 ERA in 40⅔ innings pitched.

Amid the COVID-19 pandemic, Álvarez pitched in 2020 for the champions of the independent American Association, the Milwaukee Milkmen.[9] He was the winning pitcher in Game Two of the finals against Sioux Falls, throwing seven shutout innings in mid-September.[10]

During that season Álvarez signed on August 9 with the Pittsburgh Pirates, but the contract was voided on August 16.[11]

Álvarez celebrated one of MLB's most unusual no-hitters: a 1-0 walk-off win completed on a wild pitch. His gem came against Detroit on the final day of the 2013 season. (Jason Arnold / Getty Images Sports)

Later that year, Álvarez remained active, playing for Los Tigres de Quintana Roo in the Mexican League.[12] Once you could find his tweets in @HendersonA37 and his posts at @alvarez3737 on Instagram. As he tweeted on September 27, 2020, "en este momento es importante tener jugadores de experiencia en los roster." (At this moment [MLB playoffs], [it] is important to have experienced players in the rosters.)[13]

Álvarez continued pitching for Magallanes in winter league ball the next three seasons and pitched in three games – he was 1-0 – in the 2021 Caribbean Series.

His 2022 and 2023 seasons were both in Mérida, Yucatán, pitching in the Mexican League for Los Leones de Yucatán, starting 17 games and finishing with a record of 7-4 (4.43 ERA) in 2022 and 6-4 (3.68 ERA) in 2023.

In 2024 Álvarez continued pitching Mexican League baseball, starting four games for the Saraperos de Saltillo (Norte Division) and two for the Guerreros de Oaxaca (Sur Division), for a combined 1-2 (5.40 ERA).

Álvarez clearly kept plugging away, pitching professional baseball wherever and whenever he could, into his 35th year.

SOURCES

In addition to the sources cited in the Notes, the author relied on Baseball-Reference.com and Retrosheet.org. Additional information has been contributed by Bill Nowlin.

NOTES

1   "Alvarez Participates in MLB Futures Game," milb.com, July 2, 2010. http://www.milb.com/news/article.jsp?ymd=20100702&content_id=11861122&fext=.jsp&vkey=news_t424&sid=t424.

2   "Jays' Alvarez Set for Major League debut against A's," *Toronto Star*, August 10, 2011. Thanks to Adrian Fung.

3   Michael Jong, "Henderson Alvarez Suffers Setback in Return from Injury," SB Nation Fish Stripes. https://www.fishstripes.com/2013/5/3/4296272/miami-marlins-news-henderson-alvarez-injury-shoulder-setback.

4   Juan C. Rodriguez, "Marlins Shelve All-Star Alvarez with Shoulder Inflammation," *South Florida Sun-Sentinel* (Deerfield Beach, Florida), August 1, 2014. http://articles.sun-sentinel.com/2014-08-01/sports/fl-marlins-notes-0802-20140801_1_henderson-alvarez-colin-moran-jake-marisnick.

5   Clark Spencer, "Henderson Alvarez, Named Marlins' Opening Day Starter," *Miami Herald*, March 29, 2015. http://www.miamiherald.com/sports/mlb/miami-marlins/article16857254.html

6   Drew Silva, "Henderson Alvarez Undergoes Shoulder Surgery," NBCSports.com, July 28, 2015. http://mlb.nbcsports.com/2015/07/28/henderson-alvarez-undergoes-shoulder-surgery/.

7   "Henderson Alvarez's Rehab on Pause After Shoulder Discomfort," ESPN.com, June 19, 2016. http://www.espn.com/mlb/story/_/id/16340382/henderson-alvarez-shut-oakland-athletics-due-shoulder-discomfort.

8   Jeff Todd, "Henderson Alvarez Undergoes Shoulder Surgery," mlbtradeumors.com, September 20, 2016. http://www.mlbtraderumors.com/2016/09/henderson-alvarez-set-for-shoulder-surgery.html.

9   "Deal with Pittsburgh Falls Through," rotowire.com, August 17, 2020. https://www.rotowire.com/baseball/player.php?id=11198&refer=SportsRef.

10   Curt Hogg, "Champs! The Milwaukee Milkmen Defeat Sioux Falls to Win the American Association Championship," *Milwaukee Journal-Sentinel*, September 17, 2020. https://www.jsonline.com/story/sports/2020/09/17/milwaukee-milkmen-win-2020-american-association-baseball-championship/3489912001/.

11   "Deal with Pittsburgh Falls Through."

12   https://twitter.com/HendersonA37/status/1312092257894498304. Note: as of June 2023, these two Twitter posts were no longer available.

13   https://twitter.com/HendersonA37/status/1310279029199704067.

WILSON ÁLVAREZ

BY LEONTE LANDINO

Wilson was destined for greatness.

The no-hitter he threw for the Chicago White Sox on August 11, 1991, didn't just change the course of his career—it transformed how an entire generation in Venezuela connected with baseball.

Asked about that unforgettable day over the years, Álvarez would humbly repeat: "It was a gift from God."

And truly, it seemed to be.

At just 21 years old, Wilson Álvarez became the fourth-youngest pitcher in major-league history to throw a no-hitter. He was the 13th pitcher in Chicago White Sox history to achieve the feat, accounting for the franchise's 14th hitless game. More importantly, it was the first no-hitter ever thrown by a Venezuelan in the major leagues. And incredibly, it came in just his second career start.

The baseball world in the United States first heard of Wilson Álvarez in July 1989, when the Texas Rangers gave him a spot start on July 24. But back home in Venezuela—especially in Maracaibo—his name was already familiar. He had been making headlines since childhood, starring in local Little League tournaments and becoming a symbol of hope for a baseball-crazed city.

Wilson Álvarez was born in Maracaibo on March 24, 1970, the son of William Álvarez, an upholsterer, and Ada Álvarez, a homemaker. Maracaibo is one of the most baseball-crazy corners of the world, the place where Luis Aparicio became an idol. Like so many kids growing up in Venezuela, Wilson and his siblings dreamed of making it to the major leagues. With his three brothers—William, Walter, and Willy—and his sister Wendy, baseball wasn't just a pastime; it was a way of life.

It was Wilson's mother, Ada, who made the sacrifices, week after week, driving her sons to the Santa Lucía Little League field in Maracaibo. Weekends were for games, weekdays for practice. Her dedication laid the foundation for their love of baseball.

Maracaibo is widely considered the heart of Venezuela's Little League system. It's home to the legendary *Pequeña Liga Coquivacoa*, the first Venezuelan Little League directly connected with the Williamsport, Pennsylvania-based organization. That affiliation began in 1955, thanks to Frank Poteraj, an American oil worker who committed to bringing organized baseball to the area. His initiative sparked the growth of Little League baseball throughout the country. As of 2023, 23 of the 37 affiliated leagues in Venezuela were operating in the state of Zulia. Of the five Latin American teams to win the Little League World Series, two came from Maracaibo.

Wilson Álvarez grew up in that intensely competitive environment, where talent met high expectations. Between the ages of 11 and 16, while pitching in Little League, he threw an astonishing 12 no-hitters. By then, his name was already circulating among local scouts and coaches as a top prospect.

In August 1984, as Venezuela celebrated Luis Aparicio's induction into the National Baseball Hall of Fame, a commemorative magazine was published by the National Sports Institute. Aparicio, of course, was on the cover. But on the back page was a photo of a 14-year-old left-hander named Wilson Álvarez, fresh off a 21-strikeout no-hitter in a national youth tournament.

Aparicio's Hall of Fame induction ceremony took place on August 11, 1984. Exactly seven years later—to the day and nearly to the hour—Wilson Álvarez threw a no-hitter in just his second major-league start, and for one of Aparicio's former teams: the Chicago White Sox.

Following the buzz around his amateur career, Álvarez was signed as an international free agent by the Texas Rangers on September 23, 1986. He was assigned to Águilas del Zulia in the Venezuelan Winter League, where he made one start and nine relief appearances.

It was a humbling debut: 12 earned runs in 9⅓ innings, ending his first professional season with a 0–1 record and an 11.57 ERA.

A few months later, he traveled to his first spring training in the U.S. and was assigned to the Gulf Coast League White Sox for the 1987 season. In 10 starts, he went 2–5 with a 5.24 ERA. He was promoted to the Class-A South Atlantic League with the Gastonia Rangers, where he struggled again, going 1–5 with a 6.47 ERA in six starts. His first year in pro ball ended with a combined 3–10 record and a concerning 5.2 walks per nine innings.

"Those days were tough," Álvarez later recalled. "It was hard adapting to a new culture, making new friends, the language, the food—everything. Expectations were high back home, and I felt like things weren't going in the right direction. But deep down, I believed I could pitch and get the job done."

By then, Álvarez had grown into a 6-foot-1, 175-pound frame. Quiet and shy by nature, he was often misunderstood—his calm demeanor mistaken for laziness. His first two seasons in the minors were difficult on paper, but those in the know could see the promise. He had a live fastball, and while he was still working on command and developing his curveball and slider, the raw talent was unmistakable.

Back in Venezuela, Álvarez was playing in a league that, unlike the developmental focus of the minors, was all about winning. The Venezuelan Winter League featured a fierce mix of major-league veterans, top-tier prospects, and elite compe-

Wilson Álvarez made history in 1991 with a no-hitter in just his second big league start. He pitched 14 seasons in the majors, winning 102 games.
(Courtesy Chicago White Sox)

tition, arguably more intense than rookie or minor-league ball in the U.S.

In the Caribbean, it's never just about development—it's about results.

Between 1987 and 1990, Álvarez's game was getting shaped by the competitiveness of winter baseball. He became a fan favorite with Zulia, a team managed by Manny Trillo in '87, Pete Mackanin in '88 and '89, and Rubén Amaro Sr. in 1990.

In 1989, Mackanin took the team and his star young arm to another level, winning the league title and the 1989 Caribbean Series in Mazatlán, México. Led by catcher Joe Girardi and first baseman Carlos Quintana, the team also featured top-caliber major-league prospects, including Phil Stephenson, Cris Colón, Pete Castellano, Eddie Zambrano, and major-league journeyman infielder Angel Salazar.

Playing with bright major-league prospects and for coaches like Trillo, Amaro, and Mackanin helped shape Álvarez's character. "Zulia was a very competitive team," he recalled. "Those guys played with hard-core passion for the game and for the franchise. Most of them were hometown locals just like me, and it was a matter of pride to win. It was a completely different scenario from what we were seeing in those years in the minors. The Venezuelan League was about passion. It was tough baseball. Many, many good players were there ... major leaguers, foreign players, people wanted us to win, and there was a lot of pressure and fun and they had confidence in me, which I always appreciated."

The Rangers sent Álvarez to Triple-A Oklahoma City for a brief stint in 1988, but he spent most of the season with Class-A Gastonia, where he was 4-11 but recorded a 2.98 ERA. He started 1989 in the Florida State League for the Port Charlotte Rangers, where, going 7-4 with a 2.11 ERA in the first half of the season, he showed at age 19 that his three years of professional experience were paying off. His strikeout-to-walk ratio improved, and his curveball and changeup command were effective after coming back from the Winter League. He was promoted to Double A, joining the Tulsa Drillers of the Texas League in the first week of July.

The big-league club was challenging Oakland in the divisional race, and after several years, the White Sox had a shot at the postseason. They knew their farm system was loaded with great talent from Latin America thanks to the labors of assistant GM Sandy Johnson.

Rangers general manager Tom Grieve decided to start showing off his talent pool by calling up players who could either help or become fodder for trades. In June, the White Sox called up 20-year-old Dominican outfielder Sammy Sosa. And on July 24, after just three weeks in Tulsa, Álvarez was called up to start against the Toronto Blue Jays in place of the injured Charlie Hough. The 19-year-old became the first player born in the 1970s to play in the major leagues.

Álvarez's first pitch to Junior Félix was a strike. On his fifth pitch, Félix hit a single to center field. Tony Fernández was up next, and he hit a home run to left. On a 2-and-2 count, Kelly Gruber went back-to-back deep to center field. George Bell walked. Fred McGriff got four balls in a row. Manager Bobby Valentine took Álvarez out of the game, bringing in Dominican veteran Cecilio Guante in relief.

The rookie departed after facing five batters and surrendering three hits and two walks for three runs. Having recorded no outs, he carried an earned-run average of infinity.

"Most people thought (calling up Álvarez) was because (White Sox GM Larry Himes) was at the game," Grieve told the *Chicago Tribune.* "The purpose of that callup was to win that game, and he was the best one we had for that job."[1]

"They called me up to show me so they could trade me," Álvarez declared. "I was devastated. I thought it was going to be almost impossible to get back to the majors. The next day, they sent me back down to Tulsa, and the day after, they told me I was traded to the Chicago White Sox."

Álvarez took the news badly. His confidence was hurt. The Rangers needed to add a veteran bat for the rest of the season, and the White Sox were an aging team with a poor farm system.

Chicago sent veteran All-Star Harold Baines and Venezuelan infielder Fred Manrique to Texas for Álvarez, skinny outfielder Sammy Sosa, and infielder Scott Fletcher.

A few days later, Álvarez was pitching for the Birmingham Barons of the Double-A Southern League. He pitched just six more games the rest of the season and then returned to Zulia, where his confidence returned with the comfort of playing at home.

The 1990 season offered a fresh start for the lefty, and after his solid performance in Venezuela, he was sent to Triple-A Vancouver. That year, he married Daihanna, who was pregnant; he started the season with a record of 7-7 and an ERA of 6.00. He was demoted to Double-A Birmingham by midseason.

On the personal side, his wife gave birth prematurely to their first child, a boy. After complications from a pulmonary infection, the baby died on August 11, just five days old.

"That was hard. We were so excited about the birth of the baby. I couldn't concentrate on baseball. Losing a child was something we couldn't understand, and we were both so young and hopeful that all was going to be fine with my career, our family. But it wasn't."

Álvarez finished the season with seven more starts in Double-A, going 5-1 and improving his ERA to 4.27. Birmingham pitching coach Rick Peterson helped him face his emotional struggles.

By spring training of 1991, Álvarez was coming off his best season in winter ball, having gone 3-3 in nine starts for Zulia with an ERA of 1.38, establishing himself as one of the top hurlers of the circuit at the age of 20. He looked like a veteran on the mound and was ready to prove to the White Sox that he belonged in the majors. His fastball was in the mid-90s, and he had better command of his slider and curveball. The White Sox assigned him again to Birmingham, and after 23 starts, he was 10-6 with a 1.83 ERA and 165 strikeouts in 152⅓ innings. The stuff was there, and the moment to return to the majors was getting close. The White Sox were reshaping their team, and Álvarez was in their plans.

To ensure that Álvarez was fit for the job, the White Sox called him up on August 11. He would face the Baltimore Orioles that Sunday afternoon at Memorial Stadium. It was his second major-league start.

"I couldn't believe I was getting back and pitching on the same day when we lost our baby," he said. "I had a million things on my mind, I was nervous because I was afraid that I was not going to be able to make an out like in 1989. I didn't know what to think or do because of the chance to pitch back on this level. When we arrived on the bus at the ballpark, I realized I had left my bag with all my clothes and equipment at the lobby of the hotel. The team sent a person to get my stuff, where my wife was waiting. When the bag arrived, I got dressed and ran to the bullpen with the belt in my hand to prepare for the game, and was only able to warm up for a half-hour."

That afternoon, the baseball gods were behind Álvarez. Facing a tough Orioles lineup with hitters like Cal Ripken,

Randy Milligan, Chris Hoiles, and Dwight Evans, he managed to make outs step-by-step, with his solid fastball, circle change, slider, and splitter. Everything worked just fine. The White Sox scored twice in the top of the first and Álvarez struck out the side, all three swinging, in the bottom of the inning. The White Sox scored two more runs in the second, and after walking Dwight Evans in the second, Álvarez resumed mowing Baltimore batters down. The next baserunner reached on a walk in the sixth. Álvarez walked five batters in all, and his catcher, Ron Karkovice, made an error in the seventh, but Álvarez didn't give up a hit. The White Sox defense did its part with a memorable sliding catch in the seventh inning by center fielder Lance Johnson that helped preserve the gem. Álvarez had himself a no-hitter.

"He didn't realize he was there," recalled teammate and countryman Ozzie Guillén. "I'd heard about his performance in the little leagues in Venezuela, and in Chicago, we knew him as the kid we got in the Harold Baines trade. I never got to know him until that day when we needed a pitcher and he came over for a start. I always think that he didn't believe he was pitching that day and he just let go of all his talent from the mound."[2] It was a historic achievement for a Venezuelan pitcher. The whole country watched the game on television, and the no-hitter became a national storyline of pride and greatness – a mark for a whole generation.

For the next seven days, every major newspaper in Venezuela sold out its advertising space—each page filled with congratulatory messages for Wilson Álvarez. From corporate brands to local businesses, everyone wanted to celebrate him. Even a month after the no-hitter, tributes were still visible: billboards lined the streets with his image, and graffiti on city walls offered heartfelt thank-yous. The entire country was part of the celebration.

Álvarez became only the second pitcher in major-league-MLB history to throw a no-hitter in his second major league start. He remained with the White Sox for the rest of the 1991 season and secured a spot in the starting rotation, finishing the year with a 3–2 record, a 3.51 ERA, and nine starts.

From that moment on, Venezuelan fans followed every game he pitched over the next 12 years, always hoping to witness another magical no-hitter. That historic moment became part of the collective baseball psyche in Venezuela.

After the season, Álvarez returned home to pitch for the Águilas del Zulia and was welcomed as a national hero in Maracaibo. That winter, he made history again—becoming the first pitcher in team history to win the Triple Crown, leading the league in wins (8–0), ERA (1.47), and strikeouts (64). He was named Pitcher of the Year and led Zulia to the league championship and a spot in the 1992 Caribbean Series.

Following his 8–0 record and an extraordinary year, Álvarez earned a new nickname: "El Intocable"—The Untouchable.

Álvarez began the 1992 MLB season in the bullpen for the White Sox, but struggled, largely due to control issues, walking nearly six batters per nine innings. He rejoined the starting rotation in mid-June and ended the season with a 5.20 ERA, starting just 9 of his 34 appearances. That winter, he pitched six games back in Venezuela, posting a 4.08 ERA.

By then, major-league baseball had begun monitoring and limiting the winter workloads of its Latin American players, especially those considered vital to their big-league clubs. The White Sox saw Álvarez as part of their long-term plans, and fans in Venezuela had to adjust to seeing fewer major-league stars in action during winter ball.

"I wanted to pitch every year—and all season—in Venezuela," Álvarez explained. "The White Sox felt it was risky, but also necessary to stay in shape during the offseason. For me, it was about growth, yes—but also pride. Pitching in front of my family, my friends, and for the team that gave me so much meant everything. Even with restrictions, I tried in every way to keep pitching at home."

One of the moments he cherished most was pitching in *El Juego de la Chinita*, the annual celebration game held on November 18 in honor of the Virgin of Chiquinquirá, the patron saint of Maracaibo. The tradition began in 1933, and it was during this game in 1953 that Luis Aparicio made his professional debut for Gavilanes.

"It was always special to pitch that day," Álvarez said. "It's a spiritual thing. It's the energy of the fans. The stadium is packed—more than 25,000 people, all excited, all part of the celebration that defines the city. Those games were different. It was an honor for me—and for my family—to stand on that mound and represent who we are."

In 1993, Álvarez was a full-time starter for the White Sox alongside Jack McDowell (Cy Young Award winner in 1993), Cuban-American prospect Alex Fernández, and Jason Bere. This quartet won 67 out of the White Sox's 92 victories as they clinched the AL West. Álvarez (15-8) led the starters with a 2.95 ERA.

The White Sox advanced to the ALCS against Álvarez's nemesis, the Toronto Blue Jays, who won the first two games of the series. Álvarez took the mound for Game Three.

"It was a huge game for me, for all the people behind me, and I always remembered when I could not record an out in 1989. It was time to be the face of my team and step up," he said.

Álvarez threw a real gem, a complete-game 6-1 win at SkyDome, allowing only seven hits and two walks. The win lifted morale, and Chicago won the next game, but couldn't contain the Blue Jays' offense in the final two games. The Blue Jays won the ALCS and followed with a World Series victory over the Philadelphia Phillies.

In 1994, Álvarez was named to the American League squad for the All-Star Game. He pitched the bottom of the eighth inning, retiring the side in order. For the season, he was 12-8, 3.45.

Álvarez spent 1995 and 1996 as a solid member of the White Sox rotation, starting 64 games. He improved his strikeout-to-walk rate and won 23 games (8-11 and 15-10, with ERAs of 4.32 and 4.22).

At the July trading deadline in 1997, Álvarez was 9-8 with a 3.03 ERA. The White Sox looked to revamp the team with a younger roster. It was Álvarez's final year before free agency. Rather than losing Álvarez, the White Sox traded him to the San Francisco Giants along with pitchers Danny Darwin and Roberto Hernández in a nine-player deal.

"I was not comfortable with the Giants," Álvarez said. It was a difficult change switching leagues. I struggled. I never felt comfortable in the dugout. Roberto and I got into a place where we never felt welcome. Barry Bonds was not the nicest person in the world, and he was the leader of that clubhouse. Overall, it was not a good experience."

During his time with the White Sox, Álvarez was 67-50 but lost 30 games in which the team scored two or fewer runs. After his stint with the Giants, he became one of the most sought-after lefties in baseball. The New York Yankees were a top contender for his services, but he chose to sign with the expansion Tampa Bay Devil Rays for five years and $35 million.

Álvarez recalled, "Signing with Tampa Bay was a decision my family and I made together. We had stayed in the Sarasota area after I signed with the White Sox, so being close to home was the most important factor. My daughters were in school, and the new ballpark was just a few miles away. On top of that, they offered me the opportunity to be the number-one starter in the rotation. It was a new challenge—and I embraced it."

Álvarez went on to make history as the first starting pitcher in Devil Rays franchise history, delivering the inaugural pitch at Tropicana Field. However, the season didn't unfold as he had hoped. He finished with a 6–14 record and a 4.73 ERA. As with his earlier seasons, run support was limited—perhaps unsurprisingly, given the realities of an expansion team. Still, Álvarez felt the pressure from fans, who had high expectations for both the fledgling franchise and its marquee free-agent acquisition.

Tampa Bay was an inconsistent team. The Devil Rays had signed big names such as Álvarez, Roberto Hernández, sluggers Fred McGriff and José Canseco, and future Hall of Famer Wade Boggs. The rotation was not deep, and the bullpen was inconsistent, and the team finished with a 63-99 record. The Devil Rays improved to 69-93 in their second season. Álvarez was 9-9 (4.22).

Álvarez returned to Venezuela for the 1999 winter ball season and played a pivotal role for the Águilas del Zulia, winning several key games, five of them in the postseason, to help the team reach the finals. Zulia went on to win the championship, marking Álvarez's fourth title with the club. He was then selected to start the opening game of the 2000 Caribbean Series, though he took the loss due to unearned runs.

Heading into the 2000 MLB season, expectations were high for the Tampa Bay Devil Rays. But just five days before Opening Day, Álvarez was placed on the disabled list with shoulder tendinitis. Arthroscopic surgery followed, and what was initially thought to be a short setback turned into an 18-month rehab. The recovery process cost him two seasons and forced him to essentially relearn how to throw a baseball. He made his return to the mound in 2002 but managed to pitch in only three games before June.

"It was the most frustrating time of my life," Álvarez said. "At first, I didn't think it was that bad, but the recovery stalled, and surgery became the only option. I wanted so badly to show the fans in Tampa what I could bring to the team, but my body just wasn't ready. I had to relearn how to pitch—how to gain velocity, how to move my arm. It's a long, painful process, and at times you feel like giving up. But my family supported me through everything. I gave all I had to Tampa Bay, but the injury came at the worst possible time for me and the team. I understand the frustration from the fans and the organization."

In 2002, Álvarez pitched just 75 innings across 23 games. It was less about results and more about rebuilding his mechanics and confidence. No longer the power lefty he once was, he began transitioning into a different kind of pitcher—one who relied more on command and precision than velocity.

By season's end, Álvarez had successfully reinvented himself. With a rebuilt shoulder and a new approach, he was ready for the next chapter—but the Devil Rays released him. He soon signed with the Los Angeles Dodgers, who envisioned him as a reliever. Álvarez delivered a strong performance, going 6–2 with a 2.37 ERA in 21 games, earning a spot in the bullpen as a left-handed specialist and occasional starter. In 2004, he appeared in 40 games, including 15 starts.

After re-signing with the Dodgers following the 2004 season, Álvarez faced yet another setback in 2005 when his shoulder issues resurfaced.

On August 1, despite still being under contract, he chose to retire rather than undergo another surgery.

On December 30, 2005, Álvarez took the mound one final time for Zulia. With the team already eliminated from post-season contention, he pitched one sentimental inning in front of a small crowd in Maracaibo. Wearing his iconic number 47 jersey, he retired to the side and walked off the mound for good. It was a quiet, heartfelt farewell to the game from a local hero who had reached the sport's highest stage.

After Álvarez's no-hitter, five more Venezuelan-born pitchers (as of 2017) pitched no-hit games: Anibal Sánchez in 2006 for the Marlins, Carlos Zambrano in 2008 for the Cubs, Johan Santana in 2012 for the Mets, Félix Hernández, a perfect game in 2012 for the Mariners, and Henderson Álvarez in 2013 for the Marlins. (The list should be six: Armando Galarraga lost his perfect game for the Tigers in 2010 when umpire Jim Joyce incorrectly called a batter safe at first base.)[3]) For each one of these pitchers, Wilson Álvarez was an inspiration due to both his successful 14-year major-league career and the impact the no-hitter had in a baseball-crazed country.

Wilson Álvarez was the first Venezuelan pitcher to surpass 100 wins in major-league baseball, finishing his career with a 102–92 record and a 3.96 ERA across 355 games. A 1994 All-Star, Álvarez also built a distinguished career in his home country, pitching 12 seasons in the Venezuelan Professional Baseball League with a 29–18 record and a stellar 2.49 ERA. His legacy was solidified with his induction into the Caribbean Series Hall of Fame in 2010 and the Venezuelan Baseball Hall of Fame in 2011.

After retiring from professional baseball, Álvarez began a new chapter as a mentor. He served as pitching coach for the Gulf Coast League Orioles (Rookie) near his home in Sarasota, Florida, where he lived with his wife, Daihanna, and their three daughters: Vivianna, Vanessa, and Valentina. He later returned to the Venezuelan winter league as pitching coach for Caribes de Anzoátegui, Águilas del Zulia, and Leones del Caracas, but it was with Zulia, where he remains as an all-time favorite, as part of four of the franchise's five championships, cementing his status as an icon of the club.

Reflecting on retirement, Álvarez once shared:

"When you retire, it's like all the attention you once had disappears overnight—and it never comes back. That's when a new phase of life begins, one you have to discover while you're still young."

In the 2016–17 season, Álvarez helped lead a young Águilas pitching staff to a championship under manager and former teammate Lipso Nava. The team reached the finals for the first time since 2000, defeating Cardenales de Lara in six games. At the Caribbean Series, they fell in the semifinals to Puerto Rico's Criollos de Caguas. Álvarez continued to coach, later joining Leones del Caracas, where he added another title to his résumé in the 2022–2023 season. Once again, he teamed up with Nava, who served as hitting coach under manager José Alguacil.

Álvarez also played a key role in the newly established Liga Mayor de Béisbol Profesional de Venezuela, where he earned a strong reputation for developing top-tier pitching talent.

His iconic number 47 remained one of the best-selling jerseys among fans. On December 14, 2016, Águilas del Zulia officially retired the number in a moving ceremony.

"This is the most important moment of my life," Álvarez said. "Because I'm here with my family, my teammates, my friends—and my beloved team."

His parents and siblings attended, and he delivered the ceremonial first pitch to cap off the tribute.

Outside of baseball, Álvarez ventured into music, founding 47Music, a label managed by his wife, focused on promoting new voices in the Latin pop genre.

And still today, one moment continues to echo across generations in Venezuela:

"Even after all these years, new generations of fans in Venezuela still hear the echoes of August 11, 1991—when an entire nation shouted in unison: '¡Wilson lanzó un no-hitter!'"

Álvarez simply calls it: "A gift from God."

SOURCES

This article draws on personal interviews and both on- and off-record conversations with Wilson Alvarez between 1995 and 2017.

The author also consulted ¡A La *Carga!*, the official magazine of Águilas del Zulia (Maracaibo, Venezuela: Tripleplay Sports Productions, 1997–

2002), *Baseball Zone* (Maracaibo: Tripleplay Sports Productions, March 2001), *Diario Panorama* (Maracaibo) and the *Dallas Morning News*.

In addition to the sources cited in the Notes, the author consutlted Baseball-Reference.com.

NOTES

1   Alan Solomon, "Alvarez: The Making of the Sox' No-Hit Kid," *Chicago Tribune*, August 13, 1991: B1.

2   Conversation with Ozzie Guillén about Álvarez's no-hitter, March 24, 2017.

3   See Armando Galarraga and Jim Joyce, with Daniel Paisner, *Nobody's Perfect* (New York: Atlantic Monthly Press, 2011).

LUIS APARICIO

BY LEONTE LANDINO

The name Luis Aparicio is deeply intertwined with Venezuelan baseball history. Both Luis Aparicio Ortega (Ortega) and his son, Luis Aparicio Montiel (Aparicio), played pivotal roles in elevating the game to new heights across Latin America. It is often said that speaking of one invokes the legacy of the other.

The younger Aparicio was more than just an exceptional baseball player. His endurance, defensive prowess, and speed during an 18-year major-league career earned him a rightful place in the National Baseball Hall of Fame. Yet his legacy extends beyond statistics – he became a powerful symbol of baseball's growth and cultural impact in Latin America, especially in Venezuela and his hometown of Maracaibo. Aparicio's rise to greatness marked the peak of a transformative era for baseball in the region, a sport now embedded in Venezuela's national identity.

To understand Aparicio's significance and enduring legacy, one must trace the game's origins in Maracaibo.

The emergence of baseball in Maracaibo began around the turn of the twentieth century, when American businessman William Phelps, who would later become a media mogul and philanthropist, opened the city's first department store, the American Bazaar.

While importing baseball equipment from the United States, Phelps realized that to sell his merchandise, he also needed to educate local children about the game. His interest quickly turned into passion: he became an avid supporter of baseball, teaching schoolchildren the rules of the sport, which they readily embraced. Phelps went on to serve as the first umpire for documented games and constructed Maracaibo's first baseball field, laying the foundation for the sport in the coastal city.

Beginning around 1912, baseball swiftly became a beloved pastime for people across all social classes. Multiple fields were built throughout the small urban area, and both adults and children became captivated by the game. Within a few short years, baseball had spread across the region and was soon played professionally. Fans fell in love with the sport, flocking to see the best players and teams in action. The game became so popular that it earned the nickname "el juego de las cuatro esquinas" – the game of the four corners. Baseball had truly found its stage in Venezuela.

Over time, the region saw an influx of American oil workers, whose presence helped shape the city's identity and cultural landscape, including its deepening embrace of baseball.

By 1926, a heated rivalry between the teams Vuelvan Caras and Santa Marta had captured the attention of fans and local sports media alike. It was during this era that the region's first professional baseball star emerged: Rafael "Anguito" Oliver, a talented shortstop for Vuelvan Caras. From the early days, the local media began highlighting the importance and allure of the shortstop position, thanks in no small part to Oliver's standout play.

Oliver became an icon. Two brothers were among his biggest fans – Luis and Ernesto Aparicio Ortega. Following the Latin American naming custom, they used both their father's and mother's surnames. Both were natural athletes.

Luis initially enjoyed playing soccer but ultimately turned to baseball alongside Ernesto. They both became talented infielders; however, it was Luis who emerged as the standout superstar athlete, while Ernesto, despite possessing strong skills, focused on mastering the game intellectually.

Ernesto Aparicio went on to become a respected manager, coach, and team owner, passing his deep understanding of baseball to future generations and leaving an indelible mark on the game in Venezuela.

Meanwhile, Luis Aparicio Ortega rose to national fame for his spectacular defensive plays and exceptional baseball intelligence as a shortstop. He became a role model, a master of the position, a pioneer of the sport, and one of Venezuela's first major baseball stars. He competed in the country's top professional leagues, in both Caracas and Maracaibo, and in 1934, he made history by becoming the first Venezuelan player "exported" internationally, signing with Tigres del Licey in the Dominican Republic.

That same year, Luis Aparicio Ortega and his wife, Herminia Montiel, welcomed their son, Luis Ernesto Aparicio Montiel.

Born on April 29, 1934, in Maracaibo, Luis entered a world where his father was already a national sports icon – one of the earliest stars of Venezuelan and Latin American baseball. Ortega was an all-star shortstop and widely regarded as one of the most respected players in the country's history.

Many referred to him as "an artist at the shortstop position."[1]

Luis's uncle, Ernesto, would become his lifelong mentor. In the clubhouse of Gavilanes, his father's team, young Luis began his baseball journey as a batboy.

Both his father and uncle passed down the game's fundamentals and unwritten rules. From an early age, Luis also had the privilege of learning from players of various nationalities – Cubans, Dominicans, and Americans – who brought their experience and style to Maracaibo's rich baseball scene.

Baseball was his life. Aparicio later recalled how his mother washed team uniforms at home, and how the rhythm of daily life revolved around the sport. By age 12, he was playing shortstop for a local team, La Deportiva, already exhibiting the elegance and finesse he inherited from his father.

From then on, he would play for multiple teams in Maracaibo, Caracas, and Barquisimeto, constantly moving with his family depending on the season and the location of his father's team.

That was his world: baseball, his father's stardom, his uncle's mentorship, and whatever the game brought to the family table.

In 1953, Caracas hosted the Baseball Amateur World Series, and a 19-year-old Luis Aparicio was selected to represent Venezuela. It was his first major international tournament, and he played shortstop, third base, and left field.

Although Cuba won the championship, Aparicio quickly stood out – both to fans in the stands and in newspaper headlines – as the tournament's most electrifying player. He made spectacular defensive plays and showed poise and maturity beyond his years. Spectators waved white handkerchiefs, a sign of admiration, in recognition of his speed, solid glove, and all-around performance.

All eyes were on him for the first time, but the weight of his father's name would always be on his shoulders if he chose to turn professional.

After the Amateur World Series, a moment of truth arrived: Aparicio told his parents he was leaving school to pursue a career in professional baseball. His mother was upset by the decision, worried about his future outside of academics. His father, however, offered a piece of advice that would stay with him for the rest of his life – a message that would define his path in the game.

Son, if you are going to play baseball for a living, you will have to be the number one always. You will never be a number two of anybody, always be the number one.[2]

That winter, the four best teams in Venezuela competed in the country's first national tournament. The participants: Gavilanes and Pastora from Maracaibo, and Caracas and Magallanes from the capital, rotated their games across both cities.

It was the first tournament officially played under the Winter Baseball Agreement, sanctioned by the rules and regulations of the Office of the Commissioner of Baseball and the National Association of Professional Baseball Leagues (NAPBL). This marked the beginning of a new era for professional baseball in Venezuela.

Luis Aparicio signed with Gavilanes, and his debut was scheduled for November 17, 1953, in Maracaibo. However, heavy rain forced a postponement. His debut was rescheduled for the next day, November 18 – a date of special significance in Maracaibo. That day, the city honors its patron saint, the Virgin of Chiquinquirá, with religious celebrations, music, and parades. One of the day's most anticipated traditions is the baseball game between crosstown rivals Pastora and Gavilanes.

In that game, Ortega, who also played for Gavilanes, stepped in as the leadoff hitter against Pastora's Howie Fox, a veteran of the major leagues. After the first pitch, Ortega returned to the dugout and, in a symbolic gesture, pointed to his son with his bat – signaling that it was time for Luis to take his place at the plate for his first official at-bat.

The crowd of 7,000 fans responded to this powerful and emotional moment with a 15-minute standing ovation.

They were honoring Ortega – widely known as "El Grande de Maracaibo" – for his remarkable career, his brilliance as the finest shortstop in Venezuelan baseball, and his two decades of dedication to the sport's growth in the city. At the same time, they were recognizing that a new chapter was beginning. The ovation was also for Luis, who now carried the weight of his father's name and the enormous responsibility of living up to that legacy on the field.

Aparicio, Jr., at 19 years old, grasped the situation and embraced it with maturity. "I knew the responsibility was on me. I knew about the expectations people had everywhere I stepped on a field. I just had to be great as my father, otherwise people would consider me a total deception," he said in later years. "It was destiny."[3]

Panorama, the local newspaper, wrote the next day: "Aparicio´s son's debut was patronized by the Virgin herself." For a very Catholic region, this was a big deal.[4]

Aparicio ended up being named the best shortstop of the tournament. By December, the Cleveland Indians were negotiating with him. Gavilanes's manager, Red Kress, who was a coach for the Indians, spoke with Indians general manager Hank Greenberg about signing Aparicio, but Greenberg replied that he thought Luis was too small to play baseball.

Chico Carrasquel, who was playing for Caracas and Chicago at the time, talked to Chicago White Sox general manager Frank Lane and told him about Luis, asking him to sign the youngster before someone else did. Caracas's manager, Luman Harris, also talked to Lane. Soon after, Lane sent an offer and a contract for Aparicio with a $10,000 check. Young Luis became a member of the White Sox.

Aparicio's early days in the minor leagues were difficult. His command of English was limited, and while he knew he had the talent to play in the majors, the learning curve was steep. At the time, Chico Carrasquel held the starting shortstop position for the White Sox. After spring training in 1955, Aparicio was assigned to Memphis in the Double-A Southern Association.

Frustrated and homesick, he considered returning to Venezuela and quitting the White Sox altogether. But both his father and Carrasquel persuaded him to stay, emphasizing his potential and explaining the long, often grueling path to the majors, especially for Latino players during that era.

Carrasquel, a national baseball hero in Caracas, became both a mentor and a father figure to Aparicio. That same season, Aparicio also recalled an unexpected encounter at a small bar in Memphis – meeting a then-unknown young singer named Elvis Presley.

In October 1955 the White Sox traded Chico Carrasquel to the Cleveland Indians, clearing the way for Luis Aparicio to step into the role that would define the next chapter of his career.

When Lane announced the trade, a Chicago journalist said, "You are trading your All-Star shortstop? You will need a machine to replace Chico." Lane replied, "Yes, that's precisely what we have – a machine, and his name is Luis Aparicio."[5]

Aparicio was named the American League Rookie of the Year in 1956. He was the first Latin American player to win the award. He finished with a .266 batting average and a league-leading 21 stolen bases, and also led the league in sacrifice hits. The stolen base as a strategy was becoming less and less used in baseball in those years. Aparicio revived the essence of the stolen base from the moment he reached the majors. He injected the White Sox with the game of speed, the Caribbean game, where speed is a key. He was praised for his defense, but during his first season he made 35 errors.

Luis needed to work on his throw. Venezuelan journalist Juan Vené, who covered Aparicio's entire career, recalled, "Fans were afraid to sit behind first base, and they were aware of the throw every time Aparicio was fielding a grounder because the ball often ended up in the stands."[6]

His debut met everyone's expectations at home, but he knew he needed to do more. After his first season, when he returned home with his wife, Sonia, Aparicio said, "By seeing how so many people have gathered to welcome me at the airport just to say hello and congratulations, it makes me realize that I still have a long way to go and a lot of work to do to go beyond their expectations. I need to put the name of my country and my people up high; I feel my game represents them."[7]

In 1958 Aparicio had a breakout season: He won his first Gold Glove, earned a spot in his first All-Star Game, hit .266, and led the league in stolen bases (29) for the third consecutive year. The White Sox finished in second place for the second straight year, once again trailing the powerhouse New York Yankees.

The American League landscape at the time was brutal. The White Sox were a formidable team, but the Yankees were the Yankees – a dynasty that dominated baseball in that era. There were no playoffs back then; only the team that finished first in the league advanced to the World Series.

For Chicago, that meant one more step needed to be taken. In 1959, they finally took it.

Dámaso Blanco, a former infielder for the San Francisco Giants, remembered 1959: "I went to Chicago in August 1959 with the Venezuelan baseball team for the Pan Am Games, and they took us to Comiskey Park to watch the White Sox and Luis Aparicio. It was my first MLB game ever, and I was very anxious. Aparicio hit a single in his first at-bat, and we all noticed that people started to yell: 'Go! Go! Go!' At first, we did not understand what was happening, and then our guide explained that people were rooting for Aparicio to steal second base. I can't describe how proud we felt listening to a full Comiskey Park rooting for a fellow Venezuelan and the team leader of the 'Go Go White Sox.'"[8]

That season the White Sox won 94 games and finally won the pennant. Among the keys to their success were Aparicio's basestealing skills and his defense, along with his double-play partner and close friend, Nellie Fox. For Chicago, it was a magical era. It was their first trip to the World Series since 1919.

That 1959 team was the complete opposite of the infamous Black Sox – they were fun to watch, full of energy, and united. Aparicio recalled:

> *We were so close, like a family. We enjoyed the game and the fans in Chicago so much during that 1959 season. Having guys on the team like Ted Kluszewski, Jim Rivera, Sherm Lollar, and Early Wynn was just amazing. We just had to win the league because we were good, having fun in the field, and playing very seriously.*[9]

Aparicio ended up second to his double-play partner Fox in the voting for the American League's Most Valuable Player. He stole a career-high 56 bases.

He realized no one in baseball was better than him at stealing bases.

Aparicio's speed was a key to victory. He led the team in runs scored with 98. "Before the season, Al Lopez, our manager, told me he wanted me to focus on my basestealing," Aparicio said long after his career ended. "They wanted me to spice things

The first Venezuelan Hall of Famer, Luis Aparicio, redefined the shortstop position with speed and grace. He led the AL in stolen bases for nine straight seasons and won nine Gold Gloves. (SABR / The Rucker Archive)

up in the club, and that was going to be our key to win games that season."[10]

After their great season, the White Sox lost the World Series to the Dodgers in six games. Aparicio batted .308 (8-for-26), and although he was thrilled to participate in the fall classic, he was deeply frustrated in not winning the Series.

"People were very excited in the city, because they waited 40 years to see their team in a World Series. They were disappointed, but at the same time, they treated us like winners," he recalled.[11]

This first trip to the Series made Aparicio realize how important it was to be a winner and how hard a team needed to work to win it all.

Hoping to return to the World Series in 1960, the White Sox instead slipped to third place. They fell to fourth place in 1961 and fifth in 1962.

The White Sox wanted to rebuild their team, and in January of 1963, Aparicio and veteran outfielder Al Smith were traded to the Baltimore Orioles for Ron Hansen, Pete Ward, Dave Nicholson, and Hoyt Wilhelm.

The trade came as a shock to Aparicio, but he was joining a contending team built on a foundation of power and pitching. Aparicio added a crucial element of speed to their lineup, capturing two more stolen-base titles in 1963 and 1964. With those, he extended his streak to nine consecutive seasons leading the American League in stolen bases – a record that still stood in 2025.

More importantly, Aparicio helped anchor the Orioles' defense, forming one of the greatest shortstop-third base combinations in baseball history, playing alongside future Hall of Famer Brooks Robinson.

In 1966 the Orioles captured the American League pennant. Aparicio was the spark of this club, leading the American League in plate appearances and at-bats, improving his batting average to .276, with 6 home runs, scoring 97 runs as Baltimore's leadoff hitter, and stealing 25 bases to lead the team.

He co-led the club in hits with 182 along with Frank Robinson, who finished the season with 49 home runs, 122 RBIs, and a .316 batting average, winning the Triple Crown and the MVP Award. Aparicio ended ninth in the MVP race.

Once again, Aparicio faced the Los Angeles Dodgers in the World Series, but this time, the combination of power, contact hitting, defense, speed, and superb pitching created the perfect environment for success.

The Orioles swept the Dodgers in four games, with Games Two, Three, and Four won via shutouts by Jim Palmer, Wally Bunker, and Dave McNally. "Little Louie" contributed four hits and two RBIs in the Series, including a crucial RBI double off Sandy Koufax in Game Two. His trademark defense also shined on baseball's biggest stage, helping seal each win with precision and poise.

This was the first and only World Series championship ring of Aparicio's career. He returned to Maracaibo a hero, dedicating his share of the title to his parents, who had been his most devoted supporters throughout his journey.

In November 1967, Aparicio was traded back to the White Sox, with whom he had launched his Hall of Fame career over a decade earlier. Aparicio, along with John Matias and Russ Snyder, went to the White Sox in exchange for Don Buford, Bruce Howard, and Roger Nelson.

Now a seasoned veteran, Aparicio embraced a new role as a team leader and mentor to younger players. Though his trademark speed had begun to fade, his defensive brilliance remained unmatched, and he was determined to continue contributing at a high level by sharpening his offensive approach.

Off the field, his impact was just as profound. In his early years with the White Sox and during his prime with the Orioles, Aparicio remained a fixture in the Venezuelan Winter League. After his original team, Gavilanes, folded, he joined Rapiños, a club he helped lead and sustain in the Liga Occidental until it folded in 1963. He then joined Tiburones de La Guaira in the Central League, becoming a staple every winter.

I just wanted to wear the uniform and be on the field," Aparicio said. "At that time, I wasn't financially secure despite playing in the majors. I needed the money. And La Guaira needed a name to draw fans because the early seasons were financially tough for the club."[12]

Aparicio led La Guaira to three league titles in six seasons (1964-65, 1965-66, 1968-69), and in 1967-68, he took on the role of player-manager. Though they didn't reach the finals, Aparicio's leadership was evident. That season, he mentored an emerging 18-year-old shortstop named Enzo Hernández, who would eventually make it to the majors.

In 1968 Aparicio captured his eighth Gold Glove Award and finished in the top 20 of AL MVP voting, reinforcing his elite status. In 1969 the White Sox finished fifth in the newly formed American League West Division, but back in Venezuela, big changes were brewing.

Luis Rodolfo Machado, a businessman and farmer, purchased a new franchise for Maracaibo, forming the Águilas del Zulia. He invited Aparicio Ortega to join the staff and appointed White Sox coach Bill Adair as the team's first manager. Aparicio, Jr. wanted to return to Maracaibo and play in front of his hometown crowd.

Mr. Padrón Panza, the owner of La Guaira, didn't want to let me go," Aparicio recalled. "But I asked for the trade. I wanted to be near my family and support the new team. I understood his position, and I'm grateful he eventually agreed."[13]

Águilas del Zulia debuted on October 14, 1969, while Aparicio waited for the trade to clear. Fans, unaware of the negotiations, began protesting during a game with signs asking for Aparicio, Jr., who addressed the roaring crowd personally on his first visit to the new and modern ballpark, explaining the situation and calming fans claiming for him to join the club.

By October 27, the deal was finalized, and the next day he joined Zulia as player-manager, with Adair and his father as coaches. Zulia ended its first season in last place, but its "return" to Maracaibo sparked a whole new breed of fans and the foundation for one of the most successful and iconic franchises in Caribbean baseball.

Meanwhile, in the 1970 major-league season, Aparicio delivered the best offensive performance of his career.

Back with the White Sox at age 36, he hit .313 with a .372 on-base percentage, leading the team in hits, runs, and doubles. He earned his ninth and final Gold Glove, was named starting shortstop for the AL All-Star team, and on September 25 broke Luke Appling's record for most games played at shortstop (2,219) in the first game of a doubleheader against the Milwaukee Brewers.

That year's All-Star Game, held at Cincinnati's Riverfront Stadium, went 12 innings. Aparicio and Carl Yastrzemski were the only two players to play the entire game, each logging six at-bats, joining a rare group of just 18 players in history with at least six at-bats in an All-Star Game.[14] Aparicio went 0-for-6 but made three stellar defensive plays.

In Venezuela, Águilas del Zulia thrived under Aparicio's leadership. With support from White Sox GM Eddie Short, players like Bill Melton, Walt Williams, Carlos May, and Bart Johnson joined Aparicio in Maracaibo. His mentor, Chico Carrasquel, also came aboard as a coach along with his father.

But the White Sox started rebuilding and on December 1, 1970, they traded Aparicio to the Boston Red Sox for Luis Alvarado and Mike Andrews.

However, on January 1, 1971, tragedy struck – Luis Aparicio Ortega died of a heart attack.

"It was the toughest day of my life," Aparicio said. "My father was everything – my mentor, my teacher. It was devastating, but I had to carry on. I had a responsibility to my family and his legacy."[15]

The impact was noticeable. In a new city and beginning the final stage of his career, in 1971, Aparicio continued to excel defensively, but his offense suffered a drastic decline, including a long slump of 44 consecutive hitless at-bats in May. He was widely supported by his teammates and fans, and even got a letter of support from US President Richard Nixon, encouraging him to go on.[16]

Once again, fans selected Aparicio to start at shortstop in the All-Star Game, played at Tiger Stadium, an epic matchup featuring 22 future Hall of Famers. He singled off Dock Ellis and scored a run in a 6-4 AL victory. His hitting improved; he finished with a batting average of .262 in the second half of the season.

In 1972 Aparicio's playing time was diminished by a broken finger, but he still managed to play 110 games, mostly with a cast.[17] He was selected as a reserve for his 13th All-Star Game. Then came 1973. At age 39, he returned as the Red Sox' everyday shortstop. Despite 20 errors, he maintained a solid range and was a consistent contributor. He batted .271, posted a .324 OBP,

and was used in the second spot of the lineup by manager Eddie Kasko.

Aparicio played in 131 games that season. On September 28, 1973, in the second game of a doubleheader at Fenway Park against the Milwaukee Brewers, he unknowingly took the field for the final game of his major-league career. He had a single in the seventh off Kevin Kobel and drew two walks. In the top of the fourth, he fielded a grounder from Don Money, recording one last out – his final groundball assist after more than two decades of excellence.

Across his final six seasons (1968-1973), Aparicio hit .271, appeared in the top 20 of MVP voting in 1968, 1970, and 1972, and transformed into a reliable leadoff hitter despite diminished speed.

On March 26, 1974, just before Opening Day, the Red Sox released Aparicio during spring training in Winter Haven, Florida. He still hoped to play at age 40 and believed he had more to offer.

Journalist Juan Vené recalled that moment:

"Luis was in Red Sox camp when he got the news. That night, he returned to the hotel and found a letter. It was from George Steinbrenner, owner of the New York Yankees. Inside was an open contract and a note:

You fill in the amount you want to play for the New York Yankees.

Aparicio respectfully declined. He sent it back with a short note:

Dear Mr. Steinbrenner, thank you very much for your offer. But I only get released once in my lifetime.[18]

And just like that, Luis Aparicio's legendary major-league career ended.

He returned to Venezuelan baseball, where he had been the player-manager of Zulia. Though Jack Moore managed Zulia for the 1974-75 season, Aparicio returned to training with the club later that year. On November 17, 1974, with Toby Harrah moving to third base, Aparicio resumed his role at shortstop – and also as manager.

"It was a pleasure being around Aparicio and Carrasquel," Harrah recalled. "Just watching them made the game feel simple – even though it wasn't."[19]

Luis Aparicio played his final professional game on December 23, 1974, coming in as a substitute for César Gutiérrez, who exited with an injury. In the 11th inning, with the score tied 4-4, Aparicio hit a walk-off single, giving Zulia a 5-4 win over Cardenales de Lara.

There was no tribute, no farewell ceremony. Only those present at Estadio Barquisimeto knew they had just witnessed the final at-bat of Luis Aparicio – the greatest baseball player Venezuela has ever produced.

From 1956 to 1973, no shortstop was more dominant than Aparicio, a defensive wizard who won nine Gold Gloves and redefined the position with his elegance and athleticism. He was a transformative figure in his era, using his speed to help revive the stolen base as a major offensive weapon during a time when power hitting dominated the headlines.

Aparicio was selected for 13 All-Star Games, played in two World Series, and won one. Among his many accomplishments, he achieved what he considered his most meaningful personal milestone: setting the major-league record for most games played at shortstop, 2,583. That mark was later surpassed by fellow Venezuelan Omar Vizquel, and then by Derek Jeter. Vizquel remains the all-time leader, with 2,709 games played at the position.

Over his 18-year career, Aparicio had 2,677 hits, a .262 batting average, and 506 stolen bases.

Despite his fame, adjusting to retirement was emotionally challenging. While he was financially secure and well-organized, stepping away from the game's daily rhythm left a noticeable

Luis Aparicio, the iconic No. 11, closed his journey as more than just a baseball player; he became a symbol of pride for Venezuela and a timeless legend in Chicago. Revered as the greatest player his country has ever produced, Aparicio's legacy lives on in the hearts of fans who still celebrate his exceptional skill, determination, and groundbreaking impact on the game. (SABR / The Rucker Archive)

void. During this period, Aparicio focused on family and became involved in various local community projects and national sponsorship deals.

In the early 1980s, Aparicio began a new chapter as a color analyst for Venezuelan Baseball broadcasts with Radio Caracas Televisión (RCTV). Although he appreciated the opportunity to remain connected to baseball, television wasn't his true passion. Still, it allowed him to stay close to the game when he wasn't managing.

It was during this time, while working with RCTV, that he received the news of his Hall of Fame election in 1984.

After 10 years of Hall of Fame eligibility – and thanks in part to a passionate campaign by several Hispanic sportswriters and journalists – Luis Aparicio became the first Venezuelan player to achieve the sport's highest honor: baseball immortality.

"This is a triumph of Venezuela for all Venezuelans," said Aparicio when he heard of his election.[20]

Aparicio's greatest regret was that his father did not live long enough to witness his induction into the National Baseball Hall of Fame.

In the years after his death, Aparicio Ortega was honored in multiple ways: first with his induction into the Venezuelan Sports Hall of Fame, and later with the Maracaibo baseball stadium being renamed Luis Aparicio Ortega "El Grande de Maracaibo."

When the Venezuelan Baseball Hall of Fame and Museum was established, both Aparicio Ortega brothers – Ernesto and Luis – were inducted in recognition of their foundational roles in Venezuelan baseball history.

In 1990 Luis Aparicio returned to the dugout in Venezuela. He became the first manager of the expansion franchise Petroleros de Cabimas, leading the team through its initial two seasons. After that, he returned to familiar territory with the Tiburones de La Guaira, serving as manager and coach, continuing to mentor younger generations of players.

During this period, Aparicio moved from Maracaibo to Barquisimeto, where he embraced a quieter life surrounded by family, especially cherishing time with his grandchildren and great-grandchildren.

However, Aparicio's life was forever altered by a devastating personal tragedy. His 40-year-old daughter, Sharon, was the victim of a violent crime in Venezuela, shot in the neck during a robbery at a drugstore in Maracaibo. The attack left her with severe spinal damage and permanent disabilities. Despite undergoing over three years of intensive treatment and rehabilitation, Sharon ultimately passed away due to complications from her injuries.[21]

The incident left a deep emotional scar on Aparicio. In the wake of the tragedy, he gradually withdrew from public life, prioritizing his family and stepping away from the spotlight. Though his public appearances became increasingly rare, his passion for baseball remained intact. With the unwavering support of his son, Nelson, he continued to attend major baseball events in Venezuela and abroad, quietly maintaining his connection to the game that had defined his life.

After his Hall of Fame induction in 1984, Aparicio's status in Venezuela reached mythical proportions. He was widely considered the most important and influential athlete in the country's history. His fame transcended borders, and he made regular trips to the United States to take part in autograph signings, fan festivals, Hall of Fame weekends, and All-Star Game celebrations.

In 2005 Aparicio threw out the ceremonial first pitch before a World Series game honoring his former team, the Chicago White Sox. The following year, 2006, the White Sox unveiled the Luis Aparicio statue at US Cellular Field, located in the center-field concourse. Created by artist Gary Tillery, the sculpture is part of a two-player series depicting Aparicio receiving a throw from his legendary double-play partner Nellie Fox. Aparicio attended the event with his wife, Sonia, celebrating 52 years of marriage, accompanied by his son, Luis, Jr., and daughter, Karen.

This is my biggest moment in baseball. I thank the White Sox organization for allowing me to play baseball, and I thank God for giving me the ability to play this game. The only thing I can say is baseball is so much a part of me – I even met my wife playing baseball.[22]

In 2011 Aparicio returned to the baseball spotlight as a special color analyst for ESPN International and ESPN Deportes, covering Venezuelan Winter League broadcasts from 2011 to 2013. He joined Emmy Award-winning broadcaster Ernesto Jerez and other notable Spanish-language voices, further cementing his place in the hearts of fans across Latin America and introducing his legacy to a new generation.

In 2014 the Venezuelan Winter League celebrated the 30th anniversary of Aparicio's induction into Cooperstown by dedicating the entire season to him. He was honored in every ballpark across the country, and the league announced the retirement of his iconic number-11 jersey by every team in the league – a tribute unmatched in Venezuelan baseball history.

Despite his fame, Aparicio never lost sight of his values. His integrity, humility, and leadership defined him just as much as his glove and stolen bases. He played 19 consecutive years in the Venezuelan Winter League, effectively doubling his workload year-round while maintaining elite performance in the majors, where he played fewer than 130 games in a season only once.

Perhaps his greatest legacy lies not in statistics, but in how he carried the weight of being Venezuela's icon. He embraced the social responsibility that came with fame. As a nation mired in political and economic turmoil, Venezuelans looked to their heroes, and Luis Aparicio never let them down.

In 2017 Aparicio was invited by Major League Baseball to take part in a ceremony honoring Latino Hall of Famers before the All-Star Game in Miami. He respectfully declined, stating publicly:

Thank you for the honor @MLB, but I cannot celebrate while the young people of my country are dying while fighting for freedom.[23]

That same year, he did not attend the Hall of Fame induction ceremony, using his voice and platform to condemn the Venezuelan regime under Nicolás Maduro. Aparicio had become a vocal opponent of the dictatorship that had ruled the country since 1998.

Even into his later years, Aparicio stayed connected to the game through social media, where he shared commentary and personal reflections on baseball and Venezuelan affairs. His insights carried the weight of someone who had seen it all and still stood for principle.

Each November 18, Maracaibo celebrates the anniversary of its professional debut as part of the Virgen de Chiquinquirá festivities. At Águilas del Zulia's game, Aparicio has often delivered the ceremonial first pitch, bringing the crowd to its feet in reverence.

Additionally, the Luis Aparicio Award, given annually since 2004 to the best Venezuelan player in the US major leagues, honors not only his career but also the legacy of his father, Luis Aparicio Ortega. For current Venezuelans in the major leagues, it is considered a high honor to earn the annual award. Recipients include Miguel Cabrera, José Altuve, Omar Vizquel, Johan Santana, and Ronald Acuña, Jr.

Aparicio was named Venezuela's Athlete of the Twentieth Century by both the National Circle of Sportswriters and the National Sports Institute – an honor that reflects far more than his baseball achievements. He was also awarded an honorary doctorate by the Universidad del Zulia in recognition of his lifelong contributions to Venezuelan sports and culture.

In 2012 the State of Zulia officially declared November 11 as "Día de Luis Aparicio," a public holiday celebrating the legendary shortstop. The date – 11/11 – was chosen as a symbolic tribute to the number-11 jersey Aparicio wore throughout his career, now retired across Venezuelan professional baseball in his honor.

While he is widely recognized as the greatest player ever born in the country, it was his integrity, humility, and unwavering family values that truly defined him. He became not just a national hero but a role model for generations to come, often referred to as the "godfather" of the Venezuelan shortstop dynasty that would later flourish in the US major leagues.

On April 29, 2025, Luis Aparicio celebrated his 91st birthday at home in Barquisimeto, Venezuela. Despite having suffered a mild stroke, he remained active and engaged with the game he loved. At the time, he held the distinction of being the oldest living member of the National Baseball Hall of Fame in Cooperstown.

In March 1956, the Venezuelan newspaper *Panorama* published a letter that Aparicio had written to his mother just days after learning he had made the Chicago White Sox' Opening Day roster:

To Herminia de Aparicio, Maracaibo.

Dear Mom, You are finally the mother of a big leaguer. Try to figure out what it means to me to become 'a big leaguer.'

Today, I cried alone when they told me they were sending my luggage to Chicago because I had made the big league team. Tears came out by themselves, and I just thought about Dad.

Mom, please tell Dad that my debt to him is finally paid.

Kisses. Your son, Luis.

Years later, reflecting on the promise he made to his father, Aparicio said:

When my father asked me to always be number one, I kept that in my heart. I don't think I disappointed him. I wanted him to be proud of me, and I know he was.

That's the greatest achievement of my life.[24]

SOURCES

In addition to the sources cited in the Notes, the author consulted

Verde, Luis. *The History of Baseball in Zulia* (Maracaibo: Editorial Maracaibo SRL, 1999).

Perfiles: Luis Aparicio. ESPN International. 2002-2007.

Author's personal interviews with Luis Aparicio, JuanVené, Dámaso Blanco, Angel Bravo, Luis Verde, Nelson Aparicio, and Rafael Aparicio.

¡A La Carga! Tripleplay Sports Productions, Maracaibo, Venezuela. Various televisión episodes 1998-2002.

www.eljuegoperfecto.com

www.baseball-reference.com

www.retrosheet.org

NOTES

1   Luis Verde, *The History of Baseball in Zulia* (Maracaibo: Editorial Maracaibo SRL, 1999). Vol. 1., 36.

2   Leonte Landino, personal interview with Luis Aparicio, Maracaibo, Venezuela, July 2008. Hereafter, author interview.

3   Author interview July 2008.

4   *Diario Panorama* (Maracaibo, Venezuela), November 19, 1953.

5   Carlos Cárdenas Lares, *Venezolanos en las Grandes Ligas* (Caracas: Fondo editorial Cárdenas Lares, 1990), 78.

6   Author interview with Juan Vené, Cincinnati, August 2007.

7   *Diario Panorama*, October 10, 1956.

8   Author interview with Dámaso Blanco, Cincinnati, August 2007.

9   Author interview July 2008.

10   Author interview July 2008.

11   Author interview July 2008.

12   Augusto Cárdenas, *Mi Historia … Luis Aparicio con Augusto Cárdenas* (Maracaibo, Venezuela: Cardenas Sports Media, 2012), 157.

13   Cárdenas, 160.

14   https://www.baseball-reference.com/allstar/leaders_bat.shtml.

15   Author interview July 2008.

16   Cárdenas, 131.

17   Cárdenas, 139.

18   Author interview with Juan Vené, New York, 2008.

19   Cárdenas, 164.

20   *Revista IND*, Instituto Nacional de Deportes, Caracas, Venezuela, August 1984.

21   Cárdenas, 229.

22   Scott Merkin, "Aparicio, Fox Honored with Statues," MLB.com, July 23, 2006.

23   Luis Aparicio, via Twitter, July 11, 2017.

24   Author interview July 2008.

TONY ARMAS

BY AUGUSTO CÁRDENAS

In the 2015 season, Miguel Cabrera surpassed Andres Galarraga as the Venezuelan with the most home runs in the major leagues. His 400th home run, on May 16 at St. Louis, gave to the Detroit Tigers first baseman a record that had been held by the "Big Cat" since 1997, when he eclipsed the record of the first great Venezuelan slugger, Antonio Rafael Armas Machado.

Tony Armas was born on July 2, 1953, in Puerto Piritu, Anzoátegui state, a town in eastern Venezuela, 235 kilometers (about 150 miles) from Caracas. His father, Jose Rafael Armas, was an electrician, while his mother, Julieta Machado de Armas, was engaged in household chores, taking care at home Antonio and his 12 brothers.

"My parents were able to keep me on track," Armas said. "We were a very poor family, and lived on what was achieved. My dad was a farmer too."

In a place having beautiful beaches, the Armas family also had land that they worked. "We used to plant all kinds of beans, all kinds of fruits. We were poor and planted all kinds of fruit for the sustenance of the house," Armas said. "As the oldest I was the one who was in charge of that, to load sacks of corn, pumpkin, watermelon, everything that was harvested. I think my strength came from there."

There was no Little League or the Criollitos of Venezuela in those days, no organized movements that help children and young people today to start polishing their skills. Armas began to imitate his idols playing baseball in the street with older people in his neighborhood.

"There were no baseball schools, no little-league baseball. You become a baseball player through hard work," he said. "I played *caimaneras* (baseball in the street) with adults, as everyone did in those days. I played since I was a boy, since I was in school. It is not like today, when children are born with a uniform. Right now they have coaches, all benefits that a little boy may have from birth until (he) reaches his youth. At that time, no, at that time you had to make yourself as a player."

At 17, Tony played for the first time on a team in an organized league, Deportivo Pachaquito, and began to develop his skills on defense.

"I ended up not playing the tournament," he recalled. "I started the championship, but didn't finish it, because there was a National Youth Championship, to be played in Cumaná city and as I was 17, I was called from the Double A to the youth team to go play."

Armas had an outstanding performance, starring as his team won the Anzoátegui state title. He was called to the national team to play for the World Youth Championship in Maracaibo. That was where he caught the attention of the former major leaguer Pompeyo "Yo-Yo" Davalillo, a scout for the Pittsburgh Pirates.

Davalillo, brother of the former All-Star Vic Davalillo, played in the majors in 1953 with the Washington Senators, but a broken leg shortened his career and he devoted his life to trying to recruit players from Venezuela to play in the United States.

"Pompeyo Davalillo had checked me in both the national junior and youth world championships. I also went to a world-wide Double-A championship, in Cartagena, Colombia. I didn't have much chance to play, because I was very young and we had players who were better prepared than me at that time. I did not play, but I had a pretty good time. I kept playing and in 1971 Pompeyo Davalillo arrived at my house, talked to me, said he thought I could make it to the majors, that I could go far in baseball. He spoke with my parents and that's how I started my career."

On January 18, 1971, Armas signed as a free agent with the Pittsburgh Pirates for $5,000. At the same time he signed for 30,000 bolivars to play Venezuelan winter ball with the Caracas Lions, a club that had previously featured two of his idols, Vic Davalillo and Cesar Tovar. Tovar played in the majors from 1965 to 1976 with the Twins, A's, Rangers, Phillies, and Yankees, with a lifetime average of .278; Davalillo batted .279 between 1963 and 1980 with the Indians, Angels, Cardinals, Pirates, Dodgers, and Athletics.

"I was a fan of Caracas and my favorite players were Cesar Tovar and Vic Davalillo. I also admired Joe Ferguson, a power hitter who came as a foreign player." Ferguson, who played 14 seasons in the majors with Dodgers, Cardinals, Astros, and Angels, played with the Lions in Armas's rookie year in Venezuela and batted .294 with 15 homers and 51 RBIs, an inspiration for the young prospect.

"I think they signed me because I was a good outfielder. I was not a good hitter," he said. "You learn to hit with constant work."

Pittsburgh assigned Armas to play with Monroe and with Bradenton in 1971, dividing his time between rookie ball and Class A, where he combined for a .230 batting average; it was clear he had to work harder to improve his offense.

"I was a good outfielder and I realized I had to work twice (as hard as) the Americans to keep my job. That's the way it was at that time, not like now, when someone comes to the majors with a lot of money and have to call you up. Plus there are more teams now. That is the reality of my career."

In 1972 Armas batted .266 with 9 homers and 51 RBIs in Class-A Gastonia, and in 1973 he got the opportunity to play at Double A in an unusual way, after being a batboy for almost two weeks.

"Not that I was happy with what they were doing, but actually they had a lot of players in spring training. There were about 80 players in camp and on the field there were nine. I had no chance to play," he said. "The manager of Class A needed a batboy and from among those 80 players they called my name. So I spent a week doing that. It bothered me a little bit, because I didn't go up there to collect bats. I went to earn a spot. There was a Mexican named Mario Mendoza who helped me a lot; what I did was thanks to him, because I told him I wanted to go home, I was not up there to collect bats. He told me to stay calm, that I was being observed to see what kind of character I had, whether I was spoiled. I followed his advice and stayed. The next week was all the same. We arrived on Monday and started the game the same, 'Armas, you're the batboy.' It turns out that on Wednesday, in a game between Double A and Triple A, the Double-A center fielder got injured. The manager shouted that they needed an outfielder and then he said, 'Armas, get in there.' I went in, and I stayed."

His bat began to speak for him with Sherbrooke in the Double-A Eastern League; he hit .301 with 11 homers and 45 RBIs in 84 games, despite suffering a broken arm that had him away from action several days.

The young prospect continued his rise in the organization and, after another season in Double A in 1974, he was promoted to the Charleston (West Virginia) Charlies (Triple A) in 1975. With Charleston again the next season he showed some power, hitting 21 homers, and earned a call-up to the Pirates. Armas debuted on September 6, 1976, against the Philadelphia Phillies at Three Rivers Stadium. He replaced Richie Zisk in left field in the ninth inning. He played in four games during his call-up. On October 3, in the last game of the season (the second game of a doubleheader), Armas got his first start, in the lineup as the center fielder and batting sixth. He got his first major-league hit off Pete Falcone of the St. Louis Cardinals, a single to center field to lead off the bottom of the fifth.

Falcone was locked in a pitching duel with Jerry Reuss, and the game went into the bottom of the ninth scoreless. Armas came up with a runner on second base and two outs in the bottom of the ninth and singled to right field to give the Pirates a 1-0 walk-off victory to end the season.

Still, Armas faced trying to break in to an outfield populated by Al Oliver, Omar Moreno, and Dave Parker.

"I had no chance to play, because the Pirates had many good players," he said. "At the time I was in that organization was (Roberto) Clemente, Al Oliver, Willie Stargell, Dave Parker, Richie Zisk, and I had no opportunity to climb. In 1977 (I was out of options), so they had to keep me on the roster or trade me. At the last minute, they traded me to the A's. It was there that I got the chance to show my full potential."

Armas was sent to Oakland on March 15, 1977, along with pitchers Dave Giusti, Doc Medich, Doug Bair, and Rick Langford, and outfielder Mitchell Page, for pitcher Chris Batton and infielders Tommy Helms and Phil Garner.

Oakland, a rebuilding team, relied on the talents of Armas, who hit 13 homers and drove in 53 runs in 118 games. The next two seasons, he played in only 171 games because of injuries.

"In Oakland I obviously had to work hard, because no Latin at that time had a safety spot in the big leagues," he said. "Thanks to Oakland I received the opportunity to play every day and I was able to prove myself."

In 1980 Armas was healthy and able to deploy his strength to become one of the most feared sluggers in the American League. That year he hit 35 homers and drove in 109 runs, with a respectable .279 average.

The following year, in a strike-shortened season, Armas tied three other players for the American League lead in home runs with 22. (The others were Dwight Evans, Eddie Murray, and Bobby Grich. Armas drove in 76 runs, took part in his first All-Star Game, and finished fourth in the voting for the MVP award. He was chosen by *The Sporting News* as the Player of the Year.

Thanks to Armas and Rickey Henderson, the Athletics advanced to the playoffs and swept the Kansas City Royals in the Division Series. Armas was 6-for-11 with two doubles and three RBIs. His bat cooled off in the ALCS against the New York Yankees (2-for-12 with five strikeouts); Oakland was eliminated in three games.

Armas's power caught the attention of the Boston Red Sox. He hit 28 homers for the A's in 1982 and set an AL record for the most putouts in a game by a right fielder (11, on June 12 against the Toronto Blue Jays). After the season the Red Sox acquired Armas and catcher Jeff Newman in exchange for third baseman Carney Lansford, outfielder Garry Hancock, and Jerry King.

"They wanted a player who would protect Jim Rice and they made the deal," said Armas, who was surprised by his departure from Oakland. For Boston, Armas played center field, although he wasn't a particularly fast fielder, but with Rice and Dwight Evans he helped form one of the most powerful outfields in Red Sox history.

"It was a good team," Armas said. He hit a career-high 36 homers, with 107 RBIs, topping 100 for the second time in his career, finishing with 107. Rice led the club with 39 homers and 126 RBIs, but Evans fell short with 22 homers and 58 RBIs, playing only 126 games in the final season of future Hall of Famer Carl Yastrzemski.

"It was a real experience to play with a superstar like Carl Yastrzemski was," Armas said. "I met Ted Williams in spring training and it was a great experience to meet those two legends."

Despite his power, Armas heard some boos from Red Sox fans because of his anemic .218 average and 131 strikeouts in 145 games. "At that time, Latinos and black people were not beloved in Boston. I came to Boston and they started to boo me. I spoke with my lawyer and told him to get them to trade me. I didn't want to play in Boston anymore. There was a pressure in playing for that team. They talked with me and said, 'Hey, you came over here to help Jim Rice and Dwight Evans.' 'Yes, but I can't, this way. It is very difficult to play like this.' At that time it was different from the way it would be now – if I had been signed to a $120 million contract, I wouldn't have cared if they shouted at me and booed me. But at that time you had to earn your place and play hard."

A year later the Venezuelan, led by his power, changed those boos into ovations. Injury-free, Armas played 157 of the team's 162 games and home runs steadily found their way into the stands. He finished as the American League leader in both home runs and RBIs (43 and 123). He dominated the circuit with 77 extra-base hits and 339 total bases.

"You never have those goals. Your goal is having a good year, but I never thought I would be the home-run king or the RBI champion when there were many superstars in the majors – Reggie Jackson, Jim Rice, Dave Kingman, Lance Parrish, Dwight Evans, many good players. That I could compete with these superstars made me proud, and that year, thank God, I was able to play an almost full season."

Armas's remarkable season earned him his second All-Star Game and his only Silver Slugger Award, and he placed seventh in the MVP voting.

Injuries cropped up again in 1985 and Armas was limited to 103 games; his production declined sharply to 23 homers and 64 RBIs.

In 1986 Armas got into 121 games as the Red Sox advanced to their first World Series since 1975. And if the defeat in 1975 was painful, after the famous Carlton Fisk homer in Game Six forced a deciding seventh game, the loss to the New York Mets was even worse.

"These were frustrating days for me," admitted Armas, who was the greatest home-run hitter in the American League from 1980 through 1985, with 187 round-trippers, but he hit only 11 in 1986. "In the ALCS I hurt and I couldn't play anymore, because my right ankle was swollen."

If Armas's home runs had seemed to become a constant in Boston, so had injuries. During his career he spent 12 stints on the disabled list, but no injury was as painful as the one in the fifth game of the ALCS against the California Angels at Anaheim Stadium.

In the second inning, Armas chased down a long fly ball hit by Doug DeCinces. "Many of my leg injuries were from running, but the one in the ankle was because I was hooked in the center-field fence," he recalled. "Now they are cushioned but back then, the walls were all concrete." Dave Henderson took over for Armas for the rest of the playoffs. Henderson had an immediate impact.

"I tried to play, but I couldn't anymore," Armas said. "And that's when Dave Henderson replaced me and he did a good job." Henderson's ninth-inning homer in Game Five against Anaheim spared the Red Sox a loss, and he drove in the winning run with a sacrifice fly in the 11th. Though Armas's ankle improved, Henderson made the most of his opportunity; Armas was sentenced to the bench.

In the World Series, Armas was limited to one pinch-hitting appearance in Game Seven, after 15 days without playing.

"The ankle still bothered me, but I could pinch-hit. I could not run at 100 percent," he recalled. "It was difficult, but I had a strong desire to appear in the World Series. Even if it was just an at-bat, it doesn't matter, and I appeared in the World Series, which is what anyone wants."

Armas pinch-hit for pitcher Bruce Hurst in the seventh inning with the game tied 3-3. The Venezuelan struck out swinging in what it was his last at-bat in a Red Sox uniform.

About Game Six, he was philosophical. "What happened is what happens so often in baseball. We were winning an easy game. At the end we felt champions but Bill Buckner's error left us without the victory. Then we lost the World Series," said Armas. "We lost by an error that cost us the Series. These are things that happen in baseball."

"The pitching also faltered. Roger Clemens couldn't do the job, Dennis Boyd couldn't do the job, many players didn't do the job," he said. "For me it was frustrating because I was playing every day, but then I couldn't help the team in the World Series because of an injured ankle. That's not easy for any baseball player."

After the season Armas became a free agent and, a likely victim of collusion, signed with the Angels but not until July 1,

Power-hitting outfielder Tony Armas led the American League with 43 home runs in 1984. He slugged 251 homers over 14 big-league seasons, mostly with Oakland and Boston. (SABR / The Rucker Archive)

1987. "The team owners got together and agreed to not sign free agents that year and I was one of those affected," he recalled. "I had offers from Mexico, but spent all that time practicing in Caracas with Pompeyo Davalillo, who was working with the Angels at the time. That's where I signed."

After so much downtime, Armas was sent to Triple A for the first time in more than a decade. He played in 29 games for Edmonton before returning to the majors for the last month and a half of the season. He batted .198 in 28 games.

Armas's days as a regular came to an end in California, where he was used primarily against left-handed pitchers by manager Cookie Rojas, with whom he had a difficult relationship in 1988. "I started to play against left-handed pitchers and that was hard," he said. "There was a time when I began to play every day and in a week I hit like five homers – but that's when I had the mishap with Cookie Rojas."

"One day we went to Oakland to play and Chili Davis, who was the regular, did not want to play; people were booing him, because he'd played the year before with San Francisco. Oakland was going to start Dave Stewart and they said I was not going to play because I was playing against lefties only. Then I got a chance to start playing against some righties, and I hit two home runs in that game (August 14). Rojas didn't put me to play anymore and there came all the controversy with the journalists, saying that if I was hitting well, why I did not play. He said it was because he was the manager, and I told them to talk to the manager, that if they did not play me, it was a matter of him."

From July 28 to August 14, Armas hit .440 with 4 homers and 12 RBIs over a 16-game stretch, including 11 starts, so some sportswriters suggested more playing time for the Venezuelan, even against righties.

"There was this controversy with journalists and Cookie Rojas blamed me because I spoke with the press. Once a newspaper did an article and it was sent to him in Boston and I was called to his office and he asked me why I had told the newspapers that I wasn't playing. 'Look, Cookie, I haven't talked to the press in a long time. They just are realizing what you're doing to me.' 'So you want to play?' And I got to play against Roger Clemens in Boston. I said, 'Cookie, if you think you're going to intimidate me because it is Roger Clemens, you're wrong. If he was going to give me four strikeouts, I'll get four strikeouts. If I'm going to hit him, I'll hit him.'"

And Armas homered against Clemens (two days earlier he had hit one off Bruce Hurst), and then he hit another the next day, on his return to California, against the Yankees. It was Armas's most explosive month of the year and his last major production in the majors: .386 with 8 homers and 19 RBIs in 24 games in August. Nevertheless, his differences with Rojas continued.

"It came out another article in California, after he took me out in a game for a pinch-hitter, even when I had a hit and a home run. I showered and went to the hotel. I did not talk to any journalist. When we got to California he called me to his office, and we hadn't an argument, because I'm not used to that, but he said why I had talked again to the press. 'No, no. I have not spoken to the press.' But they were already realizing who he was."

The relationship ended on September 24, when Rojas was fired as the manager of the Angels. Armas returned to the Angels the following year, his last in the major leagues.

"My third year in California was in the same role, as a pinch-hitter and playing against lefties, and because my knee was bothering me and I couldn't take it anymore, I retired. I could have played for three more years, but unfortunately the knees did not allow it."

Armas remained active in the Venezuelan Winter League, where he was already a legend for his power. He was the first Venezuelan to lead the majors in homers and RBIs, but his 251 career home runs led all Venezuelans. He was also the home-run king in Venezuelan winter ball, after hitting his 97th home run in the last at-bat of his career in the 1991-1992 season. (His mark was surpassed by Robert Perez in 2008.)

Armas played a few more seasons in Venezuela, but the knee hampered him badly and he'd have to take off a week now and again. "I thought it was better to retire than continue to suffer, but I thank God for giving me the opportunity to get where I got. Thanks to baseball I am who I am."

The home run was always Armas's calling card; it also happened to be his farewell letter. He was an investor in the Caribes de Oriente club and he was able to fulfill another dream there, playing with his brothers Marcos and Julio, all three taking up positions as outfielders.

"That was a great thing," Armas said. "It's never been written in any book. I was with the right team on the right day."

Both brothers followed in the footsteps of his older brother, but only Marcos managed to make the majors, with the Athletics for a brief period in 1993.

Tony and his wife, Luisa de Armas, had six children. The third was their son Tony Armas Jr., who played 10 major-league seasons with the Expos, Nationals, Pirates, and Mets, between 1999 and 2008.

"I have much to thank my dad for. Since my childhood he always took me to the stadiums. When you are a child you are like a sponge, absorbing all the information and always trying to imitate someone," said Armas Jr. "When I decided to play baseball, he said to me, 'I was a hitter, but if you don't want to be a hitter, don't do it.' He told me, 'Son, do what you want to do. I support you.' That was important. My parents, at that time, supported me the most."

After he stopped playing, Armas remained active in baseball, mainly in winter ball, as coach of the Caracas Lions. Tony Armas Jr. also played with the Lions. "That was special," said Armas Jr. "It was one of the most special times. I grew up in the Caracas stadium of Caracas, because he always took me there when he played. He felt the same way."

In 1998 Armas was inducted into the Caribbean Baseball Hall of Fame, thanks to his all-time home-run leadership in the Caribbean Series, with 11. In 2005 he was inducted into the

Venezuelan Baseball Hall of Fame and in 2013 into the Latino Baseball Hall of Fame. In 2009 Armas was the hitting coach for the Venezuelan team in the World Baseball Classic, working next to Andres Galarraga, who eclipsed all his home-run records in the majors. (In 1996 Galarraga hit 47 homers and drove in 150 runs with the Colorado Rockies to set the single-season marks for a Venezuelan.)

"Tony was a role model for all the boys that had power," Galarraga said. "I was fortunate to sign with the Lions and privileged to play with him in Venezuela. He taught me many things, gave me some batting tips and that kind of thing."

"I always knew that many good players would follow, because in Venezuela we had many academies and we had many players out there," said Armas. "After Galarraga came Bob Abreu, who was a complete player, Magglio Ordonez, and now Miguel Cabrera, who is even more complete. There is always someone who opens the doors."

And Armas, 62 in 2015, continued to share his knowledge with the younger generation in Venezuela, as a coach of Leones del Caracas (the Caracas Lions) in winter ball. "He loves to teach, because baseball is his life," said Armas Jr. That's never going to change with him. He ends a winter season and during the break goes directly to become a manager in the Bolivarian League with Deportivo Anzoátegui. He is always working with the boys and never stops. He's always traveling; he is never in one place. That is what he likes to do."

"Baseball has given me a lot. Now I'm giving to baseball, trying to help young people," said Armas, who still lives in his native Puerto Píritu. "I am very proud of my career, proud of baseball, and proud of what I do right now, because in my time there were no hitting coaches and I'm proud to work with so many young boys to help them become better players."

SOURCES

Author interviews with Tony Armas on November 12, 2014, and August 5, 2015. All quotations attributed to Armas come from these interviews.

Author interview with Andrés Galarraga on July 30, 2015. All quotations attributed to Galarraga come from this interview.

Author interview with Tony Armas Jr. on July 28, 2015. All quotations attributed to Armas Jr. come from this interview.

articles.latimes.com/1987-08-19/sports/sp-773_1_tony-armas

articles.latimes.com/1988-08-25/sports/sp-1345_1_tony-armas

articles.latimes.com/1988-09-01/sports/sp-4439_1_home-run

articles.latimes.com/1988-09-24/sports/sp-2381_1_interim-manager

el-nacional.com/deportes/lvbp/Antonio-Armas-puesto-acepte-recogebates_0_289171243.html

vidaydeportes.com/entrevista-exclusiva-antonio-armas

Cárdenas, Augusto. "El jonronero de Venezuela," *Diario Panorama*, December 18, 2005.

Cárdenas Lares, Carlos Daniel. *Venezolanos en las Grandes Ligas* (Fundación Cárdenas Lares, 1994).

RAFAEL BETANCOURT

BY GORDON GATTIE

Few players can transition from pitching to a nonpitching position; even fewer successfully can reinvent themselves as pitchers after rising through the ranks as position players. Rafael Betancourt is one of those few major-league position players who became successful pitchers, in his case for over a decade after starting his professional career as a shortstop.

Betancourt identified the two most difficult moments during in his career as the time when he was told to convert from playing shortstop to pitching and his 2001 elbow surgery that resulted in an 18-month absence from pitching.[1]

Betancourt was notorious for his slow pace and tedious between-pitch routine, which included incessant cap tugging and pawing at the mound.[2] In a July 2007 game, he was penalized for taking too much time to throw a pitch. Twice a ball was added to the count when the reliever exceeded the 12-second limit between pitches.[3]

Rafael Jose Betancourt was born on April 29, 1975, in Cumaná, Venezuela, a son of Rafael Betancourt Sr., who taught sociology at Universidad de Oriente in Cumaná, and Evelia Franco, who raised Rafael Jr., Francisco, and Evelyn. There were additional siblings from his father's side, Xermis and Xenás.

Rafael Jr. was raised in a middle-class home with a school-oriented mindset led by his mother, but on the baseball side one of his favorite players growing up was Cleveland Indians shortstop (and future teammate) Omar Vizquel. After high school Rafael enrolled in Instituto Universitario Isaac Newton in nearby Puerto La Cruz to study computer engineering.

On weekends Rafael would return home to play baseball for local amateur teams. One of those weekends, in May 1993, Boston Red Sox scouts conducted a tryout in Cumaná, and Rafael was one of those on the radar of several teams.

In a November 2022 interview, he explained, "My mother wanted me to go to school. She was never into baseball. She wanted us to attend school and forget about any distractions beyond education. But my brother and my father knew that I was passionate about the game and talented for my age, so they pushed me to go to that tryout."[4]

After the tryout, the boys of the family returned home with some news for Evelia. The Red Sox were offering a contract to Rafael as a shortstop.

"My mother saw our faces and she didn't even want us to talk to her," Betancourt recalled. "My father had to ask her for her blessing and support, so I could achieve my dream of becoming a professional baseball player. She really wanted me to attend school."

Betancourt signed with scout Willie Paffen of the Boston Red Sox on September 13, 1993, receiving the largest signing bonus to date for a Venezuelan-born player at $47,500.[5] Initial reports suggested that the 6-foot-2, 180-pound shortstop could run well and cover much ground. Paffen successfully lobbied for Betancourt's services among 10 other teams vying for the 18-year-old.[6]

Betancourt started his professional career in 1994 playing shortstop for the Rookie-level Gulf Coast League Red Sox. He struggled during his first season, hitting .111 with no extra-base hits in 63 at-bats and committing nine errors in 91 chances over 20 games. His offense improved the following season, as Betancourt raised his average to .256 in 168 at-bats but slugged only .286 while striking out over twice as often as he walked. His fielding improved, though he split time between shortstop, second base, and third base. The Red Sox moved Betancourt to the Michigan Battle Cats in the Class-A Midwest League. His batting average dropped to .167 in 168 at-bats over 62 games, and his .932 fielding percentage at shortstop wasn't helping him advance.

After a game in Fort Myers, Florida, the Red Sox director for minor leagues, Bob Schaffer, told the 20-year-old that the organization wanted him to try as a pitcher.

"Bob said they wanted me to pitch because they liked my arm and accuracy, and I said a straight 'no' right there. It was really tough to digest for me, as I was always the shortstop, I idolized Vizquel and wanted to be on the field always."

"Now I thank them for bearing with me, because they could have just fired me for saying no. But they were patient and asked me to trust in the process and that I would have their support. From that day all started to change and I started to make progress right away, the progress that I had not seen in my first two years," he recalled.[7]

The Red Sox converted Betancourt from shortstop to pitcher during 1997 spring training. The 21-year-old right-hander rejoined the Battle Cats as a reliever. Betancourt enjoyed more success on the mound than at the plate: He allowed no runs during an 11-game span from June 15 through July 23. Over 12 innings, he allowed only six hits, recorded 17 strikeouts, and issued no walks. The blossoming reliever earned his first two saves.[8]

Betancourt's stellar strikeout-to-walk ratio characterized his pitching throughout his career. He finished his first professional season pitching with 11 saves and 1.95 ERA over 32⅓ innings for Michigan. He recorded 52 strikeouts against only two walks; his 14.5 strikeouts and 7.8 runners allowed per nine innings led all Midwest League pitchers.[9] Years later, Betancourt admitted, "I was a good defensive shortstop, but never was a real good hitter. And Boston had Nomar (Garciaparra), so they turned me into a pitcher."[10]

That offseason in Venezuela, Betancourt worked with Boston's legendary pitcher Luis Tiant.[11] Betancourt became a father during the offseason; his daughter Raniel was born to him and his wife, Griselda, in February. Over the next two seasons, the aspiring pitcher split time between Rookie ball, Class-A Sarasota, and Double-A Trenton, maintaining high strikeout-to-walk ratios but not overpowering hitters. His 13 saves at Trenton were fifth among Eastern League relievers. However, the Red Sox released Betancourt in November 1999 and sent him to pitch in Japan for the Yokohama Bay Stars, with the understanding he would return to the Red Sox organization.[12] The Venezuelan didn't fare much better in Japan, compiling a 1-2 record and a 4.08 ERA over 28⅔ innings; he recorded 16 strikeouts and an uncharacteristically high 11 walks, then spent the latter half of the season in the Japanese minor leagues.

Boston invited the nonrostered Betancourt to spring training in 2001.[13] In mid-March, he headed to minor-league camp and spent the first six weeks with Double-A Trenton. In mid-May Betancourt's season ended with right elbow troubles. Two months later, he underwent surgery on his right elbow, transposing the ulnar nerve and stabilizing his right elbow and ulna with a metal rod inserted in his right forearm. His days with the Red Sox organization ended after his 0-1 record and 5.63 ERA over 24 innings and subsequent surgery, though his stellar 9-to-1 strikeout-to-walk ratio offered hope that he would latch on with another club. He missed the entire 2002 recovering from surgery. Betancourt believed he would return. "People probably were saying, 'He's done.' But I always had in mind that I have to come back. I needed one more chance to see if I could pitch."[14]

In January 2003 the Cleveland Indians took a chance on the former infielder by signing him to a minor-league deal.[15] The Betancourts' second child, son Rafael, was born that January.[16] During the season's first half, Betancourt split time between Double-A Akron and Triple-A Buffalo, pitching in the Akron Aeros bullpen as a middle reliever before taking over as closer on May 15. He immediately thrived in his new role, saving 13 consecutive games, and recording 16 saves with a 1.39 ERA, 75 strikeouts, and 13 walks over 45⅓ innings before his big-league promotion. After starting his professional baseball career nine years earlier, Betancourt made his major-league debut pitching for Cleveland against the Chicago White Sox on July 13 2003. He entered the game in the seventh inning, recording his first out when Aaron Rowand hit a foul popup. His next batter was future Hall of Fame slugger Frank Thomas; Betancourt struck out Thomas on four pitches. Unfortunately for the rookie, in the next inning, he allowed a leadoff single to Paul Konerko that ultimately led to the game-winning run and absorbed the loss in a 7-4 White Sox victory. Betancourt was ecstatic about his debut, commenting, "I was very excited that they used me in a tie game. I'm sorry we lost, but it was like, 'OK, the score is tied, let's go get them.'"[17] Two weeks later, Betancourt earned his first major-league victory when he pitched a scoreless 14th inning in a 3-2 Cleveland victory.[18] Two weeks after his first win,

he recorded his first save by retiring the final four batters in a 3-1 Indians win.[19] Cleveland manager Eric Wedge was pleased with his rookie's approach: "He's got a good fastball and slider. I like the way he handles himself out there and stays focused."[20] The rookie reliever took advantage of his long-awaited opportunity and became a steadfast member of Cleveland's bullpen. Over a 31-day stretch in mid-August and late September, Betancourt pitched in 15 of 26 games, compiling a 1.83 ERA over 19⅔ innings.[21]

Betancourt completed his rookie season with a 2-2 record, one save, and a 2.13 ERA in 38 innings. He struck out 36 batters and walked 13; his above-average 2.77 strikeout-to-walk ratio was among the lowest in his career. Although Cleveland struggled to a 68-94 record and a fourth-place AL Central Division finish that season, the organization felt it had a blossoming bullpen between Betancourt, a returning Bob Wickman in the closer role, David Riske, Scott Stewart, Bob Howry, and Jack Cressend.[22] One unique event in Betancourt's career occurred on August 3: in the seventh inning, he hit Marcus Thames on an 0-and-2 pitch. That game was Betancourt's 10th big-league appearance, and Thames was only the 35th batter he faced in his burgeoning big-league career. Betancourt pitched 678 more regular-season innings over 11 seasons, facing another 2,752 batters – and never hit another batter again.[23]

For the first time in his career, Betancourt made a major-league team's Opening Day roster. The 2004 Indians were optimistic that they would return to their winning ways from the late 1990s. Betancourt pitched well during the first six games, then allowed runs in his next three appearances. Wedge continued displaying faith in his control artist, first making him the primary set-up man,[24] then naming him closer on May 1, replacing Riske.[25] Betancourt earned two saves in his first three games as a closer, which included a game-ending Manny Ramirez strikeout after Boston rallied with a four-run ninth inning to pull within a single run and Ramirez represented

Veteran reliever Rafael Betancourt poses during spring training with the Cleveland Indians in 2009. He logged over 600 career appearances in the majors. (Ronald Martinez / Getty Images Sports)

the go-ahead run.[26] However, after a month in the role, Wedge shifted closer duties from Betancourt to José Jiménez because the Cleveland manager wanted Betancourt in the setup role. "Raffie has been our most consistent reliever this year. We've had him in the closer's role for almost a month, and he's only had a couple of opportunities because we're not able to get the lead to him. So I've got my best pitcher in the bullpen not pitching."[27]

After struggling through a mediocre first half, the Indians played better during the second half. From August 4 through August 14, Cleveland won 10 of 11 games with the only defeat a loss by Betancourt on a walk-off. The Indians pulled within one game of the division-leading Minnesota Twins but lost their next nine straight to fall out of playoff contention. Betancourt completed the season with a 5-6 record, four saves, a team-leading 12 holds, and a 3.92 ERA. His strikeout-to-walk ratio improved to 4.22, among the best in the American League.

Firmly established in Cleveland's bullpen, Betancourt pitched in a set-up role during the entire 2005 season. He started the season by pitching nine hitless, scoreless innings and pitched more reliably and consistently in the seventh and eighth innings. Betancourt retired 27 of the first 28 batters he faced, allowing a lone walk in his third appearance that season. Early that season he appreciated having a stable role: "I think the whole bullpen, not just me, feels more comfortable this year. We have a guy for every spot."[28]

Well-known for his control, Betancourt was evolving into a strikeout pitcher who could tempt batters to chase high fastballs while slowing the game down.[29] He spent time on the 15-day disabled list with a sore right shoulder from June 30 through July 8, then was handed a 10-game suspension for violating Major League Baseball's Joint Drug Prevention and Treatment Program from July 8 to July 18. He was the first major-league player and third in the Indians' organization to be penalized for a violation.[30] The Indians were completely surprised by Betancourt's suspension, as his body type and velocity hadn't notably changed in his three years with the organization; Cleveland was not informed what specific substance was in violation of the MLB agreement. Betancourt speculated that the issue might be related to an anti-inflammatory drug prescribed in Venezuela that would be equivalent to over-the-counter medication in the United States. "It would be like you guys going to a pharmacy here and buying Advil or Tylenol," he said.[31] Except for one bad outing, Betancourt pitched well and stayed off the DL for the rest of the season, ending his third big-league season with a 2.79 ERA and 73 punchouts over 67⅔ innings.

The year 2006 started on a high note, as Betancourt pitched for Venezuela in the World Baseball Classic, but he regressed during the major-league season. Pitching mostly in a set-up role once again, he endured a challenging first half while pitching better in the second half. Betancourt thrived while pitching at Jacobs Field in Cleveland; his 1.88 ERA there was significantly better than his road 5.79 ERA. For the third consecutive year, he spent time on the DL. During the offseason, the Betancourt

and the Indians avoided arbitration by agreeing to a one-year deal.[32] The signing paid off handsomely for Cleveland.

The 2007 season featured a dominant Betancourt all year while the Indians returned to the postseason. Betancourt made a major contribution to Cleveland's success, establishing a career-high 79⅓ innings pitched and a career-best 1.47 ERA while tying his career highs in wins (five) and reaching his second-highest strikeout total (80). He issued a career-low 1.02 walks per nine innings and allowed a career-low 5.8 hits per nine innings. His microscopic first-half 1.13 ERA increased only slightly to 1.82 during the season's second half; he pitched at least 10 innings each month and only once did his monthly ERA exceed 2.00. Betancourt again pitched primarily during the eighth inning as a set-up man, tying for the AL lead with 31 holds.[33] He walked only one batter during his first 24⅓ innings while recording 20 strikeouts. Several managers and players noticed Betancourt's effectiveness, with Detroit Tigers manager Jim Leyland praising the reliever, commenting. "He's been one of the best pitchers in the game all year. He gets no publicity, but you look at his numbers and they are remarkable. Where would the Indians be without Betancourt?"[34] Leyland was especially aware of Betancourt's pitching, as the Tigers finished in the American League Central Division's second place, eight games behind the Indians. One highlight for Betancourt that season was standing on the mound when Cleveland captured the division title. On September 23 against the Oakland Athletics at Jacobs Field with over 40,000 fans in attendance, Betancourt pitched the final 1⅓ innings for his second save, striking out Mark Ellis on a fastball to end the game.

"It was by far the most rewarding moment of my career," Betancourt said. "Closing that game, clinching the division was very special for our group since we were growing together. The emotion was hard to describe."

In the Division Series against the New York Yankees, Betancourt pitched twice, striking out three and issuing no walks over two scoreless innings. In his first four appearances during the Championship Series against Boston, pitching at least one inning in four consecutive games, Betancourt allowed one hit while delivering 6⅓ shutout innings. In Game Two he delivered the best postseason appearance in his career. Throwing 2⅓ scoreless innings when the game was tied from the seventh inning through the ninth, his shining moment was retiring Kevin Youkilis in the ninth inning with two outs and Jacoby Ellsbury representing the winning run on second base. Betancourt and Youkilis dueled during an 11-pitch at-bat to send the game into extra innings. Youkilis saw 11 straight fastballs, fouling off six consecutive 2-and-2 pitches,[35] before driving the final one into center field where the ball landed in Grady Sizemore's glove. Betancourt threw 42 pitches, striking out three while allowing one hit, giving Cleveland the opportunity to win in extra innings.[36] In the decisive seventh game, Betancourt entered the game in the bottom of the seventh with Cleveland trailing 3-2, but allowed six earned runs over 1⅔ innings and couldn't finish the eighth inning.[37] The rough outing dampened the numerous highlights from the 2007 campaign, during which he tied with Victor Martinez with the fourth-highest Wins Above Replacement (4.3 per Baseball-Reference) on the Indians.

The Indians and Betancourt once again avoided arbitration before the 2008 season. Since joining Cleveland in 2003, Betancourt had signed successive one-year contracts. Now the Indians, who experienced no player arbitration hearings from 1992 to 2007, signed Betancourt to a two-year contract with a club option for the third year. Cleveland general manager Mark Shapiro commented, "This is a great story. Knowing what Rafael has been through and how hard he worked, to see him get the security of a multiyear deal and for us to get the consistency and effectiveness we've had from him for our bullpen, it's a great story."[38] Unfortunately for both sides, Betancourt's 2008 numbers nosedived after his spectacular 2007 season. His ERA skyrocketed to 5.07 over 71 innings; his strikeout rate dipped slightly, but his walk rate more than tripled from 2007's 1.0 to 3.2 walks per nine innings. He struggled during the first half, with a 2-4 record and a 6.00 ERA over 42 innings; August was the only month when his ERA was below 4.00. Eager to prove 2007 was no fluke, Betancourt pushed himself even harder while exercising and throwing during the offseason, noting, "That's why I prepared myself in the offseason. I feel stronger than I did last year." Indians skipper Eric Wedge complimented Betancourt's drive, saying, "He doesn't take anything for granted. He doesn't assume anything. He feels like each and every day he has to prove himself all over again. He's always been like that."[39]

Focused on the coming season, Betancourt declined the invitation to play for Venezuela in the 2009 World Baseball Classic. When the season began, his ERA in his 10 April appearances was 5.40, and while the Indians found themselves in the division basement. Betancourt notably improved during May, compiling a 2.70 ERA over 16⅔ innings, then injured his right groin and missed all of June. He returned to the mound on July 9, and pitched three more games for the Indians. On July 23 Betancourt was sent to the Colorado Rockies for minor-league power pitcher Connor Graham.[40] Betancourt wasn't surprised by the trade, commenting, "You never know when this is going to happen. I've seen a lot of guys come here and leave this year. Now it's my turn."[41]

Betancourt immediately thrived in his new environment, delivering 11⅔ scoreless innings and 14 strikeouts against two walks during his first 14 appearances in a Rockies uniform. He pitched well for the rest of the season, recording a 3-1 record, a team-leading 12 holds, and a 1.78 ERA over 25⅓ innings. His 5.8 strikeout-to-walk ratio illustrated his exceptional control.[42] Betancourt solidified the bullpen and helped Colorado win the National League wild card, though the Rockies fell to the Philadelphia Phillies 3 games to 1 in the NL Division Series.

During the offseason, Betancourt decided to remain with the Rockies, signing a two-year deal.[43]

He excelled once again in a set-up role, teaming with Matt Belisle to form a highly effective one-two late-inning bridge to closer Huston Street. He established career highs with 72 appearances, 89 strikeouts and an 11.13 strikeout-to-walk ratio, second-highest in the majors. Similar to previous seasons, he pitched better in the second half of the season, evidenced by his first-half 5.06 ERA and significantly better second-half 2.08 ERA. Over the season's last two months, Betancourt's minuscule 1.52 ERA and .114 opponents' batting average over 23⅔ innings helped the Rockies make a late-season playoff push. On September 18 the Rockies were only one game behind the West Division-leading San Diego Padres. Betancourt threw 7⅓ shutout innings during the final two weeks, allowing just one hit, but Colorado lost 13 of its final 14 games – including the final eight straight – and missed the playoffs.[44] Although he delivered another solid season, similar to many pitchers feeling the effects of Coors Field, his road ERA (2.27) was lower than his home ERA (4.99).

Betancourt continued his excellent relieving the next season. Although the Rockies endured a challenging 2011, finishing with a 73-89 record, Colorado's reliable bullpen gave the Rockies an opportunity to win in the later innings. Betancourt and Belisle continued serving as effective set-up relievers for closer Street during the season's first half. When Street spent time on the DL in mid-August and late September, Betancourt filled in as closer, earning eight saves, and when Street returned, he pitched in a set-up role while Betancourt closed.[45] Betancourt's 2011 second half was even better than his 2010 second half. His subatomic 0.33 ERA over 27 innings included 39 strikeouts and only seven hits, an opponents' batting average of .080, and one walk; From August 27 through September 28, he retired 27 consecutive batters.[46] After the season the Rockies traded Street to the San Diego Padres, with the expectation that Betancourt would be the closer the next season.[47]

For the first time in his career, the resilient 36-year-old, nine-year veteran entered a season as a major-league closer. While the rebuilding Rockies struggled throughout the season, Betancourt provided stability in the bullpen. His season started well as he recorded six saves while allowing a lone run over 10 innings. He struggled in May and June, rebounded with a stellar August, and then fizzled during September. Betancourt recorded a career-high 31 saves; through the end of the 2023 season, that total is tied for seventh-highest in club history. However, Colorado endured a challenging season, dropping to the NL West Division basement on July 17 and remaining there for remainder of the season. Betancourt was 1-4 with a 2.81 ERA over 57⅔ innings, and tied with teammate Dexter Fowler for a team-high 2.6 WAR (per Baseball-Reference). He pitched equally well during the first and second halves, while his home 3.72 ERA was notably higher than his road 1.88 ERA.

After Betancourt's first full season as a closer, nagging injuries and a heavy workload affected his ability to remain healthy. In June of 2012 the Rockies in an experiment had switched from the commonly used five-man starting rotation to a four-man rotation with three "piggyback" relievers, limiting starters to 75 pitches per outing. The result was a bullpen that pitched a then major-league record 657 innings with their opponents' batting average reaching a majors-worst .274.[48] For the 2013 season, the Rockies were planning to use an eight-man bullpen with starting pitchers reaching 100 pitchers per outing. Betancourt started the season strong, saving eight games with a 1.59 ERA over 11⅓ innings in April, but as Memorial Day drew near, Betancourt's effectiveness was decreasing. He landed on the DL with a strained groin in early June. Betancourt left the DL four weeks later, pitched for six games, then went back on the DL because of an emergency appendectomy on July 19. He felt sick after a team workout, assistant trainer Scott Gehret determined he had appendicitis, and Betancourt was rushed to the hospital. Rockies manager Walt Weiss commented, "I don't think they had a whole lot of time left before that thing ruptured."[49] Betancourt's season worsened when he underwent Tommy John surgery on September 17.

After recovering for several months, Betancourt started traveling the comeback road once again.

In 2014 he pitched a few innings for the Rookie Grand Junction Rockies and Triple-A Colorado Springs Sky Sox during his rehabilitation. The following spring training as a nonroster invitee, his comeback took another detour when he was hit in the face with a line drive that deflected off his glove during an exhibition game.[50] Betancourt was a solid bullpen contributor during the first two months, then went on the DL for vertigo on June 8.[51] He returned in late June and pitched poorly during August. After six seasons and 58 saves, he was designated for assignment on August 23. He made his final appearance in the seventh inning on August 22, retiring the side in order.

Mentoring younger pitchers, Betancourt appeared in several short YouTube clips; those posted in 2012 included his experience with elbow surgery[52] and advice to young players.[53] Additional clips posted in October 2016 included short tutorials on how to throw a breaking ball[54] and how to prepare for a baseball game.[55]

Betancourt finished his 12-season career with a 38-37 won/lost record, a 3.36 ERA, and 75 saves. His high 9.5 career strikeout rate and 4.41 strikeout-to-walk ratio became a benchmark for the power and control relievers that became commonplace during the late 2010s. As of the end of the 2023 season, Betancourt remained among the Rockies' top 10 pitchers for career saves (58, seventh) and appearances (309, eighth), and his 2007 Indians season is one of the best relief seasons in Cleveland's history. The only uniform number he ever wore was number 63.

"To be honest, I was not mentally ready to hang up my spikes, but I was happy with the career I achieved," Betancourt said. "I worked very hard every day for so many years. I felt if I was not training, I was leaving something behind. Being a major-league player is a very difficult job, far from the glamour of being seen on TV or making a solid income. At 40 years old I was tired of surgeries and I thought very much about my family, so I took the decision to call it off."

In 2016 Betancourt, who was a staple in the Rockies locker room, worked as a special adviser to the Rockies general manager. After the season he moved to Miami to focus on raising his children, Raniel and Rafael, and help them on their way through college.

"It goes back to education and providing the best opportunities. My kids saw how hard the way of professional sports is. Will I support them if they want to go that route? Yes! Do I want that for them? I am not exactly sure."

Asked in 2023 if he aspired to return to baseball in some capacity, Betancourt said he was open to return at some point working as a coach or adviser. "Baseball implies a lot of responsibilities and after my playing days were done, I wanted to focus all of that into my family."[56]

Betancourt overcame an early position change from shortstop to pitcher, a potential career-ending elbow injury, and multiple DL stints to become one of the best set-up relievers during the mid-2000s. His amazing control, highlighted by only one hit batsman out of 2,787 career batters faced, complemented with strong work ethics, made him an exemplar reliever for aspiring pitchers.

ACKNOWLEDGMENTS

The author thanks Cassidy Lent for providing National Baseball Hall of Fame source material, Carl Riechers for his thorough fact-checking and recommended edits, and Lisa Gattie for her meaningful input.

SOURCES

Besides the sources cited in the Notes, the author consulted Baseball-Almanac.com, Baseball-Reference.com, Retrosheet.org, TheBaseballCube.com, and the following:

James, Bill. *The New Bill James Historical Abstract* (New York: The Free Press, 2001).

Thorn, John, and Pete Palmer, et al. *Total Baseball: The Official Encyclopedia of Major League Baseball* (New York: Viking Press, 2004).

Thanks to Leonte Landino for interviewing Rafael Betancourt for this biography.

NOTES

1   ProTips4U, "Rafael Betancourt – His Toughest Moments from Surgery to Switching Positions," YouTube.com, June 22, 2012. https://www.youtube.com/watch?v=S2VfSFTgT50.

2   Tom Withers, "Betancourt and Indians Agree to $5.4 Million, Two Year Deal," *Marion* (Ohio) *Star*, January 24, 2008: 18.

3   Sheldon Ocker, "So, Who Said There's No Clock in a Baseball Game?" *Akron Beacon Journal*, July 5, 2007: C005.

4   Leonte Landino interview with Rafael Betancourt, November 2022. Unless otherwise indicated, all direct quotations are from this interview.

5   Foreign Exchange, *Hazleton* (Pennsylvania) *Standard-Speaker*, November 17, 1993: 24.

6   Nick Cafardo, "Sox Explore Steinbach Deal," *Boston Globe*, November 17, 1993: 42.

7 Leonte Landino interview of Rafael Betancourt, May 2023.

8 Crystal Evola, "Ex-Battle Cat Realizes Big-League Dream," *Battle Creek* (Michigan) *Enquirer*, July 26, 1997: 13.

9 *2004 Cleveland Indians Media Guide* (Cleveland: Cleveland Indians Baseball Company, Inc., 2004), 92.

10 Stephanie Storm, "Aeros Closer Eases Pain," *Akron Beacon Journal*, June 3, 2003: C004.

11 Peter Gammons, "Time for Owners to Show Resolve," *Boston Globe*, January 4, 1998: 87.

12 Peter Gammons, "Duquette Has Done Worlds of Good Here," *Boston Globe*, December 5, 1999: 69.

13 Gordon Edes, "Red Sox Send Out Invitations," *Boston Globe*, February 1, 2001: 51.

14 Sheldon Ocker, "So Far, Switch to Pitching Working," *Akron Beacon Journal*, July 17, 2003: C004.

15 "Tribe Signs Four to Minor-League Deals," *Port Clinton* (Ohio) *News Herald*, February 7, 2003: 7.

16 2004 Cleveland Indians Media Guide, 92.

17 Paul Hoynes, "Laker Not as Cunning as Fans Might Think," *Cleveland Plain Dealer*, July 14, 2003: 67.

18 Burt Graeff, "Laker Delivers Late in Tribe Victory," *Cleveland Plain Dealer*, July 28, 2003: 23.

19 Burt Graeff, "Tribe Duo Pitching Perfectly," *Cleveland Plain Dealer*, August 11, 2003: 21.

20 Associated Press, "Betancourt Sparkles in Relief for Cleveland," *Bucyrus* (Ohio) *Telegraph-Forum*, August 11, 2003: 12.

21 Sheldon Ocker, "Loss to Royals Gives Indians Sick Feeling," *Akron Beacon Journal*, September 11, 2003: C005.

22 Paul Hoynes, "Ex-Rockie Jimenez Close to Deal with Tribe," *Cleveland Plain Dealer*, January 8, 2004: 44.

23 Paul Sullivan, "The Return of Incredible Rafael Betancourt Fun Facts," Fangraphs, February 2, 2015. https://blogs.fangraphs.com/the-return-of-incredible-rafael-betancourt-fun-facts/. Accessed December 15, 2021.

24 Paul Hoynes, "Faulty Pen Faces a New Challenge," *Cleveland Plain Dealer*, April 12, 2004: 25.

25 Burt Graeff, "Rafael Opens as Closer," *Cleveland Plain Dealer*, May 1, 2004: 36.

26 Burt Graeff, "Betancourt Outduels Ramirez," *Cleveland Plain Dealer*, May 5, 2004: 41.

27 Paul Hoynes, "Jimenez Gets Surprise Call to Close," *Cleveland Plain Dealer*, May 27, 2004: 47.

28 Paul Hoynes, "Betancourt Benefiting from a Set Role," *Cleveland Plain Dealer*, April 19, 2005: 31.

29 Paul Hoynes, "Sweet Relief," *Cleveland Plain Dealer*, June 7, 2005: 31.

30 Paul Hoynes, "Betancourt Suspended for Steroid Violation," *Cleveland Plain Dealer*, July 9, 2005: 38.

31 Dennis Manoloff, "Betancourt Will Try to Clear Name," *Cleveland Plain Dealer*, July 16, 2005: 41.

32 Paul Hoynes, "Tribe Signs Betancourt, Still Waiting for Davis," *Cleveland Plain Dealer*, January 17, 2007: 41.

33 *2009 Cleveland Indians Media Guide* (Cleveland: Cleveland Indians Baseball Company, Inc., 2009), 94.

34 "Blake Makes Game-Ending Homers a Habit," *Bucyrus Telegraph-Forum*, September 19, 2007: 4B.

35 Dan Shaughnessy, "Lasting Impression: Rest for the Wary," *Boston Globe*, October 15, 2007: 49.

36 Paul Hoynes, "Youkilis Just Can't Foul Up Betancourt," *Cleveland Plain Dealer*, October 15, 2007: 23.

37 Paul Hoynes, "Monster Letdown in Boston," *Cleveland Plain Dealer*, October 22, 2007: 21.

38 Chris Assenhelmer, "One Down, Blake to Go," *Elyria* (Ohio) *Chronicle-Telegram*, January 24, 2008: C1.

39 Paul Hoynes, "Miserable '08 Inspiring Betancourt Not to Repeat It," *Cleveland Plain Dealer*, March 21, 2009: 27.

40 Chris Assenhelmer, "Betancourt Traded for Power Arm," *Elyria Chronicle-Telegram*. July 24, 2009: E1.

41 Paul Hoynes, "Betancourt Not Surprised He's Sent to Rockies," *Cleveland Plain Dealer*, July 24, 2009: 28.

42 *2015 Colorado Rockies Information Guide* (Denver: Colorado Rockies Baseball Club, Ltd., 2015), 49.

43 "Rockies Reach Deal with Street, Betancourt, Two Others," *Fort Collins Coloradoan*, January 10, 2010: 8.

44 "Until Next Year," *Grand Junction* (Colorado) *Daily Sentinel*, October 4, 2010: 11.

45 "Giants Put Rockies Away in 8th," *Grand Junction Daily Sentinel*, September 18, 2011: 22.

46 *2023 Colorado Rockies Information Guide* (Denver: Colorado Rockies Baseball Club, Ltd., 2021), 222.

47 Troy Renck, "Street Sent to Padres," *Grand Junction Daily Sentinel*, December 8, 2011: 11.

48 Troy Renck, "Rox Mull Bullpen Options," *Grand Junction Daily Sentinel*, February 19, 2013: 12.

49 "Surgery Shelves Reliever," *Vancouver* (British Columbia) *Province*, July 20, 2013: 43.

50 "Betancourt OK After Scare," *Grand Junction Daily Sentinel*, March 30, 2015: 14.

51 "Third-inning Struggles Costly for Rusin, Rockies," *Grand Junction Daily Sentinel*, Jun 17, 2015: 12.

52 ProTips4U, "Rafael Betancourt – Going Through Elbow Surgery," YouTube, June 12, 2012. https://www.youtube.com/watch?v=QqZhEI106KY.

53 ProTips4U, "Rafael Betancourt – Advice to Young Players," YouTube.com, June 22, 2012. https://www.youtube.com/watch?v=Pa28znF8FNE.

54 ProTips4U, "How to Throw a Breaking Ball with Rafael Betancourt," YouTube.com, October 25, 2016.https://www.youtube.com/watch?v=74f-9KFophI.

55 ProTips4U, "Pitching Tips: How to Prepare for a Baseball Game with Rafael Betancourt," YouTube.com, October 27, 2016. URL: https://www.youtube.com/watch?v=TBAVkQDOd7M.

56 Leonte Landino interview of Rafael Betancourt, May 2023.

MIGUEL CAIRO

BY TONY S. OLIVER

Mickey Cochrane, Roger Bresnahan, and Ralph Kiner are enshrined in Cooperstown. Cecil Fielder once swatted 51 home runs in a season; Roger Maris, a still mythical 61. Nomar Garciaparra won consecutive batting titles in the American League. Shoeless Joe Jackson became an all-time great, all-time goat, or both, depending on your viewpoint. Hack Wilson drove in 191 runs in one season. Charles Comiskey had not one, but two ballparks named after him.

Yet none of these men played in more major-league baseball games than Miguel Cairo, who suited up for 1,490 contests over 17 years and for nine franchises, ranking 21st among Venezuelans as of the start of the 2024 season. Cairo logged eight campaigns with 100 or more games played and hung up his spikes with a 77.65 percent stolen-base percentage, a higher rate of success than those enjoyed by Craig Biggio, Jackie Robinson, Willie Mays, and Lou Brock during their Hall of Fame careers.

Cairo was born on May 4, 1974, in Anaco, Venezuela. Located in the state of Anzoátegui, the city is supported by the petroleum and natural gas industries. It was a banner year for major-league baseball with the Oakland Athletics three-peating as World Series champions and 185 future players coming into the world, including 12 Venezuelans, the first time the country had produced that many.[1]

As an international player (not residing in the United States, Puerto Rico, or Canada), Cairo was eligible to sign with any franchise. He agreed to a deal with the Los Angeles Dodgers as an amateur free agent on September 20, 1990. Los Angeles had a less than spectacular draft, selecting 63 players, only seven of whom made it to the majors.[2]

The trek to "The Show" was arduous for Cairo. He logged time in five different minor leagues, appearing in 642 games, and playing second base, third base, and shortstop. (He would play an additional 137 games during rehabilitation assignments after the 1998 season, for a total of 779 minor-league contests.) In 1992 he debuted for the rookie-league Gulf Coast League Dodgers at age 18 and hit .303 in 21 games to earn a promotion to the high Class-A Florida State League. Suiting up for Vero Beach, Cairo was the youngest position player on the team and four birthdays behind his peers. His youth showed as he struggled through 36 games (.224/.285/.224) before a winter of rest helped him produce a .315 line while playing 90 games as an infielder in 1993.

The Dodgers brass kept Cairo at Class A for the 1994 season but shipped him across the nation to the West Coast, where he produced a .291 batting average in 133 games with Bakersfield (California League). He found himself in San Antonio (Double-A Texas League) in 1995, penciled in for 107 games and hitting .278 but the Dodgers traded him and Willis Otáñez to the Seattle Mariners in the offseason for Mike Blowers. Blowers, who had played several years in the majors with the Mariners and the Yankees, would guard the hot corner for a single year with LA before returning to Seattle. Cairo, on the other hand, never suited up in the Northwest, instead being shipped to Toronto on December 18, 1995, as part of a four-player trade. The Blue Jays had lost hope of re-signing future Hall of Famer Roberto Alomar, so second base was up for grabs in 1996. Tomás Pérez, who had hit a respectable .245 as a 21-year-old in 1995, was Cairo's competition, though the position saw Domingo Cedeño, Felipe Crespo, and Tilson Brito on the field for the 1996 Jays.

After spending various campaigns in the minors, Cairo did not waste time on April 17, 1996, when he debuted in the majors batting second and playing second for the visiting Blue Jays. Facing the Angels' Chuck Finley, Cairo lunged at the first pitch and laced a double to left field. Joe Carter later drove him home; while it was the only run of the game for Toronto, it was the first of 504 Cairo would score in the major leagues. His aggressive at-bat set the tone for his career, as he averaged .328 when attacking the first pitch. He played one more game, April 21 at Seattle, hitting another double, before finding himself back in the minors. He played 120 games with Syracuse (Triple-A International League) and hit .277 before returning to the Blue Jays on September 4 against Kansas City once the rosters expanded. For the year, he logged six hits (only singles in September) in 27 at-bats and did not commit an error in 40 chances (22 putouts, 18 assists). After the season he was traded to the Chicago Cubs for Jason Stevenson, a right-handed pitcher who never made the majors. Cairo, on other hand, enjoyed a robust season for Triple-A Iowa (Pacific Coast League), belting 35 doubles and swiping 40 bases while hitting .279 and playing solid defense up the middle. He enjoyed a brief call-up during a series facing Houston, pinch-hitting in all three games. Cairo returned to Iowa but rejoined the Cubs once the rosters expanded, playing in 13 contests, pinch-hitting, pinch-running, handling the middle-infield positions and batting .241. The team's tandem of Shawon Dunston and Ryne Sandberg, together for more than a decade, would not return in 1998: Sandberg retired and Dunston had been traded to Pittsburgh in late August. In Sandberg's last home game, Cairo ran for him in the bottom of the fifth and scored on a Mark Grace home run. He enjoyed two at-bats in the game, picking up a single.

Although the club had some young talent on its roster (Rey Sánchez, Manny Alexander, José Hernández, and Cairo were all capable of playing up the middle and were younger than

30), the Cubs opted to sign veterans Mickey Morandini and Jeff Blauser as their double-play combination. Sánchez was traded to the Yankees and Cairo was left unprotected during the expansion draft for the Arizona Diamondbacks and Tampa Bay Devil Rays.

Having enjoyed a couple of cups of coffee, Cairo was hungry for the chance to stay in the majors for an entire year. Tampa Bay provided him the opportunity. Chosen eighth in the expansion draft, Cairo spent three years with the team. In 1998 he played at second base in 150 contests and batted a respectable .268. His consistency earned him a spot in the Topps All-Star Rookie Team along fellow Venezuelan Magglio Ordóñez. He had a seven-game hitting streak and finished third in the AL in Defense WAR (2.6). Although he had two stints on the disabled list in 1999 due a strained right hamstring, he upped his offensive contribution, hitting .295, then dropped to .261 in 2000. He enjoyed a highlight game on April 6, 2000, driving home the winning run by singling in Tony Graffanino off Héctor Carrasco. Tampa and Cairo went their separate ways in the postseason, with the now-established major leaguer being released on November 27.

After signing with the Athletics on January 7, 2001, Cairo found himself traded at the end of spring training. Oakland swapped him to the Cubs for former AL Rookie of the Year Eric Hinske on March 28, just before the season began. He slashed .285/.364/.374 in 66 games before being claimed off waivers by St. Louis. The Cardinals finished second in the NL Central Division; St. Louis shared the best record in the senior circuit with Houston, but the Astros earned the top seed via the tiebreaker system. Cairo performed admirably for the Cardinals, playing in 27 games and hitting .333 with a .576 slugging average. His bat turned cold (1-for-5) in the NLDS as the Cardinals lost to the eventual World Series champion Diamondbacks in five hard-fought games. (The Cardinals pitched better, but Arizona won the close games.)

St. Louis valued Cairo's presence and kept him for two more years, during which he played 200 games and hit .247. He appeared across the infield, both outfield corner spots, as designated hitter, pinch-hitter, and pinch-runner, displaying his versatility. He enjoyed postseason success in 2002, avenging the prior year's loss to Arizona by going 4-for-4 (three singles, a double, three RBIs, and one hit-by-pitch) in the Division Series and 5-for-13 in the NLCS against San Francisco (four singles, one home run), when the Cardinals were bounced in five games. St. Louis did not reach the postseason in 2003, finishing third in a competitive NL Central.

The 2003 New York Yankees offseason was bizarre, even by the club's standards. ALCS hero Aaron Boone injured his knee while playing pickup basketball, leaving the Yankees with a hole at third base. The Red Sox, their hated rivals, had aggressively pursued a complex trade with Texas for disgruntled shortstop Alex Rodriguez. However, Boston had its own All-Star playing the position in Garciaparra. A swap sending Rodriguez and White Sox outfielder Ordóñez to Boston, Manny Ramírez to the Rangers, and Garciaparra to Chicago was close but ultimately fell apart. New York sensed the opportunity and shuttled its incumbent middle sacker, Alfonso Soriano, to Texas for A-Rod, creating an opportunity at second base. Cairo signed a free-agent deal with the Yankees on December 19, 2003.

Although Enrique Wilson, a three-year veteran with the team, was chosen to start in 2004, his offensive struggles allowed Cairo to earn more playing time.[3] Wilson started 38 of the team's first 59 games, but his anemic bat (he was under .200 for most of the time) earned him the bench. Cairo seized the opportunity, emboldened by manager Joe Torre: "he knows how to play the game ... defensively, offensively, on the basepaths. Right now I'm going to play him for a while because I'm comfortable watching him."[4] He produced a .292/.346/.417 slash line out of the ninth spot and anchored the infield defense. He started all four games of the ALDS against Minnesota, scoring three runs, and delivered a robust line against the Red Sox in the ALCS, reaching base in all but the final game while scoring four runs on a .280/.419/.400 performance. He made a rare appearance in the league leaderboard with 14 times being hit by pitch. Though he found a place in the fans' hearts, his spot in the roster was taken by Robinson Canó, who had wrapped up a solid season split between Double A and Triple A. On October 28, a day after the Red Sox won the World Series, the Yankees granted Cairo free agency. He has fond memories of his time, telling a 2008 interviewer that "it was amazing. To get to play in a lot of full stadiums and to be a part of that organization, it was fantastic."[5]

Cairo's next team was literally across the city. The Mets offered him a one-year deal on January 10, 2005. He shared second base with Kazuo Matsui and again attained the century mark of games played. Alongside Carlos Beltrán, Mike Piazza, Tom Glavine, and former foe Pedro Martínez, Cairo nurtured the next flag-bearers for the franchise in José Reyes and David Wright. He hit .251 while defending first, second, and third bases as well as the outfield corner spots, although he spent two weeks on the DL due to the nagging hamstring issue.

Cairo's Big Apple adventures were not yet over. He switched boroughs again, leaving Queens for the Bronx, signing a free-agent contract with the Yankees on January 6, 2006. Though Canó enjoyed a robust year at the plate, hitting .342, injuries limited him to 122 games, giving Cairo an opportunity to play at second base, third base, first base, shortstop, and left field. He hit .239 but allowed the Yankees flexibility across various positions as they won yet another division title. He re-signed on January 26, 2007, and played every infield position and left field but was released on August 15. He joined the Cardinals four days later and played most of the stretch run at first base, second base, and third base. St. Louis finished 78-84, seven games behind the division-winning Cubs. The Cardinals did not offer him a 2008 contract, opting instead to use Aaron Miles, Brendan Ryan, and Felipe López as their bench infielders.

Seattle saw the promise of Cairo as a veteran presence for its crop of young players, signing him on January 8, 2008, to a one-year contract. He mentored 24-year-old second baseman

José López and 26-year-old shortstop Yuniesky Betancourt in numerous ways: as a first baseman, given Richie Sexson's nagging injuries; as a double-play partner when one of them had the night off; or as a quasi-coach from the dugout on games Cairo did not play. Betancourt noted the guidance on and off the field: "He's a player who has so many years in the league and has the experience in the infield. The things we talk about are learning how to play different hitters and what action needs to be taken."[6] The experiment, while noble, was short-lived as Seattle slumped to 61-101, 27 games off the prior year's pace. Cairo's flexibility enabled him to cross the century mark in games played as he hit .249 for the campaign. The Mariners granted him free agency on October 30, 2008, a day after the Phillies won the World Series. (Game Five began on October 27 but was suspended due to rain and completed on October 29.)

Philadelphia had won its second title in franchise history by riding a potent starting lineup but its bench was thin, making Cairo's versatility and leadership a good match. On February 15, 2009, both parties agreed to a one-year deal. But Cairo played sporadically: He pinch-hit in 19 contests and appeared on the field in eight others. In the postseason Cairo played in the Division Series and the Championship Series, going 0-for-5.

Miguel Cairo played 17 seasons in the majors, known for his versatility and professionalism. He appeared in over 1,500 games with nine teams, including the Yankees and Cardinals. (Jerry Coli / Dreamstime)

When the Phillies returned to the World Series, Cairo was left off the roster.

The Phillies declined to offer Cairo a new contract but the Cincinnati Reds picked him up on January 27, 2010. Originally inked to a one-year deal, Cairo would finish his career with the team after playing three campaigns. In 2010 he hit .290, his highest output since 2004, and produced an OBP of .353, his best mark since 2001. He committed only three errors while playing right field and all four infield positions. The Reds met the Phillies in the 2010 NLDS, with Philadelphia sweeping the three-game set as Cairo went 0-for-3 hitting for the pitcher in each contest. He re-signed during the offseason and delivered a .265 clip in 2011, his last year playing 100 games. He walloped two home runs on August 13 in a 13-1 laugher against San Diego, connecting off Tim Stauffer and Anthony Bass, driving in Jay Bruce both times. Earlier in the summer (June 19) he had homered off Toronto's Carlos Villanueva to drive in Joey Votto and win the game for the Reds, 2-1.

Cairo spent some time in the minors in 2012, rehabilitating a hamstring injury with the Dayton Dragons. His skipper was Delino DeShields, a former teammate; almost a quarter of his teammates had not been born when he signed his first professional contract. He prepared himself for this next stage of this baseball life, stating, "[W]hen you come back here, you want to make sure the kids watch you work. … I just want to make sure I'm a model for them."[7] In 2012 he slumped to .187, below the Mendoza line,[8] but the Reds still employed him in the memorable LDS against the Giants (won by San Francisco in five games after dropping the first two games at home). He pinch-hit twice and replaced Scott Rolen in the bottom of the ninth of the second game. Cairo grounded out on a 0-and-1 pitch from two-time Cy Young Award winner Tim Lincecum in the sixth inning of Game Four, closing the book on his professional career.

Cairo retired after the 2012 season. Stan Javier, himself an Energizer bunny who appeared in 1,763 games, had once told him: "Miguel, you are going to play until your body tells you can't."[9] He averaged 3.62 pitches per plate appearance, driven by a tendency to swing at the first pitch (25.7 percent) as he did in his debut. His .328 average when hitting the first pitch was his highest among all situations, though his .327 during 1-and-0 was a close second. He made solid contact (11 percent strikeout percentage) but did not walk much (5.5 percent) and created 3.9 runs per game. His OPS+ was 77 (100 is league average) due to his low patience at the plate and weak power, but he managed better numbers during the postseason (29 games, 82 plate appearances, .282 average with .394 slugging). He hit better against southpaws (.287) than righties (.255) and during the first half (.268) than the second (.259). Cairo cherished using the lumber against the Phillies, White Sox, and Indians (above .300) but could not figure out the Giants and Dodgers (sub-.200). He was sad to see the Kingdome (1.319 OPS) and Veterans Stadium (1.020 OPS) go to ballpark heaven and was giddy with excitement when Hall of Famers John Smoltz (.467) and Randy Johnson (.346) were on the mound. Mike Mussina (.226) and Martínez (.171) gave him fits, as did the half-brothers Orlando and Liván Hernández (a combined 7-for-45). He places 50th among second basemen in fielding percentage (.9841) and 51st in range factor per nine innings, above Alomar and Biggio.

Cairo played in 10 consecutive seasons in the Venezuelan Winter League, participating in four title-winning clubs. From age 19 to 21 he donned the colors of the capital's Leones before being traded in midseason to the Cardenales of Lara (née Oriente) in 1995-1996. Debuting at age 19, Cairo appeared in 33 games and hit .246.[10] The Leones boasted various big leaguers on their roster, as Omar Vizquel, Bobby Abreu, Ugueth Urbina, and Edgar Alfonzo mixed youth and experience on the 1993-1994 club, which lost the finals to the Navegantes of Magallanes. The nucleus returned in 1994-1995, and Cairo appeared in 56 of the 60 regular-season contests, lifting his average to .319 as Caracas won the league title over the Águilas of Zulia. After a slow start in 1995-1996 (14 games, .250 average), he was traded to Lara for Dilson Torres, and regained his stroke with the Cardenales, hitting a personal-high .341 and picking up a Golden Glove Award.

Cairo struggled mightily in 1996-1997, playing 47 games but managing only 43 hits in 187 at-bats for the lowest production in his Venezuelan career. He rebounded the next year, hitting .284 and .257 in 1998-1999 and then took the next year off from the winter competition. (By then, he had become Tampa's starting second baseman and thus had more mileage.)

Cairo returned to winter ball in 2000-01 with a fine season, earning the MVP award for the final series, claimed in six games by Lara. He played sporadically after that, appearing in 29 games in 2000-2001 and only five in 2002-2003.

For his career, he appeared in 348 games and hit .286 with a .351 OBP. His postseason résumé added 149 games with a .249 batting average. (Walk totals are not complete, making OBP usage less reliable.) Although correlation does not prove causation, Cairo's teams enjoyed winning records in every one of his campaigns, earning four total championships (1994-1995, 1997-1998, 1998-1999, and 2000-2001). The sole blemish in his credentials was the inability to win the Caribbean Series as Venezuela suffered through a 17-year drought between 1989's Zulia victory and the 2006 championship of Caracas. He gathered 10 hits in 53 at-bats (nine singles, one home run) and scored five runs in 14 games. He represented the country as part of the 1995 Caracas team, the 2001 Lara club, and as a reinforcement for the 1996 Magallanes roster.

Cairo had barely donned his uniform for the last time before the Cincinnati Reds named him assistant to general manager Walt Jocketty.[11] The organization had recognized his efforts in the past, nominating him to the Major League Baseball Players Alumni Association's Heart and Hustle Award, given to the player who "best demonstrates a passion for the game of baseball and best embodies the values, spirit, and traditions of the game."[12] Jocketty announced the news on February 14, 2013, declaring, "Miguel expressed an interest in retiring as a

player and becoming involved with the baseball operations side of the game. ... Our younger players will benefit from his work ethic and experience."[13]

After five seasons, the last of which saw Cincinnati fail to achieve 70 wins, Cairo rejoined the Yankees organization, accepting a role as a minor-league infield coordinator prior to the 2018 campaign.[14]

The 2019 season brought another milestone for Cairo. His son, Christian, was rated 83rd among the top 300 draft prospects by *Baseball America*.[15] A shortstop accepted into LSU's powerhouse baseball program, he credited his father for his talent and attitude: "He taught me how to be a man and how to have a work ethic. From day one to the end of the season you have to grind and be all in every game."[16] On June 4, 2019, Christian was drafted by the Cleveland Indians with the 130th pick in the fourth round of the amateur draft.[17] He finished the 2023 season with the Class-A Lake County Captains.

ACKNOWLEDGMENTS

JJ Montilla, Venezuelan sportswriter, for sharing the Venezuelan Baseball reference site "Pelota Binaria," which includes winter league statistics.

Lorenzo "Tony" Piña Cámpora, adviser to the Caribbean Baseball Association, for providing Caribbean Series statistics.

Pete Palmer and Jim Wheeler for detailed disabled list records.

SOURCES

In addition to the sources cited in the Notes, the author relied extensively on Baseball-Reference.com.

NOTES

1   http://www.baseball-almanac.com/players/baseball_births.php?y=1974.

2   https://www.baseball-reference.com/draft/?team_ID=LAD&year_ID=1990&draft_type=junreg&query_type=franch_year&from_type_jc=0&from_type_hs=0&from_type_4y=0&from_type_unk=0.

3   Matt Klassen, "The Legend of the Legendary Miguel Cairo," Fangraphs, February 15, 2013. https://blogs.fangraphs.com/the-legend-of-the-legendary-miguel-cairo/.

4   Mike Bernandino, "Cairo a Strange Fit in New York," *South Florida Sun Sentinel*, May 16, 2004. https://www.sun-sentinel.com/news/fl-xpm-2004-05-16-0405160260-story.html.

5   Associated Press, "Mariners Look to Miguel Cairo as Player-Coach," TDN.com, March 10, 2008. https://tdn.com/sports/mariners-look-to-miguel-cairo-as-player-coach/article_0ca0e441-4032-589f-a31d-a2fbbf19816d.html.

6   "Mariners Look to Miguel Cairo."

7   David Jablonksi, "Reds' Cairo a Model for Young Dragons," *Springfield* (Ohio) *News-Sun*, March 3, 2012. https://www.springfieldnewssun.com/sports/baseball/reds-cairo-model-for-young-dragons/wuNg7x8Cy6QHvSGpL9E3iN/.

8   The Mendoza Line is a term coined by a teammate of Mario Mendoza on the 1979 Mariners - usually credited to Tom Paciorek or Bruce Bochte - as a joke on the light-hitting shortstop, who typically carried an average around .200. (Though he actually finished with a career mark of .215.) http://m.mlb.com/glossary/idioms/mendoza-line.

9   "Mariners Look to Miguel Cairo."

10   http://www.pelotabinaria.com.ve/beisbol/mostrar.php?ID=cairmig001. Statistics provided via e-mail by Lorenzo "Tony" Piña Cámpora, researcher for the Dominican Republic Baseball League and adviser to the Caribbean Baseball Association.

11   Blaine Blontz, "Miguel Cairo Joins Reds' Front Office," SB Nation MLB Daily Dish, February 14, 2013. https://www.mlbdailydish.com/2013/2/14/3989334/miguel-cairo-reds-front-office.

12   https://www.mlb.com/mlbpaa/events/heart-and-hustle-award.

13   "Miguel Cairo Joins Baseball Operations Staff," MLB.com, February 14, 2013. https://www.mlb.com/news/miguel-cairo-joins-baseball-operations-staff/c-41637894.

14   Robert Pimpsner, "Miguel Cairo Joins Yankees as Minor League Infield Coordinator," February 17, 2018. https://pinstripedprospects.com/miguel-cairo-joins-yankees-minor-league-infield-coordinator-29831/.

15   Joel Poley, "Instinctual Florida SS Christian Cairo Ready for the Next Level," *Baseball America*, April 11, 2019. https://www.baseballamerica.com/stories/instinctual-florida-ss-christian-cairo-ready-for-the-next-level/.

16   Poley.

17   Rodney Page, "Calvary Christian Shortstop Christian Cairo Drafted in Fourth Round by Cleveland Indians." *Tampa Bay Times*, June 4, 2019. https://www.tampabay.com/sports/high-schools/2019/06/04/calvary-christian-shortstop-christian-cairo-drafted-in-fourth-round-by-cleveland-indians/.

ALBERTO CALLASPO

BY DARIN WATSON

For about a half-hour, Alberto Callaspo was a hero in Oakland. But ultimately, through no fault of his own, Callaspo would become a footnote in baseball history. It was rather a shame for a player who had a solid 10-year career in the majors.

The Kansas City Royals had already made the 2014 American League wild-card game memorable by rallying from a 7-3 deficit, tying the Oakland A's with three runs in the eighth inning and one more in the ninth. The teams traded zeros in the 10th and 11th innings before Oakland's Josh Reddick worked a walk to lead off the 12th. After a sacrifice bunt, the switch-hitting Callaspo stepped to the plate as a pinch-hitter, looking to send one of his former teams home for the winter. Jason Frasor's second pitch to Callaspo was in the dirt and bounced away from catcher Salvador Perez, moving Reddick to third. After a foul ball, Callaspo lined a high fastball into left field, giving the Athletics the lead again. Callaspo was stranded at first but returned to the dugout as the potential hero for the A's.

It was not meant to be. The Royals moved the game to classic status with two runs in the bottom half of the inning, earning a walk-off win in the franchise's first postseason game in 29 years and relegating Callaspo's big hit to an afterthought. The ironic element to this story was that it had been the Royals who first gave Callaspo a real chance to play in the majors, after a bit of a circuitous route to becoming a regular.

Alberto Jose Callaspo Brito was born on April 19, 1983, in Maracay, Venezuela. After attending the Institucion de Formacion in Aragua, Callaspo was signed by Anaheim Angels scouts Carlos Porte and Amador Arias.[1] The signing happened on February 16, 2001, a couple of months before Callaspo's 18th birthday.

Callaspo's first professional experience came with the Angels' Dominican Summer League team. From there, it was on to a successful minor-league career. In 2002 he made Baseball America's Pioneer League all-star team after batting .338/.374/.488 in 70 games for the Angels' Rookie League team in Provo, Utah. Not surprisingly, his manager in Provo, Tom Kotchman, later said, "He was just very, very talented. He was very advanced for his age. When you see guys at that level, you might get some inflated numbers offensively because of the light air, but the talent was definitely there."[2]

Callaspo continued to impress in 2003, playing for Class-A Cedar Rapids (Iowa) in the Midwest League and batting .327/.377/.428. That got him a number-71 ranking in Baseball America's prospect rankings before the 2004 season. Callaspo rewarded that faith with a .284/.338/.376 line for Double-A Arkansas, while also trying to adjust to the shortstop position after playing mostly second base in his professional career. In 2005, for the first time in his minor-league career, Callaspo started a season at the same level he had played at the year before, but after hitting .297/.346/.406 for Arkansas, he was promoted to Triple-A Salt Lake for the rest of the season.

Callaspo's first taste of the Pacific Coast League was a success; he hit .316/.345/.488 in 50 games for the Stingers. The prospect was gaining a reputation as a natural hitter, nearly impossible to strike out (97 K's in 1,925 at-bats from 2002 to 2005). But Callaspo was facing tough odds as a middle-infield prospect in the Angels' organization. Los Angeles already had Adam Kennedy and Orlando Cabrera at the major-league level, plus Maicer Izturis and Chone Figgins, both capable of playing second base but moved to other positions. Meanwhile, Erick Aybar and Howie Kendrick were establishing themselves as prospects at Triple-A Arkansas.[3] The Angels, with a wealth of middle-infield talent, dealt Callaspo to Arizona for pitching prospect Jason Bulger in February of 2006.

Callaspo returned to the PCL to start the 2006 season, playing for Tucson. After hitting .337/.404/.478 in 114 games, he made his major-league debut on August 6, grounding out as a pinch-hitter against Houston's Andy Pettitte. Callaspo remained in the majors, picking up 47 plate appearances and hitting .238/.298/.310 through the end of the season. He collected his first hit on August 8, a double off San Francisco's Brian Wilson. Although his first stint in the big leagues wasn't outstanding, his exceptional season for Tucson earned him Arizona's Minor League Player of the Year honors.

Arizona began the 2007 season with Callaspo on the roster, but an off-field incident in mid-May put a damper on his season. On May 10 he was arrested at his home on suspicion of assaulting his wife, Marianny Paola. The Diamondbacks placed Callaspo on the restricted list, but the charges were soon dropped. Court documents indicated that the couple had had previous disputes turn physical, but Paola, new to living in the United States, was unsure how to contact the police.[4] Once the charges were dropped and the players union filed a grievance, Callaspo was reinstated. However, batting just .206/.257/.254 on June 14, he was sent back to Triple A.

Back in Tucson, Callaspo rediscovered his hitting form, batting .341/.406/.491 in 59 games. That got him a September call-up, although he had just 19 plate appearances as the Diamondbacks managed to hold off surging Colorado for the NL West title. Callaspo did not appear in Arizona's Division Series victory over Chicago, but had two hitless at-bats in the National League Championship Series, which saw the Rockies sweep their division rivals.

Dodgers infielder Alberto Callaspo fields a grounder during a 2015 game at Dodger Stadium. A versatile switch-hitter, Callaspo played 10 major-league seasons. (Harry How / Getty Images Sports)

Once again, Callaspo found himself behind established major leaguers, this time second baseman Orlando Hudson and shortstop Stephen Drew. With the off-field issues on top of that, Arizona was willing to trade Callaspo, this time to Kansas City for pitcher Billy Buckner.

While the trade seemed like a minor one, former Royals player Kevin Seitzer, who had been Arizona's hitting coach for the first part of the 2007 season, assured Royals fans the team had acquired a good player. He told the Kansas City Star, "I liked him, and I liked his ability a lot. He's the type of guy that if he ever got into the lineup, you might not ever get him out of it. The big thing with him is, he needs to play."[5]

Seitzer was correct, as the fresh start seemed to be just what Callaspo needed. Although the Royals were using him as a utility player, he was playing a lot and hitting well, batting .290/.349/.330 through June 25. But another off-field issue arose, as Callaspo was pulled over by campus police at the University of Missouri-Kansas City and arrested for driving under the influence. The Royals placed Callaspo on the disabled list for "an unspecified ailment," and he did not return to the team

until late August. He did hit a solid .319/.371/.407 the rest of the season, giving him the inside track on the Royals' second-base spot heading into 2009.

However, he was not guaranteed the job, as there were concerns about his defense. The Royals made noises about moving Mark Teahen to second base and they signed Willie Bloomquist as additional competition for the job.[6] Teahen was the second baseman on Opening Day. But just three games into the season, Teahen was moved to right field in place of an injured Jose Guillen. Callaspo took advantage, hitting .379/.432/.545 for the first month of the season. It was a springboard to his finest year in the majors, which resulted in a .300/.356/.457 line, the first 11 home runs of his major-league career, and 41 doubles.

On the other hand, Callaspo led American League second basemen with 17 errors, despite concerns about his lack of range. Seeking a defensive upgrade, the Royals acquired Chris Getz. The Royals were unable to move Callaspo over the winter, but clearly his days in Kansas City were numbered.

Playing more often at third base in 2010, and with trade rumors swirling, Callaspo saw his offense fall off a bit. He hit .275/.308/.410 in 88 games for Kansas City before he was finally traded on July 22. Callaspo was headed back to his original major-league organization, as the Angels sent pitchers Sean O'Sullivan and Will Smith to Kansas City. Callaspo hit a disappointing .249/.291/.315 for the Angels, who had been on the fringes of contention when they acquired Callaspo and pitcher Dan Haren right before the trade deadline.

But Callaspo rebounded in 2011, with a .288/.366/.375 line that helped the Angels remain in contention for the whole season, although they ultimately missed the wild-card spot by five games. Callaspo held the Angels' third-base job for another season and half of 2013, before he was traded once again. This deal moved him up the coast, where he joined the Oakland A's for the stretch run. Callaspo hit .270/.350/.409 in 50 games to help Oakland to a division title. However, he was limited to six plate appearances in the AL Division Series loss to Detroit.

Callaspo was something of a supersub for the A's in 2014, playing three infield positions and serving as a DH for a total of 451 plate appearances. However, he hit a disappointing .223/.290/.290. Despite his big hit in the wild-card game, the Athletics let him leave as a free agent.

He signed with Atlanta, but his stay with the Braves would be brief. On May 27, 2015, Callaspo was dealt to the Los Angeles Dodgers as part of a six-player deal. He played in 60 games for the Dodgers, hitting .260/.336/.301 in 138 plate appearances before Los Angeles released him on August 27.

That was the end of Callaspo's major-league career, but not the end of his playing days. He signed with the Bridgeport Bluefish in the independent Atlantic League for the start of the 2017 season, then moved to Laguna in the Mexican League that same year. Before the 2018 season, he was traded to Yucatan, then dealt back to Laguna after just a few weeks. He was released after about a month. But Callaspo didn't give up on baseball that easily – he signed with the Welland Jackfish of the Intercounty

Baseball League in Canada for the 2021 season but was released before ever playing a game for them. He then signed with the West Virginia Power/Charleston Dirty Birds of the Atlantic League, and batted .335/.469/.461 in 429 plate appearances.

Of course, no accounting of Callaspo's career would be complete without mentioning his numerous appearances in Venezuela's Winter League. After making his debut with Caribes de Oriente in the 2006-07 season, he moved to Aguilas del Zulia for the final 13 games of the campaign. He returned to Zulia for the following three seasons, then played for Navegantes del Magallanes in three of the next four seasons (skipping the 2012-13 one), albeit for a total of 52 games. He then joined his hometown Tigres de Aragua, playing four seasons for them, including a stellar .351/.449/.442 line in 227 plate appearances in the 2017-18 season. Callaspo was part of three championship teams in Venezuela, one with Magallanes and two with Aragua. For the 2019-20 winter ball season, he signed with Vaqueros de Montería of the Colombian Baseball League, having an outstanding performance in the postseason and helping Vaqueros to win the first title for the franchise. Callaspo participated in the Caribbean Series 2020 in San Juan, Puerto Rico, representing Colombia, which went winless in five games.

For the 2020-21 winter baseball season, Callaspo signed with Tigres de Chinandega of the Nicaraguan Professional Baseball League and was released after the first month of the season, then rejoined Vaqueros de Montería. For the 2021-22 season he signed with the Cardenales de Lara, hitting .262/.373/.310 in 18 games. For 2022-23, he was back with Aragua, batting .281/.395/.344 in 28 plate appearances.

SOURCES

In addition to the sources cited in the Notes, the author accessed Baseball-reference.com.

NOTES

1 http://www.thebaseballcube.com/players/profile.asp?ID=20302.

2 Robert Emrich, "Path of the Pros: Alberto Callaspo," milb.com, March 24, 2010. https://www.milb.com/news/gcs-8101760.

3 Kevin _____, "The Alberto Callaspo Trade," AngelsWin.com, 2013. https://angelswinblog.blogspot.com/2009/05/alberto-callaspo-trade.html. (fan site).

4 Jack Magruder, "Callaspo Has History of Abuse Reports," *East Valley Tribune* (Tempe, Arizona), May 16, 2007, updated October 7, 2011. https://www.eastvalleytribune.com/sports/callaspo-has-history-of-abuse-reports/article_86ee6d77-40ff-50f8-b8dc-35deodcf5b5b.html.

5 Jeffrey Flanagan, "Royals' Trade for Callaspo May Pay Big Dividends," *Kansas City Star*, December 20, 2007: D2.

6 Sam Mellinger, "A Primer for Royals Spring Training," *Kansas City Star*, February 8, 2009: C10.

GIOVANNI CARRARA

BY JEAN CARLOS ARIAS TROISI

If there is a word to describe Giovanni Carrara during his 24 years of professional pitching, it is courage. As a starter or a reliever, it was hard to pull him from the game. Managers faced the tough task of going to the mound and asking for the ball, as Carrara showed no sign of leaving the field. His devotion to each game was evident.

Giovanni Carrara Jiménez was born in El Tigre, Anzoátegui state in Venezuela, on March 4, 1968, the youngest of five siblings. His parents were Héctor Carrara, owner of a construction company, and Omaira Josefina Jiménez. From a very young age, he showed an interest in baseball. At age 5, he joined Constructora Carrara, a local baseball team run by his mother, where he played until age 10. However, when his parents divorced, the team broke up, and Giovanni started to play for other teams, from pre-little league to junior categories.

Giovanni began as a shortstop, his favorite position because his idol was Dave Concepción. When he wasn't playing shortstop, he was pitching. At shortstop, he showed great defensive prowess. At age 15, professional organizations in Venezuela and the United States observed his development and saw special potential in him.

While participating in the Junior Category Championship in 1986, Carrara was invited to try out with Águilas del Zulia, managed by former All-Star Rubén Amaro. Manuel Lunar, a pitcher with Águilas, had urged the team to see Carrara play. At shortstop, he showcased his solid arm; however, his hitting was nothing unusual. Still, the team invited him to its preseason workouts.

On the first day of workouts, the team asked him to try pitching. After a bullpen session where he showed the potential of his arm, Águilas signed Carrara for the 1986-87 season.

In the 1986-1987 season, Carrara pitched 2⅔ innings with a 6.75 ERA. The next season he played in three games and logged his first victory on October 22, 1988, against the Tiburones de La Guaira.

In 1986, Carrara was signed by the Chicago Cubs. In 1987, he attended the Cubs' training camp, staying for the extended spring training. In May, he hurt his arm (tendinitis), and it took a full month for him to recover. The Cubs sent him to Venezuela to complete the rehab process in the Summer League. Despite recovering successfully, he did not return to the Cubs because the contract with the organization was never legally registered with the National League. As a result, Carrara spent four years (1986-1989) without being signed by any team from the majors.

Another setback occurred in 1988 when Zulia released Carrara after only 14 games pitched (1-1, 5.40 ERA). At the suggestion of Venezuelan baseball legend César Tovar, the Cardenales de Lara invited him to training camp for the 1989 campaign. Manager Domingo Carrasquel, with pitcher Luis Leal, who supported him from the beginning, told Carrasquel to keep him on the team because he would be helpful for a while. This would be the start of a prodigious career. "Luis Leal was one of the people who helped me the most during the practice with the Cardenales so that they kept me on the team," Carrara told the author.[1]

Carrara made his debut with the Cardenales on October 27, 1989, and saw action in six games, with a 1-0 record and a 4.82 ERA.

Carrara continued with the Cardenales and was part of the team that won the franchise's first title in the 1990-1991 season. He played in the Caribbean Series in Miami, leading the tournament with 15⅓ innings pitched. Those numbers were enough to convince Dominican scout Epy Guerrero to give him a chance with the Toronto Blue Jays.

After the Caribbean Series, Carrara was assigned to his first team in Organized Baseball, St. Catharines of the Low-A New York-Pennsylvania League. His days in the minors were rough, as for many Latino players, due to the discipline and struggles of the process to make it to the major leagues. Between 1992 and 1995, he pitched at least 100 innings in the minors.

Patience and effort were finally rewarded. The Blue Jays called up Carrara. He made his debut on July 29 in the Toronto SkyDome in a start against the Oakland Athletics, with Cuban Ariel Prieto as his opponent. The first hitter he faced was future Hall of Famer Rickey Henderson, who walked. His first strikeout was against Scott Brosius. After three scoreless frames, in the top of the fourth, he yielded a two-run homer to Brosius. He ended with five innings, seven hits, two doubles, a triple, a homer, five walks, and two strikeouts, but got the win in a wild 18-11 game.

Carrara appeared in 23 games in 1995 and 1996 for the Blue Jays, mostly as a reliever, starting only seven games. His record was 2-5 with an 8.20 ERA, not very satisfactory stats for a 28-year-old pitcher. On July 3, 1996, the Cincinnati Reds selected Carrara off the waiver list, joining the big-league club in August after an impressive performance with the triple-A club in Indianapolis with an ERA of 0.76 in nine appearances, six as a starter, and a record of 4-0.

He joined the rotation and got his first win as a starter for the Reds on August 23 against the Florida Marlins.

Entering 1997, he signed as a free agent with the Baltimore Orioles, getting assigned to Triple A in Rochester, but after eight games, he was released. The Reds picked up his contract and reassigned him to Indianapolis, where he ended up with a record of 12-5 and an ERA of 3.51. He spent the month of August with the big-league club, and after the season, he was released.

In 1998, after three seasons in the major-league system, Carrara signed to play in Japan with the Seibu Lions in Nippon Professional Baseball. In 33 outings (five of them as a starter), he had a 1-2 record with a save and a 4.91 ERA. "It was the toughest league in my career because it was competitive and tough with the training. You must grind from the first day of practice," he said.[2]

After his stint in Japanese baseball, Carrara suited up for Lara earlier than expected, and again his name became a staple for the rotation of Cardenales, being not only a workhorse but also a fan favorite. Lara advanced to the finals against Leones del Caracas, and Carrara's legacy reached a peak on January 29, 1999, in the fifth game of the Championship Series. Carrara pitched 6⅔ innings in perhaps one of the most brilliant relief appearances in the history of Venezuelan baseball finals.

There were several emotional moments during the game: the game-tying homer by Bobby Abreu for Caracas in the ninth, which triggered Carrara to prolong his relief appearance up to the 10th inning. "I either kill them or get killed here," he said, referring to the epic game.

Lara scored twice in the top of the 10th, and Carrara held on for the 5-3 win. Lara led the series 3-2, and his performance provided the momentum to win the third title for the franchise.

"During every inning, manager Omar Malavé would tell me he was going to pull me. I would reply: 'Listen, Omar, we are going to have a problem, you and I, if you pull me.' You take me out of this game dead," he said.[3]

In 2000, Carrara was back in the big leagues, this time with the Colorado Rockies, where he pitched in just eight games. However, it was with the Los Angeles Dodgers that he had his best major-league performances.

In 2001 and 2002 with Los Angeles, Carrara had a 12-4 record with a 3.22 ERA in 110 games (four of them as a starter). On April 20, 2002, Carrara got the first save of his career against the San Diego Padres in Dodger Stadium.

After his great season with the Dodgers in 2005 (7-4, 3.93 ERA in 72 games), Carrara was part of Team Venezuela in the 2006 World Baseball Classic. The country's fan base was very enthusiastic because it was the first national team ever assembled with MLB players, generating great expectations. Despite the great roster, the team performance was disappointing, including Carrara's, who was severely criticized despite having but one outing (against Cuba during Round 2).

"Both Robert Pérez and manager Luis Sojo, along with myself, were pointed out by the fans," Carrara told the author. "I had enough merit to be on the team in the first tournament, and Robert is, in my opinion, the best batter in the history of the LVBP and had to be there. Some people suggested that we were part of the team because of our friendship with Sojo. That hurt a lot." Carrara remembers barely pitching a game against Cuba in the second round. In two-thirds of an inning, he allowed three hits, five runs, two homers, and a walk.

September 23, 2006, was Carrara's last outing in the majors. He faced the Arizona Diamondbacks and came in relief of Elmer Dessens with one out; he gave up a single to center by Eric Byrnes but retired both Orlando Hudson and Luis González to end the inning. After the season, the Dodgers released him.

During his five seasons with the Los Angeles Dodgers, Giovanni Carrara made a significant impact as a key component of the bullpen. Appearing in 249 games with an impressive ERA of 3.32, Carrara established himself as one of the most effective and feared relief pitchers in the National League. His record of 24 wins and 11 losses, along with a WHIP of 1.24, highlighted his consistent performance and ability to manage high-pressure situations. Carrara's dominance on the mound came from his strategic approach and solid control of the strike zone, rather than sheer power. With just 255 innings pitched, he exemplified the role of a dominant reliever during an era where precision and tactical prowess were paramount, earning him a lasting reputation among Dodgers fans and peers alike.

Carrara always hoped to pitch in the majors again. He tried a comeback in 2007 in the Mexican Baseball League for Piratas de Campeche, but an injury kept him from completing the season. That same year, he signed with Nettuno of the Italian League, where he pitched for three years. "The advantage of playing in Italy is that they play during the weekends, and pitchers can only perform once," he said. "It allowed me to recover from the injury I suffered in Mexico and stay active for the Venezuelan season," he remembered.[4]

Carrara had a farewell season in Venezuela with the Cardenales de Lara. On December 20, 2009, he faced the Navegantes del Magallanes. The righty was 41 years old and became the only pitcher with 24 seasons in the history of the Venezuelan league (21 of them with Lara).

The last hitter he faced in the Venezuelan league was Elvis Andrus, who singled up the middle. The line for the last game

Carrara made his MLB debut for Toronto in 1995, and earned the win with his jersey misbuttoned. The Anzoátegui native pitched in parts of 10 major-league seasons. (Carlo Allegri / AFP via Getty Images)

of his career was two-thirds of an inning, allowing two hits and two runs.

The right-handed pitcher was a member of four championship Cardenales teams and one of three players in the league with over 50 wins and 50 saves, along with Roberto Muñoz and Luis Aponte. He closed his career with 67 wins and 56 saves, ranking ninth all-time in both categories in Venezuelan baseball, while also sporting a 2.93 ERA. He led the league in wins in 1994-95 (seven), in strikeouts in 1997-98 (64), and in ERA in 1997-98 (1.30) and 2007-08 (2.30).

Carrara's 1.205 WHIP was the third best in the history of the LVBP with at least 180 games pitched, surpassed only by stellar pitchers Diego Seguí (1.18) and Luis Mercedes Sánchez (1.196).

Carrara never earned the Carrao Bracho Award, the Venezuelan winter season's equivalent of the Cy Young Award. In 1997-98, possibly one of his best seasons in Venezuela, it was his teammate Beiker Graterol, with a record of 9-1, and a 1.67 ERA, and 50 strikeouts in 80⅔ innings pitched.

After retirement, Carrara worked in the Venezuelan Winter League as a coach. In September 2012, he was the pitching coach of the Cardenales de Lara in the Liga Paralela (Parallel League). In a published story with *El Impulso*, he said, "This was something I was hoping for since retirement. I wanted people from the Cardenales to give me the chance to go back to the organization. I am very happy for the opportunity they are giving me. I hope I can be up here (with the main team) soon."[5]

On December 22, 2013, in Estadio Antonio Herrera Gutiérrez in Barquisimeto, the club honored him by retiring his number 28, which he had worn for over two decades. "It never crossed my mind that at some point they would retire my number," he said during his remarks. "I will always be grateful for the opportunity they gave me. … I think Zulia made a mistake when they let me go because, in my second year here, we won the championship."[6]

Carrara was in the Development League with the Lara team until 2014 when he was hired by the Tigres de Aragua as a bullpen instructor. His dream of becoming a pitching coach in the LVBP seemed close, but by the end of November that year, he parted ways with the organization following the departure of manager Luis Sojo.

It wouldn't be long before Carrara found a new job, his first outside of Venezuela. In 2015, he was hired by the St. Louis Cardinals as a pitching coach for one of their affiliates in the Dominican Summer League. From day one in the organization, Carrara showed character in leading a group of talented young aspiring major leaguers. "The first thing I try to teach the minor-league guys with the St. Louis Cardinals is discipline, as I was taught by Mr. Domingo Carrasquel. Discipline and perseverance help a lot of people apart from doing things with love. He was like a father to me, teaching me about respect not only on the field but also off the field."[7]

In 2016, he became a pitching coach with the Gulf Coast League Cardinals, where he advanced to two championship finals and helped lead the team to a league title.

After appearing on the ballot for the first time in 2016, Carrara was elected to the Venezuelan Baseball Hall of Fame on August 1, 2017. He said, "I am very grateful to all the fans in Venezuela, but especially to the fans of the Cardenales de Lara, with all the people from Barquisimeto, who always supported me."[8]

Carrara's biggest regret was not attending the induction ceremony because of personal commitments. However, this didn't keep the former major leaguer from writing a speech that was read at the ceremony where he showed his gratitude to his great friends:

"To my brothers Robert Pérez and Luis Sojo, we were together through the good and the bad, supporting each other, because, as you all know, our career is not easy. One goes through difficult moments that the fans don't know about, and it is then that we, as teammates, and brothers, are there to support each other. And that is what counts the most in the life of a ballplayer: brotherhood and family, who are always there in difficult times."[9]

The right-hander's solid career was recognized not only because of the numbers he had in any league but also because of the courage and integrity he displayed with the teams he played for. Venezuelan fans always expected the best from him, and he proved it in every inning as a pitcher.

After induction, Carrara continued to carry out his role as a minor-league pitching coach for the Cardinals, as well as in the winter circuits with the Cañeros de Los Mochis and the Águilas de Mexicali in the Mexican Pacific League, in both the 2017-2018 and 2018-2019 seasons.

Carrara returned to Cañeros de Los Mochis for the 2022-23 season as a pitching coach working alongside Venezuelan manager José Moreno. They won the fourth title for the franchise in the Mexican Pacific League and represented Mexico at the 2023 Caribbean Series in Caracas, Venezuela. It was an emotional return for Carrara, who expressed his gratitude for opportunities in Mexico upon his arrival in Caracas. Los Mochis finished in third place in the tournament.

Outside baseball, Carrara devoted most of his time to his family, especially his wife, Dorien, and his two sons, Cristian Giovanni and Giovanni Gabriel. "They are the biggest accomplishment of my life," reflects Carrara, considered one of the most ferocious competitors on the mound in the history of Venezuelan Baseball.

SOURCES

All citations from this article are attributed to a personal interview of the author with Giovanni Carrara in the winter of 2023.

Apart from the sources in the Notes, the author also consulted:

Guía de Medios, *Cardenales de Lara temporada 2016-17* (Barquisimeto: Editorial Horizonte C.A, 2016).

Saer, Alfonso. *Cardenales de Lara, 50 años de pasión* (Barquisimeto: Editorial Horizonte C.A, 2015).

Interview by the author with Giovanni Carrara.

www.pelotabinaria.com.ve.

www.baseball-reference.com.

www.museodebeisbol.com.

NOTES

1   Interview by the author with Giovanni Carrara, March 2018.

2   Interview with Giovanni Carrara. March 2018.

3   Interview with Giovanni Carrara. March 2018.

4   Interview with Giovanni Carrara. March 2018.

5   *Diario El Impulso*, September 19, 2012.

6   *Diario El Impulso*, December 23, 2013.

7   Interview by the author with Giovanni Carrara, August 2017.

8   Interview by the author with Giovanni Carrara, August 2017.

9   Prensa Museo del Béisbol, "El Salón de la fama recibió a la clase 2017," LVBP.COM, December 16, 2017.

ALEX CARRASQUEL

BY LOU HERNÁNDEZ

Alejandro Carrasquel was the first native Venezuelan to play in the major leagues. When the 27-year-old trailblazer joined the Washington Senators in 1939 he was already a seasoned veteran, having pitched for years in countries throughout the Caribbean basin. The Senators that spring were housing an international contingent of players never quite seen before in major-league baseball. The camp had three Cuban players and a French Canadian–born pitcher named Joe Krakauskas. Senators owner Clark Griffith partially assessed his team, after a walk around camp, by saying, "The way things are now we sound like a row in the League of Nations."[1]

Carrasquel had gained the Senators' notice with his pitching over the previous winter in Cuba, when the right-hander had been named MVP of the Cuban winter league season. Team Cuba's manager José Rodríguez, former major-league player with the New York Giants, alerted Washington to the pitching prospect. The Senators sent scout Joe Cambria to investigate. Cambria, in an often retold account, "trailed him from the Havana park one day and got his name on a Washington contract while they were sitting on a park bench, with an interpreter between."[2]

From the mound, Carrasquel showed right off that he was a polished pitcher. He could field his position, hold runners on, and commanded a variety of pitches. Carrasquel easily made the Washington staff. There was an imposed proviso with it, however. The Senators modified Carrasquel's name to a more fan friendly–sounding "Alex Alexandra." Alejandro was nicknamed "Patón" ["big-footed"] in Venezuela for his purported size 18 shoes. Former teammate José Zardón said it began one day when Carrasquel accidentally grabbed one of Zardón's shoes. "Hey, this shoe doesn't fit. I think it must be yours," Carrasquel said. "Of course it's mine," Zardón replied. "How do you expect my shoe to fit that patón you have?"[3]

Carrasquel made his first appearance on April 23, 1939, against the New York Yankees at Griffith Stadium. He relieved starter Ken Chase with two outs in the fourth inning and a man on first base. The first three batters he faced were future Hall of Famers Joe DiMaggio, Lou Gehrig, and Bill Dickey. He retired them all, but the Yankees, ahead 6–3 when Carrasquel entered the game, won 7–4.

The *Washington Post's* Shirley Povich's game report contained some colorful but perhaps insensitive language by today's standards: "Pitching from a big league mound for the first time in his life, Alexandra – who would need only to be climbing over the side of a ship with a cutlass in his teeth to look like one of Lafitte's fiercest henchmen – gave an amazing exhibition of calm and effectiveness against the Yanks. The Venezuelan, with utter disregard for the reputation of the Yanks, surrendered only one run in the last 5 1/3 innings to the unbridled delight of the 22,000."[4]

The game marked the first appearance in the major leagues by a native of Venezuela. Alejandro Eloy Carrasquel was born in Parroquia La Candelaria, a municipality of Caracas, on July 24, 1912. He was the youngest of four children born to Alejo Carrasquero and Emilia María Aparicio, following two brothers and a sister. (Emilia María was not related to the ball-playing Aparicio family eventually rooted in Maracaibo.) A land inheritance left by Carrasquel's paternal grandmother to Carrasquel's father forced a generational surname alteration. In court papers, the inheritance was listed bequeathed to Alejo "Carrasquel," and the spelling error forced Carrasquel's father to legally change his name in order to accept the holdings.[5]

Alejandro was signed as an 18-year-old by his country's Royal Criollos team in 1930 and pitched his first professional game for the club the following spring. Over the next few years, Carrasquel played for several other teams in his homeland, and traveled to pitch in other baseball countries as he gained experience on the mound. Invited by Cuban great Martín Dihigo to join the Cuban winter league in 1938, he made the most of the opportunity, sporting an 11–6 record, with 10 complete games, and caught the eye of the Senators.

In his second major league game, on April 30, Carrasquel picked up his first save. At Yankee Stadium he was called in to relieve in the eighth inning, with two outs and the bases loaded, and Washington clinging to a 3–2 lead. Staying composed, the pitcher coaxed a fly out from Yankees second baseman Joe Gordon, and then retired the side in order in the ninth to preserve the victory.

Three days later, May 3, in another relief role, Carrasquel picked up his first win and the first by a Venezuelan pitcher in the major leagues. The historic victory occurred over the St. Louis Browns at Sportsman's Park. The Senators rallied from a six-run deficit, scoring seven runs over the final three innings of the game, to pull out an 11–10 road triumph. Hurling scoreless eighth and ninth innings, Carrasquel secured the special win.

The solid relief pitching of the rookie earned him his first big-league start on May 14. It came at home against Lefty Grove and the Boston Red Sox. Carrasquel came out on the losing end of a 5–4 score in a strenuous 12-inning battle. Tied at two after nine innings, the Red Sox reached the Washington hurler for three runs in the 12th, and the Nationals' rally in the bottom of the inning against Grove and two relievers fell one run short. Earlier in the game, Carrasquel recorded the first hit by a Venezuelan player in the major leagues when he singled off

Grove. In absorbing his first pitching loss, Carrasquel hung an 0-for-5 on heralded Red Sox rookie left fielder Ted Williams. Incidentally, the Red Sox starting lineup that day had five future Hall of Famers: Grove, Jimmie Foxx, Joe Cronin, Bobby Doerr, and Williams.

Four years later Shirley Povich recalled Carrasquel's amazing composure as a rookie. "I don't know where he learned it," Senators manager Bucky Harris told him back in 1939, "but this big fellow is smoother than any rookie who ever broke in under me."[6] The impressed Harris gave the "big fellow," who was 6'1" tall -- and weighed somewhat more than his listed 182 pounds -- three successive starts after the locked-horns effort against Grove. Carrasquel won two of them. All three starts were complete game endeavors.

On May 25, Carrasquel three-hit the Browns, 4–1, at Griffith Stadium. The pitcher gained high praise from Povich with the effort. "Certainly, Alex Alexandra is the most sensational rookie to flash across the big league scene since Bobby Feller appeared in 1936," wrote the *Washington Post's* best-known sportswriter. "That he is no flash in the pan is well established. One only has to look at his past three performances."[7]

Not long afterwards, Senators owner Clark Griffith stepped in and ended the name charade. Stripping Carrasquel of his foisted-upon Alexandra alias, Griffin announced to the press that "when a fellow comes that far, I think it's no more than right that he get all the credit that's coming to him under his own name."[8]

The sole loss in that three-game span for Carrasquel was a 3–1 defeat to the Philadelphia Athletics on May 30. Allowing only four hits and two earned runs, the Caracas-born pitcher supplied his team's only run with a long ball. At Griffith Stadium, Carrasquel tagged Athletics starter Nels Potter to register the first home run hit by a Venezuelan player in the major leagues. Following the 3–1 loss to the A's, Carrasquel plodded through several rough outings, winning only once in six more starting appearances.

Carrasquel was honored by a delegation of Venezuelans between games of a doubleheader at Yankee Stadium on the Fourth of July. Dr. Tomás Pacanins, consul general of Venezuela, introduced him and presented several gifts and a diploma from the Venezuelan Baseball Association.[9] Alex made a speech – in Spanish – but his part in the occasion has been lost in history because the vast majority of the 61,808 fans had turned out for "Lou Gehrig Appreciation Day," and Gehrig's speech and its immortal line, "Today I consider myself the luckiest man on the face of this earth," overshadowed everything else.

Carrasquel started the second game of the doubleheader, but lasted only three innings, giving up six hits and five earned runs in the Yankees 11–1 victory. His record had been 3–2, with a 2.64 ERA, following the loss to the Athletics on May 30, but his performance declined the rest of the season. He finished with a record of 5–9 and an ERA of 4.69 in 40 games. His 159 1/3 innings pitched, 17 starts, and seven complete games would

The first Venezuelan to reach the major leagues, Carrasquel debuted with the Washington Senators in 1939. His arrival marked the start of a long Venezuelan legacy in major-league baseball. (The Conlon Collection / Getty Images)

prove to be career highs, and it was his only losing record in eight major-league seasons.

As a result of his second half decline, Carrasquel needed to prove himself again to the Senators in 1940. His job wasn't made easier when he reported late to training camp. "Alejandro explained that as steamship service from South America to Cuba is irregular, because of the war, he had to take a boat from his native Venezuela to New York, a longer journey."[10] He made the opening day roster, but faltered in early relief appearances and was optioned to Jersey City of the International League on May 25. He was recalled in the first week of July, and turned things around over the second half of the season. Used exclusively in relief, he pitched only 48 innings in 28 games, and posted an overall 6–2 record, with a 4.88 ERA.

The Washington team Carrasquel reported to in 1941 was distinctively different to the one he had encountered two years earlier. Shirley Povich's pre-season report had little remaining of the flattery he had once attributed to Carrasquel's pitching: "The once-populous Latin Legion of the Nats, which for years had set up a babble of Spanish in the Washington camp, has dwindled to one slightly unwanted Venezuelan. . . .The fact that he is still being retained by the Nats is less a tribute to Carrasquel than it is a sad commentary on the state of the Washington pitching."[11]

On the year, Carrasquel duplicated his 6–2 record from the prior season and was an overall steady force working primarily out of the Senators' bullpen. His 3.44 ERA was the best of any of the club's bullpen specialists, in 96 2/3 innings of work. He started five games late in the season, his first since 1939. By the time August rolled around, his pitching seemed to have warmed the critical Povich. The scribe offered this overview of the previously marginalized pitcher, along with personal snapshots of the man: "Alex Carrasquel, who is the leading percentage pitcher in the American League with six wins and no defeats

... he's Spanish and Indian ... in his native Venezuela, he was a mechanic in a Ford factory ... he's the best fielding pitcher on the Washington club, and the best at holding runners close to bases ... he dances the rhumba and, in fact, teaches it in his native Caracas ... he's continually showing Bucky Harris a new kind of pitch and tosses up more variety of pitching than any man in the league."[12]

In 1942, Carrasquel's fourth year in the league, he had a 7–7 record in 35 appearances. Bucky Harris increased his workload and gave him 15 starts. He finished with a 3.43 ERA in 152 1/3 innings of work. On July 18, the husky pitcher tossed his first major league shutout – the first in the majors by a Venezuelan -- blanking the St. Louis Browns 3–0 on five hits and no walks at Griffith Stadium. The pride of Caracas also registered two ten-inning complete game victories during the campaign: a 3–2 win against Detroit at Briggs Stadium on June 21, and a 4–3 home win against Cleveland on September 1.

Owner Clark Griffith hired a new manager for 1943 – Ossie Bluege, a popular 18-year veteran player with the Senators – and Carrasquel had reason to be optimistic about the new season. The persevering right-hander received the following reevaluation from team beat writer Povich in a spring training column:

"With the exception of Dutch Leonard, Alex Carrasquel is now rated the most valuable item on the Nats' pitching staff. Alex, the Venezuelan, has come a long way with the Nats since that day in 1939 when he checked into the club's Florida training camp speaking the only three English words he knew, 'Me peetch gude.' Carrasquel had a rough time of it in his early years with the Nats. He wasn't a popular fellow with teammates. The fault was theirs, not his. They resented the presence of the South American. They were fed up, in fact, with all of the Latins the Washington club was importing. The 1000 per cent [sic] Americans on the club viewed the influx as bread being taken from their mouths.

"The Washington players couldn't pin anything special on Alex. They didn't like the cut of his clothes, with his fancy padded shoulders, to be sure. But the fact that he looked like a Spaniard and couldn't speak English was enough. Even the locker room attendants grumbled when Carrasquel and the other Latins sought the routine services in the clubhouse, towels, under socks, perhaps a dry sweatshirt. [The players] didn't let Carrasquel into their card games, and he was forced into the role of 'loner,' even when he was winning five games in a row for the Nats during the 1941 season. Officials of the Washington club stepped in and demanded that Carrasquel get some of the common courtesies."[13]

The Senators made a startling improvement under Bluege, finishing in second place with an 84–69 record – 13 ½ games behind the Yankees – compared to seventh place and 62–89 in 1942. The improvement began, as it usually does, with the pitching staff. Carrasquel was one of five hurlers with 11 or more wins. He started 13 games, compiling an 11–7 record, with a 3.68 ERA in 144 1/3 innings pitched. He led the team with 39 appearances, and his 11 wins were a career best. His best performance came early in the year, with a two-hit, 5–0, shutout over the Athletics on April 25.

In 1944, Bluege's team lost 90 games and dropped all the way down to the cellar of the American League. Carrasquel managed a respectable 8–7 record -- though limited to only seven starts – with a 3.43 ERA in 134 innings pitched, and once again led all team hurlers with 43 appearances. His best performance as a starter came on September 10 when he pitched a complete game to defeat the Athletics 8–2, at Griffith Stadium.

Washington was back in a pennant race once again in 1945. At the end of July the Senators were in third place at 45–41, 5 ½ games behind Detroit and only 1 ½ games behind the second-place Yankees. Carrasquel had been used sparingly, pitching only 49 1/3 innings in 20 appearances, and had lost his only start back on May 13. His record stood at 2–3, but he had a fine 2.10 ERA.

However, Carrasquel's pitching gave Washington a much-needed boost in the final two months of the pennant race. He started six games and relieved in nine others during this stretch. The first four starts were complete-game wins, including two shutouts. He lost to St. Louis 4–3 in a 10-inning complete-game start on September 5, giving up a game-tying home run to the Browns' Lou Finney with two outs in the top of the ninth. His final start was a seven-inning no-decision against the White Sox on September 9. Carrasquel finished the season with 7–5 record and a 2.71 ERA in 122 2/3 innings pitched.

Carrasquel was sold to the White Sox on January 2, 1946 for the $7,500 waiver price. Washington scribe Shirley Povich wrote in the January 31 issue of *The Sporting News* that Senators' owner Clark Griffith made his decision to cut Carrasquel loose "in a fit of high disgust" after the Venezuelan gave up the two-strike home run to Finney. According to Povich, "Griffith went to his office and immediately advised [League President] Will Harridge's office that he was asking waivers on Carrasquel. 'That was the dumbest pitch I ever saw in my 60 years in baseball,' said Griffith. 'That Carrasquel wasn't satisfied to get Finney out. He wanted to strike him out and walk off the field in a blaze of glory, and Finney was laying for it.'"[14]

It is probable that Griffith saw 1945 as his last best chance to win a pennant since all drafted players would be returning from the war in time for the 1946 season, and viewed the Carrasquel-Finney game as one particularly squandered. But it is difficult to see how Griffith could really blame Carrasquel for losing the pennant. The club went 14–8 after the September 5 game, to finish 11/2 games behind Detroit, who were 14–10 over the same span. Actually, the Senators really blew their chances when they lost three of five games to the Tigers in Washington from September 15-18, and followed up by losing three of five games to the Yankees and Athletics to close out the season.

Povich's January 31 *TSN* column also carried a paragraph heading reading, "Hit Home Runs, but Pitched 'Em Too," reviving an old erroneous claim that Carrasquel gave up too many home runs. He cited a 1939 game as an example. "Carrasquel hit a home run. It was one of the longest home runs ever hit to the Griffith Stadium left field bleachers. Eventually, he lost the game because a home run was hit against him. 'That's the trouble with Alex,' Bucky Harris [Ossie Bluege's predecessor as Senators' manager] moaned, 'You never know when he's going to hit a home run or pitch one.'"[15]

In fact, that was Carrasquel's only home run in the majors, and he lost the game 3–1 without giving up a home run. Furthermore, from 1939–45 he gave up 0.43 home runs per nine innings, compared to the American League average of 0.50.

On January 12, 1946 --less than two weeks after his waiver sale -- Alejandro was pitching in Caracas for the Magallanes Navigators. He defeated Cervecería Caracas, 5–2, in the inaugural game of the Venezuelan winter league. Eight days later, Carrasquel and Roy Welmaker of Vargas faced one another in an epic duel, in which both pitchers threw 17 innings before Carrasquel came out on top, 3–2. (Welmaker was a 36-year-old veteran of the Negro Leagues who was 22–12 in 1949 with Cleveland's Wilkes Barre Class A farm team in his first season in Organized Baseball.)

In mid-February he signed a three-year deal to play in Mexico for Jorge Pasquel's upstart Mexican League. "Pasquel paid me $3,000 cash [bonus], to sign a three-year contract calling for $10,000 a year," Carrasquel said, in an interview three years later. "I took it, for in addition to the $33,000 I was to receive in Mexico, I also was free to pitch winter baseball."[16] However, Carrasquel and others who cast their lot with Mexico at that time, were punished with lifetime suspensions by Major League Baseball, and were not permitted to play in Organized Baseball–backed winter leagues.

The league in Mexico had the option of moving a player from team to team for attempted parity purposes, and Carrasquel wound up pitching for several squads over the next three summers. From 1946–48, he pitched for Veracruz, Mexico City, and Monterrey, respectively, with an overall 44–27 record.

While in Mexico, Carrasquel met Eva Guerra of Monterrey. The couple married in January of 1949. It was the third marriage for Carrasquel. He had previously married Caracas native Elvira Estegui. That union produced a son named Jose Alejandro and a daughter christened Rita Emilia. During his time with the Senators, Carrasquel tied the knot with Virginia Catherine Johnson, a native of Takoma Park, Md, shortly after the conclusion of World War II. With Virginia, Carrasquel had two more sons: William Alejandro and Thomas Joseph Blue, the latter preferring to use the surname of his stepfather.

When the "jumpers" ban was lifted in the summer of 1949 by Major League Commissioner Happy Chandler, Carrasquel reported to the Chicago White Sox in early July, but the veteran's return to the big time was a short one. On August 5, after seeing action in only three games out of the bullpen, Alex was traded to the Detroit Tigers for pitcher Luis Aloma. The next day Detroit optioned the 37-year-old to the Buffalo Bisons of the International League. The move ended his eight-year major league career. The vanguard pitcher compiled a lifetime record

of 50–39 with a 3.73 ERA in 861 innings pitched. He appeared in 258 games, recording 30 complete games in 64 starts, along with 16 saves.

With the lifting of his organized baseball suspension, Carrasquel was able to return to the Venezuelan winter league for the 1949–50 season. After pitching two seasons for Cerveceria Caracas, the 40-year-old moundsman rejoined his original club, Magallanes, but pitched very sparingly. In 1953–54, the fading hurler made two appearances with Gavilanes of Venezuela's Occidental league. These efforts closed out his post–Major League winter pitching career in his homeland. His record of 12–20 in those five years reflected a pitcher past his prime.

Carrasquel bounced around in the minor leagues in the early 1950s and stretched out his pitching tenure until 1956. After his final season with Mexico City in the Class AA Mexican League, Carrasquel returned to the Venezuelan winter league and became a coach with the Caracas Lions. In 1958–59 he was appointed manager of the Pampero Juicers. While guiding the Pampero club to lackluster results during the 1959–60 campaign, he was involved in a serious fight with a team executive. "League officials voted a two-year suspension against Alex Carrasquel who started the season as manager of Pampero," read the winter league report of the incident. "The ban was imposed because Carrasquel allegedly slugged Eddy Moncada, breaking his jaw in two places, in a dispute which followed Carrasquel's ouster as pilot."[17] The suspension led to a players' strike, which caused a shutdown of the entire league. (The vacated season forced Venezuelan officials to send the Occidental league champion as the country's representative to the Caribbean Series for the first time.)

Carrasquel never managed in the winter league again. However, he had a personal relationship with Rómulo Betancourt, president of Venezuela, and Carrasquel returned to the diamond in the 1960s when Betancourt asked him to become the manager of the Vigilantes de Tránsito, an amateur league team. He managed the Tránsito club until shortly before his death.

The first Venezuelan major leaguer to win a game, throw a shutout, record a save, hit safely, and stroke a home run, died from diabetic complications in Caracas in 1969 at the relatively young age of 57. Two years later, the major-league trailblazer was inducted into the Venezuelan Sports Hall of Fame.[18] In 2003 Alejandro was among a group of 14 – 11 players, one owner, one umpire, and one sportswriter – selected in the inaugural class for the newly-created Venezuelan Baseball Hall of Fame.[19]

ACKNOWLEDGMENT

Special thanks to Mr. Gil Reyes for providing Venezuelan family data on Carrasquel and his post-winter league life. Additional thanks to Ms. Dana May Blue for furnishing information pertaining to Carrasquel's U.S. matrimony.

SOURCES

In addition to the sources cited in the Notes, the author also consulted 1800baseball.com, baseball-reference.com, iconosdevenezuela.com, purapelota.com, museodebeisbol.com.ve, retrosheet.org, and:

Figueredo, Jorge S., *Who's Who in Cuban Baseball 1878–1961* (Jefferson, North Carolina: McFarland & Co., 2003).

Treto Cisneros, Pedro. *Enciclopedia del Beisbol Mexicano.* 994 Segunda Edición (Mexico, D.F.: Revistas Deportivas, S.A. de C.V., 1994).

NOTES

1   "Solons Seek Interpreter," *Los Angeles Times*, February 26, 1939: A13.

2   Shirley Povich, "Nats' Man of Moods Moves to White Sox," *The Sporting News*, January 31, 1946: 2.

3   José Zardón, personal interview, March 2011.

4   Shirley Povich, "Champions Get 6 Runs in 4 Innings," *Washington Post*, April 24, 1939: 15.

5   Gil Reyes, SABR Luis Castro/Latin American Chapter, personal e-mail correspondence with author, June 17–18, 2014 and June 26–27, 2014.

6   Shirley Povich, "This Morning," *Washington Post*, March 12, 1943: 14.

7   Shirley Povich, "This Morning," *Washington Post*, June 1, 1939: 18.

8   "American League," *The Sporting News*, June 1, 1939: 10.

9   "Alexandra Feted By Countrymen in New York," *Washington Post*, July 5, 1939: 16.

10 "Training Camp Notes," *The Sporting News*, March 14, 1940: 8.

11 Shirley Povich, "This Morning," *Washington Post*, February 23, 1941: S1.

12 Shirley Povich, "This Morning," *Washington Post*, August 17, 1941: SP1.

13 Shirley Povich, "This Morning," *Washington Post*, March 22, 1943: 14.

14 Shirley Povich, "Nats' Man of Moods Moves to White Sox," *The Sporting News*, January 31, 1946: 2.

15 Povich, "Nats' Man of Moods Moves to White Sox."

16 Ray Gillespie, "Carrasquel Threatens Border to Border Jump," *The Sporting News*, March 9, 1949: 28.

17 M.J. Gordon, Jr., "King and Tovar Torrid Sockers in Lion Sweep," *The Sporting News*, November 25, 1959: 33.

18 http://www.venezuelatuya.com, accessed April 29, 2015.

19 http://www.museodebeisbol.com.ve, accessed April 24, 2015.

CHICO CARRASQUEL

BY LOU HERNÁNDEZ AND RORY COSTELLO

Alfonso "Chico" Carrasquel was the first great Hispanic defensive player in the major leagues. His play at short-stop made him as recognizable a big-leaguer as there was for several years. Carrasquel may not have revolutionized the position defensively like latter-day greats Ozzie Smith and Omar Vizquel – but he brought panache, born of his innate love for the sport and the excitement and joy he felt while on the baseball field. Some athletes, in the way they look or the way they play, are naturally appealing to the sports public at large. Carrasquel was one of them. From his minor league days, and for much of his time in the majors, the four-time All-Star was someone whom many people came to the ballpark with particular interest to watch.

In Spanish-speaking nations outside of his home country, Carrasquel was known as *El Gato de Venezuela* because of his cat-like fielding movements. As sportswriter Ray Gillespie put it, "Chico has a natural talent for putting color into his tosses across the infield by using a graceful follow-through."[1] His throws on double-play pivots also added flavor to the game, as Carrasquel said years after his retirement. He recalled that to avoid being spiked, "I was one of the first shortstops to throw the ball from second to first underhanded during double plays. Throwing the ball underhanded, the runner would have to slide or get hit with the ball."[2] Former teammate Minnie Miñoso recalled Carrasquel's defensive brilliance in this manner: "I had seen so many good shortstops, but Chico played like no one I had ever seen. Gee whiz, this guy never misses a ball! What a glove. What hands. Perfect throw to first base all the time."[3]

Alfonso Colón Carrasquel was born on January 23, 1926, in Caracas, Venezuela. He was one of 11 children and the first boy in the family of María Lourdes Carrasquel and her husband Cristóbal Colón. They lived in a canton of the capital city called *Caserio Corao*. Cristóbal worked as a laborer in a brewery in La Guaira, a town on the coast north of Caracas. María Lourdes supplemented the household income as a street vendor of home-cooked products such as *arepas* (corn cakes), which Alfonso also helped sell starting around the age of nine.

María Lourdes was the sister of pitcher Alejandro "Alex" Carrasquel, who became the very first Venezuelan in the majors in 1939. More than 300 have followed since – Alfonso was third overall after his uncle and Chucho Ramos. He was comfortable using his mother's family name instead of his father's – no doubt because of the repute associated with the name Carrasquel in Caracas. No other boy in all of Venezuela, outside of his own family, could say that he had an uncle who had played in the major leagues. Young Alfonso especially enjoyed listening to his uncle's baseball reminiscences, involving some of the game's greatest names. This was a source of pride for the boy, who (when not hustling around the neighborhood on behalf of his large family) was playing baseball.

Many members of Alfonso's extended family also played professional baseball. His nephew, also named Cristóbal Colón, made it to the majors for 14 games with the Texas Rangers in 1992. Cris was a shortstop too. Two of Alfonso's brothers, Domingo and Martín, played in the U.S. minors. So did his first cousin, Manuel Carrasquel, and three other nephews: Domingo and Emilio Carrasquel and Alfonso Collazo. Yet another nephew, Juan Muñoz, played briefly in Venezuela's winter league, La Liga Venezolana del Béisbol Profesional (LVBP).

Alfonso was a sensation in junior league ball from the age of 17. He played (and also pitched) with various local clubs, including El Triunfo, La Vega, and the team of the city's electric company, Electricidad de Caracas. When he was 19, he became a member of the team that represented Venezuela in the Amateur World Series of 1945. The following year, the country formed a professional league, which played its first season in the summer before switching to the winter. Carrasquel joined the Cervecería Caracas team. He played seven seasons with that club and eight more after it was rechristened as the Caracas Leones in 1952. He went on to play 21 total in his homeland.

In 1948, Fresco Thompson of the Brooklyn Dodgers signed Carrasquel to his first professional contract in the United States. The bonus was US$1,000. The scout traveled all the way to Caracas to secure the player. "I didn't know where he [Carrasquel] lived," Thompson said shortly after the signing. "The owner of the team didn't have his address either. I had to wait around in my hotel room…until his team played again. We got along all right once he spelled out the name 'Dodgers' on my business card. That's a universal word."[4]

After winning the Venezuelan batting title with a .373 mark (in 118 at-bats), Carrasquel reported to spring training with the Dodgers at their "atomic-age" camp in Florida in 1949. The 23-year-old – who, like many players, took a couple of years off his age for professional purposes – made his way around Vero Beach with the help of Roy Campanella, who had picked up Spanish while playing ball in the Caribbean and Mexico. But when camp broke, Campanella headed with the team to Brooklyn, and Carrasquel was shipped to Triple-A Montreal before being transferred to the Dodgers' Double-A team in Fort Worth. Shortstop was the wrong position for a Brooklyn prospect in the 1940s and '50s because Pee Wee Reese was entrenched there.

Carrasquel, as did nearly all Hispanic players of the era, faced the challenge of a new language. Montreal manager Clay Hopper did not play him because he could not speak English. Slightly more than four decades after his rookie season, Carrasquel recalled, "I was very lonely that year. I would go to my hotel room and look at myself in the mirror and say: '*Buenos días, Chico. Como estás?*' I had to talk to someone, and that someone was me. But I was determined to be a big league player. I wasn't going to let anything stop me."[5]

Carrasquel had a fine year with the bat at Fort Worth: a .315 batting average, with 6 homers and 69 RBIs. This end-of-season report delved further into the minor-leaguer's potential: "Most of the experts believe the Cats possess by far the hottest prospect in Chico Carrasquel, who is called the league's greatest postwar shortstop, and one of the finest to perform in the Texas League."[6] It was at Fort Worth, incidentally, that the infielder received the nickname "Chico" from teammates.

In October 1949, Frank Lane, general manager of the Chicago White Sox, obtained Carrasquel. The initial terms were $25,000 and two minor-league players.[7] The deal was among the best of many by the man called "Trader Frank." Just weeks after the exchange, John P. Carmichael of the *Chicago Daily News* wrote, "Lane is just as happy he got Carrasquel from Branch Rickey as if he'd taken Montreal's Sam Jethroe, for whom the Braves paid $125,000." Meanwhile, Rickey said, "It was a bad deal. It was a mistake."[8] The following year, renowned sportswriter Bob Broeg said, "Rickey reportedly has labeled [the trade] as his worst mistake."[9]

The White Sox trained in Pasadena, California, in the spring of 1950. After just a year in the minor leagues, Carrasquel was appointed the successor to Hall of Famer Luke Appling, who had been a fixture at Comiskey Park since the early 1930s. At 42 years of age, Appling had played 141 games at short in 1949, hitting .301. However, sportswriter Ed Fitzgerald later echoed a sentiment no doubt held by the White Sox brass at the time. "Appling could still hit the ball hard, but he had slowed up so badly that the White Sox pitchers weren't getting anything like the protection they deserved. It wasn't Luke's fault. It was just a case of time winning another victory."[10]

Carrasquel had a prominent role to fill and from Opening Day 1950 he measured up to the task. In his major-league debut that April 18, against Ned Garver of the St. Louis Browns, he walked in his first plate appearance and then singled in his first official at-bat. Number 17 – which he wore nearly throughout his career because there are 17 letters in Alfonso Carrasquel – also handled six chances in the field without fault. The White Sox lost at home, 5-3.

Carrasquel hit his first of 55 major league home runs on May 5, at Fenway Park, against Joe Dobson of the Red Sox. His overall play helped prompt the following mid-season prediction from GM Lane: "The new sparkle given our infield by Chico Carrasquel's play at shortstop and outfielder Gus Zernial's potential greatness at bat may enable us to finish this season in the upper division for the first time since 1943."[11] (The White Sox finished sixth in the eight-team league.)

On July 16, 1950, a mid-summer afternoon at Yankee Stadium, Carrasquel was at the center of a distinctive and significant ceremony. It was remarkable in that the honoree was a rookie who had played barely three months in the major leagues – the shower of gifts and praises he received would usually be reserved for elite players nearing the *end* of their careers. It was significant in that a Latin American player, for the first time, was receiving public esteem from North American baseball.

The tribute, or first "International Day" as *Collier's* magazine called it, occurred between games of a Sunday doubleheader that was also broadcast in Spanish throughout Latin America. The politically motivated homage was the idea of Walter Donnelly, then U.S. ambassador to Venezuela. Donnelly sought "to focus attention upon the United States as a land of opportunity for all and to combat untruths about this country with which the Communists were poisoning the minds of young Venezuelans."[12]

Carrasquel's bounty included an automobile, luggage, watch, a television set and radio, plus an array of medals (from baseball and various fraternal orders) – not to mention 16,300 Venezuelan bolivars. That sum was then equal to about US$5,000 – five times his signing bonus. Carrasquel's sister and mother were among those on hand at the New York event. Alfonso himself had just returned from Caracas a week earlier. He had taken advantage of the All-Star break to visit his wife, Marcela Rodríguez. She had given birth to a new son, Omar, born June 5. The couple had married on February 25, 1948, and welcomed their first child, Edgar, 12 months later.

Less than two weeks after "Carrasquel Day" at Yankee Stadium, Chico's team was preparing for their sixth series meeting of the season against the New York Yankees. Chicago sportswriter Edgar Munzel previewed the series. "Although the White Sox in general are sinking in the American League race like a lead weight in a millpond," wrote Munzel, "there was one among them who was definitely on the rise. In fact, he was rising to stardom so rapidly he seemed jet-propelled. The shooting star was none other than Alfonso 'Chico' Carrasquel, rookie shortstop."[13] When the story came out, Carrasquel's 24-game hitting streak had just ended.

Carrasquel finished third behind Walt Dropo and Whitey Ford in the American League Rookie of the Year Award balloting. Dropo was the clear choice, with 34 homers and a league-leading 144 RBIs. Though he pitched only half a season, Ford made a strong impression with his 9-1 record and 2.81 ERA. Carrasquel – with 4 homers, 46 RBIs, a .282 average (his best in the majors), and sparkling play at short – also finished 12th in the voting for AL Most Valuable Player.

"The only thing that keeps general manager Frank Lane from grinning all over the place," wrote Bob Broeg shortly after the season, "is a recent knee operation necessitated by Chico's habit – like that of Pepper Martin – of jamming abruptly to a stop after sprinting from the batter's box to first base."[14] The damaged knee cartilage forced Carrasquel to miss the last week of his rookie season, but he came back the next season without missing a defensive beat.

Early in the 1951 season, John C. Hoffman of *Collier's* described Carrasquel in a feature called "Chicago's Chico – Baseball's New Mr. Shortstop." "Physically, Chico suggests the late Tony Lazzeri, famed Yankee second baseman. High cheekbones betray some Indian blood and he smiles through dark-brown eyes adorning an expressionless countenance. There is good humor in his manner, and his temper is even. He walks with the stride of a panther, dresses elegantly off the field."[15]

Hoffman also depicted Carrasquel in the field. "Carrasquel plays deep at his position. His strong accurate arm permits him to stand far back. On fast grounders hit to his left or right, when he is caught off balance, he leaps high into the air after snaring the ball and throws to first base with both feet off the ground."[16] The latter part brings Derek Jeter to mind, though Jeter's range was not comparable. Carrasquel also had to deal with an occupational hazard of shortstops – he received over 100 stitches for spike wounds throughout his playing days.

At least as early as 1951, his spectacular glove work also made Carrasquel one of the first Latin American players in the United States to receive a national endorsement deal. The Nocona Athletic Goods Company, a small Texas-based manufacturer of gloves, used his photo to complement their "major league quality" products. "Chico handles the hot ones with ease using his Nokona 59 glove…made especially for him," one of the print ads (from 1954) proclaimed.

After winning just 60 games in 1950, the White Sox picked up to 81 in 1951. This included a 14-game winning streak – the first 11 on the road – from May 15 through May 30. The South Side of Chicago was infected with early pennant fever, as an Associated Press story described. "A crowd of more than 1000 rolled cheers through the LaSalle Street Station as Sox stalwarts detrained. Perhaps the loudest salvo of applause was directed at shortstop Chico Carrasquel."[17]

In July 1951, Carrasquel enjoyed what he later described as "my greatest thrill in baseball … my first All-Star Game … because I was the first Latin player to play in one."[18] The fans voted him in over reigning AL MVP Phil Rizzuto. Chico's selection was reinforced this way by *Washington Post* columnist Shirley Povich: "If you're asking how Carrasquel got into the All-Star act with a sub-.300 average, that's easy. There isn't a shortstop who's outhitting him, and there isn't a rival who deserves mention in the same inhalation with Carrasquel as a defensive man."[19] The AL's shortstop went 1-for-2, his hit (a single) coming against NL starter Robin Roberts.

The White Sox were still in first place at the All-Star break, but they soon fell out of the hunt, despite Carrasquel's continued fine play. On July 13 at Comiskey, Chico accepted 18 chances without fault in a 19-inning game against Boston. Two days later, he established a new AL shortstop record of 289 chances without an error. The streak (since surpassed by various players) reached 297. Also, on July 15, Carrasquel kept Sam Zoldak of the Philadelphia Athletics from throwing a no-hitter with a third-inning single.

In August, *Look* magazine ran a five-page feature centered around Carrasquel and how the White Sox pennant chances were tied to him. It described Carrasquel "at shortstop, covering ground like sunlight, inspiring the rest of the team to outdo itself in trying to match him."[20]

As the weekly magazine hit the newsstands, a third Carrasquel "edition," Alfonso Carrasquel Jr., made his happy arrival into the clan. Alfonso Sr. and Marcela had six children in total. Rosalia (born in October 1952) and Roberta (born in August 1956) were numbers four and five; the name of number six is not currently available. In a 2003 interview, Chico admitted to fathering other children from relationships he had with women during the 1960s. He stated that he took responsibility for all of them and that the offspring all bear his last name.[21]

Manager Paul Richards reasserted the shortstop's importance to his team and how much he wanted Carrasquel to stay in Chicago: "He's unquestionably the standout player in our lineup," said Richards. "He's so brilliant, in fact, that he pulls the whole ball club up with him, because the rest give out that extra effort to try and keep up with him. If Chico ever got homesick and jumped the ball club like Luis Garcia [a player who went home

White Sox shortstop Chico Carrasquel poses in 1951, early in a trailblazing major-league career. He became the first Latin American to start an All-Star Game. (The Stanley Weston Archive / Getty Images)

to Caracas after four days in White Sox training camp], I'd hop a plane and go down to Venezuela after him myself. And if he refused to return, I'd keep right on going."[22]

Carrasquel had made such an impact in just two years that after the season his name was even bandied about in one-on-one trade talk involving a supposedly slipping Ted Williams. (The Red Sox great had hit "only" .318 that year.) "We stopped talking about Carrasquel almost simultaneously the moment his name was mentioned," Frank Lane said in November 1951. "We'll take Williams and pay him his Boston salary, not the $125,000 given out to gullible reporters in Boston. In return, we'll gladly pay the proper and required price in player, money, marbles and bubble gum. But," added a pompous-sounding Lane, "no proper price can possibly include our All-Star shortstop, especially in a deal for a 33-year-old outfielder who couldn't play shortstop with the aid of three arms and a lacrosse racquet."[23]

A Chicago-based fan club also sprang up around the White Sox shortstop. Although the Carrasquelites may have sounded like a musical group from the emerging rock 'n' roll era, they did not do any singing – except for the praises of their idol. An initial fee of $1.00 brought a one-year membership, with an official card, monthly bulletins, an annual journal, and invitations to monthly meetings during the season. There were periodic autograph parties too, also attended by other White Sox players.

The Carrasquelites had their share of female constituents, who called themselves "Carrasquelettes." The handsome South American's appearance brought them together as much as – if not more than – his stylish play. White Sox management appreciated Chico's appeal to his feminine fans, who regularly boosted home ticket sales.

Carrasquel had signed his 1952 contract for a published $20,000, a good amount then for a third-year player and shortstop. But much to the disappointment of his boosters, their hero floundered in 1952. As the season drew to a close, Edgar Munzel was brutally frank in his criticism. "What has happened to Chico Carrasquel? The most brilliant young shortstop in baseball in 1950 has been playing like just another short fielder. Chico was hog fat last spring. He had slowed down afield and wasn't hitting anywhere near his 1950 or 1951 pace."[24] Listed at six-foot-even and a normal playing weight of 170 pounds, Carrasquel did not have enough height to distribute the excess, something he could afford even less at his position. A broken finger in late June added to the misery of an inadequately played season of 100 games. "It [the injury] eliminated the possibility that he might play himself into condition through the summer heat," wrote Munzel.[25]

Willy Miranda – a Cuban shortstop who was also known for fancy fielding, but who never hit much – subbed for Carrasquel. Over the last two months of the 1952 season, the White Sox (who finished in third place) regularly fielded a lineup of four Hispanic position players – something never seen before in major league baseball. In the infield, either Carrasquel or Miranda played alongside first-year third baseman Héctor Rodríguez.

In the outfield, Jim Rivera (a New Yorker whose parents were Puerto Rican) played next to left fielder Minnie Miñoso.

In 1953, Chicago finished third again, albeit with an improved win total of 89. Carrasquel had regained his prior form and it plainly showed. After having ballooned to 192 pounds the previous spring, he had arrived at camp at 180. The trimmer shortstop lifted his average to .279 and made only 18 errors in 758 chances. The fans voted Carrasquel onto the All-Star team over Rizzuto again (he was held hitless in two trips).

In 1954, Chicago fielded its strongest team since 1920, winning 94 games. That was still only enough for third place in the AL behind the Cleveland Indians (who won 111) and the Yankees (who won 103). Carrasquel sustained his All-Star level of play, hitting 12 homers (the most he had in any big-league season). Though he hit just .255, he drew 85 walks – contrary to the perception of Latinos as free swingers, Chico had a good eye, as befit the team's leadoff hitter. Carrasquel played in every one of the White Sox games in 1954. He was second on the team in RBIs (62) and third in runs scored (106). With the glove, he remained a standout.

That year's All-Star game had an unprecedented international scope. *Chicago Daily Tribune* writer Arch Ward, who had conceived of the Midsummer Classic in 1933, wrote that the balloting was conducted "with the cooperation of more than 200 newspapers, radio and television stations, representing the United States, Hawaii, Mexico, Puerto Rico, Cuba, Venezuela and Panama. Orestes Minoso, Chico Carrasquel and Bobby Ávila learned they have many amigos in Latin American countries by landing on the starting squad."[26] Having three Hispanics in the starting lineup was a first in All-Star play. Carrasquel, who played the entire game, was 1-for-5.

The 1951 *Collier's* article on Carrasquel had called him "Baseball's New Mr. Shortstop" – so it was ironic that there was friction between him and baseball's original "Mr. Shortstop," Marty Marion, in 1955. Paul Richards had left the White Sox with nine games to go in 1954, after signing a three-year deal to manage the Baltimore Orioles. Marion, a coach, completed the season as manager with a one-year pact to return in the same capacity.

In spring training 1955, Marion fined Carrasquel $100 for missing practice. Carrasquel was said to be ill, but reportedly, a check of his room found it unoccupied. Once the season started, Marion criticized Carrasquel's defensive play, coming out and saying his shortstop was letting fieldable balls turn into hits from lack of effort. Previously, Carrasquel's harshest critics had inferred that he "let up" when the game was decided or out of hand, that his level of play was too often equal to the competition, that only first division teams brought out his best. Carrasquel always refuted the charges by responding, "I play hard whether we are winning or losing."[27]

In spite of the criticisms, Carrasquel made the All-Star team for the fourth time in five years. Though Chico didn't match his offensive numbers from 1954, he made double figures (11) in home runs again. At Municipal Stadium in Kansas City, on

April 23, he enjoyed perhaps the finest day of his career at the plate. He sprayed five singles and scored five times in a 29-6 rout of the Athletics.

Marion decided to give Carrasquel a few days off before the All-Star Game amid worries about his play in the field.[28] It might have been an even more embarrassing message if Carrasquel had been selected to the AL All-Star squad as a starter, but even as a substitute, it still could not have felt good. After the mini-break in mid-season, Carrasquel was back in the lineup and homered in each game as Chicago swept a doubleheader from the Washington Senators.

The White Sox had another respectable year in 1955, but in the end, their 91 wins were still good enough only for third place in the AL. A month after the end of the regular season, they traded Carrasquel to Cleveland. The front office thought he had lost a step, and another Venezuelan shortstop was ready to take over: Luis Aparicio. In 2005, the Hall of Famer said, "Chico was my hero and mentor. He took me under his wing, and I'm grateful to him for making me the ballplayer that I turned out to be."[29] Several days later, another countryman, Luis Sojo, added, "When you talk about shortstops in Venezuela, you mean [Carrasquel]. He was a mentor to everyone, Aparicio, Vizquel. All the Venezuelan players wanted to play shortstop because of him."[30]

Lane was not involved in the Carrasquel deal, at least not when it took place; he had become GM of the St. Louis Cardinals. However, a Chicago newspaper report from July 1955 offers additional insight:

"Venezuelan sportswriters burn up the long distance wires to the Comiskey Park office of Frank Lane to keep abreast of Chico's moves. Lane's latest contact with south of the border journalists came when one excitedly telephoned to check a rumor that Chico was feuding with field boss, Marty Marion.

'Marion and Chico aren't having any trouble,' Frank said.

'Are you and Chico having any trouble?' the Venezuelan asked. Lane said no.

'Well, is Chico having any trouble with anybody?'

'Yes,' said Lane. 'With American League pitchers'."[31]

Carrasquel and outfielder Jim Busby brought slugger Larry Doby from Cleveland, a pretty good indication of Carrasquel's perceived value around the league. Doby was one year removed from leading the American League in home runs and runs batted in. (Busby was known more for his speed and defense.) In a stamp-of-approval quote, Indians general manager Hank Greenberg said, "By acquiring Carrasquel, generally recognized as the American League's outstanding shortstop, and Busby, a speedster, who is one of the fine fielders of the league, we believe we have improved our club."[32]

Though the shortstop regretted leaving Chicago, he welcomed the trade as a needed parting of the ways from Marion, with whom he had sparred. Chico stated that Marion had his own different way of playing shortstop and that Marion tried to change the way he played.[33] The manager said publicly, "We couldn't stir him up anymore and maybe he'll do better somewhere else." Marion took a swipe at Chico's fielding habits, saying that he would waste time by not moving toward the ball on a double play, that sometimes he would squat to field a ball and sometimes not, and that balls which he would have gobbled up the previous year were going through his legs.[34]

Carrasquel looked forward to his new team and to another major-league first: a Hispanic double-play combination with Mexican second baseman Bobby Ávila. Carrasquel believed he and Ávila would form the "best such pairing in the American League."[35]

Carrasquel had two more of his best days at the plate in 1956. On April 26, against Kansas City, he had a career-best seven RBIs (making him the second Hispanic player after Luis Olmo, and the first in the AL, to get as many in a single big-league game). On August 27, he hit two homers off Hal Griggs of the Senators, marking his only multi-homer game in the majors. Overall, though, he hit a disappointing .243-7-48 in 141 games for his new team.

In 1957, the Indians fell into the second division for the first time in 11 seasons under new manager Kerby Farrell, who replaced Al López. That July, Carrasquel got his one thousandth hit – a single against Chicago's Jack Harshman. He became the second Hispanic after Bobby Ávila to reach that milestone. Chico also got the last two of his four big-league grand slams that season. The second, also against Chicago, came on August 15. Left fielder Minnie Miñoso nearly brought the homer back into Comiskey Park "when he leaped over the left field fence and had the ball momentarily but it dropped out of his glove over the fence."[36]

Though he boosted his average to .276 for the season, with eight home runs, Chico's playing time was curtailed to 125 games. His fielding seemed to have regressed; he committed 24 errors.

The Indians hired Frank Lane away from the Cardinals over the winter in an effort to improve the club and its attendance. Lane brought in Bobby Bragan – Carrasquel's manager back at Fort Worth in 1949 – as skipper. Through 1957 and 1,099 major league games in the field, Carrasquel had made only one appearance away from shortstop (two innings at third base in 1956). In 1958, however, he began to appear at third with some frequency. Chico became more acquainted with third base than ever before after the Indians traded him to Kansas City on June 12 for Billy Hunter (who had followed Carrasquel at shortstop at Fort Worth). The Athletics had a good-fielding shortstop in Joe DeMaestri; after acquiring Carrasquel, they moved third baseman Héctor López over to second.

Shortly after joining his new team, Carrasquel tore off seven hits as the A's swept a doubleheader from the Red Sox. The infielder had five hits, including a double, in the opener, and drove in five runs for the day. Overall, though, he managed only a combined .234-4-34 line for his two clubs, a drop from his .276-8-57 marks of 1957.

As the 1958 World Series was being played, the Athletics sent the 32-year-old Carrasquel to the Baltimore Orioles in an even-up deal for Dick Williams. In Baltimore, Carrasquel was reunited with his former manager, Paul Richards, and (briefly) with Bobby Ávila. Carrasquel was the primary shortstop for the so-so 1959 Orioles. (Willy Miranda, Baltimore's starter much of the time from 1955, played sparingly in his last big-league season.) Hampered by an injury that left him with just 50% vision in his left eye,[37] he hit only .223 in 114 games, the lowest average of his career. His last appearance in the majors came at Fenway Park on September 23, 1959.

Carrasquel rejoined the White Sox in January 1960 as a free agent, but Chicago released him in late April before he played a game. He then went to the Los Angeles Dodgers organization, playing 35 games with their Triple-A team in Montreal. That marked the end of Carrasquel's career in the U.S., but he remained active in Venezuelan winter ball until 1967. In 816 regular-season games in his homeland, he hit .278 with 46 homers and 357 RBIs. He was a member of four champion teams in the LVBP with Caracas (1947-48, 1948-49, 1951-52, and 1956-57) plus another as a playoff reinforcement with Valencia (1957-58).

While still a star player in Venezuela, Carrasquel managed his Caracas Leones squad to a third-place finish in the 1957-58 winter season. Chico ended up managing in all or parts of 10 winter-league campaigns in his home country. In 1982, again as the manager of the Leones, the 56-year-old Carrasquel became the first Venezuelan to lead his national team to a Caribbean Series title. The Lions captured the bragging rights to Latin American winter ball in Hermosillo, Mexico, winning five and losing one. Carrasquel is one of 11 players to have his uniform number (17) retired by the Caracas club.[38]

For several years after retiring as an active player, Carrasquel was a scout for the Kansas City Royals and New York Mets. Starting in 1980, he also served as a broadcaster covering the Venezuelan winter league. Carrasquel became a Chicago White Sox Spanish-language radio color man from 1990 to 1996, stepping down at the age of 70. As an extended part of his radio duties, Chico represented the White Sox community relations department. The position offered the outgoing former player an opportunity to interact frequently with a new generation of Chicago fans.

In 1991, the LVBP honored Carrasquel by naming its reconstructed Puerto la Cruz Stadium after the country's first big league all-star. The stadium, home to the Anzoátegui Caribes, hosted the 1994 and 1998 Caribbean Series.

In 2003, the former shortstop was among the inaugural class of players enshrined in his country's Baseball Hall of Fame in Valencia. That January, in Caracas, Chico suffered an armed carjacking at the hands of two thugs. Luckily no one was seriously injured, including his sister, who was with him at the time.

Carrasquel, throughout his later years, stayed close to the game. His fame helped him as a tireless promoter of youth baseball in Venezuela. In 2004, he established a non-profit organization in his name to help broaden the horizons of underprivileged children in his nation. His sister, Emilia Carrasquel, remained one of the foundation's Venezuelan board members as of 2014.

One of the last public appearances for Carrasquel occurred on April 13, 2004, at U.S. Cellular Field. Confined to a wheelchair, he joined three other great Venezuelan shortstops – Hall of Famer Luis Aparicio, Dave Concepción, and Ozzie Guillén (then the White Sox manager) – in throwing out ceremonial first pitches before Chicago's home opener against the Kansas City Royals.

The fondly-remembered player, who had been suffering from diabetes, died of a heart attack on May 26, 2005, in Caracas. He was 79. He was predeceased by his first wife, Marcela, and second spouse, Conny (both women died several months apart in 2000). During a nationally televised speech, Venezuelan President Hugo Chávez declared two days of mourning for the idol. "¡Viva Carrasquel!" he shouted. Ozzie Guillén said, "I don't think he was the greatest player ever to come from the country. But to me, he was the greatest man to come from Venezuela."[39]

SOURCES

In addition to the sources cited in the Notes, the author also consulted baseball-reference.com, retrosheet.org, ChicoCarrasquel.org, purapelota.com (Venezuelan statistics), and Rich Westcott, *Splendor on the Diamond* (Gainesville, Florida: University Press of Florida, 2000).

NOTES

1   Ray Gillespie, "Veeck, in Deepest Plunge, Comes Up With a Shortstop." *The Sporting News*, October 22, 1952: 13.

2   Marcos Bretón and José Luis Villegas. *Away Games: The Life and Times of a Latin American Player* (New York, New York: Simon & Schuster, 1999), 121.

3   Tim Wendel, *The New Face of Baseball: The One-Hundred-Year Rise and Triumph of Latinos in Baseball* (New York, New York: HarperCollins Publishers, 2004), 75.

4   Harold C. Burr, "3 Rookies Brighten Brooks," *Brooklyn Eagle*, January 6, 1949: B1.

5   Dave Nightingale, "Lost in America," *The Sporting News*, August 3, 1992: 11-15.

6   John Cronley, "Texas to Send Bumper Crop to Main Tent," *The Sporting News*, September 21, 1949: 13.

7   The trade stipulated that if the minor leaguers – pitcher Chuck Eisenmann and infielder Fred Hancock – did not show enough promise to suit Rickey, Lane would take either player back and add another $10,000 to the transaction. Hancock did not live up to his billing, in Rickey's eyes, and was returned for the additional subsidy.

8   John P. Carmichael, "Sox Shaking Leg for Lane," *The Sporting News*, December 14, 1949: 10.

9   Bob Broeg, "Strong Rookie All-Stars Show .283 Mark," *The Sporting News*, November 1, 1950: 5.

10   Ed Fitzgerald, "How the White Sox Are Building a Winner," *Sport*, April 1954.

11   Jack Cuddy, "Quick-quality Farming Policy Is Paying Rapid Dividends for Chisox," United Press, July 17, 1950.

12 John C. Hoffman, "Chicago's Chico Baseball's New 'Mr. Shortstop'," *Collier's*, April 28, 1951: 24-28.

13 Edgar Munzel, "Carrasquel Zooms to Stardom as White Sox Continue to Sink," *The Sporting News*, August 9, 1950: 14.

14 Broeg, "Strong Rookie All-Stars Show .283 Mark."

15 Hoffman, "Chicago's Chico Baseball's New 'Mr. Shortstop'."

16 Hoffman, "Chicago's Chico Baseball's New 'Mr. Shortstop'."

17 "11-game Streak Has Fans Joyous," *Washington Post*, May 29, 1951: 14. Richards' squad won 15 straight road games, two short of the AL record of 17, set by Washington in 1912.

18 Rich Marazzi, and Len Fiorito, *Baseball Players of the 1950s* (Jefferson, North Carolina: McFarland & Company, 2004), 58.

19 Shirley Povich, "This Morning," *Washington Post*, July 2, 1951: 12

20 Tim Cochrane, "The Great Chicago Fire…," *Look,* August 5, 1951, 40 (five non-concurrent pages).

21 Milagros Socorro, "Alfonso Carrasquel," Analitica.com, September 12, 2003.

22 Edgar Munzel, "Chico Gives Pale Hose Chic Trick at Short," *The Sporting News*, May 16, 1951: 3.

23 Ed Burns, "Lane Bars Ted-Chico Deal," *The Sporting News,* November 21, 1951: 7.

24 Edgar Munzel, "Senor Chico Due For Plain English Winter Warning," *The Sporting News*, September 24, 1952: 8.

25 Munzel, "Senor Chico Due For Plain English Winter Warning."

26 Arch Ward, "4,272,470 Fans Pick All-Star Lineups." *Chicago Daily Tribune,* July 5, 1954.

27 Jack Orr, "Are Chico's Troubles Behind Him?" *Sport,* June 1954: 34-37.

28 Edgar Munzel, "Old Master Marty Critical of Chico's Work at Shortstop," *The Sporting News*, July 20, 1955: 16.

29 "Former White Sox Shortstop Chico Carrasquel Passes Away," MLB.com, May 26, 2005.

30 Anthony McCarron, "Sojo Fondly Remembers Carrasquel," *New York Daily News*, May 31, 2005.

31 David Condon, "In The Wake of the News." *Chicago Daily Tribune,* July 22, 1955.

32 Hal Lebovitz, "'We Needed Bat Threat at Short'–Senor," *The Sporting News*, November 2, 1955: 3.

33 "Chico Likes Lopez Better," United Press, March 19, 1956.

34 Hal Lebovitz, "Rivals Won't See Wooden Indians on Paths–Senor," *The Sporting News*, December 7, 1955: 21.

35 Gordon (Red) Marston, "Nothing Could Surprise Me Since Lane Left Chicago – Chico," *The Sporting News*, November 2, 1955: 4.

36 "Carrasquel Drives Grand Slam as Indians Beat White Sox, 5-4," *New York Times,* August 16, 1957.

37 "Chico Carrasquel Has a Serious Eye Injury," Associated Press, September 17, 1959.

38 The other 10: Pompeyo Davalillo, César Tovar, Vic Davalillo, Antonio "Tony" Armas, Baudilio "Bo" Díaz, Urbano Lugo, Gonzalo Márquez , Omar Vizquel, and Andrés Galarraga. José Luis Guaymare, "El Caballero del Béisbol," personal blog, (http://guayma.blogspot.com/2009/12/el-caballe-ro-del-beisbol.html)

39 Bob Vanderberg, "'Chico' Carrasquel, first Latin player in All-Star Game, dies at 77 [sic]," *Chicago Tribune*, May 26, 2005.

TONY CASTILLO

BY KEN FRICKE

On an October evening in Philadelphia during the fourth game of the 1993 World Series, Toronto Blue Jays left-handed pitcher Tony Castillo entered the game in the fifth inning in relief of Al Leiter with the Blue Jays trailing the Phillies 12-7, two out and Mariano Duncan on first base. Castillo induced John Kruk to ground out, then pitched the sixth and seventh innings, allowing a run in each inning. With the score now 14-9 in favor of the Phillies, the Blue Jays scored six runs in the top of the eighth inning to take a 15-14 lead, which the Toronto bullpen held, thus making Castillo the winning pitcher and the first Venezuelan-born pitcher to win a game in the World Series.

Antonio José "Tony" Castillo Jiménez was born in Quibor, Lara, Venezuela, on March 1, 1963. He began playing baseball at the age of 8 in his hometown, and from then on baseball became his passion. He left high school early to follow that dream.[1] Before turning professional, Castillo played in various state and national tournaments, always representing the state of Lara. At the age of 19, Castillo was signed by the Cardenales de Lara to pitch in the 1982-83 Venezuelan winter league (he pitched for his home-state team every winter for the next 18 seasons, missing only the 1985-86 winter season). Castillo pitched creditably during his first winter season despite some injuries, pitched briefly in the postseason tournament, then in February 1983 was signed to a contract by the Toronto Blue Jays.[2] In 1983, with the Toronto team in the rookie-level Gulf Coast League, he pitched in only one game for three innings and got the save. During the following 1983-84 Venezuelan winter league season, he pitched in one game.[3]

The 1984 season found Castillo with the Florence Blue Jays of the Class-A South Atlantic League, where he completed his first full professional season, leading the team in wins with 11; innings pitched, 137⅓; and games started, 24; and was second in strikeouts, 96. His strikeout/walk ratio was a good 1.92 and his ERA a decent 3.41. After the 1984 season, he again pitched in Venezuela and had a very fine winter league campaign, going 4-2 with a 2.06 ERA in 13 games, nine of them starts.

In 1985 Castillo pitched for the Kinston Blue Jays (Class-A Carolina League) where he went 11-7, pitching 127⅔ innings. In 35 games, 12 of them starts, he had three saves and a sterling 1.90 ERA (third best in the league for pitchers pitching at least 100 innings). He did not pitch in the 1985-86 Venezuelan winter league.

In 1986 Castillo was supposed to pitch for the Knoxville Blue Jays (Double-A Southern League), but he missed all season due to tendinitis in his left shoulder which required surgery.[4] He did manage to pitch briefly in the 1986-87 Venezuelan winter league, throwing 10⅓ innings in four games and one start.

The 1987 season found Castillo, at the age of 24, back in Class-A ball with the Dunedin Blue Jays (Florida State League), where for the first time in his career he worked exclusively as a relief pitcher. In 39 games he registered a 6-2 won-lost record with six saves and a 3.36 ERA. He allowed only two home runs in 69⅔ innings and averaged 8.0 strikeouts per 9 innings, numbers that were very good considering that he had not pitched for the entire 1986 season. Castillo returned that winter to Venezuela where he pitched 69 innings over 15 games, 13 starts, with a won-lost record of 6-4 and an ERA of 3.13.

Castillo began the 1988 season again with Dunedin, where in 30 games, all in relief, he saved 12 games and pitched to an ERA of 1.48, numbers which led to his promotion to the Knoxville Smokies of the Double-A Southern League. Castillo pitched in only five games while in Knoxville, but they were productive ones: eight innings, two hits, 11 strikeouts, one walk, two saves, and a 0.00 ERA. By mid-August, Castillo was called up to the Blue Jays, where he made his major-league debut on August 14 in Kansas City, pitching a scoreless eighth inning in a losing effort. In a book published in 1994, Castillo said, "I remember that I pitched one inning. In that moment I was nervous because I was pitching in the major leagues for the first time and I had never seen so many persons in a stadium, around 40 thousand people. Nevertheless, in my second opportunity I did not feel the same nervousness and I was more relaxed."[5]

Castillo remained with Toronto for the rest of the season. In 1988 Toronto was in a close race with Boston, Detroit, Milwaukee, and the New York Yankees for the division (they all finished within 3½ games of the eventual winner, Boston), though the Blue Jays had to finish 15-4 to get that close. Castillo gave the Toronto team a third left-handed relief pitcher (the others were David Wells and John Cerutti, who was a part-time starter). On September 3 he gained his first major-league win, pitching 2⅓ scoreless innings of middle relief against the Rangers. Overall, he pitched 15 innings over 14 games, with an ERA of 3.00. For the second straight year, Castillo pitched in Venezuela over the winter, going 5-4 in 85⅓ innings with a 2.74 ERA.

Castillo started the 1989 season with the Blue Jays and pitched, with mixed results, in 13 games through the middle of May before being sent down to Triple A. During this part of the season with the Blue Jays, his best outing came on April 16 when he pitched the final 4⅔ scoreless innings at home against Kansas City to notch the save. A couple of rough outings on May 13-14 when he gave up nine hits and seven runs, five of them earned, in 1⅓ innings ballooned his ERA to 7.71 and led to his demotion to Triple-A Syracuse.

Castillo remained with Syracuse until early August, when the Blue Jays called recalled him. Over the next three weeks, he pitched in four more games, pitching an inning or less in each, allowing no runs and lowering his ERA to 6.11. On August 24 he was traded to the Atlanta Braves with minor-league catcher Francisco Cabrera for middle-inning relief pitcher Jim Acker. Castillo remained with the Braves for the remainder of the season, appearing in 9⅓ innings over 12 games, losing one, and ending up with an ERA of 4.82. Over the winter he pitched in Venezuela, having a very fine won-lost record of 7-3 with a 3.87 ERA over 72 innings in 16 games, 12 of them starts.

Castillo, who was given a $100,000 contract,[6] spent most of the 1990 season with the Braves, except for a month from late June to late July which he spent with the Triple-A Richmond Braves working on some of his pitches, notably his curve. The 1990 season was not a very good one for the Braves as they ended up with the worst record in the majors, 65-97. However, for Castillo it was a pretty good season, as he led the Braves with 52 games pitched, 49 in relief, over 76⅔ innings, giving up 93 hits, with a won-lost record of 5-1, one save, and an ERA of 4.23. After his recall he was used as a starter for the first time in his major-league career, starting three games, winning two with no losses and a 2.51 ERA. During the 1990 season, Castillo managed the only hit, walk, and run scored of his career. On June 20 at home against the Cincinnati Reds, he walked in the third inning against Jack Armstrong and came around to score, and then on August 15 at Three Rivers Stadium in Pittsburgh, in his second career start, Castillo singled against Neal Heaton. Considering that he was the winning pitcher in that August 15 game, it was a pretty good game all around for the lefty. During the 1990-1991 winter league in Venezuela, Castillo pitched in 13 games, 10 as a starter, with a won-lost record of 6-2 and an ERA of 3.91.

Despite his success in 1990, Castillo found himself optioned to Richmond to begin the 1991 season. He remained with Richmond until mid-August, pitching in 23 games, 17 of them starts, and 118 innings, to an ERA of 2.90. Castillo was recalled on August 11 when the Braves needed a left-hander to replace the injured Kent Mercker. Over the next two weeks, Castillo appeared in seven games, pitching ineffectively, winning one and losing one with a 7.27 ERA. Shortly after Mercker returned to the Braves, Castillo was traded to the New York Mets on August 28 for the more experienced Alejandro Peña. With the Mets, Castillo pitched in 10 games, starting three, winning one game with no losses, and finished with a 1.90 ERA. He was very effective in his starts, allowing only one earned run in 15⅔ innings. In his first start for the Mets, on September 11, he threw six scoreless innings against the Cubs at Wrigley Field, getting the win in a 4-1 game. (Two pitchers named Castillo started that game: The Cubs' starter was Frank Castillo.)

Castillo spent the 1991-92 winter in Venezuela, pitching in only eight games, all starts, and working to a won-lost record of

Pitcher Tony Castillo with the Blue Jays during the 1994 season. The left-hander spent 10 years in the majors, including two stints in Toronto. (Mitchell Layton / Getty Images Sports)

1-1 with a 2.91 ERA in 43⅓ innings, the fewest innings he had thrown in a winter league in the previous four years.

The 1992 season was a difficult one for Castillo. He had been traded three times in the past three years, and then on January 22, 1992, he was again traded, along with Mark Carreon, this time to the Detroit Tigers. At the end of spring training, he was assigned to the Triple-A Toledo Mud Hens, where he spent the entire season. There he barely started to get his pitching rhythm – the trainers were attempting to change his mechanics – when, according to Castillo,[7] he broke his tibia, but the fracture was not medically detected for almost two months, at which point he was placed on the disabled list for six weeks and only returned to the Mud Hens with two weeks remaining in the season. During the season he appeared in only 12 games, starting nine, completing none, pitched in 44⅔ innings, ending up with a won-lost record of 2-3 and a 3.63 ERA. At the end of the season he was released by the Tigers. Castillo, now apparently healthy, pitched in Venezuela and had his best-ever winter season, ending up with a won-lost record of 9-4 in 15 starts, pitching 101⅓ innings, in which he struck out 79 and walked only 15 batters, ending up with a 2.22 ERA. For his outstanding winter season, he was named the Pitcher of the Year in Venezuela.[8]

However, Castillo had got a break by being on the Cardenales de Lara. Luis Leal, who had pitched his entire six-year major-league career for the Blue Jays and 14 winter seasons for Cardenales, encouraged Castillo to not give up and continue pitching, that he had had a horrible season, and that he was still young enough to make it back to the major leagues.[9] At the same time, Cardenales le Lara pitching coach Derek Bosley and manager Garth Iorg, who also managed the Knoxville Blue Jays, both sent good reports back to the major-league club. Pat Gillick, the Jays' general manager, paid a visit to Venezuela and informed Castillo that the team was interested in signing him because the Blue Jays need left-handers in the bullpen. Castillo's agent had also been talking with the Cleveland Indians. Eventually, Castillo committed to the Blue Jays and was very happy since he was very familiar with the team, its staff, and players.[10]

So, at the age of 30 Castillo started over again with the Blue Jays. He pitched sparingly in spring training and began the season with Syracuse. He pitched in one game before being called up by the Blue Jays on April 15, making his first appearance on the 17th against the Indians in Cleveland. He never again pitched in the minor leagues.

During the 1993 season, Castillo pitched in 51 games, registering a won-lost record of 3-2 with a 3.38 ERA in 50⅔ innings. He never pitched more than 2⅔ innings in any game, but was quite effective all season, maintaining an ERA between 1.08 and 2.95 throughout most of the season, until a couple of rough outings in September raised his ERA over 3.00. Castillo allowed 19 runs (all earned) during the season, but seven of those were in September. Toronto won the AL East Division title with a record of 95-67, seven games better than the second-place Yankees.

In the ALCS, the Blue Jays defeated the White Sox four games to two, Castillo pitching one scoreless inning in each of the third and fifth games. The Blue Jays defeated the Phillies in the World Series in six games. Castillo's performance during the Series was not particularly good: he was roughed up in two appearances for an 8.10 ERA, giving up six hits, one home run, and three runs in 3⅓ innings. In Game Two he entered in the seventh inning with the Jays trailing 5-3 and gave up a home run to Lenny Dykstra. Then came that wild 15-14 fourth game whenhe gave up two runs in 2⅓ innings, but became the winning pitcher when the Blue Jays overcame a 14-9 deficit by scoring six runs in the top of the eighth inning. After the World Series, Castillo returned to Venezuela for the 1993-94 winter league, pitching in nine games, all starts, with a won-lost record of 2-3.

The World Series champion Blue Jays started the 1994 season well, but May and June were hard times and by the All-Star break they were 10 games under .500, and were in third place, 16 games behind the AL East-leading Yankees when the season was shut down after the players struck on August 11. Castillo

had been exclusively a relief pitcher (as he remained for the duration of his major-league career), pitching mostly in the late innings, leading the Blue Jays in games pitched (41) and relief innings (68). He finished the season with a won-lost record of 5-2 with a 2.51 ERA, recording one save. Castillo returned to Venezuela for the 1993-94 winter league, pitching, as always, with his favorite Cardenales de Lara. There he pitched in 14 games, finishing with a record of 4-4 in 77 innings and an ERA of 2.57.

The 1995 season started about two weeks late after the strike ended. The Blue Jays finished in last place in the AL East with a record of 56-88, their worst record since the 1981 season. Castillo was the only one of the late-inning relief corps who remained healthy all season.[11] Mike Timlin, the Blue Jays closer, eventually went on the DL for elbow surgery. Castillo recorded his first save of 1995 on June 14 against the Red Sox. He led the Blue Jays in games pitched (55), games finished (31), relief innings (72⅔), and saves (13), finishing with a record of 1-5 with a 3.22 ERA. Castillo pitched in only six games (four starts) in the winter league, going 4-1 with a sterling 1.30 ERA in 27⅔ innings.

The 1996 Blue Jays finished in fourth place in the AL East with a record of 74-88. Timlin returned healthy after his elbow surgery and immediately took over the Toronto closer duties. Castillo was used anywhere from as early as the second inning to the seventh or eighth. His lone save with the Blue Jays occurred on July 11 in Milwaukee when he replaced Timlin in the ninth inning with two outs and the bases loaded and retired his one opponent.

Castillo was traded to the Chicago White Sox on August 22, but still managed to finish third on the Blue Jays in games pitched (40) and led with 72⅓ relief innings, finishing with a won-lost record of 2-3 and a 4.23 ERA.

The White Sox finished second behind Cleveland. Castillo pitched well for Chicago, with a won-lost record of 3-1 in 15 games over 22⅔ innings with one save and a 1.59 ERA. He was granted free agency on December 7 but re-signed with the White Sox four days later for $1.2 million. During the offseason, Castillo pitched in only two games, three innings, and no decisions in Venezuela.

Castillo was 34 years old when the 1997 season started. Again, the White Sox finished in second place, six games behind the Indians. Castillo led the team with 64 relief appearances, pitching in 62⅓ innings, and finishing with a won-lost record of 4-4 and a 4.91 ERA. He had a few bad outings early in the season and it wasn't until the middle of June that he lowered his ERA below 7.00, and he only got it below 5.00 on the final two days of the season, when he also recorded two of his four saves. Playing in the winter league, he again had very limited playing time, seeing action in five games, 12⅔ innings, losing his only decision. However, the Cardenales won the Venezuelan championship and Castillo got into six more games, allowing no earned runs. In the Caribbean Series the Venezuelan squad went 2-4.

The 1998 season was Castillo's last in the major leagues. Again the White Sox finished second to the Indians. Castillo's first two appearances were good ones, and his April results were fair, in 10 games pitching to a 4.26 ERA. However, in May he gave up 21 hits, including four home runs while pitching to a 10.32 ERA, and in June his ERA was 15.00. By June 19 Castillo had appeared in 25 games, giving up 38 hits (7 home runs) in 27 innings for an 8.00 ERA. He was released by the White Sox on June 21.

Castillo's totals after 10 seasons in the majors were 28-23 in 403 games. He had six starts – three each for the Braves and Mets – and closed 114 games. His career earned-run average was 3.93. Because he worked primarily as a short reliever, he had only 18 plate appearances, with just the one base hit. He did have the win in Game Four in the 1993 World Series.

Castillo pitched in both the 1998-99 and (briefly) 1999-2000 Venezuelan winter league for the Cardenales. During the 1998-99 season he pitched in 15 games, 46 innings, starting seven games, and had a won-loss record of 4-1 with a 2.35 ERA. In his last professional season, 1999-2000, he appeared in seven games, all in relief, throwing 4⅔ innings with a 5.79 ERA and no record.

Castillo pitched in 17 Venezuelan winter league seasons, all for the Cardenales de Lara, between 1982 and 1999, missing only the 1985-86 season. He had a won-lost record of 53-33, with a 2.86 ERA. He played in 12 postseasons, pitching in another 58 games, with a 16-7 won-lost record and a 2.53 ERA.

After his playing days, Castillo and his wife, Petra, remained in Quibor, his small longtime hometown. They have two children, Anthony José Jr. and Angie. He has worked in stints with teams of the Liga Paralela (Parallel League).

SOURCES

Seasonal data was obtained from the Baseball-Reference.com website, and most in-game play-by-play information was found in the box scores at the Retrosheet.org website. Venezuelan Winter League seasonal data was obtained from the Venezuelan pelotabinaria website.

NOTES

1 Carlos Cárdenas Lares, *Venezolanos en las Grandes Ligas: Sus Vidas y Hazañas*, segunda edición (Caracas: Fondo Editorial Cardenas Lares, 1994), 285. The book is the source of most of the biographical information presented here.

2 *Venezolanos en las Grandes Ligas: Sus Vidas y Hazañas*, 285.

3 Venezuelan Winter League statistics are drawn from Registro Histórico Estadístico del Beisbol Profesional Venezolano, http://www.pelotabinaria.com.ve/beisbol/mostrar.php?ID=castant001.

4 *Venezolanos en las Grandes Ligas: Sus Vidas y Hazañas*, 285.

5 *Venezolanos en las Grandes Ligas: Sus Vidas y Hazañas*, 286. Actual attendance was a little over 27,000.

6 All salary data in this article was obtained at Baseball-Reference.com.

7 *Venezolanos en las Grandes Ligas: Sus Vidas y Hazañas*, 284.

8 Registro Histórico Estadístico del Beisbol Profesional Venezolano.

9 *Venezolanos en las Grandes Ligas: Sus Vidas y Hazañas*, 284.

10 *Venezolanos en las Grandes Ligas: Sus Vidas y Hazañas*, 284.

11 *The Sporting News Baseball Guide*, 1996 Edition (St. Louis: The Sporting News Publishing Co.), 77.

ENDY CHÁVEZ

BY JON SPRINGER

He was a slender Venezuelan outfielder whose defensive skill and joie de vivre earned him a 21-year professional career, highlighted by one of the postseason's all-time most memorable plays.

A reminder of Endy Chávez's magnificent catch in Game Six of the 2006 National League Championship Series greets entrants to the left-field gate at Citi Field in New York, where the sign incudes a silhouette figure of a graceful reach into the sky – capturing the moment that Chavez's outstretched glove snared a soaring line drive by the St. Louis Cardinals' Scott Rolen that seemed destined to be a tiebreaking home run. Instead, the ball was trapped in the very top of the webbing of Chávez's glove, and safely yanked back over the fence. Chávez recovered with the presence of mind to turn it into a double play, when his relay to José Valentin caught runner Jim Edmonds hopelessly off first base, delivering a second jolt of awe to the resplendent display of larceny.

The play is further featured in the fan walk outside Citi Field, the ballpark erected just a home run north of where Shea Stadium once stood. Not that Mets fans ever need a reminder: Chávez's heroics are etched into the souls of every Mets fan and remain a signal of the breathtaking abilities that earned Chávez, never a particularly threatening hitter, a 13-year career over eight major-league organizations, along with a storied run in the Venezuelan Winter League, where he starred for the Navegantes del Magallanes for 19 seasons. The proud Venezuelan also represented his country in the World Baseball Classic tournament in 2006 and 2009.[1]

Endy de Jesus Chávez was born on February 7, 1978, in Valencia, Venezuela, to Alirio, a window installer, and his wife, Carmen, a homemaker.[2] A brother, Ender James Chávez, came two years later and followed his older sibling into pro ball, although he never cracked the big leagues. A sister, Nidi, died prematurely. Chávez described learning to hit with sticks and stones and developing skills in sandlot and youth leagues as a pitcher and a first baseman. Chávez, however, had no taste for picking balls off the ground and it was only after transitioning to the outfield, where his speed and a sense of position was a game-changer, that he forged a path to the pros.[3]

Chávez was performing in a developmental academy run by the Colorado Rockies as a teenager when Mets scouts Gregorio Machado and Junior Roman made a daring catch of their own, signing the 19-year-old to his first pro contract. Their faith was rewarded when Chávez earned the organization's Class-A Doubleday Award in 1997,[4] after the rookie flycatcher hit .277 for the Mets' Gulf Coast League Rookie franchise in Port St.

Lucie, Florida. In a short stint with Kingsport of the Class-A Appalachian League, he hit .301 with a .407 on-base percentage.

Chávez spent all of 1998 in Kingsport, where he slashed .290/.373/.430. His ascension continued at St. Lucie of the Class-A Florida State League and Capital City of the South Atlantic League in 1999, hitting .312 in more than 200 plate appearances for Port St, Lucie. In 2000 Chávez hit .298 with 20 doubles and 38 stolen bases for Port St. Lucie, whose manager, Dave Engel, compared him to a young Andruw Jones.[5]

And just like that, he was stolen away again. Kansas City in the Rule 5 Draft selected Chávez from the Mets. Considered too inexperienced to make an Opening Day roster – where rules stipulated Rule 5 draftees reside – the team in a paper transaction reassigned Chávez to New York at the end of spring training, reacquiring him the same day for a minor-league outfielder named Mike Curry.[6]

A left-handed hitter who was variously listed as 5-feet-11 and 170 pounds or 5-feet-9 and 159 pounds, Chávez had a distinct batting style that incorporated his great speed into his swing, completing the action already taking his first step toward first base. Minor-league teammates with the Kansas City organization recognized the slap-and-run approach as resembling that of the phenomenal new arrival to the big leagues, Seattle's Ichiro Suzuki and took to calling Chávez "the New Ichiro."[7]

Eyes in the organization were already open to the difference Chávez could make with his glove and his speed. "Our scouts said Chávez could play defense in the big leagues today," Royals GM Allard Baird said while explaining their decision to pluck him from the Mets despite his not having a single plate appearance above the Class-A level. "That he was an above-average runner. That he had an average arm in center field. That he could go get fly balls and that he wasn't afraid to leave his feet. That he had no fear of the wall. That he came in on the ball well."

"But," Baird added, "his bat was not major league ready. That needed to get stronger. That he played hard and wouldn't be in awe of the major league environment. So far, he's done that."[8]

That assessment would hold true throughout Chávez's career, assuring that he'd always be in demand as a player, but most often considered a utility-type deployed primarily to protect late-inning leads, pinch-hit or pinch-run, bunt runners over, and steal. Chávez was well adept in all these tasks and that made him a useful weapon and a favorite of many of his managers.

The 2001 Royals sputtered to an 18-32 start and an ensuing roster shake-up provided Chávez's first opportunity in the big leagues. He was recalled along with right-hander Kris Wilson on May 29 when struggling pitcher Brian Meadows and reserve catcher Sal Fasano were sent down to the minors.

Wearing uniform number 43 and batting ninth, Chávez started at The Ballpark in Arlington that evening, grounding out against Texas hurler Rick Helling in his first two plate appearances before lining a single to left in his third at-bat, scoring Joe Randa and scampering to second base on the play to the plate. The next day Chávez had three hits, including an RBI double, helping the Royals down the Rangers, 11-2.

Chávez, however, still needed time to solve big-league pitching. He was returned to Double-A Wichita in July after enduring an 0-for-21 skid and ending his first big-league stint hitting just .208 with a .238 on-base percentage and slugging just .234. His figures in the minors remained promising, however, logging a combined .313/.346/.375 slash line between Wichita and Triple-A Omaha that year.

Chávez was on the move three times that offseason. The Detroit Tigers in December claimed him from Kansas City after the Royals designated him for assignment, and the Expos subsequently claimed him in February 2002 when the Tigers tried the same thing.[9] Omar Minaya, the Expos' new general manager, had been among Chávez's fiercest defenders when he was a Mets prospect, and Minaya went on to reacquire Chávez once he'd returned as Mets' GM in 2005. In Montreal, Chávez was afforded the freedom needed to establish himself, as Minaya gave him the regular job in center field beginning in 2003, succeeding a promising young rival in Peter Bergeron.[10] Chávez hit .343 in 2002 in Triple-A Ottawa, climbing his way onto the organization's top prospect lists, and during a September call-up to Montreal, logged his first major-league home run, a solo blast over the right-field fence at Shea Stadium off Pedro Astacio, and was named the National League's Rookie of the Month.

Chávez logged more than 500 plate appearances in both 2003 and 2004, leading off and playing center field in most of those appearances. On June 20, 2003, he legged out an inside-the-park home run off Toronto's Jeff Tam among his five home runs that season. He hit .251 that season with a .294 on-base percentage, drove in 47 runs, and stole 18 bases. Manager Frank Robinson was patient but ultimately disappointed in his leadoff hitter, confessing to reporters that he hadn't improved over the course of the year. Playing a season split between home parks in Montreal and Puerto Rico, the Expos finished 83-79 and in fourth place in the NL East Division, 18 games behind division-winning Atlanta.

Chávez, who rehabbed a sore neck on the roster of Montreal's Triple-A franchise until mid-April, improved his performance in 2004, but the Expos, who'd lost superstar slugger Vladimir Guerrero over the offseason, sputtered to a last-place 67-95 finish that was also their last gasp as a franchise; they began a new era as the Washington Nationals beginning in 2005. Before they did, Chávez had the distinction of making the Montreal Expos' final out, grounding to New York's Jeff Keppinger at second base.

Chávez began the 2005 campaign with the New Orleans Zephyrs of the Triple-A International League as the front office acknowledged Frank Robinson's contention that he hadn't reached base enough to justify another season in the big leagues.

Chávez slashed .253/.330/.333 in New Orleans before a May 14 swap to Philadelphia for Marlon Byrd in an exchange of seldom-used outfielders. Phillies manager Charlie Manuel used Chávez mainly as a reserve for a team that contended for the NL East title but fell two games short of the division-winning Braves at 88-74. Chávez was granted free agency that offseason and lasted one day on the market before he was signed by the Mets.

The Chávez acquisition was practically lost in the bevy of high-profile signings by Omar Minaya, who returned to New York with an open checkbook that secured the services of All-Stars Carlos Beltrán and Pedro Martinez, among others. Manager Willie Randolph's fortified Mets led the NL East nearly wire-to-wire, helped along by what was the best season by far in Chávez's career. The Mets won 97 games and the NL East title by 12 games over Philadelphia. Backing up at all three outfield positions, the 28-year-old speedster hit .306 with a .348 on-base percentage, 18 stolen bases, 5 home runs, and 42 RBIs.

In the 2006 NL Division Series, the Mets dispatched the Los Angeles Dodgers in three straight games. Chávez started Game Two in right field and delivered two key singles off starter

Outfielder Endy Chávez of the Expos during spring training in 2003. Renowned for his glove, Chávez's career spanned more than a decade. (Rick Stewart / Getty Images Sports)

Hong-Chih Kuo, the first starting a rally to break a scoreless tie. His second hit set the stage for a fifth-inning uprising that added to the New York lead.

What looked to be the Mets' clearest path to the World Series in 40 years was complicated by a string of late-season injuries to its starting pitching staff. Regular-season workhorses Pedro Martinez and Orlando Hernandez each missed the series with physical ailments; slotted in their place were the talented but erratic lefty Óliver Pérez and the rookie right-hander John Maine.

The Mets drew the St. Louis Cardinals in the NLCS. The clubs split the series' opening two games in New York. In St. Louis, the Mets took two of three and so returned to Shea Stadium needing two victories.

They got halfway there in Game Six, when John Maine and four relievers scraped out a 4-2 victory. That set the stage for a winner-take-all Game Seven, a Thursday night duel between St. Louis's Jeff Suppan and Óliver Pérez of the Mets.

The Mets took the field in the top of the sixth with the score tied 1-1. Jim Edmonds drew a one-out walk as Perez faced Rolen. Perez left a first-pitch strike out over the plate and the right-handed-hitting Rolen swatted it deep into the night. Chávez, playing deep and shaded toward the left-center-field gap, turned and gave chase. Upon reaching the warning track, Chávez left his feet and reached with his right gloved hand above the eight-foot fence. Fans in the upper deck could hear the collision of Chávez's body and the fence, as his elbow bent as far as it could into the St. Louis bullpen. There was a moment where no more than a fifth of a ball could be seen trapped in the webbing of the glove. Chávez, in one of the hundreds of interviews he gave about the play, explained that his challenge at that moment was to retrieve not just the ball but the glove it then belonged to – which, between absorbing the impact of hitting the fence and the force of the arriving ball, was sliding up his hand. Countering these forces, Chávez tucked it all back into his chest as he descended to the ground. In one of the most fortuitous combinations of advertising and baseball since Cracker Jack, a slogan for the insurance company AIG on the fence where Chávez leaped read "THE STRENGTH TO BE THERE." Edmonds was well past second base, and made a game effort to retrace his steps back toward first but was way too late to beat José Valentin's relay to Carlos Delgado at first. Valentin had positioned himself where a shortstop might as José Reyes had given fruitless chase to Rolen's drive. The play took all of 12 seconds.

Writing in his 2020 book, *So Many Ways to Lose*, author Devin Gordon argues that "The Catch," as Met fans refer to Chávez's play, was the greatest single play in postseason history, coming as it did in a more crucial situation than Willie Mays' famous pursuit of Vic Wertz's long fly at the Polo Grounds in Game One of the 1954 World Series, the gold standard of postseason outfield plays. "Endy's catch should be played on a loop in an art museum," Gordon writes. "It's layered and virtuosic, the work of a grand master, each color and detail applied in just the right order, a lifetime of study and schooling and apprenticeship, all to be ready for this very moment, for this exact circumstance."[11]

One of the points Gordon makes is how Chávez's feat endures as a triumphant accomplishment despite the bitterly disappointing outcome of the game for Chávez and the Mets. By contrast, the catches that Chávez's feat brought to mind for Mets fans – game-saving grabs by Tommie Agee and Ron Swoboda in the 1969 World Series – were part of the Miracle Mets' triumphant effort. In 2006 it was missed offensive opportunities, a heartbreaking strike-three call on Carlos Beltrán with the bases loaded in the ninth inning, and another long drive to left that Chávez could only watch sail into the seats – Yadier Molina's ninth-inning, two-run shot off Aaron Heilman – that delivered the win for the Cardinals, who went on to a five-game triumph over the Tigers in the World Series and left Mets fans in a haze of cognitive dissonance.

Chávez missed 12 weeks of the 2007 season with a strained hamstring but when healthy turned in another fine season as a reserve, although the team suffered a September slump that ate away a seven-game lead in the season's final weeks, and finished a game behind surging Philadelphia at 88-74 and a game and a half out of the playoffs. Chávez added to his legend in a chilly April evening game against Colorado, laying down a surprise two-out drag bunt to drive in Shawn Green from third base with the winning run in a 2-1, 12-inning victory. An inning earlier, Damion Easley had awakened the slumbering club with a two-out pinch-hit home run to tie the game.

The 2008 Mets suffered a yet another heartbreaking finish, blowing a 3½-game division lead they'd held on September 10, finishing three games behind the Phillies and one game out of the wild card. Manager Willie Randolph was fired in a controversial move in June and replaced by Jerry Manuel, but it was an unreliable bullpen, injuries, and poor execution that ultimately did them in. Chávez for the year finished with a .267.308/.330 slash line over 298 plate appearances.

A strenuous offseason makeover, arriving just as the Bernard Madoff scandal[12] crippled the Mets' financial situation sent Chávez to a new address for 2009, as he was among seven Mets dealt away in a three-team, 12-player whopper with Cleveland and Seattle.[13]

Chávez slashed .273/.328/.342 over 182 plate appearances as a Seattle Mariner in 2009, backing up a star-studded outfield of Ken Griffey Jr., Franklin Gutierrez, and Ichiro Suzuki for a team that finished third in AL West at 85-77. But his season came to abrupt halt when he collided with teammate Yuniesky Betancourt as they pursued a shallow fly on June 19. The pair banged knees, causing Chávez's right leg to hyperextend, tearing the anterior cruciate ligament. An awkward landing then tore the medial collateral ligament on the same joint.[14]

Chávez missed all of the 2010 regular season rehabbing the injury with the Texas Rangers, with whom he signed a minor-league free-agent contract that February. Texas lost the World Series to San Francisco in five games.

The Rangers returned to the postseason again in 2011 but Chávez went hitless in five plate appearances across the club's ALCS win over Tampa Bay and seven-game loss to St. Louis in the World Series. Chávez hit .301 in 83 games as the Rangers' part-time center fielder that season.

Chávez signed with Baltimore in 2012. The Orioles under manager Buck Showalter surprised the AL East with a 93-win season and a wild-card playoff victory over Chávez's previous employer, the Texas Rangers, but lost a five-game set to the Yankees in the AL Division Series. The 34-year-old Chávez hit just .203 that season, prompting *Baltimore Sun* baseball columnist Peter Schmuck to give him a grade of D.[15]

Chávez earned better marks back with Seattle in 2013, hitting .267 as a reserve for a club that finished fourth in the AL West. On July 28 he robbed Minnesota's Chris Colabello of a three-run home run at the fence in Safeco Field in a play reminiscent of his 2006 playoff catch. Chávez returned to the Mariners again in 2014, appearing in 80 games and slashing .276/.317/.371 for manager Lloyd McClendon's third-place team. He tried out again with Seattle the next season but was released in spring training, and his 13-year major-league career ended.

Chávez stayed busy in the offseasons as a proud participant in the Venezuelan Winter League, the Caribbean Series, and in the World Baseball Classic tournament. Chants of "Endy Si! Chávez No!" were common at these events, where fans expressed their enthusiasm for the homegrown player – and their disapproval of the strife brought by President Hugo Chávez.[16] Endy had been the Venezuelan League's rookie for the year in 1999.

Chávez married Patrice Maldonado in 2015. As of 2021 they were raising five children in New Jersey: a daughter from Chávez's previous relationship, Maldonado's two sons, their own child, and an adopted niece, the daughter of Chávez's sister Nidi.[17] Daughter Joendys, born in Seattle in 2009, was the subject of a lengthy and complex international custody battle between Chávez and the girl's mother, Joelis Molina, involving authorities in the United States and Venezuela. In 2024, Chávez sued fellow Venezuelan big-leaguer Melvin Mora, alleging Mora had failed to pay a $1.2 million debt owed Chávez.[18]

In his career after major-league baseball, Chávez played independent-league ball for several years, with the Northeast League's Bridgeport Bluefish and with the Somerset Patriots of the Atlantic League. He played one season, 2017, in the Mexican League. Chávez coached the Brooklyn Cyclones, the Mets' New York-Penn League rookie club affiliate, in 2019 and later served as bench coach for the Mets' Florida State League club.

Reminders of his most famous moment are never far from Chávez, who treated his Instagram fans with a recreation in 2021 in which he is filmed leaping from his kitchen into a deep snowdrift, shoeless and shirtless, exhibiting the same exuberant joy he so often brought to fans.

SOURCES

The author would like to express gratitude to Jay Horwitz for arranging the interview with Endy Chávez. Statistics cited are from Baseball-reference.com.

A video of "The Catch" is available on YouTube at: https://www.youtube.com/watch?v=qC_5Fgii__c

NOTES

1 Stephanie Myles, "Two Expos Think of Homes," *Montreal Gazette*, February 28, 2003: 8.

2 Author interview with Endy Chávez, April 23, 2021.

3 Author interview with Endy Chávez, April 23, 2021.

4 Brian Falzarano, "Mets Notes," *Passaic* (New Jersey) *Herald-News*, September 14, 1997: 54.

5 Chuck Otterson, "Chavez a Consistent Force for Mets," *Palm Beach Post*, August 25, 2000: 191.

6 Bob Dutton, "A Peek at the Future," *Kansas City Star*, March 4, 2001: 40.

7 "Chavez Draws Ichiro Label," *Des Moines Register*, June 3, 2001: 20.

8 Jeffery Parson, "Don't Fence Him In," *Wichita Eagle*, April 15, 2001: 31.

9 Kit Stier, "Alfonzo's Back, Better Than Ever," *White Plains* (New York) *Journal News*, February 23, 2002: 20.

10 Bill Madden, "Willie Needs Minor Tweaking," *New York Daily News*, November 3, 2002: 66.

11 Devin Gordon, *So Many Ways to Lose* (New York: Harper, 2021), 296.

12 The Wilpon and Katz families, who owned the Mets, had a long relationship with the disgraced financier Bernie Madoff but argued they were victims and not beneficiaries of Madoff's ponzi scheme, which was revealed in December of 2018.

13 Geoff Baker, "Mariners GM Already Making Mark," *Spokane* (Washington) *Spokesman-Review*, December 13, 2008: 24. The Mets that offseason also let free agents Pedro Martinez and Moises Alou go, while signing closer Francisco Rodriguez. The Mets had sought relief help in the Chávez deal, with Seattle's J. J. Putz the main name acquired. Putz however pitched just 29 1/3 mediocre innings with New York; pitchers the Mets surrendered in the deal included Jason Vargas who had 11 years ahead of him in the big leagues, and reliever Joe Smith, who pitched effective relief for another 13 years.

14 Ryan Divish, "Smiling Chavez Visits Mariners' Clubhouse," *Tacoma* (Washington) *News Tribune*, July 7, 2009: B3.

15 Peter Schmuck, "Peter Schmuck's Final Grades for the 2012 Orioles" *Baltimore Sun*, October 17, 2012 https://www.baltimoresun.com/sports/analysis/schmuck/bal-peter-schmuck-final-grades-for-the-2012-orioles-20121016-photogallery.html.

16 P. Scott Cunningham, "Endy Si! Chavez No!," *Miami New Times*, March 16, 2009 https://www.miaminewtimes.com/news/endy-si-chavez-no-6530627.

17 Author interview with Endy Chávez, April 23, 2021.

18 Lauren Elkies Schram, "Ex-Mets outfielder Endy Chavez sues former MLB All-Star Melvin Mora over $1.2M investment fraud: 'I trusted him,'" *New York Post*, May 25, 2024 https://nypost.com/2024/05/25/us-news/former-met-endy-chavez-sues-mlber-melvin-mora-in-1-2m-investment-fraud/

DAVE CONCEPCIÓN

BY JOSEPH WANCHO

t's called the fall classic, and the 1975 World Series was indeed a "classic." The Series waged between the Cincinnati Reds and the Boston Red Sox was one of the more memorable championship battles, as a single run decided five of the seven games. Cincinnati shortstop Dave Concepcion entered the Series hoping that the old saying "third time is a charm" would prove true. He had been to two other World Series, losing out both times: first to Baltimore in 1970 and then to Oakland in 1972.

In 1975 Boston won Game One at Fenway Park, shutting out the Reds by a 6-0 score, and the Reds were looking to balance the ledger before the Series headed to the Queen City. It was a rainy day in Boston on October 12 for Game Two. But the inclement weather did not hinder Boston starter Bill Lee. He held the Reds to one run and was clinging to a 2-1 lead entering the ninth inning. But after Johnny Bench's leadoff double chased Lee from the game, Dick Drago and his blazing fastball moved to the hill.

After Drago retired Tony Perez on a groundout to shortstop with Bench taking third and George Foster flied to short left field, Concepcion came to bat with two outs and the tying run 90 feet away. Concepcion hit a 1-and-1 fastball into the dirt and the ball bounced high toward second base. Boston's Denny Doyle raced to his right and backhanded the ball, but it was too late for the second baseman to make a play. Bench scored the tying run, and Concepcion was on first. Red Sox fans in the Fenway Park crowd fell silent. Concepcion stole second base, sliding past the bag but getting back safely. Ken Griffey then doubled him home, and the Reds won 3-2 to even the Series. "I was just looking to make contact," Concepcion said later. "That's all you can do in a situation like that against a fastball pitcher like Drago. I knew it was a hit once I got it past the pitcher."[1]

David Ismael (Benitez) Concepcion was born on June 17, 1948, Ocumare de la Costa, Aragua, Venezuela. His father, a truck driver, was against young Dave's pursuing a career in baseball, instead hoping that he would make a living as perhaps a lawyer, banker, or doctor. After attending Agustin Codazzi High School, Dave worked as a bank teller and played for a local amateur baseball team. His coach, Wilfredo Calvino, was a scout for the Reds, and despite his father's wishes, young Concepcion signed a contract with Calvino in September 1967 and joined Tampa in the Class-A Florida State League in 1968.

Concepcion's time in the Reds' minor-league chain was brief; by the end of the 1969 season he was playing for Triple-A Indianapolis. The 21-year-old hit .341 for the Indians in 167 at-bats, and showed a high aptitude on the basepaths. "Concepcion has the best baserunning instincts I've ever seen in a youngster,"

said Indians manager Vern Rapp. "He stole 11 bases in 12 attempts and he was only with us about a month."[2]

Concepcion was promoted to the Reds for the 1970 season, but he faced veteran competition at shortstop in Woody Woodward and Darrel Chaney. When Concepcion showed up at camp, standing 6-feet-2 and weighing just 155 pounds, Pete Rose joked that he wouldn't be in danger of pulling a muscle in his legs, that instead it would have to be a pulled bone. But Rose also acknowledged, "They tell me that the kid can play shortstop with a pair of pliers."[3]

Reds rookie manager Sparky Anderson took a liking to the youngster, as did hitting instructor Ted Kluszewski. Anderson made Concepcion the starter, mostly for his defensive ability. Anderson didn't expect much offense from his young shortstop. But when Concepcion's batting average rose to .270 in May, Kluszewski commented, "I've been saying all along that the kid's gonna be a pretty good hitter."[4]

Concepcion's unexpectedly good hitting could not keep him in the starting lineup. He made 14 errors through mid-June, and Anderson replaced him with the dependable Woodward. Woodward was a valuable commodity for the Reds, able to play every infield position and play them well. He solidified the position for a while, but by the time the second half of the season began, Concepcion was back in the lineup. He made only eight more errors and batted a respectable .260 for the season. The Reds steamrolled through the National League West Division and had little trouble sweeping Pittsburgh in the NLCS, holding the Pirates to three runs in the three games. They were not as fortunate in the World Series, losing in five games to the Baltimore Orioles.

Concepcion missed most of the 1971 exhibition season with a badly sprained right thumb, and when he returned to the team in late April, he was used as a utilityman, playing second base, third base, and the outfield. He got his shortstop job back in early May but struggled at the plate that season and in 1972 with .205 and .209 batting averages. His career got an indirect boost after the 1971 season when a big trade brought second baseman Joe Morgan from the Astros. Concepcion and Morgan established themselves as one of the better keystone combinations in major-league history. As teammates with the Reds, they appeared in four All-Star Games, starting three, and won two World Series.

Concepcion was his own worst critic, and at times his being hard on himself caused subpar play to further spiral downward. Sparky Anderson decided that he needed a big-brother influence, and asked veteran Tony Perez to room with the youngster and mentor him. "He cannot stand 0-4 day. It kill him. I tell him very simple thing. 'Don't get your head down.'… 'If you don't hit now, you will next time.'… Things like this. Always I try to pick him up."[5] Perez also felt that marriage helped Concepcion settle down. (Dave and his bride, Delia, were married in 1972. They had three children, David Alejandro, David Eduardo, and Daneska.)

Whatever the reason, Concepcion emerged as a top-flight player in 1973. He was named to the All-Star team for the first time. He batted .287 and provided some punch at the bottom of the Reds' lineup. He posted the first five-hit performance of his career against San Francisco on July 5 – hit number five, in the bottom of the ninth inning, driving in the winning run.

Unfortunately for Concepcion and the Reds, his season was curtailed by an injury. On July 22 the Reds were breezing to a 6-0 victory over Montreal at home. Concepcion was having a fine afternoon with three hits and two runs scored. On first base in the seventh inning, he took off as Denis Menke hit a smash to Expos shortstop Larry Lintz. As Lintz threw Menke out at first base, Concepcion never stopped and raced to third base. As he slid into the base his left leg folded underneath him. The fibula, a long bone between the knee and ankle, was broken and his ankle was dislocated. His season was over. "It probably cost us the league championship," said Rose.[6] The Reds won the NL West, but lost to the New York Mets in the NLCS without their All-Star shortstop.

Concepcion rehabbed while playing winter ball in Venezuela. He came back healthy and began a string of four years (1974-77) in which he won a Gold Glove. In 1974 he had his first big offensive season, smacking 14 home runs and driving in 82 runs, while batting mostly sixth or seventh in the lineup. Concepcion brought another dimension to the Reds in addition to his offensive and defensive skills. Beginning in 1973 he stole 20 or more bases in six consecutive seasons, pilfering 41 in 1974.

The Reds finally reached the summit in 1975 and 1976, winning back-to-back World Series. In 1975 Concepcion hit .455

A cornerstone of Cincinnati's "Big Red Machine," Dave Concepción was a nine-time All-Star and five-time Gold Glover. He helped redefine the shortstop role during his 19-season career with the Reds. (SABR / The Rucker Archive)

in the NLCS against the Pirates but, only .179 in the tense and gripping World Series against the Red Sox. The next year he hit .357 in the Series against the Yankees with a triple and three RBIs. On a team filled with All-Stars and future Hall of Famers, Concepcion was playing at a high level at the apex of his career. Former Brooklyn Dodgers great Pee Wee Reese, a Hall of Fame shortstop himself, offered a synthesis of Concepcion as a shortstop: "Mark Belanger may be a little smoother then Concepcion. Larry Bowa is very quick. Rick Burleson is a leader type. Bill Russell has an accurate arm. But no one does everything as well as Concepcion. It's possible that no one ever has."[7]

Reds third-base coach Alex Grammas agreed with Reese's assessment. Grammas had worked with Concepcion since Dave was a rookie, helping him to hone his craft. "There are some mighty good shortstops in the league today," said Grammas. "But Concepcion is a notch ahead of them all in all-around ability because his bat is stronger and his range in the field is greater."[8] Concepcion and Grammas had such a solid relationship, that Dave's first son, David Alejandro, takes his middle name from Grammas.

Concepcion also famously used Riverfront Stadium's artificial surface to his advantage. He started to develop a pain in his throwing arm, and perfected the art of throwing the ball on a bounce off the artificial turf to the first baseman. It was extremely helpful to him on groundballs hit in the hole between shortstop and third base. "I didn't invent that throw," Concepcion said. "I saw another fellow do it. I saw Brooks Robinson do it to Lee May here in 1970. Then when my arm hurt, I decided, 'Why not try it?'"[9]

After a couple of second-place finishes, in 1979 the Reds won the NL West to cap off the decade of the 1970s, but lost the NLCS in a three game sweep to Pittsburgh. By that time, many of the cogs in the Big Red Machine had moved on. Perez was the first to go, in a deal with Montreal. Rose left via free agency in 1978, the same year Anderson was fired. Soon Morgan and Cesar Geronimo would be gone. But Concepcion could still play. "The other people move away, and all of a sudden you notice the antique work of art in the corner," Bench said of Concepcion.[10] Concepcion posted career highs in home runs (16) and RBIs (84) in 1979. He also claimed his fifth and final Gold Glove Award.

Concepcion remained the Reds' regular shortstop through the 1985 season and made the last of his eight All-Star teams in 1982. In that season's All-Star Game, in Montreal's Olympic Stadium, he hit a two-run homer off Boston's Dennis Eckersley, and was named the game's Most Valuable Player. Before he hit his second-inning homer, he spoke with All-Star teammate and fellow Venezuelan Manny Trillo of the Philadelphia Phillies, "I told Manny, 'I got a feeling I'm going to hit one out of the ballpark.' He kidded me, but I said, 'I'm gonna do it.'"[11] And he did.

Concepcion retired after the 1988 season, having played his entire major-league career with the Reds. His successor at shortstop, Barry Larkin, began his own 19-year career in 1986, and eventually was voted into the Baseball Hall of Fame.

Concepcion was inducted into the Cincinnati Reds' Hall of Fame in 2000, and his number 13 was retired by the Reds on August 25, 2007. Said Joe Morgan, "He's the greatest shortstop I've ever played with or I've ever seen."[12]

In retirement, Concepcion returned to his native Venezuela, and later managed his hometown Aragua Tigers. Later, he became an executive in a trucking business.

Concepcion continued a fine lineage of shortstops from Venezuela. He grew up idolizing Chico Carrasquel and Luis Aparicio and trying to emulate them in the field. Later, countrymen Ozzie Guillen and Omar Vizquel grew up fantasizing about playing baseball in the major leagues like their hero, Dave Concepcion. Vizquel paid homage to his boyhood icon by wearing the number 13, saying Concepcion was "the one that I liked, the one that I looked up to."[13]

SOURCES

This biography is included in the book *The Great Eight: The 1975 Cincinnati Reds* (University of Nebraska Press, 2014), edited by Mark Armour.

NOTES

1 George Vass, "The Game I'll Never Forget," *Baseball Digest*, December 1987: 86.

2 Earl Lawson, "Reds' Phenom Bears Out Latin Raves," *The Sporting News*, March 28, 1970: 11.

3 Lawson, "Reds' Phenom Bears Out Latin Raves."

4 Earl Lawson, "McCrae-Carbo Bat Platoon Is Cincy's Assault Force," *The Sporting News*, May 23, 1970: 7.

5 Si Burick, "The Making of Dave Concepcion," *Baseball Digest*, August 1974: 40-42.

6 Jim Brosnan, "Dave Concepcion: Best in the Business," *Boys' Life*, September 1975: 20-23.

7 Dick Peebles, "Dave Concepcion: Best All-Around Shortstop in the Majors," *Baseball Digest*, December 1979: 50-51.

8 Earl Lawson, "Concepcion Almost Immaculate at Shortstop," *The Sporting News*, April 26, 1975: 3.

9 Doug Feldmann, *The 1976 Cincinnati Reds: Last Hurrah for the Big Red Machine* (Jefferson, North Carolina, 2009), 41.

10 Ivan Maisel, "An All Star Comes To Light," *Sports Illustrated*, July 25, 1982: 46.

11 Maisel.

12 Kevin Kelly, "No Shorting Concepcion on This Night," *Cincinnati Enquirer*, August 26, 2007.

13 Tim Wendel, *The New Face of Baseball* (New York: Harper/Collins, 2003), 76.

OMAR DAAL

BY BILL JOHNSON

Pitcher Omar Daal's career statistics, the accepted baseline for snap judgments about a player's effectiveness, were, perhaps, misleading. A pitcher with a lifetime major-league record of 68-78 and a 4.55 earned-run average, one who relied far more on a deceptive delivery than a blazing fastball to retire hitters, might be considered something of a failure. In this case, though, that verdict is inaccurate. Over an 11-year major-league career, Daal played for six different organizations. During that time he twice finished in the top 10 in ERA and once in victories in the National League. His career ended prematurely due to arm problems, but throughout his playing career, Venezuelan Omar Daal won more games than all but two pitchers from that baseball-frenzied nation.[1]

Omar Jesus Daal Cordero was born on March 1, 1972, in Maracaibo, Venezuela. Maracaibo is the capital of the northwestern state of Zulia and the second largest city in the country. It is, like much of Venezuela, fertile baseball country, and the city alone has produced major-league pitchers Yusmeiro Petit, Wilson Álvarez, and Jhoulys Chacín.

When Omar was 2 years old his father got a job offer in Valencia, so the family moved to the capital of the state of Carabobo. His father was an avid amateur baseball player, and from early childhood, young Omar was surrounded by the game. Omar started playing Little League at age 11 at La Isabelica. His development years in junior baseball were with the team Magallanes, a formative team for Navegantes del Magallanes. He graduated in 1989 from Superior High School in Valencia but continued his baseball dream supported by both of his parents.[2]

In 1990 Daal represented Carabobo in the National Olympic Games, and after a solid performance against the Miranda team that included future Mets star Edgardo Alfonzo, a scout from the Los Angeles Dodgers and Leones del Caracas approached the 18-year-old.

According to Daal, "Flores Bolívar, the longtime scout for Leones del Caracas, approached me and introduced me to Mr. Camilio Pascual, the Latin American supervisor for the Dodgers. They invited me dinner and offered a contract. Bolívar traveled back to Valencia the next day to talk to my parents, who were always very supportive and encouraging of my baseball path and they immediately approved the terms. The following day I was signed with Caracas and the Dodgers."[3]

Leones del Caracas and the Dodgers had a working agreement in those years, allowing most of the prominent talent that Caracas scouted to be a priority for the Dodgers. This included Daal, Carlos Hernández, Roger Cedeño, Henry Blanco, and Miguel Cairo, among many players from that era. By August 24, 1990, Daal had a signed contract with the Dodgers.[4]

Daal reflected, "It was kind of a strange journey for me since I was a big fan of Aguilas del Zulia, as well as my whole family. We moved to Valencia and I grew up playing for Magallanes, and suddenly I get signed by their biggest rivals, Leones. It was funny! But they treated me so well in Caracas that I only have great appreciation."[5]

Before traveling overseas, Daal was loaned to the local Venezuelan summer league team Indios de Miranda. He became the first pitcher in the league to win the pitcher's triple crown, with 7 wins, a 1.16 ERA, and 81 strikeouts.[6] He also pitched a no-hitter. While baseball fans in Venezuela were celebrating Wilson Álvarez's no-hitter (the first for a Venezuelan in major-league history) on August 11, 1991, just a week later, on August 17, Daal threw his gem vs. Estrellas de Cagua, a game that was highlighted in all sports pages in Venezuela.[7] The name Omar Daal became a staple from that day in Venezuelan pitching.

After Daal's stint in the Venezuelan summer league, the Dodgers sent him to the Dominican Summer League, playing under former major-league infielder Teodoro "Ted" Martínez and the DSL Dodgers. The 18-year-old appeared in 17 games that summer in Santo Domingo, posting a 3-6 record and a 1.18 ERA. That winter he joined the Leones del Caracas, but managed only one full inning in three appearances.

"I wanted to be a starter. But I knew that on my first year with Caracas it was just too much to ask," Daal said. "There were so many established stars in the rotation like Urbano Lugo, Julio César Strauss, Amalio Carreño, Miguel García. I was sent to the bullpen, but I was just learning from this group with so much experience. I wanted to set my path through them and help in any way. I knew my moment would come at some point."[8]

Undaunted, Daal returned to the Dominican Summer League in 1991 and logged seven wins and a 1.16 ERA in 13 starts.[9] The DSL Dodgers fell to the DSL Blue Jays in the championship round, but Daal's confidence was visibly improved. That winter, again with Caracas, he appeared in 20 games and pitched 46⅔ innings.[10]

In 1992 Daal arrived in the United States. He made 35 appearances for Double-A San Antonio and earned a promotion to Triple-A Albuquerque, where he made 12 more. That winter, he returned to Caracas and pitched in 29 games, posting a 2.49 ERA. The combination of that winter performance, along with his first six Triple-A appearances in 1993, prompted the Dodgers to call the 21-year-old southpaw up to join the Los Angeles bullpen.[11]

An article in the *Los Angeles Times* captured the moment: "Omar Daal was asleep when he got the phone call about noon Thursday in Albuquerque. His roommate, Steve Allen, awoke him and told him that Fred Claire, the Dodgers' executive vice president, was on the phone. Daal thought he was kidding. 'Fred asked me if I could get out left-handed hitters,'... 'I said I'm ready. Daal then called his mother in Venezuela, who cried."[12]

Understandably, Daal did not speak English well. "Sure, I remember when I spoke little English," he recalled years later. "I'd go to a restaurant and somebody next to me would order rice and chicken and I'd say, 'Me, too.' Sometimes I didn't want to eat that, but I would have to. ... It was just a good thing that the catcher gave the signs with fingers."[13]

On April 23, 1993, in the eighth inning at Philadelphia, Daal made his major-league debut. He retired the three batters he faced, Darren Daulton, Wes Chamberlain, and Milt Thompson, on 11 pitches. A week later, on April 30, Daal yielded his first hit, a single by Dave Hollins, and his first home run, by Darren Daulton, and also got his first decision, a loss to the Phillies. He remained in the Dodgers bullpen for the rest of the season, and that winter returned to Venezuela to play for Caracas.

Omar and Josneil were married on November 20, 1993. Their union produced two sons, Jesús and Nicolás. Daal coached both boys on their traveling youth teams in Arizona, and Jesús was sufficiently talented to later pitch in college.

Perhaps inspired by the responsibilities of marriage, Daal sustained his enthusiasm despite bouncing between Los Angeles and Albuquerque in 1994. In LA he lowered his ERA by almost two runs from his 1993 performance, and the following winter, in Caracas, he starred with a 6-2 record and a 2.00 ERA. In 1995, still with the Dodgers, Daal seemed to lose whatever momentum he'd gained the previous year, and the team designated him for assignment. On December 15, the team traded Daal to Montreal in exchange for minor-league pitcher Rick Clelland.

Daal's Venezuelan baseball experience in the 1995-96 season was significantly more notable. That winter with the Lions, he went 10-2 with a 1.68 ERA and Caracas represented Venezuela in the Caribbean Series. The following two winters, again in Caracas, Daal was awarded the Carrao Bracho Trophy, the Venezuelan Professional Baseball League equivalent of the Cy Young Award. It represented a milestone in Daal's career, as it acknowledged him as the best pitcher in his home nation, a country that produced so many talented hurlers.

In August 1996, the Expos gave Daal his first major-league start. He tossed five scoreless innings against the San Diego Padres, striking out eight and yielding only one hit in earning a 3-2 win. He remained with Montreal, largely in relief, until June 1997, when he was optioned to Ottawa, and then waived. Toronto claimed him on July 25, but did not protect him in the expansion draft, and Arizona selected Daal in the second round.

As one of the original Diamondbacks, Daal began the season in the bullpen, but soon joined the starting rotation, and threw the first complete game in franchise history, a 5-1 win on June 16, 1998, against the Reds. Despite a 19-day stretch on the disabled list, from June 22 to July 11, due to a strained left hamstring, he managed just enough innings to qualify for the National League ERA championship consideration, and finished fifth in the

league with a 2.88 mark. *The Sporting News* noted that "Omar Daal may be the most impressive member of the [Arizona] rotation so far. ... Daal continues to confound hitters with his delivery and ability to change speeds so often. One moment he's firing an 88-mph fastball, and the very next he's throwing a 72-mph changeup that comes out of his hand with the same arm-speed and motion. Daal also has added a Luis Tiant-like motion during which he turns his back completely away from the hitter. He appears to be entering a higher echelon among N.L. pitchers."[14]

The following season Daal won 16 games and helped propel the Diamondbacks to the NL Division Series, marking the pitcher's first foray into postseason baseball in the United States. In that series, against the New York Mets, Daal started Game Three but gave up three runs and took the loss. After the season, due to severe flooding in Venezuela, Daal pitched only one inning all winter, and he feared the layoff would have

Crafty left-hander Omar Daal pitched in over 350 games across 11 big-league seasons. He led the majors in games started in 2000 and earned 68 career wins. (SABR / The Rucker Archive)

an adverse effect on his work for the Diamondbacks. "When I got (to spring training), I was worried," he said. "I thought my mechanics might not be there, since I hadn't pitched in three months. But I'm feeling strong (in spring training). It was a great idea to shut it down over the winter and rest."[15] Daal did not sit idly by, though, as reported in the *Arizona Daily Star*: "Instead of pitching over the winter, (he) pitched in. He and others in his hometown of Flor Amar [*sic*] Valencia gathered boxes of food, clothing and medicine for those caught in the mudslides. A reported hundreds of thousands died or lost their homes as a result."[16]

In 2000 Daal suffered the onset of the arm and shoulder trouble that would eventually end his big-league career. "LHP Omar Daal's first victory is proving to be as elusive as his usually impeccable control," *The Sporting News* reported. "For the first time in 69 career starts, Daal did not strike out a batter in a five-inning effort against the Phillies on April 27, and he gave up three homers for the first time since September 22, 1998." On balance, over the span he allowed 25 hits, 14 earned runs, and 9 walks in three consecutive starts.[17] His ERA soared to over 7.00, and on July 17 Arizona demoted him to the bullpen.[18] On July 26 he was sent to Philadelphia, along with Travis Lee, Vicente Padilla, and Nelson Figueroa, in exchange for Curt Schilling. In his Philadelphia debut, on July 28, he gave up two earned runs in five innings against the Dodgers and lost the 2-0 decision. Daal led the majors in losses that season, with 19. He was clearly good enough to anchor the pitching staff, as he continued to take the ball, but the losses accrued regardless.

In April 2001 Daal was named Philadelphia's Opening Day starter. On August 15 he and fellow Venezuelans Giovanni Carrara, Kelvim Escobar, and Freddy García each recorded a pitching win. It was the first time in the history of the major leagues that four Venezuelan starters recorded wins on the same day. But like a figurative duck on a pond, everything looked calm on the surface, but feet were paddling furiously below. Daal and manager Larry Bowa did not agree on the best way to use the pitcher, and the tension was impossible to ignore, despite general manager Ed Wade's denials – "I don't think it's any secret that (Daal) and 'Bo' had some rough spots the last month of the season, but I don't think that was insurmountable. ..."[19]

After the season Daal was traded back to the Dodgers, for Jesús Cordero and Eric Junge. After a moderately successful 2002 season (11-9, 3.90 ERA), Daal became a free agent and signed with the Baltimore Orioles.

The 31-year-old labored as a back-of-the-rotation starter in Baltimore, but his body betrayed him. In early July, he went on the disabled list with tendinitis in his left rotator cuff. He had "been demoted to long relief after a series of poor outings, and he made just one appearance out of the bullpen before reporting soreness in his shoulder."[20] He made it back late in the season, and on September 25, 2003, he made his final major-league appearance. He gave up seven earned runs on seven hits in just 1⅔ innings against the Red Sox, and took his last big-league loss in one final indignity.

Daal retired from major-league baseball in 2005, and for a while worked as a scout for the Diamondbacks and as an agent for his former agent Peter Greenberg.[21] In retirement, he has coached youth baseball, the East Valley Scrappers in Mesa, Arizona, and dabbled with the Venezuelan teams Navegantes del Magallanes and Tigres de Aragua. His last known residence was in Mesa, Arizona, with his wife Josneil and two children, Jesús and Nicolás. Daal is an avid golfer and focused his post-playing days in raising and coaching his children as well as helping and mentoring local youth.

AFTERWORD

Multiple attempts were made to contact Mr. Daal for additional information, but none were successful.

NOTES

1 Wilson Álvarez, with 94, and Freddy García, with 72.

2 Archivo LVBP, "Entrevista con Omar Daal, 2020," https://www.youtube.com/watch?v=KKAhh2mjioE

3 "Entrevista con Omar Daal, 2020."

4 Peter Bjarkman, "Camilo Pascual," SABR Biography Project, https://sabr.org/bioproj/person/f407403b. Accessed June 1, 2019.

5 "Entrevista con Omar Daal, 2020."

6 Diccionario General del Zulia. Omar Daal. Sultana del Lago Ediciones, 627.

7 Javier Gonzalez, Twitter, https://twitter.com/javiergon56/status/1295323652574121984.

8 "Entrevista con Omar Daal, 2020."

9 *Philadelphia Phillies Media Guide, 2001*, 203.

10 Equipos Campeones Liga De Verano Dominicana Desde El AÑO 1985 Hasta El 2018 (Dominican Summer League Champion Teams From 1985 to 2018. Online: http://www.dominicansummerleague.com/www/campeones/, accessed June 12, 2019.

11 Maryann Hudson, "Reliever Daal Gets the Call," *Los Angeles Times*, April 24, 1993. https://www.latimes.com/archives/la-xpm-1993-04-24-sp-26557-story.html. Accessed June 6, 2019.

12 Hudson.

13 *Philadelphia Inquirer*, March 9, 2001: 45.

14 *The Sporting News*, May 3, 1999: 34.

15 Jack Magruder, "Daal Feels Stronger After No Winter Ball," *Arizona Daily Star* (Tucson), April 1, 2000: 8.

16 Magruder.

17 *The Sporting News*, May 8, 2000: 29.

18 *The Sporting News*, July 17, 2000: 55.

19 Paul Hagen, "No Dilly Dallying in Unloading Omar," *Philadelphia Daily News*, November 10, 2001: 50.

20 "A.L. Reports," *The Sporting News*, July 6, 2003: 2.

21 Registro Histórico del Beisbol Venezolano, https://historylvbp.blogspot.com/2008/07/biografa-omar-daal.html. Accessed June 13, 2019.

VIC DAVALILLO

BY RORY COSTELLO

The Los Angeles Dodgers had a pair of antique dueling pistols in the late '70s. Yet despite their age, Vic Davalillo and Manny Mota were in great condition – and the fire of these small arms was often deadly. Davalillo's big-league career had seemingly ended in 1974, but after more than three years in the Mexican League, the wiry little outfielder (5-feet-7 and 150 pounds) returned at the age of 41 in 1977. He remained active in the US through 1980 and continued to play winter ball in his native Venezuela until the remarkable age of 50.

Davalillo – known as "Vítico" at home and in other Spanish-speaking lands – was a good major-league player. Although he became a semi-regular or reserve after 1968, his sixth season in the majors, he was a valuable journeyman. He won World Series rings with the Pittsburgh Pirates in 1971 and the Oakland A's in 1973. The lefty never had much power, but he made contact, batting .279 lifetime and striking out in less than 10% of his plate appearances. He was a fine pinch-hitter; he was long credited with 24 pinch-hits in 1970, and even his true total of 23 that year remains high on the list of single-season bests. Vic's 1967 Topps baseball card called him "one of the league's toughest men to get out because of his ability to go with the pitch."

This skill was really on display in the Venezuelan League, where Davalillo as of 2013 was the all-time leader in batting average at .325. He hit .400 or better three times at home and won four batting titles. He was also the lifetime leader in various other categories, including games played (1,249), base hits (1,505), and RBIs (483). In a place with a passion for baseball, Vítico is a national legend.

When Ichiro Suzuki came to the US, his slap-and-run style brought Davalillo to mind. They had other things in common. Davalillo was also very fast, a deft bunter, and a Gold Glove center fielder in 1964. His arm was another plus – in fact, Vic was a pitcher for his first four years in the pros. He continued to take occasional turns on the mound at various points during his career.

Víctor José Davalillo Romero was born on July 31, 1936. As with many ballplayers, he was long billed as being several years younger. Up through 1974, his baseball cards showed 1939 or even 1940 as his year of birth. This was finally corrected after Vic's comeback in 1977 – even though he stuck by 1939 at that time, saying, "I don't care what anyone says."[1] Also, many baseball references – both at home and in the US – show Davalillo's birthplace as Cabimas, a town in Venezuela's northwestern state of Zulia, on the shores of Lake Maracaibo. In 2006, however, he told Asdrúbal Fuenmayor, who has written several pocket biographies of Venezuelan stars, that he was actually born in Churuguara, in the neighboring state of Falcón.[2]

Víctor was the fifth of Martireño Davalillo and Angelina Romero's six children, all boys. The family moved to Cabimas a few days after he was born – and this was why the baby's birth was registered there. Martireño was a laborer, helping truck drivers to load and unload their vehicles in the oil businesses of the Maracaibo region.[3] He died around 1944.[4]

All the Davalillo brothers enjoyed baseball, but the only other one who wanted to be a pro was Pompeyo Davalillo.[5] The shortstop, who was even more diminutive than Vítico at 5-feet-3 and 140 pounds, played from 1952 through 1964 in the US, Cuba, Mexico, Nicaragua, and of course Venezuela, coming back for two final games in the winter of 1966-67. "Yo-yo" (his nickname in the US) got into 19 games for the Washington Senators in 1953 but never made it back to the majors. He suffered a broken ankle and kneecap playing at home late that year and missed the entire 1954 summer season.[6] He later became a successful manager in Mexico and at home.

Vítico started playing ball at the age of 8 with his older brothers. The lads would play numerous games a day. He was a first baseman to start with, but turned to pitching in the sixth grade; his teacher gave him a chance when the regular pitcher didn't show up.[7]

In 1956 Vítico had a chance to turn pro, but his family said no because he was too young (or so he said in 1965). He was then also studying to be a mechanic.[8] In October 1957, though, he joined the Caracas Leones of the Venezuelan League (Liga Venezolana del Béisbol Profesional, or LVBP). Brother Pompeyo had already been with the Leones for five seasons. The younger Davalillo would spend the next 16 of his record 30 Venezuelan winter seasons with this club, but he got into just nine games that season, including 17 innings in six relief-pitching appearances. He also experimented with switch-hitting, but gave it up when he realized he was losing a step running down the line to first base. The records didn't show it, Vítico said in 2007, because news reports focused only on his pitching and the fact that he was Pompeyo's brother. His batting was an afterthought then.[9]

The Cincinnati Redlegs (as they were then still known) signed Davalillo in 1958. A year before, Pompeyo Davalillo had become the shortstop for the Havana Sugar Kings of the International League, the Reds' top farm club. As he had done in Caracas, Pompeyo opened the door for his jockey-sized kid brother – and, as they told Asdrúbal Fuenmayor, at this time he altered the birthdate on Vítico's documents. "Looking more like Pompeyo's son than his brother ... Vic, who hardly weighed more than 120 pounds ... dogged his brother's footsteps into the Havana training camp. Following his introduction to O[rganized] B[aseball] by his big brother ... the olive-skinned kid was immediately shipped out to California – Visalia – as a pitcher."[10]

From 1958 through 1961, Davalillo remained primarily on the mound. Yet despite his small stature, he was not a finesse artist in the Bobby Shantz mold. With Palatka of the Florida State League (Class D) in 1959, Vic struck out 150 batters in 147 innings. His all-around ability was also attracting attention, though. In 1959, he pitched in 53 games but appeared in 73 altogether. In 1960 he pitched 52 times in 90 total games; in 1961 his mound appearances dipped to 38 in 81 games. The latter two years featured brief stints at Triple-A with Havana and (after the Sugar Kings finally left Cuba) Jersey City. Pompeyo Davalillo was still with the club.

On February 25, 1961, Davalillo was married to Luisa Ramona Barrera. She was from the city of Valera, which is about 100 miles southeast of Cabimas. For many years, though, he has been with the woman who became his second wife, Zoraida Caravallo. He fathered three children.[11]

The International League dropped Jersey City as a location in October 1961. The owner, Cuban baseball man Bobby Maduro, held onto the franchise in its new home, Jacksonville, Florida. He established a new working agreement with the Cleveland Indians, who purchased Vic Davalillo's contract. Maduro had signed Vic to the US minors back in Havana in 1958.[12] Since he was his own general manager in Jacksonville, he almost certainly was responsible for this deal too.

In the winter of 1961-62, Davalillo batted over .400 in the Venezuelan League, becoming the first man to do so for a complete season. He was 56-for-138 (.406) in 43 games – but since he fell eight plate appearances short of the required 158, the batting title went to fellow Lion Tony Curry at .346.[13] That season was also Vítico's busiest and most successful as a pitcher at home. He was 10-4 with a 2.46 ERA in the regular season, and though he lost a game in the semifinals, he had a complete-game win in the seventh game of the finals. Caracas, thanks also to two wins from playoff reinforcement Bo Belinsky, defeated Oriente.[14] The Leones then went on to represent Venezuela in the second Inter-American Series.

That was Davalillo's second Venezuelan championship; the previous year he had joined Valencia as a playoff reinforcement. Caracas made the finals six times in eight years from 1961-62 through 1968-69, winning four titles. All told, Vítico was a member of seven champion teams during his 30 winter seasons.[15] Perhaps his only regret as a player is that he never was on a team that won the Caribbean Series.[16] The tournament was on hiatus from 1961 through 1969, which deprived him of five chances.

Under manager Ben Geraghty, Davalillo made the transition to full-time outfielder with Jacksonville in 1962. He still pitched in six games, though, one reason being the International League's 20-man roster limit, which put a premium on versatility.[17] Harry Fanok, who led the International League in strikeouts that year with the Atlanta Crackers, remembered his opponent well.

"Vic Davalillo had to be the first Ichiro!" Harry said in 2010. "The guy used a big ole bat, ran like the wind, had an excellent batting eye and had a good arm.

"I remember one day [September 2] we had a doubleheader with Jacksonville. They had Vic pitch – against me! I got the win, and we were fortunate to come away with it." Davalillo had entered in the first inning of the opening game after Tommy John failed to retire a batter. He pitched seven scoreless innings and tripled in a run to help even the score at 2-2. He took the loss, though, as the Crackers scored two in the eighth. "The dude could pitch, as the score would indicate," Fanok added. "However, his calling had to be his play in the outfield and at the dish."[18]

Davalillo won the International League batting title with an average of .346, hitting 11 homers and collecting 69 RBIs. He showed speed and surprising extra-base pop, and worked to add a drag bunt to his adept push bunting and all-fields hitting.[19] The Suns finished first in the IL, then lost to Atlanta in the seventh game of the playoff finals. Fanok remembered the pennant race. "Late in the '62 season, it was going down to the wire. In a late series with them, down in Jax, I recall something that I had never seen before. Every time Vic came out on the on-deck circle, the fans would give him a standing ovation. He

A contact hitter and speedy outfielder, Víctor Davalillo played 16 major-league seasons and helped win a World Series in 1971. He was also a legend in Venezuelan winter ball, playing well into his 40s. (SABR / The Rucker Archive)

could have run for mayor down there and won! He was one hell of a ball player, that's for sure."[20]

During the season, Bobby Maduro turned down attractive offers from several big-league clubs for Vic.[21] Yet even though the Indians were on their way to a mediocre sixth-place finish, Cleveland general manager Gabe Paul did not want to call the hot prospect up. Paul, an old friend of Maduro's, said, "You know now why I didn't want to take Davalillo away from him when his team was doing so well. Hadn't Castro taken enough from him already?"[22]

Instead, under the terms of the working agreement with the Suns, the Indians claimed Davalillo for $15,000 at the end of the season.[23] Coming off a winter in which he hit .400 on the nose for Caracas – this time he got enough plate appearances to win the batting crown – Vic became Cleveland's starting center fielder in 1963. He was the eighth Venezuelan to make it to the majors. As early as May 29, the Associated Press wrote that he and Ron Hunt of the Mets "probably would win hands down if the 1963 Rookie of the Year poll were to be taken now." But just a couple of weeks later, on June 12, lefty Hank Aguirre of the Detroit Tigers broke Vic's forearm with a pitch. He missed nearly two months, and by various accounts, he was never quite the same hitter.[24] He had a tendency to step in the bucket or even bail out.

Umpire Pam Postema, who grew up in Ohio, wrote in her book, "Whenever Vic Davalillo would come up to the plate, we'd start yelling, 'Chicken! Chicken!' Davalillo would always back away from any pitch that came within a yard of him. He was so afraid of getting hit."[25]

In 1965 Bob Sudyk of the *Cleveland Press* wrote about "Davalillo's Fight Against Fear." Vic himself said, "Everybody talk about it and I begin to worry. I lose my confidence last year and I swing at everything. Then I really afraid, you know?" Birdie Tebbetts, who had also backed Davalillo as Rookie of the Year in 1963 even after the injury, returned as Indians manager in July 1964 (he had suffered a heart attack near the end of spring training). He worked closely with Vic on trying to overcome "one of the most trying times in a baseball player's life." Tebbetts talked about how Vic had lost his knack of setting up a pitcher because he was pressing. He also observed that Vic had a natural fallaway batting style against righties as well as lefties.[26] Davalillo's other notable trait at the plate was "an exaggeratedly high leg kick, perhaps the most noted since Giants great Mel Ott."[27]

The 1965 season was a successful one, as Davalillo finished third in the American League in hitting at .301 behind Tony Oliva and Carl Yastrzemski. He might have placed higher if he could have managed more than .248 against lefties. Vic was also the AL's starting center fielder in the All-Star Game, going 1-for-2. That was his only appearance in the midsummer classic, though; from 1966 onward, he was largely a platoon player. At least in the majors, Davalillo faced righties in just about 80% of his plate appearances.

It's quite likely that Vítico was more comfortable playing at home. He won his second and third Venezuelan batting titles at .351 in 1963-64 and .395 in 1967-68. He might have become the only man to win three straight in the LVBP, but his .389 mark in 1964-65 was only good enough for third that winter.[28]

Davalillo was always intensely patriotic. In June 1965 he spoke of how he wanted to win a US batting championship mainly to inspire the young boys growing up playing ball in his homeland. It seems remarkable today, but at that time there were only two Venezuelans active in the majors: Luis Aparicio and Vic.[29]

On June 15, 1968, the Indians traded Davalillo to the California Angels even-up for Jimmie Hall. He hit well for the Angels: .298, raising his average to .277 overall in the Year of the Pitcher. A quote that July summed up his approach well: "You can't get base hits if you don't swing."[30]

Vic started poorly in 1969, though – perhaps he was still getting back in form after suffering a nervous breakdown while playing in Caracas. Brother Pompeyo denied the breakdown story, though, saying that it was acute gastroenteritis.[31] Near the end of May, California dealt Vic to St. Louis for Jim Hicks. In his first at-bat for the Cards, he hit a three-run homer to ice an 11-3 win, but his .265 average with St. Louis was only enough to lift his 1969 mark to .219. He also made his only two big-league pitching appearances that year, both in the span of a week in June and July as the Amazin' Mets blew out St. Louis. Vic failed to retire any of the four batters he faced and allowed one earned run, which left him with an ERA of infinity.

In 1970 Davalillo started just 23 games while pinch-hitting in 74. Some sources still show him with 24 pinch hits that year, which ostensibly tied Dave Philley's single-season record from 1961. However, in later years the record was re-examined, and the correct total proved to be 23 – two separate scoring nuances clouded the original count.[32] At the time, Vic said, "The record isn't that important to me."[33]

In the winter of 1970-71, Davalillo won his fourth and final Venezuelan batting title at .379. While he was down there, he got the news that he had been traded on January 29 to the Pittsburgh Pirates, along with Nelson Briles, for Matty Alou and George Brunet. Alou had a very good year for St. Louis in 1971, but Brunet pitched only seven more games in the majors (though he would pitch well into his 50s in Mexico). The deal turned out very well for the Pirates, as Briles gave them three good years and Davalillo became a key reserve. He hit .285 for the world champions, even starting 14 games at first base. However, he was just 1-for-5 in his first taste of postseason play.

Vic enjoyed one of his best years in 1972 with Pittsburgh, hitting .318 in 403 at-bats and even leading the club in stolen bases. He did not fare well in 1973, though: .181 in just 83 at-bats. The Pirates brought up rookie Dave Parker to stay in July, and so Davalillo's action became even more limited.

The Oakland A's purchased Vic's contract on July 31, picking him up along with Jesús Alou and Mike Andrews for the stretch run. Although he hit just .188 in 67 plate appearances during the rest of the regular season, he saw extensive postseason action after Bill North was injured. Davalillo got into four games in the AL playoffs against Baltimore, starting two, and went 5-for-8 with a key triple in the decisive Game Five. He then played in six of seven games against the Mets in the World Series, again starting twice, though he got just one hit in 11 at-bats. After the A's won their second of three straight championships, they voted Vic a one-third Series share.

One of Davalillo's teammates in Oakland that year was José "Shady" Morales, who also became known as a pinch-hitter deluxe. Morales broke the single-season pinch-hit mark with 25 in 1976, and two years later Vic remarked (likely tongue-in-cheek), "I played one year with Morales. I taught him everything. And look what he does. He breaks my record."[34]

Davalillo remained with the A's to start the 1974 season, but owner Charles O. Finley released him on May 3 with a .174 batting average (4-for-23). There was more to the story, though; in August 1975, A's star Reggie Jackson told about it in a guest column for the *Los Angeles Times*. The team was flying home after a tough loss to the Yankees at Shea Stadium on May 1.

"The flight back to Oakland was a busy one and came to a bad end. Vic Davalillo is a good guy who goes bad when he drinks. He doesn't drink much but when he does he can't handle it. The guys tend to drink a little on the long air rides. The guy who handles the charter flights for United came to me on this flight and said Vic had had too much to drink and maybe I might do something to settle him down. ... Today when we got to the ballpark, we heard that Finley had found out and had released Vic."[35]

At the time, Davalillo was actually more displeased with manager Alvin Dark (though he was by no means alone on the club).[36] Just how much Vic liked to imbibe, though, may have been more than Reggie thought. Pirates coach Don Leppert told a story – which is subject to confirmation – about how Vic went in to pinch-hit once for the Cardinals after a heavy night out. He went into his high leg kick and landed on his backside; manager Red Schoendienst had to send in another batter.[37] In later years Dodgers manager Tommy Lasorda said, "You know, I never knew that he drank until I saw him sober."[38]

At any rate, Vítico then joined the Córdoba Cafeteros in the Mexican League. He hit very well for the remainder of 1974: .329-4-27 in 71 games. Another fine season followed with Córdoba in 1975 (.355-9-70 in 114 games) and a third with Puebla in 1976 (.333-8-63 in 123 games). Moving on to Aguascalientes for the 1977 season – brother Pompeyo was skipper – Davalillo was hitting at a tremendous clip again. He was at .384 (198-for-516) with 6 homers and 78 RBIs when he got his ticket back to the majors. Veteran baseball man Charlie Metro, then a scout for the Dodgers, told the story in his book:

"Al [Campanis, the Dodgers' general manager] said, 'Charlie, we need a left-handed pinch hitter.' Somebody said something about Davalillo down in the Mexican League. Al said, 'Go down there and take a look at him.'" Although Metro had reservations when he saw "wine bottles all over" Vic's room, he still went out and saw "Davalillo put on one of the darnedest exhibitions I'd ever seen." Metro proceeded to make "a heck

of a recommendation on him. I called Campanis and said, 'Al, this guy can help us.'"[39]

Indeed, Vic – who also served as a stopgap center fielder – went 15-for-48 (.313) down the stretch for the Dodgers. The at-bat that had lasting significance, though, was his only one in the playoffs against the Phillies. In the top of the ninth inning of Game Three, reliever Gene Garber had retired the first two men to face him. Davalillo, whose speed was still intact, saw that the right side of the infield was playing deep. He "recognized that he was being given a gift ... decided to take what was being given him ... and dragged a perfect bunt past the mound."[40] Manny Mota followed with a fly ball to left that a lurching Greg Luzinski couldn't catch; it became a double. A game-winning three-run rally ensued, propelling LA into the World Series.

Although the Dodgers lost the Series to the Yankees, Vic went 1-for-3 with an RBI in three pinch-hitting appearances. He did the same in the 1978 World Series, following a .312 performance (24-for-77) in the regular season. In its issue of June 24, 1978, *The Sporting News* pictured Davalillo (looking rather like a Venezuelan Keith Richards) and Mota on its cover, arms around each other's shoulders. "I don't care how old those two guys are," Tommy Lasorda said of his lefty-righty tandem. "They can still hit." Vic even still pinch-ran on several occasions. After one of those appearances, Dusty Baker (who had come out with a pulled muscle) said, "That's when you know you're getting old."[41]

Davalillo remained on Lasorda's squad to start the 1979 season, but in mid-June, having gone just 3-for-17 off the bench, he showed the good grace to return to Triple-A ball for the first time in 17 years. He hit .317 in 51 games for the Albuquerque Dukes, also pitching three times in relief. He then went 4-for-10 as he returned to the big club in September.

After the 1979 season the Dodgers released Davalillo. That winter, the ageless Vítico established another Venezuelan mark: he was the first to record 100 hits in a season. He batted .339 in his fourth season with Tigres de Aragua. (His long association with Caracas had come to an end after the 1974-75 season. The Leones then merged with Tiburones de La Guaira for one season to form a club called "Tibuleones" de Portuguesa.)

Vítico returned to Aguascalientes in 1980. He flirted with .400, posting a batting line of .394-6-50 in 94 games. Al Campanis reached out for Davalillo again that summer, and he reported once more to Albuquerque (.287 in 36 games, including three more mound appearances). Facing a tight race with the Houston Astros in the NL West, LA recalled the 44-year-old vet, and he got his last six big-league at-bats in September and October. His last base hit came on September 22 as he legged out an infield hit to second. The opposing pitcher was Gene Garber.

Vítico's Mexican League sojourns concluded in 1981, as he went .307-2-14 in 40 final games with Aguascalientes. For his career in that league, he finished with a batting average of .357 (782-for-2190), with 35 homers and 302 RBIs in 577 games.

His career south of the border continued, however, in the little-known Liga Nacional. This circuit was started in 1981 by ANABE (Asociación Nacional de Beisbolistas), a Mexican players' association. Founded in the wake of a strike, ANABE was described by Mexican baseball historian Jesús Alberto Rubio as "a great social movement." It faced strong opposition from the entrenched Liga Mexicana and folded during the 1986 season.[42] Davalillo was with two clubs: Lechugueros (Lettuce Growers) de León and Tuzos (Gophers) de Zacatecas.[43] If ANABE's records still exist, they would be extremely difficult to find.

Davalillo also played on at home. In 2009 he said, "It's true that before ballplayers didn't make as much in the big leagues and they supplemented their earnings in Venezuela, but the principal reason that I always came was because I loved to play here."[44] He surpassed the .400 mark once again in 1981-82, going 43-for-104 (.413) for Aragua. As late as 1983-84, he still hit .306.

After ten seasons with the Tigres, Vítico returned to the Caracas Leones. At the end of the 1986-87 season, he said, "Now's the time to retire, there are so many good kids. I'm just getting old. My legs are not the same, and I'm losing my eyes already. My bat is getting slow." Even so, he finished with a respectable performance for a man of 50: 21-for-92 (.228) in 41 games. Caracas manager Bill Plummer said, "He can still bunt for a base hit, and I've used him in the outfield some. He can still catch the ball. He's not a one-dimensional ballplayer." Plummer added of his unofficial coach, "He's a pleasure to have on the team. He's a true professional. He just goes about his business and gets the job done."[45]

Davalillo went out on a high note as the Leones won the league championship that winter. His final action as a player came in the 1987 Caribbean Series, held in Hermosillo, Mexico. That year the ballpark in Cabimas was renamed Estadio Víctor Davalillo; Churuguara's facility did the same at some point.[46] The Most Valuable Player award in the LVBP is also named for this man, who entered his nation's Sporting Hall of Fame in 1991. When Venezuela established its Baseball Hall of Fame in 2003, Vítico was part of the inaugural class in 2003.

Back in August 1980, Davalillo had said, "When I retire as a player, I don't want to get into another profession. I will become a coach. And then, after I get some experience coaching, I might become a manager. I will always be in baseball."[47] For a time after his playing career ended, he directed an amateur team in Venezuela, but he then retired fully, drawing his pension.[48] Vítico (who had made Caracas his residence several decades before) stayed active by giving baseball clinics to the young people of his homeland. In his 70s, as wiry as ever, he was still doing so. He said in 2008, "I do it with great love and passion for Venezuela."[49]

This article appeared in *Mustaches and Mayhem: Charlie O's Three Time Champions: The Oakland Athletics: 1972-74* (SABR, 2015), edited by Chip Greene.

ACKNOWLEDGMENTS

Special thanks to Asdrúbal Fuenmayor (founder of Radio Deporte 1590 AM, a Venezuelan sports radio station) and to Marcos Grunfeld of beisbolvenezolano.net for confirming biographical details. Continued thanks to Harry Fanok for his memories and to Jesús Rubio in Mexico for his input on ANABE and La Liga Nacional.

SOURCES

retrosheet.org

baseball-reference.com

purapelota.com (Venezuelan statistics)

museodelbeisbol.org (Venezuelan Baseball Hall of Fame)

Peter C. Bjarkman. *Diamonds Around the Globe: The Encyclopedia of International Baseball* (Westport, Connecticut: Greenwood Press, 2005).

Pedro Treto Cisneros, ed., *Enciclopedia del Béisbol Mexicano* (Mexico City: Revistas Deportivas, S.A. de C.V., 1998).

NOTES

1　Vic Oldest, Fairest," *The Sporting News*, September 24, 1977: 32. The 1969 *Sporting News Baseball Register* also showed 1936.

2　Asdrúbal Fuenmayor, *Víctor Davalillo* (Caracas, Venezuela: Colección de Bolsillo Radio Deporte 1590 AM, 2006). Sr. Fuenmayor confirmed by e-mail to Rory Costello that Davalillo himself was the source.

3　Asdrúbal Fuenmayor.

4　Luis Bravo, "Pompeyo: béisbol y leyenda." Web forum of Águilas del Zulia baseball club, August 1, 2010 (aguilasdelzulia.foroactivo.com/noticias-del-portal-f3/pompeyo-beisbol-y-leyenda-t383.htm). This article lists Pompeyo Davalillo's year of birth as 1928, as does his web page on the Venezuelan Baseball Hall of Fame website.

5　Francis Stann, "Vic Davalillo May Prove He Was '63's Top Rookie in '64," *Baseball Digest*, December 1963: 57.

6　Bravo, "Pompeyo."

7　Russell Schneider, "Little Vic Big Gun in A.L. Batting Race," *The Sporting News*, June 26, 1965: 3.

8　Schneider, "Little Vic," 4.

9　"Vítico Davalillo Bateaba a Las Dos Manos en Sus Inicios," Double A Baseball of Zulia blog, October 22, 2007. (beisbolaadelzulia.blogspot.com/2007_10_01_archive.html)

10　Bob Price, "Power Hitting of Vic Davalillo Dazes Sun Foes," *The Sporting News*, July 21, 1962: 37.

11　*Sporting News Baseball Register*, 1967. Juan Pazos, "Si la selecciones criollas no practican perderemos contra todo el mundo." *Diario de los Andes* (Trujillo, Venezuela), November 19, 2007.

12　Frank Gibbons, "Battler Maduro: Castro Couldn't Strike Him Out," *The Sporting News*, November 24, 1962: 37.

13　Federico Rodolfo, "Skipper Otero Nabs 4th Flag in 5 Years," *The Sporting News*, February 7, 1962: 35.

14　Federico Rodolfo.

15 Valencia – one (1960-61); Caracas – six (1961-62; 1963-64; 1966-67; 1967-68; 1972-73; 1986-87).

16 Pazos, "Si la selecciones."

17 Bill Reddy, "Davalillo Standout on Slab, in Garden," *The Sporting News*, June 30, 1962: 33.

18 E-mail from Harry Fanok to Rory Costello, December 18, 2010.

19 Price, "Power Hitting."

20 E-mail from Harry Fanok to Rory Costello, December 18, 2010.

21 "Davalillo Skein Ends at 19," *The Sporting News*, June 23, 1962: 36.

22 Gibbons, "Battler Maduro."

23 "Davalillo Skein Ends at 19."

24 Russell Schneider, *The Cleveland Indians Encyclopedia* (Champaign, Illinois: Sports Publishing LLC, 2004), 157.

25 Pam Postema and Gene Wojciechowski, *You've Got to Have Balls to Make It in This League* (New York: Simon & Schuster, 1992), 25.

26 Bob Sudyk, "Davalillo's Fight Against Fear." Reprinted in *Baseball Digest*, June 1965, 15-16.

27 David Finoli and Bill Rainer, *The Pittsburgh Pirates Encyclopedia* (Champaign, Illinois: Sports Publishing LLC, 2003), 376.

28 The other back-to-back winners are Cito Gaston (1968-69 and 1969-70); Al Bumbry (1973-74 and 1974-75); and Luis Sojo, who has done it twice (1989-90 and 1990-91; 1993-94 and 1994-95).

29 Schneider, "Little Vic Big Gun in A.L. Batting Race." César Tovar was with the Twins at the beginning and end of the 1965 season but was in Triple-A from mid-May through August.

30 John Wiebusch, "A Swinging Davalillo Puts Angels Over, 3-2," *Los Angeles Times*, July 12, 1968.

31 "Davalillo, Outfielder, Suffers a Breakdown," *New York Times*, January 9, 1969. Eduardo Moncada, "Bo Cites Threats, Packs bags After a Spat with Pilot Reyes," *The Sporting News*, January 25, 1969: 47.

32 In the seventh inning on June 7, 1970, the Cardinals batted around against the Padres, and at first Vic got credit for two pinch hits. On August 31 he had seemingly broken the National League record of 22, which had been held by Sam Leslie (1932) and Red Schoendienst (1962). However, NL statistician Seymour Siwoff, of the Elias Sports Bureau, ruled that the second at-bat on June 7 did not count as a pinch-hitting appearance. In its July 1996 issue, *Baseball Digest* quoted Siwoff. "The man cannot pinch-hit for himself," he said.

There was a debate over the double-counting – the AL had said it would credit two pinch hits in such situations. Yet ultimately, Davalillo's pinch hit on August 31 proved to be his 21st, not his 22nd. A fourth-inning double on July 27 was originally credited as a pinch hit. (See *Sporting News* box score, August 8, 1970, 41; Neal Russo, "Vic Erases All Doubt with Pinch Hit No. 23," *The Sporting News*, October 3, 1970: 9). However, Vic had already replaced Jim Beauchamp in center field in the third inning. The pinch hits he collected on September 18 and October 1 were in fact numbers 22 and 23.

33 Neal Russo, "'I'm Not a Loafer!' Cardenal Protests," *The Sporting News*, September 19, 1970: 6.

34 Gordon Verrell, "Dodgers Turning Huge Profits in Spanish Antiques," *The Sporting News*, June 24, 1978: 3.

35 Reggie Jackson, "Fighting Champs," *Los Angeles Times*, August 25, 1975: D1.

36 "Davalillo, Released, Assails Dark," *New York Times*, May 12, 1974. Ron Bergman, "Anarchist A's Find It Easy to Fault Pilot Dark," *The Sporting News*, May 25, 1974: 19.

37 Finoli and Rainer, *The Pittsburgh Pirates Encyclopedia*, 377.

38 Charlie Metro and Thomas L. Altherr, *Safe by a Mile* (Lincoln, Nebraska: University of Nebraska Press, 2002), 360.

39 Metro and Altherr, *Safe by a Mile*, 359-60.

40 Mitchell Nathanson, *The Fall of the 1977 Phillies* (Jefferson, North Carolina: McFarland & Co., 2008), 197.

41 Verrell, "Dodgers Turning."

42 For further information on ANABE and this league, see David G. LaFrance, "Labor, the State, and Professional Baseball in Mexico in the 1980s," which forms Chapter 6 of Joseph L. Arbena and David G. LaFrance, editors *Sport in Latin America and the Caribbean* (Wilmington, Delaware: Scholarly Resources Inc., 2002).

43 Ignacio Martínez Ortiz, "Entrevista y beisbol," *El Sol de Zacatecas*, (Zacatecas, Zacatecas, Mexico), March 13, 2014. E-mail from Jesús Rubio to Rory Costello, July 7, 2016, containing attestation from Mexican pitcher Fernando López.

44 "Grandes diferencias entre ayer y hoy," *Lider en Deportes* (Caracas, Venezuela), June 28, 2009: 4. (liderendeportes.com/CMSPages/GetFile.aspx?guid=6ea6f959-86b2-499e-9a9c-6d30eff27583&disposition=attachment)

45 "Vic Davalillo, 47 [*sic*], Still Going Strong," *Los Angeles Times*, February 8, 1987.

46 The Cabimas stadium hosted an LVBP team called Petroleros de Cabimas for the four seasons it existed (1991-92 through 1994-95). Later it was a temporary stadium for Águilas del Zulia. The Churuguara ballpark is a modest municipal stadium.

47 "Davalillo's Lifeblood," *The Sporting News*, August 16, 1980: 37.

48 Pazos, "Si la selecciones."

49 Eduardo Galindo. "Zona Central recibió Clínicas Béisbol y Amistad 2008." Blog of Eduardo Galindo, August 31, 2008 (eduardogalindo-producciones.blogspot.com/2008_08_31_archive.html)

BO DÍAZ

BY ANDREA LONG

Venezuelan catcher Bo Díaz played for all or part of 13 seasons in the majors, plus 14 more in his homeland's winter league. He helped the Philadelphia Phillies win a National League pennant in 1983 and was part of six champion teams with the Leones del Caracas.

Díaz made it to the majors on the strength of his defense. *The Scouting Report: 1983* remarked, "Díaz has a fine arm and can throw runners out with good consistency,"[1] and the 1985 edition continued, "Díaz is an excellent receiver with good hands and blocks the ball well."[2] He was a solid, not spectacular, hitter – but he had good power, hitting 87 home runs in the majors and 57 more in winter ball. In the winter of 1979-80, he set a Venezuelan record with 20 round-trippers, a record that lasted until 2013.

Diaz's other signal achievement was one of baseball's rarities: an ultimate grand slam.[3] The moment is etched in the memories of Phillies fans. April 13, 1983, Veterans Stadium in Philadelphia. Bottom of the ninth, two outs, Mets leading 9-6. Ace reliever Neil Allen was facing his first batter, Díaz. Longtime Phillies broadcaster Harry Kalas was calling the game. He went from calm to delirious in three seconds.

"Allen winds. The 2-and-1 pitch. A long drive. Deep left field … a grand slam! The Phillies have won the game 10-9! Unbelievable! Bo Díaz – a grand slam home run and the Phillies have won the game 10-9!"

Magical. The stuff of movies and the imaginations of baseball-playing boys everywhere.

In that moment, Baudilio José Díaz Seijas[4] must have felt light years away from his small hometown of Cúa, Miranda, in Venezuela. Born March 23, 1953, to Ángel Rosendo Díaz, a bricklayer, and his wife, Juana Angelina Seijas, Díaz was the fourth child of six. He grew up with four brothers (Francisco Eduardo, Candelario José, Ángel Rosendo, and Ramón Darío) and a sister (Ana Celina).[5] Ángel Díaz was a hard worker, but work was not always steady, money was frequently tight, and groceries were sometimes gotten on credit. They were a poor family, living in a small house, in an often-violent country, and daily life could be a struggle. With the family lacking the money to pay for bus rides to and from school or to buy the needed clothes, young Baudilio's schooling ended after the sixth grade.

With formal education no longer available to him, he eventually went to work. However, driving a forklift in a cement plant is a completely unsuitable job for a 14-year-old boy, and he soon left Cúa to join an older brother in the capital city of Caracas, 40 miles to the north. There he worked in a car wash and later a ball-bearing factory. At 17, he was slated for military service, where he would fight the guerrillas – leftist rebels who were responsible for shootings, bombings, kidnappings, and other violent activities. It was not a prospect he relished.

Still, there was baseball. Díaz came from a baseball family and was raised in that tradition. While still working in construction, his father had been an outstanding player for three different teams during the 1930s into the 1950s. Baudilio had played consistently throughout his childhood and into his teenage years.[6] And on weekends, he continued to play just as he had since joining his first Little League team at eight years old.[7] The games were loosely organized and mostly for fun, but it was during those games in 1969 that scout Willie Paffen spotted Díaz playing in a factory league. (Paffen was most likely alerted to Díaz by "legendary talent bird-dog" Francisco Rivero, who also discovered Tony Armas, Manny Trillo, and Andrés Galarraga.[8]) In December 1970, with his father's permission, he signed with the Boston Red Sox. Factory work and the specter of military service vanished.

Díaz was assigned to Class A in Winter Haven, Florida. From there he was sent to Pawtucket, Rhode Island. After playing in only one game, he moved on to Greenville, South Carolina, to Winston-Salem, North Carolina, and finally to Williamsport, Pennsylvania – five clubs in one season.[9] He spoke almost no English and had to get by with the help of any bilingual Latino player he could find. He made $450 a month and slept on cots in the clubhouses. Homesick and in pain from a knee injury sustained in his only game for Williamsport, facing the guerrillas might have seemed preferable.

Díaz reported to spring training in 1972 with his knee still badly damaged and underwent surgery to repair the cartilage, landing on the disabled list for what would be the first of many times in his career. As a result, he played just 14 games for Winter Haven that summer. In the winter of 1972-73, he began his career with the Leones del Caracas (Caracas Lions) in La Liga Venezolana de Béisbol Profesional. Díaz got 40 at-bats in 17 games that first season as the backup to the team's veteran catchers. In one of his starts that winter, on January 6, 1973, Díaz caught a no-hitter by Urbano Lugo. Remarkably, 13 years later, on January 24, 1986, he was behind the plate again when Lugo's son, also named Urbano, threw a no-hitter of his own for Caracas.

Díaz started the 1973 season in Elmira, New York. He graduated from clubhouse cots to a YMCA, which, he said, felt like a fine hotel. He bounced around the Red Sox minor-league system for four more seasons until he was called up from Pawtucket in September 1977. On September 6 he appeared in his first game for Boston and, in doing so, became the first catcher from Venezuela to reach the major leagues. After six years with Boston, he had made it. Except ... he hadn't. A significant roadblock stood in his way: future Hall of Famer Carlton Fisk. It was never going to happen for Díaz in Boston, and everyone knew it. In March 1978, he was traded to Cleveland.

As part of the trade, the Indians sent their best pitcher, Dennis Eckersley, to Boston. The expectations for Díaz were high, and manager Jeff Torborg was thrilled to have him. "The pitchers really like working with Bo. He's outstanding behind the plate," said Torborg. His strong, accurate throwing arm had earned him the nickname The Cannon, leading scout Jack Cassini to say that, "next to Johnny Bench, Díaz had the best arm he'd ever seen on a catcher."[10]

That July, Díaz had his first major-league home run, and Torborg noted that he was a better hitter than they'd given him credit for.[11] He was also, without a doubt, the best defensive catcher on the Indians roster. However, injuries plagued him still. Díaz's Achilles' heel wasn't actually his heel – it was everything else: his left ankle (sprained), his right ankle (broken, ironically, when he shifted during a slide trying to protect the left one), his index finger (broken), and his thumb (sprained), all of which led Bob Sudyk in *The Sporting News* to call him "a walking accident"[12] whose "bones resemble dry twigs."[13] Díaz was frustrated with himself, his teammates were losing patience, and the Indians may have questioned the wisdom of the trade.

Injuries notwithstanding, Díaz continued to play winter ball every year for Caracas, where he emerged as a standout. The only season in which he did not wear the Leones uniform was 1975-76, when Caracas merged with the Tiburones (Sharks) de La Guaira. For one season, a franchise called Tibuleones de Portuguesa existed. The 1977-78 season, during which Diaz caught 68 games, was the first time he played in the postseason for a Leones team that would ultimately win the championship.[14] During the 1979-80 season, the first of three consecutive championship seasons for Caracas, he broke the league home-run record of 19, which had been set in the 1972-73 season by Bobby Darwin. Díaz's record of 20 home runs, in just 247 at-bats (66 games) stood until Alex Cabrera, playing for the Tiburones, broke it in 2013. (This became a bitter pill for many Venezuelan baseball fans when Cabrera tested positive for anabolic steroids in April 2014.[15]) The Leones won another league championship in the 1981-82 season, which advanced them to the 1982 Caribbean Series. The Leones' victory in that series was only the third time a Venezuelan team had won since the tournament's inception in 1949 and was the first win for the Leones. Díaz batted .412 (8-for-19), hit two home runs, and was named the series' MVP.[16] The Leones' next league championship would not come until 1986-87, which was also the last time Díaz spent a full season with the club.

After Díaz returned to Cleveland in 1981, everything began falling into place. Starting catcher Ron Hassey injured his knee, which meant Díaz finally got a chance to play regularly. He showed what he was capable of, hitting .356 in the first half of the season with 25 RBIs and being selected for the All-Star Team, the first catcher from Venezuela ever chosen.[17] However, upon

Bo Díaz was a two-time All-Star catcher known for his strong arm and leadership behind the plate. He played 13 big-league seasons and was a beloved figure in both Venezuela and the majors. (SABR / The Rucker Archive)

Hassey's return, Díaz resumed his reserve role – an expected move but one that left him frustrated and, once again, on the back burner.

Coinciding with Díaz's part-time status in Cleveland, the Philadelphia Phillies had a problem behind the plate. As Jeré Longman of the *Philadelphia Inquirer* dryly put it, "Bob Boone and Keith Moreland were throwing out runners with the regularity of Halley's Comet."[18] This was a team with four catchers (in addition, Don McCormack and Ozzie Virgil) that still couldn't hold down the running game. In November 1981, the Phillies and the Indians did everyone a favor by orchestrating a complex trade that sent left fielder Lonnie Smith and pitcher Scott Munninghoff to Cleveland for Díaz. (Smith was dealt to St. Louis immediately.)

Calling it a "favor" may be putting too positive a spin on the way Phillies fans felt at the time. Not renowned for their tact and good humor, they were irate over the loss of the popular Smith. Bill Conlin later wrote in *The Sporting News* that Díaz had been greeted by Veterans Stadium fans "with the warmth reserved for ax murderers."[19]

Philadelphia reporters, while not openly hostile like the fans, were on the fence. In a profile for the *Philadelphia Inquirer,* Dan Coughlin described him as moody, injury-prone, slow to heal, and sensitive. On the other hand, he wrote, "Díaz is your composite major league catcher. He has a strong arm. He is smooth behind the plate. He is an acceptable hitter." Speed, however, was never among Díaz's gifts. Coughlin continued, "He is as slow as the legislative process."[20]

If Díaz was upset by the media's assessment of him or the fans' attitude, he didn't show it. And yet, he wasn't naïve; he knew the move would present challenges. Long before the days of interleague play, he was well aware of the difficulties inherent in switching from one league to the other. Furthermore, his major concern (unfounded, as it turned out) was how he would be received by the sometimes prickly Steve Carlton.[21] (By 1980, Carlton had won three Cy Young Awards and was notoriously particular about his catchers.) Still, Díaz was happy to be out of Cleveland and looked forward to a chance to play regularly. He also had manager Pat Corrales, a former catcher himself, firmly in his corner. Corrales had managed Díaz in Venezuelan winter ball in 1976-77 and had watched him over the years. Tired of seeing so many stolen bases, he had long advocated for Díaz. In the 1981 season, the Phillies caught 41 of 165 basestealers, with a third of them being picked off by the pitchers.[22] In spite of the fans' misgivings, The Cannon was clearly needed.

In time, the sportswriters and fans came to appreciate their new catcher. When Díaz, in his typical fashion, downplayed talk of having a cannon for an arm, writer Jayson Stark begged to differ. Stark took Phillies pitching to task, but praised Díaz, saying, "On Mookie Wilson's steal in the third inning, Díaz got rid of the ball as quickly as any human could do it. And when the ball got to second, it was six inches off the ground, at the right corner of the bag. A dead solid strike."[23] Later in the season when Díaz had a two-home-run game, the fans, apparently having forgiven him for being part of the Smith trade, gave him a standing ovation and demanded that he appear from the dugout.[24]

Díaz also had an attitude that was completely focused on the good of the team. He wanted to play well but would have gladly traded his personal success for the team's success. After a 7-4 loss to the Cardinals in April 1982, Díaz was described as "disconsolate" because his team was 3-11 and had lost three straight – disconsolate even though he'd gone 4-for-4 with two home runs, two doubles, and four RBIs.[25]

In September 1983, Díaz again had two home runs plus three singles in a game that he declared his greatest day, not because of his own performance, but because his team had won and clinched the NL East.[26] In the World Series that followed, he was exceptional. He started all five games and finished with a .333 average. For the Phillies, however, it was a dismal Series; they won the first game but lost the next four to the Baltimore Orioles.

During the Series, when Díaz and Baltimore catcher Rick Dempsey were squaring off against each other, an incredible story emerged from their shared past as winter-ball teammates. In an interview with the *New York Times,* Dempsey told of a game in Maracaibo, Venezuela, when he was the Leones' starting catcher, and Díaz was his backup. It was November 1973, and an on-field brawl involving Dempsey continued into the parking lot after the game. The Leones, still in their uniforms, were easy targets for an angry Maracaibo mob as the players tried to get to their cabs.

Dempsey eventually made it through the melee and got in the back seat with a few other teammates, while Díaz jumped in the front. But being in the cab offered little protection. An irate fan threw a brick through the windshield, and the broken glass cut Díaz's neck. Bleeding profusely, Díaz lost consciousness. Quick-thinking Dempsey used the catcher's pad he still had in his pocket to stanch the blood. With the crowd nearly rioting and Díaz quite possibly bleeding to death, Dempsey and the other players screamed at the cab driver to get to the hospital.[27] Twenty-seven stitches later, Díaz was out of danger, but years later, he still bore a scar on his neck from that night.[28]

Díaz returned to Caracas for the 1983-84 season but played just four games that winter. Physical troubles had appeared once again, and in 1984, he played very little in spring training due to chronic lower-back pain. He rehabbed with exercise and medication and, for the first time, admitted that an occasional rest might help him.[29] He did not, as feared, begin the season on the disabled list. In fact, he had one of the best starts of his career, hitting .295 with seven RBIs, which only made a torn ligament in his left knee especially disappointing and difficult to bear. In late April, a home-plate collision aggravated a previous injury and landed him on the DL. In early May, he had surgery to repair the knee with a projected recovery time of up to five weeks.[30] A second surgery in August on the same knee effectively ended his season. (Catcher Mike LaValliere, his Phillies teammate, once said of Díaz's knees, "They're scarred and swollen and every time he squats to catch, it makes me hurt just watching him."[31])

By late 1984 and into early 1985, the Phillies had Díaz on and off the market at various times. His frequent stints on the DL and the solid play of Ozzie Virgil seemed to make him nonessential. Publicly, Díaz said he was prepared for whatever came his way, be it Atlanta, Toronto, or Seattle, all mentioned as trade possibilities. Privately, however, he was disappointed that the Phillies considered him "so expendable."[32]

After taking off the whole winter, by spring training 1985, Díaz was rested and almost fully healed. He wanted to stay with the Phillies and wanted to play regularly. He was not interested in being the backup catcher and considered himself the starter. However, after capably stepping in for Díaz in 1984, Ozzie Virgil also considered himself the starter.[33] If Díaz had an edge, it was that the pitching staff liked him. John Denny, Jerry Koosman, and Steve Carlton all preferred Díaz to Virgil. They felt he called a better game and was a better defensive catcher.[34] In an article in the *Philadelphia Daily News,* Bill Conlin described it this way:

"[He] has quiet ways of finding out what they want from him in the way of pitch sequences, location signs and target placement. All are integral but unsung fine points. It's no secret that Bo Díaz is a member in good standing of Lefty's [Steve Carlton's] exclusive club of preferred catchers. That gives Díaz some catching clout that Ozzie Virgil lacks.[35]"

But when Opening Day 1985 rolled around, Virgil was the starting catcher and would be for all of April while the Phillies kept an eye on Díaz's progress. What followed was another run of bad luck. In a mid-April exhibition game, he was hit by a pitch that broke two bones in his right wrist. In May, while still on the DL for his wrist, he landed in the hospital with kidney stones.

By July, trade rumors were flying again. Pete Rose, now back in Cincinnati as a player-manager, made no secret of his goal to acquire his former teammate. Díaz, recovered but frustrated by his lack of playing time, was ready to go, if not to the Reds, then anywhere. "I really want to get out of here, just so I can play," he said. "I know my time for retirement is coming, but I think I can help somebody for two or three years."[36]

The Phillies were well aware of Díaz's desire to play regularly and of his frustration at not doing so. Manager John Felske, a former backup catcher himself, was particularly sympathetic. But the team was not willing to give him away. "If we're going to trade him, we're going to get quality for him. We have a quality player, and if someone wants him, we're in a position to demand what we want," Felske said.[37]

Finally, on August 8, 1985, Díaz was traded to Cincinnati.[38] Rose, Reds general manager Bill Bergesch, and his new teammates were ecstatic. "We are back in business," said shortstop (and fellow Venezuelan) Dave Concepción.[39] Upon his arrival at the Cincinnati clubhouse, starting pitcher Mario Soto hugged him like a long-lost brother.[40] And Bergesch, after praising Díaz and confirming his physical soundness, boiled it to down to this: "When you have a chance to get Bo Díaz, you must jump at it."[41]

Díaz's hitting got off to a slow start (.103 in 39 at-bats), but he adjusted well to the pitching staff. A few weeks later, in a game against the Cubs, he broke out of his slump and doubled in the game-winning run.[42] That double was the beginning of a 13-game hitting streak, the longest of his career. He finished the season batting .261 for the Reds (.245 overall). And as the focus shifted to 1986 and a shot at the pennant, the Reds knew they would start the next season with a capable defensive catcher for the first time since Johnny Bench retired in 1983.[43]

Still, in a team populated with good hitters, Díaz knew his main job was to support the pitchers and to call a strong game. (In fact, the staff ERA dropped nearly a point after his arrival,[44] and by the end of the 1989 season was at its lowest with Díaz behind the plate.[45]) Without exception, he was praised by the Reds pitching staff. Guy Hoffman recalled a time he faced a batter he didn't know how to pitch to. He deferred to Díaz, thinking, "Whatever you call, I'm going to throw." Hoffman, laughing, said, "Bo struck him out on four pitches. I didn't strike him out. Bo struck him out."[46]

Díaz – described that year as "a classic free swinger with a stance for every occasion"[47] – had a solid 1986 season as Cincinnati's primary catcher. He hit .272-10-56 in 134 games. That summer, he also set an unusual record. On June 27, in a 12-inning game against San Francisco, he threw out second baseman Robby Thompson on four stolen-base attempts, making him the first major-league catcher to throw out the same baserunner four times in a game.[48]

That winter, Díaz caught 35 games for another Leones championship team, and in 1987 he made his second appearance on the All-Star team, with *USA Today* calling him "a steady force for the first-place Reds."[49] He was the National League player of the month for July, hitting .351 with 5 home runs and 23 RBIs. But as the end of the season approached, Rose considered the possibility that he should rest his catcher more.[50] After August 5, Díaz batted .171, and when the season was over, Rose admitted that his biggest mistake that season had been overworking Díaz.[51] (Indeed, Díaz sat out the winter season and the following two as well.) Nevertheless, Díaz continued to be greatly valued by his manager, so much so that he was one of Rose's "untouchables," nine players who were off-limits as possible trades.[52]

By late July 1988, Díaz, that "classic free swinger," held a dubious distinction: he had the highest ratio of at-bats to walks in the major leagues, walking once in every 61.75 at-bats. (The MLB average was one walk per 10.88 at-bats.) "Díaz might consider being a little choosier at the plate," chided *USA Today*.[53] A week later, Rose fired back. "Bo just likes to swing. He likes to hit the ball. He might swing at one near his shoe-tops and another one over his head."[54] Later that same day, Díaz himself responded – with his bat. With two on and two out, he swung on a 3-and-0 pitch from the Dodgers' Don Sutton and drilled it over the left-field wall.[55]

More worrisome than Díaz's base-on-balls total, however, was the onset of a new physical issue, tendinitis in his right shoulder, and the return of an old one. As the season drew to a close, he once again needed surgery on his troublesome left knee to repair a small ligament tear. Díaz, who batted and threw right, saw his average drop from .270 in 1987 to .219. That was probably attributable, at least in part, to the pain in his shoulder. The knee surgery was not regarded as serious, and the Reds were optimistic that he would be strong in 1989. "His skills haven't diminished," said general manager Murray Cook. "He can still throw. He never could run. His catching is fine, and he swung the bat fine when he wasn't hurting."[56]

After unexpected visa delays for Díaz and two other players, he reported to spring training in 1989 looking fit and with only minimal lingering knee issues. However, in March he needed an emergency leave. His younger son had suddenly become seriously ill and had to have a benign tumor removed from the back of his head. Once his son was on the mend, Díaz was sent to extended spring training in Florida for a week to sharpen his skills. He didn't understand or agree with the move, which capped a very difficult spring for him.[57]

The season proceeded unremarkably with the exception of two events. In June, Díaz hit his first home run since the previous August and in doing so broke a 3-3 tie with the Dodgers. His reaction must have stunned and delighted his fans. "As it arced over the left-center-field fence, Díaz was rounding first base, shaking both hands in the air – a most unusual display of emotion from the intense, but generally unflappable catcher."[58]

Then, on July 9, 1989, Díaz played his final big-league game, though he didn't know it at the time. Once again, his left knee was the culprit, and in early August, he had his third surgery to repair it. He finished the season having played in only 43 games and with a batting average of .205. He was at the end of a two-year contract with the Reds and in November was granted free agency. He had a career batting average of .255 in the majors and a fielding percentage of .986; he'd also thrown out 34 percent of enemy basestealers. He was 37 years old and wanted to continue playing, but he remained unsigned for the 1990 season. His longtime agents, Randal and Alan Hendricks, later said that he was just too beaten up, particularly with a knee that would not cooperate, to play in 1990.[59]

In October 1990, the Cincinnati Reds were in postseason play, and Díaz was in Venezuela, playing once more for Caracas. He told a reporter, "I played hard and gave it my best in Cincinnati, and I grew to love the people of the city because they treated me well. I'm rooting for them all the way in the playoffs and the World Series."[60] As Díaz watched from 2,000 miles away, the Reds swept the Oakland Athletics in the World Series, four games to none.

Baudilio Díaz, born in a tiny house in Cúa, had worked his way to an upper-middle-class life and a two-story home in Caracas. It was there that his tragic death took place on November 23, 1990. The day was windy, and the signal from the home's satellite dish was spotty. He went to the roof and attempted to adjust the dish, which slipped and fell on him, crushing his neck and killing him instantly. He left behind his wife of 11 years, María Carolina, and his sons, Bo Daniel, 9, and Joshua, 6.

Díaz was idolized in Venezuela, and his death was a national tragedy. News crews were on the scene immediately, and just before 2:00 P.M., radio stations interrupted their regular programming to announce that he had died.[61]

Three days before his death, Díaz had quit the Leones unexpectedly amid a dispute with manager Phil Regan over Regan's use of him as a bullpen catcher. Díaz had been replaced by 23-year-old Carlos Hernández, who had made his debut with the Los Angeles Dodgers earlier that year and who had been the Leones' starting catcher for the previous two seasons. Regan felt Hernández's need to develop as a catcher was more important than Díaz's desire to prepare for a possible return to the majors. (Inconceivable as it seems, Díaz even considered the possibility of playing for another team, if it meant he could catch every day, and the rival Tigres de Aragua were calling him nonstop.)[62]

But in the end, after a major-league career that included significant tenures with Cleveland, Philadelphia, and Cincinnati, Díaz's baseball identity was most strongly tied to his native country and the Leones. His body was dressed in his Leones uniform, number 25, which the club promptly retired.[63] His December 13 funeral at the University of Caracas stadium was attended by 3,500 relatives, friends, fans, and politicians, including the president of Venezuela.

Fans and teammates throughout Venezuela and the United States grieved for the man described as tough and stoic but with a kind heart. Paul Owens, who managed Díaz on the 1983 NL championship team, said, "Bo was as nice a fellow as you'd want to meet. He was a good family man. A fine gentleman. I always admired him."[64]

"He went about his job in a very businesslike fashion," said Reds teammate Eric Davis. "When Bo wasn't playing, you knew he had to be hurt because he was so tough." Barry Larkin, another teammate, recalled, "We were young, and Bo showed us a lot of leadership. He was quiet, but he led by example."[65]

Randal and Alan Hendricks described him as a private but very happy person. "Our best memories of him are his ever-present smile when dealing with us. He was an appreciative person, which made representing him a privilege."[66]

In 2006, Díaz was inducted into the Venezuelan Baseball Hall of Fame, which called him one of the bravest players ever to play the game, given the numerous injuries he sustained during his career.[67] Sportswriter John Erardi echoed this sentiment, calling Díaz "a tough customer, a gamer who played hurt and rarely complained."[68]

Even now, the sadness of Díaz's untimely death lingers, especially for Venezuelans, and his country continues to honor him. In 2013, the Venezuelan government opened the first phase of a $5 million sports complex called Domo Baudilio Díaz. A second phase has been approved.[69] It appears, however, that construction has not started. (Given the current political and economic climate in Venezuela, this is unsurprising.)

Also, in 2013, the blog *Planeta Béisbol* featured a story from a fan who told of a game he watched as a 12-year-old between his team, the Cardenales de Lara, and the visiting Leones. The game was in 1979, and a home run by Díaz helped the Lions defeat the Cardinals. But it was after the game that the day took a memorable turn:

"As we walked back to our car, I saw the Lions' bus coming. Back then, people would throw rocks at the visiting teams' buses and yell insults at the visiting players. This happened at ballparks all over the country.

"Imagine my surprise when suddenly a bus window opened and none other than Baudilio Díaz stuck out his head. My jaw dropped when I realized he was tossing out bats, gloves, and balls to the kids who ran alongside the bus.

"That was the first time I remember seeing, in any ballpark, people applauding the visiting team's bus, especially after the visitors had beaten the home team."[70]

And in November 2013, Díaz's hometown named a ballpark for him. The dedication ceremony brought together relatives, friends, and the town's mayor to celebrate "the pride of Cúa" and to unveil a sculpture of him. He is immortalized in bronze crouched in his catcher's gear with a ball in his glove.[71]

Díaz's importance to the Leones and to baseball in the Caribbean remains undiminished. In 2019, he was selected for the Caribbean Baseball Hall of Fame.[72] And he continued to figure heavily in the Leones' media guides both as a significant part of the team's story over a 20-year period and as a record holder.[73] Over time, he has become mononymous: in much that is said and written about him, he is simply Baudilio – no last name or explanation needed.

In 1987, two years after Díaz's arrival in Cincinnati, John Erardi profiled him for the *Cincinnati Enquirer* and described his quiet, introverted ways.[74] He was warm, polite, and kind, but he was simply not a big talker and never sought to draw attention to himself. Erardi described a Reds-Astros game that resumed after a 2-hour, 20-minute rain delay:

"When only a few hundred fans remained to watch the last two innings of the game, it was suggested to [second baseman] Ron Oester that of all the players on the field, perhaps only Díaz could have enjoyed the sparsity of the crowd, and that the only way he would have enjoyed it more is if the last 200 had had the good sense to go home, too. Oester shook his head in disagreement. 'Bo wants to be appreciated,' Oester said. 'He might not come out and say it, but that is what he feels.'"

SOURCES

In addition to the sources cited in the Notes, the author used clippings from Díaz's file at the National Baseball Hall of Fame Library in Cooperstown, New York. Also helpful were Retrosheet.com, BaseballProspectus.com, and especially Baseball-Almanac.com and Baseball-Reference.com. For biographical information and background on Díaz's early life and career, the author relied heavily on the article "At Last Díaz Finds a Home," by Jeré Longman in the *Philadelphia Inquirer*, June 28, 1982.

Grateful acknowledgment to Díaz's agents, Randal and Alan Hendricks, with whom the author corresponded by email. Sincere gratitude to Rory Costello.

Díaz's statistics in Venezuelan winter ball: http://www.pelotabinaria.com.ve/beisbol/mostrar.php?ID=diazbau001

NOTES

1   Marybeth Sullivan, ed., *The Scouting Report: 1983* (New York: HarperCollins, 1983), 544.

2   Marybeth Sullivan, ed., *The Scouting Report: 1985* (New York: HarperCollins, 1985), 544.

3   Through the end of the 2022 season, this feat had been achieved 33 times. Díaz's was number 15.

https://www.baseball-almanac.com/feats/walk_off_grand_slams.shtml, accessed July 4, 2023.

4   Formal naming customs in Spanish place the mother's maiden name after the father's last name; however, the paternal family name is commonly used. As such, he is known by and will be referred to here as Díaz.

5   "Baudilio Díaz: 'El Cambao' que estableció récords en el béisbol profesional," https://globovision.com/article/especial-baudilio-diaz-el-cambao-que-batio-records-en-el-beisbol-profesional, March 23, 2017, accessed November 23, 2020.

6   "Baudilio Díaz: 'El Cambao' que estableció récords en el béisbol profesional."

7   On July 29, 1967, with his team one game away from a trip to the Little League World Series, a 6.5 magnitude earthquake occurred near Caracas. The aftermath was devastating: 240 deaths, 1,536 injuries, and $100 million in property damage. On a smaller scale, the devastation meant that a team of teenage boys could not leave the country to finish their season. https://earthquake.usgs.gov/learn/today/index.php?month=7&day=29.
John Erardi, "Ability Has Earned Respect from Teammates and Foes," *Cincinnati Enquirer*, July 5, 1987: C-6.

8   Richard Justice, "Galarraga Well-Kept Secret," *Edmonton* (Alberta) *Journal*, July 3, 1988: F2.

9   His *Sporting News* contract card shows him assigned to Winston-Salem from June 21 to July 19.

10   Russell Schneider, "Pruitt Tells Indians Not to Boo-Hoo Over Bo," *The Sporting News*, May 6, 1978: 8.

11   Bob Nold, "Indians' Hood Outstanding in 8-2 Win Against Cubs," *Akron Beacon Journal*, March 16, 1979: C-1.

12   Bob Sudyk, "Hassey No. 1 in Tribe's Mitt Plans," *The Sporting News*, November 3, 1979: 54.

13   Bob Sudyk, "Denny Makes Optimistic Pitch to Indians," *The Sporting News*, January 12, 1980: 40.

14   The Leones won the championship in 1972-73 with Díaz as part of that team, however he did not play in the postseason. He did see postseason play in 1974-75, 1975-76, and 1976-77, but the Leones did not advance past the semifinals in those years.

15   Juan Pablo Zubillaga, "PEDs, Tainted Records, and the Colorado Rockies," http://www.rockieszingers.com/2014/04/29/peds-tainted-records-colorado-rockies/, April 4, 2014, accessed March 30, 2017.

16   The Leones del Caracas are a member of La Liga Venezolana de Béisbol Profesional (LVBP) [Venezuelan Professional Baseball League]. During the years Díaz was active with the Leones, the team won the league championship in the 1972-73, 1977-78, 1979-80, 1980-81, 1981-82, and 1986-87 seasons. The Serie del Caribe [Caribbean Series] is a postseason tournament played annually in early February between the championship teams of the Caribbean winter leagues: the Dominican Winter League, Mexican Pacific League, Puerto Rican Winter League, and Venezuelan League. https://www.baseball-reference.com/bullpen/Venezuelan_League. https://www.baseball-reference.com/bullpen/Caribbean_Series.

17   https://www.baseball-almanac.com/players/player.php?p=diazbo01.

18   Jeré Longman, "At Last Díaz Finds a Home," *Philadelphia Inquirer*, June 28, 1982: 7-C.

19   Bill Conlin, "Tampering With Solid Lineup Hurts Expos," *The Sporting News*, May 24, 1982: 35.

20 Dan Coughlin, "Phils' New Bo Is No Perfect 10, but He's Improving," *Philadelphia Inquirer*, November 20, 1981: 6-C.

21 Hal Bodley, "Take Glove, Not War," *Wilmington* (Delaware) *News Journal*, February 28, 1982: D7.

22 Jayson Stark, "Smith Trade Is a Prelude for Big Deal to Come," *Philadelphia Inquirer*, November 20, 1981: 10-C.

23 Jayson Stark, "Phillies' Bo Can't Be '10' All the Time," *Philadelphia Inquirer*, April 2, 1982: 10-D.

24 Rusty Pray, "Phillies Fans Finally Accepting Competitive Bo Díaz," *Camden* (New Jersey) *Courier-Post*, May 11, 1982: 1C.

25 Jeré Longman, "Inept Phils Succumb to Cards, 7-4," *Philadelphia Inquirer*, April 25, 1982: 10-E.

26 "Phils Win NL East Crown," *Albuquerque Journal*, September 29, 1983: D-1.

27 Ira Berkow, "The Dempsey-Díaz Affair," *New York Times*, October 12, 1983: B-13.

28 "The Greatest Fans in the World?" *Lowell* (Massachusetts) *Sun*, September 16, 1977: 17. In his book *El Béisbol: Travels Through the Pan-American Pastime* (New York: Atlantic Monthly Press, 1989: 237), travel writer John Krich describes Venezuelan baseball fans as "single-minded and vicious" and points to the Díaz-Dempsey incident as proof. But he gets the story backward and has Díaz saving Dempsey's life.

29 Ray Finocchiaro, "Díaz Aching to Strike Back," *Wilmington Morning News*, March 29, 1984: C3.

30 Peter Pascarelli, "Surgery Will Sideline Díaz 3 to 5 Weeks," *Philadelphia Inquirer*, May 5, 1984: 1-C.

31 David Pietrusza, Matthew Silverman, and Michael Gershman, eds., *Baseball: The Biographical Encyclopedia* (New York: Total/Sports Illustrated, 2000), 286.

32 Jayson Stark, "Trade Talk and Knee Leave Díaz Uncertain," *Philadelphia Inquirer*, January 23, 1985: 1-F.

33 Ray Finocchiaro, "Díaz, Daulton Try to Catch Up with Virgil," *Morning News*, February 26, 1985: C2.

34 Ray Finocchiaro, "Díaz catching his share of bad breaks," *Wilmington Morning News*, April 21, 1985: C7.

35 Bill Conlin, "Scouts Find Díaz Debut Impressive," *Philadelphia Daily News*, March 13, 1985: 98.

36 Mark Whicker, "Time's Not on Díaz's Side," *Philadelphia Daily News*, July 22, 1985: 87.

37 Rich Hofmann, "Bo Holds Trading Block Party," *Philadelphia Daily News*, July 24, 1985: 89.

38 He was traded with minor-league reliever Greg Simpson for infielder Tom Foley, infielder-catcher Alan Knicely, and a player to be named later (pitcher Freddie Toliver). See Transactions: https://www.baseball-reference.com/players/d/diazbo01.shtml.

39 Greg Hoard, "Reds Elated Over Acquisition of Díaz," *Cincinnati Enquirer*, August 8, 1985: B-1.

40 Greg Hoard, "Reds' Díaz Delighted As Rumor Becomes Reality," *Cincinnati Enquirer*, August 9, 1985: D-1.

41 "Reds Deal for Díaz," *Columbus* (Indiana) *Republic*, August 8, 1985: B1.

42 "Bo Díaz and Buddy Bell 'Arrive' in Cincinnati Victory," *De Kalb* (Illinois) *Daily Chronicle*, August 26, 1985: 9.

43 Rick Van Sant, "Reds '85 Performance Spurs Dreams For '86," *St. Louis Post-Dispatch*, October 13, 1985: 4D.

44 Marybeth Sullivan, ed., *The Scouting Report: 1986* (New York: HarperCollins, 1986), 421.

45 Staff ERA with Díaz: 3.57; with Terry McGriff: 3.72; with Jeff Reed: 3.66; with Joe Oliver: 4.05 https://www.baseball-reference.com/teams/split.cgi?team=CIN&t=p&year=1989.

46 Erardi, "Ability Has Earned Respect from Teammates and Foes."

47 Sullivan, *The Scouting Report: 1986*, 421.

48 https://www.baseball-almanac.com/players/player.php?p=diazbo01; https://www.baseball-reference.com/boxes/CIN/CIN198606270.shtml

49 "National League All-Stars," *USA Today*, July 10, 1987: 9C.

50 Rick Van Sant, "Díaz Powers Reds, Rekindles Memories," *Columbus* (Indiana) *Republic*, August 5, 1987: B1.

51 "Baseball Notebook: N.L. West," *The Sporting News*, November 2, 1987: 26.

52 Greg Hoard, "Cincinnati Might Deal Parker for Pitching," *USA Today*, October 2, 1987: 5C.

53 "Time to Go for a Walk," *USA Today*, July 29, 1988: 5C.

54 "Slip in This Name Among Leaders in Slips of Tongue," *Los Angeles Times*, August 9, 1988: 2-Part III.

55 https://www.baseball-reference.com/boxes/CIN/CIN198808090.shtml.

56 Greg Hoard, "Healthy Díaz Can Solve Problem at Catcher, Reds Say," *Cincinnati Enquirer*, October 6, 1988: C-4.

57 "Reds' Díaz Not Happy in Florida," *Kokomo* (Indiana) *Tribune*, April 16, 1989: 41.

58 "Big Home Runs by Díaz, O'Neill Carry Reds 5-3," *Nashville Tennessean*, June 27, 1989: 4-C.

59 Randal and Alan Hendricks, email to Andrea Long, December 1, 2016.

60 John Erardi, "Díaz Was a Professional, with Warm Heart," *Cincinnati Enquirer*, November 24, 1990: D-1.

61 Carlos Figueroa Ruiz, "Tragedia de Baudilio Nos Enlutó Hace 25 Años," http://www.liderendeportes.com/noticias/beisbol/tragedia-de-baudilio-nos-enluto-hace-25-anos.aspx#ixzz4Lx2CWPbl, accessed October 2, 2016.

62 Carlos Cárdenas Lares, *Leones del Caracas: Crónica de una Tradición* (Caracas, Venezuela: Fondo Editorial Cárdenas Lares, 1992), 261.

63 The other 11 numbers retired by the Leones belonged to Pompeyo Davalillo, Víc Davalillo, César Tovar, Tony Armas, Urbano Lugo (the son), Gonzalo Márquez, Alfonso "Chico" Carrasquel, Omar Vizquel, Henry Blanco, Luis Aparicio (retired leaguewide), and Andrés Galarraga. http://www.leones.com/uniformes.php, accessed October 15, 2020.

64 "Satellite Dish Crushes Díaz," http://articles.philly.com/1990-11-24/sports/25929095_1_satellite-dish-bo-Díaz-baruta, accessed September 12, 2016.

65 Erardi, "Díaz Was a Professional, with Warm Heart."

66 Randal and Alan Hendricks email.

67 "Baudilio José Díaz," http://www.museodebeisbol.com/salon_fama_venezolano/detalles/2006/baudilio-jos-daz, accessed July 4, 2023.

68 John Erardi, "Díaz Dies in Rooftop Accident," *Cincinnati Enquirer*, November 24, 1990: A-1.

69 "Gobierno Nacional Inauguró Domo Deportivo-Cultural en Charallave," http://www.avn.info.ve/contenido/gobierno-nacional-inaugura-domo-deportivo-cultural-charallave, accessed September 16, 2016.

70 Frank Pereiro, "Alex Cabrera le Pide Paso al Gran Baudilio Díaz," https://planetabeisbol.com/threads/alex-cabrera-le-pide-paso-al-gran-baudilio-diaz.4180/, November 29, 2013, accessed June 22, 2017.

71 Dulce Feliciano, "Develan Estatua en Honor a 'Baudilio Díaz' en Estadio de Cúa," http://lagranciudad.net/home/develan-estatua-en-honor-a-baudilio-diaz-en-estadio-de-cua/, accessed October 3, 2016.

72 The 2019 Caribbean Series was moved at the last minute from Barquisimeto, Venezuela, to Panama City, Panama, and the Hall of Fame ceremony was postponed. Díaz and the rest of his class were inducted in 2020 alongside the 2020 members. David Venn, "5 things to know about the 2020 Caribbean Series," https://www.mlb.com/news/caribbean-series-changes-for-2020, accessed November 23, 2020.

73 *Leones del Caracas Guía de Medios 2018/2019* (Caracas: Caracas Baseball Club, C.A., 2018), 264.

74 Erardi, "Ability Has Earned Respect from Teammates and Foes."

KELVIM ESCOBAR

BY J.L. TUCUPIDO C.

San José de la Sabana might as well be a Hamlet from a Latin American magical realism novel. Is there something in its water? Or perhaps a spell cast by the village witch? The small town of Caruao, La Guaira on Venezuela's central coast is the cradle of a family tradition started by José Elías Escobar. Like the magic of compound interest, his 18 sons have continued the family dynasty, whose purebred pedigree has produced more than 20 players signed to professional contracts with major-league franchises.

Kelvim, one of José Elías's grandchildren, can claim to be the best of the crop. A versatile and smart pitcher, he played with the Toronto Blue Jays and the Los Angeles Angels of Anaheim between 1997 and 2009.[1] Armed with a blistering fastball and a cunning split finger, he earned 101 victories[2] and 59 saves[3] in the major leagues. Both totals rank among the top 10 for Venezuelan hurlers, an uncommon combination in today's specialized pitching landscape.

Kelvim José Escobar Bolívar was born in La Guaira on April 11, 1976, and developed his potential at the Oscar Santiago Escobar Stadium (oddly, no relation). At 16, he was scouted by Epifanio "Epy" Guerrero, the legendary Dominican birddog for the Cardenales of Lara and the Blue Jays, and Domingo Carrasquel, brother of Alfonso "Chico" Carrasquel. Escobar signed a contract on July 9, 1992, and immediately reported to the Dominican Summer League. Blue Jays pitching coach Mel Queen needed only one throwing session to "want to take Escobar to the United States as soon as possible to begin his career. We always knew the type of arm he had, but we did not know he would do so well in the DSL. It's a testament to his skill."[4]

In 1994, as an 18-year-old with the Gulf Coast Blue Jays, Escobar went 4-4 with a 2.35 ERA in 11 games (10 starts). He struck out 64 hitters in 65 innings and did not allow a home run. A year later, he struck out 75 opponents in 69⅓ innings in the Rookie-level Pioneer League, but walked 33 batters and gave up six home runs. The Blue Jays were nevertheless impressed, given that Escobar was roughly two years younger than his peers.

In 1996 Escobar pitched for both Class-A Advanced Dunedin and Double-A Knoxville. He struck out 157 hitters in 164⅓ innings, with a 2.75 strikeout-to-walk ratio and 12 wins. His maturity was noticed by the Toronto organization and the press: "There are some promising young arms in the minors, led by righties Kelvim Escobar and Roy Halladay, but they are a couple of years away at best," a sportswriter observed.[5] The assessment was not an indictment of the prospects' potential but rather an awareness of the Blue Jays' formidable rotation of

Roger Clemens, Juan Guzmán, Pat Hengen, and the up-and-coming Chris Carpenter.

Escobar was cold-blooded and calm under pressure on the mound, unafraid to challenge hitters with his fastball. He rose through the minors quickly, thanks to his experience in the Liga Venezolana de Béisbol Profesional (LVBP). The winter circuit boasted tougher competition than Escobar would face in the Florida State or Southern League.

Baseball America placed Escobar as the 67th-best preseason prospect. He played only eight games in the minors in 1997 (2-2, 3.72 ERA in 36⅓ innings) before being called up to the big leagues. He debuted against Baltimore on June 29, 1997, in long relief, and limited the Orioles to a pair of hits and three walks in 4⅓ innings, striking out five. His debut was the second victory by a Venezuelan hurler since 1976 as a reliever.[6]

The 21-year-old impressed his teammates and manager Cito Gaston, who quickly anointed Escobar the team closer. Right fielder Joe Carter noted, "[H]e's doing the job. He's calm on the mound and is throwing 94-95 MPH with a good forkball."[7] Pitcher Robert Person added, "I've never seen a rookie come in like that (as a closer) and grab the bull by the horns."[8]

Escobar himself was cognizant of how he reached the majors at a young age: "To me, Venezuela (LVBP) helped me dominate the minors and reach the major leagues so quickly."[9] Seasoned veterans like Luis Sojo, Gio Carrara, Edwin Hurtado, and Antonio Castillo motivated and tutored the pitcher, who benefited from the competition: "when you pitch during the finals against the Navegantes of Magallanes or the Leones of Caracas and face their lineup, with proven big leaguers like Melvin Mora, Endy Chávez, Edgardo Alfonzo, Richard Hidalgo, Carlos García, Omar Vizquel, Roger Cedeño, Bob(by) Abreu, and Henry Blanco … and then you got to the United States to play Rookie or Class A baseball, you can only imagine how I fared against those kids. I'd strike out everyone!"[10]

Escobar finished his rookie year with 14 saves and a 2.90 ERA in 31 innings. The rookie sensation arrived at the park early and worked hard. However, Escobar's versatility led to instability during his years in Toronto. Neither GM Gordon Ash nor Gaston and his managerial successors would carve out a permanent role for Escobar. He would enter a game in long relief, close in the late innings if needed, or spot-start when someone else went down with an injury. Escobar won 58 games with the Blue Jays and saved another 58, an odd statistic. He started 101 games, relieved in another 200, and struck out 744 batters in 849 innings. He swung from a 38-save season in 2022 to a 13-9, 159-strikeout, 26-start performance a year later.

The Swiss army knife would always watch the game to analyze the opposing hitters and pitchers. Though Toronto was no longer the 1992-1993 World Series-winning juggernaut, the franchise contended in the AL East. The 1999 David Wells-Clemens trade solidified Escobar as the third starter, behind Hengen and Carpenter, as Billy Koch took over the closer role. According to Escobar, Wells took him under his wing: "David Wells taught me how to pitch inside, without fear."[11]

However, Escobar's role changed again. The arrival of Halladay and Estaban Loaíza, along with the trade of Koch to Oakland, returned Escobar to the bullpen as the full-time closer in 2002. In 2003, his last year with the Blue Jays, he was a swingman: 26 starts, 15 relief appearances, 13 wins, and 4 saves.

New GM J.P. Ricciardi offered Escobar a two-year, $10 million contract. Agent Peter Greenberg, a close associate of the entire Escobar family, counseled the pitcher to test the free-agent waters. On November 24 the Angels signed Escobar to a three-year, $18.8 million deal.

Middle relief, starter, or closer? Escobar did not mind his role and was prepared to do whatever the Angels needed. Anaheim envisioned him as a starter. The team's bullpen was a veritable embarrassment of riches: Scot Shields, Kevin Gregg, Brendan Donnelly, Francisco Rodríguez, and Troy Percival. The staff even boasted Ramón Ortiz, who like Escobar could thrive in middle relief or as a spot starter.

Escobar quickly became the number two starter behind Bartolo Colón, himself a newcomer. The Latin aces led the rotation for the AL West champion Angels, who returned to the postseason after a one-year absence. Escobar started 33 games and struck out 191 hitters in 208⅓ innings. However, his teammates scored only 3.9 runs in his starts, so his team-leading 3.93 ERA produced only an 11-12 record. The club's 92 wins were no match for the 2004 Boston Red Sox, a team of destiny, which swept Anaheim in the Division Series.

Injuries hampered Escobar in 2005. Limited to 59⅔ innings during the regular season, he proved pivotal in the LDS against the Yankees. He won the second game of the series and held the Angels' lead in the third and fifth contests for closer Rodríguez. In seven innings, he allowed only one run, on a Derek Jeter home run. His luck – and Anaheim's – changed in the LCS against another Sox team. This time, it was Chicago's turn to break its decades-long World Series drought. Escobar appeared in two games (4⅓ innings, three runs, but only one earned) and lost both contests, twice bested by Joe Crede in pivotal at-bats.

As 2006 began, general manager Bill Stoneman removed any contract distractions and signed Escobar to a three-year, $28.5 million extension. The GM noted that "Kelvim was a crucial part of the success of our pitching staff. I love the idea of him being on our team through 2009."[12]

Escobar rewarded the team with a 3.61 ERA in 30 starts, a powerful one-two punch with John Lackey. The team again contended but faltered down the stretch and finished second behind Oakland. Escobar was saddled again with a losing record (11-14) despite almost three times as many strikeouts as walks.

He was even better in 2007. Escobar won a career-high 18 games (sixth highest in the AL) and lowered his ERA to 3.40. However, he faltered down the stretch after spending more of the summer limiting opponents to fewer than three runs a game. He did not garner a single vote for the Cy Young Award, which went to CC Sabathia. The Angels again met the Red Sox in the Division Series but were stymied during Boston's march to another World Series title.

The Angels and Escobar both hoped for an encore in 2008, but he experienced severe pain during the winter and rested his arm for two months. The malady proved to be worse than expected: a shoulder tear required season-ending surgery, and he had to settle for three innings with Rancho Cucamonga and two in the Arizona Rookie League during his rehabilitation.

The second year of Escobar's contract extension was not much better. In two games with Rancho Cucamonga, he dominated hitters (10⅔ IP, two hits, one run, 75 pitches in two games). He could not have been happier with the result and noted that "the doctors told me the true test for someone with my type of

Kelvim Escobar was a hard-throwing right-hander who pitched 12 MLB seasons, known for his versatility and power on the mound. A standout with the Angels and Blue Jays, he was a respected figure in both MLB and Venezuelan baseball. (Scott Halleran / Getty Images Sports)

shoulder surgery is the first 70 or 75 pitches. I did not feel any more pain than usual the next day. I woke up super happy. I threw hard, used all my pitches, had command, and even put in extra speed to overpower hitters. It couldn't have gone any better."[13]

Although he was roughed up in one start with Triple-A Salt Lake (five innings, four earned runs), Escobar returned to the big leagues on June 6 in Detroit and was a hard-luck loser. He allowed two runs in five innings against the Tigers, but Los Angeles mustered only one run in a 2-1 defeat. A solid outing – although at $9.5 million, costly for the Angels.

Escobar's future with the franchise was no longer in Scioscia's hands. Stoneman was no longer the GM, and Tony Reagins understood a sunk cost. Despite the track record of Dr. David Altchek's Hospital for Special Surgery – responsible for healing Bobby Bonilla, Bret Saberhagen, Jorge Posada, and Mariano Rivera – the Angels released Escobar on November 6, despite one year and $9.5 million left on his contract.

On December 26, 2009, the New York Mets signed Escobar to an incentive-laden contract. The franchise's medical director, Dr. Altchek, had performed the pitcher's July 2008 surgery, and vouched for his health. However, Escobar suffered from right labrum inflammation during spring training and began the season on the injured list. The discomfort did not improve, and the team transferred Escobar to the 60-day IL. He was released in November.

Despite the setback, Escobar was hopeful he could return to the major leagues: "I was close to retiring but decided against it. For a year I was away from the stadiums and baseball fields."[14] The rest, combined with a strong exercise program, kept his hope alive. While showing his form to scouts assembled by his longtime agent Greenberg, Escobar admitted "[T]his will be my last attempt to return to baseball. I've spent a lot of time in therapy and rehabilitation and it's not easy. It takes a mental and physical toll. I've had a long career. If this is the end, then so be it but I am still hopeful."[15]

The Milwaukee Brewers saw a glimmer of hope and invited Escobar to spring training in 2013. He was released on March 10, a bitter end to his comeback: "I was disappointed because they told me one thing but did another. I signed with Milwaukee because its manager (Ron Roenicke) was the third-base coach with the Angels. The GM called me personally and promised I would have a much better opportunity with the Brewers than any other team."[16] He told the author that "Terry Francona (Cleveland Indians) called me every so often to sign with them."[17]

In the end, Escobar acknowledged that his shoulder was not the same. He continued to play in Venezuela through the 2012-2013 season and in Mexico until 2013 He retired early – a premature goodbye to the game, having thrown his last major-league pitch at 33. In hindsight, surgery may have been the wrong decision. Perhaps he could have reinvented himself with lower velocity or a reduced repertoire, like Zack Greinke, Freddy García, and Félix Hernández, pitchers who remained productive after serious injuries zapped their blinding velocity.

Escobar is still beloved in his hometown, where he is known as "the monarch of the Savanah" thanks to his charitable efforts. He is active in nurturing the third generation of his family. Four-second cousins Luisangel Acuña (Texas Rangers), Maikel Garcia (Kansas City Royals), Hugo Cardona (Toronto), and Royman Blanco (Boston Red Sox) blossomed as minor-league prospects.

Escobar's sons have also sought to continue the family tradition. As of 2024, Kevin is a teenager, but baseball was not his path, while Kelvim Jr.'s time may have passed: "He hadn't pitched and when he started, playing against kids from baseball academies, he was slow to develop. However, he's quite good at basketball."[18]

Escobar and his cousins started the La Sabana Baseball Academy (Academia de Béisbol de La Sabana) in 2015. Now named after the family, the foundation has helped more than 400 children with donations of equipment and covering transportation costs for cross-province competitions. The organization is recognized by the MLB Trainer Partnership Program[19] and counts his uncle José Escobar, Ronald Acuña Sr., Víctor Sánchez, and Luis Blanco among its coaches.

Kelvim lives in Atlanta as of 2024 but remains very connected to his hometown thanks to social media and follows closely the successful career of his cousin Ronald Acuña Jr.. Had he not been blessed with baseball talent, he may have been an artist: "I consider myself a frustrated musician. I love percussion … In La Sabana, I used to play the *timbales* (the leather drums). Making a living in music is not easy, it takes time, practice and dedication and I don't have time for it."[20] Nevertheless, he has appeared in various music videos for Latin artists across various genres. He remains in love with baseball and is always open to opportunities to help a major-league franchise in baseball operations, as a scout, or as a coach.

SOURCES

In addition to the sources referenced in the Notes, the author consulted *El Emergente, Pelota Binaria, The Sporting News,* and *Baseball Reference.*

NOTES

1   During Escobar's tenure with the Angels, the club changed its name from Anaheim Angels to the Los Angeles Angels of Anaheim. Years after he retired from the major leagues, the franchise truncated its moniker to the Los Angeles Angels.

2   Seven retired Venezuelan-born pitchers have at least 100 major-league wins: Félix Hernández (169), Freddy García (156), Johan Santana (139), Carlos Zambrano (132), Aníbal Sánchez (112), Wilson Álvarez (102), and Kelvim Escobar (101). Carlos Carrasco had 107 victories as of the start of the 2024 season and remained active.

3   In 2009 only five active pitchers had at least 200 career starts and 50 career saves: Derek Lowe, John Smoltz, Ryan Dempster, Tom Gordon, and Escobar.

4   Kelvim Escobar interview with author, conducted in February 2022.

5   Rob Rains, "The Rich Get Richer," *The Sporting News,* November 11, 1996: 33-34.

6   Manuel Sarmiento was the first, on July 30, 1976. Since Escobar, two others have debuted as relievers and won their maiden game: Sergio Escalona on May 17, 2019, and Adbert Alzolay on June 20, 2019.

7   "La Estrella Invitada en Instagram: Kelvim Escobar," YouTube interview, Sojo Productions, May 13, 2020, https://www.youtube.com/watch?v=rXFjRI10AiY.

8   "La Estrella Invitada en Instagram: Kelvim Escobar."

9   "Kelvim Escobar: 'Ronald Acuña Aún Está Aprendiendo," YouTube interview, ElVillasmil 024, April 28, 2020, https://www.youtube.com/watch?v=INJ3Ai4Da8c&ab_channel=ElVillasmil024.

10 "Instagram Live: Kelvim Escobar," YouTube interview, Meridiano Oficial, April 18, 2020, https://www.youtube.com/watch?v=AlhtQ-goW8DM&ab_channel=MeridianoOficial.

11 "La Estrella Invitada en Instagram: Kelvim Escobar."

12 "La Estrella Invitada en Instagram: Kelvim Escobar."

13 Author's interview.

14 Author's interview.

15 Author's interview.

16 "La Estrella Invitada en Instagram: Kelvim Escobar."

17 Author's interview.

18 "La Estrella Invitada en Instagram: Kelvim Escobar."

19 Trainer Partnership Program MLB. The Trainer Partnership Program is a collaboration between Major League Baseball and independent trainers to help develop international baseball while addressing important issues in the international market. https://www.mlb.com/trainer-partnership.

20 Author's interview.

ÁLVARO ESPINOZA

BY GREGG OMOTH

A veteran of 12 major-league seasons, Alvaro Espinoza played a variety of roles for five different teams. He went from prospect with the Minnesota Twins to starting shortstop with the New York Yankees to utility infielder with three other teams. He is best remembered by Cleveland Indians fans as a versatile backup on the 1995 American League champions. He threw out Jay Buhner of the Seattle Mariners on a grounder for the final out in the American League Championship Series, sending the Indians to their first World Series since 1954. In a career filled with unexpected success and disappointment, Espinoza found a perfect role with the Indians as the utility infielder and team prankster. He played with a passion for the game while finding ways make it fun.

Alvaro Alberto Ramirez Espinoza was born on February 19, 1962, in Valencia, Venezuela, the country's third largest city and the hub of a 3-million-strong metropolitan area. His father, Luis, a bus driver, and mother, Matilde, raised five daughters and three sons.[1] Alvaro attended the Pedro Gual School in Valencia, where he played baseball, basketball, and soccer.[2] As a youngster, baseball was his passion; after school he played in the streets with his friends and two brothers until dark. His family was not poor, but they did not have extra money for bats, balls, and gloves. He made do with no glove, a stick for a bat, and crumpled paper taped together for a ball.[3]

On October 30, 1978, Houston Astros scout Tony Pacheco signed Espinoza as an amateur free agent to $500-a-month contract with a $3,000 bonus.[4] The Astros also signed his older brother Roberto at the same time. The Astros sent them to their rookie league team in Sarasota, Florida. Roberto spent four years in the Astros system before starting a career as a coach in multiple organizations and with the Venezuelan team in the World Baseball Classic. Alvaro spent two years in the Astros organization before being released on September 30, 1980. When he was told that they were releasing him he thought he would not be allowed to play in the United States again. He returned to Valencia, where he worked selling hot dogs out of a street cart.

Espinoza continued to play in the Venezuelan winter league, where he caught the attention of Minnesota Twins scout Hank Izquierdo.[5] He wasn't sure he wanted to play again but his father persuaded him to give it another try, and the Twins signed him in 1982. They sent him to their Class-A team in Wisconsin Rapids, Wisconsin (Midwest League), where he played in 112 games, hitting .266 while splitting time between shortstop and third base.

In 1983 the Twins sent Espinoza to Visalia of the Class A California League, where he roomed with Kirby Puckett. Espinoza credited Puckett with helping him learn English by encouraging him to watch television and repeating what he heard. Hitting .319 in 130 games at Visalia while playing solid defense, he established himself as a legitimate prospect for the Twins. At the end of the season he was named to the California League All-Star team. In the winter Espinoza returned to Venezuela to play winter ball with his idol Dave Concepcion, the Cincinnati Reds shortstop and Venezuelan hero. Espinoza credited another former major leaguer, Vic Davalillo, for helping him with his hitting during this time.[6]

In 1984 Espinoza went to spring training with a chance to win a roster spot on a Twins team that did not have an established shortstop. Even with a good spring, he lost out on his bid to win the shortstop job to Lenny Faedo and was sent to the Twins' Triple-A team in Toledo. There he was installed as the starting shortstop ahead of the Twins' other shortstop prospect, Greg Gagne. In June Espinoza went on the disabled list with 21 stitches in his leg after being spiked at second base. Solid defense was the strength of his game, while his hitting was suspect at only .233 in 104 games. The Twins called him up in September and he made his major-league debut on September 14, 1984, in a game against the Texas Rangers. He entered the game as a defensive replacement in the seventh inning at shortstop, replacing Chris Speier. This was his only appearance with the Twins in 1984; he did not get a plate appearance.

In 1985 Espinoza failed to make the big-league club out of spring training and was the last infielder sent to Toledo. The Twins found their future shortstop in Gagne, making Espinoza's route to the major leagues more difficult. He had a tough year in Toledo, hitting only .229 and reinforcing the Twins opinion that he was ready to play major-league defense but not ready offensively. In August Espinoza was called up to the majors when Gagne went on the disabled list. In his first extended chance in the majors, he hit .263 in 32 games. New Twins manager Ray Miller was impressed with his defense, providing Espinoza optimism for his chances in 1986.

In 1986 Espinoza started the season in Toledo after again failing to make the Twins roster out of spring training. On July 11 he was called up to the Twins, and remained with the team for the remainder of the season. Playing in 37 games, he split time between second base and shortstop. He hit only .214.

Espinoza remained with the Twins organization in 1987 but was sent to Triple-A Portland. A knee injury in late May forced him to miss a month. Though he had a solid year, splitting time between shortstop and third base and hitting .275, he did not receive a September call-up to the Twins. On October 15 he was granted free agency and on the advice of scout Fred Ferreira, the

New York Yankees signed him on November 17, as a six-year minor-league free agent.[7]

Espinoza spent most of the 1988 season with the Yankees' Triple-A affiliate in Columbus, Ohio. On August 4 he was called up to the Yankees and played in three games, going hitless in three at-bats, before being sent back to Columbus on August 12. He had a solid year at Columbus that was noticed by some of the Yankees front office people, who thought he could help the team the following year.

In the spring of 1989, Espinoza was invited to spring training with the Yankees with an opportunity to make the team as a utility infielder. When starting shortstop Rafael Santana went down with an injury in spring training, and the Yankees failed in their attempts to obtain another shortstop, manager Dallas Green named Espinoza the starter. He expected Espinoza to play solid defense but had limited expectations for his hitting. Espinoza's play turned out to be one of the biggest surprises for the Yankees in 1989; he had his best season in the major leagues, hitting .282 in 146 games. Batting second in the order, he was among the league leaders in sacrifices. He credited his improvement at the plate to his work with hitting coach Frank

A steady presence at shortstop, Espinoza played for five major-league clubs over 12 seasons. He was known for his glove and quiet leadership on the field. (dreammesiapeel / Dreamstime)

Howard. Manager Bucky Dent, who replaced Green in August, anticipated using Espinoza as his shortstop in 1990.[8]

Entering 1990, Espinoza was established as the shortstop and went on to play in a career-high 150 games. His offensive production was less than spectacular; he batted only .224 with 2 home runs and 20 RBIs. Espinoza did not work well with new batting coach Champ Summers, who experimented with his stance and eroded Espinoza's confidence. When Stump Merrill replaced Dent as manager and Darrell Evans became the new batting coach, Espinoza continued to struggle with the bat. He was trying too hard to drive the ball rather than making contact and moving runners along.[9] The end result was one of the worst offensive seasons for any player in major leagues in 1990.

In 1991 Espinoza was disappointed when Randy Velarde started two of the season's first three games at shortstop. This started some tension between him and manager Merrill that would carry on throughout the season. However, he quickly found himself back in the lineup as the starting shortstop, hitting .441 in the season's first 13 games. He attributed his increased production to the return of Frank Howard as the batting coach.[10] But as the season went on, his relationship with Merrill deteriorated to the point of open hostility. Late in the season, Espinoza accused Merrill of benching him so he would not meet appearance incentives in his contract.[11] He finished the season hitting .256 in 148 games, but his future with the Yankees was no longer certain.

In February of 1992 Espinoza signed a new contract with the Yankees and went to spring training competing with one of the club's free-agent acquisitions, Mike Gallego, for the starting shortstop role. After failing to trade Espinoza, the Yankees released him on March 18, in a move that saved them over $800,000. The Yankees did not believe he would be happy in a backup role after being the starter for the past three seasons. Espinoza was disappointed on being released but was also thankful for the opportunity the Yankees gave him, stating, "They gave me my chance, it was the best three years of my life. I can't say nothing bad about these guys."[12] On April 3 he signed with the Cleveland Indians and was sent to their Triple-A affiliate in Colorado Springs. He spent the season with Colorado Springs, hitting .300 in 122 games, and played in the PCL All-Star Game.

In 1993 Espinoza made the Indians' roster out of spring training as a utility infielder. He played 90 games at third base, 35 at shortstop, and two at second base. He batted .278 with 4 home runs and 27 RBIs. With his value established, he returned to the Indians for the strike-shortened 1994 season. Playing in 90 games, he split time between all infield positions, playing first base for the first time in his career.

In 1995 Espinoza's playing time was reduced because of the emergence of Jim Thome at third base and established players Omar Vizquel at shortstop and Carlos Baerga at second. His role was limited to defensive replacement and occasional pinch-hitter. With more time on the bench, he established himself as one of the team pranksters, with his favorite prank putting a bubblegum bubble on top of an unsuspecting teammate's cap and waiting for him to realize he was the victim of his prank. The Indians won the Central Division championship and faced the Boston Red Sox in the Division Series. It was Espinoza's first chance at postseason baseball. He played in Game Three as a defensive replacement for Thome at third base, getting one at-bat in the ninth inning and flying out to right field in the Indians' 8-2 win.

The Indians won the Division Series and played Seattle in the AL Championship Series. Espinoza appeared in four games, getting one hit in eight at-bats. In the World Series he played in two games, getting one hit in two at-bats. The highlight for Espinoza was a pinch-running appearance in the bottom of the 11th inning in Game Three; with no outs he scored the winning run from second base on a hit by Eddie Murray. The Indians lost the World Series to the Atlanta Braves in six games.

In December Espinoza signed a new contract with the Indians and returned to his role of utility infielder for 1996. Playing at all the infield positions, he appeared in 59 games before he was traded on July 29 to the New York Mets with Baerga for Jeff Kent and Jose Vizcaino. Playing mainly at third base, he got into 48 games for the Mets, hitting .306. He filled in at all the other infield positions for the Mets. Though he was not the primary acquisition, he outperformed Baerga with the Mets after the trade. It appeared Espinoza would have a good opportunity to play for the Mets in 1997.

He went to spring training with the Mets in 1997 but was released on March 26. The Mets decided to go with younger players with better range. On April 2 Espinoza signed with the Seattle Mariners as a utility infielder. He performed well as a backup until he suffered a bruised arm and went on the disabled list on May 30. After a short rehab stint with their Triple-A team in Tacoma, he returned to the active roster on June 13. He was hitting only .181 when the Mariners released him on July 14.

In 1998 Espinoza started his coaching career as a minor-league infield coordinator with the Montreal Expos organization. In 1999 the Dodgers hired him as manager of their Florida State League team in Vero Beach. In 2000 and 2001 he was the Dodgers' roving minor-league infield coordinator.

In 2002 he worked in the same capacity with the Pittsburgh Pirates organization.

In 2003 Espinoza returned to the major leagues as the infield instructor for the Pittsburgh Pirates. He continued in this role until the end of the 2005 season. In 2006 he was the club's roving minor-league infield coordinator. From 2007 to 2017 he worked as a minor-league infield instructor in the Yankees, Pirates, and San Francisco Giants organizations.

The father of seven children, Espinoza became a United States citizen in 2005. As of 2018 he lived in Florida with his wife, Corimar. In 2014 he was inducted into the Caribbean Series Hall of Fame. In a 12-year career in the Venezuelan League, he hit .368 in his three appearances in the Caribbean Series.

NOTES

1   Joe Maxse, "The Joker Utility Man Espinoza Helps Keep Teammates Smiling," *Plain Dealer* (Cleveland), September 14, 1995.

2   *1986 Minnesota Twins Media Guide*, 66.

3   Michael Martinez, "Promising Future With Yankees Doesn't Exclude Espinoza's Past," *New York Times,* September 12, 1989.

4   Charley Walters, "Smalley Sidelined by Injury to Foot," *St. Paul Pioneer Press,* March 26, 1985: 2B.

5   Tom Loomis, "Twins' Outfielder Battling Nerves: Eisenreich Promising in Exhibitions," *Toledo Blade,* March 18, 1984: D 3.

6   Ibid.

7   Bill Madden, "Espinoza Helping Yanks Forget Shortstop Problem," *The Sporting News,* May 29, 1989: 18.

8   Martinez.

9   Jack Curry, "Baseball: A Yankee and a Met Labor to Round Out Their Mastery of the Game; Espinoza Has to Be a More Selective Hitter," *New York Times,* March 19, 1991.

10   Jack Curry, "Baseball; Espinoza Goes Beyond His Fancy Glovework," *New York Times,* April 25, 1991.

11   Jack O'Connell, "New York Yankees," *The Sporting News,* September 2, 1991: 22.

12   Jack Curry, "Baseball; Double Play: Espinoza Goes and Gallego Is Given His Job," *New York Times,* March 18, 1992.

ANDRÉS GALARRAGA

BY BRIAN WERNER

Andrés Jose Padovani Galarraga was known as the Big Cat, or El Gran Gato, during his 19-year major-league baseball career, a career in which he became the Colorado Rockies' first big star. He looked like a slugger but what made him so popular, and helped secure his nickname, was his quickness around the first-base bag. Along the way he helped establish the Rockies' tradition of great infield defense.

Galarraga was the first of the "Blake Street Bombers" and one of the key reasons the Rockies established a major-league record for attendance during their first year and by year three were in the playoffs.

During his big-league career, he hit 399 home runs, became a five-time All-Star, two-time Gold Glove winner, and two-time Comeback Player of the Year. Most importantly, Galarraga is a two-time cancer survivor.

When his career ended in 2005, after a brief stint with the New York Mets in spring training, he had hit more home runs than any native Venezuelan (since broken by Miguel Cabrera) and was considered a national hero in his native land.[1]

Andrés Galarraga was born June 18, 1961, in the capital city of Caracas. His father, Francisco Padovani, was an Italian immigrant who painted houses for a living, while his mother, Juana, helped raise his three brothers and one sister. Orlando, Alfonso, Francisco, and sister Haide were Andrés' siblings.[2]

Andrés played sandlot ball growing up until the age of 16, when he began playing professional ball in the Venezuelan winter league. He began his career as a third baseman and catcher. It was there in 1979 that Felipe Alou first saw him play and, after getting over his "chubbiness," recommended to Montreal farm director Jim Fanning that the Expos sign him.[3]

The signing is an interesting story. According to an Alou recollection, he was friends with the Caracas manager, Oscar Minaya.[4] He brought a rooster to give him as a present and in return Oscar told him about this player named Andrés Galarraga. Alou watched him play and proceeded to call Fanning and recommend signing the young slugger. Fanning balked at the $10,000 figure Alou gave him, and while there is some discrepancy over how much Galarraga actually signed for — either $5,000 (per Alou's memory) or $1,500 according to most other reports — the Expos had him under contract as an amateur free agent.[5]

He was given the moniker "Big Cat" by his manager (and former big leaguer) Bob Bailey while playing Rookie League ball at Calgary in 1979, for his cat-like quickness and agility around the first-base bag.[6] He stood 6-feet-3 and listed at 235 pounds.

Galarraga's first impression of the United States was not all that favorable and he experienced many of the same frustrations other Latino ballplayers do when arriving in the country for the first time. According to Bob Kravitz, Andrés didn't speak a lick of English when he arrived in West Palm Beach.[7] In an interview with Kravitz years later, Galarraga remembered he was so homesick when he first arrived that he wanted to call his parents every day but only had the money to do so on a weekly basis. He was also the only Latino on his teams in Calgary and at Jamestown in the Class-A New York-Penn League.

Galarraga's road to English understanding mimicked many other Latin players' efforts in adapting to a new country and a strange language. He watched TV and he read the dictionary and newspapers to understand the language. According to Jill Leiber, Galarraga had the TV on 24 hours a day to learn English.[8] He recalled the frustration with simple day-to-day tasks such as ordering food from a menu in an American restaurant where he and his fellow Latinos had to simply point at the item to order it.

Future big leaguer Randy St. Claire was a teammate of Galarraga's at Jamestown and also helped with his English.[9]

Perhaps because of these cultural adjustments, Galarraga's career did not get off to a rousing start. In fact, he was so bad in his first professional appearance in West Palm Beach that he was demoted to Rookie League Calgary during his first professional season. He stayed in Calgary until he was promoted to the Expos' low Single-A club in Jamestown, New York, for the 1981 season.

He was back in West Palm Beach and high Single-A ball for the 1982-83 seasons before being promoted to Double-A Jacksonville in 1984. There he became the Southern League's Most Valuable Player by hitting .289 with 27 home runs and 87 RBIs. He had now also established himself as a full-time first baseman. He was promoted to Montreal's top farm club at Triple-A Indianapolis in 1985 and was named the International League's Rookie of the Year. He hit .269 with 25 homers and had 85 RBIs before being promoted to Montreal in August.

Galarraga made his major-league debut on August 23, 1985. Getting into 24 games that first year, he hit .187 with 2 home runs and 4 RBIs.

His official rookie year, 1986, was off to a promising start but he injured a knee that required arthroscopic surgery. Later in the season he also pulled a rib-cage muscle. Despite the injuries, he played in 105 games and slugged 10 home runs.

Galarraga's career took off in 1987 when he played a full season, batted .300 for the first time (.305), knocked in 90 runs and finished second in the NL with 40 doubles. The next year he fully blossomed with his first All-Star berth while being named the Expos Player of the Year. He hit .302 with 29 home runs, 92 RBIs, and 99 runs scored while leading the league in hits (184) and doubles (42).

That was to be Galarraga's high point for the Expos as he suffered through injuries and a lack of production while leading the league in strikeouts for three consecutive years (1988-90). After knee surgery again during the 1991 season and the worst batting average of his career (.219) outside of his 1985 season, he was traded in November to the St. Louis Cardinals for pitcher Ken Hill.

The 1992 season started miserably as Galarraga broke his wrist in the second game of the year. When he returned from the injury he hit only .243 with 10 home runs and 39 RBIs. He did, however, meet the man who was to transform his game and his batting approach: St. Louis hitting coach Don Baylor. Baylor liked Galarraga and when he became the Colorado Rockies' first manager for their inaugural 1993 season, he persuaded team ownership to sign the player as a free agent following his release by the Cardinals.

Toward the end of Galarraga's tenure in St. Louis, Baylor got him to alter his batting stance. This transformed Galarraga's career: He hit .301 over his last 45 games. His stance was soon to be recognizable by baseball fans everywhere for its unconventionality. Baylor persuaded Galarraga to stand so that both eyes were facing the pitcher and then stride into the pitch from that stance.[10]

Galarraga signed as the Rockies' first free agent on November 16, 1992, one day prior to the expansion draft that produced the team's first-ever roster. With him coming off two subpar seasons in succession, the Rockies were able to sign Galarraga for a mere $600,000, probably the team's best-ever free-agent signing. Galarraga's 1993 contract included $250,000 in incentives, bringing his total to $850,000.[11]

Galarraga was 31 years old and his career was about to take off as he became an immediate fan favorite in the Rockies' inaugural season. He was the cleanup hitter for the Rockies' first game, against the New York Mets on April 5, 1993. It was the first of five consecutive Opening Day starts for the Big Cat as a member of the Rockies. With his new open stance paying huge dividends, Galarraga flirted with .400 for much of the season. He was hitting .391 at the All-Star break and became the Rockies' first participant in the midsummer classic.

He ended the season with a major-league-leading .370 batting average. He knocked in 98 runs, hit 22 home runs, and finished with a 1.005 OPS, the best of his career, all of this despite missing 42 games with two stints on the disabled list. During his second DL stint, the Rockies lost a team-record 13 consecutive games, a record that still stood as of 2018.[12]

His .370 batting average was the highest by a right-handed hitter since Joe DiMaggio hit .381 in 1939.[13] Galarraga was named the Comeback Player of the Year (the first of two such selections in his career) by *The Sporting News* and finished 10th in MVP voting.

Galarraga underwent yet another knee surgery during the offseason, but also capitalized on his 1993 year by signing a $12

"El Gran Gato" crushed 399 career homers and won two NL comeback player awards. Galarraga was a five-time All-Star and batting champ in 1993. (Jerry Coli / Dreamstime)

million, four-year contract in December 1993. With incentives and bonuses, Galarraga eventually made $17.2 million over the course of the next four years.[14]

During the Rockies' second season, which was cut short at midseason by the players strike, Galarraga had an April to remember. He drove in 30 runs during the month, a National League record that Barry Bonds was to break two years later. But he broke his hand on July 28 and when the strike began on August 12, his season was over. He did lead the Rockies in home runs with 31, hit .319, and knocked in 85 runs while playing in only 103 games.

The 1995 season was to be one of the most memorable in Rockies history with the opening of Coors Field in a renovated area of downtown Denver known as LODO, for lower downtown. Galarraga played a key role in the Rockies' playoff push culminating in their first appearance in postseason play.

He was also healthy for a full season for the first time in four years and produced again with a .280 average, 31 home runs, and 106 RBIs. Galarraga also led the league in strikeouts (146) for the fourth and last time in his career.

He became part of the Blake Street Bombers that year, a reference to the location of Coors Field at the corner of 20th and Blake. The Bombers consisted of Galarraga, Larry Walker, Vinny

Castilla, Dante Bichette, and Ellis Burks. In 1995 Galarraga, Bichette, Walker, and Castilla made major-league history and tied the 1977 Dodgers with four players on a team hitting 30 or more homers in the same season.

Galarraga also made more major-league history that year by hitting home runs in three consecutive innings against San Diego on June 23 to tie a National League record. Two weeks later he went 6-for-6 with two home runs and five RBIs against Houston on July 3.[15] (His six hits in a game for the Rockies were matched by Charlie Blackmon in 2014.)

The Rockies lost to eventual World Series champion Atlanta Braves in the Division Series.

The next year Galarraga led the NL in homers with 47 and RBIs with 150. He stroked 39 doubles and had a slugging percentage of .601 while playing in 159 games, the most of his career.

The 1997 season was Galarraga's last in Colorado. He went out with a flourish, leading the NL again in RBIs with 140, scoring 120 runs (the most of his career) and being named to his third All-Star team.

Galarraga hit the most famous of his many home runs, a grand slam, on May 31, 1997, off the Marlins' Kevin Brown at Pro Player Stadium in Miami. There is no doubt where he hit the ball — it landed 20 rows up in the upper deck on a blue tarp in a closed-off section — and while initial estimates put the distance at 573 feet, it was later recalculated at 529 feet and then recalibrated 14 years later using ESPN's Home Run Tracker at 468 feet.[16] However, a recent exhaustive study of the home run by Jose Lopez and others has seemingly answered the question once and for all. Lopez and his fellow authors used the latest LIDAR technology along with a 3D mathematical model to determine that his mammoth shot probably traveled 524 feet, making it "one of the few hit prior to Statcast proven to have exceed the 500-foot distance in the history of MLB."[17]

With young prospect Todd Helton on the horizon, the Rockies said goodbye to the Big Cat after the 1997 season. He signed with Atlanta in November and earned more than $25 million during the next three years with the Braves.

His initial season with the Braves saw him play in 153 games, hit .305, knock in 121 runs, and hit 44 homers. He made the All-Star team for the fourth time. He became the first major leaguer to hit 40 home runs in two consecutive seasons for different teams.

The 1999 season was a nightmare for the Big Cat. He missed the entire season after being diagnosed with non-Hodgkin's lymphoma in spring training. It had settled into his lower back on the second lumbar vertebra. He went through five months of chemotherapy and radiation. Yet he was determined to play baseball again and went through a rigorous rehabilitation routine at the Powerhouse Gym in West Palm Beach, where he lived in the offseason.[18] It was successful and he was back to playing baseball in the spring of 2000.

In the Braves' first game he hit the game-winning home run in the seventh inning and also provided a game-saving defensive gem in Greg Maddux's 2-0 win. He played in 141 games in his comeback season and received his second Comeback Player of the Year Award by hitting .302 with 28 home runs and 100 RBIs.

After the 2000 season Galarraga asked the Braves for a two-year contract. They offered only a one-year deal and Galarraga switched leagues for the first time in his career by signing with the Texas Rangers.

His did not adapt to the American League well and, with star Rafael Palmeiro a fixture at first base, he mostly DHed and pinch-hit. After 72 games and with a .235 batting average, 10 home runs, and 34 RBIs, the Rangers traded Galarraga back to the NL and the San Francisco Giants on July 24. He finished the season with the Giants playing in 49 games and hitting .288 with 7 more homers and 35 more RBIs.

A free agent again after the season, Galarraga signed with his original team, the Montreal Expos, in the spring of 2002. At 41 years old, he played in 104 games for the Expos and saw a decline in his batting numbers. He hit 9 homers, knocked in 40 runs, and batted .260.

The decline had begun and, although he managed to hang on and play 110 games with San Francisco in 2003, Galarraga was never again the player he was before going to the American League. He hit a respectable .301 with the Giants but his power numbers were fading. He hit 12 home runs with 42 RBIs in his last full season in the majors.

After the season, Galarraga once again faced cancer. After being diagnosed with the same form of non-Hodgkin's lymphoma in November, he spent most of January 2004 at the Robert H. Lurie Comprehensive Cancer Center at Northwestern University. He went through a stem-cell transplant and chemotherapy and radiation again.[19]

Not wanting to give up his baseball career yet, Galarraga battled back from his second bout with cancer and signed a contract with the Anaheim Angels' minor-league club in Salt Lake City. He was called up to the Angels when rosters expanded on September 1. He hit his final major-league home run, the 399th of his career, while getting 10 at-bats. His last major-league appearance came on October 3, 2004, 19 years after his first major-league game.

The next season Galarraga, at 43 years old, was invited to the New York Mets' spring training. Realizing it was the end of a long and productive career, he retired officially on March 29, 2005.[20]

Galarraga's final career numbers are impressive. He finished with a .288 career average, 399 home runs, and 1,425 RBIs. He had 444 doubles, 32 triples, and 128 stolen bases — not bad for someone once considered too chubby to play professional baseball.

Galarraga and his wife, Eneyda, whom he married on Valentine's Day 1984, took up residence in West Palm Beach after his retirement. They have three children. Katherine, Andria and Andrianna.

SOURCES

In addition to the sources cited in the Notes, the author also consulted Baseball-Reference.com and the following:

Beaton, Rod. "Galarraga Says Support Makes Me Feel So Strong," *USA Today*, March 18, 1999.

Heyman, Jon. "Big Cat's Doggedness Provides Inspiration," Newsday.com, January 14, 2005.

MacDonald, Ian. "Cooperstown Bound?" *The Sporting News*, July 4, 1988.

Price, S.L. "Cat and Mouth Game," *Sports Illustrated*, March 13, 2000.

Saunders, Patrick. "Andrés 'Big Cat' Galarraga Still a Big Hit in Denver," *Denver Post*, June 5, 2013.

Tucker, Tim. "Even Schuerholz, Kasten Are Moved by Galarraga," *Atlanta Journal Constitution*, April 4, 2000.

Vecsey, George. "Sports of the Times; Galarraga Brought Angels to the Gym," *New York Times*, June 28, 2000.

York, Marty. "Expos' Unknown Superstar," *Globe and Mail* (Toronto), June 10, 1988.

NOTES

1   Carlos Frias, "Beloved Big Cat," *Atlanta Constitution*, February 6, 2000.

2   Bob Kravitz, "Rocky Mountain High: Colorado Fans are Seeing Galarraga at His Peak," *Houston Chronicle*, June 27, 1993.

3   Felipe Alou, "Fat Cat Is Big Hit at Third in Venezuela," *Rocky Mountain News* (Denver), September 25, 2003.

4   Michael Farber, "Cat Quick," *Sports Illustrated*, June 2, 1997.

5   Jill Leiber, "The Big Cat," *USA Today*, August 27, 1998.

6   Farber.

7   Kravitz.

8   Leiber.

9   Kravitz.

10 Farber.

11 Doug Pappas, Baseball Reference website/SABR; John Mossman, "Galarraga Re-Signs with Rockies," *Deseret News* (Salt Lake City), December 7, 1993.

12 Mossman.

13 Morris Eckhouse, "The Ballplayers: Andrés Galarraga," Baseball Library.com.

14 Mossman, and Pappas.

15 Owen Perkins, "Rox Reflect Fondly on Blake Street Bombers," special to MLB.com, October 19, 2007.

16 Patrick Saunders, "Rockies Legend Andrés Galarraga Talks About His Famous Homer vs. Marlins," *Denver Post,* June 13, 2015.

17 Jose L. Lopez, Oscar A. Lopez, Elizabeth Raven, and Adrian Lopez, "Analysis of Andrés Galarraga's Home Run of May 31, 1997," *Baseball Research Journal*, 46 (2), (2017): 83-90.

18 Tracy Ringolsby, "Galarraga Diagnosed With Cancerous Tumor," *Rocky Mountain News* (Denver), February 19, 1999; Frias.

19 George Vecsey, "The Princely Smile Says Galarraga, the Big Cat, Is Back," *New York Times*, February 16, 2004.

20 Pat Borzi, "Galarraga Decides to Retire to Spare the Mets Some Angst," *New York Times*, March 30, 2005.

ARMANDO GALARRAGA

BY JUSTIN KRUEGER

Armando Antonio Galarraga was born on January 15, 1982, in Cumana, Sucre, Venezuela. His mother, Mariza, was a chemistry teacher and his father, Jose (known as Pepe) was a biologist.[1] The 6-foot-4 right-handed pitcher spent parts of six seasons in the major leagues. He is best known for what transpired on June 2, 2010, at Comerica Park in Detroit.

The first 26 Cleveland Indians had gone down in order and Galarraga was on the cusp of perfection. One out was all he needed to pitch the first perfect game in the then 109-year major-league history of the Detroit Tigers and only the 21st in major-league history. With two outs in the ninth inning, the 27th batter, Jason Donald, stepped to the plate and hit a grounder between first and second base. The ball was fielded cleanly by Tigers first baseman Miguel Cabrera and tossed to Galarraga, who was racing to cover first base. He reached first base a full step ahead of Donald for the out. But shock quickly reigned for the crowd of 17,000-plus at Comerica Park as well-respected umpire Jim Joyce inexplicably called Donald safe. Manager Jim Leyland rushed the field and yelled "Jimmy! You blew it! You blew it, go look at the video!"[2] It was all for naught, though, as the call stood. Donald was safe and the perfect game was no more.

The game continued. Galarraga went back to the mound to get one more out to close out the game. He retired Trever Crowe on a groundout to end the game for his first complete game and only career shutout. It took only 88 pitches. Galarraga's dominant outing lasted all of 1 hour and 44 minutes. He was named the American League Player of the Week for his efforts. Galarraga's baseball spikes, the first-base bag and a ball from the game were donated to the National Baseball Hall of Fame and Museum.[3]

Not shockingly, what happened at the game elicited a wide range of responses: Umpire Jim Joyce upon seeing the replay acknowledged, "It was the biggest call of my career, and I kicked the shit out of it. ... I just cost that kid a perfect game."[4] Galarraga, who did not argue the call, commented after the game, "I feel sad. I just watched the replay 20 times and there's no way you can call him safe."[5] He added, "nobody's perfect." When asked about the possibility of Major League Baseball reversing the call, New York Yankees manager Joe Girardi commented, "I think it's something that baseball should look at possibly because if they do change it, it doesn't affect the game. It doesn't affect the outcome."[6] Jason Donald, the player called safe, iterated, "I didn't know if I beat the throw or not ... but given the circumstances, I thought for sure I'd be called out."[7] Calling the game, Detroit Tigers radio announcer Jim Price said, "[Donald] was clearly out and the umpire called him safe. You got to be kidding me. Wow, an absolutely horrible call."[8]

Similarly, Fox Sports announcer Rod Allen said, "He hits the base. He's out. Why is he safe?"[9]

Politicians commented as well. Michigan Governor Jennifer Granholm commented, "He was robbed. But I'll declare it a perfect game."[10] And she did via a proclamation.[11] Even Venezuelan President Hugo Chavez contacted Galarraga after the game as a show of support.[12] The next day, Commissioner Bud Selig, while agreeing that the outcome should have been different, dismissed pleas for him to reverse the call, which was not reviewable in the game, saying it would set a bad precedent. A retired pitcher who lost a perfect game on the 27th batter in 1972 via a disputed umpire call, Milt Pappas, said of Selig: "What an idiot. How the hell can [Selig] not do that? What is it, the integrity of the game? I can't believe that, after the umpire even admitted what he did. [Joyce] ruined the kid's perfect game and said so. Unbelievable. It's too bad."[13] President Barack Obama chimed in as well by siding with Selig and suggesting that baseball move to incorporate replay, as both football and basketball had done.[14] The game led to increased calls for extended replay. Through it all, Galarraga showed remarkable sportsmanship. He did not eviscerate Joyce in the media as many others did, nor did he play the victim. When asked why he did not seem mad at Joyce, Galarraga simply replied, "He probably feels more bad than me."[15]

Galarraga had a six-year major-league career beyond that career-defining night. He played for four teams, the Texas Rangers, Detroit Tigers, Arizona Diamondbacks, and Houston Astros. It was most assuredly an up-and-down career. He consistently battled elbow injuries and even had Tommy John surgery. At his best, Galarraga had a good sinker and a hard-to-hit slider. Ricky Bones taught him the slider while he was in the Montreal Expos minor-league system.[16] But he struggled with control and a proclivity for allowing the long ball, and both often got him in trouble.

Prior to making it to the big leagues, Galarraga spent seven years in the minor leagues. He was initially signed in October 1998 as a 16-year-old amateur free agent by the Expos for a $3,000 signing bonus.[17] Fred Ferreira, the Montreal Expos international scouting director who signed Galarraga, noted that he had "a winner's handshake. He wasn't scared, and very confident of himself."[18] In 1999 and 2000 he spent time in the Venezuela Summer League, a rookie-ball league operated in Major-League Baseball's academies.

Galarraga's minor-league career started in earnest at 19 years old in 2001. From 2001 through 2003 he pitched in a handful of games in rookie ball for the Gulf Coast League Expos in Melbourne, Florida. Across three seasons with the GCL Expos he won two games and lost four. He ended with an ERA of less than 3.00 in 21 games (eight starts) and 53⅓ innings pitched. Injury concerns limited his action. After two starts in 2002, Galarraga required Tommy John surgery.

Pitching for the Class-A Savannah Sand Gnats in 2004, Galarraga put together a 5-5 record with a 4.65 ERA in 110⅓ innings pitched, including his first professional complete game. In 2005 he split time between the high Class-A Potomac Nationals and the Double-A Harrisburg Senators, ending the season with a combined 6-8 record and a 3.80 ERA. At Potomac Galarraga posted a 2.48 ERA in 14 starts before earning a promotion. In 13 starts after his call-up to Double A, he posted a 5.19 ERA. After the 2005 season he was traded by the Expos-turned-Washington Nationals to the Texas Rangers along with Terrmel Sledge and Brad Wilkerson for the right-handed power-hitting Alfonso Soriano.

Coming off an injury-free season in 2005, Galarraga entered the 2006 season as the number-7 prospect in the Rangers' minor-league system.[19] The high hopes associated with moving to a new team were short-lived. As in previous seasons, he was hampered by problems with his elbow and shoulder.[20] Galarraga logged innings in 2006 at four different levels as he rehabbed from injuries: rookie ball, low A, and high A, before spending the largest portion of the season with Double-A Frisco (Texas League). For the Roughriders he posted a 1-6 record with a 5.49 ERA in 41 innings pitched. Across all levels during the season he struggled. He limped to a 1-10 record with an ERA of 5.01, pitching 70 innings.

Even with the struggles of 2006, Galarraga entered 2007 as the Rangers number-15 overall prospect.[21] It would turn out to be his most successful professional season up to that point. Posting an 11-8 record with a combined ERA of 4.14 at Double-A Frisco and Triple-A Oklahoma City, Galarraga made 26 starts, pitched 152⅓ innings, and tossed three shutouts. He earned a September call-up to the Rangers.

Galarraga addresses the media after his near-perfect game in 2010. A missed call on the 27th out sparked national debate and admiration.

(Bill Eisern / Detroit Tigers via Getty Images)

Galarraga made his major-league debut on September 15, 2007, at age 25. Appearing in relief against the Oakland Athletics, he pitched a scoreless eighth inning, allowing only a walk. (The Rangers lost the game, 7-3.) It ended up being his best outing in his short tenure with the struggling Rangers. Appearing in a total of three games, Galarraga finished with a 6.23 ERA in 8⅔ innings, allowing eight hits and six runs, and walking seven. He served up two home runs in his introduction to the major leagues, echoing his penchant for allowing the long ball over his career. He was traded after the season to the Detroit Tigers for outfielder Michael Hernandez.

Galarraga's rookie season of 2008 with the Tigers earned the best single-season statistics of his major-league career. He had 13 wins against seven losses, a 3.73 ERA, 178⅔ innings pitched, and 152 hits allowed. He set career highs for games started (28) and total games (30). He finished in a tie for fourth in the American League Rookie of the Year voting with Mike Aviles finishing behind winner Evan Longoria, Alexei Ramirez, and Jacoby Ellsbury. He finished fourth in home runs allowed in the American League as hitters knocked 28 round-trippers off him. It was the last major-league season in which Galarraga posted a sub-4.00 ERA or a winning record. He achieved a career high of 126 strikeouts. Galarraga finished eighth in the American League in WHIP (walks and hits per innings pitched) at 1.192 and was second in the league in hits allowed per nine innings pitched (7.657) and opponents' batting average (.226).

Tabbed by manager Jim Leyland to start the home opener for the Tigers in 2009, Galarraga beat his old team the Rangers, 15-2. After which he commented that it "was an honor" to start the game and "that it came against Texas made it a little better."[22] He allowed one run in seven innings of five-hit ball. Starting the season in dominating fashion, Galarraga was 3-0 with a 1.85 ERA in April. But it did not last. Galarraga lost seven games in a row before recording his fourth win of the season on June 25 against the Chicago Cubs. His ERA ballooned to 5.50 over the early-season slide. In sum, Galarraga's second season with the Tigers was a struggle. It could be easily referred to as a "sophomore slump" along with battling pain in his right forearm.

In 2009 Galarraga's record dipped to 6 wins and 10 losses with a 5.64 ERA in 143⅔ innings pitched. He allowed 158 hits, of which 24 were home runs, and a career-high 67 walks. It was, however, the only year in which Galarraga spent the entire season in the major leagues. During all of his other major-league seasons, he spent time at the minor-league level. At the close of the season, he headed back to Venezuela and played winter ball for the Leones del Caracas. He would make the same decision four times over the next five years. His pitching line in Venezuela included a 4-8 record with a 5.34 ERA in 87⅔ innings pitched. Of the 26 games in which he pitched, 18 were starts.

After a rough start to 2010 spring training, Galarraga was cut from the major-league roster and sent to the Tigers' minor-league camp. Time in the minors appeared to help. He started the season strong in Toledo, and in seven starts he posted a 4-2 record with a 3.65 ERA and an uncharacteristically low four home runs surrendered. Galarraga was called back to the Tigers to make a few starts when Max Scherzer was optioned to Toledo.[23] For the third straight season, 2010 saw Galarraga's winning percentage dip, this time to a career major-league-low .308. With the Tigers he finished with a season record of 4-9 and a 4.49 ERA, the second lowest of his major-league career. The season, however, is almost singularly (as is his career) remembered for the perfect game that was not, which has also been referred to as the "Imperfect Game," the "Galarraga Game," and the "28 out Perfect Game." Continued bouts of inconsistency on the mound led the Tigers to trade Galarraga in January 2011 to the Arizona Diamondbacks for minor-league pitchers Kevin Eichhorn and Ryan Robowski.

Galarraga started the 2011 season as a starter for the Diamondbacks. After eight starts and 42⅔ innings with a record of 3-4 and a 5.91 ERA (13 home runs allowed), he was designated for assignment. He was sent down to the Triple-A affiliate Reno Aces, where in five starts he posted a 9.26 ERA and a 1-2 record. Galarraga was released after the season.

Galarraga signed with the Baltimore Orioles in January 2012 on a spring-training invite. He was released at the end of spring training after allowing 14 hits and 9 runs in 10 innings pitched. In May Galarraga signed with the pitching-starved Houston Astros. In 24 innings over five starts with the Astros, he surrendered 6 home runs and 18 earned runs, and went 0-4. When he pitched for the Astros on August 19, 2012, it was his last appearance in the major leagues. It was an 8-1 loss to the Arizona Diamondbacks. Galarraga's pitching line was 3⅔ innings pitched, six hits, and five runs, all earned. The loss dropped the Astros to 39-83 and 35 games behind the NL Central-leading Cincinnati Reds. Galarraga was designated for assignment three days later.

By age 30 Galarraga was out of the major leagues. But he did not quit pitching. For the next couple of years, he continued pitching in the minor leagues on the hope of a return to the majors. The Cincinnati Reds signed Galarraga to a minor-league deal in January 2013. At the end of spring training he was assigned to the Reds' Triple-A affiliate Louisville Bats. Galarraga put together a 6-6 record along with a 2.98 ERA and 62 strikeouts in 84⅔ innings. After two different stints on the disabled list (blister and right elbow strain), he was traded to the Colorado Rockies for pitcher Parker Frazier on July 15. He was assigned to the Rockies' Triple-A affiliate, the Colorado Springs Sky Sox. In seven starts he went 0-2 with a 5.20 ERA. Galarraga elected free agency in November 2013. Attempting one last return to the majors, he signed with the Texas Rangers on a minor-league deal in February 2014. He was released during spring training.

Galarraga retired after the 2015 season. Asked how he knew it was time to retire, he lamented, "[M]y arm is not the same. … It's tough, but you have to realize you're not at the same level to pitch to keep going, to push, to grind. For me, it was a lot of pain in my elbow."[24] He expressed a desire to be a pitching coach, and in 2016 he was a pitching coach for the Gulf Coast League Yankees.

Galarraga's major-league record was 26-34 (.433). He pitched in 100 games, of which 91 were starts. He had two complete games and one infamous shutout. Over 542 innings pitched in the major leagues, Galarraga allowed 536 hits, including 94 home runs. He walked 226 batters and struck out 346. His career ERA was 4.78. As a hitter Galarraga batted .000. He struck out 16 times in 31 at-bats. He did, however, walk three times, scored two runs, and had one run batted in. In the minors he had a .100 batting average with two singles in 20 at-bats.

Internationally, Galarraga played winter ball for several years in Venezuela with Leones de Caracas. He debuted with them in 1999 as a 17-year-old. He also suited up for Pericos de Puebla in the Mexican League in 2015. For Puebla, in what would turn out to be his last professional stint, Galarraga went 3-3 with a 3.75 ERA over 10 starts. He pitched 50⅓ innings before being released in June 2015. He also spent time in the Chinese Professional Baseball League, playing in Taiwan with the Chinatrust Brother Elephants in 2014.

In 2011, Galarraga, umpire Jim Joyce, and author Daniel Paisner collaborated on the Grove Press book *Nobody's Perfect: Two Men, One Call, and a Game for Baseball History*. It was a look back at the baseball careers of both men as well as their shared experience on and off the field since June 2, 2010.

SOURCES

In addition to the sources cited in the Notes, the author used information from the National Baseball Hall of Fame clippings file for Armando Galarraga, baseball-almanac.com, baseballamerica.com, baseball-reference.com, mlb.com, retrosheet.org, and thebaseballcube.com.

NOTES

1 Steve Kornacki, "Armando Galarraga Perseveres Through Injuries, Trades to Become Tigers' Top Pitcher," MLive, April 21, 2009. Retrieved from https://www.mlive.com/tigers/2009/04/armando_galarraga_perseveres_t.html.

2 Amy K. Nelson, "Searching for Meaning in the Mistake," espn.com, January 9, 2011. Retrieved from https://www.espn.com/espn/otl/news/story?id=5993137.

3 Associated Press, "Bagged! Hall of Fame to Get Base, Spikes of Armando Galarraga Gem," MLive, June 8, 2010. Retrieved from https://www.mlive.com/tigers/2010/06/bagged_hall_of_fame_to_get_bas.html.

4 Associated Press, "Armando Galarraga Robbed of a Perfect Game," CBS News, June 3, 2010. Retrieved from http://www.cbsnews.com/stories/2010/06/03/sportsline/main6543410.shtml.

5 "Armando Galarraga Robbed of a Perfect Game."

6 "Armando Galarraga Robbed of a Perfect Game."

7 "Armando Galarraga Robbed of a Perfect Game."

8 "In-Game Reaction to Blown Call from Tigers Announcers," *Detroit Free Press*, June 2, 2010. Retrieved from Armando Galarraga's Hall of Fame clippings file.

9   "In-Game Reaction to Blown Call from Tigers Announcers."

10   Kathy Gray, "Granholm Declares Near-Perfect Game a Historic Moment," *Detroit Free Press*, June 3, 2010. Retrieved from Armando Galarraga's Hall of Fame clippings file.

11   Jake Sherman, "Michigan Pols Lobby Baseball on Perfect Game," Politico, June 3, 2010. Retrieved from https://www.politico.com/blogs/on-congress/2010/06/michigan-pols-lobby-baseball-on-perfect-game-027372.

12   Armando Galarraga, "Tigers Hurler Galarraga Chats with Fans," MLB.com, June 16, 2010.

13   Willie Weinbaum and the Associated Press, "Selig Won't Reverse the Call," espn.com, June 3, 2010. Retrieved from http://sports.espn.go.com/espn/print?id=5248II&type=story.

14   Mark W. Smith, "Obama: Selig Made Right Call to Hold Back Perfect Game," *Detroit Free Press*, June 8, 2010.

15   Craig Calcaterra, "Kentucky Derby DQ Brings Armando Galarraga and Jim Joyce to Mind," NBC Sports, May 5, 2019. Retrieved from https://mlb.nbcsports.com/2019/05/05/kentucky-derby-dq-brings-armando-galarraga-and-jim-joyce-to-mind/.

16   Steve Kornacki, "Armando Galarraga Perseveres Through Injuries, Trades to Become Tigers' Top Pitcher."

17   Jim Hawkins, "Detroit Tigers Pitcher Armando Galarraga Is a Most Unlikely Hero," *Oakland Press* (Troy, Michigan), June 12, 2010. Retrieved from https://www.theoaklandpress.com/news/jim-hawkins-detroit-tigers-pitcher-armando-galarraga-is-a-most/article_8471fa58-47a9-53c3-9e24-d5e354fa861f.html.

18   Amy K. Nelson, "Galarraga Ready for the Next Chapter," espn.com, June 9, 2010. Retrieved from https://www.espn.com/mlb/news/story?id=5265148.

19   Jim Callis, Will Lingo, and John Manuel, eds., *Baseball America Prospect Handbook 2007*, 447.

20   John Sickels, "Not a Rookie: Armando Galarraga," SB Nation, February 9, 2009. Retrieved from https://www.minorleagueball.com/2009/2/19/764282/not-a-rookie-armando-galar.

21   *Baseball America Prospect Handbook 2007*, 456.

22   Kornacki, "Armando Galarraga Perseveres."

23   "Armando Galarraga Perseveres."

24   George Sipple, "Armando Galarraga Retires, Wants to Be Pitching Coach, *Detroit Free Press*, December 7, 2015. Retrieved from https://www.freep.com/story/sports/mlb/tigers/2015/12/07/armando-galarraga-retires-detroit-tigers/76929124/.

RICH GARCÉS

BY BILL NOWLIN

Rich Garcés – beloved as "El Guapo" during his time as a relief pitcher for the Boston Red Sox – enjoyed a professional baseball career that saw him play minor-league ball, Venezuelan Winter League ball, independent baseball, and 10 seasons of major-league baseball.

Richard Aron Garcés Mendoza was born in Maracay, Venezuela, on May 18, 1971, a city west of Caracas on the way to Valencia and the capital of Aragua State. Other ballplayers from Maracay include Bobby Abreu, Miguel Cabrera, and Carlos Guillen.

Rich was the oldest of four children born to Fanny Maria Mendoza and Jesus Aron Garcés. His father worked in construction, building houses and other structures. Baseball was something Rich fell in love at a very early age. "I started baseball when I was 4 years old. It was just something I really wanted to do – hit the ball, catch the ball, throw the ball – to have some fun out there in the field. Since I was 4 years old, I drove my dad and my mom crazy wanting to play baseball. That's what I did."[1]

While he was still a young teenager, Rich attended a number of tryouts hosted by several major-league teams, such as the St. Louis Cardinals. After a few of them, he was starting to get a little discouraged – though he was just 16 years old. "I went to a lot of tryouts. I told my mom, 'The Minnesota Twins is going to be my last tryout. If I sign, I sign. If I don't, I'll just go back to school and continue my studying.' My mom told me, 'No, you can make it. You can make it. It's going to happen.'"[2]

Twins scout Enrique Brito noticed Garcés, and signed him about three weeks later. He had seen something in Garcés, who was an outfielder at the time. "Brito saw me throwing from the outfield. He told me, "Hey, you've got a pretty good arm. You want to throw from the mound and show me what you got?" I was so skinny. I was like 150 pounds. I was really skinny when I started. I had never pitched before, but he asked me, 'You want to try it from the mound and see what happens?' I was, 'OK, man. Let's try it and see what happens.' I threw a couple of pitches – 84, 85. ... He was like, 'You look good. You look good, man.'" Brito asked him if he could throw even a little harder, but Rich had already put in a full workout, running the 60 and throwing from the outfield. He was tired.

Brito told him he'd be coming back in 15 or 20 days and that he'd like to see him throw more from the mound. He returned, and liked what he saw. Garcés had gotten the gun up to 86 or so. Brito offered a contract for $3,500. "I told my mom, 'Hey, this is an opportunity that I have. I really want it. What do you think?' She said, "That's your future. Don't worry about me. I'll sign it for you.' I was underage. Sixteen years old. So she signed it for me. Thirty-five hundred dollars. After that, it was like, 'Okay!' I just really had one thing in my mind. This is an opportunity. If this is going to be my future, I'll take it. It didn't matter how much it was. I thought it was a good chance for, to come up here [to the United States] and play the game that I really love.'"[3]

The young right-hander was signed by Twins scout Brito on December 29, 1987. In 1988 the Twins assigned him to the rookie-ball Elizabethton (Tennessee) Twins (Appalachian League). He pitched in 17 games, starting three and closing 10. His record was 5-4 with a 2.29 ERA, and he struck out 69 batters in 59 innings.

Garcés faced acculturation problems, coming as a teenager to a country where he didn't speak the language well, and needing to adapt. Fortunately, Brito looked out for him. At one point, Garcés recalled, "They wanted me to go to Low-A ball, but I was going to be the only Latino in Low-A ball so Enrique told them no. My English was not good. That's one of the things I was really afraid of. I was going to be by myself and they didn't have any Latinos on the A-ball team. Enrique told me, 'Hey, I talked to a guy upstairs and they told me you should stay here for the rest of the year.' The next year, my velocity went up and before you know it, I was throwing 93, 94, 95. It was good."[4]

In 1989 Garcés pitched in Wisconsin for the Kenosha Twins in the Class-A Midwest League. He started 24 games, working 142⅔ innings. He was 9-10 (3.41) with four complete games and one shutout, a one-hitter against the Rockford Expos on August 27. But in 1990, the Twins converted him to a closer. In the minor leagues, he had no starts among his 62 games (56 of them finishing games). For advanced Class-A Visalia, he had a 1.81 ERA, making the league's all-star team; after 47 games with them, he was promoted to Double-A Orlando (Southern League) and worked to a 2.08 ERA over another 15 appearances. The 36 saves he recorded for Visalia and Orlando combined helped earn him the award of Rolaids relief pitcher of the year in the minor leagues.[5]

Garcés was brought to the big leagues and debuted for the Twins on September 18, 1990, in a night game at the Metrodome in Minneapolis. There was far from any pressure involved; the Twins held a 10-4 lead over the visiting Royals after eight innings. Garcés pitched the top of the ninth. He got the first two batters out, gave up a walk and a single, and then secured the third out without a runner advancing past second base.

He appeared in four more games, working two innings without a hit on the 22nd, giving up one run in two-thirds of an inning on the 26th, and then adding an inning each in two October games. His earned-run average in 5⅔ innings was 1.59. In 1990 he married for the first time.

That winter Garcés played for Aragua in the Venezuelan winter league. Despite showing well, he spent two more years in the minor leagues before returning to the majors. In 1991 he faced another challenge. In April, *The Sporting News* reported that the Twins' "closer of the future" had returned to Venezuela soon after starting the early season with the Triple-A Portland Beavers (Pacific Coast League). Twins GM Andy MacPhail said, "It's a delicate situation. We have to fine him but we don't want it to be too punitive."[6] Garcés's wife was pregnant, and he had run up some big telephone bills and he had reportedly left without informing club officials. Portland manager Russ Nixon said, "As far as I'm concerned, he's not a part of this club. I don't care if he ever comes back."[7] He had appeared in 10 games for Portland (0-1, with a 4.85 ERA). When Garcés returned after an absence of about a month, he was demoted to Orlando, where he appeared in 10 games with a 3.31 ERA. But that wasn't the story as Garcés explained it in late 2018. He said he'd had a "little confrontation" with the manager, after he was told on the very last day of spring training that they had signed someone else with more experience. He was upset, got angry, and flew home, admitting, though, "I was a kid, missing my family so much."[8]

Brito accompanied Garcés back to the States. "After that, I was fine. It was difficult for me because the language was hard. At the time, it was kind of hard to speak English. I was really frustrated at that time. But it's like anything else in life. You've got to go on. You've got to learn the language. You've got to socialize with the rest of the team. They told me, 'You've got to learn English. You've got to have communication with the catchers. With the infield. With the whole team.'" He bought some books, and a few of his teammates told him they would help teach him English. "A lot of guys wanted to help me with my English. I started learning. Everything got better."[9]

Still working exclusively in relief, Garcés spent the full 1992 season with Orlando once more and struggled there again, working in 58 games (closing 42) with a 4.54 ERA. His stock had indeed fallen. There was an expansion draft held that fall, and the Twins did not protect him. He was not selected by another team.

Garcés started the 1993 season with the big-league club in Minnesota but – even though he worked four innings in April and May without giving up an earned run – he was asked to spend the rest of the year in Portland. There he started seven games and relieved in 28. His ERA was a very discouraging 8.33. In 1994 Garcés dropped down a level to Double-A Nashville. In 40 appearances (only one of them a start), he posted a 3.72 ERA. On October 25 the Twins cut their ties to Rich Garcés and released him.

Garcés pitched winter ball again and in January, it was reported that he was "burning up the Venezuelan Winter League as a reliever," the author adding, "He ate himself out of the Twins' organization as a homesick youth, but reports indicate Garcés is in shape and throwing as hard as ever."[10]

Three months later, in January 1995, Garcés signed as a free agent with the Chicago Cubs. He pitched well for the Triple-A Iowa Cubs in Des Moines, working in 23 games with an ERA of 2.86. When Steve Buechele went on the disabled list, the Cubs called up Garcés and he appeared again in a major-league game on June 27. Over the next three-plus weeks, he pitched in seven games for the Cubs and worked a total of 11 innings, with just one poor outing. His ERA was a good 3.27, but the Cubs decided to go with Terry Adams and placed Garcés on waivers. On August 9 he was selected by the Florida Marlins.

After his first eight outings for the Marlins, Garcés was again with a 3.27 ERA and had earned his first hold, on August 28. In September he had his first decisions, both losses. Again, one bad outing cost him one of the two games and left him at season's end with a 4.44 earned-run average.

Garcés became a free agent in November, and in December signed with the Boston Red Sox. Oakland's Billy Beane was unhappy that Boston outbid him, saying, "If he keeps his weight down, he can be a force in anyone's bullpen."[11] Garcés is listed as standing an even 6 feet tall and weighing 250 pounds.

He began the 1996 season with Pawtucket, but was called up in late April and through May had borne a couple of more losses in the majors, with a 4.91 ERA. On June 7 he got his first big-league win by being the pitcher of record when the Red Sox scored four runs in the bottom of the eighth inning (on a pair of two-run homers) to take a 10-7 lead over visiting Milwaukee. Heathcliff Slocumb threw the ninth and preserved the win for Garcés.

Garcés won again on June 26, beating Cleveland thanks to another two-run homer, hit by Tim Naehring in the bottom of the 15th inning.

After experiencing some tightness in his throwing arm, Garcés spent about a month on a rehab assignment with Triple-A Pawtucket (4-0, 2.30) but returned to Boston and picked up a third win on August 20. Another injury, a strained muscle in his rib cage, troubled him in early September. He finished the season 3-2, 4.91.

In 1997, when the Red Sox broke camp, they left Garcés behind. *Boston Globe* sportswriter Gordon Edes wrote, "Word is, general manager Dan Duquette was upset that Garcés was 8 pounds overweight. … [He] apparently not only didn't lose weight in camp, he put more on."[12] He was put on the disabled list and then had a rehab assignment with Pawtucket. Garcés came up at the very end of April and – appearing in 12 games – was 0-1 (4.61) through June 1. He was placed on waivers, cleared them, was outrighted to Pawtucket, and spent the remainder of the season there, 2-1 (1.45).

By 1998 Garcés he was being called "El Guapo" (The Handsome One) by his teammates. It was also, perhaps more pertinent to the time it was first bestowed on him, "the name of the villain in the movie *Three Amigos*, whom his teammates decided he resembled." Edes said he "resembles an overripe eggplant."[13] Garcés said he was pleased to be in Boston. "I'm

Beloved by fans as "El Guapo," Rich Garcés was a reliable setup man for the Red Sox. He posted a 3.74 ERA over 10 big-league seasons.
(Courtesy Boston Red Sox)

The Red Sox got to play in the postseason, beating the Cleveland Indians in the American League Division Series. Garcés got the win in Game Four with 2⅓ innings of one-run relief in a 23-7 laugher. His fondest memory, though, was a game the team lost – Game Four of the ALCS against the Yankees. New York was leading, 3-2, in the top of the eighth, and had the bases loaded with just one out. Garcés induced Scott Brosius to pop up to second base and then struck out Chad Curtis. "That was the best game I ever had in my life. It was a dream come true, a game I'll never forget."[18]

El Guapo's 2000 season saw him set career highs, both in innings pitched (74⅔) and wins (he was 8-1 with a 3.25 earned-run average.)[19] Only Pedro Martinez and his brother Ramon Martinez had more wins for the Red Sox. Garcés was often used as a set-up man for closer Derek Lowe. The Red Sox lost him for nearly two weeks in September, due to a groin injury. They finished just 2½ games behind the Yankees. He was a very popular player with fans at Fenway Park, and with the media. "Only in a place like Boston could a middle reliever be as popular as the mayor," observed one sportswriter.[20] After the 2000 season, he was given the Tommy McCarthy Good Guy Award.

In 2001, pitching on another one-year contract that pretty much doubled his 2000 salary, Garcés again had just one loss. In June he was on the disabled list again, this time with a right hamstring pull. He won six games during the 2001 season and had an ERA of 3.90. Michael Silverman of the *Boston Herald* wrote of him in early September, "By mixing up his big-breaking curveball and tough splitter, Garcés has been a stopper in most every setup situation in which he has been used. He is particularly tough on lefthanded hitters, which is one reason the club has not fretted over its inability to acquire a reliable lefthanded specialist this year. But given his portly build, the club is leery of using Garcés on back-to-back days for fear he will break down."[21]

There was kind of a bizarre moment in August when *ESPN The Magazine* ran a poll asking "Whom do you want to win the home run race?" The winner, with 55 percent of the vote, was Arizona's Luis Gonzalez. Voters showing a sense of humor saw Rich Garcés came in second with 14.9 percent. Barry Bonds was third with 13.6 percent.[22]

Garcés's last season in the major leagues was 2002. He entered the year in something of a bad mood, because the Red Sox had declined to sign him to a multiyear deal, and declared that he wanted to be traded.[23] Garcés reported some 35 pounds lighter, but may have put most of that weight back on early in the year. He appeared in 26 games, hampered by a reported strained right hamstring in June, and was 0-1 (but with a 7.59 ERA that brought about his designation for a minor-league assignment). At one point in May, he gave up 13 earned runs in 12 appearances. In June manager Grady Little had said, "I see a kid who doesn't have a lot of confidence in his face and demeanor, like he did in the past. He used to have that bounce in his step when he got people out."[24] Garcés himself said it was another hamstring injury. Garcés declined the assignment

very happy here. I've never been as comfortable as I've been here."[14] He didn't give up an earned run in all of spring training.

Garcés's 1998 saw him with two stretches in Pawtucket (frustrating him greatly, since he had not been injured and was essentially being parked there on what his agent said was a specious rehab assignment – specious because the team had never had Garcés consult a doctor)[15] but appearing in 30 games for Boston (1-1, 3.33). Regarding Garcés's girth, teammate Vaughn Eshelman said, "You can talk about size all you want. It's what you do on the field. And the kid has a big heart."[16]

At one point Garcés was deemed "almost unhittable," but in early August had to go on the DL and he had arthroscopic surgery to have bone chips removed from his right elbow in September.[17] At the end of the year, the Red Sox released him, but three months later he was re-signed.

Garcés started 1999 with Pawtucket but just before the All-Star break was brought back to Boston and had an excellent season, mostly working as a seventh- or eighth-inning reliever. He appeared in 30 games, with an ERA of 1.55 and a final record of 5-1. The Red Sox had made a race of it, finishing just four games behind the division-leading New York Yankees, and Garcés had been a significant part of their success.

and he was formally released on August 5. Interim GM Mike Port seemed to be more than a little miffed, saying, "Different people react to challenges differently. We'll take the guys who are willing to fight the battle and be part of this."[25] Relations had apparently deteriorated. When he was let go, Garcés said that Grady Little "didn't say anything to me. One of the reasons I left [is] that they never really respected me."[26]

It was disappointing all the way around. In another article, Hohler noted that the Red Sox season somewhat fell apart due a few factors, one of them being "the complete failure" of Garcés, who had "entered the season as one of the league's premier setup men."[27]

Come November, Garcés was pitching for Aragua again in Venezuelan Winter League ball – perhaps ironically working under manager Buddy Bailey, who would have been his manager in Pawtucket had he gone there.

The Colorado Rockies were prepared to give Garcés a look, signing him in January 2003, but he failed to show up for his physical exam in Tucson, did not report, and announced his retirement through his agent in February. The Rockies released him in March. His major-league career was over. He was a good fielding pitcher, committing only one error in 69 chances (.986). He had only three plate appearances in his entire big-league career, grounding out once for the Cubs in 1995 and then batting twice in interleague play for Boston in 2001. He struck out once and grounded into a double play the other time. His career won-lost record was 23-10 (3.74).

Garcés did not pitch in Organized Baseball in either 2003 or 2004, though in November 2004 he pitched for Magallanes in the Venezuelan Winter League. He had 14 saves.

There was some drama in January 2005. Garcés went missing. A report in the January 27 *Boston Herald* said that he had been missing since the 17th and that his family hadn't heard from him. After a Magallanes game against Caracas, he disappeared. His wife, wrote Jeff Horrigan, "is said to have filed a police report. The disappearance is troubling due to the rash of kidnappings that have taken place in South American involved high-profile athletes and their families." He noted that Ugueth Urbina's mother had been kidnapped only four months earlier. Garcés's agent, Jeff Borris, was "stunned" to hear of his disappearance.[28] It was apparently not a kidnapping at all. He'd gone to a beach party. For days. "A Red Sox official with knowledge of the affair said that family problems may have been behind Garcés' absence," concluded a story in the *Globe*.[29]

On May 27, 2005, the Red Sox signed Garcés as a free agent. It was a very modest contract, said to be for about $2,500 per month. Gabe Kapler faced him in July and said he looked good, "very similar to what I've always known Rich Garcés to be."[30] He pitched three innings over three games in the Gulf Coast League (rookie league), but advanced no further and was released at the end of August.

A broken hand kept Garcés out of winter ball in 2005-06, but in 2006-07 and 2007-08, he pitched in Maracaibo for Aguilas del Zulia in the Venezuela Winter League. In the 2006-07 season, he was 3-1 (2.31) with 11 saves.

In 2007 Garcés returned to New England and worked in 36 games for the Nashua Pride, in the independent Canadian-American Association. The team was managed by former Red Sox third baseman Butch Hobson. Garcés said he was hoping to make it back to the major leagues. "That's my goal right now. I can't think about retirement right now. I'm only 35. I'm still throwing 93, 94. … There are a lot of guys 39, 40, 41 years old who are still pitching in the big leagues."[31] He was 6-4 (4.42).

The following year (2008), after another winter-league season for Zulia, Garcés pitched for Nashua in 16 more games (1-0, 3.71). He also pitched in 13 games for the Potros de Tijuana in Mexican League baseball. They were his last games in professional baseball.

His pitching career over, Garcés decided he wanted to take up coaching. "Coaching's going to be a chance to give back, to share my experience from all those years in the big leagues. And I might have a shot to get back to the big leagues. You never know. Maybe a pitching coach, maybe a bullpen coach. Whatever. I decided to be a coach and that's what I have been doing.

"I coached for Zulia for a couple of years. I worked with the Leones de Caracas for two years as the pitching coach. The third year with them, I was the bullpen coach. Last year [2017], Luis Rodriguez was the manager of the Bridgeport Bluefish here in the Atlantic League. We talked about it in the wintertime and he told me, 'Hey, compadre, why don't you come with me to the Atlantic League? I'm going to be the manager. You take care of the pitchers.'"[32]

Garcés and his second wife, Yesenia, got a place in Fairfield, Connecticut, where they live with two of his daughters. He has worked as pitching coach for the Bluefish, working also with former major-league pitcher Mike Porzio, who built an academy called The Clubhouse in Fairfield. Garcés is the academy's MLB Pitching Instructor.[33] "I'm happy, man. I'm happy. That's why I'm walking with my head high. I do what I can. I'd even go out there with a broken leg. As long as I'm pitching, it makes me happy."

In a November 2018 interview, Garcés was looking forward to returning to Fort Myers and taking part in Red Sox Fantasy Camp, which he had done for three prior years. He said he enjoyed the interactions with the campers and seeing and playing baseball with some of his old teammates.[34]

One of Rich's brothers, Jesus Garcés, was in 2018 working as a scout for the Detroit Tigers organization. Rich himself continued to credit his family for his success in baseball: "The people who helped me the most in my long career is my mom and my dad. One of my brothers was a big factor in that. He helped me in a lot of ways when I really needed it. When I was down, he was there for me."

Naturally, at the time of the interview, he expressed his hopes to continue to coach, and perhaps before too long be invited to sign on for a return trip to the major leagues, this time as a coach or instructor.

In October 2020, Garcéss began working for Denis Boucher on the coaching staff at CTEdge Baseball Academy, which maintains a complex of five fields, an indoor dome, and a full basebll field house with batting cages and the like in North Branford, Connnecticut.

SOURCES

In addition to the sources noted in this biography, the author also accessed Garcés's player file from the National Baseball Hall of Fame, the *Encyclopedia of Minor League Baseball*, Retrosheet.org, and Baseball-Reference.com. Thanks to Rod Nelson of SABR's Scouts Committee.

NOTES

1   Rich Garcés, interview with author on November 13, 2018.

2   Garcés interview.

3   Garcés interview.

4   Garcés interview.

5   "Aguilera Seeking Tendinitis Remedy," *The Sporting News*, October 1, 1990: 16.

6   Jeff Lehman, "Minnesota Twins," *The Sporting News*, April 15, 1991: 21.

7   "Falling Stock," *The Sporting News*, July 8, 1991: 36.

8   Garcés interview.

9   Garcés interview.

10 Joe Goddard, "Chicago Cubs," *The Sporting News*, January 30, 1995: 45.

11 Peter Gammons, "Red Sox Had Better Mind Their Business." *Boston Globe*, November 19, 1995: 61.

12 Gordon Edes, "Leading the Way," *Boston Globe*, March 31, 1997: 50.

13 Gordon Edes, "Garcés in Thick of Things in Pen," *Boston Globe*, March 18, 1998: 78. The nickname was reportedly first bestowed by Mike Maddux. See Sean Deveney, "The Book On … Rich Garcés," *The Sporting News*, July 10, 2000: 22.

14 "The Book On … Rich Garcés."

15 Gordon Edes, "Frustrated Garcés Wants Out," *Boston Globe*, May 6, 1998: 49.

16 Gordon Edes, "Sox Crest as They Ride Home," *Boston Globe*, June 3, 1988: 49.

17 Paul Doyle used the phrase in the June 29, 1998, *Sporting News* on page 36.

18 Gordon Edes, "Castoff Joins a Cast of Characters," *Boston Globe*, July 28, 2002: 57. What he may have forgotten is the top of the ninth, when he left with the bases loaded,after which Rod Beck gave up a grand slam to pinch-hitter Ricky Ledee. The Yankees won the game, 9-2.

19 In Fort Myers on March 14, 2000, he joined five other Red Sox pitchers in throwing a perfect game against the Toronto Blue Jays.

20 Gordon Edes, "Castoff Joins a Cast of Characters."

21 Michael Silverman, "Rotation Regains Martinez and Loses Saberhagen in a Matter of Days," *The Sporting News*, September 3, 2001: 22.

22 Tom FitzGerald, "South Korean Archers in Gutter," *San Francisco Chronicle*, August 24, 2001: 68.

23 Michael Silverman, "Boston Red Sox," *The Sporting News*, February 4, 2002: 57.

24 Gordon Edes, "Where's Guapo's Game?" *Boston Globe*, June 2, 2002: 62.

25 Bob Hohler, "Players Will OK Steroid Testing," *Boston Globe*, August 8, 2002: 69.

26 Tom King, "Pride Sign Former Sox Reliever Garcés," *Nashua (New Hampshire) Telegraph*, February 21, 2007.

27 "Sox Must Rearm for '03," *Boston Globe*, September 24, 2002: 70.

28 Jeff Horrigan, "Ex-Sox Garcés Missing," *Boston Herald*, January 27, 2005. http://bostonherald.com/redSox/view.bg?articleid=65426&-format=text.

29 "It Can Be a Dangerous Game in Venezuela," *Boston Globe*, January 30, 2005: 42.

30 Chris Snow, "Garcés Eyeing a Big Comeback," *Boston Globe*, August 5, 2005: 31.

31 Tom King, "Pride Sign Former Sox Reliever Garcés."

32 Garcés interview.

33 See The Clubhouse at http://www.theclubhousect.com/.

34 Rich Garcés, interview with author, November 27, 2018.

CARLOS GARCÍA

BY LUIS BLANDÓN

The Pan-American Highway cuts through the northern Andes state of Tachira in western Venezuela, facing Colombia.[1] The capital city of San Cristobal hovers 2,694 feet above the Torbes River, developing its own unique identity, more Colombian than Venezuelan. It was here on October 15, 1967, that Carlos Jesus García Guerrero was born.[2] During his childhood, the family moved 815 miles east to Ciudad Bolivar, a tropical city on the south bank of the Orinoco River, neighboring Guyana.[3]

García's initial baseball forays occurred in the family's backyard, where the García brothers "kept themselves entertained by playing bottle cap baseball and throwing any piece of cowhide that came into their possession."[4] As a teenager, "I did not ever think I would play baseball. With my mother, it was school first, baseball later," García once said.[5] But he played baseball while attending Escuela Bolivar.[6]

García was 14 when he watched, on television, Venezuelan shortstop Dave Concepción become the MVP of the 1982 All-Star Game. García was hooked: "It was like I was dreaming awake. I thought, 'I wish I could have the opportunity to be in one of those games.' … But at the same time, I thought, 'How can that happen?'"[7] García wore number 13 as a tribute to Concepción: "He made me dream about being a major-league player."[8]

Scouts for the Pittsburgh Pirates saw him playing softball at a local university and "ask(ed) me to play professional baseball. 'I can try,' I said.'"[9] The Pirates signed García as a non-drafted free agent on January 9, 1987. He was 19. He climbed the minor-league ladder, debuting in the majors in 1990. As he progressed, García "would find himself sitting with his nose pressed firmly against the window of the major leagues."[10] García returned home annually to play winter ball in the Liga Venezolana de Béisbol Profesional (LVBP) "for my home crowd, my friends and family and give back to Venezuelan baseball."[11] To Venezuelans, García became known as "El Almirante" (The Admiral).[12]

For the 1987 season, the Pirates sent the scrawny right-handed-throwing and -batting García to their Class-A South Atlantic League affiliate at Macon, where he was "lost in a strange land without so much as a word of English in his vocabulary."[13] Baseball was his only companion. He remembered, "[T]he first year was tough."[14] It was the first time García had left Venezuela. He was bewildered and could not read the newspapers, order food, or ask for directions. "He just wanted someone he could trust – someone who could call him and that he could develop a relationship with," said his agent, Peter Greenberg.[15] Manager Dennis Rogers was a mentor, picking up García at his home each day, and teaching García about life outside baseball.[16]

García demonstrated a work ethic and willingness to learn off and on the field. The next season the Macon franchise was transferred to Augusta and García was the starting shortstop. His play earned him a promotion to the Salem Buccaneers of the advanced Class-A Carolina League to finish the season.[17] Pirates general manager Syd Thrift saw García as "a definite major-league prospect," saying, "He'll play in the majors, and he'll play there for a long time."[18] García began the 1989 season with Salem, but in midseason was elevated to the Double-A the Harrisburg Senators (Eastern League). He began the 1990 campaign with Harrisburg performing well and earned another midseason promotion, to the Triple-A Buffalo Bisons. Teams began to ask the Pirates about García's availability in a trade. The Pirates' response was succinct: "[H]e isn't."[19] In fact García was called up to the majors on September 20, debuting that day as a pinch-hitter, collecting a single in his first major-league at-bat against Cubs pitcher Bill Long. García savored the experience, knowing "I was prepared mentally."[20]

In García's file at the National Baseball Hall of Fame, White Sox scouting reports on him from 1991 jump out. One described him as a "big man who can play SS position (with) RBI potential" and a player with the needed hands, arm and range "to be a 1st div. SS." At the plate, García was "similar to Ripken, but faster and not quite Ripken power."[21] Another scout viewed García as a prospect whose attitude was "fair," who hustled with "above av. speed and arm strength" with "fairly good hands & agility," but was "laid back on some ground balls" and his "bat contact [was] below average."[22]

As spring training opened in 1991, García was fully formed at 6-feet-1 and 185 pounds with a physique comparable to his hero Concepción. He began the season with the Bisons, endearing himself to the fans by his play on the field. In a game against the Louisville Sluggers on May 3, Sluggers starting pitcher Al Nipper was being shelled by the Bisons when in the bottom of the fifth, he hit García with a fastball "between the shoulder blades."[23] García "strolled slowly up the line" to first base.[24] Pleasantries were exchanged. When García stole second, additional vitriol spewed. Nipper motioned García to fight. García charged Nipper, landing a punch. Both were ejected.[25] García missed the next two games with a partially dislocated left shoulder after reporting tenderness, and needed surgery in the offseason to repair the damage.[26] He was called up twice by the Pirates, appearing in 12 games.

García's connection to Buffalo was cemented by more than his on-field prowess: he met Buffalo native Catherine Curran at a postgame concert by the rock band Chicago in August 1990. The couple "met through one of her friends and ex-Bison reliever Miguel García. Soon they were inseparable."[27] Catherine was a local attending the University of Buffalo with a desire to go to law school. On October 22, 1993, they married in her hometown of Lancaster, a Buffalo suburb, honeymooning in the Greek Islands.[28]

In 1992, García, still unmarried, was slated to be the Pirates' utility player, but manager Jim Leyland felt García would be better served by playing every day in Buffalo, and García was sent down. He had "a penchant for getting down on himself."[29] When asked about the demotion, García said, "[I]t's a little disappointing because I worked so hard in the spring and everything went so well. … My girlfriend is from Buffalo, so that's a good thing about it."[30]

García's best season with Buffalo resulted.[31] He was selected to the 1992 Triple-A All-Star Game. On August 30 the Pirates called up the 24-year-old García.[32] He played in the postseason, appearing in the second game of the NL Championship Series against the Atlanta Braves, going 0-for-1, playing second. It was his only postseason appearance. Though he was a member of two NL East championship teams, García "didn't feel like part of the celebration because of his limited contributions."[33]

García was at the stage that playing in Buffalo served no purpose. Jay Bell was entrenched as the Pirates shortstop. Room had to be made for García. Pirates GM Ted Simmons noted that "Carlos earned the right to play at the major league level and play every day. … We need to make room for him."[34] The Pirates traded All-Star second baseman José Lind to Kansas City, and slotted García as his replacement in 1993. García sensed this was the moment: "This is payment for six years' work in the minors. God, thank you."[35]

García represented the Pirates's future. As an everyday player, he produced. On April 16, 1993, García hit his first major-league home run, an inside-the-park stroke, off the Dodgers' Orel Hershiser. In an August 2 game against the Cubs, he led off the game with a homer and later hit a second homer. He was drilled by Bob Scanlan, precipitating a bench-clearing brawl. In the next game, in the first inning, Bob Castillo threw at García and hit him. García was unfazed: "I want to show people this is my league, too."[36] Leyland was impressed, noting that García "stood up and responded. I think he's done a hell of a job."[37]

For García, the highlight of the season was playing with Bell and admiring "how hard he works and his attitude and the way he plays the game" and being "proud that (Bell) won the Gold Glove with me playing beside him my first year."[38] García was named the Pirates' Rookie of the Year by the Dapper Dan booster club.

Success continued in 1994. García was selected as the Pirates' lone representative at the All-Star Game in Pittsburgh. He was humbled by the selection because "I never expected to make it so quickly in my career."[39] He replaced starter Mariano Duncan at second base in the fourth inning, grounding out to Cal Ripken.[40] In the sixth, he singled to center off Randy Johnson, who picked him off at first. García thought back to Concepción, reminiscing, "I try to follow his example, and be the best I can."[41]

During the offseason García had arthroscopic surgery on his left knee, delaying his start to the 1995 season. He feared the knee was not right. His habit of self-reflection and consumed him, affecting his play. Leyland assured García that his knee was fine, noting that he was "in the lineup every day."[42] Going on a torrid streak in late June (27-for-74, .365), after a June 26 win over the Cubs, García said, "[E]arly in the season I was thinking too much. Now I just go along with the pitch."[43] He had a career-high 21-game hitting streak.[44] García continued to be productive in the 1996 season, hitting .285 with 6 homers, 44 RBIs, and 16 stolen bases. He was considered one of best fielding second baseman in the NL.

After agreeing to a salary of $1.35 million for 1996, more than five times his previous $250,000, García missed games with leg injuries. On April 13, 1996, García hit what was reported as the 8,000th homer in Pirates history, a two-run slam into Three Rivers Stadium's left-field stands off the Expos' Jeff Fassero.[45] The team, though, played poorly. Changes were afoot. At the season's conclusion, Leyland left to manage the Florida Marlins. On November 14, the Pirates trimmed $6 million from payroll, trading García and two others to Toronto for six prospects. "You knew they were going to trade everybody, and I'm glad it happened now rather than later," García observed.[46] Blue Jays GM Gord Ash needed a second baseman who could defend and hit. García was 29, starting over on a new team and league.[47] "In our minds, we were trying to solidify second base. … We feel good about García," said Ash.[48] García was due to make $2.55 million.

All the hope García envisioned for 1997 dissipated during the first week of the season. Though playing solid defense, García had the worst batting average on the team, a dismal .105. Known as a conscientious teammate, García said that "I'm waiting for the perfect pitch and I want to hit it right out of Toronto now."[49] Manager Cito Gaston worked on García's mechanics and considered dropping him in the order since "you don't give up on a guy like that."[50] On April 22 García hit a game-winning two-run single off Anaheim reliever Mike James. His teammate Ed Sprague said, "[W]hat Carlos did, was big for him and the team. Everybody knew how much he wanted to show what he can do."[51]

It did not get better. The Toronto press was unforgiving. "All of a sudden the bragged-about boost in production at second base has not happened and his defence has not been notably better," commented one sportswriter.[52] By the end of May, the Blue Jays were looking elsewhere. García went from the most sought-after second baseman to "excess baggage on a team going nowhere."[53] When the Jays acquired Duncan from the Yankees to be the everyday second baseman, García noticed: "I don't see how my future could be here."[54] García "talked to Cito and he told me my problem was not my bat. It was my defence. … I was really confused."[55] An August game saw him pinch-hit and play at third, striking out in three at-bats in 10 pitches.[56] The media saw a player with "no focus. He's done as a Jay."[57]

Ash tried to deal García. The few suitors wanted the Jays to cover his salary and include a top prospect. As his playing time diminished, García's agent complained to Ash, who vented, "[I]t's a case of an agent not telling his client the whole truth. You've seen him play. If he can't handle the position at second base, how is he going to play short?"[58] A deal with the Pirates failed. García was left open to be drafted by the two expansion teams in November who showed no interest. On December 20 the Jays released him.

García had experienced a stretch of four solid seasons with Pittsburgh. There was talk of greatness. After the Pirates' salary purge and a failed tenure with the Blue Jays, his career disintegrated. The Pirates invested in García. He was a Pirates guy. In an interview with Mike Harrington of the *Buffalo News*, the writer reflected: "[Once] traded, no team would invest time in him. He was branded as a utility player going from one organization to another."[59]

On January 6, 1998, the Indians signed García to a one-year deal at a nonguaranteed $650,000 with a performance option to solve their second-base problem. García was expected to platoon with Enrique Wilson. GM John Hart initially believed García gave "more depth at second base as well as being able to fill in at short and third."[60] When the Indians signed Shawon Dunston at the start of camp to play second, García was released on March 25.[61] His career was in free fall.

Angels manager Terry Collins managed García in Buffalo and encouraged the Angels to sign him, which they did on March 30. Starting shortstop Gary Disarcina had suffered a wrist injury. García was hopeful to get a chance to play motivated, saying, "[E]very time I come to the ballpark, I expect to play."[62] He was 5-for-35 (.143) when he was placed on the injured list on May 13 for a strained right hamstring. He went on a rehab assignment to Triple-A Vancouver, batting .220 in

Second baseman Carlos García turns a double play during his All-Star era with Pittsburgh. He played for 10 seasons in the majors. (George Gojkovich / Getty Images Sports)

50 at-bats. He was designated for assignment to Vancouver, and was released on July 26.[63]

San Diego signed García as a nonroster invitee on December 27, 1998. He had been an All-Star four years earlier; now he was competing for a roster spot. García was bewildered: "Sometimes you wonder what happened to you. When you have a bad year, no one wants to give you a look. Why did everyone give up on me?"[64]

The dream lingered: "I now know I can still play. I need a place."[65] García made the 1999 Padres, starting at third base against Colorado on April 15. He went 0-for-2, grounding into a double play, and committing his second error of the season. He was batting .182. After the game the Padres designated García for assignment. Upon clearing waivers, García had the option of accepting the assignment or becoming a free agent. He accepted an assignment to the Triple-A Las Vegas Stars because "I need to play. The only way I could do it right here."[66] However, he had played his last major-league game.

"[A]lways, it's tough going back down," García said.[67] He was felled by ankle and foot injuries, playing sporadically in 78 games. He was released by San Diego after the season. He signed a minor-league deal with Anaheim on January 31, 2000, but the Angels released him on March 17. The Yankees signed García to a minor-league deal with the Triple-A Columbus Clippers. Columbus manager Trey Hillman said he was "definitely would be nice to have that veteran influence on our younger infielders."[68] Hillman said, "[I]t's a bonus having somebody who is bilingual out there."[69] The Yankees' offer represented a chance. Playing against Buffalo appealed to García.

García's role involved mentoring younger players, helping "those guys get ready, get through the different situations."[70] He was challenged by his changing role and a desire to return to the major leagues. He recognized the value of his experience: "I just want to make sure they understand the game and the way they should play the game, how they should prepare to play the game."[71]

García remained optimistic during his two seasons at Columbus, believing he had value in the major leagues as a utility player. But there was no recall by the Yankees or any other team. García played his last professional game on September 3, 2001, as Columbus defeated the Toledo Mud Hens in the season finale. His last hit, in the fourth inning, was a homer.[72]

García signed a 2002 deal with the Indians to be a coach with the Buffalo Bisons.[73] He was home living in the Buffalo suburbs with Catherine and their 4-year-old son. For three seasons García was the infield and hitting coach, translator and mentor, helping Spanish-speaking players with language and culture issues, much as Rogers, his manager at Macon, had done for him years before. García drew from his own experiences; recalling when "I came to the States and (had to deal with) two different cultures and the language barrier, but you had a chance to play baseball."[74] During the Bisons' 2004 Governors' Cup championship run, García coached a record-breaking offense achieving the highest batting average, and scoring more runs than any International League team in 50 years.[75] García "emboldened his hitters to never to quit a game," evident that the Bisons overcame seven-run deficits in four games in 2004.[76]

Mike Hargrove was hired as manager of Seattle in 2005. As a consultant with the Indians, Hargrove saw García at Buffalo "turn Jhonny Peralta into an International League MVP and make the Buffalo offense the most prolific in the IL in more than 50 years."[77] Hargrove offered García an opportunity he couldn't refuse: Mariners first-base coach and infield instructor. He said that "[b]eing in Buffalo helped me get to the big leagues as a player, and now I went back there and got to the big leagues as a coach."[78]

García developed ambitions to be a manager, "trying to learn as much as I can from [Hargrove], one of the best managers in this game."[79] In 2006 García became the third-base coach, which taught him that "whatever decision you make in the third base coaching box, everybody is going to see it."[80] Under his tutelage, the Mariners led the AL in fielding percentage in 2005 and finished in the top five overall in 2006 and 2007.

Hargrove resigned suddenly on July 1, 2007. García was shocked.[81] Hargrove's impact on García was immense: "[I] was a little insecure when I got the job but [Hargrove] just told me to go out there and not be intimidated by anybody and show what you learned in those years playing and those years you were coaching in Buffalo."[82] On December 18, García was hired as the Pirates' minor-league infield coordinator. Returning to the Pirates was a rebirth for Garcia: "I feel blessed because I have an opportunity to build up again."[83] "The more people we talked to about García, the more people raved about him," Pirates player development director Kyle Stark said.[84] With the Pirates' encouragement, García managed Navegantes del Magallanes in the Venezuelan winter league, taking the team to the league championship series in 2009.[85]

Manager John Russell selected García to be the Pirates' first-base coach and infield instructor for the 2010 season. Known for having an easygoing personality, García developed a reputation for being tough and demanding on his players, "as likely to offer a shout of encouragement through his rich Venezuelan accent, or even an embrace to someone who performs well."[86]

After Russell was fired at end of the 2010 season, García was selected to be manager of the Pirates' Florida State League advanced Class-A Bradenton Marauders. García's goal was the same as his players: make it to the big leagues, this time as a manager. Bradenton was "a way to be able to give back to an organization that has helped give me everything in my career."[87] In an interview with Marauders broadcaster Joel Goddett, García said he would help the players deal with the wear and tear playing of every day, keeping an open mind, playing hard and embracing the process. García promised "good baseball," respect for the game and the fans and a love for the game.[88] Under his leadership, the team made the playoffs in 2011. His teams were well-coached and played hard.

On January 4, 2013, the Pirates promoted García to be the manager of the Double-A Altoona Curve. García was ready:

"[I]t's a long, long road to the big leagues, and not everybody's going to make it. But I'll be able to relay to them what they need to do to get to that level."[89] García made it clear that he would hold his players accountable: "[I]f you want to play for me, you have to be able to come to the ballpark and be ready to play."[90]

After two losing seasons at Altoona, García was fired by the Pirates on September 22, 2014. "I put in (seven) years in the organization, and it really caught me by surprise," he said.[91] Pirates GM Neal Huntington said team record played no factor; it was about prospect development: "Carlos worked hard and tried to do the best he could. We just felt like it was time for a change."[92] The team completely cut ties with García without offering him a different role. Once again he was no longer a Pirate. The Pirates told him "definitely they don't feel like I was doing it in the way they wanted me to do it."[93]

García managed the Navegantes in winter ball for all or parts of seven seasons from 2009 to 2017, winning the 2013-2014 league championship.[94] The team was runner-up for three seasons. In the middle of the 2017-2018 season, he took over as manager of the Tigres de Aragua. For 2018-2019, he was the batting coach for the Tiburones de La Guaria.

García was a coach for the Venezuelan National Team in the 2013 and 2017 World Baseball Classics. He was the batting coach for the Acereros de Monclova of the Mexican League for the spring 2018 season and was promoted to manager for the fall season. The team had a 14-5 start but on July 26, García resigned for personal reasons.

After a two-year absence from Venezuelan baseball, García returned as a manager of the Navegantes for the 2020-2021 season, leading them to the semifinals sparking great national interest. It ended sourly. On January 18, 2021, García was removed as manager prior to the deciding Game Five of the semifinals against Caribes de Anzoategui after a group of players demanded his removal over a practice he called on an offday between Games Three and Four. Prior to Game Five, team President Maximiliano Branger announced that García showed symptoms of COVID-19 and was quarantined.[95] García stated: "We only have one game left to reach the final and I want to see that moment. Unfortunately, I will see it on television."[96] He watched a loss.

In September 2021 the Venezuelan Baseball Federation named García manager of the country's U-23 National Team for the 2021 World Baseball Softball Confederation's Baseball World Cup tournament. Venezuela beat Mexico, 4-0, in the finals. García reflected: "My players really wanted this world title. I've managed for quite a while, but I rarely happened to work with such an inspiring group of players."[97]

No matter where he played, coached, or managed, Buffalo was home with Catherine and their three children, Isabel, Carlos Jr., and Emanuel. "The fans were so great because they understood. You'd talk to them at card shows, and they were totally positive," García said.[98] Harrington saw other factors that tied García to Buffalo. Playing in the Buffalo in the early 1990s was like being in the majors, with attendance reaching 20,000 each night and yearly attendance over a million.[99]

At his induction into the Buffalo Baseball Hall of Fame on August 16, 2009, García stressed that "Buffalo was the trampoline for me to play in the big leagues and also to coach in the big leagues."[100] Harrington noted, "García is one of the top 15 players of the modern Buffalo Bison era and the best all-around shortstop."[101]

The Venezuelan in García is an entrenched Buffalonian, a "place where I have great memories."[102] Interwoven with Buffalo and its working-class ethos, baseball allowed García to embark on the quixotic voyage from tropical Venezuela to the weather-beaten shores of Lake Erie.

SOURCES

In addition to the sources cited in the Notes, the author consulted baseball-reference.com, retrosheet.org, mlb.com, *Baseball America*, Liga Venezolana de Béisbol Profesional, http://pelotabinaria.com.ve/beisbol/, and the Giamatti Research Center at the National Baseball Hall of Fame.

Many thanks to SABR member Tony Oliver for his assistance, to Mike Harrington of the *Buffalo News* for agreeing to be interviewed about Carlos García, and to Java Nation in Kensington, Maryland, where I researched and wrote several iterations of this biography.

NOTES

1   For a well-received history on the Pan American Highway see Eric Rutkow, *The Longest Line on the Map: The United States, the Pan-American Highway, and the Quest to Link the Americas* (New York: Scribners, 2019).

2   Spanish name customs have the first or paternal family name as García and the second or maternal family name as Guerrero.

3   Formerly known as Angostura and St. Thomas de Guyana, Ciudad Bolívar is the capital of Venezuela's southeastern Bolívar State.

4   Chad Brockhoff, "Big-League Aspirations Bring Garcia Back to Bradenton," *Bradenton Patch*, April 4, 2011. The game of bottle-cap baseball in the Dominican Republic is also called "chapita." It is the traditional game that generations played. For more see: James Wagner, "Dominican Players Sharpen Their Skills With a Broomstick and Bottle Cap," *New York Times*, October 6, 2017: Section SP, 1; A one-minute clip of chapita in Venezuela with Jose Altuve is shown at https://www.youtube.com/watch?v=_T9C9zv2lYA.

5   Bob Hertzel, "Garcia Climbing Shortstop Ladder," *Pittsburgh Press*, March 26, 1991: D1.

6   This is equivalent to a high school in the United States.

7   Paul Meyer, "Concepción's Feats Prod Pirates' Garcia, *Pittsburgh Post-Gazette*, July 10, 1994: C-8.

8   Paul Meyer, "Garcia Honoring Dave Concepcion," *Pittsburgh Post-Gazette*, April 9, 1993: C5

9   Hertzel.

10   Hertzel.

11   John Mehno, "This Fall, Bucs Really Need Some Seasoning – Around the Pirates," *Beaver County Times* (Aliquippa, Pennsylvania), September 26, 2010: C1, 13. García played in the offseason with Navegantes del Magallanes until his release in 1998. He played the following season with Tigres de Aragua.

12   The sobriquet stemmed from García's days as a player and later manager of Navegantes (Navigators) del Magallanes in the Venezuelan winter league.

13   Hertzel.

14   Hertzel.

15   Jerry Crasnick, "The Onslaught of Challenges can be Daunting," ESPN.com, March 2, 2006. Crasnick wrote of the problems García had with language, "During Carlos Garcia's tenure in Pittsburgh, he bought a gift for his wife at an upscale department store only to discover he had purchased the wrong size. When the language barrier became a problem, Garcia called [Peter] Greenberg, who resolved the dispute with the sales clerk over the phone." Greenberg and García remain close friends, and Greenberg was García's best man when he married.

16   Hertzel.

17   Macon relocated to Augusta, Georgia, for the 1988 season and became the Augusta Pirates. The team was later renamed the Augusta Green Jackets.

18   Paul Meyer, "Top Picks Not Always Top Performers in Minors," *Pittsburgh Post-Gazette*, August 8, 1988: 20. Dennis Rogers managed in the Pittsburgh and Oakland minor-league systems and was the baseball coach for 25 years at Riverside City College in Riverside, California. He was elected to the Riverside Sports Hall of Fame in 2016. See https://www.rccathletics.com/sports/bsb/coaches/Rogers-_Dennis?view=bio , accessed January 25, 2023.

19   Paul Meyer, "Garcia's Message to NL: He's a Star on the Rise," *Pittsburgh Post-Gazette*, September 26, 1993: D-11.

20   Bon Hertzel, "Garcia Climbing Shortstop Ladder," *Pittsburgh Press*, March 26, 1991: D2.

21   Chicago White Sox Professional Individual Scouting Report, "Carlos Garcia Scouting Report, 1990, June 24."

22   Chicago White Sox Professional Individual Scouting Report, "Carlos Garcia Scouting Report, 1990, July 30." *Baseball America* ranked Garcia as the number 62 prospect in baseball in 1991 and as number 45 in 1993.

23   Bob DiCesare, "Herd Cruises to Win After Stop for Brawl," *Buffalo News*, May 4, 1991: C3.

24   DiCesare, "Herd Cruises to Win."

25   DiCesare, "Herd Cruises to Win."

26   Bob DiCesare, "Garcia Out With Injury Suffered in Friday Night Brawl," *Buffalo News*, May 5, 1991: C6.

27   No relation to Carlos García; Mike Harrington, "Newlywed Garcia Knows Baseball Honeymoon's Over," *Buffalo News*, October 26, 1993: D1.

28   Harrington, "Newlywed Garcia Knows Baseball Honeymoon's Over."

29   Mark Gaughan, "Garcia Able to Put Return to Bisons in Perspective," *Buffalo News*, April 6, 1992: B1.

30   Gaughan.

31   García batted .303 with 13 homers, 70 RBIs, and a team-high 21 stolen bases.

32 When recalled, García was eighth in the American Association with a .303 average including 13 homers, 70 RBIs, and 21 stolen bases.

33 Harrington, "Newlywed Garcia Knows Baseball Honeymoon's Over."

34 Ken Wunderly, "Bucs' Money Moves Continue: Lind to KC," *Washington* (Pennsylvania) *Observer-Reporter*, November 20, 1992: B-8.

35 Paul Meyer, "Bucs' Garcia Set for Major Step," *Pittsburgh Post-Gazette*, March 11, 1993: C-1.

36 Marino Parascenzo, "After Making Right Move, Garcia Fields DD Award," *Pittsburgh Post-Gazette*, February 3, 1994: D-5.

37 Paul Meyer, "Garcia's Message to NL: He's a Star on the Rise," *Pittsburgh Post-Gazette*, September 28, 1993: D-11.

38 Alan Richman (Associated Press), "Garcia Next Great Pirate?" *Ocala* (Florida) *Star-Banner*, March 12, 1994: 5C. García batted .269 with 12 homers in 141 games. He finished ninth in Rookie of the Year voting and was named to the Topps All-Star Rookie Team.

39 Paul Meyer, "Garcia Is Pirates' Lone All-Star Player," *Pittsburgh-Post Gazette*, July 4, 1994: D-1.

40 Duncan was acquired by Toronto during the 1997 season, replacing the benched Garcia at second.

41 Meyer, "Concepción's Feats Prod Pirates' Garcia.".

42 *Latrobe* (Pennsylvania) *Bulletin*, May 10, 1995: 15.

43 "Pirates 8, Cubs 6," *Gadsen* (Alabama) *Times*," June 27, 1995: B6.

44 For the 1995 season, García hit .294 with 6 homers and 50 RBIs.

45 Paul Meyer, "Wagner Has Yet to Give Up a Run," *Pittsburgh Post-Gazette*, April 14, 1996: E-1; *2014 Altoona Curve Media & Information Guide* (Altoona, Pennsylvania: Lozinak Professional Baseball, LLC, 2014), 12. https://www.scribd.com/document/216902093/2014-Altoona-Curve-Media-Guide. Accessed April 10, 2020.

46 Paul Meyer, "Payroll Savings Plan: Garcia, Merced, Plesac to Toronto for Six Prospects," *Pittsburgh Post-Gazette*, November 15, 1996, B-1.

47 "Rating the Trade," *Toronto Star*, November 15, 1996: E7.

48 Mark Zwolinski, "Jays Shore Up Lineup in Nine-Player Deal," *Toronto Star*, November 15, 1996: E1.

49 Mark Zwolinski, "Garcia Certain Patience at Plate Will Soon Pay Off," *Toronto Star*, April 8, 1997: B5.

50 Zwolinski, "Garcia Certain Patience at Plate Will Soon Pay Off,"

51 Mark Zwolinski, "Jays' Garcia Finally Delivers," *Toronto Star*, April 24, 1997: B8.

52 Richard Griffin, "Rocket Draws a Crowd as He Bids for Milestone," *Toronto Star*, May 22, 1997: C5.

53 Richard Griffin, "Confused Garcia on Way Out," *Toronto Star*, August 22, 1997: C3.

54 Griffin.

55 Griffin.

56 Griffin. García ended the season batting .220, a drop-off of .65 points with anemic power numbers in 103 games played.

57 Griffin.

58 Griffin.

59 Interview with Mike Harrington of the *Buffalo News* on October 30, 2020.

60 Associated Press, "Tribe Turns to Garcia to Help at Second Base/ Veteran Hit .220 with Toronto Last Season," *Akron Beacon Journal*, January 7, 1998: B3.

61 Sheldon Ocker, "Garcia Released as Wilson Stays," *Akron Beacon Journal* (online), March 26, 1998: E3.

62 Chris Foster, "DiSarcina Sees Wrist Specialist," *Los Angeles Times*, April 9, 1998.

63 Kevin Aceet, "Finley Not at Wit's End Yet," *Orange County Register* (Santa Ana, California), July 27, 1998: C6.

64 Bill Center, "For Two Padres, Spring Follows a Fall. Once Coveted, Garcia, Owens Now Competing for the Last Roster Spot," *San Diego Union-Tribune*, March 26, 1999: D1.

65 Center.

66 Mark Anderson, "Rossy Returns to Fill Void Left by Injured Shortstops," *Las Vegas Review-Journal* (online), April 27, 1999.

67 Anderson.

68 Scott Priestle, "Pitcher Breaks Hallowed New Ground in Yankees Camp," *Columbus Dispatch*, March 27, 2000: 5E.

69 Scott Priestle. "Playing The Field May Turn Into Adventure," *Columbus Dispatch*, April 5, 2009:5.

70 Priestle, Playing The Field May Turn Into Adventure

71 Priestle, Playing The Field May Turn Into Adventure

72 Stephanie Storm, "Clippers Pitcher Sees Season End Just a Little Too Soon," *Columbus Dispatch*, September 4, 2001: 07E. It was the final game played in Ned Skeldon Stadium in Toledo, Ohio.

73 The Buffalo Bisons team was the Triple-A affiliate of the Pirates from 1988 to 1994 and the Triple-A affiliate of the Cleveland Indians from 1995 to 2008.

74 Amy Moritz, "Latin Rites: Carlos Garcia Smooths Transition for Bisons' Spanish-Speaking Players," *Buffalo News* (online), August 25, 2003.

75 The 2004 Buffalo Bisons had a team batting average of .297.

76 Interview with Mike Harrington.

77 Mike Harrington, "Garcia Follows His Dream to Seattle," *Buffalo News*, July 24, 2005: C8.

78 Harrington, "Garcia Follows His Dream to Seattle."

79 Harrington, "Garcia Follows His Dream to Seattle."

80 "Garcia's Aggressive Coaching From Third Works," *Altoona Mirror*, June 6, 2013.

81 Mike Harrington, "Garcia Survives Bump," *Buffalo News*, July 11, 2007: D3.

82 Harrington, "Garcia Survives Bump."

83 Mike Harrington, "Here's Hope for Long-Suffering Bucs Fans," *Buffalo News*, August 23, 2009: B7.

84 John Perrotto, "Pirates Notes: Thrilled with Garcia," *Beaver County Times*, December 30, 2007.

85 For the 2009-10 season García set the league record for most wins with 41 and received the Alfonso "Chico" Carrasquel award as Manager of the Year.

86 Dejan Kovacevic, "Looking for Meaning in 2010," *Pittsburgh Post-Gazette*, April 4, 2010: D-8.

87 Chad Brockhoff, "Big League Aspirations Bring Garcia Back to Bradenton," *Bradenton* [Florida] *Patch*, April 4, 2011.

88　"Meet the Manager: Carlos Garcia with Joel Goddett," www.bradentonmarauders.com, January 7, 2001. See https://www.youtube.com/watch?v=2bzwAaxwT78. Accessed June 20, 2020.

89　"Ex-Pirate All-Star Named Curve Manager," *Altoona Mirror*, January 5, 2013.

90　"Ex-Pirate All-Star Named Curve Manager."

91　"Pirates Part Ways with Garcia," *Altoona Mirror*, September 22, 2014.

92　Bill Brink, "Pirate Notebook: Altoona Manager Garcia Fired," *Pittsburgh Post-Gazette*, September 23, 2014: E-5.

93　"Pirates Part Ways with Garcia."

94　In the 2014 Caribbean Series, the team reached the semifinal, losing to Indios de Mayagüez of Puerto Rico's Liga de Béisbol Profesional Roberto Clemente. The champions were the Mexican Pacific League's Naranjeros de Hermosillo.

95　Andriw Sanchez, "Magallanes sin Carlos García: el Almirante Problemas de Salud," Triángulo Deportivo - TIC Televisión: January 18, 2021. See https://triangulodeportivo.com/2021/01/18/magallanes-sin-carlos-garcia-el-almirante-problemas-de-salud/, accessed May 6, 202; See also https://twitter.com/ElExtrabase/status/1351306658283216897?s=20, accessed May 7, 2021.

96　Mari Montes and Daniel Alvarez, "Carlos García: Separado, Pero no Alejado de la Nave," *El Extrabase*, January 19, 2021. The García quote is a translation from Spanish to English.

97　WSBC.org, "Managers Enrique Reyes, Carlos García Comment on Final of the WBSC U-23 Baseball World Cup," October 3, 2021. https://u23bwc.wbsc.org/en/2021/news/managers-enrique-reyes-carlos-garcia-comment-on-final-of-the-wbsc-u-23-baseball-world-cup, accessed October 20, 2021.

98　Harrington, "Newlywed Garcia Knows Baseball Honeymoon's Over."

99　Interview with Mike Harrington.

100　Mike Harrington, "Garcia Great for Herd as Player, Coach," *Buffalo News*, August 16, 2009: Blog. As of August 1, 2021, García was one of 101 members of the Buffalo Baseball Hall of Fame. For more, see https://www.milb.com/buffalo/history/hall-of-fame.

101　Interview with Mike Harrington. The modern era of the Buffalo Bisons commenced in 1985 with its return to the Triple-A American Association. In the interview, Harrington wondered aloud why no team had hired García as a hitting or fielding coach given his success in Buffalo and Seattle.

102　Mike Harrington, "Garcia Grateful for Shot with Yankees," *Buffalo News* (online), May 16, 2000; Carlos García's Instagram page can be accessed at https://www.instagram.com/carlosgarcia13oficial/?hl=en.

FREDDY GARCÍA

BY TONY S. OLIVER

Mark Langston, Mike Campbell, John Halama, Carlos Guillén, Freddy García, Brad Halsey, Dioner Navarro, Javier Vázquez, Alberto González, Steven Jackson, Ross Ohlendorf, Luis Vizcaíno. These dozen men were traded, in different transactions, for Hall of Famer Randy Johnson. While they share a bond, their major-league careers took different paths. Several would play in the World Series; some in All-Star Games; a few in the Caribbean Series; and others in the World Baseball Classic. Only one – García – would win a game in all four competitions, a feat unmatched as of 2024 by any other player in baseball history.

García was born on October 6, 1976, in Caracas, Venezuela. The year produced four other big- leaguers: Kelvim Escobar, Ramón Hernández, Alex Prieto, and Liu Rodríguez, a bumper crop of talent for the South American nation. Up north, the Cincinnati Reds would win their second consecutive World Series, sweeping the Yankees in their first postseason of the George Steinbrenner era. Fidel Castro's Cuba had been shut down as a baseball factory; Puerto Rico and the Dominican Republic had taken its place. Farther south, agents Peter and Edward Greenberg saw an opening in Venezuela and focused their attention there; at one point, 80 percent of their clients were from the country.[1]

Two days after turning 17, Freddy signed with the Houston Astros. Unlike many of his peers, García began his professional career not back home, but rather in the United States. The Astros assigned him to the Gulf Coast League; he appeared in 11 games and showcased a 6-3 record with a 4.47 ERA. The team featured seven would-be major leaguers, with García and his countryman Guillén the only ones of consequence. The tandem spent the winter with the Navegantes of Magallanes, for whom García appeared in five games; his statistics were far from inspiring: He allowed 21 baserunners in 13⅔ innings.

The Class-A Midwest League was García's home in 1996. Quad Cities won its division, with García providing a sparkling 3.12 ERA in 60⅔ innings, almost a full run better than the 3.94 league average. At 19, he was more than two years younger than his adversaries, but he handled the pressure quite well; however, his winter experience was not quite as successful; he pitched in only three games, all in relief, allowing six baserunners in 2⅔ frames.

Houston was inspired by his prior success and sent García to the Florida State League's Kissimmee club in the spring of 1997. The Cobras won their division and led the league in ERA; Freddy and future big-leaguer Wade Miller provided a formidable one-two punch with a 20-10 combined record. Perhaps concerned with his youth, the Astros kept him at high

A rather than promote him to the more advanced circuits. He tasted his first real success with Magallanes, pitching in 17 games (five starts) and allowing 3.20 runs per game. His control was spotty; he walked 19 while fanning 25. Garcia's "true outcome" (strikeouts, walks, and home runs allowed) performance robbed fielders of two out of three chances, raising his pitch count and prompting questions of his focus.

In 1998 García hurled 133⅔ innings for the Texas League's Jackson team and the Pacific Coast League's New Orleans franchise, striking out almost a batter per inning, but his potential was pitted against Houston's "win-now" mindset. In the Pacific Northwest, the Seattle Mariners were a franchise at a crossroads. From their inception in 1977 until 1994, they had enjoyed only two winning seasons. The 1987 draft brought reason for joy as Seattle chose Ken Griffey Jr. with the first pick; "The Kid," as he would be known, was a blue-chipper; a true "can't-miss prospect," and as of 2024, one of only four top selections enshrined in Cooperstown (Harold Baines, Joe Mauer, and Chipper Jones being the others). In 1995 the Mariners overcame a 13-game deficit on August 2 to tie, and then defeat, the California Angels in a one-game tiebreaker for their first Western Division crown. A young core of Griffey and Alex Rodríguez joined veterans Edgar Martínez and Randy Johnson for another two winning seasons before Johnson demanded a trade in the summer of 1998. Seattle had gambled by looking at the cards on its hand – a two-time MVP in Griffey, a two-time batting champion in Martínez, and the third youngest batting champion in history (Rodríguez), two rubber-armed, inning-eating left-handed veterans – Jamie Moyer and Jeff Fassero – and traded Johnson for three rookies (Guillén, García, and Halama).

The Big Unit was an absolute beast for Houston, winning 10 out of 11 decisions down the stretch as the team crossed the century-win mark for the first time. The fairy tale ended against eventual NL champion San Diego, and Johnson bolted for Arizona in the offseason. García, on the other hand, won three games for Tacoma and earned a spot in the Seattle 1999 rotation. He sought more winter work and appeared in 15 games for the Navegantes but again struggled to keep the opposition off the bases, highlighted by a 1.641 WHIP.

Seattle's future seemed bright, with a brand-new ballpark, Safeco Field (later renamed T-Mobile Park) replacing the monstrous granite monolith known as the Kingdome. *Baseball America* anointed García as the 61st best prospect entering the 1999 season.[2] Manager Lou Piniella entrusted García as the third starter; all García did in return was lead the team in wins (17) and strikeouts (170) and finish second in Rookie of the Year voting and ninth in Cy Young Award balloting. He debuted at home on April 7 against the White Sox in front of 21,050 fans eager to see the centerpiece of the Johnson trade. García did not disappoint; pitching 5⅔ innings, he scattered seven hits, walked two, struck out five, balked once, and allowed two runs, making for a nice assortment of outcomes from his 94 pitches. He struck out his first batter, Ray Durham, but was harmed by his countryman Magglio Ordóñez's double to score Frank Thomas in the first. The Mariners provided Garcia with five runs and García earned the win, pitching a perfect fifth inning and getting two outs in the sixth before being replaced by José Paniagua to the cheers of the Seattle faithful.

On August 7 García earned a hard lesson as the defending (and eventually repeating) Yankees visited Safeco. Although García hurled a complete game, struck out 10, and allowed only three hits, he was bested by Andy Pettitte, Mike Stanton, and Mariano Rivera, none of whose 11 baserunners crossed the plate. Scott Brosius's sacrifice fly to score former Mariner Tino Martínez was the difference in a 1-0 beauty. Although the team dipped to a 79-83 record, optimism was in the air.

García's April 2000 record (2-1) belied some ugly figures. He gave the team 18 innings but was hit hard; 14 runs were charged to his totals. On April 21 he injured his knee while covering first base and landed on the disabled list; he was far from alone, as the snake-bitten Mariners had previously lost Moyer and Martínez. John Mabry and Mike Cameron would also miss time.[3] After 17 strong rehabilitation frames, García returned to Seattle on July 7, delivering six innings in a 3-2 loss to the Dodgers. He was both durable and valuable the rest of the way, ending 9-5 for the 91-71 club. García opened the first game in the Division Series but the White Sox hammered him for four runs on six hits and three walks. In the type of irony only baseball can sometimes provide, the last batter he faced was Durham, whom he had struck out in his first start. The Mariners, however, won both the game and the series in a 3-0 sweep.

The Yankees had been dominated by García's stuff the prior summer; he was nothing short of spectacular in the Championship Series. In the series opener, he struck out eight and scattered two walks and three hits in 6⅔ innings. His teammates crossed the plate twice, giving him the needed support, as the Mariners took a one games to none lead. The Yankees won the next three games, putting the Mariners on the brink of elimination, but García was once again on the mound on Game Five in Seattle. Pitching five innings, he allowed two runs and seven hits, leaving the game with a 6-2 lead his mates would not relinquish. The Yankees closed the Series two days later, but the baseball world would take notice of Seattle's new ace.

Despite the disappointment of the prior October, the Mariners began 2001 on a roll. The team had lost Rodríguez to free agency but landed Japanese superstar Ichiro Suzuki, who like Madonna, Prince, or Liberace would soon become famous enough to go by one name and win both the Rookie of the Year and Most Valuable Player Awards. The club roared to a modern record 116 wins, with García contributing a career-high

18 wins, 238⅔ innings, and a 3.05 ERA. He finished third in the Cy Young Award voting, and joined teammates Suzuki, Bret Boone, John Olerud, Martínez, Cameron, and Kazuhiro Sasaki in front of the hometown fans for the All-Star Game. Throwing only seven pitches, García retired Chipper Jones, Jeff Kent, and Rich Aurilia in the third inning. The junior circuit scored in the bottom half, giving him the win while Sasaki earned the save in the ninth.

The juggernaut faced the dangerous Indians in the 2001 League Championship Series and García was given the ball in the first contest. Although he struck out eight, he allowed four runs on a string of seven well-placed singles, two doubles, and two walks. His mound opponent, Bartolo Colón, scattered eight baserunners across eight innings, baffling the Mariners with 10 punchouts. The duo had a rematch in Game Four with reversed roles; although both went six-plus innings, it was García who earned the win by allowing one earned run (an additional one unearned) on four hits, one walk, and five strikeouts. Seattle went on to win Game Five and earn a rematch against New York.

Three runs separated the two franchises but ultimately the Yankees prevailed, four games to one. García was a hard-luck loser in Game Two; the second inning was his downfall, as a Brosius double scored Tino Martínez and Jorge Posada; Brosius

Freddy García won 156 big-league games and was a two-time All-Star. He helped the White Sox win the 2005 World Series. (Jerry Coli / Dreamstime)

himself would score later on Chuck Knoblauch's single. The Mariners answered with a pair in the fourth but that was all the scoring the game would see.

In 2002 Oakland and New York won 103 games, Anaheim 99. The Mariners won 93 and stayed home during the postseason. A regression from the mean was to be expected, and García was not an exception. He won 16 games, but his ERA grew to 4.39 though he recorded 181 strikeouts; his record through June (11-5) earned him another All-Star nod. While he did not pick up the win, no one else did either; the 73rd midsummer classic ended as a 7-7 tie when both teams ran out of pitchers. García retired the side in the bottom of the 11th to some boos; he had entered the game in the prior inning and had even picked up an at-bat. Perhaps frazzled from the exercise, he went 5-5 the rest of the year as Seattle was surpassed by both Oakland and Anaheim and missed the postseason.

The next year proved to be disappointing as the Mariners again finished 93-69 but failed to reach the playoffs. García experienced his first losing record in the major leagues, winning 12 games but losing 14. His ERA increased to 4.51 and his control was spotty; he hit 11 batters, unleashed 11 wild pitches, and walked 71. The Mariners were inconsistent in their run support; while they averaged 4.41 runs during his starts, they scored two or fewer in 15 of his games while crossing double-digits in five others. Nevertheless, Garcia's ERA was north of 5.00 for most of the season before he closed September with 27 strong innings (3 runs, 15 hits, 20 strikeouts).

García's hard luck continued in 2004 as he started 15 games for the Mariners. Despite a 3.20 ERA over 107 innings, he was 4-7 before Seattle traded him to the White Sox. He and batterymate Ben Davis went to Chicago for prospects Mike Morse and Jeremy Reed and catcher Miguel Olivo. Although Garcia allowed more runs with the White Sox, he increased his strikeout performance and went 9-4 the rest of the way, for a combined 13-11 season, his fourth consecutive double-digit-win campaign. Chicago was in its first year with Ozzie Guillén as manager and García felt comfortable with his countryman at the helm. The relationship was beneficial in 2005, when the White Sox broke their 88-year drought atop the baseball world, winning the World Series with a dominating 99 regular-season wins and a 13-1 romp over their October rivals.

García pitched to a 3.87 ERA in 33 starts, picking up 14 victories along the way. The team had solid pitching, with Mark Buehrle, García, Jon Garland, and José Contreras all surpassing 200 innings and 30 starts. Given the team's dominance, García pitched in only one game in each of the postseason series but grew stronger as the leaves fell. He provided five acceptable innings against Boston (three runs), a complete game against the Angels (two runs), and then a masterful seven frames against the Astros (seven strikeouts, four hits, three walks) in the World Series clincher, winning all three games for a storybook October.

If García was on cloud nine after winning a ring, he soon leapt to a 10th one. After years of discussion, a multinational competition modeled after the soccer World Cup was finally a reality. The World Baseball Classic occupied the attention of the sport's fans everywhere, and Venezuela was no exception. Twenty-five of the team's 30 members were current major leaguers; All-Stars were at every position.[4] Placed in Pool D, the country dropped its first game against the powerhouse Dominican Republic, 11-5. As Italy had blanked Australia 10-0, the second contest became a must-win, and manager Luis Sojo called upon García. The pitcher dominated the Europeans (and American-born players representing "the old country" like Mike Piazza and Frank Menechino), allowing one walk and one hit while striking out seven in 3⅓ innings. Under WBC rules, strict pitch counts were in effect, so García picked up the win despite throwing only 61 pitches.[5] Venezuela advanced to the second round with a 2-0 victory over Australia but found itself in a proverbial "group of death" with the Dominicans, the Cubans, and the Puerto Ricans. Once again Venezuela dropped the first game, 7-2 against Cuba, but rebounded with a 6-0 win over host Puerto Rico. García took the mound for the series finale, a loser-goes-home affair against the Dominican Republic. Thousands of fans from both sides were present at the Hiram Bithorn Stadium and they witnessed a beauty as the teams were tied, 1-1, after six innings. The starters, Daniel Cabrera and García, were both lifted after four innings. García had allowed one run in the first frame before the Venezuelans tied it. Kelvim Escobar provided a solid three innings but was charged with a loss as Alberto Castillo scored an unearned run.[6]

The 2006 edition of the White Sox dropped to third place in its division with a solid yet unspectacular 90-72 record. The Twins and Tigers won 96 and 95, respectively, with the latter winning the pennant. García delivered another strong season, leading the team in innings pitched (216⅓) en route to 17 wins and a 4.53 ERA. Controversy surrounded him in early May, as the Venezuelan newspaper *Líder* reported that he had tested positive for marijuana during the WBC.[7] While this merited a two-year ban from the International Baseball Federation, it had no effect on his major-league status and no action was taken. García did not miss a single start, winning his last four, with a masterful performance on September 13. Facing the Angels on the road, he took a perfect game into the eighth inning before allowing a single to Adam Kennedy on his 100th pitch. García did not second-guess himself: "I threw the right pitch," he said, noting that his 8-1 career mark at Angel Stadium gave him confidence.[8] Although he was not as dominant six days later – this time he allowed two walks alongside one hit – his pristine eight innings helped the White Sox defeat the Tigers and pull his club within 4½ games of the wild-card spot; it was the closest they would get before finishing five games off Detroit's pace.

On December 6, 2006, the White Sox surprised their fans by trading García to the Phillies for Gavin Floyd and Gio González. Philadelphia was a team on the rise, with a trio of All-Stars in the infield (Chase Utley, Ryan Howard, and Jimmy Rollins). The team needed pitching, as the rotation was slated to feature now 44-year-old Moyer and hot 23-year-old prospect Cole

Hamels. García had earned a reputation as a big-game pitcher during his stay in Chicago to go along with his durability. He had thrown six consecutive 200-inning seasons, each with 30 starts. Though he would enter the season as a 30-year-old with over 1,600 professional innings pitched, the Phillies allegedly relied on Chicago's medical staff reports.[9] They paid dearly for their oversight, as García suffered through a miserable, injury-riddled campaign, starting 11 games and posting an unsightly 5.90 ERA. Though he attempted to play through his ailments, he eventually capitulated and visited pitching savior Dr. James Andrews to repair his labrum.[10] Philadelphia had surrendered two prospects and $10 million for exactly one win.

Since García was set to enter the free-agent market, his arm troubles undoubtedly cost him a fortune. Rehabilitating for most of 2008, he signed a short-term deal with Detroit that showed initial promise: His first game in almost a year yielded five solid innings, facing 18 batters, yielding one run on two hits, striking out three while issuing one walk. Six days later he was rocked by Kansas City, allowing five runs in five innings. A last start against the White Sox was inconclusive; he did not figure in the decision despite hurling five more frames of two-run ball. His season line was 1-1 with a 4.20 ERA on the strength of 206 pitches, and the Tigers declined to bring him back. García sought extra work back home in the 2008-2009 campaign, throwing seven ineffective innings (4 runs, 10 baserunners) for Magallanes.

The New York Mets signed García in early 2009 but released him before the end of April after a disappointing stint with their Triple-A affiliate Buffalo (11 innings, 10 runs). He was at a crossroads but a familiar location would soon beckon him to return. Chicago reached out to García and both sides agreed to a deal. He went back to basics and spent time with Bristol of the Appalachian League, Kannapolis of the South Atlantic League, and Charlotte of the International League before the White Sox recalled him. He appeared in nine games down the stretch, averaging roughly six innings per contest with a respectable 4.34 ERA.

Named the fourth starter, García entered 2010 with certainty for the first time in a few years. He gave the team a solid 157 innings, good for a 12-6 record on a 4.64 ERA. He surpassed 100 pitches five times, including an August 27 matchup against the Yankees (seven innings, one earned run). Little did he know it was far from just a late-season game but rather an unexpected audition. Though the Yankees won 95 games and earned the wild card, their pitching was suspect in the LCS vs. the Texas Rangers. Eager to return to the World Series, the team inked García to a one-year, incentive-laden deal and he proved to be a wise investment for 2011, contributing 12 wins and a 3.62 ERA in 26 games. He was handed the ball in the Division Series, an odd five-game affair that the Yankees dominated batting- and pitchingwise but lost, as Detroit won the close games and New York won the blowouts. García gave up three earned runs in 5⅓ innings but Max Scherzer dominated the Yankees bats to win the second game of the series. This was a different version of García; on the wrong side of 30, he relied on his other pitches rather than attempt to overpower everyone with his fastball. In a 2011 interview, he cited a "new attitude; you have to, 'cause that's your job and you gotta get people out."[11] Earlier in his career, Moyer had prompted him to "take it easy, breathe … you got the stuff" but the bravado of youth (and a strong fastball) had carried him to success.[12] Guile and experience now accompanied García on the mound.

The Yankees brass eagerly brought García back in 2012, but the magic was gone. He pitched his way out of the rotation with a 12.51 April ERA. His next 10 games as a reliever were the opposite; a sparkling 1.56 ERA in 17⅓ innings, but injuries to New York starters returned him to the rotation and he opened 13 games with a 4.67 ERA before wrapping up the year in the bullpen. His emotional apex was a July 24 contest against the Mariners; he shared the mound with the young fireballer Félix Hernández, who wore uniform number 34 in honor of García. In an episode pitting the ghosts of Christmas past and Christmas present, the all-time Venezuelan wins leader (García) was bested by the heir apparent (Hernández) in a 4-2 affair.

As 2013 began, García was looking for employment. A few clubs inquired about his services, and the Padres signed him on January 28. He was released at the end of spring training, but quickly found a suitor in Baltimore. He was ineffective as the Orioles' fifth starter, starting 10 games and allowing 34 earned runs in 53 innings. Atlanta purchased his contract for the stretch run, and his second foray into the National League was much more successful than his first; García allowed five runs in 27⅓ innings for the Braves, helping them to the division title. He was pitted against Clayton Kershaw in the last game of the LDS, with both pitchers throwing six frames of two-run ball. The Dodgers bullpen proved to be stronger, and Los Angeles won the series.

García still had a lot of baseball left in him. In 2014 He joined the Chinese Professional Baseball League in Taiwan, inking with the EDA Rhinos, following in the footsteps of Manny Ramírez, who had played in 49 contests the prior year.[13] The siren song of his homeland proved irresistible, and he suited for the Tigres of Aragua in the 2014-2015 season, his first appearance in six years. He was on the mound for 27 innings (regular and postseason), allowing eight runs en route to a 2-1 mark.[14]

After a few weeks of rest and eager to prove his value, García signed with the Mexican Baseball League's Olmecas of Tabasco for the 2015 season, catching the eye of the Dodgers brass, who offered him a contract with its Triple-A affiliate. He performed poorly and returned to Tabasco before turning his season around with the Sultanes of Monterrey. Overall in Triple A he threw 76⅓ frames with a 4.38 ERA with an impressive 51/11 strikeout/walk split. Perhaps suffering from fatigue, he struggled with Aragua in eight starts, yielding a 5.17 ERA in the regular season. All was forgotten, though, as the Tigres won the Venezuelan title with García starting one game in the playoffs, giving him the opportunity to perform on a grand stage: the 2016 Caribbean Series.

Former major leaguer Eddie Pérez led the Venezuelan team and put great responsibility on the right-hander's broad shoulders: "Freddy is our guy. To me, he's the right guy at the right time. Freddy has pitched in situations bigger than this, better and in worse."[15] The Dominican Republic hosted and dedicated the event to Hall of Famer Juan Marichal. García announced his retirement at the conclusion of the series; he started game one against Puerto Rico's Cangrejeros of Santurce and pitched six innings while allowing only one run to earn a tough victory.[16] Aragua met Mexico's representatives, the Venados of Mazatlán, in the tournament final but lost a heartbreaker when Jorge Vázquez homered to break a 4-4 tie in the ninth inning. García was named to the all-tournament team for his performance, the eldest statesman of the group.

In 2016 Monterrey requested his return, and García appeared in five games. Although his control was impeccable (7/1 K/ BB ratio), he was hit hard with a 5.01 ERA. Nevertheless, he won two games as the club was an offensive juggernaut with a league-leading .464 slugging percentage en route to a 72-39 record and the northern division title. He sat out the winter but made a triumphant return to Aragua in November for 2017. At the ripe age of 41, he announced his intention to retire at season's end and, against all odds, enjoyed his best Venezuelan season. Winning four games with an 11-1 K/BB ratio for Aragua, he earned the Comeback Player of the Year Award.[17] Earlier in the season, the All-Star game was dedicated to him; Edgar Navega, president of the Unique Association of Venezuelan Professional Baseball Players (Asociación Única de Peloteros Profesionales de Venezuela), announced the honor by stating, "Freddy García has been a pitcher who has gifted many great moments to both baseball and Venezuela; for a long time he was the pitcher with most major-league wins."[18]

The Tigres made the postseason but bowed out during the round-robin; the eventual champion Caribes of Anzoategui picked him up as a reinforcement for the finals and García contributed 8⅔ innings in two starts. The triumph afforded García another shot at the Caribbean Series title; the bitter taste of the 2016 defeat still stung: "[I]t would be wonderful. … You know, I tried doing it two years back and we lost in the last inning against México. In short series like these, a team can go on a streak. … A lot of things can happen."[19] The event was bittersweet as its original location, Venezuela, was changed to México due to the unrest in Venezuela. García started game two against the Águilas Cibeañas but struggled early, allowing three runs in 4⅔ innings. He left with the lead and his teammates put on an offensive show, crossing the plate 15 times.

As the seasons changed, Yucatán was impressed and persuaded García to sign with the Leones. Starting five games, he went 2-2. His 5.32 ERA looks lofty, but the league is offense-oriented; the average mark was 5.06 during the 2018 campaign. He followed up his performance with 14⅔ innings in the 2018-2019 Venezuelan season, although his start in the finals was rocky (two innings pitched, four runs allowed, six baserunners). Upon his retirement from the major leagues, García was the career

leader among Venezuelans in wins (156), games started (357), and innings pitched (2,264), but he has since been surpassed by Felix Hernández in all three categories.

García has earned his place in the nation's Mount Rushmore of pitchers, alongside Santana (51.08 WAR), Hernández (50.34 WAR), and Carlos Zambrano (38.32 WAR).[20] García's numbers were remarkably consistent: His home ERA, 4.13, was a shade lower than his road mark of 4.18. Batters hit .258 off him during both the first and second halves of his seasons. He was very effective when the bases were loaded, limiting hitters to a .521 OPS and no grand slams. In 181 of his career games – almost half of his tally – hitters were less successful on his 101st and subsequent pitches, with their average dropping to .235. Beyond the success against the Angels, he was dominant in interleague games, going 25-11 with a 2.84 ERA in 43 starts.

With over 3,000 career innings pitched in the major, minor, and winter leagues, García appeared on the 2019 National Baseball Hall of Fame ballot but did not garner a single vote, and was dropped from future consideration by the baseball writers.

ACKNOWLEDGMENTS

JJ Montilla, Venezuelan sportswriter, for sharing the Venezuelan Baseball reference site Pelota Binaria, which includes winter league statistics.

Pete Palmer and Jim Wheeler for detailed disabled-list records.

NOTES

1 Peter J. Schwartz, "Baseball's Best Agents," *Forbes,* June 22, 2007. https://www.forbes.com/2007/06/20/mlb-greenberg-baseball-biz_cz_ps_0622baseballagents.html#11f2825c19fc.

2 http://www.thebaseballcube.com/prospects/byTeam. asp?T=26&Src=BA.

3 "Mariners Overcome Injuries," *Los Angeles Times,* April 22, 2000. https://www.latimes.com/archives/la-xpm-2000-apr-22-sp-22373-story.html.

4 https://www.baseball-reference.com/bullpen/2006_World_Baseball_Classic_(Rosters)#Venezuela.

5 http://mlb.mlb.com/wbc/2009/stats/boxscore.jsp?gid=2006_03_08_itaint_venint_1.

6 http://mlb.mlb.com/wbc/2009/stats/boxscore.jsp?gid=2006_03_14_venint_domint_1.

7 "Sox Downplay Garcia Marijuana Report," *Chicago Tribune,* May 2, 2006. https://www.chicagotribune.com/news/ct-xpm-2006-05-02-0605020277-story.html, May 2, 2006.

8 Mark Gonzales, "García Flirts with Perfection as White Sox Beat Angels," *Chicago Tribune,* September 13, 2006. http://www.chicagotribune.com/sports/cs-060913soxgamer-story.html.

9 "Freddy García: Damaged Goods?" *Seattle Times,* June 19, 2007. https://www.seattletimes.com/sports/freddy-garcia-damaged-goods/.

10 "Shoulder Surgery Ends 2007 Season for Phillies' García," ESPN, August 30, 2007. https://www.espn.com/mlb/news/story?id=2997866.

11   Steve Serby, "Serby's Sunday Q&A with … Freddy García," *New York Post*, May 15, 2011. https://nypost.com/2011/05/15/serbys-sunday-q-a-with-freddy-garcia/.

12   Serby.

13   Jay Jaffee, "Former All-Star Freddy García to Play Professionally in Taiwan," SI.com, April 18, 2014. https://www.si.com/mlb/strike-zone/2014/04/18/freddy-garcia-signs-with-team-in-taiwan.

14   http://www.pelotabinaria.com.ve/beisbol/mostrar.php?ID=garcfre001.

15   "Freddy García Reportedly Will Call It a Career After 15 Major League Seasons," Fox Sports, February 7, 2016. https://www.foxsports.com/mlb/story/freddy-garcia-retiring-after-15-seasons-in-the-majors-020716.

16   https://www.mlb.com/gameday/puerto-rico-vs-venezuela/2016/02/01/459926#game_state=final,game_tab=box,game=459926.

17   http://www.pelotabinaria.com.ve/beisbol/premios.php.

18   "Juego de las estrellas será en homenaje a Freddy García," meridiano.com, November 22, 2017. http://www.meridiano.com.ve/beisbol/beisbol-venezolano/168510/juego-de-las-estrellas-sera-en-homenaje-a-freddy-garcia.html.

19   Rubén Castro, "Freddy García vive su última Serie del Caribe con Venezuela," ESPN Deportes, February 3, 2018. https://espndeportes.espn.com/beisbol/seriedelcaribe2018/nota/_/id/3945916/freddy-garcia-vive-su-ultima-serie-del-caribe-con-venezuela.

20   As of the end of 2020.

ALEX GONZÁLEZ

BY ADAM FOLDES

In the annals of baseball dating back to when it first became a game played by professionals, historians and fans alike always tend to remember the walk-off home runs that ended a World Series; examples of this include Bill Mazeroski off Ralph Terry at Forbes Field to win the 1960 World Series for Pittsburgh[1] or Joe Carter off Mitch Williams at the SkyDome to win the 1993 World Series for Toronto.[2]

However, what fans tend not to remember are the walk-off home runs that either extended the World Series for another game or changed the momentum of the World Series itself. The 1991 Series was extended when Kirby Puckett of the Twins hit a home run off Atlanta's Charlie Liebrandt to win Game Six in the Metrodome (punctuated by Jack Buck's call "And we'll see you ... tomorrow night!"[3]) Another home run that changed the tide of a World Series occurred in the 2003 World Series, which pitted the New York Yankees against the Florida Marlins.

The Yankees had taken back home-field advantage by winning Game Three in Miami, and seemed poised to take a three-games-to-one Series lead after mounting a ninth-inning rally off Marlins closer Ugueth Urbina to tie the game, 3-3. Going into the bottom of the 12th, the score remained 3-3 and Marlins shortstop Álex Gonzalez led off the inning against Yankees starter Jeff Weaver. On a 3-and-2 pitch, Gonzalez, who that year had set a career high with 18 home runs, hit a ball that barely cleared the left-field wall to tie the World Series, two games apiece.[4]

Alexander Luis Gonzalez was born on February 15, 1977, in Cagua, the capital of the Sucre Municipality and part of the larger city of Maracay in Venezuela. Gonzales was the oldest of five children born to Claudio and Maryuri Gonzalez, who were both amateur athletes. Claudio played amateur baseball as an outfielder and Maryuri played competitive softball for 16 years.[5] Alex was noticed for his talent as early as 1987, when he was introduced to Dave Concepcion, whose son David Alejandro was on Gonzalez's little league team. Concepcion later remarked that while his son was a better hitter, Gonzalez was far and away the better fielder.[6] In order to continually improve, Gonzalez would throw a ball against a concrete barrier in his backyard. Gonzalez was also a standout basketball player and when he was 12 had played on the youth national team of Venezuela in both sports. When Gonzalez chose baseball, he shocked many people around him, who did not know where his passion lay, and while Gonzalez claimed that his parents saw that the talent he had on the diamond exceeded the talent he had on the hardwood, nobody knew what Gonzalez would do until he signed with the Marlins.[7]

The impetus for Gonzalez to sign a major-league contract came from the signing of a childhood neighbor, future All-Star Bobby Abreu, by the Houston Astros. Gonzalez wanted to emulate Abreu. He had a tryout with Marlins scout Levy Ochoa on April 15, 1994. A student at the prep school Liceo Ramon Bastidas in Turmero, Gonzalez had class examination the same day as the tryout. He wrote his name on the test paper, picked up his equipment bag, left the classroom, and went out to the ball field. Ochoa, who later signed future major leaguers Hanley Ramirez and Juan Perez among others, hit Gonzalez balls he thought were impossible to get, but the youngster got them anyway. Impressed, Ochoa offered him a contract and three days later, on April 18, 1994, the 17-year-old Gonzalez signed a contract with the Marlins.

Like most international free agents from Latin American countries, Gonzalez first began playing in the Dominican Summer League, for the DSL Marlins. During his first foray into professional baseball, Gonzalez hit .238 in 66 games with 4 home runs and 39 runs batted in.

The next year, 1995, Gonzalez played in 53 games for the Marlins' Gulf Coast Rookie League team in Melbourne, Florida, under longtime minor leaguer Juan Bustabad. After batting .294 with 2 home runs and 30 RBIs, he was promoted to the Brevard County Manatees of the Class-A Florida State League. Gonzalez struggled in 17 games, hitting barely above the Mendoza line[8] at .203.

In 1996 a separated shoulder limited Gonzalez to 25 games, split among three teams: the Gulf Coast League Marlins, the Kane County Cougars of the low-A Midwest League, and the Portland Sea Dogs of the Double-A Eastern League. Gonzalez hit a combined .306.

Gonzalez spent the full 1997 season with the Sea Dogs, who, under manager Fredi Gonzalez, finished first in the Eastern League's Northern Division. Batting .254 with a then career high of 19 home runs, he was named the shortstop on the end-of-the-year Eastern League All-Star team.

At the end of 1997, Marlins owner Wayne Huizenga, who was looking to sell the team, ordered that the Marlins payroll be slashed. The club held a fire sale that led to the trading of players Moisés Alou, Robb Nen, Gary Sheffield, Bobby Bonilla, Al Leiter, and Kevin Brown among others. The Marlins, who had won the World Series in 1997, finished 1998 with a record of 54-108, 52 games behind the NL East champion Atlanta Braves and dead last in the major leagues, behind even the expansion Arizona Diamondbacks and Tampa Bay Devil Rays. The depletion of talent on the Marlins offered Gonzalez an opportunity. On his way to being named the top prospect in the

International League by *Baseball America* for his season with the Triple-A Charlotte Knights (.277, 10 home runs), he was called up to the Marlins on August 25 and played a pivotal role in the game that night at St. Louis. In the top of the eighth, with the Marlins leading 3-2, Gonzalez got his first major-league hit, and it was a big one: a solo home run off Cardinals starter Donovan Osborne. The hit was crucial because the Cardinals scored a run in the bottom of the inning, so Gonzalez's homer was the deciding run in the Marlins' 4-3 victory. decisive. In his 25-game call-up, Gonzalez batted only .151 with three homers; one was a 13th-inning walk-off shot on September 26 off Ricky Bottalico that broke up a scoreless tie.

After the season the Marlins traded starting shortstop Edgar Renteria to the Cardinals for a package of prospects. The ensuing 1999 season brought a series of highs for Gonzalez on both the professional and personal levels. It was also a year in which Gonzalez learned what it truly meant to play in the major leagues.

The Marlins were in rebuild mode under new manager John Boles and needed their young players, including Gonzalez, now the starting shortstop, to help them improve. Paired with double-play partner Luis Castillo, the 22-year-old Gonzalez played in 136 games and batted .277 with 14 home runs and 59 RBIs. He led all National League rookies in hits with 155 and in runs scored with 81. The team had a 64-98 season but Gonzalez was named to the National League All-Star squad, only the second rookie shortstop to be so named at that time.[9]

But Gonzalez's defensive performance (27 errors) and overall attitude left something to be desired. His dour look and attitude not only got him a nickname from Kevin Millar – Sea Bass – but also got him benched by Boles. He also got yelled at by fellow Venezuelan Ozzie Guillen, who was wrapping up his National League career with the Braves. After Gonzalez failed to run out a groundball in a late-season game, Guillen told Braves pitcher John Smoltz to drill Gonzalez the next time he came up to bat.[10] Gonzalez was, however, named to both the *Baseball Digest* and Topps All-Star Rookie teams and finished fifth in the National League Rookie of the Year voting.[11]

There was a positive: Gonzalez was being noticed and admired by 16-year-old Venezuelan shortstop phenom Miguel Cabrera.[12] When it came time to decide where he wanted to play professional baseball, he not only turned down the Los Angeles Dodgers and New York Yankees, but rejected offers in excess of $2 million to sign with the Marlins for $1.8 million. He cited both the proximity of Miami to his home city of Maracay and also his admiration for Alex Gonzalez.

Off the field, Gonzalez had something to celebrate on June 30, when his longtime partner and later wife, Johanna Josely, gave birth to their first child, Alexander Luis Gonzalez Jr.

After the 1999 season, Gonzalez returned home to Venezuela and played in the Venezuelan winter league, for Leones del Caracas. In a game in Caracas on November 7, he suffered a hairline fracture in his forearm when he was hit by a pitch, and

was in a cast for a month before having his forearm placed in a removable splint.

The injury in Venezuela was a harbinger of things to come for Gonzalez in 2000. While the Marlins had what could be considered a successful year, finishing 79-82 and in third place, Gonzalez had an injury-marred season, and when he did play he did not set the world on fire. A sprain of the medial collateral ligament cost him two months. He played in only 109 games and hit .200 with 42 runs batted in. And his poor play on defense (19 errors) did not improve. He later said that his poor play on offense was what contributed to his bad defense.[13]

The Marlins were optimistic going into the 2001 season but chaos descended. In early June manager Boles was fired for losing control of the team after he was publicly criticized by pitcher Dan Miceli, who questioned his baseball acumen because Boles never played in the majors. Miceli also went on to question the quality of the Marlins coaching staff.[14] Boles was replaced by Hall of Famer Tony Perez, who managed the team the rest of the season. The team finished fourth in the division. Gonzalez personally felt that Boles had placed undue pressure on him, causing him to underperform in 2000; he also felt that the coaching staff had wanted him to change his personality and had held him to a different standard than everybody else, something which Boles disputed.[15] Despite the chaos of the 2001 season, Gonzalez improved his batting average by 50 points, to .250. He still had his problems in the field, however, making 26 errors.

The 2001 offseason brought a lot of changes to the Marlins organization, and these changes benefited Gonzalez. Commodities broker John Henry bought the team from Huizenga, for $158 million. Henry had hoped to move the Marlins into a baseball-only stadium, but a preliminary agreement fell through and Henry looked to sell the team. He sold it to Montreal Expos owner Jeffrey Loria and bought the Boston Red Sox. Loria in turn sold the Expos to Major League Baseball.[16]

GM Dave Dombrowski moved on to the Detroit Tigers and was replaced by Larry Beinfest. Most of the 2001 Montreal Expos coaching staff was brought in. New Marlins manager Jeff Torborg told Gonzalez that regardless of what happened under the previous regime, he had a clean slate and that the only thing that they wanted from him was for him to hustle and play the game hard.[17]

Hitting just .225, Gonzalez dislocated his left shoulder, during their 10-5 loss to the San Francisco on May 18 when diving for a grounder hit by Giants left fielder Barry Bonds and was ruled out for the rest of the 2002 season.[18] During the year Gonzalez and Johanna, now his wife, gave birth to a second son they named Johander.[19]

After the season the Marlins added a number of players who would be instrumental in their 2003 season. The big move was signing catcher Ivan Rodriguez as a free agent.[20]

The way the Marlins began the 2003 season had fans thinking it was another lost year. With the team 16-22, they fired Torborg and replaced him with Jack McKeon in mid-May.[21] Gonzalez's biggest backers stayed in their positions – infield and first-base coach Perry Hill and third-base coach Ozzie Guillen.

Under McKeon's leadership, the Marlins seemingly came out of nowhere, going a league-best 75-49 and winning a wild-card slot. Gonzalez contributed out of the eighth spot in the batting order, hitting .256 in 150 games, with career highs of 18 homers and 77 RBIs. Under the tutelage of Hill, he decreased his errors from 26 in 2001 to 16 in 2003.

The Marlins' magical run continued in the postseason. They topped out the Giants in the Division Series, the Cubs in the Championship Series, and the Yankees in six games to win the World Series. In each of the playoff rounds, Gonzalez played a pivotal role. In Game Two of the NLDS, with the game tied 5-5 in the top of the sixth, he hit a one-out single off Joe Nathan, advancing Jeff Conine to second base; they scored the tiebreaking runs on a double by Juan Pierre, leading to a 9-5 Marlins win. In the next game Gonzalez drew a walk in the 11th inning off Giants closer Tim Worrell and he and Juan Pierre scored the

A slick fielder, González played 13 major-league seasons and hit the walk-off double in Game 4 of the 2003 World Series. He starred with the Marlins and Reds. (Michael Bush / Dreamstime)

tying and winning runs on a single by Ivan Rodriguez. In the NLCS, the Marlins came back from a three-games-to-one deficit to defeat the Cubs; in Game Seven, Gonzalez contributed to the Marlins' win by doubling in their final two runs, which had turned a 7-5 Marlins lead into a 9-5 lead in a game they eventually won 9-6.

In the World Series, in addition to his walk-off homer in Game Four, Gonzalez hit a two-out double off José Contreras to tie Game Five. He scored the game- and Series-winning run in Game Six, on a two-out fifth-inning single by Luis Castillo, breaking a scoreless tie as the Marlins won 2-0.

In the 2003 offseason, in order to ensure that Gonzalez would remain in Miami, the Marlins re-signed him to a two-year deal through 2005. In 2004, though the Marlins finished in third place, Gonzalez played in all but three games. He topped his career high in home runs with 23 and drove in 79 runs. But his batting average dropped 24 points .232. Defensively Gonzalez stayed consistent.

The 2005 season was Gonzalez's eighth and last in Miami. In 130 games, his batting average improved to .264, but he hit only five home runs and had 45 RBIs. For the third year in a row, he limited his errors to 16.

During the 2005 offseason, the Marlins slashed payroll again. Gonzalez signed a one-year contract with the Boston Red Sox, again replacing Renteria, who had been traded by the Red Sox to the Atlanta Braves. The move to Boston reunited Gonzalez with two former Marlins teammates, Mike Lowell and Josh Beckett.

In 111 games with Boston, Gonzalez hit .255 with 9 home runs and 50 RBIs. He made only seven errors. But events off the field cast a pall over Gonzalez's season. In September of 2006, Gonzalez's wife, Johanna was pregnant with the couple's third son, a son they would name Johan; when she went into labor two months early, Johan had an undersized trachea and a number of other underdeveloped organs. This led to multiple surgeries for their son, which at the time were deemed successful.[22]

Gonzalez had wanted to sign again with the Red Sox, but he could not come to terms with them and left for a deal that would provide better financial security for his family and their rising medical costs. He agreed with the Cincinnati Reds on a three-year, $14 million contract that also provided a mutual option in 2010.[23]

The first year of the deal seemed to be beneficial. Gonzalez played in 110 games for the Reds and batted .272 with 16 homers and 55 RBIs. Defensively, he made 16 errors. All of these stats paled when, on July 13, 2007, after surgery to elongate his trachea, Johan stopped breathing in his sleep and lapsed into a coma, unresponsive with little or no brain activity and being kept alive by a respirator.[24]

Johan was transferred from Miami to Cincinnati Children's Hospital. While he spent every hour he could with Johan when he was not on the ball field, Gonzalez said that in the field all he could think about was his son, contributing to a decline in second-half play, especially defensively.[25]

Hoping to rebound in 2008, Gonzalez suffered a fractured kneecap, the fracture was discovered by Reds team doctor Dr. Timothy Kremcheck after Gonzales complained of a sore knee at the Reds spring training camp, which at the time was in Sarasota, Florida.[26] The injury ruled him out for the season. In 2009 his defensive play was solid, but he batted only .210 with little power. The Reds placed him on waivers after the trade deadline. With Gonzalez making close to $5 million a year, unsurprisingly he went unclaimed. When he cleared waivers, the Reds traded him to the Boston Red Sox along with $1.1 million for Kris Negron.[27] Back in Boston, in the midst of a pennant race, Gonzalez stabilized the shortstop position, making only one error while hitting .284 in 44 games. His contribution helped the Red Sox clinch the wild card. For only the second time in his career, Gonzalez was heading back to the postseason. The Red Sox were swept in the ALDS by the Angels; Gonzalez hit .167.

The Red Sox declined the team option that had been in his original contract and Gonzalez once again found himself a free agent. He stayed in the American League East, agreeing to a one-year, $2.75 million contract with the Toronto Blue Jays, with an additional $2.5 million team option for 2011.[28]

On July 11, 2010, Gonzalez was hitting .259 with 17 homers and 50 RBIs when the Atlanta Braves traded their starting shortstop, Yunel Escobar, and pitcher Jo-Jo Reyes to Toronto for Gonzalez, pitcher Tim Collins, and infielder Tyler Pastornicky.[29] During the rest of the season in Atlanta, Gonzalez played in 72 games and contributed a batting average of .240 with 6 home runs and 38 RBIs. His play helped contribute to the Braves capturing the wild card. Gonzalez was 3-for-15 with two RBIs in the four games against the victorious San Francisco Giants.

The Braves picked up his option for 2011 and the now 34-year-old Gonzalez, hit .241 with 15 home runs and 56 RBIs, while posting a fielding percentage of .981 (12 errors).

The Braves had highly rated prospect Andrelton Simmons waiting in the wings along with Pastornicky, so after the season Gonzalez signed a $4.25 million one-year deal with the Milwaukee Brewers for 2012. In a game against the Giants on Saturday, May 5, Gonzalez suffered a torn tendon in his right knee, sliding into second base during a 5-2 loss to the San Francisco Giants.[30]

The Brewers brought Gonzalez back for 2013 and hoped that he could provide some veteran guidance to a club that was two years removed from an appearance in the National League Championship Series. But he played in only 41 games, at shortstop but also at first base and third base. He managed a .177 average with one final home run and eight runs batted in before the Brewers released him on June 3 to make room for the newly acquired Juan Francisco.[31]

While Gonzalez, went unclaimed the rest of the season, he hoped to jump-start the end of his career by continuing to play for Leones del Caracas in the Venezuelan winter league. His .310 batting average got the attention of the Baltimore Orioles, who signed him to a minor-league deal with an invitation to spring training.[32] But in late March Gonzalez was traded to the Detroit Tigers for Steve Lombardozzi, reuniting him with Dave Dombrowski and Jim Leyland.[33]

In what turned out to be his final year in the major leagues, Gonzalez delivered the game-winning hit in the ninth inning on Opening Day against the Kansas City Royals, but he played in only eight other games before the Tigers released him on April 20.[34]

The release brought a close to Gonzalez's 17-year major-league career, but he did continue to play some winter-league ball, until, after 16 years of playing with Leones, he retired as a player at the age of 41 on December 13, 2018.[35]

After a year away from baseball, Gonzalez was brought back to the game when in February 2019 he was named as the manager of the Palm Beach Marlins in the Collegiate League of the Palm Beaches.[36] As of 2021, he was still serving in that capacity; the team is also led by general manager and his former double-play teammate with the Marlins, Luis Castillo.[37] Also in 2021, Gonzalez was named the head baseball coach at the Sagemont School, where he had been an assistant since 2018 in Weston, Florida.[38]

NOTES

1   Anthony McCarron, "Ralph Terry, Yankees Pitcher Who Gave Up Bill Mazeroski's 1960 World Series Homer, Has a Message for Indians' Bryan Shaw," *New York Daily News,* November 3, 2016. https://www.nydailynews.com/sports/baseball/yanks-pitcher-gave-maz-homer-message-indians-shaw-article-1.2857282.

2   Evan Rosser, "Touch 'Em All, Joe," Sportsnet; October 23, 2008. https://www.sportsnet.ca/baseball/mlb/joe-carter-home-run-blue-jays-1993-world-series/.

3   Aaron Gleeman, "On this day in 1991: And We'll See You … Tomorrow Night!" *NBC Sports HardBall Talk;* October 26, 2010; https://mlb.nbcsports.com/2010/10/26/on-this-day-in-1991-and-well-see-you-tomorrow-night/.

4   Jack Curry, "Gonzalez Homers and Marlins Walk Off," *New York Times,* October 23, 2003. https://www.nytimes.com/2003/10/23/sports/baseball-gonzalez-homers-and-marlins-walk-off.html.

5   Juan C. Rodriguez, "Baseball Spoken Here," *South Florida Sun Sentinel,* June 10, 2003; https://www.sun-sentinel.com/news/fl-xpm-2003-06-10-0306100017-story.html.

6   "Alex Gonzalez," *Columbus Dispatch,* March 12, 2007; https://www.pressreader.com/usa/the-columbus-dispatch/20070312/283429187110424.

7   "Baseball Spoken Here."

8   https://www.mlb.com/glossary/idioms/mendoza-line.

9   *Florida Marlins 2001 Media Guide,* 118.

10   "Baseball Spoken Here."

11   https://www.baseball-reference.com/bullpen/1999_National_League_Rookie_of_the_Year_Award.

12   David O'Brien, "Marlins Sign Prospect Cabrera," *South Florida Sun-Sentinel,* July 3,1999. https://www.sun-sentinel.com/news/fl-xpm-1999-07-03-9907030435-story.html.

13   "Baseball Spoken Here."

14   Robert Dvorchak, "Manager Fired for Losing Control," *Pittsburgh Post-Gazette*, May 29, 2001. https://news.google.com/newspapers?id=LOhRAAAAIBAJ&sjid=b3ADAAAAIBAJ&pg=6506,5397012&dq=joe-breeden&hl=en.

15   Rodriguez

16   Murray Chass, "Owners Give Approval to Sale of the Red Sox," *New York Times*, January 17, 2002. https://www.nytimes.com/2002/01/17/sports/baseball-owners-give-approval-to-sale-of-the-red-sox.html.

17   "Baseball Spoken Here."

18   Associated Press, "Giants' Bonds Make Splashy Move," *Los Angeles Times*, May 19, 2002. https:// www.latimes.com/archives/la-xpm-2002-may-19-sp-nlsep19-story.html.

19   Amy K. Nelson, "Alex's Ordeal," ESPN.com, October 6, 2009. https://www.espn.com/boston/columns/story?columnist=nelson_amy&id=4537575.

20   Juan C. Rodriguez, "Marlins: No Extra Money," *South Florida Sun Sentinel*, November 19, 2002. https://www.sun-sentinel.com/news/fl-xpm-2002-11-19-0211190111-story.html.

21   Associated Press, "Report Marlins Fire Torborg, Hire McKeon," *Los Angeles Times*, May 11, 2003. https://www.latimes.com/archives/la-xpm-2003-may-11-sp-bbnotes11-story.html.

22   "Alex's Ordeal."

23   "Reds Sign Shortstop Alex Gonzalez," MLB.com, November 20, 2006. http://cincinnati.reds.mlb.com/content/printer_friendly/cin/y2006/m11/d20/c1743913.jsp.

24   "Alex's Ordeal."

25   "Alex's Ordeal."

26   Associated Press, "Reds shortstop diagnosed with broken left knee," ESPN.com, February 29, 2008. https://www.espn.com/mlb/spring2008/news/story?id=3270963

27   Tony Massarotti, "Sox Acquire Alex Gonzalez," Boston.com, August 14, 2009. https://www.boston.com/sports/extra-bases/2009/08/14/sox_acquire_ale.

28   "Gonzalez Agrees to 1-year Deal with the Blue Jays," *Sports Illustrated*, November 26, 2009. https://www.si.com/mlb/200/11/26/gonzalez.

29   Charles Odum, "Braves Acquire Alex Gonzalez from Blue Jays," *San Diego Union Tribune*, July 14, 2010. https://www.sandiegouniontribune.com/sdut-braves-acquire-alex-gonzalez-from-blue-jays-2010jul14-story.html.

30   Al Yellen, "Brewers' Alex Gonzalez Has Torn ACL," SB Nation, May 7, 2012. https://www.sbnation.com/2012/5/7/3005403/alex-gonzalez-torn-acl-brewers.

31   Mike Axisa "Brewers Acquire Juan Francisco from Braves; Release Alex Gonzalez," CBS Sportscom, June 3, 2013. https://www.cbssports.com/mlb/news/brewers-acquire-juan-francisco-from-braves-release-alex-gonzalez/.

32   Associated Press, "Alex Gonzalez Signs with the Orioles," ESPN.com, February 3, 2014. https://www.espn.com/mlb/story/_/id/10398437/baltimore-orioles-sign-infielder-alex-gonzalez-minor-league-deal.

33   "Tigers Acquire Alex Gonzalez," ESPN, March 24, 2014. https://www.espn.com/mlb/story/_/id10664922/detroit-tigers-deal-alex-gonzalez-baltimore-orioles. See also Associated Press, "Tigers release Alex Gonzalez," ESPN.com, April 20, 2014. https://www.espn.com/mlb/story/_/id/10811835/detroit-tigers-release-alex-gonzalez.

34   "Tigers Release Alex Gonzalez." He was 5-for-30 with two RBIs.

35   Andriw Sanchez Ruiz, "Alex Gonzalez: I Couldn't Leave Without Saying Goodbye to the Lions Fanatic," LVBP.com, December 13, 2018. https://www.lvbp.com/7192_alex-gonzalez-no-me-podia-ir-sin-despedirme-de-la-fanaticada-de-leones.

36   CLPB Staff, "PB Marlins Excited to MLB Standout Alex Gonzalez as Head Coach," clpbbaseball.com, February 20, 2020. https://www.clpbaseball.com/pb-marlins-excited-to-mlb-standout-alex-gonzalez-as-head-coach/.

37   Palm Beach Marlins - The Collegiate League of The Palm Beaches - team roster | Pointstreak Sports Technologies

38   Adam Lichtenstein "Former Marlins shortstop Alex Gonzalez takes over at Sagemont and what to look for this high school baseball season" *South Florida Sun Sentinel*, February 13, 2021. https://www.sun-sentinel.com/sports/highschool/baseball/fl-sp-hs-sagemont-gonzalez-20210214-x5agrvykovaltlad-p4nba3lezi-story.html

CARLOS GUILLÉN

BY PAUL HOFMANN

A versatile player who played all four infield positions and left field, Carlos Guillén is among a long line of excellent shortstops from Venezuela that includes Chico Carrasquel, Hall of Famer Luis Aparicio, Dave Concepción, Ozzie Guillén, and Omar Vizquel. At 6-feet-1-inch and 215 pounds, Guillén did not look like a prototypical shortstop. When he first arrived in the United States at the age of 19, "his cheeks were chunky and he looked to many of his teammates as if he was more of a batboy than a ballplayer."[1] Seventeen years later, after a career that was both limited and defined by 11 visits to the disabled list, the three-time All-Star retired as one of the best shortstops in Detroit Tigers history.

Carlos Alfonso Guillén was born on September 30, 1975, in Maracay, Venezuela. Maracay, the capital city of Aragua State, is located in north-central Venezuela, approximately 90 minutes southwest of Caracas. The city is an industrial center that produces paper, textiles, chemicals, tobacco, processed foods, soap, perfumes, and baseball players. In addition to Guillén, notable players like Concepción, Miguel Cabrera, Bobby Abreu, José Altuve, Elvis Andrus, Martín Prado, and Aníbal Sánchez all hailed from Maracay.

He is one of the two children of DeGuillén and Maria Guillén. DeGuillén worked for an agricultural company as a supervisor of a truck farm that grew bananas, beans, mangos, green peppers, potatoes, and lettuce. Maria was a schoolteacher. Including his sister, Olegmary, the family shared a first-floor apartment.[2] By all accounts the family was middle class and Guillén did not struggle as much as many other young ballplayers who came out of Latin America.

Growing up, Carlos loved animals and spent as much time with pets as he did playing sports. "Dogs, cats, a tortoise, peacocks," Guillén told Lynn Henning of the *Detroit News*.[3] Had he not gone into baseball, he said, he would have been a veterinarian.

Carlos was an all-around athlete who played soccer, basketball, volleyball, and baseball. His versatility as an athlete was one of the reasons the Houston Astros signed him as an undrafted free agent on September 19, 1992. Not yet 17 years old, he was allowed to continue his education and his amateur career in Venezuela for two more seasons before the Astros brought him to the United States.

Guillén was 19 years old when he began his professional career with the Gulf Coast League Astros in 1995. Freddy Garcia, a fellow Venezuelan, was also a member of the GCL Astros and the two made their way through the minor leagues together. After hitting .295 with two home runs, 15 RBIs, and 17 stolen bases in 118 plate appearances, Guillén was ranked number 74 on *Baseball America's* top-100 prospect list heading into the 1996 season.

Guillén started the 1996 season with the Quad Cities River Bandits of the Class-A Midwest League. The 20-year-old shortstop was off to a fast start and the team was 22-12 when he suffered a season-ending dislocation of his left shoulder making a diving attempt to stop a ball hit up the middle.[4] Guillén finished the year with a .330 average, 3 home runs, 17 RBIs, and 13 stolen bases in 29 games. Despite his limited action, Guillén's success did not go unnoticed. *Baseball America* ranked him as the number-27 prospect prior to the 1997 season.

Promoted to the Jackson (Mississippi) Generals of the Double-A Texas League for the 1997 season, Guillén appeared in 115 games and finished the season with a batting average of .254, 10 home runs and 39 RBIs. A converted outfielder, Guillén struggled defensively and committed 35 errors in the 109 games he played at shortstop.

During his time in Jackson, Guillén shared how he struggled with the English language and the challenges it created on and off the field. He often relied on second baseman Carlos Hernández

to interpret and translate for him. "Sometimes I'm scared," Guillén told the *Jackson Clarion-Ledger*. "I don't speak too good. Carlos Hernandez … he help me a lot."[5]

Fast-forward to 2010 and Guillén had become a leading advocate for organizations to have one Spanish interpreter per team. After Chicago White Sox manager Ozzie Guillén drew national attention for pointing out that Asian players had interpreters but Latin players did not, Carlos Guillén stressed the challenges Latin players had in learning English. "It's not easy for us to come here and survive. How do you explain the way you feel?" he said. "It's hard for you guys to understand what we are saying. And the communication is the key to everything," Guillén said as he explained that English classes offered to Latin players were not an effective solution.[6]

Guillén continue to advance through the Astros' minor-league system and was given a taste of Triple-A baseball at the end of 1997 season. In three games with the American Association's New Orleans Zephyrs, he hit .308 (4-for-13).

Growing up, there was a family that lived on the third floor of the Guilléns' building. They had a daughter named Amelia. Carlos and Amelia were childhood friends and later developed a romantic relationship. The couple were married in 1997 and had three children, Alfonso, Isaac, and Camelia.[7]

Guillén started the 1998 season with hopes of being promoted to the Astros, who were contending for the National League Central Division championship. He was enjoying a solid season in New Orleans (.291, 12 home runs, 51 RBIs), when on July 31 he, Garcia, and a player to be named later were traded to the Seattle Mariners for left-handed pitcher Randy Johnson.[8]

Garcia and Guillén reported to the Tacoma Rainiers, the Mariners' Pacific Coast League affiliate, for the remainder of the PCL season. With the presence of Álex Rodríguez at shortstop in Seattle, Guillén, who played shortstop exclusively in New Orleans, was shifted to second base. In 24 games with the Rainiers, he hit .228 with one home run and four RBIs.

An end-of-season callup, Guillén made his major-league debut on September 6, 1998, at the Kingdome in Seattle. He started at second base and batted ninth. He went 1-for-3 against Baltimore Orioles starter Mike Mussina, an RBI single in the eighth. The Mariners mustered little other offense that evening and lost the game, 5-2.

Guillén was hitting .333 when his season ended on September 17, establishing a pattern of injuries that would plague him throughout his career. He injured his left knee as he tumbled after making an acrobatic catch of a pop fly off the bat of A's shortstop Miguel Tejada in short center field. Mariners manager Lou Piniella ominously told reporters, "It's more than a sprain, but we don't know yet."[9] Later it was confirmed that Guillén tore his posterior cruciate ligament.

After rehabbing the knee throughout the offseason, Guillén started the 1999 season with a bang. On Opening Day he hit his first major-league home run, off the White Sox' James Baldwin. Batting in the leadoff spot, Guillén deposited a 3-and-2 offering from the right-hander over the right-field fence in the bottom of the third. The solo home run tied the score, 1-1, before the White Sox scored one in the fourth and two in the fifth, sixth, and seventh innings to roll to an easy 8-2 victory.

When Rodriguez went down with a knee injury on April 6, Guillén was moved to the left side of the infield to fill the void at shortstop. On April 10, during just his third start at shortstop, Guillén's season ended abruptly when he suffered a severe right knee injury during a collision with the A's Tony Phillips on a run-down play. The injury, a torn anterior cruciate ligament and torn cartilage, was thought to be career-threatening.

After the game Piniella spoke to the severity of the 22-year-old Guillén's injury. "We expect him to be out quite a while," Piniella said. "We don't know exactly what the prognosis will be, but it is not going to be good. It's a shame because he is a good young player."[10]

Guillén again battled his way back during the offseason and established a Mariners franchise record for hits in spring training to win the starting third-baseman job.[11] He got off to a slow start, batting only .083 in the team's first eight games of 2000, when a strained hamstring landed him on the disabled list for the third consecutive year. After returning to action on April 28, he continued to struggle. He was batting just .143 when he was optioned to Tacoma.

Guillén rediscovered his batting stroke in Tacoma. In 24 games with the Rainiers he hit .299 with 2 home runs and 11 RBIs before being recalled in early July. Guillén's recall from Tacoma proved to be good timing for the Mariners. In just his second game back, Rodriguez suffered a concussion that kept him out of the lineup for much of the month allowing Guillén to move over from third to shortstop. Guillén continued to hit after his return to Seattle. In his final 67 games, he hit .289 with 7 home runs and 37 RBIs and finished the year batting .257.

The Mariners finished the season with a record of 91-71, a half-game behind the AL West winner Oakland A's, earning a wild-card spot in the playoffs. The Mariners faced the Chicago White Sox in the American League Division Series. Guillén didn't see any action until Game Three. With the Mariners leading the series two games to none, he entered the game as a pinch-hitter with the score tied 1-1 in the bottom of the ninth inning, runners at the corners, and one out. After fouling off the first pitch, Guillén pushed a line-drive drag bunt past a diving Frank Thomas at first base to score pinch-runner Rickey Henderson from third and send the Mariners to their first-ever American League Championship Series.

After the game reporters asked a smiling Guillén if he had ever had a bigger base hit. "Never, no," he replied. "I just thought that I could hit a soft groundball to Frank Thomas at first base, and make it difficult for Frank to throw to home, and Rickey could score and we could win this game."[12]

Guillén made two appearances in the ALCS against the New York Yankees. He started at third base in Game Four and went 0-for-3 as the Yankees shut out the Mariners 5-0. He also started at third base in Game Six and went 1-for-2 with two walks, including a fourth-inning, two-run home run down the right-field line off Orlando Hernández that gave the Mariners a 4-0 lead. The Yankees rallied for a 9-7 victory to win the American League pennant.

Before the start of the 2001 season, Rodriguez signed a lucrative contract with the Texas Rangers. His departure gave Guillén the opportunity to become the Mariners' everyday shortstop. Acknowledging that he had big shoes to fill, the team's new shortstop told reporters during spring training, "I can't try to replace Alex Rodriguez. I can only play as well as Carlos Guillén can. Alex is one of the best. He played well, but I think I can, too."[13]

Guillén once again got off to a slow start in 2001. Entering play on May 10, he was batting only .183. He hit .282 during the remainder of the season and finished with an average of .259 with 5 home runs and 53 RBIs as the Mariners, led by Japanese-import Ichiro Suzuki, won the American League West with a record of 116-46. The team's 116 victories tied the major-league record held by the 1906 Chicago Cubs.

Guillén missed the last nine games of the regular season when he was diagnosed with pulmonary tuberculosis, which eventually landed him in a Seattle area hospital and required him to have surgery to stop "minor bleeding" in one of his lungs.[14] He had missed several games because of nosebleeds and had been battling the ailment for a few months prior to his diagnosis. The illness caused him to miss the ALDS against the Cleveland Indians, which the Mariners won, three games to two.

Versatile and clutch, Guillén was a key figure in Detroit's resurgence in the mid-2000s. He earned three All-Star selections as a Tiger. (Tom Hauck / Getty Images Sports)

Guillén returned to action and appeared in three games of the ALCS against the Yankees. Guillén started Game One at shortstop and went 0-for-3 before being lifted for pinch-hitter Stan Javier in the bottom of the ninth of the Yankees' 4-2 victory. In Game Three he pinch-hit for Suzuki in the top of the eighth and stayed in the game at shortstop as the Mariners blew out the Yankees, 14-3. Guillén started at shortstop, singled twice and scored a run in Game Five, a 12-3 Yankees victory that ended the Series.

Guillén got off to a quick start in 2002. He hit .337 for the month of April and was batting .306 when he was hit by a pitch while attempting to bunt in a May 31 game in Baltimore and suffered a bruised finger. The injury kept him out of the lineup for eight games.

Four days after his return to the lineup, in the early-morning hours of June 14, Guillén was pulled over doing 89 mph in a 60-mph zone and arrested on suspicion of drunk driving in Clyde Hill, Washington. He pleaded not guilty to the DUI charge and later entered a guilty plea to a misdemeanor charge of first-degree negligent driving. The judge ordered him to perform 100 hours of community service and speak about the dangers of alcohol abuse.[15]

Guillén slumped late in the season, hitting just .209 with 1 home run and 11 RBIs, over his last 34 games. He finished the year with an average of .261, 9 home runs, and 56 RBIs.

The 2003 season was another injury-plagued campaign for Guillén. In early July he missed eight games due to a strained groin. The nagging injury cost him another six games later that month and he eventually landed on the disabled list, causing him to miss an additional 23 games. The injury forced the Mariners to acquire shortstop Rey Sanchez from the New York Mets to fill the void at short. When Guillén returned, he was moved to third base for the rest of the season. Limited to 109 games, he finished the year with a .276 average, 7 home runs, and 52 RBIs.

During the winter meetings, the Mariners signed Guillén to a one-year, $2.5 million contract that included up to $900,000 in performance bonuses.[16] Yet the Mariners continued to shop the oft-injured Guillén during the offseason. When attempts to trade him to Cleveland for Omar Vizquel fell through, the Mariners signed free-agent shortstop Rich Aurilia and traded Guillén to the Detroit Tigers for minor-leaguer Juan González and shortstop Ramón Santiago on January 8, 2004.

On the surface the deal appeared to be a relatively minor one that included the two teams swapping shortstops. González was an added infield prospect who at 22 years old failed to impress the Tigers at Class-A Western Michigan and toiled in the minor leagues for 10 years with six different organizations. Santiago played in only 27 games with the Mariners during the 2004 and 2005 seasons, batting a combined .170 with just two RBIs before returning to the Tigers as a free agent in 2006. Santiago played with the Tigers until 2013. The deal turned out to be one of the best trades in Tigers history.

The Tigers were coming off a 2003 season in which they finished with a dismal record of 43-119, one of the worst records in modern baseball history. Guillén was among the new faces general manager Dave Dombrowski brought in to turn the Tigers' fortunes around.

The 2004 Tigers improved 29 games over the previous year and finished the year with a 72-90 record. Guillén's breakout season was one of the reasons for this dramatic improvement. He hit .318 with 20 home runs and a team-leading 97 RBIs in 136 games, and was named to his first American League All-Star team. He was the only nonpitcher for either team not to appear in the All-Star Game.

Guillén was on pace to break the club record of 105 RBIs for a shortstop, held by manager Alan Trammell, when his season came to an end on September 11. He injured his right knee when he slid into third base as he unsuccessfully tried to advance from first to third on a base hit. Two and a half weeks later, Guillén underwent knee surgery to repair a torn ligament in his knee.

After another offseason spent rehabilitating yet another injury, Guillén and the Tigers entered 2005 optimistic that they would be able to improve on the previous year's finish. He was hitting .355 on June 7 when he suffered a strained left hamstring that cost him 15 games. He missed another 39 games in August and September when tests on his surgically repaired right knee showed weakness in his quad muscle.[7] Limited to 87 games, Guillén finished the season with a career-high .320 average, 5 home runs, and 23 RBIs.

The Tigers' high hopes for 2005 came to fruition in 2006 when the team finished 95-67 and captured the American League's wild-card spot under new manager Jim Leyland. Guillén was vital to the Tigers' success. He established career highs in games played (153), runs scored (100), doubles (41), and stolen bases (20). He also matched his career-high .320 batting average, established a year earlier, and added 19 home runs with 85 RBIs as he finished 10th in voting for the American League MVP Award.

On August 1 Guillén became the 10th Tiger to hit for the cycle when he accomplished the feat against the Tampa Bay Devil Rays. He hit an RBI triple in the second, a solo home run to left-center to lead off the third, and a single in the sixth, and legged out a double to right in the eighth. He was the first Tiger to hit for the cycle on the road since Hall of Famer George Kell did it against the Philadelphia Athletics on June 2, 1950. As impressive as his regular season was, he saved the best for the postseason.

Guillén went 8-for-14 (.571) in the Tigers' three-games-to-one upset victory over the Yankees in the Division Series. He hit safely in all four games and had a game-tying solo home run in the top of the sixth inning in Game Two and an RBI double in the bottom of the fifth of the Tigers' series-clinching victory in Game Four.

In the Tigers' four-game sweep of the Oakland A's in the Championship Series, Guillén went only 3-for-16 with a run scored and a double. But for the first time in his career, Guillén was headed to the World Series.

The Tigers dropped the series to the St. Louis Cardinals in five games. Guillén was one of the bright spots for the Tigers. He hit .353, collecting 6 hits in 17 at-bats. In Game Two, a 3-1 Tigers victory, he went 3-for-3 with a double, triple, and RBI. He finished the 2006 postseason with a batting average of .362.

Guillén remained healthy for the entire 2007 season. In 151 games he hit .296 and had career highs in home runs (21) and RBIs (102). That summer, Guillén saw his first action in an All-Star Game when he entered the game to play shortstop in the bottom of the fifth and replaced teammate Iván Rodríguez in the seventh spot of the American League batting order. Guillén grounded out to second in the top of the sixth and led off the top of the ninth with another groundout to second as the American League dropped a 5-2 decision to the National League at AT&T Park in San Francisco.

In 2008 the 32-year-old Guillén began to show the cumulative effect of the long list of injuries suffered throughout his career. Given his diminished mobility, the Tigers attempted to switch him to first base and first baseman Miguel Cabrera to third to start the season. The experiment was short-lived.

Guillén appeared in his final All-Star Game in the American League's 15-inning, 4-3 marathon victory at Yankee Stadium. He entered the game as a pinch-hitter for Joe Crede in the bottom of the eighth and struck out and stayed in the game to play third base. He was intentionally walked in the bottom of the 10th, led off the bottom of the 12th with a double to left, and lined out to short in the bottom of the 14th.

After missing a handful of games in August due to a stiff back, Guillén played his final game of the season on August 25. Later it was determined that the inflammation was coming from a nerve root in his lower back. While he did not require surgery, the injury required an extended period of rest that ended a disappointing season for Guillén. Limited to 113 games, he batted .286 with 10 home runs and 54 RBIs, far below what the Tigers had projected for their All-Star shortstop.

Guillén started 2009 splitting time as the team's left fielder and designated hitter. He was off to a slow start when on May 5 he was placed on the disabled list with inflammation in his right shoulder, an injury he suffered earlier in the season when he crashed into the left-field wall trying to make a catch. When he went on the disabled list, he was hitting just .200 with six RBIs.

The injury caused Guillén to miss 68 games. He returned to the lineup as the team's designated hitter on July 24 and played both ends of the doubleheader against the White Sox, with a solo home run in the nightcap. He bounced back offensively and by mid-August he made it back to left-field. He finished the year with a .242 average, 11 home runs, and 41 RBIs.

Guillén appeared in even fewer games in 2010. He was hitting .311 to start the season when he landed on the disabled list again and missed more than a month with a strained hamstring. When he was activated in late May, he returned to the infield as the team's second baseman. His season came to an end on August 16 when he hurt his knee while turning a game-ending double play against the Yankees. Initial tests indicated the knee suffered no major damage and he was diagnosed with a bruised knee. Later he learned he had suffered a season-ending microfracture that required surgery. In 68 games he hit .273 with 6 home runs and 34 RBIs.

Still recovering from the microfracture surgery he had the previous fall, the switch-hitting Guillén spent the first half of the 2011 season on the disabled list. He played his first game of the season on July 16, but was placed back on the disabled list on August 13 with a sore left wrist. He returned to the lineup on September 3, but played only six games the rest of the season, including his final game on September 18, which he left in the fourth inning with a strained right calf. Limited to 28 games, Guillén hit .232, with 3 home runs, and 13 RBIs.

Guillén failed to return to the Tigers lineup during the regular season and was ineligible for the postseason. The Tigers beat the Yankees in the ALDS, three games to two, and lost to the Texas Rangers in the ALCS, four games to two.

The 2011 season brought an unceremonious conclusion to Guillén's Tigers and major-league career. After being granted free agency by the Tigers following the 2011 season, Guillen signed as a free agent with the Seattle Mariners in February 2012. After reporting to spring training, Guillén voluntarily retired on March 6, stating he was unable to return from the injuries that plagued him in 2011. In eight seasons with the Tigers, Guillén hit .297 with 95 home runs and 449 RBIs. In his 14-year major-league career, during which he conservatively missed 750 games due to injury, he hit .285 with 124 home runs and 660 RBIs.

Guillén was a nonroster invitee to the Mariners' spring training in 2012. Unable to recover from a series of injuries he experienced in the final years of his career, Guillén announced his retirement in March 2012. "It's a tough decision for me, for my family, for everybody because I tried so hard to come back," Guillén said. "I've been through a lot of injuries," he said, explaining that the body tells you when it is time to quit.

Guillén remained active in baseball. In 2016 he was named general manager of the Venezuelan Baseball Team that competed in the 2017 World Baseball Classic. His tenure as GM was surrounded by controversy. In November of 2016, Guillén asked manager Omar Vizquel to resign as team manager. Supported by many star Venezuelan players, Vizquel refused to resign and asked Guillén for an explanation. Eventually the two made peace and Vizquel stayed on as manager. Guillén said, "There was some miscommunication. These situations happen among teams and you try to keep them within the clubhouse, so to speak. The important thing is we're here."[18]

Asdrúbal Cabrera, who also publicly feuded with Guillén, was not as not as fortunate and was eventually removed from the team's star-studded roster. The team finished a disappointing eighth in the WBC with a record of 2-5.

As of 2021 Guillén owned the Carlos Alfonso Guillén (CAG) Baseball Academy in Maracay. The academy, which hosts three dozen amateur baseball players at a time, has worked to develop prospects to meet the rigors of the game both on and off the field. Guillén summarized the mission of the academy in simple terms: "Baseball is not easy. If you teach those kids what they're gonna face when they sign (to play) professional baseball and they prepare themselves, there's going to be more baseball players in the big leagues."[19]

He and his wife split time between their homes in Miami and their native Venezuela. Together they operated the Venezuelan Chamos Foundation, a charitable organization they established when Guillén played for the Tigers.

SOURCES

In addition to the sources cited in the Notes, the author also relied on Baseball-reference.com and Retrosheet.org.

NOTES

1   Dan Holmes, "Carlos Guillén Made a Name For Himself as One of Detroit's Best Shortstops," Vintage Detroit Collection, May 15, 2016. https://www.vintagedetroit.com/blog/2016/05/15/carlos-guillen/.

2   Lynn Henning, "Hurts, but So Good: Injury-Ravaged Guillen Remains Model Tigers Teammate," Detroit News, August 10, 2011. Retrieved from https://www.pressreader.com/usa/the-detroit-news/20110810/281994669172098.

3   Henning.

4   Steve Batterson, "Bandits Rally for Win," Quad City Times (Davenport, Iowa), May 17, 1996: 27.

5   Robert Falkoff, "Gens' Guillen Depends on DP Partner Hernandez as Translator," Jackson (Mississippi) Clarion-Ledger, June 30, 1997: 15.

6   Steve Kornacki, "Tigers' Carlos Guillen, Ramon Santiago Stress Importance of Latin Players to Learn English," Michigan Live, August 3, 2010. Retrieved from https://www.mlive.com/tigers/2010/08/tigers_infielders_carlos_guill.html.

7   Henning.

8   Left-hander John Halama was sent to Seattle to complete the trade on October 1, 1998.

9   Associated Press, "Injury Sidelines Seattle Prospect," Lansing (Michigan) State Journal, September 18, 1998: 23.

10   Associated Press, "Mariners: Jaha Puts on Display at Plate for A's," Spokane (Washington) Spokesman-Review, April 11, 1999: 41.

11   Larry LaRue, "Sharing the Pain," Spokane Spokesman-Review, April 25, 2000: 23.

12   Matt Glade, "Mariners: Guillen's Drag Bunt Sends 48,000 Safeco Fans into Delirium," Longview (Washington) Daily News, October 7, 2000: 10.

13   "Guillen Fills Gigantic Shoes," Greenfield (Indiana) Daily Reporter, March 13, 2001: 16.

14   "Guillen, Battling TB, Undergoes Minor Surgery to Stop Bleeding," Spokane Spokesman-Review, October 3, 2001: 14.

15   Angelo Bruscas, "Gullen Will Speak Out on DUI: M's Shortstop Sentenced to Community Service," Seattle Post-Intelligencer, March 5, 2003. Retrieved from https://www.seattlepi.com/news/article/Guillen-will-speak-out-on-DUI-1108953.php.

16   Tim Korte, "Mariners Ink Aurilia to One-Year Deal, Ship SS Guillen to Detroit," Longview Daily News, January 9, 2004: 20.

17   Gene Guidi, "Gullen on DL with Weak Quad," Detroit Free Press, August 18, 2005: 52.

18   Jorge L. Ortiz, "After Heated Dispute, Venezuela's Omar Vizquel, Carlos Guillen Unite for WBC," USA Today Sports, December 6, 2016, retrieved from https://www.usatoday.com/story/sports/mlb/2016/12/05/after-heated-dispute-venezuelans-omar-vizquel-carlos-guillen-unite-wbc/95023128/.

19   Andy Patton, "Detroit Tigers Shortstop Carlos Guillen May Have Retired in 2012, But He's Still Very Active in the Venezuelan Baseball Community," Motor City Bengals, June 21, 2018. Retrieved from https://motorcitybengals.com/2018/06/21/detroit-tigers-now-carlos-guillen/.

OZZIE GUILLÉN

BY GERARD KWILECKI

Ozzie Guillén was born to compete. The competition and motivation to win were the forces that drove the 5-foot-11 shortstop and future manager to put on the uniform every day. The fiery and combative personality was on display every game. He often vocalized his opinions; making controversial statements to the press became his trademark, much to the dismay of management. Often Guillén's comments would make it on the internet and in newspapers. Victims included former players, like future Hall of Famer Frank Thomas and White Sox general manager Ken Williams. Even the local press in Chicago was not immune from outbursts. His Gold Glove, clutch hitting, and work ethic helped him enjoy a 16-year major-league career. His aggressive nature and knowledge of baseball led him to a World Series title as the manager. But he was unable to manage his mouth and temper his comments. That inability eventually drove him out of baseball.

Oswaldo José Guillén Guillen Barrios was born on January 20, 1964, in Ocumare del Tuy, in northern Venezuela. Guillén's mother, Violeta, was a school principal. Ocumare del Tuy is known for its warm and clear climate. The average temperature is 64 to 83, with 60 days of rainfall annually: ideal conditions for playing baseball. Ozzie's childhood was not easy. He witnessed criminal activity in many forms. His formal education lasted until the seventh or eighth grade. The only outlet was baseball. The weather was perfect and it was his ticket out of poverty. Ozzie was determined to prove the doubters and naysayers wrong, by making it to the major leagues in the United States. The drive to prove people wrong was what propelled him to keep striving for the next step.

The person who had the most profound influence on Guillén's young life was Ernesto Aparicio, a longtime youth baseball coach and the uncle of Hall of Fame shortstop Luis Aparicio. Ernesto saw Guillén play and wanted to instruct him. Aparicio was the only teacher who could reach Ozzie. Guillén was not a great student, he only wanted to play baseball. All of his teachers reported to his mother about his lack of coursework. His teachers flunked him, and he turned to the prospect of playing professional baseball. Guillén had something that could not be taught and it made a huge impression on Aparicio: his love of the game.

Ozzie was signed by the San Diego Padres on December 17, 1980, a month shy of his 17th birthday. He was assigned to the Padres Gulf Coast League rookie team for the 1981 season, one of several teenagers on the team. He played in 55 games, finishing the season with a .259 batting average in 189 at-bats. Each year he moved up the Padres minor-league system, and played the entire 1984 season for the Padres' Triple-A affiliate,

the Las Vegas Stars. The next step was breaking camp with the big-league club in spring training 1985. Before that could happen, Guillén's career took a different path.

The Padres were coming off a 92-win season and a trip to the World Series in 1984. Even though they lost to the Detroit Tigers in five games, the plan was to add pieces to win it all in 1985. They had future Hall of Famer players Tony Gwynn and Goose Gossage, along with a veteran-laden team. They felt they needed one more ace to get them over the hump to win the first championship for San Diego. The Padres wanted a proven starting pitcher while the White Sox wanted a young player to take over at shortstop. The clubs hooked up for a seven-player trade on December 6, 1984. The Padres acquired starting pitcher LaMarr Hoyt and two minor leaguers, and the White Sox received two pitchers, a utility player, and one young shortstop who had yet to play a major-league game: 20-year-old Ozzie Guillén.

The Chicago White Sox were coming off a disappointing fifth-place finish in 1984, going 74-88 and finishing 10 games out of first place. They were managed by future Hall of Fame manager Tony La Russa. The shortstop for the 1984 team was Scott Fletcher. The White Sox wanted an upgrade at the position, and also wanted to dump salary. Owner Jerry Krause had roots as a baseball scout and he had watched Guillén play at Las Vegas. Krause[1] said, "He's as smart a young player as I have ever seen."[2] He liked what he saw. He liked his hustle and the way he played the game.

Guillén married Ibis Cardenas in 1983. They had three sons. Ozzie Jr. was born in 1985, followed by Oney in 1986 and Ozney in 1992. Ozzie Jr. earned his MBA and went to work for Cisco Systems. Oney was drafted in the 36th round by the White Sox in the 2007 amateur free-agent draft. He played two seasons of minor-league baseball before he retired and became a scout. Ozney was drafted by the White Sox in 2010, but retired as a player after five seasons of independent-league baseball. He managed the Houston Astros' short-season affiliate in the New York-Penn League in 2019.

Ozzie Guillén made the 1985 White Sox in spring training. He joined three future Hall of Fame players – Carlton Fisk, Harold Baines, and Tom Seaver. Guillén's style of play earned him comparisons to two Venezuelan shortstops who had storied major-league careers, Luis Aparicio and Dave Concepción. Guillén idolized both; he chose the number 13 in honor of Concepción. Guillén was in the starting lineup on Opening Day, April 9, 1985, leading off and playing shortstop. The White Sox were playing at Milwaukee. He got his first major-league hit in the top of the ninth off Brewers pitcher

Ray Searage, a bunt single to first base. His first professional hit defined Guillén's hustling style of play. He finished the game 1-for-5 at the plate, while making two putouts and getting three assists at shortstop in a 4-2 win over the Brewers in front of 53,027 fans.

The White Sox finished the 1985 season in third place in the American League West Division, six games behind the eventual World Series champions Kansas City Royals. Their 85-77 record was an 11-win improvement over the previous season. Guillén won the Rookie of the Year voting, receiving 72 percent of the first-place vote. He finished with a .273 batting average, one home run, 33 RBIs, and 134 hits in 150 games.

While Guillén was fast becoming a Chicago fan favorite, he was also gaining a reputation for being a talker. His teammate and future White Sox manager Robin Ventura said Guillén was "nonstop, never shuts up. He's talking to me, he's talking to umps, he's talking to fans, he's talking to the base runners."[3] The talker reputation would follow Guillén for the rest of his career, as both a player and a manager.

Guillén was considered a free swinger at the plate. In his rookie season he struck out 36 times and drew only 12 walks. The next season, in 547 at-bats, he struck out 52 times and again drew only 12 walks. Jim Fregosi, who managed Guillén for the White Sox from 1986 to 1988, considered him the "best defensive player I've ever seen," adding, "Nobody reads a groundball like Ozzie."[4] However, Fregosi wished his star shortstop would be more "disciplined and not swing at every pitch."[5] Guillén finished his 16-year career with 511 strikeouts and only 239 walks. However, in a testament to the way he played the game, his 511 whiffs constituted less than 8 percent of his at-bats.

Guillén spent 13 seasons with the White Sox, from 1985 to 1997. He suffered torn ligaments in his right knee in a collision with teammate Tim Raines in the 13th game of the 1992 season. A pop fly in short left field by the Yankees' Mel Hall in the top of the ninth inning sent Guillén back and Raines racing forward. They collided, allowing Hall to reach second base. Guillén left the game with his knee in tatters. Guillén's season was over. Before the 1992 season he had made the All-Star team three times (1988, 1990, and 1991). He earned a Gold Glove in 1990. His career can be defined by two halves, one before the injury and one after the injury.

Guillén's playing career with the White Sox ended after the 1997 season. His contract called for an automatic club option for $4 million for 1998 if he reached 550 plate appearances, with a $500,000 buyout. At age 34, he finished the season with 527 plate appearances, batting .245 with 120 hits, 4 home runs, and 52 runs batted in. He still maintained his excellence in the field, committing only 15 errors in 570 chances, for a .974 fielding percentage. The White Sox chose the buyout. Guillén signed with the Baltimore Orioles on January 29, 1998. He appeared in 12 games for the Orioles, playing shortstop and third base. He went 1-for-18 and was released on May 1. Guillén signed with the Atlanta Braves on May 6. The Braves were looking for a utility player, one who could come off the bench.

Guillén spent the rest of the 1998 season and all of 1999 with the Braves. He provided veteran leadership while playing all of the infield positions. He made his first World Series appearance in 1999 for the Braves versus the New York Yankees, going 0-for-5 in three games in the Yankees' sweep. The Braves released Guillén after 2000 spring training, and he immediately signed a free agent contract with the Tampa Bay Rays. He played in 63 games for the Rays, mostly at shortstop. He signed with the Rays for the 2001 season, but decided to retire to begin his coaching/managing career.

Guillén finished his 16-year playing career with 1,764 hits, 28 home runs, 619 runs batted in, and a .264 batting average. His calling card, his glove, defined his career. He made only 222 errors in 8,468 chances for a .974 fielding percentage, while playing one of the busiest positions on the field.

The next chapter of Guillén's career started in Montreal. He became a coach for the Expos in 2001, then the next season joined Jack McKeon's Florida Marlins, and was their third-base coach in 2002-03. The 2003 team won the World Series over the New York Yankees.

Guillén was ready to take his next step: managing. While the Marlins shocked the baseball world by beating the 101-win Yankees team, the Chicago White Sox finished second in the AL Central Division with an 86-76 record under six-year manager, Jerry Manuel. The White Sox made the playoffs only once under Manuel. They finished first in 2000, but lost to the Seattle Mariners in the Division Series. Manuel was voted Manager of the Year in 2000 but the team missed the playoffs he next three seasons. Ken Williams, Guillén's former teammate and now the club's general manager, was looking to breathe some new life into a White Sox team that had not been to the World Series since losing to the Los Angeles Dodgers in 1959.

Guillén had an interview set with Williams for the end of October 2003. He was in the middle of the World Series as the third-base coach of the Marlins, so some in the press thought his chances were not good to get the White Sox job. Others were being considered for the job – former Blue Jays manager Cito Gaston and other former managers Wally Backman, Buddy Bell, and Terry Francona. Guillén learned that Kenny Williams was leaning toward hiring Cito Gaston and became irate and wondered if "he was wasting his time if Williams' mind was already made up."[6] Gaston was the manager of the Toronto Blue Jays, winning back-to-back World Series titles in 1992-93. Guillén and Williams had a heated exchange discussing the managerial opening and Williams's leanings toward Gaston. Guillén's fiery personality changed Williams's mind. Williams felt his personality was just what the White Sox needed. Guillén was named the White Sox manager on November 3. Guillén became the first Venezuelan manager in the major leagues.

It did not take long for Guillén to raise eyebrows. His first game as manager was Monday, April 5, 2004, versus the Kansas City Royals. It was Opening Day game at Kansas City in front of 41,575 fans. The White Sox built a 7-3 lead going to the bottom of the ninth. The bullpen could not hold the lead, surrendering six runs in the bottom of the ninth and giving the Royals a 9-7 win. Guillén addressed his team, and told them to "go out and get drunk, do whatever … forget about this game."[7] He thought it was an innocent comment, but it was picked up by the press. Guillén did not apologize for the comment, saying he just wanted his players to forget about the game and be ready to play the next day. The comment may have worked, for the White Sox won the next game. The White Sox finished the 2004 season with an 83-79 record, earning a second-place finish in AL Central, nine games behind the Minnesota Twins. However, no one expected the season that lay ahead. The 2005 White Sox were ready to make history and Ozzie Guillén was ready to take his team to the next level.

The main theme for the 2005 White Sox was respect. Guillén felt the team needed to go earn it on the field. He always felt he and his teams were not getting the respect they deserved. Guillén first wanted the team to pick up his 2006 option before the 2005 season started. The team eventually did so in late May. Ken Williams made some trades and moves, setting the pieces in play for a historic 2005 run. The team had let longtime outfielder Magglio Ordóñez walk in free agency at the end of the 2004 season. He and Guillén did not get along. Guillén and Ordóñez had an exchange of words in the early part of 2005,

The fiery shortstop became a World Series-winning manager with the White Sox in 2005. Guillén played 13 major-league seasons, mainly in Chicago. (Jerry Coli / Dreamstime)

which garnered a lot of front-page press. Ordóñez felt Guillén was behind the White Sox decision not to re-sign him. He called Guillén his "enemy."[8] The White Sox traded outfielder Carlos Lee to the Milwaukee Brewers for another outfielder, Scott Podsednik. Guillén also had an exchange of words in the press with Carlos Lee. This was be a pattern in Guillén's life. He would lash out in the harshest way if he felt a player was not hustling, not giving everything, and was not loyal.

The 2005 White Sox finished first in the AL Central Division with a record of 99-63. It was a dramatic turnaround from the previous season. All the pieces were in place and everything clicked. Guillén's White Sox swept the defending World Series champion Boston Red Sox in the Division Series, then defeated the Anaheim Angels four games to one in the Championship Series. They squared off against the Houston Astros in the World Series. The surprising Astros were led by future Hall of Fame sluggers Craig Biggio and Jeff Bagwell. They also had six-time All-Star Lance Berkman filling in for an injured Bagwell. The Astros pitching staff was led by All-Stars Roy Oswalt, Andy Pettitte, and Roger Clemens, and closer Brad Lidge. The White Sox swept the Astros in four games with Joe Crede, Jermaine Dye, and Paul Konerko providing the offense. The pitching staff was led by Mark Buehrle, José Contreras, and closer Bobby Jenks. The White Sox had finally reached the top of the mountain with their scrappy manager. But a quick rise to the top could only mean a quicker fall.

Guillén was named the American League Manager of the Year by *The Sporting News*. He was the fifth White Sox manager to win the award. There was some discord, though: Guillén skipped the team's visit to the White House. Chicago Mayor Richard Daley felt Guillén should go to the White House. However, Guillen said he had already set his Venezuelan vacation for the same time as the White House visit. White Sox Chairman Jerry Reinsdorf defended Guillén, saying he had done everything asked of him after the World Series.

The next offseason story was Frank Thomas. Thomas was declared a free agent on November 8, 2005. He and general manager Williams did not get along, especially since his last contract with the White Sox contained a "diminished skills" clause. As the controversy unfolded in the press, Guillén took Williams's side.

Over the offseason the White Sox made several additions and had several departures. In addition to Frank Thomas, they traded Aaron Rowand to the Phillies and added future Hall of Fame designated hitter Jim Thome. They finished the 2006 season in third place in the Central Division with a record of 90-72, six games behind the division champion Minnesota Twins. The 2007 season was a disappointment: The White Sox plummeted to a record of 72-90. They rebounded in 2008 with a first-place division finish but lost to the Tampa Bay Rays in the Division Series. The 2009 season ended in another losing record (79-83) and a third-place finish. The 2010 team improved to 88-74 and a second-place finish. But Guillen was nearing an end to his time with the White Sox. The only question was how ugly it would get.

There had been tensions brewing between Guillén and Williams. They included many squabbles and disagreements. Guillén wanted a contract extension and raise. However, Reinsdorf was unwilling to give one given the sub-.500 season they were about to conclude. (The team finished 78-82.) Even Guillén's son, Oney, made comments on social media criticizing the front office. They cost Oney his job in the White Sox scouting department. The Miami Marlins were about to finish the 2011 season in fifth place in the National League East with a 72-90 record. They had gone through three managers during the season. They were looking for a new voice in the clubhouse, and contacted the White Sox about Guillén's availability. The Marlins and White Sox agreed on a trade in late September 2011 as the season neared an end. The Marlins sent two minor-league players to the White Sox for Guillén. Guillén became the manager of the Marlins for the 2012 season.

Guillén was introduced as manager of the Miami Marlins on September 28, 2011. He signed a four-year, $10 million contract. Guillén inherited a team composed mostly of veterans with a few young players. He persuaded veteran pitcher Mark Buehrle to join the Marlins from the White Sox. Veterans Carlos Lee, Hanley Ramirez, Carlos Zambrano, and Aníbal Sánchez anchored the team along with young stars Giancarlo Stanton, Nathan Eovaldi, and Logan Morrison. Guillén was the third-base coach when the Marlins won the 2003 World Series. It was hoped that he would find happiness, stability, and peace with the Marlins, having been given a long-term contract he so desperately craved. However, the honeymoon with the Marlins would be short and he quickly began to wear out his welcome.

Guillén sat down with *Time* magazine during spring training. The magazine's article was published on April 9, five days after Opening Day. Guillén covered a wide range of topics, from baseball to bullfighting to politics. Most of his comments did not raise any concern. However, it was his comments on Fidel Castro that gained headlines. "I love Fidel Castro … I respect Fidel Castro. … You know why? A lot of people wanted to kill Fidel Castro for the last 60 years, but that (expletive) is still here."[9] This comment created a firestorm and many called for Guillén's resignation. The outrage was especially high in the Miami Cuban community, many of whom had risked their lives to escape the communist regime. The Marlins suspended Guillén for five games. Guillén apologized for his comments, asking for forgiveness. The apology was not enough to stop the protests at the Marlins ballpark and calls for the Marlins to fire him. This was just the beginning of a trying year for Guillén and the Marlins.

The Marlins brought in a number of free agents to bolster the team. They also opened a brand new $634 million ballpark. The Marlins were 41-44 at the All-Star break, in fourth place and nine games out of first place. The season did not get better. The Marlins finished with their worst record in 13 years, in last place in the National League East with a 69-93 record, 29 games behind the first-place Washington Nationals. Players were making negative comments in the press about their opinionated managers. The final nail in Guillén's job as manager came when he criticized Marlins owner Jeffrey Loria. Guillén said, "If Jeffrey doesn't think I'm doing the job I should do … it's not the first time he's fired a manager. Look yourself in the mirror and ask why so many (expletive) managers come through here."[10] Needless to say, the comments were not taken favorably. Guillén was fired on October 23, after just one season on the job. The Marlins still owed him $7.5 million on his contract. The disappointing season along with his comments earlier in the season about Castro made for an easy decision for the Marlins at the end of 2012.

Ozzie Guillén will be remembered as player who hustled, played the game the right way, and played like an underdog with a chip on his shoulder. He loved the game of baseball. Playing baseball was all he ever wanted to do. He was able to carve out a 16-year major-league career. He wanted to transition to coaching, hoping one day to manage. He got his big break, taking the reins of the White Sox. He led them to their first World Series championship since 1917. He was opinionated and everyone knew his style. However, it was his opinions and brash attitude that prompted his downfall and cost him his jobs as manager. Only time will tell if this is how is he is remembered.

Guillén has said he wants to get back into baseball. He has granted some interviews and has shown a level of maturity and contrition. He has done some television work and coaching in the Venezuelan Baseball League. He has made some appearances at the annual SoxFest festivities. His son, Ozney, has been working in baseball, most recently with the Astros.

SOURCES

In addition to the sources cited in the Notes, the author consulted Baseball-Reference.com and the following:

Greenstein, Teddy. "Reinsdorf Bored with Issue, Says Guillen's Done 'Everything' Thus Far," *Chicago Tribune*, February 10, 2006.

Price, S. L. "War of the Words," *Sports Illustrated*, March 20, 2006: 74-81.

Rogers, Phil. "Guillen Won't Sell Himself Short," *Chicago Tribune*, March 2, 1997.

NOTES

1   Krause would go on to fame as the owner of the Chicago Bulls and the architect of their championship run in the 1990s.

2   Brett Ballantini, *The Wit and Wisdom of Ozzie Guillen* (Chicago: Triumph Books, 2006), 18.

3   Richard Hoffer, "Heeeere's Ozzie," *Sports Illustrated*, April 6, 1992: 93-95.

4   Hoffer.

5   Hoffer.

6   Ballantini, 25-26.

7   Scot Gregor, "Guillen Not Apologizing for 'Drunk' Comment," *Chicago Daily Herald,* April 8, 2004.

8   Ballantini, 52.

9   Ken Rosenthal, "This Time Guillen Has Gone Too Far," foxsports.com, April 9, 2012. https://www.foxsports.com/mlb/story/ozzie-guillen-should-be-suspended-by-miami-marlins-for-fidel-castro-comments-040912.

10 Sport Xchange. "Guillen's Comments Anger Marlins Owner," *Chicago Tribune*, September24, 2012. https://www.chicagotribune.com/sports/whitesox/ct-xpm-2012-09-24-chi-guillens-comments-anger-marlins-owner-20120924-story.html.

CARLOS HERNÁNDEZ

BY TONY S. OLIVER

Baseball has always been a game of figures, scenarios, and probabilities. While more than 19,000 men have worn a major-league uniform since 1876, tiny Donora, Pennsylvania, has somehow given us two of the greatest players of all time: Stan Musial and Ken Griffey Jr. Five Hall of Famers were born on May 14, despite each of the calendar's 365 days having an identical chance.[1] The DiMaggio and Alou families could stock an entire outfield without asking cousins to don a glove, but even those clans fall short of the Delahantys, who somehow produced five big leaguers at the turn of the nineteenth century.

And three ballplayers shared not just a name – Carlos Hernández – but also a birthplace, Venezuela. Two were active at the same time, with the third debuting the season after the first duo retired. The eldest of the trio, Carlos Alberto Hernández Almeida, was born on May 24, 1967, in San Félix, the old town of Ciudad Guyana, the largest city in the state of Bolívar. He enjoyed a decade in the major leagues as a catcher with the Dodgers, the Padres, and the Cardinals, earning a reputation as a defensive stalwart and beloved teammate.

Reggie Otero, a scout for the Dodgers who enjoyed a cup of coffee with the 1945 Cubs, discovered Hernández in Venezuela. On October 10, 1984, he signed with Los Angeles as an amateur free agent a few months after his 17th birthday. In hindsight, the day may have proved prophetic: It was the day the San Diego Padres won the second game of the World Series. The franchise would wait 14 long years to return to the fall classic, this time with Hernández in uniform. Hernández described his first baseball memory, as "fun … having fun out on the streets with my friends. In Little League, I played third, short. … I never caught as a youth."[2] He idolized Antonio "Tony" Armas, with whom he shared a Caracas clubhouse for seven consecutive years.[3]

Hernández also appeared in four games for the Leones of Caracas alongside another teenage prospect, Omar Vizquel, who would become the all-time Venezuelan leader in major-league games played, at-bats, and hits.[4] Sadly, Gonzalo Márquez, who signed Hernández to Caracas, died in December 1984. A true legend, Márquez played 20 consecutive seasons for the Leones (except for the 1975-1976 campaign with Magallanes) along with 76 games with the Cubs and Athletics.[5]

In the spring of 1985, the Dodgers assigned Hernández to the rookie-level Gulf Coast League and played him at the corner infield spots; none of the four catchers on the roster would reach the majors. Hernández was "just playing around, in the bullpen. … They saw my natural technique, lacking instruction. … My life changed; never had I even entertained the thought of catching. Manager Joe (José) Alvarez and batting coach

Leo Posada (uncle of Jorge) saw me and asked me to don the catcher's gear. I was hit by balls … quite honestly, fear … so I took the equipment home and called my dad. He said, 'It's up to you.' I asked my roommates and had one pitch, another one swing and miss so I could see the trajectory of the ball and lose the fear. Next day, I said, 'Joe, I'm ready! Give me a chance to show you the ball won't hit my chest. From there onwards, the rest is history. I fell in love with the position and even now, as a broadcaster, I imagine myself catching those games."

Hernández returned to the rookie team in 1986 as the main backstop, appearing in 39 games behind the plate and producing 64 hits in 205 at-bats. "More than my arm, the team saw the love that I'd devoted to the position … almost as if I'd caught for a long time." After taking the prior winter off, Hernández again wore Leones' colors, appearing in 14 games and hitting .400 but more importantly having a front-row view of Venezuelan catching pioneer Baudillo "Bo" Díaz as the club won the league championship. Díaz, the first Venezuelan-born catcher to play in the major leagues, was highly regarded in the country. The two-time major-league All-Star (once in each league) held the Venezuelan league record for home runs in a season (20, in 1979-1980) until Alex Cabrera bested him in 2013-2014, and owns a distinction that may never be equaled: He caught no-hitters 14 years apart by father and son, Urbano Lugo senior (1973) and junior (1987).[6]

Hernández enjoyed the West Coast sunshine in 1987 with Bakersfield of the advanced Class-A California League. He backed up Luis López, who was a notch higher in the prospect chart and had a stronger bat. Forty-eight games familiarized him with the pitching staff, many of whom would join him on subsequent ballclubs. Eager to get more work, he came back to Caracas and appeared in 20 games; the franchise repeated atop the circuit.

Bakersfield remained home for the 1988 campaign, with Hernández hitting .309 in 92 contests, but the team struggled to a .500 record as many of his former teammates jumped to the Double-A level. Hernández managed a .976 fielding percentage. He was called up to Albuquerque of the Triple-A Pacific Coast League for four games during which he went 1-for-8. Eager to continue polishing his skills, he appeared in 30 games with Caracas, hitting .234. One of his teammates, a right-handed pitcher who spent 13 years in the Venezuelan League but did not reach the majors, shared his name, making for a peculiar battery pairing Abbott and Costello would have loved. Hernández recalled a time when "I caught, Carlos pitched, and another Carlos Hernández was at the plate" though it may have been Carlos Quintana, whose maternal last name is also Hernández.

Having performed at the Single-A level, Hernández was slotted as the main backstop for the San Antonio Missions (Double-A Texas League) in 1989. He played in 99 games (95 on the field) and hit an even .300 to earn another Triple-A promotion, this time for 16 at-bats (three hits, two walks). He continued his hot bat with the Leones, batting .287 in 53 games as the marquee franchise won another championship.

The Dodgers had won two World Series titles in the 1980s, besting the Yankees in 1981 and the Athletics in 1988. Though Steve Sax, Fernando Valenzuela, and Pedro Guerrero were on both teams, only Mike Scioscia was a regular for the two-time champions. By 1990, Tommy Lasorda's trusted lieutenant had appeared in over 1,000 career games behind the plate and second-stringer Rick Dempsey was a 40-year-old veteran. The franchise had some young backstops in its farm system, including Mike Piazza, who would enjoy a Hall of Fame career. Hernández had competition, but he ensured that the Dodgers noticed by

Catcher Carlos Hernández began his big-league career with the Dodgers and Padres. He later mentored young pitchers during Houston's rebuild. (Otto Gruele Jr. / Getty Images Sports)

averaging .315 in 52 games with Albuquerque while backing up Darrin Fletcher, who caught 103 games and hit .291.

On April 20, 1990, when the Dodgers hosted the Astros, Lasorda gave Scioscia the night off, giving the 22-year old Hernández his initial taste of the big leagues. Penciled in as the seventh hitter, he shepherded veteran Tim Belcher through seven innings against a Houston ballclub mixing up-and-coming stars (Craig Biggio and Ken Caminiti) with on-their-way out 1980s stalwarts (Glenn Davis, Bill Doran). Belcher threw 103 pitches but allowed round-trippers to Franklin Stubbs and Davis. Hernández came to the plate three times; his first hit, a double off Jim Deshaies, was sandwiched between a fly out to right field and a groundball to shortstop. Alfredo Griffin drove him home on a single to center field which was thrown wild by Eric Yielding back to the infield for an unearned run. Hernández carries the ball with him in hopes DeShaies will sign it but acknowledges, "I always forget! I remember hitting well in Triple A. … I was looking for a lefty who threw changeups. … I thought, 'Wow! I have to look for my pitch.'"

Hernández thus became the fourth Venezuelan to catch a major-league baseball game. While many of his countrymen regard him as the second, behind Díaz, two others briefly squatted behind the plate before him: César Tóvar, who appeared in every position for the 1968 Minnesota Twins, and Toby Hernández, whose entire major-league career comprised five defensive innings and two at-bats for the 1984 Toronto Blue Jays.

Hernández wore number 41 as assigned but would inherit number 26 from Alejandro Peña, a number he had used in Venezuela. He would appear in nine more games (10 total), garnering 20 plate appearances, scoring two runs, and reaching base safely on three singles after the initial double. He scored another run and drove in a single teammate, raising no eyebrows with the lumber. His defensive numbers were better: He was errorless with one stolen base allowed, four caught-stealing runners, two wild pitches, and one passed ball against his record. His catcher's ERA was 3.27, almost half a run better than the Dodgers' full-year mark, but the club ended in second place behind eventual World Series champion Cincinnati.

Hernández has warm memories of Scioscia, who was not concerned about the youngster usurping his position. "When I made it to the majors, the first one to give me tips was (Mike) Scioscia. He knew me from the time I signed and always invited me to train. He nicknamed me 'El Torito' (the little bull) since I was not tall but stocky and liked to hit the weights. I learned how to become tough by watching him, blocking the plate. He was not only a teammate but also a mentor. He would say: 'Carlos, go check out the video. … What do you think about that pitch, why was a sinker ball called, etc.' He was an immense influence; he taught me to be calm, just like he always was, and to observe."

The Dodgers kept Hernández at Albuquerque to start 1991 but he had nothing left to prove at Triple A. He hit .345 with the Dukes, a team laden with young talent: John Wetteland, Henry Rodríguez, José Offerman, Raúl Mondesí, Eric Karros, and

Tom Goodwin all logged time in New Mexico before making their mark in the big leagues. The Dodgers called him up in the summer for a five-game stint; he got into three contests as a late-inning defensive substitution, pinch-hit without taking the field in San Diego, and started a game in Montréal. His five appearances yielded one sacrifice fly and one hit by pitch. September brought another call-up as the Dodgers and Braves fought for the National League West crown and Hernández appeared in nine games as a defensive substitution before starting on the last day of the season. The game may have been inconsequential: Atlanta had already clinched the division and Los Angeles played most of its prospects. However, the lineup was filled with his Albuquerque teammates: the future of Los Angeles. Hernández led five pitchers to a complete-game shutout of San Francisco in Candlestick Park, giving the Dodgers brass confidence to entrust him as the main backup option for Scioscia. The franchise blessed his continued participation in the winter circuit and Hernández produced a .290 average for the Leones.

The 1992 Dodgers stumbled to a last-place finish, losing 99 games, the worst tally for the franchise since the 1908 Superbas. The club was in the difficult stages of the rebuild, with a collection of past-their-prime players no longer performing while the younger crew was not quite ready for prime time. Karros provided some pop, hammering 20 home runs while winning the Rookie of the Year Award. Hernández started 47 games (and played in 22 others), and enjoyed two eight-game hitting streaks. Pitchers had a 3.82 ERA with him behind the plate, almost three-quarters of a run higher than with Scioscia. With no October plans, he sought the extra practice of Caribbean baseball and played in 45 games for Caracas, again sharing duties with Henry Blanco.

Los Angeles was a full 18 games better in 1993, reaching .500 after the abysmal prior season. Scioscia had retired; the Piazza era officially began as the one-time 62nd-round pick took the National League by storm, terrorizing pitchers with power (35 round-trippers) and contact (.318 batting average) en route to a unanimous Rookie of the Year Award. Hernández received 102 plate appearances and contributed a .253 average. The Dodgers took full advantage of their catchers' vigor as the tandem caught all 162 games (no other player appeared behind the plate) and the team boasted of the senior circuit's third best ERA. For the first time since 1985, Hernández sat out the Venezuelan league campaign.

While dark clouds circled the spring of 1994 as the player strike loomed, Los Angeles entered the season with great expectations. Another prospect, Mondesí, was ready to take over the right-field position and provide Karros and Piazza with some lineup protection. The juggernaut Braves had moved to the redesigned Eastern Division, removing the biggest obstacle to the Dodgers' advancement. While the team underperformed and managed to finish only two games above .500, that was sufficient in the mediocre NL West. Piazza played in 107 games and avoided the sophomore jinx, producing an OPS of .910 and

guiding the hurlers to a 3.96 catcher's ERA. Hernández's season had started on the disabled list due to a lower back sprain and he was unable to get into a groove; his offensive production fell to .219/.231/.344 and he caught a few blowouts (a 5-13 loss vs. Colorado and a 4-16 defeat vs. Houston). The back pain was a harbinger for the rest of his career, as the discomfort would never cease and ultimately sap him of power and agility. Hungry for more baseball, Hernández played in a career-high 55 games for Caracas during the winter, hitting .218 as the team won yet another title; this would be his last crown.

The 1995 season was bittersweet for Hernández. Its start was delayed by the ongoing strike until future Supreme Court Justice Sonia Sotomayor's injunction against the owners paved the way for the game's return. Once again backing up Piazza, Hernández suffered through his worst season by managing a minuscule .149 average in 103 plate appearances. Los Angeles was once again the cream of the West, but had fierce competition from the Colorado Rockies, who reached the postseason as the wild card in only their third year. The Reds swept the Dodgers in the NLDS with Piazza playing every single inning; Hernández was thus deprived of playoff baseball in the grandest of stages. He rejoined Caracas and provided a solid bat (.277 average) along with his customary dependable glove during the 1995-1996 Venezuelan league season.

Riding high from his winter foray, Hernández entered 1996 again as the backup to Piazza but found himself losing playing time to veteran Tom Prince, who had been acquired the prior year. His back was again problematic and he played in only 13 games, his lowest tally since his 1990 call-up. His season was effectively shut down on May 16 after he caught a 4-2 Dodgers victory over the Phillies. He singled in four at-bats, unaware that he would never again wear the team's blue-and-whites. He shook off the doldrums with a robust .282 performance in 38 games for the 1996-1997 Caracas club.

Having been granted free agency after the 1996 World Series, Hernández quickly found a new club a scant two-hour drive from Chavez Ravine. The defending division champion Padres had distributed catching duties among John Flaherty, Brad Ausmus, and Brian Johnson but had parted ways with the latter two. Hernández responded with his finest offensive season (percentage-wise), slashing .313/.328/.448 and gunning down 43 percent of would-be thieves, 11 percentage points above the 1997 league average, despite missing almost a month with a calf injury. In the offseason, San Diego traded Flaherty to Tampa Bay for Andy Sheets and Brian Boehringer, promoting Hernández to starting catcher for the first time in his big-league career. He wore number 9 in honor of Posada, a number he still keeps "even to play bocce ball."

In 1998 the team rode a career season from Greg Vaughn (50 home runs, third in the league behind Mark McGwire and Sammy Sosa), solid numbers from Wally Joyner and Tony Gwynn, and dominating performances from Kevin Brown, Andy Ashby, and Trevor Hoffman to the franchise's second Word Series appearance. Only Gwynn remained from the 1984 team and the uniforms were no longer mustard brown, but magic was in the air and 2.56 million of the San Diego faithful passed the Qualcomm Stadium (née Jack Murphy) turnstiles to cheer the Padres. Hernández proved durable, playing in a career-high 129 games and contributing 9 home runs and 52 RBIs. He fielded at a .992 clip, good for fifth in the NL (behind Javier López, Scott Servais, and former teammates Johnson and Ausmus), while placing second in range factor per nine innings and fifth in catcher's ERA (minimum plate appearances caught).[7]

He thrived in the postseason, going 5-for-12 in the LDS against the Astros and appearing in all four games. The 1998 NLCS pitted Hernández against fellow Venezuelan Eddie Pérez, the Braves' standout backup catcher who enjoyed his finest offensive season. Although they did not start the same games, both enjoyed significant playing time, as Hernández appeared in all six contests while Pérez did so in three. Hernández collected six hits in 18 at-bats, bringing his average to .367 in the postseason, tops on the team. The New York Yankees, who won a franchise-record 114 games in the regular season, dispatched the Padres in stunning fashion, with Hernández going hitless in his two starts but swatting a single in Game Two (entering for Greg Myers) and Game Three (entering for Jim Leyritz). His 2-for-10 performance was disappointing but also in line with the team's showing.

The 1999 Padres could not sustain the momentum, dropping to fourth place on a 74-88 record. The club lost vocal ace Brown and on-field cheerleader Caminiti to free agency, creating massive holes in the dugout, with an even bigger loss behind the plate once training camp began. "Baseball breaks our heart. It is designed to break your heart. The game begins in the spring … and leaves you to face fall all alone." Although the late Commissioner Bart Giamatti was referring to the game's synchronicity with the four seasons, his evocation of misfortune was flipped for Hernández, whose 1999 season crumbled not in the fall, like the Padres' title hopes the prior year, but rather in the spring.

No strangers to tragedy, the Greeks gave us the myth of Achilles, whose body was invulnerable except for his now-namesake heel. Many athletes have succumbed to the drastic injury to the calcaneal tendon, with rehabilitation ranging from six months to a year and success not being guaranteed. Decreased explosiveness in movement is likely, and basketball players dread the damage; Kobe Bryant was never the same after rupturing his Achilles' tendon at age 34, and Kevin Durant ruptured his during the 2019 NBA finals.[8] In baseball, Ryan Howard saw his career forever changed on the last play of the 2011 NLDS.[9]

For a catcher, who spends half the game squatting and stretching the ligaments, the injury can cause chronic discomfort. Hernández spent the entire year in the disabled list while rehabilitating his injury and played 16 games with the Leones during the Venezuelan Winter League, backing up Henry Blanco. He returned to the majors on Opening Day 2000, catching all nine innings of the Padres' 2-1 loss to the Mets. He collected two singles and even attempted to steal a base; his former teammate

Piazza gunned him down with Rey Ordóñez applying the tag: "That must have been a missed hit-and-run … but maybe I let Mike throw me out, since he was my friend."

Hernández played in 58 of San Diego's first 103 games before being traded at the deadline to the Cardinals with prospect Nate Tebbs, who would not reach the majors. The Padres were moving in a younger direction, having entrusted catching duties to Ben Davis and Wiki González; in return, they received Heathcliff Slocumb, who would retire at year's end, and prospect Ben Johnson, who would break into the big leagues in 2005. Years later, Cardinals and Padres fans were treated to an intriguing "what if" scenario, per Derrick Goold of the *St. Louis Post-Dispatch*: Albert Pujols, then a minor leaguer at Peoria, was considered as part of the deal, before the Cardinals decided to part with Johnson instead.[10]

Hernández joined a St. Louis team on its way to the postseason and played well, hitting .275 while starting 15 games to backup starter Mike Matheny. The trade proved to be fortuitous as Matheny sliced his finger with a hunting knife and missed the postseason.[11] Pressed into full-time duty, Hernández delivered three hits in the NLDS against Atlanta and a further four versus the Mets in the NLCS. Although the Redbirds did not reach the World Series, Hernández finished his career by appearing in all eight of his team's playoff games.

Hernández hung up his spikes with a .253/.298/.354 slash line (an OPS+ of 76) in 488 regular-season games. He cherished the postseason, hitting .299 (20-for-67) in 22 games. For the better part of his career, he played through two herniated discs; "I had gone home before reporting to Caracas and was fielding groundballs and always felt pain in my back, despite therapy and exercise. Surgery (in 2000) effectively ended my career. … I needed cortisone twice a week during my time with St. Louis. Although I'd had knee and shoulder surgeries, and the 1999 Achilles' surgery … the back was the big thing." He numbered Quilvio Veras, Plácido Polanco, Pedro and Ramón Martínez, José Offerman, José Hernández, Pedro Astacio, and José Vizcaíno among his favorite teammates, with a special mention for Mariano Duncan, who "helped my wife and me when we made it to the majors."

At the end of the 2020 season, Hernández ranked 17th among Venezuelan players in games Tóvar, Pablo Sandoval, and Eduardo Escobar all caught at least one and played more games than Hernández but were predominantly fielders at other positions. Upon his retirement, he was second on the list –behind only pioneer Díaz – but has since been surpassed by the healthy crop of Venezuelan backstops he inspired. He was surprisingly effective against Hall of Famer Tom Glavine (11-for-30, two home runs, 1.024 OPS) and Greg Maddux (5-for-10, 1.145 OPS) but could not figure out Chan Ho Park (1-for-14) or Darryl Kile (1-for-13).

After a winter of rest, Hernández returned to Venezuela for one last winter campaign, once again backing up Blanco for Caracas. In his 15 seasons, all with the league's most storied franchise, he played in 433 games with batting (.257) and slugging (.349) numbers similar to those of his major-league career. The postseason added a further 114 games with a .255 average, winning titles in 1986-1987, 1987-1988, 1989-1990, and 1994-1995. The last one holds a special place in his memory, as Caracas had to defeat both Maracaibo (Zulia) and Magallanes. "We had to win two games to get to the Caribbean Series and Omar Daal had to pitch both."

In 2004 Hernández ventured across the border from his second home in San Diego, managing the Toros of Tijuana to the Mexican Baseball League playoffs.[12] The 16-team league, not to be confused with the Mexican Pacific League which plays during the fall and winter, serves as a summer league on par with the International League and the Pacific Coast League. However, its teams are not affiliated with specific major-league franchises.[13]

His curiosity piqued, Hernández answered the call of the Caracas ballclub in the winter of 2006. Although the franchise had won both the Venezuelan title and the Caribbean Series the prior winter, it stumbled out of the gate to an 11-21 mark. Skipper Carlos Subero was fired on November 21 and Hernández steered the ship for the last 30 games (18-12). The team made the postseason but did not win the league.[14] He remained at the helm for the 2007-2008, but the team's 29-34 register prevented it from joining the playoffs.

Hernández returned to the Padres organization in 2005, serving as the club's bullpen catcher and Latin American instructor/roving catcher instructor.[15] Arizona poached him from the Padres, and he spent three years as the Diamondbacks' catching coordinator. However, his ties to San Diego were strong and he would soon share his baseball wisdom in a new capacity.

The franchise, acknowledging its large Latin fan base, decided to complement its bilingual radio narration with Spanish television broadcasts via FoxDeportes and tapped Hernández as a color analyst, the 2021 season marked his 10th in the role.[16]

Hernández moonlights as one-half of the Spanish-language radio broadcast team with Eduardo Ortega on XEMO 860 AM. He remains a beloved figure in San Diego thanks to the magical 1998 Padres season. Despite no longer wearing the tools of ignorance, he finds it hard to rid himself of the mindset. "My mentors were John Roseboro, Roy Campanella, Scioscia, Kevin Kennedy. … Kevin said, 'Catchers don't cry.'" He has grown accustomed to the role behind the microphone, acknowledging that "baseball has changed a lot, especially in game situations … how to tie a close game. … It's difficult for me, at 52, to reset my mind; I'd prefer people to focus on how to win today's game. I am happy since I have been able to learn a different aspect of my life."

Hernández is poignant when describing the state of baseball in his native Venezuela. The nation's major-league output has been directly correlated with its economic well-being. As the Chávez (and now Maduro) regime implements its socio-economic ideas, the siren song of major-league baseball offers a respite: "The country is suffering from all sides … and one of its hopes is for its sons to become baseball players. People are doing what they can to seek a better future. It's the only opportunity for their children, whereas once they could have other options via education. Baseball has always been our number-one sport; what better way for a kid to support his family than through baseball. To me, that's the main reason we're having so many big-league ballplayers."

Hernández does not solely reflect on the maudlin reality; he also seeks solace in what it could have been. "My dream was always to open up an academy in my hometown. We (my contemporaries) never thought of living in the United States; we always thought of returning like the Dominicans and Puerto Ricans. … Having played in the majors meant I was indebted to many people and to give the youth a good baseball school. Sadly, I don't think I'll be able to fulfill that, and it'll forever be a pain in my soul."

ACKNOWLEDGMENTS:

Vanessa Domínguez, coordinator of business communications for the San Diego Padres, for connecting me to Carlos Hernández

Carlos Hernández for graciously agreeing to a phone interview

Pete Palmer and Jim Wheeler for detailed disabled list records

SOURCES

In addition to the sources cited in the Notes, the author relied extensively on Baseball-Reference.com

NOTES

1   Bill Francis, "May Day: More Hall of Famers Born on May 14 Than Any Other Day," https://baseballhall.org/discover/hofers-born-on-may-14.

2   Carlos Hernández, telephone interview, August 1, 2019. Unless otherwise indicated, all quotations directly attributed to Carlos Hernández come from this interview.

3   http://www.pelotabinaria.com.ve/beisbol/tem_equ.php?EQ=LEO&TE=1984-85.

4   As of the conclusion of the 2020 season.

5   http://www.pelotabinaria.com.ve/beisbol/mostrar.php?ID=marqgon001.

6   http://museodebeisbol.com/salon_fama_venezolano/detalles/2006/baudilio-jos-daz.

7   Qualifying requirements: 0.67 Gm and Chances/Team Game (fielding). https://www.baseball-reference.com/leagues/NL/1998-fielding-leaders.shtml.

8   James O'Connell, "As Kevin Durant Waits for the Worst, Here's How NBA, NFL, MLB, and NHL Players Returned from Torn Achilles," New York Daily News, June 11, 2019. https://www.nydailynews.com/sports/basketball/ny-sports-basketball-kevin-durant-achilles-injury-20190611-bmob-63p66rgdzakj2ggshy4n5i-story.html.

9   Associated Press, "Ryan Howard Has Torn Achilles," October 10, 2011. https://www.espn.com/mlb/playoffs/2011/story/_/

id/7078557/2011-nlds-philadelphia-phillies-1b-ryan-howard-torn-left-achilles-tendon.

10   Derrick Goold, "A Scout, a Backup Catcher, and the Trade That Would Have Changed Cardinals History," *St. Louis Post-Dispatch*, June 22, 2019. https://www.stltoday.com/sports/baseball/professional/goold-a-scout-a-backup-catcher-pujols-the-trade-that/article_575051b8-1cd4-5a32-9c5f-021fddb42cdd.html#1.

11   Craig Barnes, "Matheny Injury Leaves Painful Memories," *South Florida Sun-Sentinel,* April 1, 2001. https://www.sun-sentinel.com/news/fl-xpm-2001-04-01-0103250400-story.html.

12   https://www.baseball-reference.com/register/league.cgi?id=89861b95.

13   https://www.milb.com/mexican/about/equipos.

14   http://www.leones.com/historia.php.

15   http://sandiego.padres.mlb.com/content/printer_friendly/sd/y2005/m11/d28/c1273165.jsp.

16   https://www.gaslampball.com/2012/3/27/2906971/sources-former-padres-catcher-carlos-hernandez-to-be-color-analyst.

ENZO HERNÁNDEZ

BY NELSON JULIÁN MORALES ÁLVAREZ

In his time, Enzo Hernández was a special player for fans of Venezuelan baseball. Both Hernández and David Concepción were thought of as successors to Alfonso "Chico" Carrasquel and Luis Aparicio, and Venezuela began to be seen as the cradle of the shortstop.

Enzo Octavio Hernández Martínez was born on February 12, 1949, in the hamlet of El Guasimo, near Valle Guanape, Anzoategui State, on the farm of his grandfather Pedro Rafael Valera, the popular "Don Rubito." His parents were Ricarte Hernández and Ramona Martínez de Hernández, who lived in a nearby town, San Tomé. When Enzo was barely a year old, his father was a nurse employed in the hospital of the Mene Grande Oil Company. Enzo began high school at the Liceo Briceño Méndez, and then attended Liceo Guanipa, but he left school after signing at age 17 with Los Tiburones de La Guaira in Venezuela and the Houston Astros.[1] La Guaira is a coastal city about 30 km (18.6 miles) from Caracas. The team typically plays its home games in Caracas.

Hernández had only played baseball as a street game before 1959, when Francisco Pinto, an important former Venezuelan amateur player, organized a children's championship that gave 10-year-old Enzo the opportunity to start playing organized baseball. He played in the 1959 national championship, in Maturin, Monagas state. Two years later, he was selected to represent Anzoátegui state in the national championships. There was no organized baseball for young adolescents, but at age 16, he joined the AA team of the Mene Grande Oil Company. His play earned him a position with the highest-level amateur team in the 1965 national games in Barcelona, capital of Anzoátegui. Alfonso Carrasquel selected him for the team. Enzo told author Carlos Cárdenas Lares, "Before I got to training, I was told that Alfonso was interested in me. I had gone as a second baseman, but I did not like the position very much because I had never played it. Later, I told Alfonso that I did not really play that position, but shortstop since I was 9 years old, so he put me in the shortstop and, although many people criticized him, Anzoátegui's shortstop in those nationals was me."[2]

In 1966 Hernández continued playing top-level amateur baseball and after he appeared at the national games, he was signed by Tiburones de La Guaira. As he told Cárdenas Lares, "The people of La Guaira had seen me in Maracay and they went to look for me in Puerto La Cruz, where I had moved with my family. They took me to Catia La Mar, to the Mamo military base. There I was practicing the team and they signed me for 3,000 or 5,000 bolivars."[3]

Five thousand bolivars was equivalent to $1,162 US at the time. Hernández was signed at the same time by Tony Pacheco, a scout for the Houston Astros. In his first year in the United States, he was sent to the Cocoa Astros of the Class-A Florida State League. He appeared in 129 games and it was a difficult year: He batted only .187 and made 39 errors. It was a tense time and he worried that he would be released.

He added, "With only a little to finish the season, the manager [Walt Matthews] called me. I was scared … but it was to send me to Houston for a few days to see the big-league games, while the Instructional League began. It was positive for me. As Tony Pacheco told me, if after having hit .180 in Class A they did that, it was because they saw something special in you."[4]

Starting at age 18 with the Tiburones de La Guaira in the 1967-1968 season, his luck could not be better – the team's player-manager was Luis Aparicio. Aparicio already had 12 major-league seasons as a shortstop with the Chicago White Sox and Baltimore Orioles, had been Rookie of the Year in 1956, had seven Gold Gloves and nine consecutive seasons leading the American League in stolen bases. Aparicio was looking for a shortstop who would allow him to take a breather. Enzo played in 32 of the team's 60 games, finishing with a .235 batting average. Aparicio was in 40 games at either shortstop or third base.[5]

In 1968 the Astros assigned Hernández to the Greensboro Patriots of the Class-A Carolina League, where he played in 89 games, batting .226 with 38 errors. He got into three Triple-A games for Oklahoma City of the Pacific Coast League. He still needed work to improve his game.

In Venezuelan League winter ball, the Tiburones made Hernández the regular shortstop in 1968-69. Aparicio appeared in only 15 games and was no longer manager. Hernández was largely on his own. Although he batted just .228, he was more solid defensively, playing alongside experienced quality players such as Remigio Hermoso at second base and José Herrera at third. The Tiburones won their fourth Venezuelan Professional Baseball title in the team's first seven years. It was Enzo's first great professional triumph.

In December 1968, while playing in Venezuela, he was traded by the Astros. He was sent to Baltimore along with Cuban pitcher Miguel Angel "Mike" Cuellar and a minor-league player for Curt Blefary and another minor leaguer. In 1969, Cuellar became the first Latin American player to win the Cy Young Award as the best pitcher in the American League (shared with Denny McLain). The Orioles wanted Hernández as a backup to their shortstop, Mark Belanger, coming off his first full season as starter.

The Orioles placed Hernández with the Dallas-Fort Worth Spurs of the Double-A Texas League, but he played in just two games before being assigned to the Miami Marlins of the

Class-A Florida State League. He became a much more selective hitter with good contact, and had above-average speed and solid defense. He was a difficult hitter to strike out in 1969, with just 17 strikeouts in 425 plate appearances. He stole 26 bases in 30 attempts and hit for a career-high .247.

The Orioles added Hernández to their 40-man roster and invited him to spring training with the big-league club in 1970. His first 42 games were with Dallas-Fort Worth, where he hit .282. Promoted to the Triple-A Rochester Red Wings (International League), he hit .266 in 100 games, with 17 stolen bases, 61 runs scored, 39 RBIs, and only 22 strikeouts (one every 19 plate appearances). In addition, he perfected the bunt as a weapon that gained him 12 successful sacrifices to advance the runners. But Mark Belanger, who had succeeded Aparicio with the Orioles, seemed set at shortstop.

The 1969 expansion added two new teams in each league. One of the expansion teams was the San Diego Padres, managed by Preston Gómez, the first Latin-American named as manager for a full season in the big leagues. He hadn't been satisfied with the work of the shortstops he'd had and kept his eye on Hernández.

"Hernández could solve our shortstop problem for years to come," Gómez told *The Sporting News*.[6] In December 1970 the Orioles and Padres executed a six-player trade. Hernández, Fred Beene, Tom Phoebus, and Al Severinsen went to the Padres for Pat Dobson and Tom Dukes.[7]

That winter, Enzo played his fourth season for the Tiburones de La Guaira, won his second title with the team and went to his first Caribbean Series. The Tigers del Licey won the Series in Puerto Rico in February 1971.

To win the job as starting shortstop for the Padres in 1971, Hernández had to beat out both the Quisqueyano Rafael Robles and Tommy Dean, who had played the most Padres games in their two-year history. He won the job. Dean remained as backup. Gómez had his new shortstop.

Hernández debuted on April 17, 1971, against the St. Louis Cardinals in San Diego. He wore number 11 on his back, a tribute to his idol and mentor Aparicio. Tom Phoebus started for the Padres; future Hall of Famer Steve Carlton for the Cardinals.

Hernández batted eighth. His first big-league at-bat came in the bottom of the second, with the Cardinals up 1-0. He drew a base on balls. In the bottom of the fourth inning, the Cardinals holding a 2-0 lead, he got the first of his 522 major-league hits. Carlton shut out the Padres, 4-0.

In most of his 143 games in 1971, Hernández batted leadoff. He finished his first season with a .222 batting average, 21 stolen bases, 54 walks, 34 strikeouts, and 12 sacrifice hits. He had become the first Latin American shortstop to steal more than 20 bases in the National League. The only other Latin rookie to steal at least 20 bases was his mentor, Luis Aparicio, who had stolen 21 bases in 1956.

In the Venezuelan Professional Baseball League, Hernández played his fifth consecutive season with the Tiburones de La Guaira. He reported late and played in just 24 of the team's 60 games. It was the first time in three seasons that he finished with fewer than 200 at-bats in Venezuela, but in both 1970 and 1971, he had batted more than 500 times in US baseball. He joined the Tiburones de La Guaira in their eighth consecutive final.

For the 1972 Padres season, Hernández began as the team's regular shortstop. After a last-place finish in 1971 and a slow start in 1972, ownership replaced Preston Gómez on April 27, 1972, with Don Zimmer. One of the best allies Hernández had in his career left the team. Zimmer had Hernández bat in eighth place more games than not. Zimmer also frequently pinch-hit for him later in games, some 45 times in all. Consequently, he had more than 200 fewer at-bats, He hit for a .195 average, but even with so many fewer plate appearances, he stole 24 bases, bettering his own mark for most bases stolen by a Latin American shortstop in the National League. Hernández also led the league as the most efficient base stealer, succeeding 89 percent of the time. Base stealing was coming back as an offensive weapon; Lou Brock led the league with 63.

That winter, Hernández was reunited with Preston Gómez, who was named as manager of the Tiburones. Enzo had one of his best campaigns in Venezuelan league baseball, but La Guaira's string of eight consecutive seasons reaching the league finals was snapped.

The 1973 Padres season was a difficult one. Hernández appeared in just 70 games, with 247 at-bats, hitting .223 with 15 steals. He had begun to suffer some injuries. Through June 13, he had hit leadoff in almost every game and was hitting .240 with 15 stolen bases, but problems with back pain took him out of the lineup until July 26. When he came back, he was subpar, getting into only 17 games and hitting .149, Derrel Thomas ended up playing shortstop in most of the games when Enzo was out.

Hernández played in Venezuela again in the winter, under Preston Gómez as manager. He demonstrated he had returned to health and finished with the best batting average of his career (.285 with 14 steals). His team finished first in the regular round, and were regarded as favorites for the semifinals, but a player strike brought about a premature end to a season that had looked very promising. Hernández came back to the United States, strengthened and facing a new manager: John McNamara.

The 1974 season was perhaps the best of Enzo's career as a big leaguer. He achieved personal bests in hits (119), runs batted in (34), runs scored (55), and stolen bases (37).[8] He was named Player of the Week in the National League for the week of August 4-11, the first Latin player to earn the honor.

From their inception through 1974, the Padres had always finished last in the West Division, but the farm system began to bear fruit. Dave Winfield had come up and Randy Jones became the first Padres pitcher to win 20 games. Veteran players like Willie McCovey, Bobby Tolan, and Tito Fuentes played well, and the team finished 71-91, in fourth place.

Hernández hit .218 in 116 games, again often pinch-hit for later in games. Nevertheless, he stole another 20 bases and led all of baseball with 24 sacrifice hits. He was the first Latino player in the National League with at least 20 steals and 20 sacrifice hits in the same season.[9]

In Venezuelan ball, Hernández played for a different team. From 1962 until at least 2019, Caracas had two teams play at the stadium of the Ciudad Universitaria de Caracas, the Leones del Caracas and the Tiburones de La Guaira, both sharing a stadium. The university and teams could not come to agreement on the amount of rent in 1975-76. Consequently, the teams merged and played in another city, Portuguesa, as the Tibuleones. Enzo played in 64 games with 240 at-bats, 18 runs scored, and 17 RBIs. His batting average was the lowest of his career in Venezuela, .213.

The Padres told Hernández in spring training that he'd have to compete to win the shortstop slot; he needed to hit better, and thus put himself in a better position to be able to use his base stealing skills. Hector Torres played a few more games than Hernández in their first couple of months, but Torres hit only .143 during June. Randy Jones also was said to have told manager Dick Williams that he wanted Enzo at shortstop when he was on the mound. As noted, Jones was a 20-game winner. In 1976 he won 22 games and the first Cy Young Award for the franchise.

Despite some back pains in mid-September, Hernández played in 113 games, and hit for a career-best .256 batting average.

His back problems kept him out of Venezuelan ball, save for six games. He spent most of 1977 on the disabled list. Without San Diego's approval, he underwent back surgery. Though the operation was successful, he was released after only seven games.

Hernández rested during the 1977-1978 season in Venezuela. In April 1978 the Los Angeles Dodgers signed him to a minor-league contract, and he was sent to the Triple-A Albuquerque Dukes. He was called up to the Dodgers in mid-August and appeared briefly in four games, with only three plate appearances. There were his last games as a big leaguer.

Hernández had played over eight seasons, with 2,612 plate appearances, 522 hits, 129 stolen bases, and 83 sacrifice hits. He was successful in 79.6 percent of his stolen-base attempts (129 steals in 162 attempts).

With the Tiburones Hernández played his 11th season and seemed to have fully recovered from his injuries. He played in 62 games and batted .251 in 231 at-bats. For the first time in its history, La Guaira failed to reach the semifinals, finishing last in the regular round.

At this point, Hernández simply disappeared from public sight; there were no announcements of his retirement. Since he was only 29 years old, many expected his return, but new players came along and Hernández remained out of the public eye.

Enzo continued his life in the city of El Tigre in eastern Venezuela with his wife (since 1972), Ellys, and their two daughters, Ellys Maria and Janet Virginia. The Hernández family dedicated themselves to running a pharmacy that they had in partnership with Dr. Antonio Caraballo, Enzo's father-in-law.

On January 13, 2013, Enzo Hernández took his life at his home. He had been suffering acute depression and a reported

Known for his defense, Hernández set a Padres record with 595 assists in 1971. He spent seven seasons in the majors. (SABR / The Rucker Archive)

decline in health. Bruce Markusen in an article in *Fangraphs* noted a number of recent suicides among former baseball players. He wrote, "Hernández' passing did not create major headlines, but it has stirred a reaction from me on two different fronts. The first involves a broader issue, one that seems to be becoming more prevalent in our society. If the preliminary reports of suicide are true, Hernández becomes the fourth former big leaguer to take his own life in the last two years, after Mike Flanagan, Hideki Irabu, and Ryan Freel. If we go back a little further, former major league infielder Keith Drumright committed suicide in 2010, and retired pitcher Brian Powell took his own life in 2009. So that is six suicide deaths in the past four years."[10]

The cause of death was an apparent overdose of prescribed painkillers.[11]

Markusen added, "[T]hese suicide deaths should not be completely ignored. The Alumni Association and the Baseball Assistance Team do terrific work with ex-players during their retirement years, but that is not always soon enough for some players. Perhaps Major League Baseball (or the Players' Association) should look further into the ways that players are prepared for their post-playing careers. Do players receive counseling, during their careers, about how to make the eventual move from ballplayer to real life? Are most major leaguers ready for the next part of their lives once their careers have ended?

What are the financial difficulties faced by players, especially those who played a good portion of their careers before free agency and never made big money?"[12]

SOURCES

In addition to the sources cited in the Notes, the author relied on Baseball-Reference.com and www.pelotabinaria.com.ve. Most of the Venezuelan baseball statistics mentioned in the work were taken from the latter source.

NOTES

1   http://destellosdelamemoria.blogspot.com. Personajes de mi pueblo: Enzo Hernández. Por José "Cheo" Salazar.

2   Carlos Cárdenas Lares, *Venezolanos en las Grandes Ligas, sus Vidas y Hazañas,* Segunda edición (Caracas: Fondo editorial Cardenas Lares, 1994), 126-130.

3   Cárdenas Lares.

4   Cárdenas Lares.

5   Daniel Gutiérrez, Efraím Álvarez, y Daniel Gutiérrez G., *La Enciclopedia del Béisbol en Venezuela* (Caracas: Liga Venezolana de Beisbol Profesional, 2006), 149-209.

6   Bruce Markusen, "Cooperstown Confidential: Farewell to Enzo Hernández, Fred Talbot and Sports Watch," fangraphs.com, January 18, 2013. https://tht.fangraphs.com/cooperstown-confidential-farewell-to-enzo-hernandez-fred-talbot-and-sportsw/.

7   Markusen.

8   In 1974 Dave Concepción set the new record for stolen bases by a Latin American shortstop, with 41.

9   In the American League, Cuba's Armando Marsans stole 46 bases for the St. Louis Browns in 1916 and sacrificed 23 times, Luis Aparicio had stolen 51 and sacrificed 20 times in 1960, and in 1972 Bert Campaneris stole 52 bases, sacrificing 20 times.

10   Markusen.

11   George Voutiritsas, "15 Baseball Players You Didn't Know Took Their Own Life," *The Sportster.com,* July 13, 2017. https://www.thesportster.com/baseball/15-baseball-players-you-didnt-know-took-their-own-life/.

12   Markusen.

RAMÓN HERNÁNDEZ

BY TONY S. OLIVER

Why didn't Jeremy Giambi slide?

Hindsight is always crystal clear, much to the chagrin of involved parties. The Yankees mystique built upon a century of dominance over major-league baseball. The ill-advised enthusiastic wave by third-base coach Ron Washington, perhaps blind to actions outside his tunnel of vision. The cruel spectacle of a slow runner attempting to score from first base as the team's best opportunity to mark the scoreboard.

In the heat of the moment, everyone thought Giambi would score. The 55,861 fans in attendance; the Oakland Coliseum employees; virtually all the Athletics and Yankees; and the millions who watched on television and subsequent replays. They have all conveniently forgotten the wicked caroms in Oakland's spacious right field, almost signaled by divine intervention or surgical precision; the wild throw by Shane Spencer, whose effort missed not one (Alfonso Soriano) but two (Tino Martínez) cutoff men; and the fact that Mike Mussina had already registered two outs so Giambi was moving on contact by Terrence Long.

Only a few souls were not clouded by enthusiasm. Jorge Posada, the catcher, and Derek Jeter, the architect, who wore the pinstripes, and whose attention was centered only on the moving baseball. Kerwin Danley, the home-plate umpire, who was impartial. And Ramón Hernández, the on-deck batter, who frantically signaled his oblivious teammate as the ball, against conventional logic, made its way to Posada's mitt a split-second before Giambi crossed the plate. "I saw it all unfold," Hernández told the author. "I was yelling at him to slide. From my vantage point I saw it all unfold, but that's baseball for you: a player in a position he typically wouldn't be, throwing out a slow runner at the plate in a one-run game."[1]

While Hernández would play more than 1,500 major-league games, most fans recognize his silhouette on the lower right corner of the ill-fated play. For Hernández, a quiet, unassuming catcher whose livelihood was earned wearing the mask, it's just fine.

Ramón José Hernández Marín was born on May 20, 1976, in Caracas, Venezuela, to a middle-class family. His father worked as a systems programmer and his mother was a social worker. Four other countrymen born in the same year (Kelvim Escobar, Alex Prieto, Freddy García, and Liu Rodríguez) made it to the major leagues. He fell in love with baseball at an early age, passionately picking up the bat and attempting to hit left-handed with fellow children from his neighborhood, frenzied by béisbol in a manner typical of his countrymen.

Hernández was scouted by a few teams but was ultimately signed as an amateur free agent on February 18, 1994, by the Athletics on the recommendation of Ubaldo Heredia, who enjoyed a brief, 10-inning cup of coffee in 1987 for the Montréal Expos. Oakland was Hernández's favorite team as a youngster, given the bravado of the late 1980s/early 1990s clubs: "Rickey Henderson, Dave Parker, José Canseco, Mark McGwire, Carney Lansford … those teams just had attitude."

Though he saw himself as an infielder, another player did not attend the tryout, so Hernández was asked to catch and impressed the team with his throwing ability. He was encouraged to play in the Dominican Republic summer league, an offer he eagerly accepted, with his club winning the Santo Domingo central division.[2] He flashed his promise, hitting .246 but displaying good plate discipline by drawing 18 walks to reach base in a third of his appearances.[3]

By then, fully committed to the position, Hernández began tracking the exploits of Eddie Pérez and Carlos Hernández, the flag-bearers of Venezuela backstops. "Both of them helped me during the winter league," he recalled, "by giving me suggestions and tips on how to play the game."

Oakland had taken the baseball world by storm in the late 1980s. The franchise developed young stars Canseco, McGwire, and Walt Weiss alongside veterans Dave Stewart, Lansford, and a reborn Dennis Eckersley to three consecutive World Series appearances and one trophy. By 1993, injuries, trades, and performance drops had led to a losing record, the first of six in a row. Backstop Terry Steinbach, a former All-Star Game MVP, entered his age 32 season in 1994 and was rumored to want to play with his hometown Twins. Although the club had many needs, bulking up its catcher corps was paramount, and Hernández fit the part.

Hernández began his professional career in the 1995 Arizona Rookie League. Despite being a fresh-faced 19-year-old, he hammered hurlers at a .364 clip with a 1.105 OPS, claiming the league's MVP Award.[4] Appearing in 31 games at catcher, 13 as first baseman, and six at third base, he committed 12 errors. However, the Athletics liked his defensive makeup enough to install him as the main backstop for their 1996 Midwest League affiliate, the West Michigan Whitecaps. The heightened competition brought Hernández's batting to a more pedestrian .255 but his keen eye at the plate earned 69 walks, good for a .355 OBP and a spot in the all-star team.[5] Baseball America rated him as the organization's fifth-best prospect, ahead of future compadre Miguel Tejada.[6] The young farmhands would rise through the Oakland ranks together and eventually become godfathers to each other's children, Alexia Tejada and Ramón Jr: "We're united by a beautiful friendship since we were in the minors."[7] He also appeared on his first baseball card, with Bowman ("the home of the rookie") including him in its base set with number 220, a stoic shot as the appears to return the baseball to the pitcher.

In 130 games for Visalia and Double-A Huntsville in 1997, Hernández had an .858 OPS with 19 home runs. He was named to the all-star team for a third consecutive year and punished the Class-A (advanced) California League with Visalia, though pitchers retaliated by beaning him nine times in 86 contests.[8] The Southern League provided tougher, as his hitting shrank to .193 after a call-up.

Meanwhile, in the major leagues, a triumvirate of Brent Mayne (.289 in 85 games), George Williams (.289 in 76 games), and Izzy Molina (.198 in 48 games) shared the position for the A's before turning it over to Mike Macfarlane and A.J. Hinch in 1998. *Baseball America* rated Hernández as the game's 74th-best prospect, and he responded with a .296/.389/.445 slash line.[9] Come the beginning of 1999, he was regarded as the heir-apparent with *Baseball America* anointing him as the Athletics' seventh-best prospect.[10] He began the season with the Vancouver Canadians (Triple-A Pacific Coast League, 77 games, .261) before Oakland recalled his services. His years in the minor leagues were a lesson in more than just baseball, as he had to navigate "living on my own, getting to the stadium, staying with host families" alongside many players, some of whom would become his big-league teammates.

"I was in awe of the stadiums when I first arrived in the major leagues," said Hernández, though he disguised his wonder well. Debuting on June 29, 1999, in front of 11,762 spectators, he played every one of the dozen frames required to finish the contest. Three Hall of Famers – Ken Griffey Jr., Edgar Martínez, and Tim Raines – suited up for the game and managed but one hit; Hernández swatted two, both off Mariners starter John Halama. With Raines on first base after drawing a walk, Hernández bunted toward Seattle third baseman Russ Davis, who was perhaps unfamiliar with the rookie. Though the A's loaded the bases, they failed to score and trailed by the slimmest of margins until the seventh inning. In his third plate appearance, Hernández hammered a line drive to left-center field to score Jason Giambi. Although Seattle scored in the 12th inning for the win, Hernández astutely guided four hurlers – starter Mike Oquist, and relievers Doug Jones, Billy Taylor, and T.J. Mathews – through 157 pitches, impressing not only his teammates but also the coaching staff.[11]

Hernández followed his debut with a three-hit effort that included his first home run, off Dámaso Marte in the eighth inning of a 14-5 A's win. He punished the Mariners with a walk, a single, and a double in addition to this round-tripper. He boasted a .831 OPS in 19 games, all starts, through July 25, but a collision at home plate against the Royals landed him on the disabled list. Returning on August 27, he caught most of the team's remaining games, providing a robust .279/.363/.397 line as the young A's finished second in their division with an 87-75 record, 21-19 in the contests he appeared in. His 40 appearances would be the fewest he would enjoy until his final year in the big leagues. He fielded 299 chances and authored

274 putouts, with 19 assists, five double plays, and six errors for a .980 fielding average. He caught 26 percent of would-be base thieves but sabermetrics calculated a -1 total zone catcher runs above average.

In 2000, firmly entrenched as the on-field general, Hernández played in 143 games and yielded a .241/.311/.387 line. The team won 69 of his 118 starts, with Hernández driving in 62 runners in 479 plate appearances. Despite a putrid start (he finished April with a .164 average), the front office was committed to his development, and he shepherded the staff to 91 wins and the division title. The Yankees awaited in the postseason with Roger Clemens starting the first game against the A's Gil Heredia. Hernández deftly led the veteran hurler through a serviceable start (three runs in six frames) and connected for two hits off Clemens; a single in the fifth and a double in the sixth, both of which enabled Eric Chávez to score. Though the A's lost the next two games, Hernández had a hit in each. He could not figure out Clemens in the rematch, but his teammates did as the Yankee ace was roughed up (six earned runs in five innings) while Barry Zito and a trio of relievers scattered eight hits for only one run. The decisive fifth matchup was doomed from the start as Heredia failed to get out of the first inning; Andy Pettitte, while far from sharp (five runs in 3⅔ innings) handed the lead to the vaunted pinstripe bullpen corps, which limited Oakland to three hits the rest of the game. For the series, Hernández led the team with a .375 average and .912 OPS but went home empty-handed.

Hernández would improve his hitting in 2001, setting new highs in runs (55), hits (115), doubles (25), and home runs (15) while turning a league-high 15 double plays from behind the plate. The A's won 102 games but it was good only for second place as the Seattle Mariners tied a major-league-record 116 victories initially set by the 1906 Chicago Cubs. Oakland again met the Yankees and pushed the New Yorkers to the limit before falling in in five games. Although Hernández struggled (no hits, one walk, four strikeouts in 11 plate appearances), he guided the pitchers to a 2.86 ERA and 1.159 WHIP and played a secondary role in baseball immortality. The young Athletics were up 2-0 against the Yankees, buoyed by two victories in the always-daunting Yankee Stadium, making the third game truly pivotal. Much has been written about the contest, played less than five weeks after the harrowing events of 9/11. "Our dugout was on the third-base side, and we had a great view of Terrence hitting that ball into the corner. I thought Jeremy would score. I knew he would score," laconically said Oakland manager Art Howe.[12] Washington, whose left arm could have been injured by his enthusiastic waving of Jeremy Giambi, recalled "the throw is way over everything … so I'm winding Giambi and I'm sure we're going to tie the game. And then Derek goes over and gets that ball."[13] Hernández did what he could to help Giambi, yelling at his teammate to slide and putting both hands out, palms down, and vigorously pushing toward the ground – the universal baseball sign to slide.[14] Unfortunately for Oakland, it was not meant to be. Jeter, whose unofficial mantle as the Yankees captain was not made official until 2003, may have earned the title with that play. Ever humble, he deflected praise by stating, "I've seen it a lot. I was where I was supposed to be. ... I'm not supposed to throw it home, but that's where I'm supposed to be. I've never been one to sit down and sing my own praises. I'm happy it was a big moment for us. Maybe years from now, but I've just never sat down and looked at it like that."[15]

Hernández remained durable in 2002, appearing in 136 games and again showing exemplary plate discipline. Although this batting average of .233 was pedestrian, his OBP was a solid 80 points higher (.313) and his Defensive WAR (1.7) was seventh in the American League.[16] The A's enjoyed a remarkable 20-game winning streak to revalidate their division title and avoided the Yankees by matching up against the Central Division champion Twins. The teams were evenly matched and finished the five-game series with identical ERA (4.50) and similar OPS (.833 for the A's, .829 for Twins). Minnesota slipped by, 5-4, in the last game, again breaking the Oakland fans' hearts. Hernández managed one hit in 17 at-bats, extending his postseason malaise.

He appeared in the 2003 All-Star Game as a reserve thanks to a strong first half. Playing in 80 of the team's first 93 games, he blistered opposing pitchers with a .364 average (.984 OPS) in March and April. Although he cooled off in May and June (.205 and .250, respectively) he caught teammate Mark Mulder, Brendan Donnelly, and Keith Foulke during his four innings in the midsummer classic. He replaced Posada on the field as part of a double switch and grounded out on his only at-bat, becoming the second Venezuelan to appear at catcher. (Bo Díaz, in 1981 with Cleveland and 1987 with Cincinnati, was the first.)[17]

Hernández finished the season with a .273/.331/.458 line with 21 home runs, 78 RBIs, and 70 runs scored, but the team once again flamed out in the postseason, this time in five games against Boston. Hernández reached base five times, with three singles and two walks, driving two runs, including the game-winner in the first game with an expertly executed bases-loaded bunt in the bottom of the 12th inning. It appeared he had reached a zenith, but the franchise was in transition. Jason Giambi had left during the 2001 postseason and Tejada was rumored to be departing during the offseason, his asking price untenable to the small-market franchise. Before the shortstop signed with Baltimore, Hernández was traded to the San Diego Padres along with Terrence Long for Mark Kotsay on Thanksgiving eve. He found out about the trade while watching ESPN's SportsCenter: "All of a sudden I see the ticker with my name and then my picture is on the screen. A few minutes later, my agent called and told me I was traded. 'Yes, I know that. ... I saw that on television! Twenty minutes later, Billy Beane called me to let me know. I was not mad, though I figured perhaps our time had passed.'" A streak of four straight postseason berths ended as Mulder, Zito, and Tim Hudson all left Oakland in subsequent seasons, leaving Chavez as the sole link to the early 2000s clubs.

The 2004 Padres improved by 23 games over the prior year's edition, which was still coming to grips with Tony Gwynn's retirement. Hernández established career highs in on-base average (.341) and slugging average (.477) despite playing in only 111 games due to a 29-game stint on the disabled list with a strained left knee. For the first time since 1999, he did not reach the postseason, though he would return a year later thanks to his .290 average. Hernández did not reach the century mark in appearances in 2005 as his left wrist was first sprained and eventually required surgery. Returning on September 7, he caught fire over the last 23 games with a .349 average as the Padres won the Western Division title. Though they lost the Division Series to St. Louis in three straight, Hernández tore the cover off the ball: five hits, including a home run, along with two walks for a 1.266 OPS, a masterful performance as he entered the free-agent market on October 27, the day after the World Series ended.

The Orioles' Javy López had succumbed to age and injuries, dropping from 150 games with a 127 OPS+ in 2004 to 103 contests (28 as the designated hitter) and a 106 OPS+ effort in 2005. With one more year in his deal, the club needed a long-term replacement and Hernández was a good fit. Entering his age-30 season, with a solid career progression and the endorsement of Tejada, Hernández signed a four-year deal on December 13, 2005. The move was savvy for Baltimore, as López struggled to

An All-Star in 2003, Hernández hit 169 home runs over 14 big-league seasons. He was a consistent offensive threat behind the plate. (Jerry Coli / Dreamstime)

start the campaign and was traded to Boston, where he finished the year and his career.

In 2006 Hernández played in 144 games and reached career bests in home runs (23), RBIs (91), doubles (29), and slugging (.479) while leading the league in catching assists with 69. Perhaps more tellingly, he won over the Oriole alumni and his teammates as he was the franchise's nominee for the Heart & Hustle award, given to "an active player who demonstrates a passion for the game of baseball and best embodies the values, spirit, and traditions of the game."[18] His next campaign was not as productive as he visited the disabled list twice (once for a left oblique strain and once for a groin injury), limiting him to 106 games and slicing his slugging prowess by almost 100 points (.382). The Orioles, mired in the 10th of what eventually became 14 consecutive losing seasons, selected Matt Wieters in the June amateur draft. Wieters, a future four-time All-Star, took over the position in 2009.

Hernández's last year with Baltimore (2008) was solid if not remarkable. He stayed healthy, appearing in 133 games and contributing a .257/.308/.406 line, but the club was still stuck in neutral. On December 9 the Orioles exchanged his contract (one year remaining) for a trio of Reds: Ryan Freel, Brandon Waring, and Justin Turner.

The Reds were themselves mired in a long streak of losing seasons, but Hernández focused on steering the pitchers. Now 33, he suffered a power outage (only 5 home runs and 13 doubles) during the 2009 season. After appearing in 77 of the team's first 88 contests, he underwent surgery on his left knee to clear out damaged tissue, returning in late September for a few games. Ryan Hanigan handled the dish during his absence, setting up a mentoring relationship that would last throughout Hernández's Reds career.

In 2010 there was a return to form. Hernández established career highs in average (.297) and on-base percentage (.364) but missed games due to knee and back pain. The Reds returned to the postseason, battling the Phillies in the Division Series, but were swept in three games. Hernández played in all three contests, starting two, and contributing one hit in seven at-bats. Unbeknownst to him, it was his last major-league playoff appearance. Impressed with his contributions, the franchise re-signed him to a one-year deal on November 15.

Though buoyed by the success of the prior year, the 2011 Cincinnati club regressed to a 79-83 mark. Hernández hit well (.282/.341/.446) and sent Opening Day fans home in a frenzy with a walk-off three-run home run against the Brewers on March 31. Discussing his career, he was philosophical: "I don't care if people talk about my teams being of low quality. Even better; when those teams start winning, I feel more satisfied because I arrived into a team in need of help. When one sees those improvements, one cannot help but feel satisfied."[19] When discussing the young Oakland aces Hudson, Mulder, and Zito, he stated. "Those pitchers prepared very well ... We both prepared well, and two heads think better than one. ... There was no guessing when it was time to pitch, that helped us win many games and reach the playoffs many times."[20] Thinking about his future, Hernández thought he could play "without any injuries, three or four more years. Right now, I go year-by-year. If I feel good and there are interested teams, one comes back until one no longer wishes to play baseball."[21] Hanigan took copious notes as Hernández led the senior circuit with a .998 fielding average, committing only one error in 658 innings behind the dish.

On November 30, a month after the 2011 season ended, Hernández signed a two-year contract with the Rockies.[22] Colorado's slugging prospect Wilín Rosario was targeted as the starter, but the team understood the value of a veteran to help the youngster acclimate to the big leagues. Hernández took pride in his mentor role, sharing, "[A]s a catcher, you have to be proud of the way you work with pitchers. I know everyone watches how you hit, but the main thing you can do as a catcher to help your team win is call the best game you can. I think I can help our starters go deep in games. It's a great responsibility. … I want to teach him everything I can teach him. I know he is going to be the future of our organization."[23] Hernández's body resembled the classic children's game "Operation" with injuries to his left hamstring, left shoulder, left hand, and right elbow through the punishing season. Rosario played in 117 games and clubbed 28 home runs (.843 OPS, 109 OPS+) while Hernández appeared in 52 contests with a .217/.247/.353 line.

The Rockies designated Hernández for assignment on March 28, 2013, eventually trading him to the Dodgers for Aaron Harang and $4.25 million a few days into the season.[24] With Los Angeles, he backed up starter A.J. Ellis, appearing in 17 games (at first base, as the designated hitter, as a pinch-runner, and as the backstop) and hitting a meager .208/.291/.438.

June 12, 2013, was a great day to play baseball. Almost 42,000 souls packed Chavez Ravine to watch the surprisingly first-place Diamondbacks battle the Dodgers. This early-season contest was, on paper, no more memorable than the other 14 with which it shared the calendar, though the two teams would finish one-two in the standings. Sadly, no Pulitzer Prize winner was in attendance, commissioned by the *New Yorker* to cover Ted Williams's last game. John Updike's "Hub Fans Bid Kid Adieu" has long been considered a classic piece of baseball writing, combining rich, vibrant prose with the historical significance of Williams's final game. The Red Sox suffered through a miserable season, ending 65-89 (seventh out of eight teams in the American League) prompting Williams to decide not to travel with the team to New York for the season finale and instead treat the Fenway faithful to his goodbye. Shockingly, only 10,454 patrons saw him hammer a Jack Fisher pitch into center field for this 521st round-tripper.

Almost 53 years later, Hernández would also smash a dinger in his last at-bat, a solo shot on Heath Bell's first pitch.[25] Unlike Williams, Hernández had not determined that the game would be his last. However, it provided symmetry; like his debut, almost 14 years earlier, this contest went 12 innings, with his team losing though Hernández played every frame. Two days later, the Dodgers designated him for assignment; on June 22, he was released. The Blue Jays offered him a contract with Triple A-Syracuse but released him on July 9 after only five games.

Hernández attempted to return in 2014, scoring a spring-training invite with Kansas City. He did not catch much due to a knee injury, though he hit .391 in 23 spring at-bats.[26] He opted out of his contract on March 30 but remained with the club to work out, hoping another team would show interest.[27]

Much like dozens of his fellow big leaguers, Hernández did not take offseason vacations but instead returned home to Venezuela for winter ball. He began with a new franchise, the Pastora de Occidente, cutting his teeth with professionals many years his senior. In two seasons, he totaled 54 games and 29 hits, two of which were for extra bases. The team moved to los Llanos with Hernández starring in 293 contests from 1997-1998 through 2006-2007, averaging .300 with .445 slugging. He garnered several awards, including all-star selections in 1999, 2000, and 2002.[28] His individual best was 2001-2002, when he led the league in batting average (.376) and kept the hot bat into the playoffs (.392), receiving the *Baseball America* Winter League Player of the Year award.[29] He tasted local glory twice once Pastora was eliminated and the eventual league champion Tigres de Aragua selected him as a "refuerzo" (reinforcement) playing in the 2004-2005 and 2006-2007 finals.

The club, renamed the Bravos (Braves) after its move to Margarita Island, enjoyed Hernández's services for one more year (2007-2008) though he played in only four regular-season contests and an additional 15 postseason games. As his body took the toll of more than a decade of professional baseball, Hernández sat out the next three years before returning in 2012-2013 with Magallanes. The franchise was enticed by "(his) bat which will help our offense increase its numbers with runners in scoring position."[30] In three years, he delivered a .265 average in 71 games, but provided the Navegantes faithful one of their all-time classic moments. Hernández single-handedly routed the Caribs (Caribes) of Anzoategui in 2013-2014 while playing only three contests, batting 8-for-11 with 3 home runs and 10 runs batted in, including a three-run dagger in the decisive fifth game of the finals, cementing his MVP award.[31]

Hernández announced his retirement on December 27, 2014, effective at the conclusion of the season.[32] His 16-year career produced 416 hits in 422 regular-season games and a .289/.312/.415 slash line with 234 safeties in 208 postseason contests. His numbers increased as the games mattered most, as evident by a .931 OPS in five final series.

Baseball lovers lucky enough to live in the Antilles have been privy to a thrilling yearly competition: the Caribbean Series. Though the participating countries have varied, the Dominican Republic, Mexico, Puerto Rico, Venezuela, Cuba, and Panama have sent their league champions seeking regional supremacy. Hernández played in various editions, always as a refuerzo for the league champions: "Once upon a time, every Latin player wanted to play in the Caribbean Series. In Venezuela, I would often play first base or designated hitter. An American player may have played that role in the regular season, but he was eager

to return home, so the winning club would pick from the best of the natives, so I was glad to be selected."

Venezuela hosted the 2002 event, with both Hernández and his A's teammate Tejada donning their national colors. Tejada hit .435 but Hernández won the batting crown with .526, proving both had put the 2001 postseason heartbreaker behind them. But Mexican the representative Tomateros (Tomato Growers) of Culiacán captured the title.[33]

The 2006 Caribbean Series was truly crowning for Hernández, who won the MVP and the triple crown of the tournament, hitting .542 (13-for-24) with three home runs and eight runs batted in. His 27 bases also led the campaign, which was held in Venezuela (Maracay and Valencia, marking the first time two cities had shared hosting duties). He became the first player to hit for the cycle in the tournament history during Caracas's 17-1 triumph over the Mexican representative, the Venados (Deer) of Mazatlán.[34] "In my first at-bat, I hit a rocket to right-center field. … The center fielder tripped and the ball just caromed back to second base. Since it was the first game of the series, my adrenaline was just pumping so I kept running until I reached third. Later in the game, I told Marco Scutaro, 'I need the home run…' and connected on a good pitch." The Leones swept the competition with an unblemished 6-0 record, providing Venezuela with its first title since 1989.[35] Hernández's total bases and hit totals were each one shy of the competition's all-time best.[36]

In 2014, playing for Magallanes, Hernández drove in three runs for the club's 8-5 victory over the Azucareros (Sugar Cane Cutters) of Villa Clara.[37] With Cuba's return after more than half a century, the tournament was played under a different format, with teams playing each other twice and the top four advancing to a single-elimination playoff. Hernández contributed a home run in Venezuela's victory over Puerto Rico's Indios (Indians) of Mayaguez. Hernández was again named to the all-tournament team for his performance, an honor he humbly acknowledged by stating, "I am just trying to help the team, it's no longer Magallanes but rather Venezuela."

At the conclusion of the 2019 Caribbean Series, Hernández had connected for seven home runs, tied with Robert Pérez, Tony Batista, Carlos Baerga, and Rico Carty for fifth most all time in the competition.[38] He also boasts of 163 at-bats, a .282 batting average, .466 slugging average, 46 hits, 76 total bases, and two batting titles, equaling Manny Mota's mark.[39]

After years of discussion, Organized Baseball agreed on its first ever "world cup" tournament. Eager to display its mettle beyond the Caribbean series, Venezuela boasted two major leaguers behind the plate for the inaugural World Baseball Classic, held in 2006. Hernández shared duties with young slugger Víctor Martínez, with the former going 6-for-22 and the latter 3-for-15.[40] The country lost its first game against the Dominican Republic but recovered by blanking Italy and Australia. Hernández, playing first base against the Europeans, provided a single and a double.[41] As the designated hitter against Australia, he clubbed a home run in the second inning and later added a single.[42] In the second round, Venezuela fell again to the Dominicans and to the Cubans but defeated Puerto Rico, bowing out with a combined 3-3 record.

For the 2009 WBC, the Venezuelans used a triumvirate of catchers; Hernández (7-for-19) was joined by Henry Blanco (5-for-10), and Max Ramírez (2-for-10).[43] Hernández reached base in every game he played, providing an insurance run against Puerto Rico with a round-tripper in a thrilling second-round game. Venezuela reached the semifinals, losing to eventual runner-up South Korea, 10-2.

By 2013, a new generation of his countrymen had reached the majors; Miguel Montero and Salvador Pérez wore the mask. The nation was placed in a tough draw; it lost to powerhouses Cuba and Puerto Rico before picking up a victory against Spain. Hernández pinch-hit in the bottom of ninth against Puerto Rico, but the at-bat was finalized by Montero, who struck out.[44]

While Hernández did not participate in the 2017 edition, he still ranks second (behind Miguel Cabrera, and tied with Bobby Abreu, Carlos Guillén, Magglio Ordoñez, and Endy Chávez) among Venezuelans in WBC games played, a mark he holds dear: "Playing for Venezuela was amazing … the highest level of competition. … To play for the country was a great honor, something I could not accomplish in Little League. It's a different feeling to play with your country's name on your chest."[45]

At the conclusion of the 2024 season, Hernández ranked 18th among Venezuelan-born major-league players in games played (1,526), 24th in hits (1,345), and 31st in WAR (21.9). Among his catcher brethren, he is the all-time leader in games caught, with 1,447, or 95 percent of his total. (He also appeared at first base, designated hitter, third base, and as a pinch-hitter and runner.) With the bat, he enjoyed facing Mark Petkovsek (.636), Francisco Cordero (.556), Donnelly (.545), Tim Wakefield (.310, three home runs in 45 plate appearances), Clemens (.333), and 2019 Cooperstown inductees Roy Halladay (.318), Mussina (.280), and Mariano Rivera (.300). He confessed, "I liked to face Clemens; he was a competitor, fierce and cocky, he wanted to attack." He loathed the matchup against soft-tossing lefty Jamie Moyer: "I could not figure him out … soft flies or groundouts most of the time," he recalled, confirmed by a 6-for-41 line (.146 average) but Hideo Nomo (0-for-10) and Esteban Loaiza (0-for-21) also proved to be his nemeses. As a testament to his durability, as of 2021 he was 22nd in all-time putouts by a catcher, ahead of Hall of Famers Yogi Berra, Bill Dickey, Mickey Cochrane, and Roy Campanella.

Hernández reached six divisional series though his clubs were unable to advance to the League Championship Series. He slashed .211/.268/.289 in 86 plate appearances but he caught fire in 2000 with Oakland (.912 OPS) and 2005 with San Diego (1.265 OPS). He enjoyed catching Hudson, noting, "I may have missed two of his games throughout our time in Oakland. We grew up together in the organization. He always had great movement. One time, Greg Myers was assigned to Hudson and he could not do it well. I think he lost a fingernail or two."

Although he was not known as a home-run hitter, Hernández slugged seven grand slams in his career, good for a third-place tie with Ordóñez and José Altuve, trailing only Andrés Galarraga and Abreu among Venezuelan major leaguers.[46] His 162-game average (.263/.327/.417) was solid for a catcher, and his 12-year peak (2000 through 2011, ages 24 to 35) yielded eight campaigns with double-digit home runs, six seasons with OPS+ between 107 and 119, an offensive WAR of 22.4, and a four-year span leading the American League in total games caught (2000-2003). Behind the plate, his Oakland staff reduced its ERA in every one of his years, a feat he repeated during this time in Baltimore.

Once retired, Hernández was keen to remain in the dugout. He joined the Tiburones (Sharks) of La Guaira for two seasons (2015-2016, 2016-2017) as a bench coach. Magallanes offered him the same position, which he eagerly accepted for the 2017-2018 campaign: "It's an excellent organization, from the executives to the players, the batboy and the office workers."[47] However, the prize was to manage a club, and once an opportunity arose with Aragua, Hernández pounced, becoming the Tigres manager on March 26, 2018. Though he had not played for the franchise during the regular season, he had been selected by the club as a reinforcement in the 2004-2005, 2005-2006, and 2006-2007 playoffs. The honeymoon was short-lasted as a poor start saw the team mired in seventh place (10-14 record), and Hernández was fired on November 12, 2018.[48] His former Baltimore teammate Oscar Salazar commanded the team to a 23-16 record the rest of the way, losing to Caracas in the first round of the postseason.

Hernández's next role grooming players did not take long. The Diablos Rojos (Red Devils) of Mexico City, one of the 16 teams in the Triple-A Mexican Baseball League, approached him about the bench-coach position. Though Hernández had not played professionally in Mexico, he was ecstatic about the opportunity: "Baseball in Mexico is as loved a sport as soccer. … I've heard it's a very good league, I see a lot of talented young players, it's very high-quality baseball."[49] His Caribbean Series experience in 2001 (held in Culiacán) and 2005 (hosted in Mazatlán) gave him an appreciation of the fans' enthusiasm for the game. The Diablos Rojos led the Southern Division with a 67-49 record but lost in the semifinals to the Leones of Yucatán.

Hernández remains cherished in Oakland given his role in the team's early twenty-first-century renaissance. The A's honored both Hernández and Zito in 2017, welcoming them back to the Coliseum in a game against the Braves: "It's great, it brings back old, great memories in this ballpark. This is the team I signed with, the team I came up to the big leagues with and the team I loved to watch when I was a little kid."[50] Zito added, "we had such a chemistry as a battery back then. I didn't have to shake, ever. He just put down what I wanted to throw, and it's pretty rare to get into sync to that level. And it was like that for years."[51] Hernández took the opportunity to communicate his goal: "I've learned a lot. That's what I want to do in the future, hopefully to be a coach in the major leagues and a manager. I'd love to do that. I love to help players and I love to be on the field."[52] He eagerly awaits the opportunity, regardless of whether it comes in the minors or the majors: "You have to focused and take care of each individual player to help him improve. … You have to earn their trust, and I like to teach." Given his track record, most teams ought to listen.

ACKNOWLEDGMENTS

Ramón Hernández for graciously agreeing to an interview with the author.

Carlos Hernández for connecting the author to Ramón Hernández.

SOURCES

In addition to the sources cited in the Notes, the author relied extensively on Baseball-Reference.com and Retrosheet.org.

NOTES

1   Author interview with Ramón Hernández on November 14, 2019. Unless otherwise specified, all direct quotations from Hernández stem from this interview.

2   Dominican Republic Summer League Official Statistics, http://dominicansummerleague.com/www/jugadores-en-grande-ligas/.

3   https://www.baseballamerica.com/players/18374/ramon-hernandez/.

4   http://www.thebaseballcube.com/extra/awards/history.asp?Award=Ariz-MVP.

5   http://www.thebaseballcube.com/extra/awards/history.asp?Award=Ariz-MVP.

6   http://www.thebaseballcube.com/prospects/byTeam.asp?T=21.

7   "Serie del Caribe Unió a los Compadres Ramón y Tejada," *Diario Libre,* February 9, 2006, https://www.diariolibre.com/deportes/serie-del-caribe-uni-a-los-compadres-ramn-y-tejada-CRDL87532.

8   http://www.thebaseballcube.com/extra/awards/history.asp?Award=Ariz-MVP.

9   http://www.thebaseballcube.com/prospects/byYear.asp?Y=1998&Src=BA.

10 http://www.thebaseballcube.com/prospects/byYear.asp?Y=1998&Src=BA.

11 https://www.baseball-reference.com/boxes/OAK/OAK199906290.shtml.

12 John Hickey, "Jeter Returns to the Scene of the Flip," *San Jose Mercury News,* June 26, 2012, https://www.mercurynews.com/2014/06/12/derek-jeter-returns-to-scene-of-the-flip/

13 "Jeter Returns to the Scene of the Flip."

14 https://www.youtube.com/watch?v=ApoJk9X7Vto.

15 Bryan Hoch, "Flip Play in Oakland Iconic Moment in Derek Jeter's Career," MLB.com, June 13, 2014, https://www.mlb.com/news/flip-play-in-oakland-iconic-moment-in-derek-jeters-career/c-79619840.

16 Wins Above Replacement, or WAR, is calculated using a formula accounting for a position player's performance across offensive and defensive metrics. While FanGraphs and Baseball Reference use the same framework, their estimates for the inputs may vary, and the total WAR may also be slightly different. This biography relies on the Baseball Reference version of WAR. For more information,

consult https://www.baseball-reference.com/about/war_explained_position.shtml.

17 2003 Major League Baseball All-Star Game box score, https://www.retrosheet.org/boxesetc/2003/B07150ALS2003.htm.

18 https://www.mlb.com/mlbpaa/events/heart-and-hustle-award.

19 Gustavo Hidalgo, "Ramón Hernández Tiene Espacio Bien Ganado en las Grandes Ligas," Béisbol007 Blog, April 13, 2011, https://beisbolnew.wordpress.com/2011/04/13/ramon-hernandez-tiene-un-espacio-bien-ganado-en-las-grandes-ligas/.

20 Hidalgo.

21 Hidalgo.

22 "Rockies Agree to Two-Year Contract with Catcher Ramon Hernandez," MLB.com, December 12, 2011, https://www.mlb.com/news/rockies-agree-to-two-year-contract-with-catcher-ramon-hernandez/c-26147438.

23 Arnie Stapleton (Associated Press), "Rockies Catcher Embraces Role as Mentor," *Colorado Springs Gazette,* February 28, 2012, https://gazette.com/news/rockies-catcher-embraces-role-as-mentor/article_d947b630-59eb-5011-9a2e-44426f7a19b8.html.

24 Mike Axisa, "Rockies, Dodgers Swap Ramon Hernandez for Aaron Harang," CBS Sports, April 6, 2013, https://www.cbssports.com/mlb/news/rockies-dodgers-swap-ramon-hernandez-for-aaron-harang/.

25 https://www.baseball-almanac.com/feats/feats18.shtml.

26 https://www.baseballamerica.com/players/18374/ramon-hernandez/.

27 https://www.rotoworld.com/baseball/mlb/player/16777/ramon-hernandez.

28 http://www.thebaseballcube.com/extra/awards/history.asp?Award=Ariz-MVP.

29 http://www.thebaseballcube.com/extra/awards/history.asp?Award=Winter-POY.

30 "Ramón Hernández con los Navegantes del Magallanes," Béisbol007 Blog, May 4, 2010, https://beisbol007.blogia.com/2010/050405-ramn-hern-ndez-con-los-navegantes-del-magallanes.php.

31 José Alfredo Otero, "Magallanes Campeón 2013-2014," ADN Magallanero, January 28, 2018, https://adnmagallanero.wordpress.com/tag/ramon-hernandez/.

32 Alex Ulacio, "Gracias Ramón Hernández," Desde el Bullpen, December 28, 2012, http://desdeelbullpen.blogspot.com/2014/12/gracias-ramon-hernandez.html.

33 http://www.seriedelcaribe.net/articulos/bateo-lideres-en-cada-serie/.

34 Rafael Carvajal, "Hernández Más Valioso y Triple Coronado," La Serie del Caribe, February 8, 2006, https://web.archive.org/web/20061106061701/http://www.laseriedelcaribe2006.com.ve/.

35 Alex Sternberg, "Leones de Venezuela, Justo Campeón del Clásico Caribeño," *La Nación,* February 8, 2006, https://www.nacion.com/puro-deporte/leones-de-venezuela-justo-campeon-del-clasico-caribeno/SED7PFIRXBAFBB37N22RLT2STI/story/.

36 https://web.archive.org/web/20200121032952/http://www.seriedelcaribe.net/articulos/bateo-los-mejores-de-una-serie/

37 "Magallanes Inició con Triunfo en la Serie del Caribe," *Dossier Político,* February 3, 2014, https://dossierpolitico.com/vernoticias-anteriores.php?artid=138838&relacion=&tipo=Noticias&categoria=1.

38 Norvi Guerra, "Serie del Caribe: Los 10 Jugadores con Más Jonrones en la Historia del Torneo," 12up.com, January 29, 2019, https://

www.12up.com/es/posts/6283528-serie-del-caribe-los-10-jugadores-con-mas-jonrones-en-la-historia-del-torneo.

39 http://www.seriedelcaribe.net/articulos/lideres-de-por-vida-bateadores/.

40 World Baseball Classic Statistics, https://www.worldbaseballclassic.com/stats/

41 http://mlb.mlb.com/wbc/2009/stats/boxscore.jsp?gid=2006_03_08_itaint_venint_1.

42 http://mlb.mlb.com/wbc/2009/stats/boxscore.jsp?gid=2006_03_09_venint_ausint_1.

43 World Baseball Classic Statistics.

44 http://mlb.mlb.com/wbc/2013/gameday/index.jsp?gid=2013_03_09_purint_venint_1&mode=box.

45 World Baseball Classic Statistics.

46 https://www.baseball-almanac.com/hitting/higs1.shtml.

47 "Me Gustaría Estar con Magallanes: Ramón Hernández," *El Fildeo,* March 19, 2019, https://web.archive.org/web/20190331110359/ https://elfildeo.com/lvbp/ramon-hernandez-navegantes-magallanes-lvbp-entrevista/6714/2019/

48 David Méndez, "Ramón Hernández Fue Despedido por Tigres," Tigres de Aragua Baseball Club, November 12, 2018. https://tigresdearaguabbc.com/nota/3159/ramon-hernandez-fue-despedido-por-tigres.

49 Javier Sedano, "Ramón Hernández Aportará Experiencia en Diablos," Puro Béisbol, March 4, 2019, https://www.purobeisbol.mx/lmb/ramon-hernandez-aportara-experiencia-en-diablos/.

50 Susan Slusser, "Ex A's All-Stars Ramon Hernandez, Barry Zito Return to Coliseum," *SF Gate,* July 1, 2017, https://www.sfgate.com/athletics/article/Ex-A-s-All-Stars-Ramon-Hernandez-Barry-Zito-11261239.php.

51 Slusser.

52 Slusser.

RICHARD HIDALGO

BY TOM HAWTHORN

Richard Hidalgo's career was notable for short bursts of remarkable performance. For the New York Mets, he once hit home runs in five consecutive games. For the Houston Astros, he had extra-base hits in 10 consecutive games. In September 2000 he recorded one of the greatest monthlong hitting performances ever, batting .477 for the Astros, a club mark that would last 17 years until bettered by José Altuve, a fellow Venezuelan.

The streaky hitting was reflected in Hidalgo's yearly averages. He had some stellar campaigns, including a superb season in 2000 when he smacked 42 doubles and 44 home runs with 122 RBIs and a .314 batting average, all career highs. Just two seasons later, he hit only .235 with just 17 doubles and 15 homers. After that disappointing season, he suffered a gunshot wound to his left forearm during a botched carjacking in his homeland. He recovered from the injury to post solid numbers in 2003 before his production began a steady decline, though he still showed occasional pop at the plate.

In the outfield, Hidalgo displayed a strong right throwing arm, accumulating 81 outfield assists in 967 major-league games over nine seasons. While playing in the minors in Davenport, Iowa, he set a franchise record of 23 outfield assists for the Quad Cities River Bandits in 1994. Sixteen of those came in the first half of the season, after which few opposing runners tested the teenager's arm. When the *Quad-City Times* newspaper selected an all-time team on the 60th anniversary of minor-league baseball in Davenport, Hidalgo was named to the outfield alongside Dante Bichette (1985) and Oscar Taveras (2011).[1]

His career was limited by serious knee trouble, for which he had surgery on his left kneecap, and a succession of nagging injuries, including to his hip and groin. He also suffered a hernia and even tonsillitis, as well as a scary bout with dengue fever.

Richard José Hidalgo (pronounced *HUH-dahl-go*) was born on June 28, 1975, in Caracas, but grew up in nearby Guarenas, Miranda, which has produced such major leaguers as Ozzie Guillen and Juan Rivera. (Hidalgo's Venezuelan baseball club cites Guarenas as his birthplace.)[2] While the state of Miranda is known for its agricultural output, including cacao, coffee, sugarcane, citrus, and vegetables,[3] the city of Guarenas, population 200,000, has become a working-class bedroom community to Caracas. Many residents work in the national capital, about 27 miles to the west.

Hidalgo was raised by his mother, Basilia, who stayed at home to raise sons Richard, Pedro, Luis, and Joel, while his stepfather, Antonio, supported the family as best he could from a job at a gas station.[4]

"We were very poor, very poor, poor, poor," Hidalgo recalled. "We didn't have enough to eat. At lot of times, we just ate rice and butter. Sometimes bread or bananas. Hardly ever meat."[5]

Hidalgo has said he dropped out of school after Grade 5. He signed a professional contract as a nondrafted free agent just four days after his 16th birthday. It was his ambition to escape poverty through baseball. As his salary increased as he moved up the Astros system, he had enough money to move his family from Guarenas to Valencia.

"Where we used to live, there were many people who were killed, a lot of violence, and sometimes we went hungry," he said. "I grew up and saw all this, and that gave me more strength when I signed at 16 with Houston. It gave me more reason to work hard so I would be able to help my family and take them out of there."[6]

After 51 games of rookie ball with the Gulf Coast Astros in Kissimmee, Florida, during which he hit .310 in 184 at-bats, Hidalgo spent the 1993 season in North Carolina with the Asheville Tourists of the South Atlantic League. He stole 21 bases but was caught 13 times. At just 18, he joined the River Bandits. At 6-feet-3, he was still lean, though in time the right-handed batter filled out his frame to 220 pounds. In Iowa, he became a star in the Astros system.

"It's all business to Richard when he shows up at the park," said River Bandits manager Steve Dillard. "He's willing to work to get better and as long as he maintains that attitude, the sky is the limit for him."[7]

One of the Bandits coaches was César Cedeño, a former Gold Glove outfielder for the Astros, whose responsibilities included ensuring that Spanish-speaking players such as Hidalgo had support on and off the field while playing and living in American communities.

"He has helped me a lot," Hidalgo said. "He has showed me how to hold the ball differently and get it to the base better."[8]

Two seasons of Double-A ball in Mississippi with the Jackson Generals of the Texas League earned Hidalgo a promotion up the ladder to the Triple-A New Orleans Zephyrs. The parent Astros called him up for 19 games at the end of the 1997 season. He batted .306 and knocked two homers. He started in two games of the National League Division Series, but was hitless in five at-bats. The Astros were swept in three games by the Atlanta Braves.

Hidalgo returned to Venezuela to play winter ball, only to be stricken with hemorrhagic dengue fever after being bitten by a mosquito. He suffered from severe joint and back pain, as well as vomiting, losing eight pounds during a 10-day recuperation in a Caracas hospital.

"My insides felt so bad," he said. "I was weak, had a high fever. At one time I was thinking, 'Oh god, I'm going to be dead.'"[9]

Back home in Venezuela, Hidalgo also met his biological father, known to him only by the nickname Quintin, who sought him out when Richard was a rising, and potentially wealthy, baseball star.[10]

At spring training in 1998, Astros manager Larry Dierker offered a candid assessment of the prospect. "Beautiful guy, great attitude," he said. "Everybody loves him. ... I think Richard can be an above-average guy, a guy that if he gets a regular job, needs to improve and could make the All-Star team a couple of times." The manager considered Hidalgo to be a potentially premier player, though not a superstar.[11]

With Derek Bell solidly ensconced in right field, Hidalgo was platooned in center with Carl Everett. In May he recorded a four-RBI game with a double and a homer to defeat the Brewers in Milwaukee. He ended the month on the disabled list with a separated right shoulder after crashing into an outfield fence in unsuccessful pursuit of a Larry Walker grand slam. The injury

A power-hitting outfielder with a cannon arm, Hidalgo clubbed 44 homers in 2000. He played for the Astros, Mets, and Rangers. (Craig Melvin / Getty Images Sports)

needed surgery and he had a rehabilitation stint with New Orleans. He finished the season hitting .303 for the Astros.

A forgettable 1999 campaign (.227, 56 RBIs, 15 HRs) was followed by his breakout 2000 season, during which he enjoyed a 29-game span in which he hit .477 and scored 38 runs. His OPS (on-base average plus slugging average) in that time was 1.486. Only three players have ever had a better OPS month: Joe DiMaggio (1.487 in July 1937), Lou Gehrig (1.501 in June 1930), and Babe Ruth (five times).[12]

Before the 2001 season, Hidalgo signed a four-year, $32 million contract, after which he struggled at the plate, batting just .275 and .235 in successive seasons.

On the evening of November 21, 2002, Hidalgo, back home in Venezuela, was sitting in his truck awaiting a friend when he was shot during an attempted carjacking. A 9mm bullet tore through his left forearm, injuring muscle though missing bones, ligaments and tendons. He drove himself to a hospital[13] in Valencia, where he was treated before recuperating at home.[14]

The outfielder bounced back with solid numbers for the Astros in 2003 (.309, 28 homers) for which he was named the team's most valuable player. After 58 games with Houston in 2004, he was hitting just .256 and, perhaps more worrisome, his power seemed to have evaporated, as he had just four homers. On June 17 he was traded to the Mets for right-handed pitchers Jeremy Griffiths and David Weathers.

"I know what he can do," Mets manager Art Howe said. "He's a run-producer, an outstanding right fielder. He hasn't played on a regular basis. He'll get that opportunity here. It's a fresh start for him. I know he's a good middle-of-the-order hitter."[15]

The Mets intended for Hidalgo's bat to offer protection for power hitters Mike Piazza and Cliff Floyd. Hidalgo responded by hitting eight home runs in his first 16 games with the Mets, including setting a club record by hitting homers in five consecutive games. Three of those games included a July 4 long weekend Subway Series against the New York Yankees. The Mets swept the series, as Hidalgo homered off Mike Mussina, José Contreras, and Felix Heredia. While he hit just .228 for the Mets in 324 at-bats, Hidalgo's 21 homers in a half-season were second-best on the club, trailing only center fielder Mike Cameron's 30. Piazza hit 20 and Floyd 18.

A free agent at the end of the season, Hidalgo returned to Texas by signing with the Rangers. He ran a hot streak in May with 8 homers and 18 RBIs in 18 games before slumping badly at the plate.

A free agent at the end of the season, Hidalgo signed a minor-league contract with the Baltimore Orioles only to leave spring training in 2006 when his wife was hospitalized with an illness.[16] He signed a minor-league contract with Astros in 2007 and played with the club in spring training but was released after refusing a minor-league assignment. He never returned to the majors after leaving the Rangers. His major-league career totals include a .269 batting average, 560 RBIs, and 171 homers.

In the minors, he hit 62 homers in 2,615 at-bats with a .282 batting average.

The Long Island Ducks, an independent minor-league team, enjoyed Hidalgo's services for 30 games in 2008, while he also played in two games for the Sultanes de Monterrey in the Mexican league in 2009.

Hidalgo was a year-round player, as he returned to his native land in winter to patrol the outfield for the Navegantes del Magallanes.

In the 1996-97 finals, he hit .600 with a slugging average of .900, including one home run and six RBIs. He was named series MVP as his Navigators claimed the championship over the Caracas Lions (Leones del Caracas). He was just 21.

The outfielder spent 16 seasons in the Venezuelan Winter League. He hit 76 doubles and 56 homers with 218 RBIs. He scored 239 runs. His 411 hits gave him a career league average of .278. In 2017 Hidalgo was inducted into the team's hall of fame, known in Spanish as the Salón de la Fama de los Navegantes del Magallanes.[7]

Hidalgo settled in Florida, where he owned a house in Dr. Phillips, an affluent suburb of Orlando. He owned a second home nearby on farmland on which he raised ponies, horses, goats, and chickens. In 2008 neighbors objected to Hidalgo's plans to build a baseball facility for youth, as well as for his own training, including batting cages. "It won't be quiet anymore," one resident complained to local television station WFTV. "This is country out here. We like it that way."[18]

After being rejected, Hidalgo revised his plans five years later after doubling the size of his farm to 9.13 acres. The new proposal included a baseball field, three batting cages, a gymnasium with bathrooms, and parking for a training facility to accommodate up to 10 athletes and three coaches for daytime training. He got an exemption from the property's agricultural zoning from Orange County as long as he met 16 conditions. In the end, it appears the facility was never built.

Hidalgo played a total of 16 seasons with Navegantes del Magallanes in Venezuela, and retired in the 2011-12 season as the franchise leader in home runs with 56. On October 30, 2011, Magallanes held a retirement ceremony for Hidalgo prior to its game against rivals Leones del Caracas, where the former outfielder was honored by his peers and the team's front office. He said, "It's hard to look at myself in the mirror and say it's over."[19]

Since his retirement, Hidalgo has acted as hitting coach for Magallanes for several years. In 2022 he joined the coaching staff for Tiburones de La Guaira along with manager Henry Blanco.

Hidalgo has three sons – Richard, Ricky, and Renny, who was signed on July 2, 2019, as an international free agent with the Miami Marlins. An outfielder, Renny was still playing in the Marlins' minor-league system in 2024. In September 2023, Navegantes del Magallanes announced the signing of Renny Hidalgo for the Venezuelan Winter League.[20]

SOURCES

Thanks to Leonte Landino for supplying information about Richard Hidalgo's more recent years.

NOTES

1   Steve Batterson, "Q-C All-Time Team Rich in Talent," *Quad-City Times* (Davenport, Iowa), June 28, 2020: B4.

2   "Clase 2017," Sitio Oficial de los Navegantes del Magallanes, https://magallanesbbc.com.ve/salon.php. Accessed December 29, 2023.

3   Britannica, The Editors of Encyclopaedia, "Miranda," *Encyclopedia Britannica*, July 2, 2015, https://www.britannica.com/place/Miranda-state-Venezuela. Accessed December 29, 2023.

4   Kathleen O'Brien, "Happy to Be Any Place but Home," *Fort Worth* (Texas) *Star-Telegram*, February 27, 2005: 62.

5   O'Brien.

6   O'Brien.

7   Steve Batterson, "Hidalgo Has Given Bandits Big Assist," *Quad-City Times*, August 21, 1994: 3S.

8   Batterson, "Hidalgo Has Given Bandits Big Assist."

9   Mike Berardino, "Just Happy to Be Here," *South Florida Sun-Sentinel* (Deerfield Beach, Florida), March 14, 1998: 19C.

10 O'Brien.

11 Berardino.

12 "A Good Month's Work" [graphic], *Boston Globe*, September 10, 2023: C7.

13 O'Brien.

14 Jose de Jesus Ortiz, "Astros Richard Hidalgo Shot in Left Arm During Carjacking in Venezuela," *Houston Chronicle*, November 22, 2002. www.chron.com/sports/astros/article/Astros-Richard-Hidalgo-shot-in-left-arm-during-2099084.php. Accessed December 26, 2023.

15 Joel Anderson, "Astros Trade Hidalgo to Mets for 2 Pitchers," *Victoria* (Texas) *Advocate*, June 18, 2004: 2B.

16 Jeff Zrebiec, "Hidalgo Likely Won't Return," *Baltimore Sun*, March 7, 2006: C7.

17 "Clase 2017."

18 "Neighbors Try to Stop Former Pro Baseball Star's 'Field of Dreams,'" wftv.com, January 29, 2008, https://web.archive.org/web/20120813101959/https://www.wftv.com/news/news/neighbors-try-to-stop-former-pro-baseball-stars-fi/nJpBR/. Accessed December 30, 2023.

19 https://mendoza-inning10.blogspot.com/2011/10/richard-hidalgo-se-despidio-entre.html.

20 https://magallanesbbc.com.ve/2193_magallanes-firmo-al-prospecto-renny-hidalgo.

CÉSAR IZTURIS

BY KATIE MURRAY AND BILL NOWLIN

Venezuela is known for producing oil, coffee, cocoa – and shortstops. Joining a long tradition of *campocortos venezolanos* who include Ozzie Guillen, Luis Aparicio, and Omar Vizquel (to whom he is often compared), César Izturis quickly made a name for himself in the majors. During his career, which spanned 13 seasons (2001-2013) and saw him play in 1,310 major-league games, the right-handed switch-hitter was primarily known for his solid glove. He received the Gold Glove Award in 2004 and was named to the National League All-Star team in 2005.

César David Izturis was born on February 10, 1980, in Barquisimeto, Venezuela, the third of six sons. One of his brothers, Maicer Izturis – born only seven months after Cesar – played in 11 big-league seasons, debuting with Montreal in 2004.

Their father, also named Cesar, earned a living working at the local farmers' market in the Cerrito Blanco section of Barquisimeto and transporting mangoes and "pineapples and tomatoes and whatever else had ripened" from open market to open market in his 1954 Chevy pickup truck, often on the road for three or four days at a time. Maicer arrived unexpectedly, brought home in the pickup truck, "a 2-month-old boy, born along his regular route, by a woman he'd met who was not his wife."[1] Maicer was welcomed, by the elder Cesar's wife, Elidez, who "managed the emotional strain of the unexpected arrival, the third of what would become six sons."[2] It was a marriage that endured. In 2005 both parents traveled together to Southern California to visit the two major leaguers.

Cesar, the father, had been a baseball fan himself, but it was always a struggle to provide for the family. "My kids," he said, "were always the worst-dressed kids." They had to borrow gloves from others when they played ball, but they were clearly exceptionally talented and not only played in local leagues but were at one point recruited by a local baseball school that waived tuition."[3]

Notes David Haugh, "He's the guy who signed for $40,000 after growing up borrowing gloves from friends who had more money. He's the guy who learned how to catch bad-hop grounders by practicing on the taped-together balls his dad used to hit him and his brothers."[4] At 16, he was discovered by Chico Carrasquel's nephew, Toronto Blue Jays scout Emilio Carrasquel.

A student at Lara High School, Izturis was signed by the Blue Jays as an undrafted free agent on July 3, 1996.[5]

Izturis began his pro career in 1997 with the St. Catharines (Ontario) Stompers in the short-season New York-Penn League. The 17-year-old split his time in the field between second base (40 games) and shortstop (30 games), batting just .190 with 11 RBIs, but he scored 32 runs.

His next two seasons saw him take incremental steps up the ladder, advancing to the low Class-A Hagerstown Suns (South Atlantic League) in 1998 and then the Advanced-A Dunedin Blue Jays in the Florida State League in 1999. With Hagerstown, he got in a full season's work – 130 games – batting .262 (with a .297 on-base percentage), scoring 56 runs and driving in 38. Almost every game was at shortstop. In 1999 at Dunedin, he hit .308 (.337 OBP) with 77 runs scored and 77 RBIs. He played shortstop in 84 games and second base in 45.

The Blue Jays jumped Izturis to Triple A for 2000, as shortstop with the International League's Syracuse Chiefs. Facing a higher level of pitching, he was more challenged at the plate and hit just .218, but he excelled at fielding.

Izturis was back with the Chiefs in 2001 and had adjusted at the plate, hitting .292 in 87 games. In the field, he again split his time as in 1999, with about two-thirds of the games at shortstop and the rest at second base.

Izturis's 2001 season was most notable, though, for his major-league debut. That came on June 23 at Boston's Fenway Park. Izturis had been called up after Alex Gonzalez strained his left shoulder and pitcher Lance Painter had been designated for assignment. Manager Buck Martinez had Izturis play shortstop and batted him ninth in the order. He singled to left field off starter Frank Castillo in his first big-league at-bat, scoring two batters later on a two-run single by Homer Bush, part of a seven-run inning that gave the Blue Jays a 7-3 lead and the edge they needed in a 9-6 win.

Izturis's first RBI came a week later, when the Red Sox played at SkyDome. With the Blue Jays losing 7-3 in the bottom of the ninth, he doubled down the left-field line off Derek Lowe, driving in a run, then scoring two batters later on a double by Alex Gonzalez. The final score was Boston 7, Toronto 5. His first home run came against the visiting Montreal Expos, a two-run inside-the-park home run off Guillermo Mota.

Izturis stuck with the team through the end of July, batting .253. He returned to Syracuse for August, then came back to the Blue Jays after the International League season was over. He appeared in 15 September games, upping his average to .269. He had 9 RBIs and scored 19 runs. The Blue Jays finished third in the AL East. An assessment near the end of the season said that Izturis might replace Bush at second base in 2002, at a lower salary, that he could steal bases like Bush, "but he's a slap hitter who shows little patience at the plate and lacks Bush's power." That said, he had "impressed the club with steady performances and an ability to learn from mistakes."[6]

At the Winter Meetings in mid-December, Izturis was traded to the Los Angeles Dodgers, along with pitcher Paul

Quantrill, for prospect Luke Prokopec and minor-leaguer Chad Ricketts. The Blue Jays had traded several players, shedding $24 million in salary. Izturis was least among them in salary but the team apparently felt he needed another year at Triple A.[7]

Izturis spent the next five seasons playing for the Dodgers.

After a fourth season of winter ball in Venezuela, he had a very strong spring training in 2002 and the "speedy Izturis [was] considered a good bet to beat out incumbent Alex Cora."[8] He did indeed win the starting role at shortstop, Dodgers manager Jim Tracy saying Izturis could "bring some energy, some speed and the potential to create more run-scoring opportunities to the top of the lineup."[9]

Izturis averaged over 150 games of playing time in the years 2002-04, and saw his batting average improve each year, from .232 to .251 to .288. His RBI totals increased as well, from 31 to 40 to 62. Late in 2003, it was observed that Izturis hit about 60 points higher when batting right-handed but he was making progress from the left side.[10] Over the course of his career, he hit .263 batting right-handed against lefties and .249 batting left-handed against righties.

In his fourth game with the Dodgers, on April 5, 2002, Izturis doubled, singled, and tripled against the visiting Colorado Rockies.

After his second season with the Dodgers, in 2003, Bill Plaschke of the *Los Angeles Times* wrote, "Cesar Izturis may be the best young shortstop in the National League."[11] Then his 2004 season was his best: Working with new hitting coach Tim Wallach, Izturis posted the third-highest batting average on the team and ranked fourth in RBIs.[12] He also stole 25 bases. In midseason, Plaschke called him "maybe the league's most improved player not named Adrian Beltre."[13]

It had always been Izturis's defensive play that kept in the lineup in prior years, since his earliest days in the minor leagues. In 2004 his work at shortstop was recognized when he was awarded a Gold Glove, the first Dodgers shortstop to win a Gold Glove since Maury Wills in 1962.

In Izturis's first three seasons, the fortunes of the Dodgers improved each year as well. Under manager Tracy, the team finished third in 2002, second in 2003, and first in the NL West in 2004. The Dodgers faced the St. Louis Cardinals in the 2004 National League Championship Series, losing three games to one. Izturis played in all four games, hit a single his first time up and a double the next, but then went 1-for-15 for a .176 postseason average. It was his only time in postseason baseball. He handled all 20 fielding chances without an error.

Maicer Izturis had made the majors in 2004, debuting on August 27 and playing in 32 late-season games for the Montreal Expos. The last game that saw the Expos and Dodgers play each other had been August 26. Maicer was traded to the Los Angeles Angels of Anaheim in November, so the only time the two brothers might face each other in a game would be in interleague play.

After the 2004 season, Cesar Izturis signed a three-year deal with the Dodgers for a reported $9.9 million. His 2005 season

started off very strongly on offense. He was batting .333 at the end of April and .342 at the end of May. He began to struggle in June, "hampered by a sore right hamstring."[14]

The two brothers lived 90 minutes away from each other in Southern California. On June 25, 2005, César and Maicer faced each other when the Dodgers played the Angels. "When I go on the field, he's my first enemy,' Maicer said with a broad smile. 'After the game, we'll go back to being brothers.'"[15] Cesar played the full game at Angel Stadium and was 0-for-4 at the plate. After the sixth inning, Maicer came in to play third base. He did not bat, and no play involved the two of them. The next day, though, both played the full game, Cesar going 0-for-4 but Maicer enjoying a 3-for-4 day. He drove in the third run in a 5-3 Angels win. Jeff DaVanon's triple was "followed by a single by Maicer Izturis that looped over the head of his brother, Dodger shortstop Cesar, who was playing in to cut off a run."[16]

Cesar had been named as a reserve to the National League All-Star team, but did not play. He spent the first two weeks of July on the disabled list. What proved to be a sprained back

Gold Glove shortstop César Izturis began his career with Toronto and shined in Los Angeles. He was an All-Star in 2005. (Scott Halleran / Getty Images Sports)

troubled him in the latter half of August, and he played his last game of the season on August 22. The day he was due to come off the DL for the back, he had an MRI of his right elbow. The diagnosis led to Tommy John ligament replacement surgery in September.

With recovery time expected to take until nearly the summer of 2006, the Dodgers acquired Rafael Furcal at shortstop. Izturis did return in June, after rehabbing with Class-A Vero Beach and then in 15 games for Triple-A Las Vegas. More often than not, he played third base on his return.

In mid-July, Izturis was criticized for choosing to attend the birth of his daughter Daniella, by cesarean section, because he missed four games.[17] Major League Baseball at the time offered no accommodations for paternity leave.[18]

At the end of July, after 32 games with the Dodgers, Izturis was batting .252. At the trade deadline a week later, he was traded to the Chicago Cubs for Greg Maddux. "The Cubs are going to have a pretty good shortstop for a long time," declared manager Ozzie Guillen. Cubs fans eagerly anticipated the double-play combo of Izturis at short and Ronny Cedeño at second, but some lamented his shaky offense: "He doesn't walk and he doesn't hit for power."[19]

The Dodgers were in fifth place at the time of the trade; they finished tied with San Diego and entered the playoffs as the wild-card team. Maddux contributed, with a 6-3 mark. The Cubs had been fifth in the NL Central; they finished last, in sixth place.

Izturis hit .233 for Dusty Baker's Cubs in 22 games. He missed three weeks with a strained hamstring.

In 2007 Izturis played shortstop for the Cubs, batting .246 through July 15, Roger Cedeño moving to second base. Izturis's contract was sold to the Pittsburgh Pirates on July 19. Playing again for manager Jim Tracy, now with Pittsburgh, Izturis hit .276 for the Pirates in 45 games.

The Pirates declined to exercise the option they held for 2008 and Izturis signed a one-year deal with the St. Louis Cardinals in November. His reception remained ambivalent since he was replacing fan favorite David Eckstein, another small-statured shortstop with a great glove. Columnist Bernie Miklasz remarked, "The Cardinals like his glove, but others say he's slipped defensively." Dan O'Neill wrote, "Why do people get bent out of shape about the Cardinals' signing of César Izturis? It's not like winning championships with a light-hitting, sharp-fielding shortstop is a foreign concept. For reference, see Dal Maxvill, 1967 and 1968."[20] Izturis batted .263 in 135 games, with 24 stolen bases.

A free agent after the 2008 season, Izturis played for the Baltimore Orioles from 2009 through 2011. In 2009 he was out from June 4 to July 10 after needing an appendectomy. Appearing in 114 games, he batted .256. In 2010 he played in 150 games, but with less productivity at the plate, hitting .230.

Izturis got into only 18 games for Baltimore in 2011. He was out from May 13 to August 5 with a right elbow injury and then from August 8 to the end of the season with a left groin strain. He hit .200.

Izturis spent the end of his career bouncing from team to team. In December 2011 he signed a minor-league contract with the Milwaukee Brewers, but he made the team out of spring training. After he appeared in 57 games, batting .235, Milwaukee placed him on waivers. On August 6 the Washington Nationals claimed him. They designated him for assignment 11 days after he had arrived in Washington.

In January 2013, the Cincinnati Reds signed Izturis to a minor-league contract. Once again, he made the team and he appeared in 63 games. He got 129 at-bats and hit .209 with 11 RBIs. He signed a minor-league deal with Houston in January 2014, but was released in March. In September 2015 he joined the Cardinales de Lara of the Venezuelan Professional Baseball League and played with them for two seasons.

Izturis is among the six players who have played for every team in a single division; he and 1960s Phillies outfielder Ted Savage share the distinction of playing for every team in the NL Central.[21]

Maicer's career saw him play from 2005 through 2012 for the Angels, batting .276 over those eight seasons. He played in 107 games for the 2013 Toronto Blue Jays, and then a final 11 games in 2014. His career batting average was .269, with 334 RBIs to Cesar's 312.

Izturis's son, also named César, signed with the Seattle Mariners in 2017 and as of 2023 was still an infielder in the Mariners' farm system. In 2021, Izturis was living in Barquisimeto with his wife Liliana and their children César (b. 1999) and Daniella (b. 2006). César Izturis Jr. played for the Mariners' minor-league team, the Modesto Nuts in 2021. (He opted to return to Venezuela for his high school career so that he could start his professional baseball career sooner as an international free agent).

César is close with his half-brother Maicer. Another half-brother, Julio Izturis, has played in the San Francisco and Toronto farm systems. In 2015 César and Maicer opened a baseball academy in Barquisimeto. Several of its graduates have played in the minor leagues. As of 2024, the Academia de Béisbol Izturis was still going strong.[22]

César Izturis' career was marked by strong defense, shaky offense (he finished with a .254 career batting average), and a reputation as a positive presence. Though he hopped from team to team, he was generally seen as a drama-free, affable mentor to upcoming players, especially his fellow Venezuelans.

NOTES

1   Tim Brown, "Truckload of Talent," *Los Angeles Times*, July 11, 2005: D1.

2   Tim Brown.

3   Tim Brown.

4   David Haugh, "César Izturis, His New Cubs Career Off and Running, Doesn't Regret Wrangle with Dodgers After Missing

Games Following His Daughter's Birth," *Chicago Tribune,* August 2, 2006, https://www.chicagotribune.com/news/ct-xpm-2006-08-02-0608020214-story.html.

5   Rod Nelson, of SABR's Scouts and Scouting Committee, points out that in the *1998 Minor League Digest* (Baseball Blue Book), Blue Jays cross-checker Mike Russell was also credited with signing Izturis.

6   Tom Maloney, "Gonzalez Shows a Potent Bat in the No. 2 Spot," *The Sporting News,* October 1, 2001: 59.

7   Ken Rosenthal, "Let's Separate the Deal Deals from the Duds," *The Sporting News.* December 24, 2001: 57. Within three years, wrote Ross Newhan, the trade, pulled off by GM Dan Evans, "turned out to be a steal." Ross Newhan, "Hailing Cesar, Whose Fame Is a Two-Sided Issue," *Los Angeles Times,* October 5, 2004: D5.

8   Mike DiGiovanna, "Don't Sell Him Short," *Los Angeles Times,* March 9, 2002: D4.

9   Mike DiGiovanna, "In the Short Run, Izturis Is Tracy's First Choice," *Los Angeles Times,* March 26, 2002: D1.

10 "Los Angeles Dodgers," *The Sporting News,* September 1, 2003: 73,

11 Bill Plaschke, "Evans Still Has A Little Work Remaining," *Los Angeles Times,* December 12, 2003: D1.

12 On beginning to work with Wallach, see Ben Bolch, "Izturis Has Been a Hit at the Plate," *Los Angeles Times,* April 29, 2004: D7, and Ben Bolch, "Players Embrace Wallach's Message," *Los Angeles Times,* May 13, 2004: D8.

13 Bill Plaschke, "L.A. Team That Gets the Concept," *Los Angeles Times,* July 23, 2004: D1. Near the end of the season, columnist T.J. Simers enthused about the success the Dodgers had had as a "miracle," asking, "How do you explain trading away left-handed-hitting Dave Roberts, a base stealer, and going with Cesar Izturis, maybe the worst left- handed hitter in baseball since Tom Lasorda posted a career .071 batting average, only to find he has developed into one of the best leadoff men in baseball?" T.J. Simers, "You Can't Spell Miracle without Lima," *Los Angeles Times,* September 26, 2004: D2.

14 Dave Curtis, "Martinez Will Pass on the All-Star Game," *New York Times,* July 8, 2005: D2.

15 Greg Ball, "Izturis brothers finally have showdown," *San Diego Union Tribune,* June 24, 2005, https://www.sandiegouniontribune.com/sdut-izturis-brothers-finally-have-showdown-2005jun24-story.html.

16 Steve Henson, "Sweeping Message by Angels," *Los Angeles Times,* June 27, 2005: D1.

17 David Haugh.

18 One writer who criticized MLB was J.A. Adande: "Izturis Case Shows How Baseball Drops the Ball," *Los Angeles Times,* July 23,2006: D2. Izturis had missed the birth of his son six years earlier and didn't want to miss this one. See David Haugh.

19 Dave Studeman, "Ten Things I Didn't Know Last Week," *Hardball Times,* August 3, 2006, https://tht.fangraphs.com/ten-things-i-didnt-know-last-week29/.

20 "How César Izturis Replaced David Eckstein at Shortstop," Retrosimba.com, November 28, 2017 https://retrosimba.com/2017/11/28/how-César-izturis-replaced-david-eckstein-at-shortstop/.

21 Bryan Grosnick, "The Players Who Have Appeared for Each Team in a Division," February 19, 2016, *Bleacher Report,* https://www.beyondtheboxscore.com/2016/2/19/11064018/every-team-division-mark-mclemore-ted-savage-kelly-johnson-steve-finley-matt-herges-César-izturis.

22 The academy website provides more information: https://www.instagram.com/academiaizturis/?hl=es.

RAMÓN MONZANT

BY RICHARD BOGOVICH

n the minor leagues, Ramón Monzant won 61 games and lost only 25, spanning 784 innings, for a .709 record. No minor leaguer who hurled at least 1,000 innings ever came close to that rate.[1] Alas, he was merely mediocre for the New York and San Francisco Giants of the National League, for whom he pitched in 106 games over six seasons from 1954 to 1960. Chronic homesickness for his native Venezuela seemed as plausible an explanation as any for his inability to find consistent success against NL teams.

Ramón Segundo Monzant y Espina was born on January 4, 1933, in Maracaibo, Venezuela,[2] to Ramón Monzant y Almarza and the former Corina Espina y Moran. Maracaibo is a large city close to a gulf of the Caribbean Sea, and is the capital of the state of Zulia. Church records show the elder Ramón was baptized in late 1907. He had two younger sisters, but the second died very young. Corina was baptized in 1913, and she apparently had at least nine older siblings, plus two younger ones. The younger Ramón had a sister named Nora Graciela and a brother named Nelson. Two-year-old Nelson died in 1940.

A profile of Monzant late in his career reported that his father was an office worker, and that Ramón junior attended school for six years. During his youth he played some basketball and plenty of baseball. He gravitated toward the latter simply because "that's what all the fellows were doing," he said in 1960. He played third base and considered himself "a good hitter," but his manager decided his powerful throws could make him an effective pitcher.[3] Earlier, in 1958, Monzant said his change of position was of necessity. "I had to become a pitcher because my throws from third were too hard for our first baseman," he said.[4] His team was called the Royals, and the manager who moved him to the pitching mound was Heberto Camacho.[5]

However, in mid-1954 Monzant told one sportswriter he actually didn't play baseball before age 16. "Then I play all the time," he said. "Good game, lots of fun." It's possible Monzant only meant he started in an organized league at 16, because otherwise he would've had just three years of experience before his professional debut in the United States. "I learn to pitch myself," Monzant said, playing what he called "kid baseball,"[6] which may have meant Camacho wasn't cut out to be a pitching coach. Regardless, the aforementioned profile of Monzant late in his career did refer to him spending only two seasons in amateur baseball prior to a tryout camp he attended in the United States.[7]

Monzant played with the Orange Victoria and Crosley amateur clubs in Maracaibo, but also traveled between 100 and 300 miles for additional experience. He played on the Deportivo Rubio team in distant San Cristóbal, and with a team in Carora. A very important step in Monzant's development was connecting with the Navegantes del Magallanes in the Liga Venezolana de Béisbol Profesional. Though there may be no evidence of his actually playing with that team during the winter of 1951-1952, owner Carlos Lavaud enrolled Monzant in a baseball school in the United States directed by Lou Haneles, a minor leaguer from 1936 to 1949.[8]

Haneles, who could speak Spanish, owned the Florida School of Baseball at Williston, about 100 miles north of Tampa. Paul Florence, a veteran scout of the Cincinnati Reds, watched Monzant pitch a game there in mid-February of 1952. Shortly after the Reds opened their spring-training camp in Tampa on February 25, Florence arranged for Haneles to present Monzant to Cincinnati manager Luke Sewell for a 10-day tryout. "Believing that the boy might be as capable as Haneles touted him, and that if he was some other club would try to wean him away, Red officials threw a cloak of secrecy around him," *The Sporting News* reported. "He did have good stuff, especially a puzzling letup ball, while warming up with a catcher." Monzant's tryout with the Reds ended after just two innings at the end of an eight-inning intrasquad game on March 7.[9]

Catching for Monzant was Hobie Landrith, who had played just eight games of a 14-year major-league career. Monzant struck out the first batter he faced, Hank Foiles. Next, career minor leaguer Bob Wilson hit a double. Monzant then issued three straight walks, followed by two hit batsmen. He finally retired a second batter before Foiles batted again, with the bases loaded, and swatted a triple. Wilson was then the third out. Monzant pitched well in his second inning but was cut the next day.[10]

On March 17 a team from Shelby, North Carolina, of the Class-D Western Carolina League began a few weeks of spring training in Tampa.[11] Monzant eventually joined them. The Shelby Farmers played few exhibition games in the Tampa area, and newspaper coverage was minimal.[12]

The Farmers weren't affiliated with any major-league team that season, nor were four of the league's five other franchises. Managing Shelby was Dave Coble, a catcher who had played 15 games for the Phillies in 1939. Only five players in the entire league ever had major-league experience.[13]

During the regular season, Monzant made his professional debut on April 22, 1952. It was Shelby's second game and their home opener. They hosted the Rutherford County Owls at night before 2,500 fans. Monzant entered in the seventh inning with the score tied, 6-6. He gave up a run in the eighth but his teammates rallied for three in the bottom half, which produced the final score, 9-7. While winning in his debut, Monzant gave up three hits in three innings and offset a walk with five strikeouts.[14]

Through June 6, Monzant had a record of 6-4 in 11 games, with 68 strikeouts in 81 innings.[15] He won 10 of his next 13 decisions to end the regular season with a record of 16-7. His seventh win, on June 16, was a 3-0 four-hitter.[16] Monzant hurled another shutout on September 1 in the first game of the Farmers' postseason semifinal series, 7-0. He scattered six hits and struck out 11 Owls.[17]

In the finals, which went the full seven games against Lincolnton, Monzant allowed only three hits but lost the third game, 1-0, on an unearned run. Three days later, with the Farmers down three games to one, he hurled a 4-2 complete-game victory. On September 15 he pitched the final 3⅓ innings of the finale and helped Shelby win the crown by a score of 4-3.[18]

A significant milestone for Monzant occurred shortly before September 11, when the New York Giants purchased him for an undisclosed sum that one North Carolina sportswriter said was "the highest price ever paid for a Western Carolina League player."[19] The scout involved was Willie Duke, a recent player-manager for a few minor-league teams in North Carolina.[20] On September 19 Monzant signed with the Knoxville Smokies, the Giants' affiliate in the Class-B Tri-State League. "We paid out a good-sized chunk of money for Monzant," Smokies business manager Jack Aragon said.[21]

Monzant returned to Venezuela to play for Magallanes that offseason, and he was one of six pitchers on manager Lázaro Salazar's Opening Day roster.[22] Over the season, other pitchers included Johnny Gray and John Mackinson, both future major leaguers, plus John Hetki, who played eight years in the majors between 1945 and 1954. Monzant was among the four-team league's pitching leaders with five wins and two losses.[23]

By early February of 1953, Monzant was on the roster of the Leafs of Danville, Virginia, the Giants' affiliate in the Class-B Carolina League (instead of Class-B Knoxville).[24] In early April he was among nine pitchers working out with the Leafs in Melbourne, Florida. He was described then as a "Ewell Blackwell type of hurler."[25] Blackwell's SABR biographer described him as "a long, lanky side-arming right-hander."[26]

Monzant's high points during the regular season included three-hitters about five weeks apart. In Fayetteville on May 13, he limited opposing batters to one run on three hits. In his three-hitter at home on June 18, he handcuffed Greensboro, 3-0.[27] In early July his record was 12-4, and he received the second-most votes for the league's all-star teams.[28]

At the end of the regular season, Monzant had a record of 23-6, led the Carolina League with 232 strikeouts, and was named the circuit's most valuable player. On September 8 he was the winning pitcher in Danville's first semifinal playoff game, and on September 14 he hurled a 1-0 shutout in the first game of the finals. He lost a start, but Danville ultimately won the championship, four games to two.[29]

Danville's newspaper soon reported that seven players were promoted for the following season. However, only Monzant made the big jump to Minneapolis in the Triple-A American Association. Only one of his Danville teammates later played in the majors, future NL President Bill White, who was a year younger than Monzant.[30]

That offseason, Monzant went home to play with Magallanes again. He set three league records, 13 strikeouts in a game, 132 in a season, and 15 wins.[31]

Monzant was married around then. His wife, according to 1956 international travel records, was Rita Monica Diaz de Monzant. She accompanied him to the United States in March of 1954, and apparently remained with him at least through midyear. "She speaks no English and Ramon very little, but they do all right," wrote *Minneapolis Star* sportswriter Bob Beebe. "Ramon has no trouble with the signs on the diamond and the waiters seem to understand his signals in the restaurants."[32]

In the early days of summer, Monzant had a record of 7-3 for the Minneapolis Millers, with an earned run average of 3.91 and 74 strikeouts in 99 innings. On June 26, at age 21 and in just his third pro season, the Giants brought him up. Manager Leo Durocher started on July 2, 1954, at Pittsburgh.[33] Monzant became just the eighth player born in Venezuela to make it to the majors, only one of whom that season, Chico Carrrasquel of the White Sox, was still active at that level.[34]

The Giants had a record of 48-23 while the Pirates had the opposite, 23-48. Forbes Field held 9,603 fans that day. The first batter Monzant faced was shortstop Gair Allie, who struck out looking. Across Monzant's first three innings he faced the minimum nine batters. He walked two Pirates but each was erased by a double play. The fourth inning went very differently. Allie led off with a single, and a few batters later, the Pirates had the bases loaded and a run scored, with one out. Monzant then induced a pop fly for the second out, but Durocher pulled him after Dick Cole's two-run double. Pittsburgh scored once more before the inning ended, and Monzant was charged with four earned runs. However, the Giants eventually won, 9-5.

Monzant pitched five more times for the Giants that month, all in relief. In those four innings there were no earned runs against him, and his ERA decreased to 4.70, but in two appearances he didn't retire a batter. In late July he was returned to the Millers, with whom he spent the remainder of the season.[35] He went 4-4 in his second stint, to finish at 11-7, and his ERA increased somewhat, to 4.42.

Monzant was back with Minneapolis at the start of the 1955 season. On May 30, with a 7-1 record, he was on a plane to rejoin the Giants in the midst of a homestand.[36] He started against the Chicago Cubs on June 3 but didn't finish the third inning and was the losing pitcher. The final score was 4-1, and he gave up three earned runs. His projected start on June 9 was rained out, so his next appearance was a start in Chicago on June 16.[37] He gave up only two earned runs in seven innings but the Giants scored only once. After a few relief outings and one more start, he ended June with a record of 0-4 and an ERA of 8.56. At home on July 6, he picked up his first victory in the majors after an unremarkable inning of relief against the Phillies. At home on August 17, he hurled his first complete game, vs. the Brooklyn Dodgers, and the Giants won, 5-1. In September he had a complete-game loss followed by a complete-game win, and he lowered his ERA to 3.99 by the season's end. His record was 4-8. The Giants played their finale on September 25, and international travel records listed him on a Venezuelan airline that same day.

In early March of 1956, Giants manager Bill Rigney was furious that Monzant missed a deadline for reporting to spring training. Monzant supposedly said he was "very tired," and soon Rigney softened his tone. Monzant then denied fatigue and invoked his mother's poor health. It was later specified that she had a fractured spine. International flight records show that on March 14 he arrived in New Orleans. It turned out that her back injury wasn't so severe, and she helped persuade her son to report to the Giants.[38]

Monzant made his regular-season debut with two innings of relief on April 25, in the Giants' seventh game. He then started the second game of a doubleheader at home, against Philadelphia on April 29. He was masterful. The Phillies scored an unearned run in the first inning on a walk, an infield error, and a single, and then were hitless. In the fifth inning he struck out the side and in the sixth he induced three infield popups. He struck out nine Phillies and walked five on his way to a final score of 8-1. He finished the one-hitter in 2 hours 15 minutes. Afterward, he contrasted Rigney's style with Durocher's:

The other fellow, he used to tell me 'do this,' 'do that,' whenever I came back to the dugout after an inning. He would holler to me from the bench while I was pitching. Bill, he doesn't say anything. He just lets me pitch like I want. It is a different feeling. I feel more relaxed out there.[39]

Monzant didn't pitch in a Giants game again until two weeks later, due to a sore arm.[40] He struggled in relief outings on May 13 and 26. International travel records show that his wife and their first child, infant son José, arrived around mid-May, but their presence didn't boost his performance.

On June 7 Monzant happened to test his arm in Minneapolis when the Giants played an exhibition game against the Millers. Monzant gave up one hit, one run, and no walks in four innings. However, his inability to strike out any of the Millers was unsettling.[41] He was a pinch-runner on June 12 and 13 in Chicago, but that concluded his major-league service during 1956. By June 19 he was back with Minneapolis, but didn't make a road trip due to his arm.[42]

Monzant was scheduled to start for the Millers on July 1, but a sore foot delayed that two days. On July 3 he fared well until he gave up three earned runs in the sixth inning and exited with one out. He suffered a 3-2 loss. He started again on July 8 but was lifted after giving up a single to the opposing leadoff man. "Monzant's ailing shoulder and/or jammed toe acted up again," a Twin Cities sportswriter explained. He started one more time, on July 22, and was pulled after two walks to begin the fourth inning.[43] Across those three outings and 8⅓ innings he yielded 12 hits, three walks, and five earned runs.

One of the earliest Venezuelans in the majors, Monzant debuted with the New York Giants in 1954. He pitched parts of five big-league seasons. (National Baseball Hall of Fame)

He also had five strikeouts.[44] The team held out some hope as late as August 17 that he could recover. Minneapolis was in the American Association playoffs after its regular season ended on September 9, but on September 6, Monzant, his wife, and their son left for Venezuela.

Monzant avoided the minors during the next two seasons, but his initial outing for the Giants in 1957 wasn't until the second half of June. He still hadn't shown up for spring training a week into March, but the Giants reportedly assumed his arm remained sore. Monzant soon explained that his mother had surgery for a brain condition in December and that her recovery was slow. In fact, she passed away on April 2, with him there.[45]

Monzant arrived in New York by May 8, about 20 games into the regular season. The Giants didn't put him in a game until another exhibition game in Minneapolis, on June 17. He pitched well in three innings against the Millers. "I could have gone a few more innings if Rig wanted me to," Monzant said.[46] Rigney then used him in Chicago against the Cubs on June 22. His following appearances were also mostly in relief, and through July he was mostly mediocre, with an ERA below 5.00

just briefly. He lost his only two starts, on July 23 and September 22, though in the latter he gave up no earned runs. He ended 1957 with a record of 3-2 in 24 games and an ERA of 3.99. On September 29 he became the last man to pitch in a National League game for the New York Giants.

For the 1958 season, the Giants relocated to San Francisco. Unchanged was criticism of Monzant for being late for spring training. In mid-March Rigney chose to comment on a related pattern with Monzant:

I had him at Minneapolis. He'd always break well from the barrier and rack up about an 8-1 record and then The Lion in New York [i.e., Durocher] would roar and demand to know why Ramon was hidden away in the minors when the Giants could use him. So, off to the big city would go Ramon and pretty soon he'd be back with me; frustrated, disgusted and homesick. The next season Ramon jumped off to a 9-2 lead, and again The Lion roared. When I told Monzant Durocher wanted him again, Ramon's eyes lit up wide and he cried: "Me no go. Stay here with you. Me happy here. Me no go to New York. Me go home. Me happier there.' Well, Ramon finally gave in and back to the Giants he went. And back to me he came again.[47]

Through February 13, 1958, Monzant was on Venezuela's team in the Caribbean Series. Two days earlier, he helped beat Cuba's team, 8-1, in San Juan, Puerto Rico. Venezuela finished last in the four-team tournament.[48] On March 6, Monzant "finally arrived" at spring training, "late for the fifth time in as many years," one San Francisco sportswriter noted.[49] Late that month, an Associated Press article about Monzant said this time he was at least "well under the spring curfew he'd missed in the past." Still, the writer said that in the previous four years he had "presented a variety of excuses" (perhaps unaware his mother's death was one reason). "Sure, it helps to be here early," Monzant conceded. Looking forward, he said, "I can do much better as a starter. I look for my best year this season. If I pitch every four days, my arm would be better."[50]

Through June 10, Monzant was deployed as a starter in 12 of his 13 games. He went 4-5 with a 4.93 ERA. His four victories were all complete games. The most impressive was his third start, a 2-0 four-hit shutout against the Chicago Cubs at home on April 25. "My fast ball inside and my slider were working good, and I did not walk a man," he said, grinning. "First man up I hit but after that no free passes." By mixing in sliders, he notched three strikeouts against eventual 1958 MVP and Hall of Famer Ernie Banks. "But for the rest I give the fast ball." Monzant said.[51] He struck out four other Cubs.

Monzant pitched 30 more times after June 10, but only four were starts. He finished with a record of 8-11 plus a save, and had a 4.72 ERA. That was his only time in the majors when he was active from Opening Day until the finale. That year also became unique when his photo appeared twice in the Topps baseball card set. In addition to his own card, a photo of Monzant was mistakenly used on teammate Mike McCormick's card.[52]

On February 6, 1959, Monzant announced he would be a holdout unless the Giants boosted his pay by $3,000, to $10,000.

Club vice president Chub Feeney said the contract they'd sent him about week earlier did offer more money. "Maybe we were a little low on the first one," Feeney admitted. "He pitched a lot of innings for us last year and we gave him a raise." It so happened that on February 8 Monzant shook off two losses in the Venezuelan playoffs to hurl a 1-0 three-hitter in the decisive seventh game, which sent Oriente into the Caribbean Series as Venezuela's entry. "Hundreds of jubilant fans swarmed on the field in Caracas after the final out," M.J. Gorman, Jr. wrote in *The Sporting News*, "and Monzant was carried off in triumph."[53]

On February 21, 1959, Monzant asked for his release, and said he'd "already wasted six years in pro ball." Feeney responded promptly. "We won't give him his release. He could then sign with any other club," he said. "If he persists, he will be placed on the voluntary retired list." That was on the eve of spring training. San Francisco sportswriter Bob Stevens said Monzant "would become the first Giant in modern times to get mad enough to quit."[54]

Initial reports of the differing salary levels must have been inaccurate, because in mid-March Monzant was said to have agreed to a contract for $11,500, though a potential sticking point was his insistence on a tax-free advance of $5,000. The Giants said that wouldn't be possible, and on March 24 Monzant said he'd stay home and work for an oil company. One theory was that loud booing of him during some home games was a big factor. However, teammate Al Worthington drew attention to the fact that Monzant and his wife, who still knew no English, had two children by that point and weren't getting to see him for eight months a year. "I don't blame him for hanging 'em up," Bob Stevens responded.[55]

Monzant didn't sign a new contract with the Giants until November 12, 1959. Atop the first sports page of the *San Francisco Chronicle* the next day, spanning the full width, a headline proclaimed, "Monzant Will Rejoin Giants in 1960." Not long afterward, Bill Rigney commented. "I always thought Monzant was going to be a great pitcher. I think his trouble is that we rushed him along too fast when he first joined the club. One thing about Ramon, he knows how to pitch – more than some who have been in the majors a lot longer. He may benefit by laying out last year and I look for him to come back strong."[56]

On March 2, 1960, Monzant once again reported late for spring training. *San Francisco Examiner* sportswriter Walter Judge said Monzant offered no particular reason for being tardy. "I just wanted a rest," the pitcher said. "He hardly could have been tired from winter league play," Judge replied. "He pitched only 21 innings."[57]

On April 25 Ramón Monzant made his 1960 regular-season debut, in St. Louis. It was the Giants' 11th game. He relieved in the eighth inning, right after the Giants pounded Bob Gibson to take a 9-7 lead. The first two Cardinals grounded out, but pinch-hitter Carl Sawatski swatted a homer to deep right field. Monzant then struck out pinch-hitter George Crowe to end the frame. A pinch-hitter batted for Monzant in the top of the ninth. Neither team scored, and the 9-8 victory improved the

Giants' record to 8-3. That turned out to be Monzant's final inning in the major leagues.

Monzant hadn't been mentioned in the *Chronicle* or the *Examiner* from Opening Day until that inning of work, so readers received no explanation for his disuse in the first 10 games. That remained true until May 12, when those dailies announced that he was assigned to the Giants' Triple-A farm team, Tacoma of the Pacific Coast League. The Giants faced a deadline for reducing to 25-player rosters.[58]

On May 24 Monzant was the subject of a long, anonymous article in the *Tacoma News-Tribune*. The writer began by pointing out that Monzant had no personal connection to the Tacoma team's leadership, nor "any sentimental attachment" to the state of Washington. "However, it shouldn't be assumed he's the unfriendly type. He isn't at all," the writer continued. Naturally, Monzant wanted return to the NL as soon as possible, but that didn't create a bad attitude toward his new team.[59]

Monzant's season ended prematurely on August 4, at home. He pitched a scoreless eighth inning in relief and singled to lead off the bottom half. When he advanced to second base on a passed ball, his spikes caught awkwardly and he dislocated an ankle, which Tacoma sportswriter Ed Honeywell said "is sometimes more serious than a fracture." Tacoma general manager Rosy Ryan was said to be "considerably upset" by the injury. "Monzant was a major league relief pitcher and probably the most valuable man on our staff," Ryan declared.[60] Monzant pitched 80 innings in 40 games for Tacoma. He went 4-3 with a 3.38 ERA.

In February of 1961, the Tacoma club remained optimistic that Monzant would return, and still tried to woo him in April. Tacoma may have given up by mid-June, when his injury the previous August was described as a broken ankle that hadn't healed properly.[61] In March of 1962, Monzant announced his retirement due to injury, albeit to his *arm*, though that broken ankle was also noted.[62]

Late in 1962, *The Sporting News* reported Monzant's early success in Venezuela's Occidental League, "pitching with Pastora this season on loan from Oriente of Venezuela's Central League. The arrangement was worked out so he could retain his job with a local brewery."[63] One of his comeback games received coverage back in Tacoma.[64] A year later it was reported that Monzant signed again with the Pastora club,[65] but infrequent mentions of him later that decade in US newspapers tended to be in reminiscences of the 1950s.

Ramón Monzant died on August 10, 2001, at age 68. By 2007 he became one of the first 20 baseball players in the Venezuelan Sports Hall of Fame.[66] It's possible a big reason his pitching success in Venezuela and the minor leagues never materialized in the NL was casual xenophobia that was easier to shrug off where there was less pressure. What seemed like exaggeration of his accent and imperfect English in newspapers at times certainly could have reflected a widely dismissive attitude toward foreign players. Similarly, there were three instances each in the *San Francisco Chronicle* during the spring trainings of 1958 and 1960 when Monzant's reasons for arriving late were belittled as involving "banana boats," in a context considered derogatory in recent decades.[67] One example in March 1960 may have been an attempt to be clever. "Ramon Monzant of Venezuela, a banana boat rider, also arrived late but not because of officialdom," wrote longtime *Chronicle* sportswriter Art Rosenbaum. "He explained that 'the boat with the banana she said manana.'"[68] It's questionable that Monzant would have actually said this, partly because international travel records accessible via Ancestry.com show he arrived in Miami a week earlier by airline. In any event, it couldn't have been easy being the only player from his country in the NL during the second half of the 1950s.

SOURCES

The primary source for statistics throughout is baseball-reference.com.

NOTES

1   Kevin T. Czerwinski, "Legendary Minor League Records," April 5, 2005, https://www.milb.com/news/gcs-377.

2   J.G. Taylor Spink, ed., *Baseball Register* (St. Louis: C.C. Spink & Son, 1956), 214.

3   "Monzant Wants to Show That He's Big Leaguer," *Tacoma* (Washington) *News-Tribune*, May 24, 1960: C-7.

4   "Monzant Impresses Bill Rigney, Slated for Regular Mound Stint," *Danville* (Virginia) *Bee*, March 27, 1958: 2-D.

5   Manolo Rodriguez, "Una Gran Figura Aporta Venezuela Para el Beisbol Mayor: Monzant," *La Prensa* (San Antonio, Texas), July 11, 1954: 7.

6   Tom Briere, "Kid Venezuelan Hurler Takes 7-3 Mark to Giants," *The Sporting News*, July 7, 1954: 9.

7   "Monzant Wants to Show that He's Big Leaguer."

8   "Una Gran Figura Aporta Venezuela Para el Beisbol Mayor: Monzant"; Carlos Cárdenas Lares, *Venezolanos en las Grandes Ligas*, 2nd ed. (Caracas: Fondo Editorial Cárdenas Lares, 1994), 40. For at least three of Haneles's minor-league seasons he was that rarest of catchers, a left-hander.

9   "'Ten-Day' Trial Lasts Two Innings," *The Sporting News*, March 19, 1952: 21. A few years later, this school was apparently known as the Bill Virdon Baseball School, based on an ad in *The Sporting News*, December 11, 1957: 30. A claim in it read, "900 players from our camp have signed contracts since 1946 including Danny O'Connell (Giants) and Ramon Monzant (Giants) from our 1952 class." The school was "Operated by National Baseball Placement Bureau." O'Connell made his major-league debut in 1950 and served in the military during 1952, so he presumably wasn't in the 1952 class with Monzant, contrary to one interpretation of that sentence in the ad.

10 "'Ten-Day' Trial Lasts Two Innings"; Pete Norton, "Reds Invade Sarasota for Tilt With Bosox," *Tampa Morning Tribune*, March 8, 1952: 11, 13. There were several indications that a few rules were ignored during this informal game. Contrasting the detailed play-by-play with the box score (in which the inning-by-inning subtotals flipped the two teams) seems to indicate that the other team skipped over their fifth-place hitter in that informal game. Also, Monzant was pinch-hit for in the bottom of the seventh but

stayed in the game. What's more, Bob Wilson apparently pinch-hit for both squads, and a second player was also in both lineups. This Bob Wilson was presumably Robert Alexander Wilson, born in Piedmont, Alabama, who spent three seasons in Cincinnati's farm system. For the record, Monzant was credited as the winning pitcher despite blowing a five-run lead because his side came right back with a four-run rally to produce the final score of 9-6.

11   "Shelby Club Opens Camp Here Today," *Tampa Morning Tribune*, March 17, 1952: 15.

12   Despite the minimal coverage, a box score was printed of Shelby's loss to the Class-B St. Petersburg Saints on March 29. See Bob Hudson, "Saints Trounce Farmers, 7 To 1," *St. Petersburg Times*, March 30, 1952: 25. The starting pitcher for the Farmers was reportedly named Julio Ramon. Was it just a coincidence that that surname matched Monzant's first name? Though the Farmers' regular-season roster in 1952 at baseball-reference.com had no player with a surname anywhere close to Ramon, it's possible he was trying out and soon was cut. Also, a minor-league pitcher named Julio Ramos, not Ramon, was active at that time, but all of his regular-season pitching from 1950 through 1952 was for teams in Texas in Class B, two rungs above D. It's worth noting here that Shelby's roster for 1952 at baseball-reference.com might be incomplete. The pitcher for Shelby in its third game was named Rainey, but there's no such name on the roster. See Lawrence Smith, "Farmers Blast Hickory," *Hickory* (North Carolina) *Daily Record*, April 24, 1952: 2, 13. In fact, an Opening Day preview mentioned three other Farmers, Bill Lowder, Oscar Del Calvo, and Rush Gold, who aren't on the baseball-reference.com roster. See Sandy Grady, "'Nobody Loves Nobody' In Cozy Western Carolina," *Charlotte* (North Carolina) *News*, April 21, 1952: 18.

13   Only one of the six franchises is listed as being affiliated with a major-league club at https://www.baseball-reference.com/register/league.cgi?id=2e4c3a74. On each roster accessible from this web page, boldface denotes the very few future or former major leaguers.

14   "Shelby Tops Owls, 9 to 7 on Nine Hits," *Hickory Daily Record*, April 23, 1952: 2, 9. In the box score's batting order he was "Munvant" (with a hitless at-bat), while beneath the line score he was "Monvant" four times. Thanks to Martin Otts of the Patrick Beaver Memorial Library in Hickory, North Carolina, for providing newspaper coverage of Shelby's early games.

15   "Minor Averages," *The Sporting News*, June 18, 1952: 38.

16   "Lincolnton, Shelby in Tight Race," "*Asheville* (North Carolina) *Citizen-Times*, June 22, 1952: D5. "Wright's .381 Remains Best in Western," *Greensboro* (North Carolina) *Daily News*, June 22, 1952: sports, 9.

17   "Shelby, Lincs Win Openers," *Greensboro Daily News*, September 2, 1952: 2, 3; Ronald Kiser, "Cards Rap Mauraders [*sic*] by 6 to 2," *Gastonia* (North Carolina) *Gazette*, September 2, 1952: 8.

18   "Lincolnton Tops Shelby by 1-0," *Greensboro Daily News*, September 10, 1952: 2, 5; "High School Football," *Greensboro Daily News*, September 13, 1952: 2, 3; "Shelby Takes Shaughnessy in WC Loop," *Asheville Citizen*, September 16, 1952: 15

19   Irwin Smallwood, "Tar Heel Sports," *Greensboro Daily News*, September 12, 1952: 4, 1.

20   Smallwood. See also "Ray Monzant Giant Now," *Charlotte Observer*, September 12, 1952: 18-A. The latter article was accompanied by a photo of Monzant from the waist up, wearing a Farmers jersey.

21   "Smokes Sign Venezuelan," *Knoxville* (Tennessee) *News-Sentinel*, September 19, 1952: 10. Aragon, who was born in Cuba, was a pinch-runner in his only major-league game, for the Giants in 1941.

22   Antonio Lutz, "Venezuela Pro League Opens with 4 Teams," *The Sporting News*, October 15, 1952: 33.

23   Antonio Lutz," Magallenes Club Slides From Top to League Cellar," *The Sporting News*, December 3, 1952: 34; Antonio Lutz, "Schenz' .355 Wins Bat Title in Venezuela," *The Sporting News*, March 11, 1953: 32. Lutz provided regular updates in other editions of *The Sporting News*. Monzant's other teammates included Dick Whitman, a six-year National Leaguer from 1946 through 1951, who hit .371 for Magallanes but didn't have enough plate appearances to qualify for the batting average title, and Jesus "Chucho" Ramos, whose major-league career consisted of five hits in 10 at-bats (.500) across four games with the Cincinnati Reds in 1944.

24   "46 Players Are Formally Placed on Danville Leafs' 1953 Roster," *Danville Bee*, February 5, 1953: 2, 8.

25   Walter Christianson, "Leaf Positions Still Not Fixed but Formidable Team Is Forecast," *Danville Bee*, April 6, 1953: 11.

26   Christianson. See also Warren Corbett, "Ewell Blackwell," https://sabr.org/bioproj/person/ewell-blackwell/. Monzant was likewise compared to Blackwell by Moses Crutchfield: "Bucs, as Flag Contender, Pass 1952 Gate," *Greensboro* (North Carolina) *Daily News*, July 5, 1953: sports, 6.

27   "Cards, Buc Win; Highlanders Lose," *Raleigh* (North Carolina) *News and Observer*, May 15, 1953: 18; Earle Hellen, "Pats Seek to Slow Bur-Gra Flag March Tonight," *Greensboro* (North Carolina) *Record*, June 19, 1953: B-4.

28   Earle Hellen, "Recording Sports," *Greensboro Record*, July 7, 1953: B-8.

29   "Danville Pitcher Is Named Most Valuable Player," *The Robesonian* (Lumberton, North Carolina), September 9, 1953: 12. "Radulovich, Buddin, Hussey Cop Carolina League Honors," *Durham* (North Carolina) *Morning Herald*, September 13, 1953: II, 5; "Pirates Drop Opener to Leafs, 6-4; Play Here Tonight," *Burlington* (North Carolina) *Daily Times-News*, September 9, 1953: 8; "Monzant Hurls Leafs to Win Over Luckies in First Game," *Burlington Daily Times-News*, September 15, 1953: 2; "Luckies Top Danville, 5-1," *Raleigh News and Observer*, September 18, 1953: 24; "Rosser Led Pitchers With 2 Wins; Collins, Gilbert Paced Hitting," *Danville Bee*, September 21, 1953: 2, 12.

30   "Seven Leafs Promoted; Monzant Goes to AAA Minneapolis Club," *Danville Bee*, September 24, 1953: 4, 5. Bill White was promoted to Sioux City, Iowa, in the Class-A Western League.

31   Lou Hernández, *The Rise of the Latin American Baseball Leagues, 1947-1961* (Jefferson, North Carolina: McFarland & Company, Inc., 2011), 336-337.

32   "Members Of 1953 Leafs Now on Roster of Higher Class Clubs," *Danville Bee*, March 29, 1954: 10; Bob Beebe, "Beebe's Scrapbook," *Minneapolis Star*, April 29, 1954: 38; Bob Beebe, "Monzant to Giants in Cash Purchase," *Minneapolis Sunday Tribune*, June 27, 1954: Sports, 1. The latter article included a photo of Rita helping her husband pack. For Rita's full name after their marriage, see international travel records dated May 13 and September 6, 1956, accessible via Ancestry.com. See also Manolo Rodriguez, "Una Gran Figura Aporta Venezuela Para el Beisbol Mayor: Monzant," *La Prensa:* July 11, 1954: 7.

33   Bob Beebe, "Monzant to Giants in Cash Purchase," *Minneapolis Sunday Tribune*, June 27, 1954: Sports, 1; "Moryn Called Up by Brooks; Monzant May Go for Giants," *Minneapolis Morning Tribune*, June 29, 1954: 26; Tom Briere, "Kid Venezuelan Hurler Takes 7-3 Mark to Giants," *The Sporting News*, July 7, 1954: 9.

34   See https://www.baseball-almanac.com/players/birthplace.php?loc=Venezuela, which is sortable by Debut Year.

35 Bob Beebe, "Giants Recall Worthington; Send Monzant,"
    Minneapolis Star, July 28, 1954: 36.

36 Bob Beebe, "Monzant Has Real Chance in Majors, Says Rigney,"
    Minneapolis Star, May 31, 1955: 30. Sid Hartman, "The Roundup:
    Lundeen Recalls Feats of Monzant," *Minneapolis Morning Tribune*,
    June 1, 1955: 22.

37 Jim McCulley, "Diamond Dust," *New York Daily News*, June 11,
    1955: 19c.

38 Jim McCulley, "Rigney to Throw Book at Missing Monzant," *New
    York Daily News*, March 2, 1956: 25c; "Monzant Is Excused," *New
    York Times*, March 3, 1956: 13; "Monzant Denies Reports," *New York
    Times*, March 4, 1956: S9; "Monzant Will Join Giants," *Minneapolis
    Morning Tribune*, March 12, 1956: 26; Joe King, "N.Y. Reporter:
    Assist by Mom Brought Giant Hurler in Fold," *San Francisco
    Chronicle*, March 18, 1956: 4H.

39 "Monzant Takes Dig at Lippy," *Boston Traveler*, April 30, 1956: 27.

40 Jim McCulley, "Giants Think EF Fences Can Cure Hitting Woes,"
    New York Daily News, May 11, 1956: c20.

41 Tom Briere, "21,832 Watch Giants Defeat Millers 6-4," *Minneapolis
    Morning Tribune*, June 8, 1956: 24.

42 "Terwilliger, Stephenson in Lineup," *Minneapolis Star*, June 19,
    1956: 12B.

43 "Double Triumph First for 'Fireman' Paine," *Minneapolis Morning
    Tribune*, July 2, 1956: 20; Bob Beebe, "Monzant Hurling Pleases
    Stanky," *Minneapolis Star*, July 4, 1956: 1D; "Millers Must Halt
    Denver Drive Now," *Minneapolis Star*, July 9, 1956: 13B; Tom Briere,
    "Millers Win 10-1, Lose 3-2," *Minneapolis Morning Tribune*, July
    23, 1956: 24.

44 "Miller Figures," *Minneapolis Star*, August 23, 1956: 11B.

45 Louis Effrat, "Gomez' Absence Irritates Giants," *New York Times*,
    March 7, 1957: 49; Louis Effrat, "Antonelli, Mays Among Giants
    With Minor Arm Troubles," *New York Times*, March 8, 1957: 32;
    "Monzant's Mother Dies," *New York Times*, April 3, 1957: 49.

46 Jim McCulley, "Diamond Dust," *New York Daily News*, May 8,
    1957: 80; "Monzant Earns Spot With Giants," *Minneapolis Morning
    Tribune*, June 18, 1957: 14.

47 Bob Stevens, "Tris Speaker at Home in LA's 'Unusual Climate,'" *San
    Francisco Chronicle*, March 19, 1958: 2H.

48 "Monzant Pitches Caribbean Win," *San Francisco Examiner*,
    February 12, 1958: II, 7; "Cuba Defeats Puerto Rico in Caribbean
    Final," *St. Louis Post-Dispatch*, February 14, 1958: 6B.

49 Walter Judge, "Giants' Kids Wallop Vets in 7-2 Tilt," *San Francisco
    Examiner*, March 6, 1958: II, 7, 11.

50 "Monzant Impresses Bill Rigney, Slated for Regular Mound Stint."

51 Will Connolly, "'Best Game Ever,' Says Monzant," *San Francisco
    Chronicle*, April 26, 1958: 1H.

52 Tim Jeninks, "Walter Moved Quick and Horace Jumped to
    Candlestick," December 5, 2018, https://sabrbaseballcards.
    blog/2018/12/05/walter-moved-quick-and-horace-jumped-to-can-
    dlestick/.

53 "Giants Hope to Satisfy Monzant," *San Francisco Chronicle*, February
    7, 1959: 1H; M.J. Gorman Jr., "Monzant Rips Goat Label to Star
    in Finale," *The Sporting News*, February 18, 1959: 26. Monzant's
    baseball-reference.com entry provides limited stats for one of his
    Venezuelan winter league seasons, 1958-1959. He went 8-9 for the
    Oriente team and struck out 109 batters in 136 innings.

54 "Monzant to Giants: 'I Want Out,'" *San Francisco Examiner*,
    February 22, 1959: 18; Bob Stevens, "S.F. Won't Release Monzant;
    Varsity Reports Today," *San Francisco Chronicle*, February 23,
    1959: 1H, 3H.

55 Walter Judge, "Worthington in Fold; Monzant Is Ready to Sign,"
    San Francisco Examiner, March 17, 1959: II, 8, 10. "Monzant Decides
    to Stay Home," *San Francisco Examiner*, March 25, 1959: 4, 2. Bob
    Stevens, "Giants Lose Homer Battle," *San Francisco Chronicle*, March
    31, 1959: 1H, 4H.

56 Bob Stevens, "Monzant to Pitch for S.F. Again," *San Francisco
    Chronicle*, November 13, 1959: 1H, 2H. The banner headline
    "Monzant Will Rejoin Giants in 1960" was some inches away from
    Stevens' article containing the details. See also Jack McDonald,
    "Guessers Bat .000 Dropping Names in Giant Swap Hopper," *The
    Sporting News*, December 2, 1959: 25.

57 Walter Judge, "Monzant Rejoins Giants; Arm OK," *San Francisco
    Examiner*, March 3, 1960: 4, 1.

58 "Monzant, Rookie Shipped to Tacoma," *San Francisco Chronicle*,
    May 12, 1960: 35.

59 "Monzant Wants to Show That He's Big Leaguer."

60 Ed Honeywell, "Tacoma Beats Seattle but Loses Monzant," *Tacoma
    News-Tribune*, August 5, 1960: 21; Dan Walton, "Sports-log," *Tacoma
    News-Tribune*, August 6, 1960: 8.

61 Ed Honeywell, "Giant Hurlers Sign Papers," *Tacoma Sunday News
    Tribune*, February 26, 1961: C-18; Ed Honeywell, "Between Bounces,"
    Tacoma News Tribune, April 29, 1961: 8; Dan Walton, "Sports-log,"
    Tacoma Sunday News Tribune, June 11, 1961: B-11.

62 "Monzant to Quit Diamond," *Tacoma News-Tribune*, March 5,
    1962: 14.

63 Olaf E. Dickson, "Monzant, Aparicio Spark Flag Contenders With
    Flashy Feats," *The Sporting News*, November 17, 1962: 29.

64 Dan Walton, "Sports-log," *Tacoma Daily Ledger*, November
    16, 1962: 23.

65 Dan Walton, "Sports-log," *Tacoma News Tribune*, November
    4, 1963: 16.

66 William F. McNeil, *Black Baseball Out of Season: Pay for Play Outside
    of the Negro Leagues* (Jefferson, North Carolina: McFarland &
    Company, Inc., 2012), 184-185.

67 For example, this term caused players to revolt in 1993 against Iowa
    Wesleyan College football coach Charlie Moot. One player said that
    among Moot's most derogatory comments was, "I'll ship (you) home
    on the banana boat," directed at a player from Samoa. See Jeff Olson,
    "Hard-Nosed Football and a Player Revolt," *Des Moines* (Iowa)
    Sunday Register, April 25, 1993: 1D, 13D. As an example outside of
    sports, in 2002 a jury in West Palm Beach, Florida, awarded $30,000
    to a Cuban-American employee of the local sheriff's department
    after a retaliatory demotion by a supervisor who had said Cubans
    were "good for rowing" and "worked on banana boats." See Bill
    Douthat, "Sheriff's Employee Awarded $30,000 after Demotion,"
    Palm Beach (Florida) *Post*, November 28, 2002: 2B.

68 Art Rosenbaum, "Overheard: Now Batting – United Nations," *San
    Francisco Chronicle*, March 6, 1960: 33, 37. An example from two years
    earlier was penned by Bob Stevens, "Giants Open Spring Camp
    Drills Today," *San Francisco Chronicle*, February 24, 1958: 1H. A
    sportswriter in Tacoma also "got into the act," as the saying goes, at
    least one time: Ed Honeywell, "Giant Hurlers Sign Papers," *Tacoma
    Sunday News Tribune*, February 26, 1961: C-18.

MELVIN MORA

BY MIKE HUBER

t takes only one swing to hit a home run. It takes two teams to play the game. Three strikes and you're out. Four balls will mean a walk. Unfortunately, there aren't many times in baseball when the number five sticks out. Melvin Mora may be the exception, though. Although he had a successful 13-year career in the majors, he is probably better known as the first major leaguer whose wife had quintuplets.

Mora was born in Agua Negra, Venezuela, on February 2, 1972. He had one brother and one sister. When he was only seven years old, Melvin "witnessed his father, Jose, being murdered by a man who mistook him for someone else."[1] Playing organized sports, Mora was determined to escape the violence that had claimed his father's life and make it to the big leagues.

Mora was a natural athlete. He attended primary school in Agua Negra and Libertador High School in Valencia, Venezuela, graduating from the latter. Before he played baseball, he was an amateur boxer in Venezuela.[2] From 1981 to 1990, Mora also played soccer for the Venezuelan National Soccer League. As he spent more and more time on the baseball diamond, his sister, Sunirde, competed in track and field. She went on to the University of Mayaguez in Puerto Rico on a track scholarship.

On March 30, 1991, the 5-foot-10-inch, 160-pound Mora signed with the Houston Astros as a non-drafted free agent. He spent his first season in professional baseball in the Astros' instructional camp in the Dominican Republic. A year later, the Astros assigned the 20-year-old Mora to their 1992 rookie team in the Gulf Coast League. Although he batted only .222 in 49 games, he led the team with 16 stolen bases. The next year found him assigned to the Asheville Tourists in low Class-A ball (the South Atlantic League). He started exhibiting power, hitting two home runs. Further, the Astros organization experimented with Mora at different positions. In addition to playing in the outfield, he played every infield position and even threw two-thirds of an inning (one hit, no runs). By 1994 he had advanced to the Osceola Astros in the advanced Class-A Florida State League and batted .282 with 8 homers and 24 stolen bases (both team highs). He was primarily an outfielder, although he saw action at second base and third base.

Mora continued to impress the Astros organization, and in 1995 he started the season with the Triple-A Tucson Toros, but after only two games (in which he batted 3-for-5), he was sent down to the Jackson Generals in the Double-A Texas League. He hit .298 and was a starting outfielder for Jackson. By 1997, Mora was again splitting time between the outfield and third base, now playing for the New Orleans Zephyrs in the Triple-A American Association.

In the offseason, he was granted free agency from the Astros, and he began 1998 with the Mercuries Tigers of the Chinese Professional Baseball League in Taiwan. He hit .335 with 34 runs scored and 11 RBIs. The New York Mets organization took interest and signed Mora, now 26 years old, on July 25, assigning him to the St. Lucie Mets in the Florida State League. Within four weeks he was promoted to the Triple-A Norfolk Tides.

From 1992 to 1998, Mora had spent seven seasons in the minor leagues before he received his first invitation to major-league spring training in 1999. He proceeded to prove he belonged, hitting .421 in the Grapefruit League,[3] yet he was sent back to the Tides.

After two months in Norfolk, the Mets called him to the majors, and Mora made his debut in the big leagues on May 30, 1999, in a game against the Arizona Diamondbacks. Manager Bobby Valentine put him at shortstop, batting eighth in the lineup. He was 0-for-3; all three at-bats ended in fly outs to the outfield. He spent the next two months being used primarily as a pinch-hitter and pinch-runner. On July 6, in his 20th game, he pinch-hit for Robin Ventura and collected his first major-league hit, a single to center. Three weeks later, on July 25, Mora made his first start, playing center field against the Chicago Cubs. Again, he was 0-for-3, but he collected a bases-loaded walk in his first at-bat of that game, which resulted in his first career run batted in. He spent the month of August playing for Norfolk but was then called back to New York, to be eligible for the post-season. He made 66 game appearances for the Mets in 1999, with five hits in 31 at-bats.[4] New York added Mora to its postseason roster and he batted .429 (6-for-14) in the six-game National League Championship Series against Atlanta. (The Mets lost the series in six games.)

A season later, Mora became the Mets' everyday shortstop when Rey Ordonez was sidelined with a broken forearm. He blasted his first major-league homer on April 20 in the bottom of the 10th inning off Milwaukee's Curt Leskanic, giving New York a 5-4 victory. On July 6, 2000, Mora celebrated an offday by getting married. The Mets had finished a series against the Marlins in Florida and did not have to be back in New York until the 7th. His wife, Gisel, had a daughter, Tatiana, and Mora adored the instant family. However, just before the 2000 trade deadline, Mora was traded with pitchers Leslie Brea and Pat Gorman and infielder Mike Kinkade to the Baltimore Orioles for shortstop Mike Bordick. Mora had split his time with the Mets between the outfield and shortstop, and Baltimore was looking for someone to replace Bordick at short. Mora hit safely in 15 of his first 19 games with the Orioles, displaying a .413 batting average. In the offseason, he returned to Venezuela and won a home-run-hitting competition in Caracas, defeating Andres Galarraga, Richard Hildago, Magglio Ordonez, Edgardo Alfonzo, and Bobby Abreu. Mora received a trophy and $7,000, which he donated to the Hospital San Juan de Dios.

On July 28, 2001, Mora was waiting to board a flight from Anaheim when Gisel gave birth to quintuplets at Johns Hopkins Hospital in Baltimore. Daughters Genesis Raquel (1.51 pounds), Jada Priscilla (1.88 pounds), and Rebekah Alesha (1.88 pounds), and sons Matthew David (2.01 pounds) and Christian Emmanuel (2.48 pounds) became five new additions to the Mora family. The quintuplets were born 3½ months before their due date. All the names were chosen from the Bible. "I'm happy. God has blessed us. All of the babies are doing fine," Mora told reporters two days later.[5] When the new father visited his locker before the game, a package of 68 diapers was stuffed into the top compartment. Soon folks were describing his family as baseball's version of the Brady Bunch with "Mora the merrier."[6] Interestingly, Mora and his wife were initially told to expect twins. Early in the pregnancy, Gisel was rushed to a hospital in Fort Lauderdale, Florida, after experiencing massive bleeding. Doctors performed an ultrasound, and Gisel was told she would instead have quintuplets and all were safe. Melvin had been out in the parking lot praying. When he came into the hospital, he found his wife laughing. The babies were safe. Mora recalled, "I thought, 'What's going on?' Then the nurse congratulated me five times. I didn't know whether to laugh or smile or what."[7]

Mora had played 124 of the first 137 games of the season before injuring his left elbow on September 3 against the Oakland Athletics. Mora had the rare feat of getting two hits in the same inning in a May 9 game at Tampa Bay. He then went on a tear at the plate, and in a 43-game stretch during May and June, he went 52-for-146, including a season-high eight-game hitting streak.

On April 25, 2003, Mora was batting .250 with only 10 hits in his first 14 games. Over the next three months, he had gone from struggling utility player to the leading hitter in the American League and a spot on the junior circuit's All-Star squad. A nine-game stretch in May saw him get 22 hits, and he put together a 23-game hitting streak. He was selected as a reserve for the midsummer classic in Chicago, telling reporters, "I'm excited for the way my career is going. I've worked hard all season. I think I deserved it."[8] At the All-Star break, Mora was batting .349 with an on-base percentage of .443. Primarily playing in the outfield, Mora hit .379 in May and .355 in June. He had led the American League in batting from July 12 until the end of the season. Mora tried to become the first Oriole to win a batting championship since 1966, when Frank Robinson batted .316 as part of his Triple Crown season. At the end of July, Mora had been batting .325. But he missed all of August due to injury and September saw his average drop to .317. The American League's leader for the season was Boston's Bill Mueller (.326).

In January 2004, Mora followed up his breakout season by signing a three-year deal with Baltimore. The Orioles made him their everyday third baseman, a position he occupied for the

Two-time All-Star Melvin Mora was a mainstay in Baltimore's lineup during the 2000s. He had six seasons with 15+ home runs. (Nick Laham / Getty Images Sports)

next six seasons. He delivered on his end of the bargain, batting .340 with 27 home runs and 104 runs batted in (all career highs) in 2004. The .340 mark was second to Seattle's Ichiro Suzuki (.372). Mora's .419 OBP led the American League. He also won a Silver Slugger Award and was named Most Valuable Oriole. Further, he was named third baseman on *The Sporting News* AL All-Star Team and AL Silver Slugger Team. In May 2004, Mora claimed American League Player of the Month honors. His average had surpassed Ken Singleton's previous Baltimore record of a .328 batting average in 1977. In the offseason, Mora established the Melvin Mora Foundation to fund educational, medical, and other needs in his native Venezuela.[9]

In 2005 Mora earned his second election to the American League All-Star team. He led the Orioles and matched his career high with 27 home runs. He batted .319 with 22 RBIs over his final 24 games of the season.

In 2006 Mora announced that he was stepping out of the inaugural World Baseball Classic after being asked to play center field rather than third base for Venezuela, a position he had not played since 2003. He told the press, "I cannot go to that competition to try and play something that I don't know how to play."[10] In the midst of a contract negotiation, he added, "This is not spring training. It's a big competition. And as everybody knows, I'm trying to negotiate my contract here. If I don't agree with the Baltimore Orioles, I'm going to be a free agent. But not as a center fielder – as a third baseman."[11] The Venezuelan manager wanted 22-year-old Miguel Cabrera to play third base for the national team.

Later that spring, on May 19, the Orioles agreed with Mora to terms on a three-year contract extension that would keep him with the team through 2009. The new deal guaranteed Mora $25 million and included an option for a fourth year. At the time of the signing, he was batting .288 with 7 home runs and 20 runs batted in in 40 games. He played 155 games in 2006, finishing the campaign with 16 home runs, 83 RBIs, and a .274 batting average. His production had slipped a bit in 2006 and 2007, as he hit 16 and 14 homers respectively and batted .274 each year. However, in August 2008, Mora again earned American League Player of the Month honors. He finished the season with 23 round-trippers and 104 runs batted in, batting .285.

After only five regular-season games in 2009, Mora was placed on the disabled list with a strained left hamstring on April 15 (retroactive to April 13). He was activated from the 15-day disabled list after he failed to catch a plane to begin a rehabilitation assignment. He was eligible to return April 28, and the Orioles wanted him to test his leg in a rehab stint with Triple-A Norfolk, but Mora never got the chance. "I tried to go to the airport and then there was traffic everywhere," Mora said. "I tried to catch the next one, and the next one goes [through] Dallas, and I had to be at the ballpark at 6 o'clock."[12] He then told manager David Trembley that his leg was fine and that he had already run on it, so the Orioles placed him in the starting lineup against the Anaheim Angels. He went 3-for-5 with two runs batted in, but the O's fell to the Angels, 7-5.

Mora became a free agent in November 2009, when the Orioles did not pick up his $8 million option for 2010. Mora had spent 10 seasons with Baltimore. He ended his Baltimore tenure (1,256 games) in the top 10 in many team offensive categories, playing third base in a Sunday afternoon game (October 4, 2009) at Oriole Park at Camden Yards against the Toronto Blue Jays. He was removed for pinch-hitter Justin Turner in the bottom of the sixth. When the inning ended, Mora stepped out of the dugout and acknowledged a standing ovation. He had played 807 games at third base for Baltimore, second only in franchise history to Hall of Famer Brooks Robinson.

Mora signed a one-year, $1.275 million with Colorado. After a solid season with the Rockies, he signed a one-year, $2 million contract with the Arizona Diamondbacks. However, he injured his neck in a car accident while in spring training. He appeared in only 42 regular-season games, splitting time as a third baseman and a pinch-hitter. At the end of June, he was batting .228 with only two walks (a .244 on-base percentage), and the Diamondbacks released him on June 29.[13]

So, in December 2011, Mora announced his retirement from baseball. He was five weeks shy of his 40th birthday. At a news conference in Valencia, Venezuela, Mora said, "It's a very difficult decision because this has been my life, but it's time to do it. I've been in this for many years and it's time to dedicate myself to my family. I've had a beautiful career that I will always remember."[14] In 13 seasons with four teams, the two-time All-Star had played every position but catcher and pitcher. Two weeks later, he told reporters he was interested in a minor-league deal, as long as it was for an East Coast team. He wanted to remain close to his family, who still lived north of Baltimore. But no offers came.

On April 20, 2015, the Baltimore Orioles announced that Mora had been selected for enshrinement in the Orioles Hall of Fame, along with outfielders Gary Roenicke and John Lowenstein and longtime scout Fred Uhlman Sr. The new inductees were honored at an August 2015 luncheon at Oriole Park.

Two years later, on May 10, 2017, Melvin Mora was naturalized as a United States citizen. He thanked the country that gave him the opportunity to follow his dreams and play baseball.[15] He holds dual citizenship in both the US and Venezuela. His children had become dual citizens in 2013.

Mora appeared on the Baseball Hall of Fame ballot in 2017, but he didn't receive any votes. However, he did accomplish one thing that no other Hall of Famer ever did. On July 18, 2008, Mora hit a two-run home run "off the very TOP of Camden Yards' 70-foot-high foul pole," which stands 333 feet down the left-field line.[16] He told the *Baltimore Sun*, "I just prayed it was a home run. I didn't want to have to take another swing." And Matt Monagan of the *Sun* wrote, "You shouldn't have needed to take another swing, Melvin. If you had retired after this at-bat, who could've blamed you? You were on top of the foul pole. You were on top of the world."[17]

ACKNOWLEDGMENTS

The author thanks Liam Davis, public relations intern for the Baltimore Orioles, for sharing Melvin Mora's pages from the 2001-2009 Baltimore Orioles Media Guides (and his page in the 1999 New York Mets Media Guide). A number of the articles cited come from Mora's file at the Giamatti Research Center at the National Baseball Hall of Fame.

SOURCES

In addition to the sources cited in the Notes, the author consulted Baseball-Reference.com and Retrosheet.org.

NOTES

1   Jim Armstrong, "Mora a Five-Tool Player off the Field," denverpost.com, March 23, 2010. This article was part of Mora's file at the Giamatti Research Center at the National Baseball Hall of Fame. Accessed June 2019.

2   "Melvin Mora," 2000 *New York Mets Information Guide*: 152.

3   "A Christmas Miracle," *New York Post*, December 23, 1999. Found online at https://nypost.com/1999/12/23/a-christmas-miracle-met-melvin-mora-became-a-playoff-hero-when-his-rocket-arm-and-timely-bat-nearly-led-amazins-past-braves-but-to-a-young-orphan-boy-in-flood-ravaged-venezuela-hes-about-to-becom/.

4   In 82 games at Norfolk in 1999, Mora thrived, batting .303 with eight home runs.

5   Roch Kubatko, "Proud Mora Gets High-five for Quints," SunSpot.net, July 31, 2000.

6   Armstrong.

7   Armstrong.

8   "Newfound Patience Transforms Orioles' Mora into All-Star," *USA Today*, July 9, 2003.

9   "Melvin Mora," *2005 Baltimore Orioles Information Guide*, 130.

10   "Mora Out of Classic," *USA Today*, February 27, 2006.

11   "Mora Out of Classic."

12   "Mora Inserted into O's Starting Lineup," espn.com/mlb/news/story?id=4108570, April 28, 2009. Accessed July 2019.

13   "Melvin Mora Retires After 13 Seasons," espn.go.com/espn/print?id=7406121&type=story, December 30, 2011.

14   "Melvin Mora Retires After 13 Seasons."

15   Eduardo A. Encina, "Orioles Hall of Famer Melvin Mora on Becoming U.S. Citizen: 'I finally did it,'" *Baltimore Sun*, May 10, 2017. Story and video online at baltimoresun.com/sports/orioles/bal-orioles-hall-of-famer-melvin-mora-becomes-u-s-citizen-in-baltimore-20170510-story.html. Accessed July 2019.

16   Matt Monagan, www.mlb.com. February 2, 2018. See story and video at https://www.mlb.com/cut4/the-night-melvin-mora-did-the-impossible-and-homered-off-the-top-of-the-foul-pole.

17   Monagan. The Orioles won the game, 7-4, over the Detroit Tigers.

MAGGLIO ORDÓÑEZ

BY LUIS BLANDÓN

The kids had no access to actual ballfields. The streets of Coro were the diamond. The ball came in different shapes. Bases were parked cars or street signs. The game was continually interrupted by cursing pedestrians and honking cars. The object of the game was to win, with one major caveat: Avoid hitting any windows. Magglio Ordóñez was one of those kids. He never forgot the windows.

Ordóñez was a major leaguer for 15 seasons (1997-2011), playing for the Chicago White Sox and Detroit Tigers. His path from Coro, Venezuela, to the majors was paved with struggle and perseverance. Known for consistency, he hit 294 home runs, had 1,236 RBIs, and a .309 batting average. Ordóñez had seven seasons of 100 RBIs or more and four 30-homer seasons.[1]

An unassuming player off the field, in some ways baseball's Clark Kent, Ordóñez was transformed once in uniform. The man who "discovered" him in 1991, White Sox scout Oscar Rendón, knew what he found: "It's not a surprise for me what he has done. I always said he was going to hit like crazy someday."[2]

Magglio José Ordóñez Delgado was born on January 28, 1974, in Caracas, Venezuela, to Maglio and Albertina. He was the youngest of seven children, born to Spanish and indigenous Indian ancestry. His father "gave me an extra 'g' for luck," Ordóñez recalled.[3] Ordóñez named his own son Magglio and first daughter Maggliana with the extra "g" to continue the tradition.

Ordóñez grew up in Coro, a port city of 195,000 on the northern coast of Venezuela.[4] The seasonal climate made baseball an all-year activity. His father was a cab driver who owned a construction business. Ordóñez encouraged his son's passion for baseball, giving him his first bat and glove when he was nine years old.[5]

Here began his love of hitting: "You would throw to your buddies, and they throw to you. We hit good balls, taped-up balls, anything round."[6] Ordóñez said: "My dad always wanted me to play in the big leagues. When I was 13, 14, I didn't like to play because I was hanging out with my friends. But my dad told me to play because I was a good player."[7] While at Coro Falcón High School, Ordóñez worked several jobs; his first was washing cars: "I make a little bit. Save the money and spend it on a movie or whatever."[8]

Ordóñez's life in Organized Baseball began when he caught the notice of the Houston Astros scouts, who invited him to their academy when he was 16. His roommate was Melvin Mora. The Astros tried Ordóñez as a catcher but cut him due to inadequate fundamentals. But Mora knew his friend had talent and reached out to White Sox scout Oscar Rendon, who had been following Ordóñez.[9]

The two met on May 18, 1991. "He was crying about [being cut]. His eyes filled with water. But I knew he could play," Rendon said.[10] Rendon had Ordóñez bat, catch hundreds of fly balls, and throw. The sound of his bat stood out. Rendon signed Ordóñez to his first professional contract that day, a $3,500 bonus plus $500 a month. "I took my first plane ride to Santo Domingo for the White Sox. My mom was crying, 'My little boy is going away," said Ordóñez.[11] Ordóñez was 17 years old.

After initially playing in the Dominican summer league, Ordóñez played for Sarasota in the short-season Gulf Coast League in 1992. His play did not scream "touted prospect."[12] For the 1993 season, Ordóñez was with the low Class-A Hickory Crawdads. He was unimpressive, batting .216 in 84 games with 3 homers and 20 RBIs.[13]

The White Sox kept Ordóñez in Hickory for the 1994 campaign. The now 20-year-old played for manager Fred Kendall, whom he credited with making him the player he became: "He's like a daddy to me; I like to play for Kendall."[14] When interviewed at Hickory, he apologized for his English, which he picked up from watching ESPN's *Sports Center* and reading the closed captions.[15] Ordóñez was selected to start in the 1994 South Atlantic League All-Star Game. At season's end, he was selected to the league's 16-man all-star team along with Jermaine Dye.[16]

A first-base coach for Hickory in 1994, Paul Casanova had been a Cuban-born journeyman catcher in the major leagues.[17] Casanova held close relationships with young Latin players like Ordóñez. When Ordóñez's hand was hurt by an inside pitch, Casanova noticed a flaw in his batting stance. Casanova taught him to hold it correctly: "Ever since he learned to hold the bat knuckle-to-knuckle, the ball has been jumping off his bat," Casanova said.[18]

Promoted to the Prince William Cannons of the High-A Carolina League in 1995, Ordóñez had a good year with 12 homers and 65 RBIs. He was selected to the Carolina League all-star team as a starter.

Playing for the Double-A Birmingham Barons in 1996, Ordóñez met batting coach Von Joshua.[19] Joshua had played 10 seasons in the majors.[20] He noticed that Ordóñez's stance changed constantly as he "tried to be Willie Mays one day, and Carl Yastrzemski another, Hank Aaron another."[21] Joshua worked on Ordóñez's footwork and hands, teaching him to be consistent with his batting stance.

Joshua kidded constantly, "*Cambio esta stance, tu está muerta.*"[22] Ordóñez hit .263 under Joshua's tutelage; he broke out in 1997 when he hit .329 for the Triple-A Nashville Sounds. "Von was the main guy who pushed me and taught me to be a big leaguer," he told a reporter.[23]

Any team could have had Ordóñez after the 1996 season when the White Sox did not place him on their 40-man roster, leaving him available in the 1996 Rule 5 Draft. But no team picked him. The White Sox promoted Ordóñez to Nashville in 1997 but were not convinced he was ready for that level or even had a future. However, Ordóñez dominated the American Association, crediting his offseason work: "[L]ast year I didn't feel comfortable. But playing winter ball in Venezuela, I learned how to hit the breaking ball."[24] Ordóñez was one of three co-MVPs in the Triple-A All-Star Game but stayed behind as other outfielders were called up to Chicago. Ordóñez fought through his disappointment, leading the league in hitting and being named MVP.

From a distance, Ozzie Guillén watched Ordóñez: "He's not a first-round draft choice, and he has an ugly Latino name. He has to do twice as much as someone else to get an opportunity."[25] The two became teammates when Chicago finally called Ordóñez up to the majors.[26]

Ordóñez made his major-league debut on August 29, 1997, vs. Houston. Starting in right field and batting eighth, Ordóñez hit a bloop single off Ramon García into right-center for his first major-league hit.[27] His first home run came in his second game, a two-run shot over the left-field wall in the seventh inning off Houston's José Lima. On September 1, Ordóñez hit his first pinch-hit homer, a two-out game-winning blast, in the top of the ninth off St. Louis reliever Tony Fossas. "Sometimes it just happens," said Ordóñez, while Fossas concluded, "[T]his is definitely the worst thing that happened in my career."[28]

Ordóñez was expected to platoon in right field in 1998 with Ruben Sierra, but in spring training, he caught the notice of manager Jerry Manuel. Teammate Frank Thomas said: "If he keeps swinging the bat like that, we're going to have a very dangerous lineup" (along with Albert Belle and Robin Ventura).[29] Ordóñez was an everyday starter in right.[30] His .282 batting average in 1998 was the lowest of his career until his final year, 2011, when he batted .255.[31]

Ordóñez strove to drive in more runs in 1999. He drove in his 50th run in his 57th game, prompting teammate Ray Durham to say, "[H]e's an RBI machine."[32] Ordóñez's swing was described as "sweet as anything this side of Count Basie."[33] Ordóñez was selected to his first major-league All-Star Game. On August 26, he reached the 100-RBI mark for the first time with a two-run popup double down the right-field line in the top of the seventh during a 9-7 loss to Tampa Bay. He topped his 1998 RBI total of 65 on July 8, finishing with 117 (the first of four consecutive 100-RBI seasons) and 30 homers.

For the next four seasons, Ordóñez was one of the elite batters in the American League, hitting over .300 each season, driving in 100 RBIs each year except 2003, when he had 99. He hit 32, 31, 38, and 29 homers respectively from 2000 to 2003. The White Sox made the playoffs in 2000 but were swept in the ALDS by Seattle. Ordóñez went 2-for-11 with one RBI.

Playing in the shadow of Thomas and the Cubs' Sammy Sosa, he was Chicago's "best-kept secret since deep-dish pizza went national."[34] After making $425,000 in 2000, Ordóñez agreed to a three-year, $29.5 million deal before the 2001 season.

In 2001 Ordóñez became the first player in the American League to hit at least .300 with 40 doubles, 30 homers, 100 RBIs, and 25 stolen bases in a season.[35] The 2002 season saw Ordóñez drive in 100 for the fourth consecutive season.[36]

In the months leading to the 2004 season, Ordóñez was part of the framework of the failed Álex Rodríguez trade from Texas to Boston. The White Sox were going to trade Ordóñez to Boston for Nomar Garciaparra, opening the Boston shortstop slot for Rodríguez. The trade failed. When Ordóñez found out about the proposed trade, his relationship with the front office was damaged.

Efforts at a contract extension were rebuffed by Ordóñez as general manager Ken Williams was told by his agent that Ordóñez "wanted to play his free agent out and find out his value on the open market."[37] The length of the deal was an obstacle as the White Sox were set on four years, and Ordóñez sought a five-year, $75 million deal. He was 30 years old. "[T]his is going to be my last big contract and I have to take advantage of that," Ordóñez emphasized, noting that when he turned 35, all he would be offered were one-year contracts.[38] This was perhaps his last chance at a life-altering deal, and he was willing to leave Chicago to get it.

Ordóñez was due to make $14 million in 2004. The lack of an extension started speculation that he might be traded before the deadline. His durability and all-around play were not an issue as Ordóñez had started 157 games and ranked 14th in innings played in the American League in 2003 with 1349⅔ and committed just two errors.[39]

With a .311 average, 8 homers, and 34 RBIs in the first 42 games, the 2004 season appeared to be on par with past Ordóñez performances. But on May 19, he collided with Willie Harris on a popup to short right field, missing a game with a left-knee bone bruise. On May 25, in the seventh inning of a game against Texas, Ordóñez felt something strange in his knee on a swing. He missed seven games and was placed on the disabled list for the first time in his career. He had arthroscopic surgery on June 5 to repair a slight meniscus tear.[40]

After the surgery, Ken Williams announced, "Magglio's not going anywhere. We're trying to win this thing."[41] Going after the pennant would be worth it, even if they lost Ordóñez to free agency and received only draft compensation or nothing.

Ordóñez returned to the lineup on July 9 after missing 37 games. However, the knee was sore, and his mobility was slowed. He didn't play after July 21; it was announced on August 24 that Ordóñez was out for the year.[42] Williams said Ordóñez "hasn't been able to do much. If it doesn't start to improve, he may have to undergo some sort of surgical procedure."[43] It was believed that the Harris collision was a factor. What was believed to be a bone bruise and a minor tear was now feared to be a potential degenerative condition.[44]

Ordóñez was a six-time All-Star and 2007 AL batting champ. He helped lead the Tigers to the World Series in 2006. (Brian Bahr / Allspo via Getty Images)

Ordóñez switched agents to Scott Boras. He also traveled to Vienna, Austria, to have Dr. Wolfgang Schaden perform ultra-wave therapy surgery for edema in his injured knee. The surgery was not approved in the United States.[45] The White Sox were not pleased by this action, convinced the knee issue was more serious than what the Ordóñez camp indicated. Mistrust between the parties deepened. Chicago began preparing for life without Ordóñez, who announced his free agency after the World Series ended. He was not offered arbitration by the White Sox.

The Tigers offered a five-year, $75 million contract with two option years at $15 million a year. No other team came close, due to concerns about his knee. Tigers general manager Dave Dombrowski and owner Mike Ilitch were apparently not that concern about his health. Ordóñez signed the richest contract given to any player in Tigers history.

During negotiations, Ilitch and Ordóñez met in a Miami country club. Ilitch recalled, "[W]e spent two hours together and his agent said, 'What do you expect from Magglio?' I used to carry a ring in my pocket, and it was a Red Wings ring from the Stanley Cup championship. I pulled it out and said, 'I want to get one of these rings, but I want it to be a World Series ring.'"[46] "When you have an owner that's committed to you and respects and believes in you, it feels good," Ordóñez said.[47] He wanted to erase the memory of the 2004 season. Now a Tiger and part of the Motor City, Ordóñez said, "I drive a Mercedes. I might have to get a Chrysler."[48]

The high hopes for 2005 were damaged by an injury Ordóñez incurred early in the season. He played three games to start the season, going 0-for-10 with no RBIs when he was diagnosed on April 27 with an exercise-induced sports hernia, necessitating surgery. Returning on July 1 against the Yankees, Ordóñez got his first hit as a Tiger, a homer off Randy Johnson. He played 82 games with a .302 batting average, 8 homers, and 46 RBIs.

Ordóñez witnessed his old team win the 2005 World Series over Houston. "It's hard to see your teammates win the World Series. You spent your whole career there and left one year early," he said.[49]

In 2006 Ordóñez wanted to prove that the last two seasons, despite the injuries, were a fluke. With new manager Jim Leyland, expectations were high. In his first 119 at-bats, Ordóñez collected 9 homers and 23 RBIs. Selected to his fifth All-Star squad, he felt vindicated: "I promised myself that I was going to be the same player, or better."[50] The Tigers won the AL Central championship. Ordóñez pointed to Leyland for the team's success: "He is the main reason we're doing so good. He makes you focus on every game. … He doesn't let you sleep."[51]

Ordóñez hit a walk-off ninth-inning three-run homer on a fastball inside by Oakland's Huston Street over the Comerica left-field wall in Game Four of the 2006 ALCS, sending the Tigers to their first World Series in 22 years. "That was an unbelievable moment for the city, for the fans," he said. "When you hit that, you don't think, you just enjoy. It was so loud. You just want to touch home and score and celebrate."[52] But the World Series ended in disappointment. The Cardinals defeated the Tigers in five games. Ordóñez went 2-for-19 with no extra-base hits or RBIs. There were no more World Series appearances for him.

Ordóñez had his best season in 2007, leading the American League with a .363 batting average and 54 doubles coupled with 28 homers and 139 RBIs.[53] At season's end, Leyland left a handwritten note for Ordóñez: *The best single-season performance I've seen. Love you. Your manager, Jim Leyland.*[54]

In 2008 Ordóñez continued to be a productive full-time player, though his power numbers began to decline: 21 homers, but with 103 RBIs. In 2009 the numbers fell to 9 homers and 50 RBIs.

Ordóñez played for Venezuela in the 2009 World Baseball Classic. In the games played in Miami, he was subjected to intense catcalls by Venezuelan fans for his support of Hugo Chavez's socialist agenda for Venezuela. In South Florida, where he resided in the offseason, Ordóñez was the rare baseball Chavista. His teammates said this vitriol from his countrymen affected him.

As the 2009 season began, Ordóñez started slowly with diminished power. In the spring he had learned his wife, Dagly, was diagnosed with thyroid cancer. The focus that made him the player he was had vanished. "You hear about cancer and do not pay attention to it until it happens to you. My wife needed two surgeries and some mild treatment. It wasn't easy on us. It's your life, and that is more important than baseball. It's family first," he recalled.[55]

Ordóñez struggled at the plate. As the season progressed, he was benched and then platooned. There was talk of waiving Ordóñez if Ilitch consented. By August, Dagly was in remission, and Ordóñez's vaunted focus came back; he batted .401 the rest of the season. Ordóñez hit a game-tying home run in the top of the eighth inning in the one-game playoff against

Minnesota to decide the AL Central Division crown, but the Tigers ultimately lost in extra innings. "The weight came off my shoulders. It made me more relaxed," Ordóñez said.[56] On September 15, by reaching base on an error, he had enough plate appearances over the past two seasons to vest his option for the 2010 season.

In 2010 Ordóñez came into spring training aiming to regain the pop in his bat. "Since the first day of spring training, the bats sounded a lot louder. He looks great," said Leyland.[57] On April 29 against Minnesota, a sharp single off Carl Pavano in the fourth gave him 2,000 career hits. Ordóñez became the sixth Venezuelan to reach this milestone.[58] Coming into the July 24, 2010, game versus Toronto, Ordóñez had been limited to designated hitter as he tried to heal a sore right ankle. In the third inning, trying to score from first on Miguel Cabrera's double, he broke his right ankle sliding into home. "I saw his right foot go in the wrong direction," said teammate Johnny Damon.[59]

He required surgery, but the ankle caused him problems for the rest of his career. "They have put three screws in his ankle. He's got three tight screws and I have got one loose screw," said Leyland.[60] When he was injured, Ordóñez was batting .303 with 17 doubles, 12 homers, and 59 RBIs.

In December the team declined to exercise the option year on Ordóñez's contract and paid him the $3 million buyout. Ordóñez wanted to return: "There are so many reasons. ... Detroit is everything, man."[61] On December 17, Ordóñez signed a one-year, $10 million contract to return as a Tiger. He had offers from other teams for more years, but loyalty to Ilitch guided his decision.

The 2011 season was marked by injuries, decline, and uncertainty. Ordóñez was 11 homers short of becoming the 80th member of the 300-homer/2,000-hit club, but it was not meant to be. Playing in only 92 games, he batted .255 with 5 homers and 32 RBIs. Ordóñez was platooned. In July he considered retirement: "When I was playing, I didn't enjoy the game. And I play with my heart."[62] Leyland informed Ordóñez that the team was not going to offer him a contract for 2012. His time as a Tiger was coming to an end. He did rebound, hitting .365 after August 13, and played a role in the Tigers winning the AL Central Division pennant. His last career homer was a two-run shot in the fifth inning on September 1 during an 11-8 loss to Kansas City. He played his last regular-season game on September 27, 2011, when he went 2-for-3 with three RBIs. He fell six short of the 300-homer mark.

Playing in his third postseason in 2011, Ordóñez had been complaining of discomfort in his surgically repaired ankle. He went 5-for-11 in the Division Series vs. the Yankees with two hits in the Game Five clincher. In Game One of the Championship Series vs. Texas on October 8, 2011, Ordóñez took an intentional walk in the fifth; then rain caused a second stoppage in play. During the delay, Ordóñez experienced a flare of pain in the right ankle. Leyland said later that after X-rays were taken, "a situation [was evident] there that is not conducive to playing the rest of the year."[63] Ordóñez had refractured the ankle in the same location. Tigers athletic trainer Kevin Rand said that since the initial fracture was horizontal instead of vertical, "fluid pushed its way into the bone and led it to cracking in the same place."[64]

There was very little interest in Ordóñez from major-league teams. He wanted to play a 16th season in the majors. The reinjured ankle and his age were factors. Ordóñez was clear that he would not accept a minor-league deal. Spring training came and went. He was home working out as Boras attempted to get him a contract. On March 25 the 37-year-old Ordóñez hinted on Twitter that he was nearing retirement: *Estoy muy [c]erca de mi retiro.*[65]

On June 3, 2012, Ordóñez formally announced his retirement. The Tigers held a ceremony at Comerica Park on a sunny afternoon before the game. "I thought he was somebody who could make a big contribution to our club because we didn't have a leader at the time," said Ilitch.[66] Leyland wept about Ordóñez's impact: "He was a good soldier. ... He was a treat because he wasn't high-maintenance."[67]

Ordóñez wanted to play, but his body had other ideas. "It's hard to retire. I'm going to miss it always, but this time was going to come. I am glad that it was today," he said.[68]

Ordóñez was known for his quiet charitable endeavors. He established the $2,500 Ordóñez Family Scholarship, awarded annually to a Southwest Detroit High School senior.[69] He donated $100,000 to the American Red Cross to help those affected by the 2010 Haitian earthquake. He funded a baseball field for inner city youth in southwest Detroit. The city dedicated the Magglio Ordóñez Field on July 23, 2010.

Ordóñez moved to Puerto la Cruz, an oil town in Venezuela, with Dagly and their children, Magglio, Jr., Maggliana, and Sophia.[70] His son was a 38th-round draft pick by the Tigers in 2014.[71]

Ordóñez was a vocal supporter of Venezuelan President Hugo Chavez and his successor, Nicolás Maduro. Ordóñez appeared in a 2009 television political commercial stating that "the best of the revolution and socialism is yet to come."[72] In 2013, under the banner of Chavez's United Socialist Party, Ordóñez announced his candidacy and was elected on December 8 as the mayor of Juan Antonio Sotillo municipality with 52 percent of the vote.[73] He served one term. "I like it because you help people," Ordonez said. "It's hard because our economy is 100 percent based on oil. And the oil [price] right now is low. It's hard to respond to the demand that the people have when the economy is struggling."[74]

Ordóñez had played winter ball for Caribes de Anzoátegui in Puerto la Cruz of the Venezuelan Professional Baseball League. He became a co-owner of the team on May 14, 2013.[75] During his ownership, the Caribes have won three titles (2014-15, 2017-18, and 2020-21).[76] Ordóñez's number 33 was retired by the team.

With many of his teammates from the 2006 team, Ordóñez returned to Detroit for the 10th anniversary of the World Series on September 24, 2016. He threw out the ceremonial first pitch before the game against Kansas City. "I used to come here and say I would never play in Detroit, never," Ordóñez said. "Look at it now, I love Detroit."[77]

When it came to National Baseball Hall of Fame voters, Ordóñez was not an all-time great, worthy of a vote. In 2017, his first year of eligibility, Ordóñez accrued only three votes and was dropped from the ballot.

Living back in Venezuela, one thing has changed from childhood: Ordóñez no longer fears breaking windows. He can now afford to replace them.

ACKNOWLEDGMENTS

To my wife, Teri, for her unearthly patience with me, her invaluable input, and her copy-editing talents.

Special thanks to the Columbus Memorial Library of the Organization of American States in Washington, D.C., for their use of their collections and archives to examine the Venezuelan newspapers in their repository.

SOURCES

In addition to the sources cited in the Notes, the author consulted baseball-reference.com, retrosheet.org, mlb.com, youtube.com, *Baseball America*, *Diario Las Americas* (Miami, Florida), and the Detroit Tigers and the Chicago White Sox media guides and website.

NOTES

1   Ordóñez ended his career with a .309 batting average over 15 seasons with 2,156 hits, 294 homers, and 1,236 RBIs. He fell six home runs short of the exclusive 300-homer/2,000-hit club. He was six-time All-Star (1999-2001, 2003, 2006, and 2007). He won three Silver Slugger Awards (2000, 2002, and 2007).

2   Teddy Greenstein, "Quiet Star with a Loud Bat," *Chicago Tribune*, July 29, 1999: 4-10. In various newspaper articles dating back to 1994, Rondon's first name has been given as Alberto as well as Oscar.

3   "All About Magglio," *Detroit Free Press*, April 4, 2005: 17G.

4   A UNESCO World Heritage Site, Coro is the capital of Falcón State and the second oldest city in Venezuela, founded on July 26, 1527.

5   Jo-Ann Barnas, "Ordonez: Stays True to his Roots," *Detroit Free Press*, July 30, 2006: 5D.

6   Steve Kornacki, "Ordonez Great Balance Is Key to Hitting Success," *Grand Rapids* (Michigan) *Press*, March 1, 2009: C10.

7   Barnas.

8   George Sipple, "My First Job," *Detroit Free Press*, May 28, 2006: 39.

9   Greenstein, "Quiet Star with a Loud Bat."

10 "Quiet Star with a Loud Bat."

11 Barnas.

12 Ordóñez batted .180 in 38 games, with a single home run and 14 RBIs.

13 When he arrived at Hickory, Ordóñez was listed at 5-11,150 lbs., a far cry from the 6-0, 215 lbs. athlete he grew into by 1997.

14 Jeff Hawkins, "Ordonez Learned the Game on the Streets," *Hickory* (North Carolina) *Daily Record*, June 18, 1994: 1B. Kendall played for San Diego Padres (1969-1976), Cleveland Indians (1977), Boston Red Sox (1978), and again San Diego (1979-1980). He managed in the Chicago White Sox organization between 1992 and 1995 and served as major-league coach for eight seasons between 1996 and 2007 for the Detroit Tigers, Colorado Rockies, and Kansas City Royals.

15 Hawkins. See also Bonnie DeSimone, "Ordonez: Sox's Star Byword: Perseverance," *Chicago Tribune*, March 30, 2003: 3-9.

16 "'Bat': Ruben Rivera Named Best in SAL," *Greensboro* (North Carolina) *News and Record*, August 28, 1994: C1. Ordóñez ended the season with 144 hits, 11 homers, 69 RBIs, and a .294 average. The White Sox signed Dye in 2005 to replace Ordóñez, who left in free agency to Detroit.

17 Paul Casanova played in the major leagues from 1965 to 1974 for the Washington Senators and Atlanta Braves.

18 Jeff Hawkins, "Ordonez Now an All-Star," *Hickory Daily Record*, June 18, 1994: 5B.

19 Ordóñez achieved career highs playing for Birmingham in homers (18), doubles (41), and RBIs (67) while hitting .263.

20 Von Joshua was an outfielder who played for the Los Angeles Dodgers, San Francisco Giants, Milwaukee Brewers, and San Diego Padres from 1969 to 1971, 1973 to 1977, and 1979 to 1980.

21 John Lowe, "Maggnum RBI," *Chicago Tribune*, April 4, 2005: 17G.

22 DeSimone. Translated, Joshua was telling Ordóñez, "Change this stance and you're a dead man." The correct grammatical Spanish phrasing is *"Cambia este stance, tu estás Muerto."*

23 "Maggnum RBI."

24 Maurice Parker, "Ordonez Raises Level of Play," *Nashville Tennessean*, June 22, 1997: 3.

25 Phil Rogers, "In Ordonez, Sox May Have Another Valued Venezuelan." *Chicago Tribune*, July 31, 1997: 4-25.

26 Ozzie Guillén later managed Ordóñez with the White Sox in 2004.

27 MLB, "Magglio Ordoncz's First Big League Hit," *YouTube*, posted July 22, 1998: https://www.youtube.com/watch?v=o8tmGbRjqkM, accessed April 28, 2025. In the brief call-up, Ordóñez batted .319 with 4 home runs and 11 RBIs.

28 Jim Salter (Associated Press), "Newest Sox Comes Through in the Pinch," *Northwest Herald* (Woodstock, Illinois), September 2, 1997: C-1. At the end of the season, Ordóñez was on the list exempt from being selected in the expansion draft to stock the Tampa Devil Rays and Arizona Diamondbacks.

29 Teddy Greenstein, "In the Running, Literally, for a Bench Job," *Chicago Tribune*, March 5, 1998: 4-5.

30 Ordóñez played in 145 games his rookie year, batting .282 with 14 homers and 65 RBIs.

31 Ordóñez was named to the 1998 Topps Rookie All-Star Team.

32 Teddy Greenstein, "Quartet Shows All-Star Potential," *Chicago Tribune*, June 17, 1999: 4-10.

33 Joel Stevenson, "Sweet Swing Matures in Chicago," *Northwest Herald*, June 24, 1999: Sports-6.

34 Paul Sullivan, "Shining as Brightly as the North (Side's) Star," *Chicago Tribune*, July 7, 2000: 4:3.

35 Paul Sullivan, "Ordonez: AL's Secret Superstar," *Chicago Tribune*, March 24, 2002: 3:3. Since Ordóñez accomplished this feat, four additional; American League players joined him to hit at least

.300 with 40 doubles, 30 homers, 100 RBIs, and 25 stolen bases in a season: Alfonso Soriano (2002), Jacoby Ellsbury (2011), Mookie Betts (2016), and Bobby Witt, Jr. (2024).

36 With his .317 batting average, Ordóñez hit 29 homers and fell one shy of another 30-100 season in 2003.

37 Steve Rosenbloom, "Don't Make Williams Say It Again," *Chicago Tribune,* January 30, 2004: 33-16.

38 Bob Foltman, "Sox, Ordonez Try Hard on a New Deal," *Chicago Tribune,* April 14, 2004: 4-4.

39 "Catching Numbers," *Chicago Tribune,* March 30, 2004: 33-26.

40 Bob Foltman, "Surgery for Ordonez," *Chicago Tribune,* June 5, 2004: 3-1.

41 Dave van Dyck, "Williams' Pledge: No Ordonez Trade," *Chicago Tribune,* June 12, 2004: 3-1.

42 Ordóñez played in 52 games batting .292 with 9 homers and 37 RBIs.

43 Bob Foltman, "To No One's Surprise, Ordonez Out for the Year," *Chicago Tribune,* August 25, 2004: 4-4.

44 The knee injury hindered his play causing pain when he threw and ran, affecting his ability to change directions.

45 David Waugh, "Recovery Time Said to Be Cut in Half," *Chicago Tribune,* January 19, 2005: 4-5. Dr. Schaden was a world-renowned specialist in the use of ultra-shock-wave therapy using a device called Ossatron. The surgery in Austria involved shock-wave therapy which caused microfractures in the bone to stimulate blood flow to the injured area and accelerate healing, Dr. Schaden also performed a surgery to repair Ordóñez's posterior torn meniscus.

46 James Schmehl, "Detroit Tigers Star Magglio Ordonez Celebrated in Teary-Eyed Retirement Ceremony," mlive.com, June 3, 2012, https://www.mlive.com/tigers/2012/06/detroit_tigers_magglio_ordonez_1.html, accessed May 8, 2025.

47 Paul Sullivan, "Sox GM 'Was Burying Me,' Said Ordonez," *Chicago Tribune,* February 7, 2005: 3-3.

48 Krista Latham, "Ordonez Super Signing for '05," *Detroit Free Press,* February 8, 2005: 4E.

49 John Lowe, "Only Pain Ordonez Has Is Chicago Blue," *Detroit Free Press,* February 20, 2006: D-1.

50 John Lowe, "Magglio Ordonez – The All-Star Pick Tops His List of Five," *Detroit Free Press,* July 11, 2006: 1D.

51 John Lowe, "Ordonez: The All-Star Pick Tops List." *Detroit Free Press,* July 11, 2006: 5D.

52 Kyle Beery, "Ordonez Returns to Detroit for '06 Anniversary," mlb.com, September 23, 2016. See https://www.mlb.com/news/magglio-ordonez-returns-for-2006-anniversary-c202969730, accessed January 10, 2025.

53 Ordóñez was the ninth Tiger to win a batting crown and the first since Norm Cash in 1961.

54 John Paul Morosi, "Tigers: End Season with 13-3 Victory," *Detroit Free Press,* October 1, 2007: 6B.

55 Steve Kornacki, "Ready to Bounce Back," *Flint* (Michigan) *Journal,* February 28, 2010: B6.

56 "Ready to Bounce Back."

57 Chris Iott, "Tigers: Bondsman Gets First Win Since 2008," *Grand Rapids Press,* April 11, 2010: C3.

58 The five Venezuelans to reach the 2,000-hit mark before Ordóñez were Omar Vizquel, Luis Aparicio, Andres Galarraga, Dave Concepcion, and Bobby Abreu.

59 ESPN.com News Services, "Ordonez Will Be Out 6-8 Weeks," ESPN.com, July 24, 2010. See https://www.espn.com/mlb/news/story?id=5407591, accessed December 9, 2024.

60 Steve Kornacki, "Leyland on Ordonez Surgery," *Muskegon* (Michigan) *Chronicle,* August 27, 2010: B1.

61 Steve Kornacki, "Ordonez: Outfielder Wanted to Return," *Grand Rapids Press,* December 18, 2010: D2.

62 James Schmehl, "Ordonez Expects to Play in 2012," *Muskegon Chronicle,* January 12, 2012: B5.

63 ESPN, "Magglio Ordonez to Miss Rest of Playoffs," ESPN.com, October 9, 2011. See https://www.espn.com/au/mlb/playoffs/2011/story/_/id/7081244/2011-ace-detroit-tigers-lose-magglio-ordonez-outfielder-injuries-ankle, accessed December, 9, 2024.

64 Chris Iott, "Leyland Bemoans Loss of Ordonez for the Playoffs," *Grand Rapids Press,* October 11, 2010: C5.

65 Chris Iott, "All Stitched Up and Ready to Go," *Muskegon Chronicle,* March 27, 2012: B4. Translated into English, "I am very close to my retirement."

66 Schmehl, "Detroit Tigers Star Magglio Ordonez Celebrated in Teary-Eyed Retirement Ceremony."

67 David Mayo, "Leyland Reflects on Ordonez's Stellar Career," *Grand Rapids Press,* May 31, 2012: C1.

68 Schmehl, "Detroit Tigers star Magglio Ordonez Celebrated in Teary-Eyed Retirement Ceremony."

69 For more on the scholarship, see https://cfsem.org/wp-content/uploads/2018/02/Ordonez-Scholarship-Overview.pdf.

70 Ordóñez met his wife, Dagly, while playing winter ball in Puerto la Cruz. Ordóñez's son remained in the Miami area to finish his schooling at American Heritage in Plantation, Florida.

71 "Magglio Ordonez, Jr. Suspended for Drug Use," Fox Sports, September 9, 2015. See https://amp.foxsports,com/stories/mlb/tigers-prospect-magglio-ordonez-jr-suspended-for-drug-use, accessed April 28, 2025. Ordóñez, Jr., was suspended for 50 games for testing positive for a second occasion for a drug of abuse on September 8, 2015, and was released by the Tigers.

72 Paul Kix, "The Morning According to Us: Magglio and Hugo Chavez," ESPN.com, March 16, 2009. See https://www.espn.com/espnmag/story?id=3984227, accessed May 3, 2025. Ordóñez appeared in a television ad in February 2009 supporting a proposal by Chavez to eliminate term limits for the president and other elected officials through a constitutional amendment. Voters approved the proposal in a February 15 referendum.

73 The municipality in eastern Venezuela, population 27,000, is named after the nineteenth-century Venezuelan leader Juan Antonio Sotillo.

74 Beery, "Ordonez Returns to Detroit for '06 Anniversary."

75 Brian Manzullo, "Ordóñez, Guillen Keeping Busy," *Detroit Free Press,* February 9, 2015: B5.

76 During his ownership tenure, the team has appeared in six league finals (2013-14, 2014-15, 2017-18, 2019-20, and 2020-21).

77 Beery, "Ordonez Returns to Detroit for '06 Anniversary."

EDDIE PÉREZ

BY TONY OLIVER

Catchers, like musicians, use both two hands for their craft: the gloved one captures the ball while the other acts as a conductor's baton to guide the action. Johnny Bench, arguably the best player to don the tools of ignorance, stated, "The catcher is in the middle of everything. He sees it best."[1] The statement is both literal and figurative; not only is he the sole defensive player with a frontal view of the mound, but it is his guidance that traditionally starts every micro-battle between hitter and pitcher. Braves fans – both the ones in the South and those who were raised on "America's Team" during their TBS heyday – were privy to a clinic in the late 1990s thanks to Eddie Pérez.

Born on May 4, 1968, Eddie was blessed with a comfortable upbringing in then-prosperous Venezuela. For most of the second half of the twentieth century, the country's vast oil reserves afforded a standard of living envied by its Latin American neighbors. Growing up in Ciudad Ojeda in the state of Zulia, he and his siblings enjoyed the allure of baseball without the sport representing a one-way ticket out of poverty: "My family loved baseball. … All my brothers and my dad played. I don't recall specifically when I started."[2] His father worked for in the oil industry as a shore captain and his mother stayed at home with the children. (Both parents now reside in Atlanta.)

Although the Águilas of Zulia played in Maracaibo, only 90 minutes across the namesake lake, Eddie rooted for the Tigres of Aragua, who played more than seven hours away, near the capital city of Caracas: "My dad took me to see two games. Zulia played against Aragua and I preferred the latter, even though people rooted for the Águilas." Later he lived out two dreams, playing 10 winter-league seasons with his favorite club before winding down his active career at home: "Aragua traded me to Zulia, which hurt me a lot; it was a transition, but I liked playing at home, seeing my family and friends on the stands."

Perez was mesmerized by the exploits of Davey Concepción, the National League's premier shortstop during the 1970s and a vital member of the fearsome Big Red Machine. In the days before cable broadcasts, a "game of the week" was the main drug to fuel the country's baseball addiction, and appearances by Cincinnati were appointment television. Concepción was the heir to "Little Louie" Aparicio, whose Spanish nicknames focus on his stature on the diamond: "El Grande" and "El Rey David." Much like Puerto Rican players wearing number 21 in honor of Roberto Clemente despite being born after his tragic death, Aparicio's contribution to the fertile grounds of Venezuelan baseball has bloomed for generations after his retirement. As Aparicio's number 11 and Concepción's 13 were popular, Eddie opted to split the difference and choose number 12.

Prior to Cal Ripken and Alex Rodriguez, shortstops were hardly tall, and Eddie had grown to 6-feet-1 by his teens. Eddie did not have to look far to determine a position to play: His father was a celebrated amateur catcher. In the major leagues, Baudillo "Bo" Díaz had replaced Bench behind the plate in Cincinnati, giving Venezuelans another established big-league hero. Though Eddie and Bo never met, they share a connection via Carlos Hernández, Eddie's contemporary behind the plate in the big leagues. Díaz played with Hernández in Venezuela and the latter, in turn, shared some of those tips with Pérez.

At the tender age of 7, Eddie was turning enough heads to play his first children's Campeonato Nacional. Blessed with the twin graces of natural ability and a patient father who taught him the fine art of catching, he progressed through the youth levels to star in the 1986 Big League World Series tournament in Fort Lauderdale, Florida. Venezuela lost its first game against Taiwan but then reeled off eight consecutive victories to win the tournament. Eddie earned Most Valuable Player (MVP) honors with seven home runs and 16 runs batted in.[3] The event, held from 1968 through 2016, picked up where the Little League World Series ended, affording 15- to 18-year-old youth the opportunity to showcase their talents in front of scouts. It was Venezuela's first and only title, prompting joy in the state capital of Maracaibo and a massive opportunity for Eddie, but his decision was far from easy.

In the days before cell phones and email, messages were relayed via landline telephones and intermediaries; his performance in Fort Lauderdale garnered Eddie some scout interest and the chance to further impress the scouts. "The Aguada Tigres gave me a tryout; about 50 or 60 kids showed up, 10 of whom were from Zulia, like me. I was the only one signed. Since I was underage, my dad said: 'Here's the deal, $15,000 is more than I've ever earned in a year. That means nothing, though: It's your decision.'"

Having finished high school, Pérez was planning to enroll in college like his older siblings and weighed the pros and cons of leaving Venezuela to prove his mettle in the United States. "My dad asked if I was sure if I wanted to sign the contract. My brothers criticized me – 'Are you crazy?' they would say." He remembers his father cautioning him how life would change: While he would indeed be playing baseball, he'd have to cook for himself, launder his clothes, and handle a host of other domestic duties typically glossed over by scouts spinning tales of stardom and riches. Pedro González, himself a former major leaguer with the Yankees and Indians, gave Pérez an honest opinion of the opportunity: While the $15,000 offered by Atlanta was a sizable sum, Eddie also had an offer with his favorite club, the Tigres de Aragua, for 200,000 bolívares, (about $10,700, 18.7 bolívares being worth $1 in early 1986).[4] "It was both luck and a blessing to follow my dad's footsteps (playing catcher). Eight years in the minors, always as a backup, followed by 11 years in the big leagues and another 10 as a coach. Every career has obstacles and I never gave up. Moreover, the franchise taught me not just to be a good ballplayer but also a good person, off the field and with the community. I've been with them more than 30 years."[5]

Ultimately Pérez decided to follow his dreams. After signing with Atlanta on September 27, 1986, he packed his bags for the Gulf Coast League, where he started the 1987 campaign. Playing with future big leaguers Derek Lilliquist, Keith Mitchell, and Ben Rivera, Pérez appeared in 31 games and fielded at a .980 clip while hitting .202. The team finished last with a 20-43 record but gave the 19-year-old his first exposure to life outside of Venezuela.

It was a slow climb for Pérez. He amassed 721 games in the minors across the Gulf, Class A, Double A, and Triple A affiliates of the Braves franchise. The 1988 season saw him at Burlington of the Midwest League, with another last-place finish; 1989 at Sumter of the South Atlantic League, with a club 1½ games out of the cellar; 1990 split between Sumter and Durham (Carolina League), where both clubs posted winning records; 1991 between Durham and Greenville (Southern League). The 1992 and 1993 seasons were spent at Greenville and 1994/1995 at Richmond (International League) before Pérez got the much-desired call from Atlanta. From 1987 through 1995, he played 698 games in the minors, garnering 2,456 plate appearances and producing a .246 batting average. (After establishing himself in the majors, Pérez played 23 minor-league games in 2001 and 2006 during rehabilitation assignments.)

On September 10, 1995, he debuted in the major leagues in Miami, pinch-hitting in the getaway game of a series against the Marlins. Although the Braves were six weeks away from winning the World Series, they lost that contest 5-4 in extra innings. Greg Maddux started but pitched only one inning, as Atlanta manager Bobby Cox gave work to six other hurlers in preparation for the extended postseason (this was the first campaign with the Division Series, since the 1994 strike canceled the playoffs). With the score tied, 4-4, Mark Wohlers' spot was up in the 10th inning and Pérez was summoned to bat against Terry Matthews. He recalled the game fondly, stating, "I was happy in the big leagues after so many years in the minors. In the last game of the series, I was asked by Bobby Cox to bat and I struck out." He caught Pedro Borbón Jr. for two innings and witnessed former Brave Terry Pendleton cross the plate for the Marlins win.

Of the 139 major-league baseball players whose first career at-bat produced a home run, four have been Venezuelans: Keibert Ruiz (2020), Willson Contreras (2016), Gerardo Parra (2009), and Alex Cabrera (2000).[6] Pérez narrowly missed being the first, leaving the yard for his first hit during his first start (and second plate appearance) on September 15, 1995. While Atlanta had already clinched the NL East (and ended up winning by a comfortable 21-game margin), the game was far from meaningless. Pérez recalls not just the game but the circumstances with flawless details: "Pat Corrales called me and said: 'I have good news and bad news: You're starting but you're catching John Smoltz, who had been struggling.' Javy López told me 'good luck.' … Charlie O'Brien said good luck too, but stay calm, call your game. Smoltz shook me off twice: Barry Larkin hit a home run and Hal Morris doubled. He struck out 11 batters in eight innings pitched and (Greg) McMichael closed."

Starting behind the plate for the first time, Pérez hit seventh in the batting order and recorded 12 putouts, one assist, and one double play. Pérez connected off veteran left-hander Mike Jackson in the seventh inning to drive home David Justice. The play provided to be difference maker as the Braves beat the Reds 3-1 in front of 31,882 fans for Smoltz's 11th victory of the season and McMichael's second save. The first of Pérez's 40 career round-trippers was particularly memorable: His boyhood idol Concepción was on hand during one of his appearances at Riverfront Stadium. They met and shook hands after the game. During Pérez's phone call to his parents' home, it was hard to figure out which accomplishment pleased him more: "The game ended, and I was so happy, calling my family from a pay phone and when I left the stadium I ran into Davey who was there signing autographs. He came over. … I couldn't believe it, this was my dream, my first hit, and meeting Davey. I still have the ball."

For the season, Pérez appeared in seven games and had four hits in 13 at-bats; he struck out twice, did not walk, and collected a double in addition to the earlier home run. He pinch-hit, started another game at catcher supporting Steve Avery, pinch-ran, and played first base for half a game. As the backstop, he tallied 25 innings with no errors, two assists, and two double plays; the starters yielded only two runs in 18 innings over the two games he started, demonstrating a facility to call the game. The Braves opted not to include him in the postseason roster, choosing the regular-season tandem of O'Brien and López for all three rounds. The Braves, however, liked what they saw from Pérez and declined to offer O'Brien an extension after the World Series, making Pérez the heir to the second catcher spot on the roster.

The 1996 and 1997 seasons brought plentiful action for Pérez. As the backup catcher, he played in 141 total games, collecting 373 at-bats and 81 hits, 25 of which were for extra bases. He tasted the postseason in both years, playing in 10 games but reaching base only twice, on a hit against the Dodgers in the NLDS and a walk against the Cardinals in the National League Championship Series, both in 1996. The Braves, so-called team of the 1990s, played good baseball against the Marlins and the Yankees but could not best their foes in the fall.

In 1996 Pérez saw action in 68 games, 39 as a starter. The Braves were 26-13 with his name in the starting lineup. He had a six-game hitting streak and at one point reached based in eight consecutive games. The back-of-the-baseball-card statistics did not tell the whole tale; as the Braves knew, his game-calling abilities provided value beyond his offensive output. Braves pitchers compiled a 3.02 ERA when he was their backstop, more than half a run better than starting catcher López. The next year, his batting average dipped by 41 points (from .256 to .215) while his OPS dropped by more than 100 points (from .697 to .594). His handling of the staff continued to be exemplary, with a catcher's ERA of 3.24 as the Braves led the league with a 3.18 mark.

The 1998 campaign yielded batting highs for Pérez. Appearing in 73 games and garnering 206 plate appearances, he hit .336 with a .404 OBP and a .537 slugging percentage. Pérez attributed his success to a sound mindset: "I want to remain here, and I need to hit. If I don't, I won't stay. Great hitting catchers like Javy and (Mike) Piazza were there … so I focused on hitting." While his lumber was white-hot, his focus on the mound did not waver; Braves pitchers allowed a scant 2.60 runs per nine innings when he was on the lineup. Atlanta's starters combined for 88 victories with Glavine picking up 20, Maddux earning 18, Kevin Millwood and Smoltz tying at 17 and Denny Neagle winning 16 as the team's fifth starter. The juggernaut finished the campaign at 106-56, establishing a franchise record.

Pérez also found an unlikely source of hitting prowess: Maddux. "Few people know this, but Maddux knows more about hitting than pitching. He wouldn't talk more unless asked. … In LA, I said if I don't hit, I am not sure I won't catch you again. He said try to hit to third base. That day I had three hits. I asked him why he hadn't told me before; he said, 'You never asked.'" Beyond Maddux, Pérez sought hitting tips from Chipper Jones, former teammate Fred McGriff, and fellow Venezuelan Fred Manrique. He was consistent throughout the year, overcoming a 1-for-8 start with three multihit games in April to reach .385 by month's end. His average dipped below .300 for only a fraction of July. Although Atlanta swept the Cubs in the NLDS, the Braves fell to the San Diego Padres in the NLCS in six games. Pérez collected three hits against the Friars and one against the Cubs, establishing personal postseason marks he would shatter the next year. The sole hit against Chicago was decisive, an eighth-inning grand slam off Rod Beck to give the Braves and Maddux the win.

The 1999 season saw Atlanta seek an elusive second World Series title en route to its seventh consecutive division championship. (The Braves accomplished the task during 14 consecutive seasons, a major-league record, although one aided by the cancellation of the 1994 postseason since they trailed the Montréal Expos.) Pérez appeared in a career-high 104 games due to his former minor-league roommate Lopez's season-ending injury in late July. Though he hit a pedestrian .249, his on-base average and slugging both improved by 21 and 39 points after his playing time increased in August and September. Despite the extra games and the sweltering Georgia summer, Pérez logged a 3.55 catcher's ERA on 3,182 opponents' plate appearances, the second-best mark in the majors for backstops with such workload. He powered to Braves to a World Series appearance by hitting .500 while slugging .900 against the Mets in the NLCS. Pérez

was voted the series MVP, echoing his 1987 amateur accolades. Had fans been told before the series began that a catcher would win the award, most would have guessed future Hall of Famer Piazza, who donned the mask for the Mets. However, Piazza was not in a groove, going 4-for-24 during the six-game affair.

While expectations were high for the World Series (a rematch of the 1996 fall classic), Atlanta could not answer the Yankees, who swept the Braves en route to their third title in four years.

With López back to full health in 2000, Pérez returned to full-time backup duty. He suffered through right-shoulder injuries in consecutive seasons, suiting up for only 32 combined games in 2000 and 2001.[7] The Braves nevertheless won the NL East but failed to advance to the World Series, dropping three straight contests to the Cardinals in the 2000 NLDS and a tough five-game series against eventual champion Arizona in the 2001 NLCS. Pérez watched the postseason from home while nursing his injuries.

The 2002 season saw Pérez switch leagues for the first time, after the Braves traded him to Cleveland for a player to be named later (Jason Fitzgerald) on March 28. Eight days earlier, Atlanta had shipped Paul Bako and José Cabrera to Milwaukee for Henry Blanco. A fellow Venezuelan, Blanco was two years younger than Pérez and had averaged close to 100 games for the Brewers in the prior two seasons. He played until age 41 in the majors, appearing in 971 games (914 as the catcher), a representative of the strong Venezuelan catching corps that followed Pérez. Steve Torrealba, a second-generation Venezuelan major leaguer, played a handful of games for the Braves as well in 2002, having debuted in the big leagues the prior October against the Marlins by replacing Pérez in the ninth inning and singling in his first at-bat. Though Pérez was leaving the Braves, his mark on the franchise was well-felt and his countrymen had set up a club behind the plate.

With the 74-88 Indians, Pérez appeared in 42 games in 2002. While the team was 18-24 in games he played, they were 16-18 in his starts, proving his ability to manage the pitching staff, as attested by his 4.37 catcher's ERA, three-quarters of a run better than starting backstop Einar Díaz's 5.18. The Indians were in transition, fielding a team with veterans like future Hall of Famer Jim Thome, Omar Vizquel, Ellis Burks, Bartolo Colón, and Chuck Finley, alongside youngsters CC Sabathia and Milton Bradley. Pérez backed up Díaz but also provided tutelage to a young Víctor Martínez, who was beginning his career in the majors. Pérez knew his stay with the Indians would be short-lived, given the promise of Martínez and the presence of a younger option, Josh Bard, on the roster.

The 2003 season brought him back to the National League with the Brewers, who were in the 11th of a brutal stretch of 12 consecutive losing seasons. Pérez was the main catcher for Milwaukee, appearing in 107 games and slashing .271/.304/.420 while playing his customary solid defense. The Brewers improved their 2002 mark by 12 games, though their pitching worsened by almost a third of a run. Pérez hit his second (and last) career regular-season grand slam in San Diego, victimizing Carlton Loewer on May 28 in the first inning of an 8-6 loss, and his only career walk-off round-tripper, against Cincinnati's Scott Williamson on May 17. His batting average reached .316 in the summer, but he fell into a slump to finish the year.

The Brewers did not offer Pérez a contract for 2004, granting him an opportunity to reunite with the Braves. Although only Chipper Jones and John Smoltz remained from the 1990s core, Pérez welcomed the opportunity to show the ropes to young prospect Brian McCann, who would enjoy seven All-Star seasons with the Braves. Pérez played in 74 games, collecting 39 hits (15 of which were for extra bases) as the Braves reached the NLDS in 2004. Atlanta lost a hard-fought series to the Astros in five games, three of which Pérez entered as part of a double switch. He was hitless in three at-bats.

Baseball is at its core a game of matchups. Every manager seeks an advantage, no matter how small, against his opponent. Often the pendulum swings in unexpected ways, as was the case of Randy Johnson and Pérez. By the time both met on May 18, 2004, Pérez boasted of a 6-for-13 batting line against the Hall of Fame-bound lefty. In their last matchup, he was tasked with a seemingly impossible feat: pinch-hit against the Big Unit as Johnson attempted to pitch a perfect game. "I think I hit .400 or .500 vs. RJ. I was surprised that day that I wasn't in the starting lineup since Bobby liked to play the hitters with strong history. I was watching the game and Pat said, you're going up, and I grabbed the bat. Everything was working for Randy; I could see how he was dominating all our hitters. One of my most memorable at-bats … perfect games are so hard to do." Facing a 98-mph fastball, Pérez struck out to end the game.

The 2005 season proved to be tough for Pérez. After appearing in 15 games through May 18, he did not see action until the end of the year due to tendinitis in his right shoulder. Brian McCann established himself as the regular during his absence, wrapping up the season with a .745 OPS as a 21-year-old and helping the staff finish sixth in NL ERA. Pérez's curtain call came on September 27, 2005, during a 12-3 blowout against the Rockies. He pinch-hit for Danny Kolb and grounded out on a 2-and-1 pitch from Randy Williams. He had made his final on-the-field appearance on May 14, starting behind the plate and guiding Mike Hampton to two innings of work and Adam Bernero to three frames before yielding to Johnny Estrada.

The Braves signed Pérez to a minor-league deal on January 6, 2006, and he did not return to the majors. He appeared in 13 games for the Southern League's Mississippi Braves and provided a veteran presence for prospect Jarrod Saltalamacchia. He played an unofficial role assisting his former teammate Jeff Blauser, who managed the team. The franchise was transitioning; it would experience its first losing season since 1990, failing to make the postseason. During Pérez's years with the Braves, the team played deep into every October, but the next playoff trip would not come until 2010.

To watch Pérez catch Maddux was akin to seeing a world-class ballet performance between favorite partners. Baseball players in general are creatures of habit but pitchers are more inclined to seek the comforts of routines. The sabermetrics explosion has given us statistics like pitch framing and catcher's ERA to better measure the defensive contributions of catchers. Savvy pitchers, though, have long trusted their feelings, recollections, and overall easiness by "feel." Like a nervous animal prognosticating an earthquake, *they just knew.* During their tenure with the Braves, Maddux and Pérez teamed up for 832⅓ innings, dozens of wins, and hundreds of moments that could serve as clinics for players and fans alike.[8]

On June 17, 1996, Pérez found himself in the starting lineup for Maddux's start. He tripled and supported Maddux's eight innings with zero walks and only four hits allowed. The relationship clicked to such a degree that the rest of the campaign saw a marked difference in the pitcher's effectiveness: His 1.89 ERA in Pérez's 114 innings caught was about half of regular López's 3.44 ERA in 131 innings. While the proper calculation and recording of catcher's ERA was not yet en vogue, the organization took

Catcher Eddie Pérez was World Series MVP in 1999 with the Braves. He later became a respected coach in Atlanta. (Icon Sportswire via Getty Images)

notice and made Pérez the starter for Maddux's starts the rest of the year despite the more potent bat of López.

Maddux's exploits are legendary, and readers wishing the stories were apocryphal may be surprised. While the tandem had played together during 1994 and 1995 spring training, the decision to pair them was made by Cox, who noticed the ace's level of comfort with the team's backup catcher. Unlike other positions, where starters are expected to play 95 percent of the games, a starting catcher may average 120 to 130 starts to account for the wear and tear on the body and the "always-on" concentration before, during, and after the game. While a position player must account for the opposing pitcher's "stuff," a catcher must prepare for every single one of the other team's players.

Pérez himself was eager to praise Maddux. From the way he caught the ball to the way he held it in the right hand, Maddux was always providing signals on his preferred methods. Seemingly insignificant gestures like the way he touched his cap – typically a signal between hitters and third-base coaches – gave Pérez clues on what Maddux was thinking. The pitcher's 1994-1995 partner in crime, O'Brien, had departed for Toronto during the 1995 offseason. The organization knew, from the small sample of 1994/1995 spring training games and a batch of September contests, that Pérez was ready to fulfill two roles: overall backup and Maddux's catcher. Although the baseball fan saw their connection only on the field, they also spent time in the dugout, going over hitters and observing the intricacies of the opponents' lineups. Pérez took the opportunity to ask Maddux questions about each situation for future reference: "Umpires would often ask me how come Maddux never pitched a no-hitter. I would say he didn't want to. ... He purposely wanted batters to have some hits off him so he could dominate them the next time."

Pérez never took the opportunity for granted, but he worked hard to ensure that the Braves star was comfortable on the mound. "I never heard that Maddux demanded me as his catcher," Pérez said. "It was Bobby's decision. It started in the 1994 spring training, he seemed at ease with me. In 1995 spring training I caught a lot of his games too and Bobby noticed. I think it also had to do with ensuring Javy had a day off and I had a day to play that was scheduled. Communication between Maddux and me was important; he wanted us to sit together and talk about the game and a lot of people didn't see that. Perhaps Maddux told Bobby, I don't know. Maddux was different, I learned quickly, and Charlie O'Brien helped me tremendously. When we first started, he'd tell me what to throw – a lot of people didn't know it. I had to learn fast; in a month I picked up and wanted to call the game. He shook me off three times, and I asked him how we did. He jokingly said it was three times too many. I learned a lot from him that has helped me not only as a player but also as a coach."

Pérez's favorite anecdote about Maddux: "In 1998 we were discussing the opposite team, going over batter by batter, how to pitch to each in individual situations. Against Jeff Bagwell, nothing inside, everything outside. In the seventh or eighth, we were ahead 8-0, Bagwell came up with the bases empty. Maddux said inside and I was annoyed; I always wanted to be on the same page as Maddux. He shook me off three times and said inside. I thought he was crazy. ... Bagwell hit a massive foul shot and Maddux still asked for it inside. Next pitch, home run, a long shot. I was mad and asked him why, he said we'll talk later. Maddux pitches eight innings and then Wohlers picked up the save in the ninth. In the dugout I was mad at him and he said, 'In two months, Bagwell will come up and seek that pitch.' Two months later, in Houston, Bagwell came up with two men on base, we were up 3-1 in the seventh inning, Bagwell sought the inside ball, but Maddux pitched three outside changeups to strike him out. I was happy celebrating and thought he'd be mad as he didn't like such emotions during the game. ... So he pulled me aside and said, 'Remember two months ago? The pitch we threw him?' I didn't recall at the time, but thought about it, and then remembered the prior pitch."

Has the anecdote been embellished? Perhaps, but much like a myth, it has plenty of historical origins. Rob Neyer tried to verify it and found one instance of its possible occurrence.[9] He concluded that the story wasn't as "good" as originally called, but one might beg to differ. Maddux "allowed" the round-tripper to Bagwell while staked with a four-run lead early in the game, rather than in the later innings. This attests to the pitcher's confidence in his stuff, his catcher, and his team's offensive prowess. The comeuppance did not occur late in a playoff game, but rather early in one (first inning). But the result was the same: Bagwell chased a pitch Maddux knew he'd be seeking.

Like many Latin American players, Pérez could not resist the siren song of winter baseball. He returned to Venezuela for 12 straight campaigns (1987-1988 through 1998-1999), playing in 420 regular-season games and another 72 in the postseason. He won two Golden Gloves (1993-1994 and 1994-1995) and was selected as the league's MVP (known as the Vitico Davalillo Award) in 1994-1995. Aragua won 34 games and lost 26, placing second in team ERA (2.78) and third in team batting (.262). The magic did not carry over to the round-robin: Aragua finished last with a 3-9 mark as their bats and arms grew cold.[10] (Winter Leagues in the Caribbean typically begin in November and go through January, so they are titled after both years.)

After the 1996-1997 season, Pérez was traded to Zulia, where he would finish his playing career. His lifetime numbers (.254 average in 1,564 at-bats) are eerily similar to his major-league tally of .253 in 1,525 at-bats.[11] While his playing career in the winter leagues did not result in a league title, Pérez was able to play with many major leaguers, including Concepción for the latter's final three campaigns in the Venezuelan circuit.[12] However, Pérez's voyage into the Venezuelan record books did not stop with his retirement.

Bitten by the coaching bug with Atlanta, Pérez was tapped to lead the Zulia team in 2008-2009 and 2009-2010, posting a 61-66 regular-season record and a 9-18 mark in the postseason. He returned in 2014-2015, compiling a 35-28 line good for third place. More than 20 major leaguers played for the team, including fellow Venezuelan catcher Sandy León, who established himself as a "pitcher's catcher" for the Boston Red Sox.

In 2015-2016 Pérez moved to the Aragua franchise. Though the Tigres had won the title in 2003-2004, 2004-2005, 2006-2007, 2007-2008, 2008-2009, and 2011-2012, they'd been led by a foreign-born manager. Pérez managed the club to the Venezuelan Winter League title, become the first *criollo*, or Venezuelan, to achieve the goal for the franchise.[13] The team became the runner-up in the Caribbean Series, losing a tough final game to México's Venados of Mazatlán.

"Specialist" is sometimes a backhanded compliment in baseball. Stone-gloved hitters are often derided as "DH's in waiting." Lefty-One-Out-Guys (LOOGYs) are lambasted for lengthening the game and slowing its pace. Charlie Finley even employed a "designated pinch-runner," the much-derided Herb Washington who would not enjoy a single plate appearance but appeared in 105 major-league games and scored 33 runs.

Historically, shortstops and catchers have seen their defensive value weighed above their offensive contributions. Paradoxically, the pendulum is swinging away from shortstops and toward catchers as more complex and definite metrics to value fielding contributions gain popularity among fans and front offices. General managers have, perhaps belatedly, recognized catchers' contributions beyond passed balls and caught-stealing percentage to include pitcher effectiveness, once thought to be the sole responsibility of hurlers. Yet while Joe Tinker and Ozzie Smith have gained Cooperstown immortality thanks to their leather exploits, catchers with similar careers (Bob Boone, Jim Sundberg, Jason Kendall) have been all but ignored by voters.

Catchers are like teaching assistants, their entire livelihoods providing an apprenticeship not enjoyed by the other positions. Yet this trait is often missed by even hard-core fans. The Milwaukee Brewers' classic logo combined a "B" for Brewers and a "M" for Milwaukee into a silhouette of a catcher's mitt that many missed, much like the contribution of the masked men.

Catchers are the second least represented position in Cooperstown, with only 20 immortalized with a Hall of Fame plaque. (The fewest are the 19 third basemen.) Only two backstops have made it in their first year of eligibility, Bench and Iván Rodríguez. Not Yogi Berra (second year). Not Roy Campanella (seventh year). Not Bill Dickey (11th year). Not Piazza (fourth year). Catchers are unlikely to spend 20 years in the majors as their wear and tear is evident even if they switch positions in their older years (as Bench and Berra did), so their opportunity to amass counting statistics like hits and runs is limited, making their offensive numbers less impressive than those of their teammates.

Their job is never done; every game has a post-mortem to discuss what worked, what did not, and what should change. While other positions receive such scouting updates, they do not generate the due diligence expected of the catcher, whose view includes not just the pitcher and his mechanics but also the placement of the fielders. Given that only 70 percent of plate appearances yield a play on the field, their position plays an outsized role in the outcome of a game.[14]

Like a Sherpa, the catcher guides the pitcher through the game, but his responsibility changes as the game progresses. The average 2018 major-league game saw 4.5 hurlers take the mound; yielding new personnel, new conversations, new signs, and new strategy.[15] These tasks were added to the time squatting behind the plate, catching 100-mph balls, handling wild pitches and foul tips, focusing on the baserunners, and ensuring that the pitcher's confidence is strong regardless of the scoreboard. A baseball card, often focused only on hitting prowess, cannot adequately capture the catcher's performance, which is much more correlated to the team's winning percentage than to any other measure.

After the 2006 season, the Braves offered Pérez the role of bullpen coach, understanding that his wealth of knowledge would be integral to the young roster. The Braves finished 2006 with a 79-83 record, the first losing campaign since 1990. Pérez kept the role for a decade (until 2016), seeing the team both rise and fall again in the NL East. He was shifted to the first-base job on May 17, 2016, and kept the position until the end of 2017, bringing a total of 11 full seasons as a member of the Braves' major-league coaching staff.[16]

Pérez's son Andrés was drafted by Atlanta in the 36th round of the 2016 amateur draft.[17] Buoyed by the robust support network of American collegiate sports and academics, the 6-foot-7 Andrés received a scholarship to the University of North Georgia.[18] Pérez the elder recognized the opportunity but was quick to highlight the reality: "It is different than in Venezuela. There I would have gone to study and forgotten about baseball. My son can play and study. Had he been in Venezuela, I would suggest he take the $5,000 or $20,000 given the reality of the country."

Pérez enthused about the new wave of his countrymen reaching the major leagues, although as a proud Venezuelan, he is heartbroken about the main catalyst. As of the conclusion of the 2024 season, 488 Venezuelans had played in the major leagues, with almost three-quarters of them reaching the "Big Show" after Pérez's debut. While Vizquel, Andrés "The Big Cat" Galarraga, Díaz, Aparicio, and Chico Carrasquel reached the baseball pinnacle before Pérez, younger stars like José Altuve and Miguel Cabrera have followed in his footsteps. In the spring of 2017, Pérez beckoned the call of the motherland by serving as the bench coach for the Venezuelan team in the World Baseball Classic.

"There'll be lots more (Venezuelan players) due to the (political) situation. Before, one could be doing OK with a college education especially in the oil industry. Fandom has always been there, people love baseball. It was easier for us to make a living, especially in the West, all of life's necessities." As Pérez and the author spoke on the phone in early 2019, the United States and dozens of other countries had recognized Juan Guaidó as the legitimate president of Venezuela, triggering a showdown with Nicolás Maduro.

Pérez's catching exploits emboldened Victor Martínez and Salvador Pérez, perennial All-Stars at the position. At the end of the 2024 season, Pérez's career placed him 15th among Venezuelan catchers players who have caught at least 75% of their appearances. Ever humble, he downplayed his role in fomenting the boom of his countrymen in the major leagues. Only one (Díaz) predated him in the majors. While playing for the Indians in 2002, Pérez mentored Martínez, a decade younger and still unpolished behind the plate. Pérez recalled telling Indians skipper Charlie Manuel, "V-Mart will be your top catcher" and Martínez himself, "I am not a fraction of the player you will be." But above all, he credited Díaz, who "opened the doors with the great job he did, may he rest in peace."

As Venezuela's economy has collapsed, the possibility of a middle-class life has all but disappeared. Inflation reached one million percent in 2018, rendering the bolívar almost worthless and forcing those with means to subsist by turning to the black market for their needs.[19] Players who fail to reach the majors may not have a good education as a backup plan. Though Pérez wished the younger generation the best of luck, he said he was deeply concerned about the underlying conditions: "Some schools have 12- to 14-year-olds with poor education. Education has worsened for the younger generation; the baseball schools don't cover education."

Pérez garnered another milestone in 2014 as he became an American citizen, cementing his ties to the Atlanta area and the franchise that has employed him for almost three decades.[20] Prior to the 2019 season, Pérez was named a special adviser for player development, granting him oversight of the next generation Braves while they make their way through the system.[21]

From his new perch, Pérez counseled the Braves' farmhands and the system within the major leagues. "Working with the Braves, I am focused on ensuring they don't just play well but also learn English. … We'll soon pass the Dominicans (in percentage of major-league players). Venezuelan players seek that better future, just like Dominicans did. There will be lots of great players, representing Latin America and Venezuela, but it saddens me to see the younger players struggle to read. (The major leagues) must do a better job." He left the role in 2022 and has since returned to the Braves' coaching staff.

ACKNOWLEDGMENTS

Eddie Pérez for graciously discussing his career via a phone interview.

Greg McMichael, Atlanta Braves director of alumni relations, for connecting the author to Eddie Pérez.

JJ Montilla, Venezuelan sportswriter, for sharing the Venezuelan Baseball reference site Pelota Binaria, which includes winter league statistics.

Pete Palmer and Jim Wheeler for detailed disabled-list records.

SOURCES

In addition to the sources cited in the Notes, the author relied extensively on Baseball-Reference.com.

NOTES

1   brainyquote.com/authors/johnny_bench.

2   Eddie Pérez, telephone interview, January 29, 2019. Unless otherwise indicated, all quotations directly attributed to Pérez come from this interview.

3   Robert Lohrer, "Broward Loses Big League Title," *South Florida Sentinel* (Fort Lauderdale), August 17, 1986. sun-sentinel.com/news/fl-xpm-1986-08-17-8602180967-story.html.

4   govinfo.gov/content/pkg/GOVPUB-T63_100-dd1437db9d97161a1d6cd294515 1dd6c/pdf/GOVPUB-T63_100-dd1437db9d97161a1d6cd294515 1dd6c.pdf.

5   govinfo.gov/content/pkg/GOVPUB-T63_100-dd1437db9d97161a1d6cd294515 1dd6c/pdf/GOVPUB-T63_100-dd1437db9d97161a1d6cd294515 1dd6c.pdf.

6   As of the conclusion of the 2018 season: baseball-almanac.com/feats/feats5.shtml.

7   Associated Press, " Braves' Perez May Miss Season," *New York Times*, March 22, 2001. nytimes.com/2001/03/22/sports/plus-baseball-braves-perez-may-miss-season.html.

8   Tom Ley, "Here's an Awesome Story About Greg Maddux," Deadspin.com, January 8, 2014. deadspin.com/heres-an-awesome-story-about-greg-maddux-1497441759.

9   Rob Neyer, *Rob Neyer's Big Book of Baseball Legends: The Truth, the Lies, and Everything Else* (New York: Touchstone, 2008), 14-16.

10 pelotabinaria.com.ve/beisbol/temporadas.php?TE=1994-95.

11 pelotabinaria.com.ve/beisbol/mostrar.php?ID=pereeduoo2.

12 pelotabinaria.com.ve/beisbol/mostrar.php?ID=concdavoo1.

13 Mark Bowman, "Perez Eyeing Venezuelan Winter League Title," MLB.com, January 21, 2016. mlb.com/braves/news/braves-eddie-perez-eyeing-winter-league-title/c-162485118.

14 Mike Axisa, "MLB's Biggest Problem Is Not Pace of Play and It's Only Getting Worse in 2018," CBSSports.com, April 15, 2018. cbssports.com/mlb/news/mlbs-biggest-problem-is-not-pace-of-play-and-its-only-getting-worse-in-2018/.

15 Jim Albert, "Historical Look at Pitcher Usage," January 28, 2019. baseballwithr.wordpress.com/2019/01/28/historical-look-at-pitcher-usage/.

16 atlanta.braves.mlb.com/team/coach_staff_bio.jsp?c_id=atl&coachorstaffid=120407.

17 David O'Brien, "Eddie Perez's Son Drafted by Braves in 36th Round," *Atlanta Journal-Constitution*, June 11, 2016. ajc.com/sports/baseball/eddie-perez-son-drafted-braves-36th-round/PaN3SAsQzLVtLzgKdpMTYL/.

18 ungathletics.com/roster.aspx?rp_id=3060.

19 Reuters, "IMF Projects Venezuela Inflation Will Hit 1,000,000 Percent in 2018," Reuters.com, July 23, 2018. reuters.com/article/us-venezuela-economy/imf-projects-venezuela-inflation-will-hit-1000000-percent-in-2018-idUSKBN1KD2L9.

20 Michael Cunningham, "Braves Coach Perez Becomes American Citizen" *Atlanta Journal-Constitution*, August 14, 2014. ajc. com/sports/braves-coach-perez-becomes-american-citizen/ YvxtkUA6bXj9L4A9MaO6LJ/.

21 mlb.com/braves/team/front-office.

ROBERT PÉREZ

BY J.L. TUCUPIDO C.

The numbers just don't make sense. A pedestrian .254 batting average, 8 home runs, and 44 RBIs in six years in the majors simply *shouldn't* belong to Robert Pérez. One can only wonder why one of Venezuela's most beloved baseball players did not enjoy greater success in the big leagues despite a professional career that spanned more than a quarter-century.

Though Pérez was not blessed with the five tools, he possessed a tireless work ethic. A natural athlete, he willed his 6-foot-3, 205-pound frame to outperform his innate abilities and reached the major leagues in 1994, as the clash between owners and players left the nation without its beloved pastime.

Robert Alexander Pérez Jiménez was born on June 4, 1969, in Guayana City, the most populous city in Bolívar state. His parents, homemaker Luisa Jiménez and amateur boxer Jesús "Negro Blanco" Pérez, already had two children, Odalis and Richard, and would later welcome a fourth, Robinson. The elder Pérez instilled a love of sports into his brood, and the quartet was famous in its Vista del Sol neighborhood for their athletic exploits.

Odalis boxed in the Seventh Pan American Games (Mexico City, 1975) in the lightweight class. Richard ran like a gazelle in the 100-meter dash, boxed, played soccer, and tried out for the Lara Cardenales of the Venezuelan Winter Baseball League (LVBP, for Liga Venezolana de Béisbol Profesional). Robert always preferred baseball but was also talented on the volleyball court and the soccer pitch. As a child, he rooted for La Guaira: "I was a fan of the Tiburones (Sharks). At home we'd listen to the games on the radio, back in the era of Oswaldo Blanco, Aurelio Monteagudo, Norman Carrasco, Alfredo Pedrique, and Juan Francisco Monasterios."[1]

On May 1, 1989, Robert signed as an international free agent with the Toronto Blue Jays. He pocketed a $1,500 signing bonus. Almost 20, he would have been considered too old by today's standards, but not in the 1980s, when Venezuela had not yet emerged as a baseball hotbed, and major-league franchises sought only prospects already under contract to a winter league team.

Pérez was scouted by Epifanio "Epy" Guerrero, who signed 52 Latin American players, including 17 Venezuelans, during his bird-dog career, mostly with the Cardenales and the Blue Jays. He benefited from the tutelage of Domingo Carrasquel, Alfonso "Chico" Carrasquel's brother, and a former star in his own right. Carrasquel would teach Pérez more than just baseball: "I've always tried to be an upright citizen thanks to Domingo Carrasquel," said Pérez. "He instilled the value of responsibility, work ethic and morals."[2]

A year prior, Pedro Millán and Carrasquel had noticed the youngster and took him to Barquisimeto, capital of Lara province. Carrasquel recalled "the passion, given (Pérez's) humble background. Urged by Pedro, I went to Ciudad Piar to see Pérez. I saw him practice and saw a fundamental trait: the hunger to play baseball, the desire to make himself into a ballplayer. I saw a love for baseball."[3] The sage Carrasquel's track record proved he was rarely wrong in his assessments; Pérez grew to consider him as a father figure.

Pérez did not disappoint. He was named the MVP of the Dominican Summer League (DSL) and Rookie of the Year of the LVBP in 1989-90. The following spring, he played with the St. Catharines Blue Jays of the New York-Pennsylvania League. He was soon promoted to Myrtle Beach of the Class-A South Atlantic League and batted .269 in 73 combined games.

In 1991 he was promoted to the Class-A Advanced Florida State League. He slashed .302/.338/.401 in 516 plate appearances with Dunedin. After a four-game stint with Triple-A Syracuse, the Blue Jays added him to the 40-man roster.

Pérez received a coveted invitation to spring training in 1992, though the starting left-field job was held by veteran Candy Maldonado. Derek Bell was seen as the heir apparent, but Toronto was sufficiently impressed by Pérez's potential to assign him to Double-A Knoxville to start the season while Shawn Green and Carlos Delgado, other heralded prospects, returned to Dunedin. The Blue Jays won their first World Series while Pérez averaged .261 in 526 plate appearances for Knoxville. His nine home runs foreshadowed a potential problem with insufficient power.

In 1993 Pérez improved to .294 with Syracuse but was passed over for a September call-up to the big leagues while both Delgado and Green enjoyed cups of coffee. During the season, Toronto employed six left fielders, including Rickey Henderson, acquired during the stretch run from the Oakland Athletics.

Henderson returned to Oakland in the offseason. Toronto sought to promote within its ranks rather than a sign a free agent. Rob Butler, Juan de La Rosa, and Pérez were the contenders, but none impressed: "Before leaving Florida, left field has to be settled. The two front-runners, Robert Perez [*sic*] and Rob Butler, did not take the bull by the horns, and Delgado was moved into the spot. It remains to be seen if Delgado's quick process in the outfield will continue."[4]

Pérez returned to Syracuse and lifted his average to .304 but hit only three home runs. Delgado struggled and Mike Huff, signed before the season as a backup, played a plurality of games in left field. Toronto was rumored to be interested in Larry Walker, but the Canadian native was not traded by Montreal.

It appeared Pérez was not in general manager Pat Gillick's sights. A long season, however, brings unforeseen opportunities.

Toronto played .500 ball most of the year and the club gave its youngsters a look. Pérez debuted on July 20, 1994, with 48,162 fans in attendance. He replaced Joe Carter in right field in the top of the seventh inning. The Jays led the Twins, 7-0, and Pérez flied out against Rick Aguilera in the eighth. Earlier that day, Syracuse manager Bob Didier shared the good news: "He told me I was going to play, that I'd been added to the roster, to take care of anything I needed since the flight to Toronto was leaving soon. The minors are the price you must pay to reach the major leagues. Everything was high class."[5]

Pérez was the starting left fielder on July 29 against Baltimore. In his fourth trip to the plate at Oriole Park at Camden Yards, he singled in the ninth inning off Mark Eichhorn for his first major-league hit. He finished the season 1-for-8 in four games.

Pérez understood his battle against other young players eager to prove their talent. The strike canceled 47 games, and, as the offseason progressed, threatened to wipe out 1995. Green, Butler, and Pérez decamped to Venezuela and new GM Gord Ash dispatched Mel Queen, his player development director, to evaluate their progress: "Outfielders Shawn Green and Robert Pérez, who figure to battle for the starting left-field job, are hitting over .300 for their Lara team and will soon be joined by Rob Butler, another Blue Jays outfield prospect. Mel's more pleased with Green's outfield play than necessarily the bat. We know he's going to hit."[6]

Green was indeed the apple of Toronto's eye. After free agent Walker spurned the Jays for the Rockies, Carter shifted to left field and Green took over right. The lanky lefty was fifth in the 1995 AL Rookie of the Year voting thanks to his .509 slugging average. Meanwhile, Pérez demolished the International League. He led the league with a .343 average[7] and again joined the Blue Jays, this time when rosters expanded in September.[8]

Toronto could not deny Pérez a roster spot in 1996. The question was whether he would surpass Huff as the fourth outfielder. Pérez broke camp with the team and appeared in 86 games, 48 as a starter. He had a solid .354 on-base percentage and a .327 batting average, but only 12 of his 66 hits were for extra bases. Hitting coach Willie Upshaw exhorted Pérez to alter his swing to produce more power, but Pérez was concerned about a slump and reduced playing time. The franchise relented but remained concerned about this weakness. Despite his five home runs in 191 at-bats with Lara in the 1996-97 LVPB, Toronto signed free agent Darrell Whitmore to compete for a bench role.[9]

Pérez spent most of his time on the bench in 1997. He played in 37 games (20 as a starter) and hit only two home runs: June 13 off the Phillies' Ricky Bottalico and August 20, against Nelson Cruz of the White Sox. His .192/.192/.346 slash line did not augur a return.

The 29-year-old Pérez entered 1998 as a third-year player and Ash was unwilling to commit to his development any further. Pérez was waived on March 29 and claimed by Seattle a day later. The Mariners, however, flipped him to Montreál in exchange for Raúl Chávez. He was a valuable pinch-hitter and spare outfielder for the Expos, but a left wrist injury cost him a month of playing time. His performance suffered upon his return, and, unable to protect Vladimir Guerrero Sr. in the lineup, he was released on September 29, 1998.[10]

Pérez tried his luck in Japan. In 1999 he signed a contract with the Orix Blue Wave and shared the outfield with the phenomenal Ichiro Suzuki during the latter's next to last season in Japanese baseball. It was a rough transition for the Venezuelan: "I was very frustrated in Japan. They'd bring me up and send me down. I wasn't prepared for the culture shock. It was hard and I wanted to leave halfway through the season."[11]

Pérez returned to North America in 2000, again with the Blue Jays organization. He played with the Double-A Tennessee Smokies and finally generated power, with 19 home runs and 92 runs batted in. While those numbers did not excite Toronto, they caught the attention of the New York Yankees, who invited him to spring training in 2001.

Though a starting job was unlikely, Pérez was happy to wear the pinstripes. He started four consecutive games during Bernie

Longtime slugger in Venezuela, Robert Pérez represented his country in the 2006 WBC. He had brief MLB stints with the Blue Jays and Expos.

(Matthew Stockman / Getty Images Sports)

Williams's bereavement leave for his father's funeral. After two weeks on the bench, the organization chose to send Pérez to the minors: "They called me into the office and Brian Cashman and Joe Torre were there. They said they were happy with my performance (4-for-15 in six games), but they needed to make a move and they chose me. They wanted to send me to Triple A and said they'd call me up at the first opportunity. They even offered me more money to go to the International League. I said 'absolutely not!' I signed my release papers because I wanted to stay in the majors, I felt good."[12]

The Yankees placed Pérez on waivers on June 12 and the Milwaukee Brewers promptly claimed him. He hit .333 in 84 at-bats with Triple-A Indianapolis and was called up to the parent club. He started on July 1 against Houston (0-for-4) and pinch-hit the next day (0-for-1). He languished on the bench and was again demoted to the minors. Regular, consistent playing time continued to evade him.

In 2002 Pérez split time between Indianapolis (43 games, .197) and Columbus (84 games, .275) in a return to the Yankee organization. However, neither club promoted him to the majors.

At 32, Pérez still had a lot of baseball left to play, though few would have imagined he would last an additional 13 years. He continued to play in the LVBP, and was a resourceful import in the Mexican (2003, 2006, 2007, 2008, 2009), Korean (2003, 2004, 2007), and Italian Leagues (2011). He was the third-oldest player on Team Venezuela for the 2006 World Baseball Classic. Father Time was seemingly the only obstacle he couldn't overcome and Pérez retired at age 45.

In his early 50s, Pérez remained a baseball lifer. He has served as the hitting coach of the Cardenales, the Tiburones, and the Navegantes (Navigators) of Magallanes. He worked in the same capacity with the Venezuelan youth national team, winner of the 2020 U-23 Baseball World Cup in Mexico. Since 2022, he has been the bench coach of the Miranda Líderes (Leaders) in the nascent Liga Mayor de Béisbol Profesional (LMBP, Major Professional Baseball League), a summer circuit started in 2021.[13]

In 2015 the LVBP Finals MVP Award was named in Pérez's honor, a fitting tribute given his record 11 home runs in the finals (tied with Tony Armas Sr.) Regarded as one of the finest right-handed batters produced by Venezuela, Pérez's name is a fixture in the LVBP record books. As of 2024, he was the all-time leader in career RBIs (736), doubles (221), games (1,300), extra-base hits (382), and runs scored (625). He won five Gold Gloves in 27 seasons (behind only Vic Davalillo's 30) and is third in the HR list with 125 home runs. (He broke Armas's record before his own was surpassed by Alex Cabrera and Eliézer Alfonzo.) Pérez is one of only six players to reach 1,000 hits and one of 20 to hit three home runs in the same game; he is the only one to have accomplished the feat twice. He was deservedly elected to the LVBP Hall of Fame in 2021.[14]

Pérez founded the Robert Pérez 51 Academy (RP51, after his LVBP uniform number) in June 2015 to focus on the development of Venezuelan prospects. He has four daughters (Roberit, Gabriela, Melani, and Yulihed) and two sons (Robert Jr. and Hedbert). Robert Jr. has followed his father's footsteps: Signed with the Seattle Mariners as a 16-year-old, he began the 2024 season with the San Antonio Missions, San Diego's Double-A affiliate. Like his father, the son is a right-handed outfielder, and played with the Cardenales in 2023-2024, coached by his father.

Despite a 27-year career on three continents, Pérez carries a chip on his shoulder: "I wasn't a regular in MLB but if I'd had the chance to play every day, maybe I would've shown what I could do, like I did in the Venezuelan league. I had the talent and the physical condition to shine in the majors, but I am proud to have played in the big leagues with several teams. I respect baseball and everything God has given me."[15]

SOURCES

In addition to the sources cited in the Notes, the author consulted Baseballreference.com, ESPN.com, Newspapers.com, MLB.com, Pelotabinaria.com.ve, Sabr.org, Radiofeyalegrianoticias.com, YouTube, Instagram, and Twitter.

NOTES

1   "Robert Pérez con la Guaira," Tiburones de la Guaira website, September 21, 2018, https://www.tiburones.net/nota/3968/robert-perez-con-la-guaira.

2   "Robert Pérez cumple 51 años y sigue siendo la leyenda más prominente de los Cardenales," El Extrabase, June 4, 2020, https://elextrabase.com/2020/06/04/robert-perez-cumple-51-anos-y-sigue-siendo-la-leyenda-mas-prominente-de-cardenales/.

3   W. Duarte, "51: Más que una Leyenda Robert Pérez (Robert Pérez" More Than a Legend," WD Productions, Barquisimeto, Venezuela, 2016.

4   Steve Milton, "Offense-Rich Jays Will Be There Again in October," The Sporting News, April 4, 1994: 74.

5   "Robert Pérez," Latin World Sports, Venezuela 2018.

6   Steve Milton, "Weekly Reports: Toronto Blue Jays," The Sporting News, November 21, 1994: 45.

7   Though other hitters had a higher average, they did not garner the required plate appearances to qualify for the batting title. In second place, behind Pérez, was Yankees prospect Derek Jeter.

8   Associated Press, "Transactions," Salina (Kansas) Journal, September 2, 1995: 12.

9   Tom Maloney, "Weekly Reports: Toronto Blue Jays," The Sporting News, January 27, 1997: 50.

10   Stephanie Myles, "Trade Talk Has Been Quiet Despite Available Talent," The Sporting News, August 3, 1998: 31.

11   Luis Sojo, "La Estrella Invitada: Entrevista especial con Robert Pérez," Sojo Productions, 2020, https://www.youtube.com/watch?v=4NJiUDlrIxA

12   "Sports in 60 seconds. Yankees Make Moves," Chicago Daily Herald, June 13, 2001: 58.

13   Eudo Torres, "Viene la segunda edición de la Liga Mayor de Béisbol Profesional," Radio fe y alegría noticias, February 22, 2002, https://www.radiofeyalegrianoticias.com/viene-la-segunda-edicion-de-la-liga-mayor-de-beisbol-profesional/

14   "Roberto Pérez: Una Pared Negra de la Fama", Museo de Béisbol
     YouTube Page, https://www.youtube.com/watch?v=IvMAd-Q-PSo-
     &ab_channel=MUSEODEBEISBOL

15   "La Estrella Invitada."

TOMÁS PÉREZ

BY JAY HURD

When asked in 2015 about his earliest baseball memory, Tomás Pérez replied, "Caimaneras," referring to Venezuela's "improvised baseball game, without referees, in which players are chosen spontaneously, which usually takes place in the streets, in the schoolyards or in some field…"[1] He recalled that his parents were angry that baseball, a game, interfered with his education; but he commented, simply, that "I didn't like studying."[2] Indeed, baseball was his calling, and in time, with reluctant support from his parents, he played in the Venezuelan Professional Baseball League and in the US major leagues, and for all baseball fans in Venezuela, Pérez is known simply as "Tomasito" (Little Tomás).

Tomás Orlando Pérez Garcia was born on December 29, 1973, in Barquisimeto, the fourth largest city in Venezuela. His father, Tomás Pérez Duarte was his baseball coach at Escuela Barquisimeto, his high school, and a longtime amateur player in local leagues. His mother, Adde Garcia Pérez, faithfully followed Pérez's amateur and professional career as a homemaker.

After years of caimanera, and after causing "astonishment by his catches in shorts when he was 18 years old,"[3] he joined the expansion Petroleros de Cabimas team of the Venezuelan league for the 1991-1992 season. With that team, he appeared in one game, had three at-bats, and had one hit. Also in 1991, on July 11, the National League's Montreal Expos signed the 5-foot-11, 185-pound Tomás as an amateur free agent. First steps for further development were playing with the Dominican Summer League Expos in 1992. Tomás, a switch-hitting infielder, appeared in 44 of the season's 71 games and batted .305. For the next 23 years, Pérez played baseball for minor-league teams, major-league teams, and Venezuelan Professional Baseball League teams.

Pérez had established himself as a dependable infielder in the Venezuelan league and in the same seasons worked to improve his game through more Rookie baseball with the Gulf Coast League Expos, based in West Palm Beach, Florida, in 1993. After playing in 52 games, at shortstop, of a 58-game season, he returned to the Venezuelan league's Petroleros de Cabimas team. He remained with that team until 1997; in latter years, the team's name changed to Pastora de Occidente. In the meantime, his major-league career began to take hold. For the 1994 season, with the Burlington (Iowa) Bees, Class-A affiliate of the Expos, he played second base and shortstop in 119 games of a 137-game season, batted .262 with 8 home runs and 47 RBIs, and was selected as a league All-Star. Rather than make the expected leap to the Expos' Triple-A affiliate Ottawa Lynx, however, he was selected in the Rule 5 draft on December 5, 1994, by the California Angels.[4] In turn, the Angels sold Pérez's contract to the Toronto Blue Jays for cash considerations.

Added to the Blue Jays' roster, Pérez made his major-league debut on May 3, 1995. In the bottom of the 10th inning, in a tie game with the Chicago White Sox, he had his first major-league at-bat, his first major-league hit, and his first major-league RBI, driving in Ed Sprague with the game-winning run.[5] He went on to appear in 40 more games that season, alternating between second base, third base, and shortstop.

The next season, 1996, became Pérez's official rookie season. When he was called up to the Blue Jays from the Triple-A Syracuse Sky Chiefs at the end of May, the *Windsor* (Ontario) *Star* noted that Pérez "was back to his usual self: strutting around the dugout and clubhouse displaying a cocky confidence that spoke – I'm a major leaguer."[6] As in the previous season, the switch-hitting Pérez alternated infield positions – this time with most playing time at second base. He completed the 1996 season with a .251 batting average, 19 RBIs, and 15 errors – 11 at second base and 2 each at third base and shortstop. In 1997, still with the Blue Jays, he appeared in 40 games, with most of his time spent at shortstop – he committed only three errors, between shortstop and second base. For the 1996, 1997, and 1998 seasons, Pérez split playing time between the Blue Jays and Syracuse. This back-and-forth from major-league team to minor-league team became a pattern throughout his career.

Pérez married his girlfriend, Andrea Carolina, in 1998. They welcomed their first daughter, Paola Valentina, in 2002. He had been living in the United States since 1993 and said that he wanted his daughter to attend "high school and college" in the states. His parents and sister visited for one month each year.[7]

In early March 1999, the Toronto Blue Jays removed Pérez from the major-league roster and sent him outright to Syracuse.[8] On March 30 they traded Pérez to the Anaheim Angels for switch-hitting infielder-designated hitter Dave Hollins and cash. The Angels sent Pérez to their Triple-A affiliate, the Edmonton Trappers of the Pacific Coast League. There, he played in 83 games.

After the season the Angels released Pérez, and he signed a Triple-A contract with the Philadelphia Phillies with an invitation to spring training. Phillies general manager Ed Wade said, "Everybody I've talked to has raved about what we've seen from Tomás and [middle infielder Félix Martínez]."[9] Wade had not at first agreed with assistant GM Rubén Amaro about signing Pérez. Wade had heard that Pérez might be a problem, "…selfish and a bit of a hot dog."[10] However, Wade admitted in the spring of 2002 that he had been incorrect. He was now "pretty high on Tomás Pérez" and acknowledged that he "brings a lot of life to the game and a lot of life to the clubhouse. … The

A clubhouse favorite, Pérez played every position except pitcher and catcher. He had a 12-year major-league career with five clubs. (Lisa Blumenfeld / Getty Images Sports)

Pérez began the 2000 season with the Triple-A affiliate Scranton-Wilkes Barre Red Barons. An impressive stretch of hitting led the Red Barons to a winning streak. After a sixth straight multihit game, he said, "It's the first time I've had a stretch like this."[15] In August his contributions in Triple A were rewarded as the Phillies, under manager Terry Francona, called him up.[16] He saw minor-league baseball only once more during his time with the Phillies – this a two-game rehab stint with Double-A Reading after sustaining an injury in a March 2002 exhibition game against the New York Yankees that sidelined him for several weeks.[17]

Pérez's 12-year major-league career did not interfere with his career in Venezuela. Manager Larry Bowa observed: "Pérez is known for playing an entire winter ball season in his native Venezuela. Not all big-league bench players are willing to do that."[18] The *Allentown Morning Call* in December of 2002 termed Pérez the most productive Phil playing winter ball, noting that his .326 batting average ranked him eighth in the league.[19] From 1997 through 2002 Pérez played with the Caribes de Anzoátegui club, based in Puerto Cruz, Venezuela. He did not know at this time that this same team would become a storied part of his baseball career.

Pérez's major-league career included numerous season highlights. On July 24, 2001, he became the second Phillies player (the first was Steve Jeltz, in 1989) to hit a home run from each side of the plate in a game. Of his feat, Pérez said, "It feels great, one for my mom (Adde) and one for my wife (Andrea). My mother has seen me play a lot in Venezuela, but this was only the second time in the big leagues."[20] On December 20, 2001, Pérez signed a contract with the Phillies for $475,000, plus performance bonuses.[21]

The next season, 2003, may be regarded as Pérez's best year in baseball. He played in 125 games, had 79 hits for a .265 average, 5 home runs, and 33 RBIs; and he played each infield position. On September 9 he and Jason Michaels each hit a grand slam in an 18-5 win over the Atlanta Braves.[22]

One of Pérez's more notable games came on May 28, 2004, at home against the Atlanta Braves, when he hit a game-tying double in the eighth, and then a walk-off homer in the 10th.

In the first World Baseball Classic, from March 3 to March 20, 2006, Pérez was on the Venezuela team. Soon after Venezuela had been eliminated from the tournament, he returned to the Phillies and by mid-March he realized that only one bench position remained open, and his job was in jeopardy. When the Phillies made a late-night trade for David Dellucci, and with Alex Gonzalez and Abraham Núñez having already made the team, Pérez became the man to be released. In his six seasons with the Phillies, he played in 504 games, batted .249, with 20 home runs and 128 RBIs, and committed only 24 errors.[23]

Fans and teammates alike were unhappy to see Pérez, the prototypical Phillies "Bench Dog,"[24] leave. The Pie Man was gone. "Tomás Pérez was just one of those guys who gave you a lot more than what you saw on the stats page," a sportswriter commented.[25] Teammate Ryan Howard said, "I will miss

utility infielder has exceeded all expectations, providing clutch hitting and fielding. He has even pitched."[11]

Phillies bullpen coach Ramon Henderson said of Pérez's defense, "He was young and immature. ... He was pushed to the big leagues early [with Toronto in 1995]. He didn't have people tell him the truth and say, 'Cut out the [junk] and play baseball. Perhaps age, marriage and fatherhood" helped him mature. His second daughter, Alejandra Cristina, was born in August 2005; on the night of her birth, he "left the ballpark during batting practice ... to be with his wife."[12] Indeed, soon after joining the Phillies in 2000, through the 2005 season, Pérez became – despite an earlier reputation as having "an attitude problem" – a favorite of Phillies teammates and fans as a clutch hitter and prankster [aka the Pie Man.][13] Pérez became the official shaving cream or whipped cream pie-to-the-face-guy with the Phillies early in his career there. "Although he has no exact criteria, Pérez usually saves that honor for the teammate who gets the game-winning hit or comes up with a game-saving defensive play or pitch."[14]

the pies in the face."[26] And catcher Mike Lieberthal, another frequent pie victim, added, "He is one of my favorite players I ever played with. He was not only a good player, but he kept everybody loose and is one of the best personalities I have ever been around."[27] Broadcaster Harry Kalas said he regarded Pérez as "the Phillies' secret weapon."[28]

Pérez wasn't without a job long. Shortly after his release, he signed with the the Tampa Bay Devil Rays. In 99 games he split time between each infield position, and left and right fields committing, in total, only eight errors. In this, his only season with the Rays, he hit .212. On July 29 he tied the major-league record with four doubles in a 5-for-5 game, leading Tampa Bay to a 19-6 rout of the New York Yankees.[29]

The following seasons were chaotic for Pérez. In October 2006 the Devil Rays released him. He signed with the Chicago Cubs on January 24, 2007. Soon after, the Cubs sent him to the Los Angeles Dodgers for future considerations. He played 36 games with the Dodgers' Triple-A affiliate, the Las Vegas 51s of the Pacific Coast League. On May 26, 2007, the Dodgers traded him to the Chicago White Sox for minor-league pitcher Dwayne Pollok. He finished the season, appearing in 88 games, with the Charlotte Knights of the Triple-A International League. Released at the end of the season, Pérez signed with the Houston Astros in November. In 2008 he played in 79 games for Round Rock Express of the PCL and eight games for the Astros; his final game with the Astros and, as it happened, in major-league baseball, was April 21, 2008. He was designated for assignment a few days later.[30] On March 13, 2009, he signed with the Colorado Rockies for what turned out to be an 18-day stint; he was released on April 1.[31]

His major-league career ended, in 2011 Pérez signed a one-year contract with the Italian Bbc Grosseto team. However, due to an elbow injury, the Grosseto team waived him on March 6, 2011. His attentions, which he had split between major-league baseball, the minor leagues, and the Liga Venezolana de Béisbol Profesional, could now focus on longtime goals – namely, reaching more than 1,000 hits in the Venezuelan league, playing all nine positions in one nine-inning game, and coaching and managing.

Pérez played 24 seasons in the Venezuelan Winter League and became one of nine players in the league to reach the 1,000-hit milestone. From the 1991-1992 season to the 2014-2015 season, he played for five teams in the Venezuelan league: Petroleros de Cabimas, later Pastora de Occidente; Caribes de Oriente (later Anzoátegui); Leones del Caracas; Navegantes del Magallanes; and Cardenales de Lara, and with Team Venezuela in the 2014-2015 Caribbean Series.[32] He retired after the 2014-2015 season.

In his 12-year major-league career, Pérez had only one season in which he played more than 100 games (2003 with the Phillies). He played with four major-league teams – the Blue Jays, the Phillies, the Devil Rays, and the Astros; and many more minor-league teams – two Rookie, one Class A, one Double-A, and six Triple-A. He appeared in one World Baseball Classic on the Venezuelan national team. During major-league and minor-league offseasons, he played 24 seasons in Venezuela. His 1,010 hits are sixth all-time in the Venezuelan league (inspired by his longtime idol and "father in baseball,"[33] Luis Sojo, who had 1,007 hits); He played all nine positions in a single game with Caribes de Anzoátegui. During his career, Pérez and other Venezuelan ballplayers, faced the reality that because of political unrest their home cities and home nation had become unsafe for themselves and for their families and friends. Pérez hired bodyguards for himself and his family. He said. "It's a big problem. … You have to worry about two things … playing baseball and protecting your family."[34] Pérez's wife , was "victimized when her SUV was vandalized when she took the couple's newborn baby to the doctor," another article reported.[35]

Pérez has said he would like to become a manager. Having "flipped the switch"[36] from player to coach, he wants to learn, he wants to share his knowledge, and he wants to give back to his teachers, including Venezuelan-born Alfredo Pedrique and Omar López. "If at any time a team gives me the chance and confidence to transmit all my knowledge in a position of such responsibility as that, it will be well received. … This is not new to me. In the United States with the Atlanta organization, I had already been a coach, but in Venezuela I am making my debut in these struggles and the experience is definitely different. You really have to know how to be a coach in this league."[37]

Pérez has worked with the Atlanta Braves since 2015 and in 2024 is a batting practice pitcher with the Braves. Of note, he pitched to Freddie Freeman in the 2018 All-Star Game Home Run Derby; and, when, on November 2, 2021, the Braves won their first Word Series in 26 years, Pérez was one of three Venezuelan-born coaches on the team – the other two being Eddie Pérez and José Yépez.

NOTES

1   "Origins of the Word 'Caimanera.'" Posted August 21, 2020. http://blog.com/banesco-origenes-la-palabra-caimanera.

2   Ignacio Serrano, "Me fue bien como pitcher, nunca me hacieron carreras" (I did well as a pitcher, they never gave me races). *El Emergente*, https://www.elemergente.com/2015/02/me-fue-bien-como-pitcher-nunca-me.html.

3   Serrano.

4   Jeff Blair, "Expos Axe Benavides; Pick One, Lose Four in Draft," *Montreal Gazette*, December 6, 1994.

5   "Blue Jays 8, White Sox 7," *Baltimore Sun*, May 4, 1995,

6   "Baseball on the Wire," *Windsor* (Ontario) *Star*, May 31, 1996.

7   Mandy Housenick, "Phillies Pieman Perez Is More Than a Clown," *Allentown* (Pennsylvania) *Morning Call*, July 18, 2004. https://www.mcall.com/news/mc-xpm-2004-07-18-3560505-story.html.

8   "Transactions," *Philadelphia Inquirer*, March 5, 1999.

9   "Phils' Anderson Knows His Job's in Jeopardy" *Lancaster* (Pennsylvania) *Intelligencer Journal*, March 2, 2000.

10   Bob Brookover, "Pérez Gives Off Sparks," *Philadelphia Inquirer*, May 31, 2002.

11 "Pérez Gives Off Sparks."

12 Dana Pennett O'Neill, "Bell Hears It from Fans, but Declines to Give It Back," *Philadelphia Inquirer,* August 8, 2005.

13 Jim Salisbury, "Prankster and Player, Pérez a Phils Favorite," *Philadelphia Inquirer,* April 1, 2004.

14 Housenick, "Phillies Pieman Perez Is More Than a Clown."

15 Randy Showmanski, "Barons Keep Rolling," *Scranton* (Pennsylvania) *Tribune.* May 29, 2000.

16 Bob Brookover, "Retooled Lineup Delivers More Punch," *Philadelphia Inquirer,* August 12, 2000.

17 He was injured by "a hard takeout slide by Shane Spencer." Rob Maadi, "Pérez Hurt; Punto Gets Call," *Scranton Times-Tribune,* March 26, 2002.

18 Salisbury, "Prankster and Player, Pérez a Phils Favorite."

19 "Winter League Update," *Allentown Morning Call,* December 3, 2002.

20 Paul Hagen, "Phillies Use a Full Nelson to Slice Braves' Lead to 1," *Lancaster New Era,* July 25, 2001.

21 "MLB Transactions," http://mlb.com/mlb/transactions/?c_id=phi&year=2001&month=12.

22 "Phillies Pound Braves with Two Slams," *Sunbury* (Pennsylvania) *Daily Item,* September 10, 2003.

23 Matt Rappa, "Former Phillie Still Swinging Away Down in Venezuela," *Baseball Talk Philadelphia,* December 30, 2014. https://www.philliedelphia.com/2014/12/former-phillie-tomas-perez-still-swinging-away-down-in-venezuela.html.

24 Robert Gordon and Tom Burgoyne, *Movin On Up: Baseball and Philadelphia Then, Now, and Always (*Mooretown, New Jersey: Middle Atlantic Press, 2004), 237.

25 Kevin Lagowski, "The 2000 Philadelphia Phillies: A Crash Course in Tomas Pérez," *Section215.* https://section215.com/2020/05/30/2000-philadelphia-phillies-tomas-perez/.

26 Jenn Zambri, "Phillies History: Shaving Cream Pies," *Phillies Phollowers,* July 12, 2010, https://mlblogsphilliesphollowers.wordpress.com/?s=tomas+perez.

27 Zambri.

28 Jim Reeser, "'Hard to Believe' Beloved Harry Kalas Is Gone," *Wilkes-Barre* (Pennsylvania) *Citizens Voice,* April 14, 2009.

29 Associated Press, "This Date in Baseball," https://apnews.com/article/12b: Shaving72ae2c35ac82596795b843777c950.

30 "Transactions, Baseball, American League." *Port Huron* (Michigan) *Times Herald,* April 25, 2008.

31 "Tomás Pérez, Career Transactions." *Baseball America.* https://www.baseballamerica.com/players/23556/tomas-perez/.

32 Pelota Binaria. Tomas Perez. https://pelotabinaria.com.ve/beisbol/mostrar.php?ID=peretom001.

33 "Tomasito in the History of the LVBP," *ElImpulso.com.* Regions of Lara and Barquisimeto, Venezuela, October 23, 2014. https://www.elimpulso.com/2014/10/23/tomasito-en-la-historia-de-la-lvbp/.

34 Bart Jones, "Unsafe at Home," *Newsday* (Long Island, New York), February 5, 2005. https://www.newsday.com/sports/unsafe-at-home-1.548975.

35 Kevin Baxter, "Foreign Baseball Players' Family Face Threat of Kidnapping," *Tiger Boards Archive,* January 24, 2005. https://www.tigernet.com/forums/thread.jspa?threadID=71456.

36 "Tomás Pérez Continues to Learn as a Coach," LVBP.com. https://www.lvbp.com/3905_tomas-perez-sigue-aprendiendo-como-coach.

37 Atlanta Braves Official Website. https://www.mlb.com/braves/roster/coaches. Accessed December 16, 2021.

JUAN RIVERA

BY TONY S. OLIVER

Correlation is *not* causation, as statisticians never fail to state, but it's hard to tell which one was at play as Gene Michael and the Yankees brass enjoyed freedom from George Steinbrenner during the Boss's suspension. Although originally issued as a lifetime ban by Fay Vincent in 1990, it was lifted after less than three years by the effete commissioner. The interregnum gave the baseball operations group enough leeway to develop the core of the late-1990s Yankee dynasty: Jorge Posada, Derek Jeter, Andy Pettitte, Mariano Rivera, and Bernie Williams. By the end of the decade, with fan favorite Paul O'Neill on the wrong side of 30, the Yankees expected Juan Rivera to ease into the right-field position once patrolled by Babe Ruth, Roger Maris, and Reggie Jackson, whose numbers adorned Monument Park. Instead, Rivera joined David Justice, Félix Jose, Lance Johnson, Karim García, Raúl Mondesi, Shane Spencer, John Vander Wal, Gerald Williams, David Dellucci, Rubén Sierra, Bubba Crosby, and Kenny Lofton as the Yankees employed a carousel of players as stopgap measures in right field before signing Gary Sheffield prior to the 2004 campaign.

While Rivera would enjoy over 1,000 regular-season games in the majors and 36 others in the postseason, he never reached the lofty expectations placed upon him by baseball experts. His 162-game averages (.274/.323/.443, 102 OPS+) were respectable but misleading, as he never came close to playing a full season.

Juan Luis Rivera was born on July 3, 1978, in Guarenas, a city on Venezuela's coast that has produced two other big leaguers, Ehire Adrianza and Giomar Guevara, though neither enjoyed as long a career as Rivera. Former minor leaguer Raúl Ortega scouted the tall, lanky outfielder and brokered a deal with the Yankees on April 12, 1996, a few weeks before Rivera graduated from high school. He was quickly assigned to the Yankees' Dominican Summer League affiliate, where he rubbed shoulders with his peers in 10 games (18 at-bats, three singles).[1] He enjoyed the comforts of home the next season, playing for the Maracay Number 2 club of the Venezuelan Summer League and flashing good speed (12 stolen bases) and plate discipline (16 strikeouts in 142 at-bats, with 12 walks for a .331 on-base percentage).[2]

The Yankees deemed Rivera ready for higher competition in 1998; he abused the Gulf Coast League, slugging .557 with good plate discipline (26 walks to 27 strikeouts) and was briefly promoted to the short-season New York-Penn League (5-for-18 in six games). He faced tougher competition the following year, playing in advanced Class A for the Florida State League Tampa Yankees (.725 OPS in 109 games), and appeared on his first major-league baseball card thanks to the 1999 Topps "Bowman" set, which often heralded "rookies" more than a year

away from reaching the majors. The front of cardboard #386 pictures Rivera exiting the batter's box after making contact, while the back reflected his odd arrangement: He "played two summers under contract to New York prior to making official professional debut."[3] The new century saw his OPS increase to .783 with Tampa and earn a promotion to the Double-A Norwich Navigators (.226 in 17 games). He increased his average to .320 in 2001 and triggered a promotion to Triple-A Columbus (.327 in 55 games), prompting the Yankees to call him up as rosters expanded.

Rivera made his major-league debut on September 4, 2001, as a defensive replacement for O'Neill. The Yankees, trailing the Toronto Blue Jays by nine runs, opted to give their veterans some rest for the stretch run; little did they, or the world, know that a scant week later the sport would experience its longest nonstrike stoppage due to the 9/11 attacks. Rivera picked up one at-bat, popping out to first base. Eighteen days later, on September 22, he again entered the game in place of a regular (Williams) and enjoyed one plate appearance, in which he lofted a fly ball to right field. In the pinstripers' next to last game of the regular season, he went hitless in two at-bats against Tampa Bay to finish the season 0-for-4. The Yankees opted not to add him to the postseason roster for any of their postseason series.

As the 2002 campaign began, Rivera was tabbed as the 67th best prospect by *Baseball America*.[4] He began the season with Columbus, where he produced a .325/.355/.502 line and New York called him up for a two-game cameo in early summer. On June 5, against Baltimore, he rapped his first major-league hit, a double off Travis Driskill, and also walked on six pitches against Orioles closer Jorge Julio. Two days later, against the Giants, he played the entire game but failed to reach base in three plate appearances. The Yankees recalled him on August 31 and he appeared regularly down the stretch, collecting his first home run against Tampa Bay on September 19 and finishing the season with a .265 average in 31 games. This time, New York added Rivera to the postseason roster and he played all but two innings of the division series against Anaheim. The favored Yankees could not stop the Angels, destined to win their first World Series; Rivera contributed three hits and two runs in what would become a familiar postseason setting.

Despite Rivera's limited time in the majors, *Baseball America* was still high on his potential, upping the ante by citing him as the 55th best prospect in the minors, and tops for the franchise as 2003 began.[5] While he did not break camp with the team, he returned to the Bronx on May 23 and contributed a .266/.304/.468 line over 185 plate appearances, including a six-game hitting streak and a two-home-run game on September

27. His power disappeared in October, as he had just one double among five hits in 10 games (four in the ALDS, two in the ALCS, and four in the World Series).

On December 13, 2003, the Yankees – outpitched in the World Series by the young Marlins –traded Rivera and fellow homegrown prospects Nick Johnson and Randy Choate for Expos right-hander Javier Vázquez. Although the Montréal franchise was expected to leave the city, it would play the 2004 season in Olympic Stadium and, for the second straight year, in Puerto Rico's Hiram Bithorn Stadium for selected series. (On September 29, 2004, Major League Baseball officially announced the franchise relocation, the first since the second iteration of the Washington Senators departed for Arlington, Texas, and became the Rangers before the 1972 campaign.)

Rivera played in 134 games in 2004 – his career-best until 2009 – patrolling all three outfield spots and as the designated hitter. While the 67-95 Expos did not give their fans much to cheer about, Rivera entered the record books by clubbing two home runs in one inning on June 19, with his blasts off White Sox pitcher Arnie Muñoz generating six runs.[6] As of the conclusion of the 2020 season, the feat had occurred only 63 times in major-league history, making it only one-sixth as frequent as a no-hitter.[7] He became the first Venezuelan-born player to accomplish the deed, although he has since been joined by Magglio Ordóñez and Pablo Sandoval. For the season, he hit .307 with an .829 OPS, generating two wins above replacement. His Canadian work visa did not need renewal, as the soon-to-be Nationals traded Rivera and Maicer Izturis to the Anaheim Angels for José Guillén.

Anaheim became the scene of Rivera's best memories. He spent six years with the team, reaching the 100-game mark in four of them. While the Angels did not return to the World Series, the remaining nucleus of the 2002 champions was still productive enough to reach the postseason in 2005, 2007, 2008, and 2009. In his first year with the franchise, Rivera played in 106 games, generating an OPS+ of 104. He was too aggressive on the bases, being caught stealing nine times while successfully pilfering only one bag. In the postseason he faced his old team, the Yankees, and contributed six hits and one walk in the five-game win by the now-renamed Los Angeles Angels of Anaheim. He played in three of the five Championship Series contests against the White Sox, who were en route to their first title since 1917.

While settled in the Angels outfield in 2006, Rivera reached career bests in batting average (.310), on-base-percentage (.362), and slugging average (.525). The club did not reach the postseason and Rivera returned to Venezuela to play winter ball. Sliding on December 22, he broke his left tibia, making 2007 a lost season.[8] The injury cost him all but 14 games (.737 OPS) and four plate appearances (one walk, one hit) during the Red Sox' sweep of the Angels in the 2007 Division Series.

Perhaps still suffering the lingering effects of the injury, Rivera did not raise his 2008 numbers to prior levels: In 89 games he had a .720 OPS, the lowest since his second Yankee campaign. He reached base four times in 11 plate appearances against the Red Sox in the Division Series, which the Angels lost in four games. His best season came in 2009, as he reached his zenith of games played (138), plate appearances (572), hits (152), home runs (25), runs (72), and runs batted in (88) with an .810 OPS. The ghosts of playoff pasts came revisited, as the Angels again faced the Red Sox (Division Series) and the Yankees (Championship Series). Covering left field, Rivera had 36 plate appearances and reached base in eight of them.

Rivera's 2010 numbers took a backward step; he played in 124 games and slashed .252/.312/.409; the Angels did not reach the postseason. The club traded him to Toronto with Mike Napoli on January 21, 2011, for Vernon Wells, whose seven-year, $126 million contract had become a massive albatross for the Blue Jays.

With a 70-game sojourn in Toronto, Rivera became one of 56 players to suit up for both Canadian teams. Although the Expos had by now spent several years in Washington, some of the franchise's prior players were still active in the major leagues.[9] Curiously, many Venezuelans abound in the short list (Raúl Chavez, Omar Daal, Darwin Cubillan, Izturis, Fred

Rivera played 12 seasons in the majors and topped 20 home runs twice. He started his big-league career with the Yankees and Expos. (Rick Stewart / Getty Images Sports)

Manrique, Robert Pérez). Perhaps due to the change of scenery, Rivera struggled at the plate, with his slugging dropping to a career-low .360. The Blue Jays sold his contract to the Los Angeles Dodgers on July 12, 2011. The move energized him, as he slugged the first pitch from the Arizona Diamondbacks' Joe Saunders to deep left field for a debut home run. Playing left field, right field, and first base for the rest of the season, Rivera hit a collective .258/.319/.382 and re-signed with the Dodgers on November 3, 2011.

Rivera suffered an injury on May 8, 2012 and spent almost four weeks on the disabled list, impacting his timing at the plate. Returning on June 4, he was inserted into the starting lineup and continued to cover left field, right field, and first base as the lineup needs demanded. Like many players whose careers did not reach their full promise, Rivera did not expect his October 3, 2012, at-bat to be his last.[10] The Dodgers and Giants played a Wednesday afternoon game in front of 34,014 at Dodger Stadium. Los Angeles was nine games behind its archrivals, who would win a second World Series in three years. Clayton Kershaw tossed eight masterful frames for this 14th victory and manager Don Mattingly lifted his starting first baseman, Adrián González, at the start of the eighth, slotting Rivera in his place. Kershaw, ever efficient, did not give the veteran a chance to field (two strikeouts and a fly out put away San Francisco) and neither did Kenley Jansen, who retired the side on identical methods (a fly ball and two strikeouts). Rivera, however, took two balls on the bottom of the eighth against Jean Machi before smashing the third offering to deep center field for a two-run blast.

A possible reunion loomed, as the Yankees invited Rivera to 2013 spring training, but he did not make the team and was released. Arizona inked Rivera to a minor-league deal on April 30, 2013, and he was assigned to Triple-A Reno. In 96 games as the Aces' left fielder, he collected 109 hits but his power numbers (17 doubles, 10 home runs) were uninspiring and the Diamondbacks did not call him back to the majors. Only 34 years old, Rivera expected to have more opportunities during the offseason, but they did not materialize.

Beyond his playing time in North America, Rivera also played 13 seasons in the Venezuela winter league, slashing .305/.328/.474 in 395 games with the Tigres of Aragua, the Caribes of Anzoátegui, and the Navegantes of Magallanes.[11] He won a Venezuelan League Gold Glove award in 2001-2002 and appeared in 110 additional postseason contests, increasing his output to .312/.330/.520.[12] In three instances his club won the circuit's title (Aragua in 2003-2004, Magallanes in 2012-2013 and 2013-2014) with the last final series being a veritable showcase of his talents (1.177 OPS in five games).[13]

Rivera wore his country's colors on the international stage on two occasions. Nearing his prime in 2006, he was chosen as the nation's starting left fielder in the 2006 World Baseball Classic. In five games, he had 13 at-bats and two singles; he scored three runs for the team before it was eliminated in the second round.[14]

While the WBC garnered the attention, a second international tournament provided professional players a chance to provide their mettle on the global stage. The 2012 World Baseball Softball Confederation Premier12 was hosted by Taiwan and Japan. Venezuela faced a tough draw in Group B alongside Japan, the United States, and eventual champion South Korea; its 2-3 record tied with Mexico but the latter owned the tiebreaker given its 6-4 win over Venezuela. Rivera was eager to join the team, noting that "this is an opportunity to wear the country's uniform for the second time and that obligates me to work even harder, to ensure the name of Venezuela stands tall."[15] However, he struggled at the plate, hitting 4-for-18 and drawing three walks.[16]

Rivera's career is riddled with what-ifs. Had the Yankees provided him regular playing time, he could have blossomed into a valuable piece of their puzzle, much as Brett Gardner did in the 2010s. His leg injury cost him not only most of the 2007 campaign, but also the chance to prove that his 2006 breakthrough season was not a fluke. He particularly enjoyed hitting against Eric Milton (4-for-10, 1.500 OPS), Kenny Rogers (7-for-12, 1.500 OPS), Mark Buerhle (three home runs), Cliff Lee (four homers), and Jarrod Washburn (three homers), while he could not figure out Roy Halladay (0-for-14), Justin Verlander (0-for-13, one walk), and Jamie Moyer (2-for-18).[17] Among Venezuelans through the conclusion of the 2020 season, he was number 38th in career games (1,058), 41st in runs (425), 35th in hits (950), and 19th in home runs (132) in the major leagues.

SOURCES

In addition to the sources cited in the Notes, the author relied extensively on Baseball-Reference.com.

NOTES

1   Dominican Summer League Statistics, https://www.baseballamerica.com/players/24534/juan-rivera/.

2   Venezuelan Winter League Statistics, https://www.baseballamerica.com/players/24534/juan-rivera/.

3   Juan Rivera Baseball Cards, https://www.tradingcarddb.com/ViewCard.cfm?sid=1300/cid/225396/1999-Bowman-386-Juan-Rivera.

4   Baseball America 2002 Prospects by Organization, http://www.thebaseballcube.com/prospects/years/byYear.asp?Y=2002&Src=BA.

5   Baseball America 2003 Prospects by Organization, http://www.thebaseballcube.com/prospects/years/byYear.asp?Y=2003&Src=BA.

6   Montréal Expos vs. Chicago White Sox, June 19, 2004, box score, https://www.retrosheet.org/boxesetc/2004/B06190MON2004.htm.

7   Ed Eagle, "Players with Two Home Runs in an Inning," MLB.com, April 9, 2019. https://www.mlb.com/news/two-home-runs-in-an-inning-c266221190.

8   Associated Press, "Angels' Rivera Breaks Leg in Winter Game," ESPN.com, December 22, 2006, http://www.espn.com/espn/wire?-section=mlb&id=2706891.

9   Multi-franchise players: Montréal Expos and Toronto Blue Jays, https://www.baseball-reference.com/friv/multifranchise.cgi?level=team&t1=TOR-TOR&t2=MON-WSN&t3=--&t4=--.

10 Los Angeles Dodgers vs. San Francisco Giants, October 2, 2012, box score, https://www.baseball-reference.com/boxes/LAN/LAN201210030.shtml.

11 Juan Rivera Venezuelan League Statistics, http://pelotabinaria.com.ve/beisbol/mostrar.php?ID=rivejua001.

12 Juan Rivera Venezuelan League Statistics.

13 Juan Rivera Venezuelan League Statistics.

14 World Baseball Classic 2006 Statistics, https://www.worldbaseballclassic.com/stats/. Box scores accessed on March 2, 2021, via archive.org/web.

15 "Rivera y Nieve se Unieron al Equipo Criollo del Premier," Meridiano.com, https://meridiano.net/beisbol/beisbol-venezolano/113102/especialistas.html

16 World Baseball Softball Confederation (WSBC) Premier2012 Statistics, https://premier12.wbsc.org/en/2015/stats/general/team/VEN.

17 Selected Batter-Pitcher Matchups for Juan Rivera, Retrosheet.org, https://www.retrosheet.org/boxesetc/R/MU0_rivejo01.htm.

FRANCISCO RODRÍGUEZ

BY ANDY STURGILL

On Wednesday, September 18, 2002, the Anaheim Angels[1] and Oakland Athletics faced off in the third game of a four-game set in Oakland. The two teams were locked in a tight battle for supremacy in the American League West Division as the season reached its final weeks. The A's won this game, 7-4, to pull into a tie with the Angels for first place with identical 95-57 records. Oakland won again the next day to pull into first place for good, ultimately winning the division by four games over the 99-63 Angels. The Angels' record was good enough to capture the American League's lone wild-card berth.

While the game on September 18 marked the last time the A's trailed the Angels in the division race, it was perhaps most notable for a seemingly minor event that took place in the bottom of the eighth inning. Making his major-league debut, 20-year-old Francisco Rodríguez entered the game to pitch the inning for Anaheim, facing four batters, allowing one hit, and striking out two in 16 pitches.

The lanky right-hander appeared in only four more games over the remainder of the regular season, but opened some eyes by not allowing a run and striking out 13 in just 5⅔ innings. Unexpectedly added to the Angels' postseason roster, Rodríguez announced himself with authority to the baseball world with a dominating run through the 2002 playoffs, amassing a 5-1 record with 28 strikeouts in 18⅔ innings in 11 appearances as the lockdown set-up man for closer Troy Percival. The Angels captured their first World Series title, winning in seven games over the San Francisco Giants. A pitching star was born.

That star went on to become one of the most dominant, consistent, and reliable relief pitchers in baseball for the next 15 years, along the way making six All-Star teams and leaving the game with the majors' fourth-most career saves.

Francisco Jose Rodríguez was born on January 7, 1982 in Caracas, Venezuela, the capital city of the South American country, and grew up in Maracao, a parish about 25 kilometers southwest of Caracas. Just a few months after his birth, his parents, Francisco Rodríguez and Isabel Mayorca, split up and turned him over to his paternal grandparents, Juan and Isabel Rodríguez, to raise him. His father lived with him and his grandparents intermittently in his first few years, but moved out for good when the younger Francisco was 4 years old. His mother also lived in Maracao while Rodríguez was growing up, but was distinctly uninterested in her son. When he attempted to visit her, she turned him away quickly. "When you're seven or eight years old, you want to see your mom," he said. "I still ask myself, Why? Why wasn't she there, even for 10 minutes?"[2] Rodríguez has 13 "siblings" – six via his father, four from his mother. Three uncles that he grew up with he calls brothers.[3]

Rodríguez spent his formative years living in a two-bedroom apartment with those paternal grandparents, whom he called Mom and Dad; the apartment frequently served as home for various other family members. "We were poor," Rodríguez recalled in 2002. "I never had new shoes or new T-shirts. But we were all together."[4] Growing up on the streets of Maracao, Rodríguez acquired the nickname Nene Fran (Baby Fran), a name that continued to resonate in the area even after his star turn in the major leagues.[5]

Rodríguez often tagged along to baseball games played by his uncles, imitating the action on the field. A stranger approached his grandmother and suggested that she enroll him in a baseball school. The stranger, Graciano Ravelo, operated one such school, and accepted the seven-year-old to the academy. The Graciano Ravelo Baseball School was a ramshackle operation founded by Ravelo, a scout for the Texas Rangers, in the 1970s to help develop baseball talent and also help keep kids in Caracas out of trouble. The school was over an hour away from Maracao via public transportation; since Rodríguez couldn't afford the small monthly fee, Ravelo waived it.[6]

When he was 15 years old, Rodríguez was a well-known shortstop and pitcher. He was only 5-feet-8 and 155 pounds, but his fastball was still regularly recorded above 90 mph. In 1998 Ravelo attempted to sign Rodríguez for the Rangers for a bonus of $120,000, but Rodríguez decided to wait before committing to a professional team. After a strong showing while pitching for the Venezuelan national team in a youth tournament, he was showered up with offers from several clubs that dwarfed the $120,000 the Rangers had put on the table. In September 1998 the Anaheim Angels signed the 16-year-old Rodríguez to a contract with a $900,000 signing bonus, the largest the franchise had ever given to an international prospect at that time. The bonus money allowed him and his family to leave the crowded two-bedroom apartment in Maracao for a four-bedroom apartment in the more affluent La Urbina section, east of Caracas. It also allowed Rodríguez to purchase a 1998 Ford Explorer – one with an Angels decal on the windshield to uniquely identify its owner.

Rodríguez reported to the Angels camp in Arizona in the spring of 1999 for his first professional season but returned home in April to be with his ailing grandfather. He was slated to travel back to the United States on April 25, and before leaving was given a word of instruction by his grandfather.

"Don't come back here if something happens to me," Juan Francisco told his grandson. "You stay there and show them you can play baseball."[7] Juan Francisco died within minutes of Francisco's flight leaving for Arizona.

As a 17-year-old new to professional baseball and the United States, Rodríguez split his season between 12 appearances with the Butte Copper Kings of the Rookie Pioneer League and one appearance with the Low-A Boise Hawks of the Northwest League. He made 10 starts in his 13 games, going a combined 2-1 with a 3.49 ERA and 75 strikeouts in 56⅔ innings pitched. In the 2000 season, still just 18 years old, Rodríguez advanced to the Lake Elsinore Storm of the High-A California League. Still working primarily as a starter, Rodríguez posted a 2.81 ERA and again struck out well over a batter per inning (79 strikeouts in 64 innings pitched). The combined performances and raw stuff displayed before turning 19 years old led *Baseball America* to rank Rodríguez the minor leagues' number-71 prospect before the 2001 season.[8] A 2001 season that saw Rodríguez struggle to a 5.38 ERA as a starter at High-A Rancho Cucamonga set the stage for the whirlwind of 2002.

While working as a starting pitcher during his first three seasons in professional baseball, Rodríguez often experienced elbow and shoulder tendinitis that would cause pain on the days after he pitched and limited his progress and on-field performance. His focus and concentration also seemed to wander while he pitched only about once a week. In the winter between the 2001 and 2002 seasons, the Angels organization decided to give Rodríguez a try as a reliever.

The move worked. After three seasons of performances that ranged between all right and pretty good, Rodríguez became dominant out of the bullpen. He began 2002 at Arkansas of the Double-A Texas League, and overwhelmed the competition. He posted a 1.96 ERA, and his previously strong 3-to-1 strikeout-to-walk ratio grew to 4-to-1, all while his hits allowed per nine innings dropped from 10.1 at Rancho Cucamonga in 2001 to 6.7 in 2002. By mid-June Rodríguez had accomplished all that there was to do at Double A and was promoted to Triple-A Salt Lake City. His performance at Triple A was nearly identical to what he had done at Arkansas, and when the Salt Lake season ended in early September Rodríguez was called up to the Angels.

After a few weeks of inactivity, Rodríguez made his major-league debut in that September 18 game at Oakland. Four months shy of his 21st birthday, he did not appear in another minor-league game until more than a decade later. He pitched in four more games before the end of the regular season and didn't allow a run while striking out 13 and allowing three hits in 5⅔ innings. Along the way he tied Nolan Ryan's Angels record by striking out eight consecutive hitters, a streak that covered his first four career major-league appearances and was snapped by an intentional walk.

On the last day of the regular season, Angels manager Mike Scioscia summoned Rodríguez into his office and gave him the surprising news that he would be a part of Anaheim's playoff roster. "We liked his composure, his mound presence, his stuff," said Bud Black, the Angels pitching coach. "We started to say, 'Hey, this guy can have an impact.'"[9]

Rodríguez's inclusion on the Angels playoff roster was a source of some controversy and deep examination of the eso-

terica of roster rules. Major-league rules at the time required a postseason-eligible player to be on a team's active 25-man major-league roster before September 1.[10] Rodríguez was called up on September 15, two weeks after the cutoff. However, the eligibility rules did allow for injury replacements, Angels pitcher Steve Green had Tommy John surgery the previous offseason and was on the disabled list all season. When it came time to compile their list of 25 eligible players for the playoffs, the Angels replaced Green with Rodríguez. It was perhaps not in line with the spirit of the rules, but was clearly within the letter of the rules, so Rodríguez was in.[11]

Playoff baseball did not start off well for either the Angels or Rodríguez. They led the New York Yankees 5-4 in the eighth inning of Game One at Yankee Stadium, only to see three relievers (Ben Weber, Scott Schoenweis, and Brendan Donnelly) give up four runs in the bottom half of the inning on the way to an 8-4 loss. The next night Rodríguez entered the postseason cauldron in the sixth inning with the Angels up 4-3. He had two outs with a runner on first and then got ahead of Yankee leadoff hitter Alfonso Soriano 0-and-2. Soriano crushed the next pitch over the left-field fence to put the Yankees up 5-4.

Expecting to be removed from the game after giving up the lead, Rodríguez instead responded to Scioscia's confidence in him by returning to the mound for the seventh inning and breezing through the Yankees' Jason Giambi, Bernie Williams, and Robin Ventura in only 11 pitches. The Angels scored three in the eighth and another in the ninth while the bullpen this time held the line and the Angels evened the series at a game apiece with an 8-6 victory.

From that moment forward, Rodríguez was nearly untouchable in the postseason. The Angels played 16 games in defeating the Yankees, Minnesota Twins, and San Francisco Giants and capturing their first World Series title. Rodríguez pitched in 11 of the games, throwing 18⅔ innings with a 1.93 ERA, allowing only 10 hits and striking out 28 of the 70 batters he faced. On a team with decent starting pitching and a deep and effective bullpen, Rodríguez found himself responsible for locking down the crucial seventh and eighth innings ahead of closer Troy Percival. Rodríguez's dominant performance in the role evoked memories of young Mariano Rivera's work setting up John Wetteland as the Yankees captured the World Series crown in 1996. His dominance and strikeout-rich appearances led to him being dubbed "K-Rod," a takeoff on the nickname of Texas Rangers star Álex Rodríguez and using the baseball shorthand for strikeout in place of a first initial. "Sometimes I have to pinch myself to see if this is real," Rodríguez said during the playoff run. "Am I really in the playoffs? Am I really pitching almost every day? I pinch myself and it hurts, so, yes, this is real."[12]

Dominating the best hitters on the major leagues' biggest stage could have been attributed in part to Rodríguez's newness, and the hitters not having seen him previously. But it was his raw pitching stuff that was most responsible for his success and the Angels' confidence in him. "He has an easy, smooth but powerful delivery," Angels pitching coach Bud Black said. "The fastball comes out of his hand with so much life, and there's such tremendous snap to his slider that it's a wipeout pitch."[13]

When it was all said and done, Rodríguez became the first pitcher to earn his first major-league win in postseason play and the youngest to win a World Series game, and he tied Randy Johnson's record of five wins in a single postseason set just the year before.[14] His postseason success catapulted him to fame in Venezuela. Upon his return to the country after the triumph over the Giants in the World Series, he found hundreds of fans and a swarm of photographers waiting for him at the airport. His Venezuelan winter league manager declared, "He's a bigger name than the president (Hugo Chávez) right now."[15]

Despite his postseason heroics and ascent to the top of the baseball world, Rodríguez entered the 2003 season still officially a rookie. On the eve of the 2003 season, he said, "I look forward to trying to prove I can do this season what I did then. I don't feel like a rookie; I don't feel like a veteran, I feel like a player."[16] *The Sporting News* reported that "at least one general manager, and some scouts, have quietly wondered if Rodríguez is strong enough to avoid arm problems, given his maximum-effort delivery and a tendency to throw across his body."[17]

The start of the 2003 season did not serve as a continuation of the 2002 playoffs for Rodríguez. He allowed earned runs in three of his first four outings, and his ERA rested over 5.11 at the end of action on May 25, the result of a very mediocre 22 appearances. However, from that point forward, Rodríguez posted a 2.20 ERA over his final 42 games, cementing his role as the primary setup man for Percival. Finishing the 2003 season with a 3.03 ERA and more strikeouts (95) and fewer hits allowed (50) than innings pitched (86), K-Rod proved that he was no flash in the pan.

As good as Rodríguez was in 2003, he was markedly better in 2004. Entering the season as an established player with no questions about whether he could contribute for a full season, Rodríguez lowered his ERA more than a full run to 1.82 and increased his strikeout total by 28 in nearly the same number of innings as in 2003. Used in the closer's role around Percival's injuries, he also recorded 12 saves. Rodríguez was selected to his first All-Star Game, in which Yankees manager Joe Torre used him to get the final two outs of the eighth inning to set up Mariano Rivera for the ninth. At the end of the season, Rodríguez finished tied for fourth in the American League Cy Young Award voting. (The winner was the Minnesota Twins' Johan Santana.) The Angels returned to the playoffs but were swept by the Boston Red Sox in the American League Division Series.

After the 2004 season, with Rodríguez fully entrenched as a dominant late-inning presence and Troy Percival 35 years old and dealing with chronic injuries, the Angels were content to allow Percival to leave for the Detroit Tigers via free agency and move Rodríguez into the closer's role. Thus began one of the most prolific four-year runs of any major-league relief pitcher.

From the time he ascended to the Angels closer role in 2005 until he left the team after the 2008 season, Rodríguez averaged 69 appearances, 60 games finished, and 48 saves per season, all while striking out nearly a third of the batters he faced. He made two more All-Star teams and had two more top-four finishes in the Cy Young Award balloting.

The crown jewel of Rodríguez's run as the Angels closer was in 2008, when he set a single-season record with 62 saves, besting the previous mark of 57 established by Bobby Thigpen of the Chicago White Sox in 1990. The combination of Rodríguez's durability, effectiveness, and the Angels team winning 100 games with a much narrower than expected run differential meant that Rodríguez had no shortage of close games to try to nail down. During this stretch the Angels averaged 94.5 wins per season and made the playoffs three times, but were unable to return to the World Series.

As Rodríguez had worked his way into the upper echelon of major-league relief pitchers, he also had developed a reputation as a fiery and demonstrative figure on the mound. "He's a melange of pirouettes, fist pumps, and primordial screams," a sportswriter observed in 2008. "Francisco Rodríguez is perhaps the most demonstrative pitcher in the majors, punctuating his strikeouts and saves with clenched fists and roars."[18] In an environment as staid and traditional as baseball, not everyone loved Rodríguez's showiness. In 2009, Yankees reliever Brian Bruney referred to his celebrations as a "tired act,"[19] a comment that led to a brief media war of words between the two and an on-field confrontation during batting practice before a game.

After the 2008 season, Rodríguez hit the free-agent market at the height of his powers. He was coming off a historic season and was just shy of his 27th birthday, younger than most players who reach free agency. He parlayed his situation into a three-year, $37 million contract with the New York Mets, a team coming off back-to-back late-season meltdowns due in large part to a faulty bullpen. After wearing jersey number 57 throughout his

Rodríguez burst onto the scene in the 2002 playoffs at age 20. He finished with 437 saves — fourth most in major-league history. (Brian Bahr / Getty Images Sports)

Angels tenure, he reversed the digits and took number 75 with the Mets, as multi-Cy Young Award-winning pitcher and fellow Venezuelan Johan Santana had taken the number 57 when he joined the team a year earlier.

Despite the high hopes and high expectations, the deal never worked out for either side. After averaging more than 90 wins for the three seasons before Rodríguez arrived, the Mets never reached the 80-win mark in the three seasons Rodríguez spent with them. Rodríguez pitched well but was not the same dominant force he had been in Anaheim. His highest save total with the Mets was 35, and his strikeout numbers declined even as his ERA increased. As the team struggled, employing a high-priced closer was especially unpleasant for the Mets, a franchise whose finances were destroyed not long after they signed Rodríguez following the revelations of the team's exposure to losses in financier Bernie Madoff's fraud.[20]

Perhaps an appropriate symbol of Rodríguez's time with the Mets was a game at Yankee Stadium against the Mets crosstown rivals on June 12, 2009. The Mets led the Yankees 8-7 heading to the bottom of the ninth and Rodríguez was summoned from the bullpen to close the game out. The Mets were 31-27 and were four games behind the defending World Series champion Philadelphia Phillies. This was a game a big-money closer has to finish off for his new team. Rodríguez retired Brett Gardner for the first out before allowing a single to Derek Jeter. He then struck out Johnny Damon on a 3-and-2 pitch for the second out, as Jeter stole second base. The Mets intentionally walked Mark Teixeira, putting the potential winning run on base to face Alex Rodríguez, struggling in his return from offseason hip surgery that caused him to miss the first month of the season. Pitcher Rodríguez fell behind in the count, 3-and-1, but appeared to get out of trouble when A-Rod popped the pitch up behind Mets second baseman Luis Castillo. Castillo, who had won two Gold Gloves with the Florida Marlins, had the ball lined up for the game-ending catch. He dropped it. Jeter easily scored the tying run and Teixeira, running hard from first base, followed with the game-winning run. Francisco Rodríguez stood with both hands on his head, stunned at what he had just witnessed. From the moment Castillo dropped the popup to the end of the season, the Mets went 39-64, while the Yankees went on to win the World Series. The game was Rodríguez's first blown save with the Mets.

Worse than any individual struggle or team performance during his time in New York were some of the nonbaseball headlines Rodríguez made. In August of 2010 he was arrested after he assaulted his girlfriend's father following a game at Citi Field. The Mets suspended him for two games, but during the incident he suffered a torn ligament in the thumb on his pitching hand that required season-ending surgery. A few months later, Rodríguez was back in court for violating a protective order by sending dozens of text messages to his girlfriend, also the mother of two of his children. He pleaded guilty to attempted assault and disorderly conduct and was sentenced to a year of anger-management counseling.

In 2011, with the Mets out of the playoff race in mid-July Rodríguez was traded to the Milwaukee Brewers for two players to be named later. Milwaukee desperately needed bullpen help ahead of closer John Axford, and Rodríguez pitched to a 1.86 ERA in 31 appearances as Milwaukee captured the National League Central Division crown. Rodríguez returned to the postseason for the first time since his last season with the Angels in 2008. He allowed one run in five innings over five appearances, helping the Brewers defeat the Arizona Diamondbacks in the National League Division Series before falling to the eventual World Series champion St. Louis Cardinals in the National League Championship Series.

A free agent again, Rodríguez re-signed with the Brewers for 2012, posting a 4.38 ERA in 78 games, again setting up for Axford. This was the first of four consecutive seasons (2012-2015) that Rodríguez re-signed with Milwaukee on one-year deals, an arrangement interrupted only by a deadline trade to the Baltimore Orioles in 2013. He regained his old closer's role for the Brewers in 2014 and '15, posting 44 and 38 saves respectively and earning a selection to the National League All-Star team in both seasons.

In September 2012 while with the Brewers, Rodríguez was arrested in Wisconsin on suspicion of domestic violence, this time for allegedly striking his 23-year-old girlfriend, the mother of one of his children, at their shared home. After the alleged victim and a member of the household staff who witnessed the incident returned to Venezuela without cooperating with the prosecutor, the charges were dropped in late November. In addition to the three children with the two women connected to his arrests, Rodríguez had at least three children with two women prior to his 2002 major-league debut, with two living in Phoenix and one in his hometown in Venezuela.[21]

Rodríguez's run with the Brewers finally came to an end in the offseason between 2015 and 2016 when he was traded to the Detroit Tigers. He produced a solid 2016 season before an abysmal first half in 2017 in which he posted a 7.82 ERA. At 35 years old with declining strikeout ability, the Tigers released Rodríguez in late June, ending his major-league career. He was quickly signed and released by the Washington Nationals in the summer of 2017 and went to camp with the Philadelphia Phillies in the spring of 2018 but was released a week before the season began.

Hoping to continue his career, Rodríguez spent the 2018 season with the Long Island Ducks of the independent Atlantic League and 2019 with the Aceros de Monclova of the Mexican League. He pitched well enough while playing alongside a number of other former major leaguers hoping for one more bite at the big-league apple, but not well enough for a big-league team to sign him.

At the height of the COVID-19 pandemic in the spring of 2020, Rodríguez told a Venezuelan journalist that he hoped to make a comeback to the major leagues that year at age 38. Despite his pitching background and the fluid and expanded rosters during 2020's disjointed season, no team signed Rodríguez and his career was effectively over.

Rodríguez left the major leagues with a 52-53 record, 10.5 strikeouts per nine innings, and a 2.86 ERA in 948 games, all in relief. His 437 saves are fourth on the all-time list, behind only Mariano Rivera, Trevor Hoffman, and Lee Smith, all Hall of Famers.

After 16 seasons in the major leagues, Rodríguez appeared on the Hall of Fame ballot for the first time in 2023. He earned 10.8 percent of the vote in his first year of eligibility, enough to remain on the ballot but far short of the 75 percent needed for election, and indeed even far short of Lee Smith's lowest percentage of the vote (29.9 percent). While Rodríguez did pitch about 300 fewer career innings than Smith, he put up better marks in ERA, ERA+, WHIP (walks plus hits per inning pitched), strikeouts per nine innings, strikeout-to-walk ratio, and hits allowed per nine innings. He also far outshines Smith in the postseason, where Smith had an ERA over 8.00 in only four games.

Ultimately, Rodríguez will be remembered for the highs with the Angels in the 2002 postseason and his magical 2008 campaign, and conversely for all the ways his promise turned sour on and off the field after he left Anaheim. He's hardly the only major-league baseball player with a complicated story.

NOTES

1   The franchise was known as the Anaheim Angels from 1997 to 2004, the Los Angeles Angels from 2005 to 2015, and adopted the current Los Angeles Angels moniker beginning with the 2016 season.

2   Stephen Cannella, "Bienvenido, Nene Fran," *Sports Illustrated*, November 18, 2002: 60-63.

3   T. Christian Miller, "His Rise Has Been as Fast as His Fastball," *Los Angeles Times*, October 22, 2002. https://www.latimes.com/archives/la-xpm-2002-oct-22-me-rodriguez22-story.html. Accessed December 4, 2023.

4   Cannella.

5   Cannella.

6   Different 2002 sources list the fee differently, either $3 or $7 per month. In any event, the fee was small, and Ravelo waived it because Rodríguez couldn't afford to pay it. Different sources also describe the journey to the Ravelo academy differently, from a 60-minute bus ride to a 90-minute train ride. The point here is that the academy was not easy for Rodríguez to get to.

7   Cannella, "Bienvenido, Nene Fran."

8   At 71, Rodríguez was ranked just ahead of Carl Crawford. Josh Hamilton and Josh Beckett were ranked number 1 and number 3, respectively.

9   Cannella.

10   As of the 2023 playoffs, to be eligible for inclusion on a postseason roster a player only had to be with an organization by September 1 of that year, not necessarily on the active major-league roster. Rosters had also expanded to 26 players.

11   Rob Neyer, "K-Rod Is Great, But He Really Shouldn't Be Here," ESPN.com, https://www.espn.com/mlb/columns/story?columnist=neyer_rob&id=1449436. Accessed 12/4/2023.

12   Miller, "His Rise Has Been as Fast as His Fastball."

13   Miller.

14   In the 2023 postseason, Nathan Eovaldi also won five games.

15   Cannella, "Bienvenido, Nene Fran."

16   Stan McNeal, "Starting Over at the Top," *The Sporting News*, March 31, 2003: 25.

17   McNeal.

18   Matt Hurst, "Angels' Rodríguez Remains Unapologetic, Defiant," *Riverside* (California) *Press-Enterprise*, June 6, 2008. https://www.seattlepi.com/sports/baseball/article/angels-rodriguez-remains-unapologetic-defiant-1275852.php. Accessed December 4, 2023.

19   Harold Friend, "Brian Bruney Blasts Francisco Rodríguez," BleacherReport.com, https://bleacherreport.com/articles/198987/brian-bruney-blasts-francisco-Rodríguez. Accessed December 4, 2023.

20   In 2009 Madoff was convicted of defrauding investors of billions of dollars (prosecutors estimated $65 billion) and was sentenced to 150 years in federal prison. Nicholas Reimann, "Bernie Madoff Dies in Federal Prison at 82." Forbes.com, https://www.forbes.com/sites/nicholasreimann/2021/04/14/bernie-madoff-dies-in-federal-prison-at-82/?sh=3c2712823fad. Accessed January 11, 2024.

21   Cannella, "Bienvenido, Nene Fran."

LUIS SALAZAR

BY JUSTIN KRUEGER

"I never have fear of the ball."[1] It's a sentiment that Luis Salazar has been known to iterate about his love of baseball and it's also a good way to sum up his playing career. He was willing and had the skill to take the field as needed. In his 13 years as a major-league utilityman he manned nine positions (including designated hitter), lacking only time as a catcher. In the minor leagues he played every position except pitcher.

Over time Salazar's versatility as a platoon fielder would prove invaluable; as was his throwing arm. Together they allowed him a 13-year career in major-league baseball. He spent the first five years with the San Diego Padres (1980-1984) before being traded to the Chicago White Sox, where he spent two years (1985-1986). This was followed by a second stint with the Padres (1987). Salazar then signed as a free agent and played a year for the Detroit Tigers (1988). He returned for yet a third stint with the Padres, which lasted three-quarters of a season (1989) before he was traded to the Chicago Cubs at the trade deadline. He played with the Cubs the remainder of his career (1989-1992).

Luis Ernesto Salazar Garcia was born on May 19, 1956, in Barcelona, Venezuela. He grew up in Lecheria, a coastal city 200 miles east of Caracas, the nation's capital. As a boy he would often come home from school and immediately head out to play baseball. He recalled, "My family would be looking for me … and I'd be down the block playing street ball with the other kids."[2] It was a common occurrence. Eventually scouts began to notice him. He was originally signed by the Kansas City Royals as an amateur free agent on November 29, 1973, at age 17. At 5-feet-9 and 180 pounds he was not a physically imposing presence. It was his fielding and arm that grabbed the attention of scouts. His hitting was more hit-or-miss.

The Royals sent the 18-year-old Salazar to the rookie-ball Gulf Coast League Royals for the 1974 season. He played two games before heading home. He was homesick and did not speak English.[3] The Royals released him. Back in Venezuela, Salazar played winter ball at the behest of a coach who felt he might have the ability to make a career out of baseball if he kept at it.[4] Salazar eventually signed with the Pittsburgh Pirates in November 1975. He began the 1976 season in Low Class A with the Niagara Falls Pirates of the New York-Pennsylvania League. In 42 games he batted .238 with one home run and 17 RBIs. It was not a particularly sterling start to a professional career. The next two seasons were spent with the Salem Pirates of the Advanced Class-A Carolina League. Over the two seasons, Salazar batted .270 and .292, with 14 home runs, 37 doubles, and 9 triples. Showing decent speed, he swiped 22 bases on 29 attempts in 1978.

In 1979 Salazar was promoted to Double A, the Buffalo Bisons of the Eastern League. Starting the season as an extra outfielder, he became part of the starting lineup when left fielder Larry Littleton was called up to the Triple-A Portland Beavers. Salazar became an everyday outfielder for the Bisons and had his best offensive season in professional baseball, batting .323 with 27 home runs, 86 RBIs, and a .515 slugging percentage, the only time in his career he had a slugging average over .500 (and, with 119 strikeouts the only time he had more than 100 whiffs in a season). His offensive surge that season was in stark contrast to his previous year, when he hit only three home runs with 49 RBIs. Explaining the change, Salazar said, "[In] the past, I always tried to pull the ball and hit home runs. Now I've learned to hit to right."[5] It also did not hurt that he played in the friendly offensive confines of War Memorial Park, known unlovingly as "The Rockpile" for its dilapidated look.[6] Reflecting on Salazar's approach at the plate, Bisons manager Steve Demeter commented, "Luis is not a picture-book hitter. He will look terrible on one swing and then hit the next pitch out of the park."[7] Preston Gómez, a former major-league manager, offered a similar observation while scouting at the Caribbean Series in February 1985. He said of Salazar that he "swings at too many bad pitches. I'd like to see him be more selective. I think he swings too hard. He should realize he's not a home run hitter."[8]

After his breakout season with Buffalo, Salazar was promoted to the Triple-A Portland Beavers (Pacific Coast League) for 1980. On August 4 of that season he was traded, along with teammate Rick Lancellotti, to the San Diego Padres for Kurt Bevacqua and a player to be named later (Mark Lee). The trade was made as Portland was hosting Hawaii, the Padres' Triple-A affiliate. Salazar merely walked to the other clubhouse and suited up for his new team, the Islanders. The next day, August 5, he delivered a two-out single in the 12th inning that put the Islanders up 7-6 and secured their victory. After spending some time with the Islanders, Salazar was called up by the Padres.

Salazar, 24 years old, made his major-league debut on August 15 at San Diego Stadium with the Padres hosting the Houston Astros. He ran for Broderick Perkins in the eighth inning of a 20-inning, 6-hour and 17-minute marathon that the Astros won, 3-1.

During that season, playing in 44 games for the Padres, Salazar made a good first impression by batting .337 in 169 at-bats with 7 triples (a career high), 25 RBIs, and a career-high .372 on-base percentage. His speed was on display again as he stole 11 bases in 13 attempts.

Over the next 12 seasons, Salazar put together a solid, if unspectacular, journeyman career. He was never named to an All-Star team, but often received the praise of those he played with or under. Padres general manager Jack "Trader Jack" McKeon traded for him three times. To which McKeon said, "that's a compliment to a player … when you keep getting them back."[9] Tony La Russa, Salazar's manager on the White Sox, said, "He's just a good-natured, good-hearted man who has a way of bringing people together."[10] Salazar was no offensive juggernaut, nor did he ever win a Gold Glove. But he was a valuable piece; a tradeable commodity for his versatility in the field, and a good guy to have in the clubhouse.

Flexibility in the field was Salazar's calling-card. He was a super utility-player. Nearly two-thirds of his time on the field (863 games) was spent playing third base. He also played over 100 games at left field, shortstop, and center field. For his career he accumulated a .956 fielding percentage. In 1982, his first season as the starting third baseman for the Padres, he had a career-high 29 errors. It was also a season in which he tied Mike Schmidt in leading National League third basemen by turning 28 double plays.

Eight seasons in Salazar's career he played in over 100 games. His season high for games played was 145 in 1982. That year he also set season highs with 127 hits and 62 RBIs. (He matched the RBI figure in 1988 while with the Tigers.) In three other seasons Salazar had hits in the 120s (121 in 1981 and 124 in 1983 with the Padres, 122 in 1988 with the Tigers). A fifth season of over 100 hits was 1990, when he had 104 hits with the Cubs. His season-high home-run total was 14, in 1983 and 1991.

Salazar was the Opening Day third baseman for the Padres in 1982 and 1983. The 1982 season was his high-water mark for walks and stolen bases: 23 walks and 32 stolen bases in 41 attempts. Team-wise, the 1984 season, Salazar recalled, "was a great year. You can never forget it. The best time of our lives."[11] The Padres won the National League West Division title with a record of 92-70, 12 games ahead of the Atlanta Braves and the Houston Astros. They went on to win the pennant, three games to two against the Chicago Cubs. In the World Series he went 1-for-3 as the Padres lost to the Detroit Tigers in five games.

Individually, though, the 1984 season was a struggle. Salazar lost his position as the regular third baseman with the Padres' acquisition of Graig Nettles. He battled injury for the first time in his career: a muscle injury in his rib cage. In 93 games, Salazar batted .241, the lowest of his career, with 3 home runs and 17 RBIs in 228 at-bats. And he was moved into a part-time role. During the 1984 winter meetings, Salazar was traded with Ozzie Guillén, Tim Lollar, and Bill Long to the White Sox for LaMarr Hoyt and minor leaguers Kevin Kristan and Todd Simmons. Salazar welcomed the trade. "I was beaten down last year and I must get my confidence back," he said. "Last year, the Padres pinch-hit for me in the third and fourth innings and it hurt. I went to Jack McKeon at the end of the season and asked him to trade me somewhere to get the pitcher he needed. I'm not a part-time player."[12]

Salazar's 1985 season was better in terms of offensive output. The change to the American League seemingly suited him well. In 122 games with the White Sox, he hit 10 home runs with 45 RBIs, 18 doubles, and 14 stolen bases. His batting average was .245. But he lost the starting third baseman's job to Tim Hulett, and after the season he had knee surgery. Team physician Richard Corzatt hoped that "with the combination of surgery and rehabilitation," Salazar could play at some point in 1986.[13] He did return briefly during the 1986 season, but only for four games in August.

After the season Salazar was released by the White Sox. The Padres signed him again. Getting 189 at-bats over 84 games, Salazar batted .254. Again, his offense caused concern. Only 8 of his 48 hits went for extra bases (three home runs and five doubles). Despite his flexibility in the field, his offensive struggles continued and he was released after the season.

Signing with the Tigers in February 1988 meant a return to the American League. In September Tigers manager Sparky Anderson commented to *Baseball Digest*, "I never thought we'd get this much out of him. We wouldn't even be a .500 club without him." Personally it was an offensive resurgence for Salazar as he hit 12 home runs and tied his single-season high for RBIs with 62. He batted .270 in 452 at-bats, his most since 481 in 1983.

Barely 13 months after signing, Salazar was traded back to the Padres for Mike Brumley. It would be his third stint with the team. Salazar commented, "I know that third base is the weakest part of this team. … That is where I play the best. But even if I don't play, I will not complain. I'm just glad to be back home." His old-now-new teammate Tim Flannery recalled how Salazar (in the early 1980s) used to walk from his house to Jack Murphy Stadium where the Padres played their home games. It was about a two-mile walk. "I remember driving down the highway and seeing this figure on the side of the road and – zoom –as soon as I'd pass him I'd realize, 'I know that guy,' … I'd stop the car, turn around, drive back, open the door and shout, 'Get in the car, Louie.'"[14] Salazar echoed a similar sentiment, noting, "This is my team. These are my people."[15] It was nice to be back in San Diego.

The return home, however, was short-lived. At the trade deadline in 1989, Salazar was sent with Marvell Wynne to the Cubs for Calvin Schiraldi, Darrin Jackson, and Phil Stephenson (the player to be named later). Cubs manager Don Zimmer commented on the acquisition of Salazar, by then known as a versatile infielder with a streaky bat: "He's the type of guy, when he gets a hot bat, he can do some damage."[16] In his three-plus seasons with the Cubs, it was a thought often proved true.

After the trade in 1989, Salazar batted .325 in 26 games. In the National League Championship Series against the San Francisco Giants he batted .368 (7-for-19). He smashed a triple and a home run, and had the only two RBIs of his postseason career. For his career, Salazar batted .333 in postseason play (9-for-27). Over his last three-plus seasons he put together solid personal offensive numbers (.293, .292, .237, with 32 home runs). Then in his mid-30s, Salazar did not have the same speed of his youth, and was caught stealing six times in 10 attempts. On June 11, 1991, he had the only multi-home-run game of his career. Both home runs came off Bud Black of the San Francisco Giants. He played his last major-league game on October 4, 1992. He went 0-for-3 as the Cubs defeated the Montreal Expos, 3-2. After the season the Cubs granted him free agency, effectively serving as his retirement from playing baseball.

Salazar's major-league statistics were 1,302 games played, 4,101 at-bats, 1,070 hits, 94 home runs, 438 runs scored, 455 RBIs, 117 stolen bases, 33 triples, a .261 batting average, a .293 on-base percentage, and a .381 slugging percentage. He was known for his defensive ability and flexibility in the field. And on occasion he flashed offensive skills. He also played several seasons of winter league ball in Venezuela.

Salazar coached or managed in the minor leagues in a variety of different levels after retiring as a player. He spent two years in the Brewers farm system managing the Class-A Beloit Snappers in 1996-1997, and was the hitting coach for Triple-A Louisville in 1998-1999 and for Triple-A Indianapolis in 2000. He spent the 2001 season as a coach for the Brewers. After the 2001 season he began an eight-year association with the Dodgers. He managed the Gulf Coast League Dodgers in 2002-2005 and the Vero Beach Dodgers in 2006. In 2007-2008 Salazar was the hitting coach for the Double-A Jacksonville Suns, and in 2009 he served in the same capacity for the Double-A Chattanooga Lookouts.

Salazar was inducted into the Hispanic Heritage Baseball Museum Hall of Fame on August 14, 2010.

After a year out of baseball, Salazar sent his résumé to five major-league teams with the hope of getting back into coaching. The Atlanta Braves were the first to respond with a job offer for the 2011 season. Kurt Kemp, the Braves farm director, noted Salazar's strong love of baseball as part of the reason he offered Salazar a managing position 30 minutes after their interview.[17] During spring training in 2011, Salazar, who was to manage the Class-A Lynchburg Hillcats, was coaching with the Braves before the minor leaguers reported for camp to help familiarize himself with the big-league club. On March 9 he was standing on the top step of the first-base dugout directing comments to Nate McLouth about fielding and positioning when he was hit in the face by a Brian McCann line drive. He fell back and landed face-first on the concrete floor of the dugout. It was a five-foot drop.[18]

The game was delayed 14 minutes as Salazar lay unconscious bleeding from his mouth, nose, and face. Some thought he might be dead. He did not regain consciousness until after he was taken in a helicopter to Orlando Regional Medical Center. Players Chipper Jones and Rodrigo López and Braves first-base coach Terry Pendleton said it was the worst baseball accident they had ever seen.[19] Catcher David Ross commented, "It was one of the scariest things I've ever witnessed on a baseball field. For a minute, it entered my mind that he was dead."[20] Former Braves manager Bobby Cox said, "I thought he was dead. I

was in a booth upstairs, and I saw him go down and he wasn't moving. There was blood everywhere."[21]

Salazar suffered no brain damage in the fall. But he suffered several facial fractures, and after several surgeries and the removal of his left eye, Salazar made his managerial debut for the Hillcats on April 15, barely a month after the accident. He commented that his debut with the Hillcats "was my biggest thrill in baseball ... bigger than my big-league debut as a player. It was so important to me to get back in the uniform. And now, I wake up every day and thank God I'm still alive, and for giving me another chance to do this job. I feel lucky."[22] To another journalist he said, "They're not going to take baseball away from me."[23]

Reflecting on the incident, which could have very well been much worse, Salazar commented, "I'm very fortunate to be alive. ... God gave me a second chance in this life, and I'm going to take advantage of it."[24] After four years as manager of

A versatile utility man, Salazar played 13 MLB seasons and later coached in the Braves organization. He overcame losing an eye in 2011. (Jerry Coli / Dreamstime)

the Hillcats, he moved to the Carolina Mudcats for the 2015 season. The stint was followed by two years as manager of the Mississippi Braves in 2016-2017. During the 2017 Arizona Fall League, Salazar managed the Peoria Javelinas to the championship. After the 2018 season as manager of the Florida Fire Frogs of the Florida State League, Salazar was dismissed from his position. It was his last coaching position in professional baseball.

SOURCES

In addition to the source material cited in Notes, the author used information from the National Baseball Hall of Fame clippings file for Luis Salazar, and consulted baseball-almanac.com, baseball-reference.com, retrosheet.org, mlb.com, and thebaseballcube.com.

NOTES

1   Tyler Kepner, "A Manager Turns Misfortune Into a Lesson," *New York Times*, May 4, 2011. Retrieved from https://www.nytimes.com/2011/05/05/sports/baseball/05kepner.html.

2   Anna Katherine Clemmons, "'I'm Lucky to Be Alive,'" espn.com, April 28, 2011. Retrieved from https://www.espn.com/mlb/news/story?id=6442017.

3   "'I'm Lucky to Be Alive.'"

4   "'I'm Lucky to Be Alive.'"

5   Tony Violanti, "Salazar Leads Rampaging Bisons," *Buffalo News*, July 14, 1979.

6   The ballpark was also the one in which field scenes for *The Natural* were filmed in 1983.

7   "Salazar Leads Rampaging Bisons."

8   "Salazar Leads Rampaging Bisons."

9   Bill Plaschke, "For McKeon, Salazar, Baseball's Lovelier the Third Time Around," *Los Angeles Times*, March 26, 1989. Retrieved from https://www.latimes.com/archives/la-xpm-1989-03-26-sp-1065-story.html.

10 Dave Sheinin, "Looking on the Bright Side," *Washington Post*, June 29, 2011: D1, D7.

11 Barry M. Bloom, "After Tough Road, Salazar Gets to Feel Joy of Title," *MLB News*, November 19, 2017. Retrieved from https://www.mlb.com/news/luis-salazar-gets-to-feel-joy-of-afl-title-c262180504.

12 Mike Kiley, "Salazar Feels Confident Sox Got Best of Trade," *Chicago Tribune*, February 8, 1985. Retrieved from https://www.chicagotribune.com/news/ct-xpm-1985-02-08-8501080240-story.html.

13 "Saturday's Notebook," *Orlando Sentinel*, October 13, 1985.

14 "For McKeon, Salazar, Baseball's Lovelier the Third Time Around."

15 "For McKeon, Salazar, Baseball's Lovelier the Third Time Around."

16 Andrew Bagnato, "Cubs' Salazar Warms Up with Weather," *Chicago Tribune*, July 4, 1990: 1.

17 "A Manager Turns Misfortune Into a Lesson."

18 Scott Miller, "Near-Fatal Swing Haunts Brian McCann but Made Accidental Victim an Inspiration," *Bleacher Report*, September 16, 2016. Retrieved from https://bleacherreport.com/articles/2658292-near-fatal-swing-scarred-brian-mccann-but-made-unintended-victim-an-inspiration.

19 David O'Brien, "With Salazar Hospitalized, McCann Playing with Heavy Heart," *Atlanta Journal Constitution*, March 11, 2011.

20 "'I'm Lucky to Be Alive.'"

21 "Near-Fatal Swing Haunts Brian McCann but Made Accidental Victim an Inspiration."

22 "Looking on the Bright Side."

23 Associated Press, "Home Opener 'Emotional' for Luis Salazar," CBC.ca, April 15, 2011. Retrieved from https://www.cbc.ca/sports/baseball/home-opener-emotional-for-luis-salazar-1.1060127.

24 Associated Press, "Luis Salazar Returns to Braves Camp," espn.com, March 23, 2011. Retrieved from http://sports.espn.go.com/espn/print?id=6250099&type=story.

JOHAN SANTANA

BY BRYAN LAKE

A GPS search for "middle of nowhere" might lead you to Tovar, Venezuela, a town of roughly 42,000 people located more than a mile up in the Andes. It is an unlikely birthplace for a Cy Young Award winner, but in a ballpark in Tovar there is a proud sign that says, "Welcome to the territory of Johan Santana."[1]

Johan Alexander Santana was born on March 13, 1979, the second of five children born to his mother, Hilda, and his father, Jesus, an electrician. Young Johan dreamed of becoming an engineer.[2] It seemed like a reasonable career path for a kid who wasn't even the most talented baseball player in his own family – that designation went to his older brother, Franklin.[3]

Johan's baseball career almost ended before it started after his coach sent him home from his first youth league baseball practice for being improperly dressed.[4] The next day, however, he got a better reception when he arrived wearing the uniform of his father, a semipro infielder.[5]

Santana started out as a right-handed shortstop but he was moved to the outfield after his coaches figured out that he was a natural lefty.[6] By his mid-teens Santana was nudged to the pitching mound because of his cannon left arm, and at a tournament the teenage fireballer caught the attention of Andres Reiner, a Houston Astros scout.

Reiner wanted to sign Santana. He asked the Astros' front office for funds to make the 350-mile journey to visit the pitching prospect and his family, but big-league players were on strike at the time, so the Astros were being fiscally conservative. The answer came back to Reiner: No.

But Reiner was nicknamed Bulldog for a reason. He kept asking for the money until the Astros' general manager, Bob Watson, used his personal expense account to cover the trip.[7] Watson later recalled, "Johan wasn't in one of the more populated areas of Venezuela. He was off the beaten path. If it wasn't for Andres, it's very, very likely Johan might not have been seen."[8]

After a 10-hour drive, Reiner found himself knocking on the door of the Santana family home. Santana's father wondered who Reiner was and Johan said, "Dad, that's the man who was there at the tournament."[9] Reiner mesmerized the young southpaw with a picture of the Astros' spring-training complex in Florida. "I had never seen four or five diamonds together," Santana recalled. "It made an impression. It was beautiful."[10] Johan's family was impressed, too, and they urged him to sign with the Astros.

Separating from his family was difficult for Santana. He recalled, "I was crying. I said, 'I don't think I can do this.' But then I told myself that I was going to do it for my family."[11]

The Prospect

Santana started out in the Astros' training academy. The days were long and grueling. Practice began at 7:30 A.M., afternoons were spent in the gym, and evenings were filled with English classes (in which Johan excelled) and other life-skills courses.

Santana began the 1997 season pitching for the Astros' Gulf Coast League affiliate, and by 1999 the 20-year-old left-hander had worked his way up to the Michigan Battle Cats in the Class-A Midwest League. His numbers for the season were mediocre: an 8-8 record with a 4.66 ERA. He struck out almost a batter per inning, however, and his strong arm drew the attention of Jose Marzan, who was managing the Minnesota Twins' affiliate in the Midwest League.

"He didn't have much other than a fastball," Marzan recalled,[12] but that was enough for him to recommend that the Twins select Santana in the Rule 5 draft, in which the Twins had the first pick. Although they really wanted Santana, the Twins were able to select Jared Camp and flip him for Santana and cash in a trade with the Florida Marlins, who drafted Santana from Houston but wanted Camp (a fellow minor-league pitcher who ended up never reaching the majors).

As a Rule 5 draftee, Santana had to spend the entire 2000 season in the big leagues with the Twins. Having never pitched above Class A, Johan wasn't ready – and it showed. He pitched poorly (a 6.49 ERA) and wildly (5.7 walks per nine innings). In 2001 Santana was back again with the Twins. He spent three months on the disabled list and otherwise pitched sparingly and unimpressively.

In 2002 Johan was cut from the Twins' big-league spring-training camp and assigned to Triple-A Edmonton. The team did not know if he had a future as a starter or reliever. The club's general manager, Terry Ryan, said, "I can't tell you what he's going to be, as much as I have seen him."[13] *Baseball Prospectus* was more certain about Santana, writing in 2002 that his "likely career is as a lefty specialist."[14]

Santana's future and his role were uncertain, but a mere 18 months later, after a sudden and stunning transformation, everyone knew exactly what he was: the best pitcher in the American League.

The Sudden Ace

The Twins sent Santana to the minors with instructions to work on his changeup. Neither he nor the Twins could have predicted how much both the pitcher and the club would profit from that suggestion. Working with Edmonton pitching coach Bobby Cuellar, Santana developed complete mastery of – and total confidence in – his changeup. He threw the pitch again and again in bullpen sessions and games until it looked identical to his fastball coming out of his hand. "I was challenging myself and forcing myself to take command of that pitch," Santana recalled.[15]

Suddenly, he was unhittable. Pairing a 94-mph fastball with a 76-mph changeup, Santana made hitters look as if they were swinging bananas instead of bats. In one game he struck out 16 batters and by the end of May he had piled up 75 strikeouts in just 48⅔ innings. The Twins had seen enough to bring him back to Minnesota.

Santana proved to be just as dominant facing big-league batters. After striking out three times against Santana, the Oakland A's Adam Piatt said, "I couldn't tell the difference between his fastball and his changeup at all. His fastball had late life. He was tough to figure out."[16] Santana's sizzling fastball and cotton-soft changeup were such a devastating combination that his third pitch, a good slider, was often an afterthought.

Santana spent the remainder of the 2002 season swinging between starting and relieving for the Twins, making 14 starts in 27 appearances. He excelled in both roles, posting a 2.99 ERA and leading the team with 137 strikeouts in just 108⅓ innings. When asked if he was a strikeout pitcher, Santana said hitters

Two-time Cy Young winner Johan Santana threw a no-hitter and led the league in strikeouts three times. He was MLB's top pitcher in the mid-2000s. (Jerry Coli / Dreamstime)

were "striking out themselves. They are swinging the bats. I'm just throwing the ball."[17]

The following year in spring training, Santana's relationship with the Twins became seriously strained. The friction arose when Twins starter Eric Milton got injured. The Twins first promised Milton's rotation spot to Santana, but then they picked up veteran starter Kenny Rogers and demoted Santana to the bullpen. Santana was so angry he considered asking for a trade, but he calmed down, accepted his role, and set out to prove his value. "I looked at it as a challenge," he recalled. "I was just waiting to show they were making a big mistake by having me in the bullpen."[18]

Santana pitched well in a few emergency starts, and by midseason he was a permanent fixture in the starting rotation. Permanent and dominant. In the second half of the year he went 8-1 with a 3.13 ERA. When the playoffs rolled around, the Twins selected him to start Game One of the ALDS against the Yankees. He was the unquestioned ace of the team.

Soon he would be the ace of the league.

The Best of the Best

By 2004 Santana's fluttering changeup was perhaps the most lethal weapon in baseball. He honed it in bullpen sessions, working relentlessly to make it indistinguishable from his fastball by alternating the two pitches, over and over, instead of throwing a series of each.[19]

Seattle Mariners second baseman Bret Boone said, "He's the only guy I know who at times has a 20-mile-per-hour difference between his fastball and changeup. Usually guys have a 10-mile-per-hour difference."[20] And former Cy Young Award winner Frank Viola, commenting on Santana's historic 2004 season, said, "I've never seen a pitcher make hitters look as foolish as Johan did with his changeup."[21]

In 2004 Santana swept all first-place votes and won the American League Cy Young Award unanimously. He started the season slowly – by the end of May his ERA was an ugly 5.61 – but he gained steam in June and didn't lose a game after July 11, finishing with a 20-6 record. He led the American League in old-school stats like ERA, strikeouts, and opponents' batting average, as well as new-school categories like ERA+, FIP, and WHIP. Yankees manager Joe Torre was among those who were amazed by Santana. "Sandy Koufax used to put up numbers like that," Torre said. "Those numbers don't exist anymore."[22]

The Twins rewarded Santana with the biggest contract in team history: a four-year deal worth $40 million. It was a smart baseball decision for the Twins to lock up their ace, but it was also a good business move because attendance jumped noticeably when Santana pitched at home.[23]

Santana held up his end of the bargain in 2005, making 33 starts for the Twins and posting a 2.87 ERA and a league-leading 238 strikeouts. Poor run support left him with a 16-7 record, though, and in an era when pitcher wins were a critical factor for many voters, Johan finished third in the AL Cy Young vote behind winner Bartolo Colon, who had 3.48 ERA but led the league with 21 wins.

Santana's performance in 2006 left no doubt about who should win the AL Cy Young. He was unquestionably the best pitcher in baseball. He tied with Chien-Ming Wang for most wins (19) and led both leagues with a 2.77 ERA and 245 strikeouts. He was the first pitcher in 21 years to top the majors in victories, ERA, and strikeouts. He once again received every first-place Cy Young Award vote, becoming only the fifth pitcher to win the award unanimously more than once. Johan was so superior to his competition that *Baseball America* named him not just the best pitcher in the major leagues but the best *player*, period.[24]

Transitions

In 2007 Santana's fastball lost a little zip and the speed difference shrank between his heater and his changeup. He gave up a career-high 33 home runs and his 3.33 ERA was his highest since 2001. But even though he regressed slightly from his 2004-2006 peak, Santana still had a season for which many players would sell their souls: he made the American League All-Star team, finished fifth on the Cy Young ballot, and won his first Gold Glove.

He also had perhaps the most dominant performance of his career.

On August 19, 2007, more than 36,000 fans witnessed Santana's electrifying performance against the Texas Rangers at the Metrodome in Minneapolis. It was obvious early that he had great stuff, with five strikeouts in the first two innings and 11 K's after five. He didn't record any strikeouts in the sixth inning but struck out the side in the seventh and again in the eighth. The crowd roared louder with each punchout, reaching a crescendo when Santana buzzed a 93-mph fastball past Jarrod Saltalamacchia to finish the eighth inning. After recording a team-record 17 strikeouts, Santana was spent. He doffed his cap to the thundering crowd and let closer Joe Nathan finish off a 1-0 victory.[25]

In his eight overpowering innings, Santana threw 112 pitches and didn't shake off catcher Mike Redmond a single time. He threw only four sliders – his other 108 deliveries were nothing but bullet fastballs and butterfly changeups that had Rangers hitters flailing helplessly. Texas shortstop Michael Young, who went down swinging three times against Santana, said, "That was as good as I've seen his changeup, and that's saying something."[26] Recalling the magical day years later, Twins outfielder Torii Hunter said, "I didn't get a single ball in center field. I was bored. I could have brought a lawn chair."[27]

*　*　*

Santana may have been in total control on the mound, but his frustration with the Twins' front office boiled over in the summer of 2007 when the club traded three-time All-Star second basemen Luis Castillo for a pair of prospects and didn't make any moves to improve the team. During Santana's time with the Twins they had won several division titles but had struggled to advance in the playoffs. "Why waste time when you're talking about something that's always going to be like that?" Santana said. "It's never going to be beyond this point. It doesn't make any sense for me to be here, you know?"[28]

Santana had a year left on his contract and a no-trade clause, but at the end of the 2007 season he indicated he was open to a change of scenery. He said he loved everything about the Twins, but "if I have to go somewhere else, and it's for the better, I'll do it. I won't have any problems with that."[29]

During the offseason, Santana's agent and the Twins exchanged contract-extension offers that were significantly different in size.[30] Then, after endless rumors and speculation, the Twins traded Johan to the New York Mets, who inked him to a six-year $137.5 million deal, the largest contract ever given to a pitcher.[31]

The kid from the middle of nowhere was going to the Big Apple.

*　*　*

Santana was welcomed as a savior in New York, the man who could have stopped the Mets from collapsing at the end of the 2007 season, when they blew a division title despite holding a seven-game lead with 17 games left. Santana was aware of the expectations he faced in New York, but he took it in stride. "Pressure is part of the game," he said on the first day of the Mets' spring-training camp. "I know what I have to do, so I'll be fine."[32]

Santana proved he had reason to be confident in 2008 as he topped 200 strikeouts for the fifth straight season, led the National League in innings pitched and ERA, and came in third on the NL Cy Young ballot.[33] And when his team needed him the most, he was the definition of an ace, going 4-0 in September with a 1.83 ERA to keep his team in playoff contention. In his second-to-last start, he threw 125 pitches over eight innings to secure a big win over the Cubs. He then insisted on pitching on three days' rest against the Marlins, firing another 117 pitches in a complete-game three-hit shutout to pick up a crucial victory. What made the performance even more remarkable was that Santana did it with a torn meniscus in his left knee that required offseason surgery.

Unfortunately for Santana, it was neither his last nor his most serious surgery during his time with the Mets.

Woe-Han and No-Han

Santana pitched well for the Mets in 2009 and 2010, making 54 starts and posting a 3.05 ERA, but both seasons were cut short by surgeries. In September 2009 he had bone chips removed from his elbow. He recovered and was effective for most of the 2010 season,[34] but he was forced to leave an early September start after throwing only 65 pitches. A couple of days later the

Mets said Santana's left pectoral area was sore but the shoulder in his pitching arm was fine.[35]

It wasn't.

"WOE-HAN! Shoulder surgery will end Santana's season" blared the headline in the *New York Daily News*.[36] Rather than rest to heal a pectoral strain, it turned out that Santana needed surgery to repair a tear in the anterior capsule of his left shoulder. It was a serious injury and the timeline for his return to the mound was uncertain. Santana missed the entire 2011 season, but he worked diligently to rehab his shoulder and he willed himself to become the Mets' Opening Day starter in 2012.

Post-surgery Santana was a different pitcher. His formerly blazing fastball was now an 88-mph fast-enough-ball. Santana knew he couldn't blow speedballs by hitters anymore, but he still had his parachute changeup and he knew how to pitch. "I know my fastball is not like it used to be," he said, but "pitching is about keeping hitters off balance."[37]

Despite diminished velocity, Santana was still very effective, and he had an impressive 2.75 ERA when he took the mound for his 11th start of the season on June 1, 2012, against the St. Louis Cardinals. It was the 8,020th game in the history of the Mets franchise, and despite having had more than their fair share of dominating pitchers through the years, not once had a Mets hurler tossed a no-hitter. Time and again they came close – there were 35 one-hitters in franchise history – but they never had a no-hit game, and it seemed unlikely to happen that night with St. Louis visiting New York. In addition to Santana's ongoing recovery from surgery, the reigning World Series champion Cardinals came into the game second in the National League in runs scored and leading the league in batting average, on-base percentage, and slugging percentage.

Santana started out the game with shaky command and didn't seem to have good stuff. He walked two batters with one out in the second inning, but he stuck out the next two hitters to get out of the jam and then he started rolling. After Santana got through his seventh hitless inning, however, his pitch count was 107. He returned to the dugout and, as he shared with reporters after the game, his manager, Terry Collins, "told me that I was his hero and that was the end of it. I told him I was not coming out of the game."[38]

He stayed in.

On his 118th pitch of the night, Santana issued a walk with two out in the eighth inning. Collins jogged out to the mound as the crowd booed, had a brief conversation with Santana, and then jogged back to the dugout to cheers. "I just couldn't take him out," Collins said later. "I just couldn't do it."[39]

Johan finished the eighth inning with his no-hitter intact and then took the mound in the ninth with 27,000 Mets fans roaring for him. He started the inning by inducing looping liners to center field and left field to pick up two outs. Next up in the batter's box was David Freese. Santana quickly put himself in a three-ball, no-strike hole, but he got a called strike on his fourth delivery and then Freese pulled the next pitch foul to bring the count full.

With the crowd frenzied and his manager fretting, Santana prepared to throw his 134th pitch of the night. He stared at his catcher, Josh Thole, and shook off the sign. At this historic moment, there was only one pitch Santana wanted to throw: his trusty, legendary changeup. The pitch floated in and dove over the plate. Freese swung and missed. Bedlam erupted. Santana's teammates mobbed him as the scoreboard flashed "No-Han."[40]

In the clubhouse after the game Santana stood in the middle of his teammates and told them they had made history together. It was a moment Santana never expected to happen. "I don't even think I've thrown a no-hitter in video games," he said. "I never had it in my mind that I would throw a no-hitter. Never."[41]

*   *   *

As euphoric as everyone was after Santana's no-hitter, Terry Collins was filled with anguish about the man he had once described as "by far the greatest competitor I've ever been around."[42] The manager was painfully aware of the potential toll that Santana's 134 pitches may have taken on his repaired and rehabbed shoulder. "I'm very excited for him," Collins said, "but if in five days his arm is bothering him, I'm not going to feel very good."[43]

The Mets gave Johan a couple of extra days of rest before his next start, against the Yankees, but the Bronx Bombers still blasted four home runs off him, including three in a row. He continued to struggle for several weeks before going on the disabled list with a sprained ankle. After he returned, he was worse. The man who threw the first no-hitter in franchise history became the first Mets pitcher to give up six or more runs in five consecutive starts.[44] Finally, in late August the Mets announced that Santana would be out for the rest of the season due to inflammation in his lower back.[45]

A Shooting Star Fades Away

During spring training in 2013, Santana experienced weakness in his throwing shoulder and did not pitch in any exhibition games. Then came the terrible news: In late March the Mets announced that he had another tear in the anterior capsule in his left shoulder – the same injury that caused him to miss the entire 2011 season.[46]

He had thrown his last pitch for the Mets.

After recovering from a second shoulder surgery, Santana threw for scouts in the spring of 2014. His fastball didn't exceed 81 mph, but the Orioles gave him a chance and signed him to a minor-league deal.[47] Unfortunately, he tore his Achilles' tendon during an extended spring-training game, ending his season. In 2015 Johan had another aborted comeback with the Blue Jays, after which he settled into his life in Florida, filling his days with his foundation[48] and his family (his wife, Yasmile – whom he has known since he was 9 years old – and their three children).

After hinting at other comebacks, Santana finally announced that he was officially retired when he was inducted into the Twins Hall of Fame in 2018. That same year he was also eligible for the National Baseball Hall of Fame for the first time, but he didn't receive the minimum 5 percent of the vote necessary to stay on the ballot. Although widely recognized as the best pitcher in baseball at his peak, his prime years simply didn't last long enough in the minds of many Hall voters.[49]

Santana's career was filled with sharp contrasts and rapid transitions. Venezuela to the United States. Class A to the majors. Reliever to starter. Unknown to ace. Mild Midwest to frenetic New York City. Invincible to incapacitated. And, of course, fastball to changeup. He was a fierce, gritty, determined competitor who would – and literally did – pitch until his arm was ruined.

It's easy to recall the vision of Santana in his prime – his left arm a whip at the end of his smooth, compact delivery as he fired fastballs and floated changeups and flummoxed the best hitters of his generation. The kid from nowhere could've more than held his own against anyone anywhere.

Update in 2025, by Leonte Landino:

Santana has remained close to the game, living near the Minnesota Twins' spring training complex in Fort Myers, Florida, where he regularly serves as a special instructor during preseason camps. In the winter of 2024, his legacy was immortalized with his induction into the Latin Baseball Hall of Fame in Punta Cana, Dominican Republic—joining a prestigious class that included Félix Hernández, Andruw Jones, Alfonso Soriano, and Alex Rodríguez.

"This is for Venezuela—because Venezuela is amazing," Santana declared, his voice breaking through a wave of emotion and thunderous applause.[50] Among his countrymen, Santana is revered as the greatest pitcher in Venezuelan baseball history, a title he holds in a respectful and ongoing debate with fellow legend Félix Hernández.

NOTES

1 Daniel Cancel, "Santana's Hometown Awaits His Next Move," *New York Times*, January 24, 2008.

2 Sean Deveney, "Twins Ace in Hole Is Santana," *Chicago Tribune*, October 3, 2004.

3 "Remote Town Deals Twins an Ace – Santana Still Has Soft Spot for Home in Venezuela," *Houston Chronicle*, September 15, 2004.

4 "Remote Town Deals Twins an Ace."

5 "Remote Town Deals Twins an Ace."

6 Peter Botte, "Johan Throws 'Em Curveball, From Shortstop to Ace of AL," *New York Daily News*, October 5, 2004.

7 Jack Curry, "Scout Listens to His Instincts, Not to His Boss, and Uncovers a Star," *New York Times*, January 31, 2008.

8 Curry, "Scout Listens to His Instincts."

9 Charlie Devereux, "Venezuelan Children Flock to See Santana on His Trip Home," *New York Times*, December 13, 2009.

10 Mel Antonen, "Santana Relishes Role; Dream Ride Takes Pitcher from Venezuela to Twins Bullpen to Starting Rotation," *USA Today*, July 27, 2004.

11 Antonen, "Santana Relishes Role."

12 La Velle E. Neal III, "A Change for the Better; Johan Santana Has Used his Outstanding Off-speed Pitch to Become a Blossoming Star," *Minneapolis Star Tribune*, September 5, 2003.

13 La Velle E. Neal III, "Camp Report; Santana Is Cut from Major League Camp," *Minneapolis Star Tribune*, March 15, 2002.

14 Jay Jaffe, "Johan Santana Won't Make the Hall of Fame, but His Career Creates a Unique Measuring Stick," *Sports Illustrated*, December 21, 2017 (available at https://www.si.com/mlb/2017/12/21/johan-santana-hall-fame-ballot-2018).

15 Dane Mizutani, "For Twins Legend Johan Santana, Memories Will Live On at Target Field," *St. Paul Pioneer Press*, August 3, 2018.

16 Jeff Fletcher, "Twins Catch Breaks Against A's, Mulder; Oakland Hits Into Three Rally-Killing Double Plays Against Santana," *Santa Rosa* (California) *Press Democrat*, July 4, 2002.

17 La Velle E. Neal III, "Santana Provides Big Boost," *Minneapolis Star Tribune*, June 8, 2002.

18 Chuck Johnson, "It's Unanimous: Santana Deserves Rotation Spot," *USA Today*, November 12, 2004.

19 Brian Costa, "Santana and His Baseball Are in a Serious Relationship," *Wall Street Journal*, April 5, 2012.

20 Albert Chen, "A SUDDEN ACE," *Sports Illustrated*, August 30, 2002. (https://www.si.com/vault/2004/08/30/8184296/a-sudden-ace).

21 Patrick Reusse, "Peers Provide Warm Reception; Jim Perry and Frank Viola, Past Cy Young Award Winners for the Twins, Are Happy to Have Johan Santana Join Their Exclusive Group," *Minneapolis Star Tribune*, November 12, 2004.

22 John Powers, "His Heat Is Stifling; Twins Santana Sizzled Through the Second Half," *Boston Globe*, October 5, 2004.

23 Patrick Reusse, "Purse Strings Loosen, and Fears Lessen," *Minneapolis Star Tribune*, February 15, 2005.

24 La Velle E. Neal III, "American League Cy Young Award; Two Out of Three: Not Bad," *Minneapolis Star Tribune*, November 17, 2006.

25 Highlights of Santana's 17-strikeout performance can be seen at https://www.youtube.com/watch?v=xK32meADvjg.

26 Phil Miller, "So Close to Perfect: Santana Whiffs Team-Record 17: Cuddyer Hits Solo Homer for Twins' Only Run," *McClatchy-Tribune Business News*, August 20, 2007.

27 Phil Miller, "Santana, 'Equalizer' Are Honored," *Minneapolis Star Tribune*, August 5, 2018.

28 Joe Christensen, "Santana's Unhappiness Doesn't Bode Well for Twins; The Two-Time Cy Young Winner Says He Might Not Have a Future with the Team Because It Won't Do What It Takes to Win a Title," *Minneapolis Star Tribune*, August 1, 2007.

29 La Velle E. Neal III, "Twins; The Offseason: Has Johan Santana Made His Final Start as a Twin?" *Minneapolis Star Tribune*, October 2, 2007.

30 Joe Chistensen, "Do the Math: Twins, Santana a Long Ways Off," *Minneapolis Star Tribune*, November 22, 2007.

31 Ben Shpigel, "It's Official: Santana and Mets Have a Deal," *New York Times*, February 2, 2008.

32 Gerry Fraley, "Santana Raises the Bar: Mets' Newest Savior Goes About His Business with Quiet Confidence," *USA Today*, February 19, 2008.

33   Winner Tim Lincecum trailed Santana slightly in innings and ERA but had far more strikeouts. Second-place finisher Brandon Webb trailed Santana in all three categories but led the NL with 22 wins.

34   Santana also hit his only career home run on July 6, 2010, against Cincinnati. Video available at https://www.youtube.com/watch?v=TU2phKSZEeI.

35   Mike Puma, "Santana on Track to Make Next Start," *New York Post*, September 5, 2010.

36   "Woe-han! Shoulder Surgery Will End Santana's Season; Beginning of 2011 in Doubt," *New York Daily News*, September 11, 2010.

37   "Woe-han!"

38   Mike Puma, "50-Year Wait Finally Ends, Santana Delivers Amazin's First No-hitter," *New York Post*, June 2, 2012.

39   David Lennon, "Collins Hopes He Can Share Santana's Joy," *Newsday*, June 2, 2012.

40   The complete broadcast of Santana's no-hitter is available at https://www.youtube.com/watch?v=rZrpSpMLBSc. A shorter video that is limited to the 27 outs of his gem can be found at https://www.youtube.com/watch?v=5bGvwhz6MW4.

41   Derrick Goold, "No-hitter*, *Santana Throws Gem with Help of Missed Call; Mets 8, Cardinals 0; New York's Franchise First Comes at Expense of the Redbirds," *St. Louis Post-Dispatch*, June 2, 2012.

42   John Harper, "Could Be Start of Something: Never-Back-Down Santana Looks Like Pitcher of Health," *New York Daily News*, April 6, 2012.

43   Lennon, "Collins Hopes He Can Share Santana's Joy." Years later in a *Sports Illustrated* feature, Collins called Santana's no-hitter "the worst night I've ever spent in baseball." In the same article, Santana said, "Even if an army had come to get me, I couldn't have come out of the game." Phil Taylor, "No-No Regrets: Johan Santana Would Not Alter a Thing. Terry Collins Might," *Sports Illustrated*, June 1, 2015 (available at https://www.si.com/mlb/2015/05/31/johan-santana-no-hitter-anniversary-new-york-mets-terry-collins).

44   Mike Puma, "No More Johan; Mets Shut Down Santana for Rest of Season," *New York Post*, August 23, 2012.

45   "No More Johan."

46   Ken Belson, "Santana's Year Appears Over Before It Begins," *New York Times*, March 29, 2013.

47   Eduardo Encina, "Santana deal expected soon: 2-time Cy Young Award winner would go to minors for rehab; Orioles," *Baltimore Sun*, March 4, 2014.

48   https://johansantanafoundation.org/

49   For a thorough examination of Santana's Hall of Fame candidacy, see Joe Posnanski, "In short, Santana makes for a curious Hall case," January 19, 2018 (available at https://www.mlb.com/news/hall-of-fame-case-johan-santana-c265053106).

50   Salón de la Fama del Béisbol Latino. XI Induction ceremony. https://www.youtube.com/watch?v=s2d6Tw6KaoA&t=77s

MARCO SCUTARO

BY AUGUSTO CÁRDENAS

From a very young age, he never took anything for granted. He always had to fight to open the doors to success. And he did everything to compensate for the effort his mother made since he was a child, when she accompanied him on a trip of more than an hour from his native San Felipe to the city of Barquisimeto so he could practice his favorite sport: baseball.

Marco Scutaro Hernández, born October 30, 1975, always had to go the extra mile to get noticed. From his beginnings in his native San Felipe, Yaracuy state, to his mature years in the major leagues.

Scutaro played the last two categories of Little League Baseball, at 14 years old, in Barquisimeto, a city 46 miles from San Felipe.

"I went to Barquisimeto, where the competition was a little better. I never saw myself with much of a chance, but something told me to keep training, to see what happened," he recalled. "And well, from that time on, the idea (of playing professionally) began to creep into me. Everything I did, I did it for my mother."[1]

Nélida Hernández, a housewife of Spanish origin, and Donato Scutaro, barber and an an Italian immigrant, had four children, two girls (Maribel and Kathy) and two boys (Piero and Marco), Marco being the youngest of all.

In 1993, at the age of 18, Marco suffered the loss of his mother from brain cancer, and before saying goodbye to her he made a promise to her that he would be a professional baseball player.

"I promised her. She was very sick," he said. "I promised her when she was in bed, about to die, and that was my inspiration."

His mother always supported him in his attempt to sign, and although she was unable to see her son fulfill his dream, she showed him the way. Her routine on school days was to pick him up at school, serve him lunch, and then take him to the San Felipe bus station so he could travel to Barquisimeto to practice, returning later to pick him up except on game days, when he stayed in Barquisimeto. On one occasion he had to sleep in the ballpark because he finished late and couldn't find transportation back.[2]

The sacrifices he made to achieve his goal were many, especially because of the many setbacks he had.

For a month he traveled to Maracay to practice at the New York Yankees academy, returning to his home in San Felipe on the weekends. There he met Tony Armas, Jr., as well as other players who signed with the organization, such as René Pinto, Víctor Valencia, and Jaime Torres.

"After a month, the boss arrived who was going to see all the players. It was an academy with many players," Scutaro recalled. "They start to play the game and I wasn't playing. It was at the Tigres de Aragua stadium (José Pérez Colmenares).

The bosses get behind home plate and start checking everyone. I was waiting for my opportunity, warming up."

Scutaro was left alone in the dugout. Everyone had seen action except him.

"And those people said, 'This is the last pitch, the last batter.' I turned around, my tears came out, I took off my shirt, left it there and went to San Felipe," he said. "Do you know what it is to be a month in an academy and not even be looked at?" Despite being disheartened, he did not lower his head. He kept insisting and continued attending tryouts.

"Once I asked a scout from Colorado to sign me for free and he said no," he said. "On another occasion, a friend from San Felipe who had signed with Oakland lent me his uniform, to see if they would notice me, and I went to a tryout in Puerto Cabello. The tryout ended and I asked if they were not going to check me out, and the scout told me that they did not check released players. Since he saw me in the Oakland uniform, he thought I was released. I couldn't hit a thing."

Scutaro's luck changed when he approached the academy of former Venezuelan major leaguer Luis Aponte, who played with the Boston Red Sox (1980-1983) and the Cleveland Indians (1984).

"He didn't invite me, I went to ask him for permission to see if he would let me practice. I told him that he didn't have to pay for my lodging or food. That what I wanted was to practice to get into shape. And that's how the adventure began."[3]

With the support of his sister Kathy, he was in Barquisimeto at the academy of Aponte, who was a scout for Cleveland.

Two weeks after Scutaro's arrival, the head of scouts for Latin America, Winston "Chilote" Llenas, made an appearance and was the first to notice the future infielder's abilities.

"He saw me catching groundballs and it seems that I caught his attention. He approached me while I was catching groundballs and asked me where I was from," he said. "It seems that he told Luis Aponte to leave me for the next show, which was months later in Puerto La Cruz. They left me for the next show and I continued there training and running on my own."[4]

And it was in Puerto La Cruz that Scutaro finally managed to capture the attention of the Cleveland scouts at the showcase.

"You know when they are watching you and I looked like the circus monkey. I did everything so that they would see me, because I was already going on 18 years old," he recalled. "I was 17, and I had already gone through too many tryouts and I said, after this, if nothing comes out, I don't know what I was going to do, but I said, 'This is the chance.' And well, the signing happened, thank God."[5]

Finally, on July 26, 1994, Scutaro fulfilled the promise he made to his mother on her deathbed and became a professional baseball player with the Cleveland Indians.

"Like everyone who pursues that dream, it was quite difficult. In my case, I would dare to say that it was a little more difficult than usual, because I was not a player with excellent conditions. It cost me a lot. I went to countless tryouts and they never said anything to me. They didn't even look at me," he acknowledged. "At that time, the last thing I thought about was a bonus. What I wanted was to sign and they gave me $3,500."[6]

Scutaro began his professional career in 1995 in the Venezuelan Winter League with Caribes de Oriente, a club managed by Aponte. But he took his first steps in the United States in 1996 with Columbus of the Class-A Sally League, standing out for his ability to hit by hitting 25 extra-base hits, including 10 home runs, with 66 runs scored and 45 RBIs in 85 games.

"When I played in Columbus, Georgia, I didn't know anything about anything. What I knew was how to play and it was the easiest thing. You were impressed with everything, because you come from your culture, from your town, and playing baseball was the easiest thing, but simple things, like ordering food, communicating, even when the coaches tried to teach you something, you didn't understand. You just said, 'Yes, yes.'"[7]

The following season, 1997, he again excelled with the bat with Kinston of the high-A Carolina League and hit 10 home runs among his 103 hits in 97 games. That earned him a 21-game stint with the Triple-A Buffalo Bisons.

"In those years, being invited to spring training or playing in Triple A was very difficult, because they had a very good team," said the then rookie, at a time when the Indians had his idol, Omar Vizquel, in their infield, as well as Jim Thome, Carlos Baerga, Tony Fernández, and Matt Williams.[8]

In 1998 Scutaro was a Double-A Eastern League all-star after hitting .316 with 27 doubles, 11 home runs, and 62 RBIs with the Akron Aeros. He finished with another internship in Triple A, a circuit in which he played full-time in 1999 with the Bisons until August 30, 2000, when he was traded to the Milwaukee Brewers along with Richie Sexson, Kane Davis, and Paul Rigdon for Jason Bere, Bob Wickman, and Steve Woodard.

"There were about three games left to finish the season, I was in Buffalo, New York, and I was already preparing to return to Venezuela, and it turns out that I had to travel from Buffalo to Indianapolis, the Triple-A branch of Milwaukee, with the luck that that team went to the playoffs and we won everything," said Scutaro. "At that time, there was a World Series, which was the champion of the International League, in Triple A, with the winner of the Pacific Coast Leagur, and it was played in Las Vegas."[9]

In 2001 Scutaro played again in Triple A, with the Indianapolis Indians, and batted .295 with 87 runs scored, 43 extra-base hits, and 50 RBIs in 132 games. Not only was he not considered for promotion to the major leagues, but in April 2002 he was placed on waivers by the Brewers and was taken on April 5 by the New York Mets.

"Milwaukee put me on waivers and I said, 'If I didn't make it to the major leagues with Milwaukee, here on this team with (Roberto) Alomar at second base and (Rey) Ordóñez at shortstop, even less so here (with the Mets).'"[10]

And far from lowering his head, Scutaro found a large group of Venezuelans who made him feel at home immediately, including one who helped him play a position that would be key in his future.

"In Triple A I remember that there was a group of Venezuelans who had a great time. There was (Jorge) Velandia, Felipe Lira, 'Manacho' (Oscar Henríquez), and (Carlos) 'El Tapón' Hernández," he recalled. "I started to fight and things started to go really well for me. There they started to put me to play in various positions and I thank Velandia a lot, because he taught me to play shortstop. He was very intelligent to play shortstop. With Cleveland I practically played second and third base, but they never put me to play shortstop."[11]

Scutaro continued to hit in Triple A in 2002, this time with the Norfolk Tides, a club with which he had a .319 average, with 20 doubles, 7 home runs, 39 runs scored, and 25 RBIs, before receiving the long-awaited call to the major leagues.

"After more than seven years of fighting in the minor leagues, I was always waiting for that day. I remember, it was a Sunday, entering the apartment the phone rang. ... My wife, Marinés, always picked up, because they always called her from her home in Venezuela. When she picked up the phone I saw her face, as if shocked. I said to her, 'What happened?' She said, 'It's the manager.'"[12]

Bobby Floyd, his manager in Norfolk, was on the phone to inform him that he had to report to the Mets. His wife, Marinés García, whom he married that same year, was anxious to know the reason for that call.

"I knew there could be two pieces of news, one bad or one good, but I wasn't thinking about that, because I was playing well. When that man said those magic words, my heart started racing, and Marinés noticed, because she was looking at me. That's when the screaming and crying started."[13]

At 26 years old, Scutaro traveled to Cincinnati on July 20 to join the Mets in the series against the Reds and had his first contact with his new manager, Bobby Valentine, in the hotel bar, where he tried to start a conversation with him.

"What are you doing here?" Valentine asked him, when the rookie insisted on approaching him.

"They just brought me up," replied Scutaro, who had been called up to replace the injured Joe McEwing.[14]

On July 21 he made his debut at Cinergy Field in Cincinnati as a defensive replacement at second base, entering the lineup for first baseman Mo Vaughn. In his only at-bat, in the ninth inning against Danny Graves, he flied out to left field in the Mets' 9-1 loss to the Reds.

The next day in New York, he got his first hit, against the Montreal Expos, a pinch-hit triple in the seventh inning that broke a two-run tie and gave the Mets a 5-2 victory.

The 23,655 people present at Shea Stadium chanted his name after his hit off pitcher Tomo Ohka.

"It's a great feeling. There's no explanation for the feeling," Scutaro said. "I couldn't ask for anything better."[15]

After his call-up, Scutaro, who was an All-Star in the International League that year, played 27 games with the Mets, then 48 more in 2003 before being claimed on waivers by the Oakland Athletics on October 9, 2003.

The Venezuelan knew that with his new team he would start another season in Triple A, but a shoulder injury that took second baseman Mark Ellis out for the season opened the doors to a starting role in Oakland.

"That year (2004) I was going back to Triple A. When I got to spring training they already had their team made and you know what's coming when they give you that very high (uniform) number," said Scutaro. "But I think that God's timing is perfect, and The Man kind of looked down. ..."[16]

Scutaro played a full season in the major leagues for the first time and in 137 games, 123 of them at second base, he had respectable numbers: .273 batting average with 32 doubles, one triple, 7 home runs, 50 runs scored, and 43 RBIs. But the numbers did not guarantee him a place on the team in the 2005 season.

"My surprise is that after that full year, the following year they were going to send me to Triple A. From the first day of training, a month and a half before the start of the season, they told me that I possibly would not make the team, for X reasons, because I did not take walks, for this, for that. ... Imagine six weeks getting up early, always thinking about that, and the hardest thing of all is that I knew I could play, because they

had given me the chance and I proved it to them. But these are decisions that you cannot control and that is the most frustrating thing about all this."[17]

Scutaro ended up making the team as a utility player and played in 118 games, 81 of them at shortstop and 30 at second base, also playing in the outfield.

In the winter of 2006, Scutaro lived two memorable moments in his career, winning the Caribbean Series with Leones del Caracas and later representing Venezuela in the first World Baseball Classic, where he had the opportunity to play with his childhood idol.

"Omar Vizquel was my idol, the one I always looked up to and wanted to imitate. When I was in the minor leagues, in Cleveland, the first thing I did was go to the major-league stadium to watch him play."[18]

Scutaro played in the first of his three World Baseball Classics in 2006, also participating in the 2009 and 2013 editions.

After playing for his country, Scutaro returned to the A's to fill the same utility role for the 2006 season, in which he played his first postseason, and 2007, his last in Oakland before being traded to the Toronto Blue Jays on November 18, 2007, for Kristian Bell and Graham Godfrey.

"Toronto is an organization that I loved playing for and I have to thank them for giving me the opportunity to play every day. The year I came (2008) I was in the utility role, but the following year they gave me the opportunity to play every day for that organization."[19]

With John Gibbons as his manager, Scutaro began the 2008 season playing at third base, replacing the injured Scott Rolen, and then continued playing every position in the infield and outfield for a then-career-high 145 games.

The following season, in 2009, Cito Gaston, who had replaced Gibbons as manager in July 2008, gave him the starting shortstop job, so he was able to take advantage of the lessons he had from Jorge Velandia in his years in the minor leagues with the Mets to show that he was an everyday player and to get rid of the utility label that he had had since he went up to the major leagues.

"That year was key for me. They gave me the chance to play and it is totally different when you get to the stadium and you know that you are going to be in the lineup. You know that if you don't get a hit, tomorrow you are going to have another chance."[20]

As a starting shortstop, he made only 10 errors in 143 games, leaving personal bests so far in the offense, with averages of .282/.379/.409, 100 runs scored, 162 hits, 35 doubles, 12 home runs, 60 RBIs, 235 total bases, 14 stolen bases, and 90 walks, which allowed him to reach free agency as a coveted player.

On December 4, 2009, Scutaro signed a two-year, $12.5 million contract, with an option for a third year, to be the starting shortstop for the Boston Red Sox.

"Thanks to the opportunity that Toronto gave me, because they let me play, I was a free agent at the perfect time. Boston needed a shortstop, there were negotiations with other orga-

Scutaro was named 2012 NLCS MVP after helping the Giants to a World Series title. He was known for his gritty, clutch play. (Jason O. Watson / Getty Images Sports)

nizations, and the reason I wanted to play for that team was because we were going to have a chance to win."[21]

In his first year he set new personal bests in games (150), at-bats (632), hits (174), and doubles (38), while in 2011 he hit .299 in 113 games, seeing his performance diminished by discomfort in his right shoulder.

Despite coinciding in the lineup with Hall of Famers like David Ortiz and Adrian Beltre, as well as great players like Dustin Pedroia, Victor Martinez, and Kevin Youkilis, Scutaro was not able to taste a postseason in Boston.

"Unfortunately, in the years I was there, as a team we did not win, but I have always said that in Boston, when you win, it must be very, very good, and when you lose it is very, very ugly, because of the fans," he said. "Unfortunately, it was not my best experience playing there as a team, because we could not win in a big market."[22]

The Red Sox picked up Scutaro's option for a third season in 2012, but on January 21 he was traded to the Colorado Rockies for pitcher Clayton Mortensen.

After a slow start to the season in Colorado, Scutaro was regaining his offensive rhythm, acting primarily as a second baseman, but before the trade deadline on July 27, he was traded to the San Francisco Giants for Charlie Culberson and cash, making an immediate impact in the Bay Area.

In just 61 games he hit .362, with 40 runs scored, 20 extra-base hits, and 44 RBIs, with a career-high of seven RBIs in a game, thanks to a grand slam on August 8 against the Cardinals in St. Louis. His contribution was key to the Giants capturing the National League West Division, with an eight-game lead over the Los Angeles Dodgers.

Although Scutaro barely hit .150 (3-20) in the Division Series, the Giants defeated the Cincinnati Reds in five games to advance to the National League Championship Series against the St. Louis Cardinals, whom he once again destroyed offensively.

Scutaro had a dream Championship Series, despite suffering a spectacular collision at second base with Matt Holliday in a double play that took him out of action in the second game, and that in the future would mark his destiny.

But the adrenaline kept him in the lineup and his bat heated up, taking home the series MVP title by batting .500 (14-for-28), with six runs scored, three doubles, and four RBIs, helping the Giants return to their second World Series in three years by beating the Cardinals in seven games, after being down in the series 1-3, being the main protagonist with an iconic image before capturing the 27th out that took them to the fall classic, opening his arms savoring the rain falling at AT&T Park in San Francisco.

"At that moment, what I did was open my arms, look up, and thank God. That was a blessing," he said. "It was an unforgettable experience and memory that I will carry with me until the last day of my life. I remember exactly the last out (a fly ball by Holliday to second base), when it was raining, I grabbed the ball and hid it in my pocket, celebrating with the boys on the infield, and I clearly remember someone from Major League

Baseball coming up to me and whispering in my ear, you were the MVP. You can imagine that emotion inside."[23]

In the World Series, against the Detroit Tigers, Scutaro once again played the hero in the four-game sweep. In Game One, he went 2-for-4 with two RBIs, and in Game Four he also had two singles, including the hit that broke a tie in the 10th inning and gave the Giants a 4-3 victory at Comerica Park to win his long-awaited World Series ring.

"In that at-bat, I was thinking about bringing in that run, because it was so cold. And I wanted to finish that game, because the next day it was going to be colder and Verlander was going to pitch," he said of his at-bat against Phil Coke with Ryan Theriot running on second base that ended up leading to the World Series title.[24]

"It was something inexplicable, because it was something you had dreamed of for so many years, winning a World Series, and at the same time you feel like a weight has been lifted off your shoulders, because you achieved your goal. From then on, what comes next is celebrating."[25]

On December 7, 2012, Scutaro signed a new three-year, $20 million contract with the Giants and started the 2013 campaign in full force, hitting .316/.367/.400 with 2 home runs, 22 runs batted in, and 37 runs scored in the first half, earning his only All-Star selection, though he didn't get into the game.

On June 11 he was hit by Tony Watson and suffered an injury against the Pirates. He played on through September 15, batting .297, but and underwent surgery on September 27 that finished his season.[26]

And although in 2013 he was able to play without any major physical problems, in 2014 "the drama began" due to his back problems, caused mainly by a collision with Matt Holliday on October 15, 2012, in the second game of the NLCS against the Cardinals.

"Literally what I felt was that someone grabbed my leg and pulled it away from my hip. I had a deep pain between my groin and my hip. I think I got off cheap at that moment, I don't know how I didn't break my knee or ankle. I was able to keep playing, but two innings later I felt a pain in a nerve in my leg and asked to be taken out. I think that that collision brought us closer as a team, because they saw the desire I had to keep playing. It was something beneficial for the team, but in the long run it wasn't for me," he said about his clash with Holliday.[27]

"A kind of spur formed between two discs in my spine, because I kept playing without fully healing. I spent a long time avoiding surgery."

At the end of the 2013 season, he was already feeling discomfort in his hip, and in 2014 the pain was so intense that he received five cortisone injections in a span of four weeks.

Scutaro began the season on the disabled list and was only able to briefly return to the field in July, when he played the last five games of his career.

"Months went by, I was trying to come back and come back, and it was hard. I left my house with the intention of competing and when I got to the stadium and swung, I felt that pain and it turned me off. I was fighting with that until one day I got to the stadium and said, 'I'm not going to do this anymore, unfortunately.' I hid in the bathroom, shed a couple of tears, and that was the day I accepted that I couldn't do it anymore. After that, I kept trying, but deep down I knew I couldn't. After I stopped playing, it was worse. I couldn't even tie my shoes and my wife had to put my socks on. I told her to call the doctor so they could operate on me."[28]

On December 19, 2014, Scutaro underwent back surgery and on January 28, 2015, the Giants released him, but on June 17, he was re-signed symbolically, collecting the $6 million remaining on his previous contract, so that he could officially retire as a member of the organization, using its facilities and training staff for his rehabilitation "in hopes of maintaining a quality of life and being pain-free with his family."[29]

After his retirement, Scutaro has remained away from baseball, living in Weston, Florida, with his wife, Marinés, and their three children, María Verónica (born 2002), María Valeria (2005), and Marco (2011), enjoying other passions such as horseback riding and hunting.

"I am grateful to God for the career he gave me," said Scutaro, a man who was synonymous with perseverance to play 13 seasons in the majors when no one wanted to sign him for free. "When you set a dream and go for it, the work, perseverance and dedication will pay dividends later. Everything you do in this life requires sacrifice, not everything will come easy, and my advice is to work harder than everyone else and do things with love, because at the end of the day, if your dream doesn't come true, you can look in the mirror and sleep peacefully because you gave it your best."[30]

SOURCES

In addition to the sources cited in the Notes, the author consulted baseball-reference.com, MLB.com, espn.com, nytimes.com, and sfchronicle.com.

NOTES

1   "Talk Beisbol. Episodio 4- Marco Scutaro Pt 1," May 13, 2020. https://www.youtube.com/watch?v=LqWKdr2JuDI&t=2192s. All direct quotations attributed to Marco Scutaro come from this interview unless otherwise noted.

2   He recalled, "Once I even had to sleep in the Barquisimeto stadium. I remember that time the security man took out a piece of cardboard and I had to lie down where they served the beers, because we left the stadium too late. We had to stay in the stadium."

3   "Las Barajitas de Luis. Marco Scutaro T1-EP 3: Marco Scutaro y sus barajitas," January 23, 2023. https://www.youtube.com/watch?v=hXD2yoUxsbE.

4   "Las Barajitas de Luis. Marco Scutaro."

5   "Las Barajitas de Luis. Marco Scutaro."

6   "Las Barajitas de Luis. Marco Scutaro."

7   "Las Barajitas de Luis. Marco Scutaro."

8   "Las Barajitas de Luis. Marco Scutaro."

9   "Las Barajitas de Luis. Marco Scutaro."

10 "Las Barajitas de Luis. Marco Scutaro."

11 "Las Barajitas de Luis. Marco Scutaro."

12 "Las Barajitas de Luis. Marco Scutaro."

13 "Las Barajitas de Luis. Marco Scutaro."

14 Michael Morrissey, "New Met Scutaro calls on Bobby V.," *New York Post*. July 20, 2002. https://nypost.com/2002/07/20/new-met-scaturo-calls-on-bobby-v/.

15 Associated Press, "Scutaro an Immediate Hit," *Middletown* (New York) *Times Herald-Record,* July 23, 2002. https://www.recordonline.com/story/sports/2002/07/23/scutaro-immediate-hit/51167442007/.

16 "Las Barajitas de Luis. Marco Scutaro."

17 "Las Barajitas de Luis. Marco Scutaro."

18 "Las Barajitas de Luis. Marco Scutaro."

19 "Las Barajitas de Luis. Marco Scutaro."

20 "Las Barajitas de Luis. Marco Scutaro."

21 "Las Barajitas de Luis. Marco Scutaro."

22 "Las Barajitas de Luis. Marco Scutaro."

23 Interview with the author, October 22, 2022.

24 Interview with the author.

25 Interview with the author.

26 Alex Espinoza, "Banged-up Scutaro to sit out remainder of season," MLB.com, September 24, 2013. https://www.mlb.com/news/giants-infielder-marco-scutaro-to-sit-out-remainder-of-season/c-61618578

27 Interview with the author.

28 Interview with the author.

29 John Shea, "Marco Scutaro Re-Signs with Giants – Not to Play, Though." *San Francisco Chronicle,* June 17, 2015. https://www.sfchronicle.com/giants/article/Marco-Scutaro-re-signs-with-Giants-more-of-a-6333473.php.

30 "Las Barajitas de Luis. Marco Scutaro."

LUIS SOJO

BY RICHARD CUICCHI

From 1996 to 2003, the New York Yankees featured the Core Four (Derek Jeter, Jorge Posada, Mariano Rivera, and Andy Pettitte) and Bernie Williams as they collectively propelled the Yankees to six World Series in eight years, including four championships. The Yankees also had Luis Sojo, who wasn't of the same caliber talent-wise as those five All-Stars but was nonetheless an important part of those dynastic teams.

The only seasons Sojo played as a regular were in 1991-92 as the second baseman with the California Angels and in 1995 as the shortstop with the Seattle Mariners. It was as a role player with the Yankees that he gained notoriety during his 13-year career. He never made an All-Star team, but his value to the Yankees was best evidenced by the fact that they traded for or signed him as a free agent six times. He collected as many World Series championship rings as the Core Four during 1996-2003.[1] His highest annual salary with the Yankees was $800,000, not in the millions like those of many of his Bronx teammates; yet he demonstrated that he merited every penny of it and possibly more.

Sojo was valuable to the Yankees as a versatile, dependable utility player. Manager Joe Torre liked having him around. Sojo made the most of his role by playing multiple infield positions, filling in for teammates when they needed a day's rest, coming in as a late-inning defensive replacement, or making a pinch-hit appearance when the rest of the bench had been depleted. In the clubhouse he was a favorite of his better-known teammates. The Yankees thought enough of Sojo to twice sign him for the final month of the season.

Luis Beltran Sojo was born to Ambrosio and Cristina Mayorca de Sojo in Caracas, Venezuela, on January 3, 1965.[2] His father was a cab driver while his mother took care of the home duties. The family lived on Barrio 24 de Julio in Petare, a section of Miranda state, which holds a big portion of the Venezuelan capital city.

In this populous, working-class area, Luis grew up playing "chapitas," the Venezuelan version of stickball that has been popular with children for the last 50 years – a street game that many current professional baseball players thank for helping them develop eyesight and hand-eye coordination. In chapitas, the batter uses a wood broomstick to hit a flying metal bottle-cap, which takes a lot of precision to do.

By going to school, playing chapitas, and working as a drinking water delivery boy, Luis spent his childhood idolizing former major-league shortstop and fellow Venezuelan Dave Concepción. Sojo said of the member of the Big Red Machine of the mid-1970s: "He was my hero, and he's what got me thinking about being a professional ballplayer. He was the big guy in Venezuela, and at that time we didn't have as many big-league players from Venezuela as we do now. He's the guy that really inspired me."[3]

In January 1986 Sojo was signed by Dominican baseball scout Epy Guerrero, who was working for the Toronto Blue Jays at the time.[4] Guerrero ultimately signed more than 50 Latin-American major leaguers. Guerrero gave Sojo a bonus of $2,000. Luis used the money to buy a new kitchen, a washing machine and some home goods for his mother. "After that I only had 5,000 bolivares left, which I used to buy some new clothes for me, then I was broke again," he recalled.[5]

Sojo was 21 years old when he made his professional debut in the Dominican Summer League in 1986. The next season was his first in the United States, with Class-A Myrtle Beach. Two years later, he jumped straight to Triple-A Syracuse to start the season. He made his major-league debut on July 14, 1990, with Toronto and appeared in 33 games that season. He singled and drove in a run his first time at bat.

In making a relatively quick ascent to the majors, Sojo faced difficulties adapting to life in the United States. "The adjustment was very difficult, especially not being able to speak English," he said. "It's tough being by yourself here, especially the first couple of years, you're very depressed. You just have to get into the country and learn from experience."[6]

In 1990 Sojo played in left field his first five games but then was used as an infielder, often coming in during the late innings for defensive purposes. He batted .225 and drove in nine runs.

After the 1990 season, Toronto made two significant roster changes that would contribute to two World Series championships. The Blue Jays acquired Roberto Alomar and Joe Carter in a trade with San Diego and received center fielder Devon White from California in a trade involving Sojo.

Sojo was the starting second baseman for most of the 1991 season with the seventh-place Angels, but he didn't provide much offense. After starting the season with Triple-A Edmonton in 1992, he joined the Angels in late May and showed significant improvement (.272, 7 home runs, 43 RBIs). One of his season highlights included a 10th-inning two-run home run in the first game his parents saw him play in the majors.[7]

The Angels traded Sojo back to Toronto after the 1992 season for Kelly Gruber, who had been a two-time All-Star and helped the Blue Jays win a World Series. There were questions at the time about why Toronto traded Gruber for the marginal Sojo. It was ultimately revealed that Gruber had begun suffering from a degenerative disk condition in his neck that he kept secret during the prior year.[8] Gruber's major-league career ended during 1993 because of the injury.

The Blue Jays won their second consecutive World Series in 1993, but Sojo played in only 19 games and was not on the postseason roster. He was granted free agency after the season and signed with the Seattle Mariners. He secured the starting shortstop job in 1995. In the biggest moment of his career to that point, he had a key hit (a bases-clearing double on which he also scored on a throwing error) in a one-game playoff between the Mariners and the Angels that clinched the AL West title for the Mariners.

However, 19-year-old phenom Alex Rodriguez had started to get more playing time in 1995. He won the shortstop job coming out of spring training in 1996, relegating Sojo to a utility infielder role and ultimately making him expendable. Sojo was put on waivers in mid-August of 1996, and at that point he thought his career might be over.[9] But the New York Yankees claimed him, because manager Joe Torre was looking for someone to give shortstop Derek Jeter rest down the stretch. Torre wasn't comfortable using his current backup infielders, weak-fielding Mariano Duncan and light-hitting Andy Fox, in that role.[10]

At age 31, Sojo's career was finally about to get a lot more interesting. When he failed to claim a starting job with the Yankees, he adopted the attitude necessary for a backup player. "You have to have a strong mind to have that (bench) role," Sojo said. "No doubt in my mind that I want to play every day when I wasn't, but you have to prepare yourself for every time you go out there and do the best you can."[11]

Sojo took advantage of his opportunities at second base, as well as backing up Jeter, as the Yankees won the AL East Division by four games over Baltimore. When they advanced to the World Series against Atlanta, Sojo appeared as a substitute in five games, getting three hits in five at-bats. The Yankees won their first fall classic since 1978 in six games.

Torre wound up using four players at second base in 1997, with Sojo playing in 77 games (51 starts). He had his best major-league batting average (.307). However, in mid-August he suffered a fractured left forearm and missed the remainder of the regular season as well as the playoffs.[12]

Sojo was slated by Torre to be the starting second baseman in 1998 until the Yankees acquired Chuck Knoblauch from Minnesota. With the addition of the four-time All-Star, Torre had to explain to Sojo that he wasn't going to get many at-bats; but he needed Sojo to be ready to play when called on to substitute.

"I got a call from Derek Jeter in January 1998 after I found out they had signed Knoblauch," Sojo said. "I was trying to get out of the Yankees and find some place where I could play regularly. I was so pissed after they promised me they would give me the starting job on second base. Jeter said, 'Luis, don't do anything crazy, man, I have a friend here with me who wants to talk to you. Suddenly on the other side of the phone I heard: 'Hey Luis, this is George Steinbrenner!' I was like: 'Who?' I hung up. I was like, stop making fun of me. Then again, the phone rang and it was the Boss himself and he said: 'Hey Luis, stop being pissed, man, I know how you feel the way the situation

was treated, but the guys want you on the team, so I will give you two years. How much money do you want?' So seriously, I said, 'Give me five minutes and I'll call you back.' I grabbed the phone, I called my agent and told him, 'Hey man, how are you? I'm calling you to tell you that you are fired from representing me.' I called back Jeter and Steinbrenner and said, OK, now we can talk.' So, Mr. Steinbrenner rewarded me with a $1.9 million contract which I took without hesitation."

Sojo said he got sound guidance from Yankees bench coach Don Zimmer that a good attitude as a role player would allow him to spend a lot of years with the team.[13] Zimmer's counseling turned out to be valuable advice for Sojo's future.

When Jeter went on the injured list in early June, Sojo filled in as the everyday shortstop. The Yankees wound up having one of the best seasons in their storied history, as they won 114 regular-season games. Their postseason was a cakewalk: They lost only two of their 13 games, including a sweep of the San Diego Padres in the World Series. Sojo played in only one postseason game, as a defensive replacement in the Championship Series.

Sojo and the 24-year-old Jeter developed a mentor-pupil relationship early in Jeter's career. They frequently sat together in the dugout and talked about game situations. Known for his defensive abilities, Sojo taught Jeter various fielding intricacies.[14] As a result, Jeter would credit Sojo as one of the primary teammates from whom he learned the most.[15]

Learning from his own experiences from his first few pro seasons, Sojo also took new Latin players under his wing in the clubhouse, in order to ease their transition to the big leagues. He helped them overcome the language barrier and assimilate with the other players on the team. "I like to talk to the young guys," Sojo said, speaking not only of the Latin players who made it to the Bronx, but of prospects from his native Venezuela. "That's the way I am. I like to make it easier for everybody. The most important thing is to stay together, and for us to win."[16]

The Yankees repeated as division champions in 1999, with Sojo playing in 49 regular-season games (33 starts). They dominated again in the postseason, losing only one of 12 games, including a sweep of Atlanta in the World Series. Sojo played sparingly (one at-bat) in the League Championship Series against Boston. When his 72-year-old father, Ambrosio, died during the LCS, Torre requested a special exemption to allow a substitute for Sojo while he was to miss the first two games of the World Series to attend his father's burial in Venezuela. Torre had been concerned about Knoblauch's defensive play (26 errors during the regular season) and felt he needed Sojo's availability as a defensive replacement. After the request was denied by Commissioner Bud Selig, Torre decided to leave a roster spot open for him when he returned.[17] As it turned out, the Yankees didn't need Sojo, because they swept the Braves. Sojo wound up making an appearance in Game Four.

The Yankees released Sojo after the 1999 season, and he signed with the Pittsburgh Pirates, where he played a similar utility role in 2000. However, the Yankees thought enough of him to reacquire him in early August after Knoblauch went on the injured list. When the Yankees were struggling at midseason, former Yankees teammates Jeter and Williams had approached GM Brian Cashman about getting Sojo back on the roster.[18] It turned out to be one of the most valuable player transactions the Yankees made that season.

Sojo played well in Knoblauch's place, hitting .288 with 17 RBIs in 34 games. The Yankees won the division by 2½ games over Boston. Sojo then saw his most action in a postseason, playing in 15 games. The Yankees defeated Oakland in the Division Series, Seattle in the Championship Series, and the New York Mets in five games as they captured their third consecutive World Series championship. In the World Series, Sojo provided the two-out game-winning RBI single in the ninth inning of Game Five off Al Leiter. Sojo said after the game. "This is the happiest day of my life."[19] He collected 11 hits and 9 RBIs during the postseason.

Rookie Alfonso Soriano took over the Yankees' second base spot in 2001, and once again Sojo was relegated to the backup role at all of the infield positions. He had the worst offensive season of his career, batting .165 and barely playing during the last month of the season. Sojo was surprised that Torre put him on the postseason roster. In deciding on him for the final spot, Torre said, "I felt more comfortable with an experienced guy, especially someone who has been with us for six years and has participated in what we have accomplished."[20] The Yankees captured their fourth consecutive pennant in 2001 but were defeated by the Arizona Diamondbacks in seven games in the World Series. Sojo delivered an RBI single in Game Six.

Sojo talked openly about retirement during the World Series, expressing a desire to eventually return as a coach or manager.[21] The Yankees granted him free agency after the season, but two months later he signed with them for the fifth time. However, the 37-year-old didn't make the team coming out of spring training, having lost his utility role to switch-hitting Enrique Wilson. Torre and Sojo's teammates were sad about his departure, praising his ability to get a clutch hit after sitting on the bench for days and his presence in the clubhouse with the younger players. Bernie Williams said, "He's the ultimate team player." Torre told Sojo the Yankees wanted to keep him in the organization.[22]

Sojo jumped at a chance to replace Stump Merrill as the manager of Double-A Norwich at midseason in 2002, and the team wound up winning the Eastern League title.

The 2003 season turned into a bizarre one for Sojo. He served as a special instructor for the Yankees in spring training, but then had a stint of 22 games as a player in the Mexican League. He hit a run-scoring single in the Yankees' Old-Timers Game.[23] The Yankees added Sojo to the major-league staff as a special-assignment instructor in late June, but he wasn't allowed to sit in the dugout during games, because the team was at its limit of six coaches. He was the Yankees' first Hispanic coach since Jose Cardenal in 1999, and his main job was to smooth the path to stardom for second baseman Soriano, who was still learning how to play the position.[24] The Yankees surprisingly activated Sojo in September for insurance when Jeter suffered a rib-cage injury, but he played in only three games. Torre couldn't put Sojo on the postseason roster because he had been activated after the deadline. The Yankees won their fifth pennant in six years, but lost to the Florida Marlins in the World Series.

Always a favorite of Torre, Sojo took the Yankees' third base coaching job in 2004 and 2005. He continued in the Yankees organization by managing Class-A Tampa and the Yankees' Gulf Coast League affiliate for eight seasons between 2006 and 2017.

Sojo maintained his ties to his native country throughout his career and became one of the biggest stars and one of the most impactful players in the Venezuelan League history, becoming the historical face of the Cardenales de Lara franchise, based in Barquisimeto, a city that considers Sojo its son. With the Cardenales he won five batting titles: 1989-90 (.351); 1990-91 (.362); 1993-94 (.375); 1994-95 (.376); and 1999-2000 (.346).[25] Sojo was a four-time champion as a player with Cardenales.

Sojo won five World Series rings, including four with the Yankees. He delivered the go-ahead hit in Game Five of the 2000 Series. (Jerry Coli / Dreamstime)

Sojo managed the Venezuelan entry in the World Baseball Classic three times (2006, 2009, and 2013), taking third place in 2009. He spent time as a manager in the Venezuelan League, first as player-manager with the Cardenales, then won the title and represented Venezuela in the Caribbean Series with the Navegantes del Magallanes, and also managed the Tigres de Aragua. Sojo has also managed the Toros de Tijuana in the Mexican League, the Caneros de Los Mochis and Aguilas de Mexicali in the Mexican Pacific League, and the Tigres del Licey in the Dominican Winter League. He was a part-owner of Astronautas de Chiriqui of the Panamanian Baseball League, winning a title and representing Panama in the Caribbean Series.

Sojo is a member of the Venezuelan Baseball Hall of Fame and the Caribbean Series Hall of Fame.

In 2018 Sojo summed up his major-league career: "Being on that (1998) team was the best thing that happened to me in all the years I've been in baseball. After playing for the Blue Jays in 1993, I was really close to retiring. I told my wife that I had enough. I had a lot of injuries, and I was frustrated. Then I went to Seattle where I had my best year as a player in 1995. I got put on waivers in 1996, and that was disappointing. I didn't know what I had to do to stay in the big leagues. When I got to the Yankees, I not only got an opportunity to stay in the big leagues for a while, but I was also winning. I still can't believe that we won 125 (including postseason) games that season and that I ended up playing on two more championship teams after that. It was a great run."[26]

Sojo had hit the proverbial jackpot when he landed with the Yankees after being claimed off waivers in August 1996. It could be said he was in the right place at the right time. Better known for his defensive skills, he was an average player, who could have wallowed in relative obscurity had he continued to play for practically any other major-league team. Instead, he developed into an important role player between 1996 and 2003 and wound up sharing the glory with many All-Stars. His worth transcended his games played and batting average.

Sojo and his wife, Zuleima, have three children, two daughters, Lesluis and Lyz, and a son, Luis.

SOURCES

In addition to the sources cited in the Notes, the author consulted Baseball-Reference.com. Thanks to Leonte Landino for contributing valuable information.

NOTES

1   Jeter, Posada, Pettitte, and Rivera won a fifth World Series in 2009, after Sojo retired as a player.

2   Helene Elliott, "Sojo Hits One to Paste Up in Family Album," *Los Angeles Times*, August 24, 1992: C9.

3   Mike Henry, "Amigo de Todos," *Yankees Magazine*, Vol. 19, Issue 5, August 1998: 48.

4   Helene Elliott, "Lacking Influence: Angels Trying to Re-Establish Their Ties to Major Talent Source – Latin America," *Los Angeles Times*, March 31, 1991: C6.

5   Luis Sojo interview by Leonte Landino on February 8, 2021. Unless otherwise indicated, all quotations attributed to Sojo come from this interview.

6   Henry, "Amigo de Todos."

7   Elliott, "Sojo Hits One to Paste Up in Family Album."

8   Dave Cunningham, "California Angels," *The Sporting News*, February 8, 1993: 33.

9   Alfred Santasiere, "Perfect Fit," *Yankees Magazine*, April 2018: 168.

10 Lyle Spatz, *Yankees Coming, Yankees Going* (Jefferson, North Carolina: McFarland & Company, 2000), 296.

11 "Sojo's Time to Shine," *Yankees Magazine*, Vol. 18, Issue 4, July 1997: 6.

12 Jack Curry, "Sojo Optimistic on Return Despite Breaking Forearm," *New York Times*, August 15, 1997: B13.

13 Santasiere.

14 Lawrence Rocca, "Derek Jeter Heart of the Yankees," *Baseball Digest*, July 1999: 26.

15 "Derek Jeter Baseball Profile," *Baseball Digest*, June 2000: 59.

16 Peter Caldera, "Following in His Footsteps," *Yankees Magazine*, Volume 19, Issue 4, July 1998: 46.

17 Buster Olney, "Sojo's Absence Presents Challenge for Yanks," *New York Times*, October 23, 1999.

18 Joe LaPointe, "Sojo Gets the Call and Delivers Again," *New York Times*, October 27, 2000: D6.

19 LaPointe.

20 Steve Popper, "Sojo Gets the Call," *New York Times*, October 11, 2001: S4.

21 Buster Olney, "Sojo Ends Retirement for Chance with Yankees," *New York Times*, January 9, 2002: D7.

22 Tyler Kepner, "The Show Comes to an End for the Yanks' Sojo," *New York Times*, March 29, 2002: D2.

23 Joe LaPointe, "Glory Days Are Here Again, *New York Times*, July 20, 2003:8, 3.

24 John Levesque, "Yankees Make Use of Sojo's Mojo," *Seattle Post-Intelligencer*, August 7, 2003. https://www.seattlepi.com/news/article/Yankees-make-use-of-Sojo-s-mojo-1121287.php. Accessed August 12, 2019.

25 *2009 World Baseball Classic Media Guide*, 174.

26 Santasiere.

CÉSAR TOVAR

BY RORY COSTELLO

In the late 1960s and early '70s, César Tovar was a fixture at the top of the Minnesota Twins lineup. The speedy, enthusiastic little Venezuelan (5-feet-9 and 150 pounds) came up as a second baseman, but he could handle just about any spot – he is perhaps best remembered today as one of the four players to play all nine positions during the course of a single big-league game.[1] Yet that game in 1968 was just one of 1,488 in a respectable 12-year major-league career. Tovar, who mainly played the outfield, hit .278 with 46 homers and 226 stolen bases. He was a great favorite of manager Billy Martin, another peppery little player, who loved all-out competitors.

Tovar played on after his final year in the majors, 1976. He was in Mexico during the summers of 1977 and '78; he also wound up playing in 26 seasons in the Venezuelan winter league, second only to Vic Davalillo's 30. Neither before nor since has Venezuela had a one-two table-setting duo to compare with "Pepa e Burra" and "Vítico," who were winter teammates for 19 straight years. (Tovar's raunchy nickname – it refers to the genitals of a she-donkey! – was cleaned up as "Pepito" or "Pepi."[2]) César started in 1959, after his first professional summer, and finally hung it up at the age of 45 after two final games in the winter of 1985-86. He was part of eight champion teams at home and ranks high among the lifetime leaders in various categories.

César Leonardo Tovar was born on July 3, 1940, in Caracas, the capital of Venezuela. His family name – which is properly pronounced "toe-VAR"[3] – is that of his mother, Justina Tovar. She and César's father, Francisco "Frank" Pérez, lived together but were never married. Frank, who worked in construction, and Justina had three children, all boys. César's older brother was named Pedro and his younger brother was Alfonzo. Neither of them was involved with sports – but their father was a ballplayer. As César said in 1967, he was "a good second baseman. In Caracas he played on the same amateur team with Chico Carrasquel. When my father quit playing, he gave me his glove. I used it for a long time."[4]

Young César came to baseball around the age of 8. As a lad he also helped the family's finances by shining shoes. "Sometimes I made around $10 or $12 a day. People would come and ask for me because I did a good job." César's earnings bought him a glove before he inherited his father's.[5]

Tovar attended Escuela Nacional Franklin Delano Roosevelt in Caracas. At 15, he became friends with another future Venezuelan big leaguer, Gustavo "Gus" Gil. They played sandlot ball together, and Gil noted, "César always played the game hard." On New Year's morning in 1959, Gabe Paul, general manager of the Cincinnati Redlegs, signed them both. Gil got a $2,000 bonus. Tovar got nothing.[6]

Gabe Paul told the story himself in 1968. "I went to see Gus Gil in a morning workout. He insisted on bringing Tovar along. Gil was the man we wanted. I thought he was a great one. He wanted his buddy Tovar signed, too. César showed nothing, but I signed him to get Gil."[7] The Reds' top farm team in those days was the Havana Sugar Kings. Havana owner Bobby Maduro had been friends with Paul since the early '50s and the Sugar Kings had a sizable following in Venezuela.

Tovar's first pro season, with Geneva of the New York-Penn League (Class D), was not that auspicious. He batted .252 in 87 games, with 3 homers and 41 RBIs. In the winter of 1959, he joined the Caracas Leones of La Liga Venezolana del Béisbol Profesional (LVBP). He became Rookie of the Year and spent 16 seasons with that club, winning championships in five of them.[8]

The young infielder's second summer in the US was more promising. With Missoula of the Pioneer League (Class C), he hit .304/12/68, including 10 triples. The local writers, sportscasters, scorers, managers, and umpires voted him to the league's 1960 All-Star team.[9] As a reward, he spent two games with Triple-A Seattle. On a personal level, César also married Beatriz Veitia on December 10, 1960.

Yet for reasons at present unknown, Tovar had to step back down to Geneva in 1961. He stole 88 bases in 100 attempts to lead the league, shattering the New York-Penn League record in the process. He batted .338 with 19 homers and 78 RBIs. He was named to both the league and Class D All-Star teams, a feat he repeated in 1962 with the Rocky Mount Leafs of the Carolina League (Class B). He led that league in batting at .329, to go with 10 homers and 78 RBIs.

Nonetheless, it appeared Tovar would have a hard time progressing through the Reds' system. In 1963 the big club in Cincinnati had a new second baseman: Pete Rose, who became National League Rookie of the Year. Future major leaguer Bobby Klaus was at Triple-A San Diego and Gus Gil was at Double-A Macon. The organization sent Tovar on loan to the Twins; he played for their Triple-A farm team, Dallas-Fort Worth. There too, manager Jack McKeon had veteran Jim Snyder at second base, so Tovar became a utilityman for the first time, playing shortstop and the outfield while hitting .297/11/49. "He has to be in the lineup and he has to be my leadoff man," McKeon worried, "but where do I play him?" After seeing him in the outfield, the skipper said, "It's amazing. He gets a great jump on the ball – as if he had always played out there."[10]

Tovar also made two good friends in the Twins organization in 1963. One was Billy Martin, who that year was a minor-league instructor in spring training and took César under his wing. Another was his roommate, Tony Oliva, from Cuba, who became his teammate for seven-plus seasons in Minnesota. That year César and Beatriz added twin boys Jhonny Gustavo (named for Gus Gil) and Edgar José to their family. César Augusto had been born in 1961.

Tovar returned to the Reds chain in 1964 and played for San Diego, which won the Pacific Coast League pennant. He hit .275/7/52 while playing third, short, second, and the outfield. During the pennant series against Eastern Division winner Arkansas, opposing manager Frank Lucchesi said, "Tovar killed us with his great plays in the field as well as his bat."[11]

On December 4, 1964, the Twins traded pitcher Gerry Arrigo (coming off his best big-league season) to Cincinnati to get Tovar. Minnesota owner Calvin Griffith had wanted Tommy Helms, but the Reds wouldn't part with him, and Griffith said the Twins "had to pay through the nose" for Tovar. Scouting reports at the time labeled César an "adequate" second baseman who was "not considered outstanding on the double-play pivot."[12] Minnesota was thinking about him at third base as well as second.

Manager Sam Mele gave Tovar a long look at second base during spring training 1965 in a competition with light-hitting Jerry Kindall. Martin, a former second baseman and by then the Twins' infield coach, became César's tutor again.[13] Tovar made the Twins roster to open the 1965 season, becoming just the ninth Venezuelan to reach the majors. It seems remarkable today, but at that time only two more of his countrymen were active at the top level, Luis Aparicio and Vic Davalillo. In his debut on Opening Day at Metropolitan Stadium, playing third base, Tovar went from goat to hero. He dropped a Joe Pepitone popup in the ninth inning, allowing the tying run to score – but in the 11th inning he came through with a two-out game-winning single.

César appeared in just nine games with just 13 at-bats through mid-May. Near the end of the month, the Twins sent him down to Triple-A Denver as they reached the 25-man roster limit. After he performed well (.328/11/50), the big club recalled him in September. He was not eligible for the postseason, but he never played in the minors again.

In April 1966 Tony Oliva said, "Tovar plays the game hard. He runs, he chases down groundballs, dives at the ball, steals bases. And he sure can hit."[14] Tony was right. The following seven summers with Minnesota, 1966 through 1972, were the heart of Tovar's big-league career. He averaged 153 games played and 653 plate appearances per season over this period – indeed, from 1967 to 1971 he never appeared in fewer than 157 games. As the table-setter for the likes of Tony Oliva and Harmon Killebrew, he averaged 166 hits and 92 runs scored a year. In 1970 he led the American League in doubles (36) and triples (13). Tovar followed up with a career-best 204 hits in 1971 – the best one-year total by any Venezuelan until Magglio Ordóñez got 216 in 2007.

Tovar received MVP votes in each year from 1967 to 1971. In fact, when Carl Yastrzemski finished one vote short of unanimous American League MVP honors during his Triple Crown season in 1967, the 20th first-place ballot went to Tovar

(.267/6/47). Minnesota beat writer Max Nichols defended his choice, saying, "He played six positions for the Twins and I saw him win games for them at all six positions. We didn't have the best of player relations on our club, but Tovar never got mixed up in any of the clubhouse politics. He kept plugging away, no matter where they put him, and to me he did a tremendous job. If I wanted to be a 'homer,' I would have voted for Harmon Killebrew. But Tovar was my choice and, if I had to do it all over again, I'd vote for him again."[15]

"I would've voted for him too," said Billy Martin, who became the Twins' manager in 1969.[16] In his 1981 book, *Number 1*, Billy said, "Tovar was my little leader. He was the guy who got everyone going. When I wanted him to push Leo [Cárdenas] a little bit or if Rod [Carew] was getting down and I needed someone to give him a boost, I'd get César to do it."[17]

Tovar was never known as an outstanding fielder at any of his positions, but thanks to his speed he covered a lot of ground wherever he played. "He can play center field as well as anyone," said Cal Ermer, who managed him at Denver in 1965 and with the Twins in 1967 and '68. In the infield, "He's too rigid with his hands in fielding groundballs," said Billy Martin, who spent a lot of time in practice with César. Tovar himself said he that he was very tense when he first came to the majors.[18] When Rod Carew arrived in 1967, however, the Twins had an outstanding young second baseman. Though Tovar played a lot of third base in 1967-68, his focus after that became the outfield.

Tovar did not walk as much as one would like in a lead-off hitter. His on-base percentage was .335 for his career, peaking at .356 in both 1970 and 1971. Yet despite his moderate walk totals (a high of 52 in 1970), he often got on base another way – he was hit by a pitch 88 times in his career. As new Twins manager Bill Rigney put it in 1970, "He does not mind sticking an elbow out."[19] A related anecdote came from 1974 and the Venezuelan Winter League. Umpire Armando Rodríguez (the first Latino ump in the majors) called each ball that hit Tovar's arm a strike because he knew what César was doing. Once Tovar got hit in the back and Rodríguez sent him to first base because he was truly hit. After the game, Tovar said, "I have to recognize that the guy has class."[20]

Although Tovar was small, he was muscular and tough-bodied. He was also a very good contact hitter who struck out in only 7% of his plate appearances in the majors. In this vein, Tovar holds a record along with Eddie Milner: They each had the only hit in five one-hitters. Tovar was the spoiler in gems by Barry Moore (April 30, 1967); Dave McNally (ninth inning, May 15, 1969); Mike Cuéllar (ninth inning, August 10, 1969); Dick Bosman (August 13, 1970); and Catfish Hunter (May 31, 1975).[21] There might have been a sixth, but he made the last out in Vida Blue's no-hitter (September 21, 1970).

Tovar's best season for stolen bases was 1969, with 45. Over his career he was successful 68% of the time when stealing, somewhat lower than ideal, especially in a leadoff hitter. Both he and Rod Carew had the skill and daring to steal home, though – in fact, they did it in the same inning against Mickey

Lolich and Bill Freehan of the Detroit Tigers on May 18, 1969. On August 23 at Metropolitan Stadium, César also stole home on the front end of a triple steal. Billy Martin's club was remarkably aggressive on the basepaths that year, pulling off that feat four times.

The Twins won the AL West in both 1969 and 1970, but each time, the Baltimore Orioles swept them in three straight playoff games. Baltimore's superb pitchers kept Tovar off the basepaths in 1969, as he went 1-for-14 with one walk. He did better in 1970 (5-for-13) but scored just two runs.

Tovar played all nine positions on September 22, 1968. The Twins were trailing the league-leading Detroit Tigers by 26 games at the time, and Calvin Griffith thought it would be a good promotional stunt. (The game drew a modest crowd of 11,340 to Metropolitan Stadium). He started the game on the mound – his scoreless inning featured a strikeout of Reggie Jackson, plus a walk and a balk – then went behind the plate. He then moved counter-clockwise around the infield, followed by a trip across the outfield from left to right.[22]

On November 30, 1972, the Twins traded Tovar to the Philadelphia Phillies for outfielder Joe Lis and pitchers Ken Reynolds and Ken Sanders. The Twins were willing to let him go because "his figures slipped some in 1972, partly due to a

One of MLB's most versatile players, Tovar played all nine positions in one game in 1968. He stole 226 bases and hit over .300 twice. (SABR / The Rucker Archive)

shoulder injury when he was hit by a pitch."[23] The Phillies wanted César to play third base – a position he had not manned since 1968 – because they had traded Don Money.[24] They weren't sure if young Mike Schmidt was ready, and indeed he did struggle in 1973, hitting just .196 before emerging as a star. General manager Paul Owens also wanted Tovar on hand in case Mike Anderson couldn't hold down the starting center-field job. "Tovar gives us all kinds of things," said Owens. "He's a team leader. He's an outstanding basestealer, which will help [shortstop] Larry Bowa in his learning process. But most important, he gives us maneuverability."[25]

Tovar played 97 games for the Phillies in 1973 (.268/1/21), missing most of July after knee surgery. That December the Texas Rangers purchased Pepi's contract, as his longtime backer had been clamoring to get him. "When Billy Martin became the Rangers' manager last September, he made one immediate request: 'Get me César Tovar.'" Billy added, "I didn't want him back just because I had him before. That'd be foolish sentiment. I wanted him because of his leadership and his hustle and his ability. He's always played for me – given 100 percent – and I know he will.

"The little guy can beat you so many ways – his bat, his feet, his brains, his hustle."[26]

Tovar rebounded nicely in 1974 (.292/4/58 in 138 games, with 629 plate appearances), playing mainly center field and left field. There was also an amusing footnote to that season. According to Mike Shropshire's 1996 book about the 1973-1975 Rangers, *Seasons in Hell*, there were rumors that Pepito had three wives in three different countries. In 1975 he played less in the field and served more as a designated hitter.

Billy Martin was fired in July 1975. On August 31 the Oakland A's purchased Tovar. Although they already had a healthy lead in the AL West, owner Charlie Finley still wanted a player to help in the final month of the season. Mike Shropshire wrote, "According to speculation, it would be Tovar's job to goad [Bert] Campaneris to get off his ass."[27] The A's placed Angel Mangual, who had been with Oakland since 1971, on irrevocable waivers.[28] Tovar was on the postseason roster and appeared in two playoff games against the Red Sox, going 1-for-2 with two runs scored.

In the winter of 1975-76, Tovar's career at home took a turn as the Caracas Leones merged with Tiburones de La Guaira. For one season, a franchise called "Tibuleones" de Portuguesa existed. When Tovar returned to Oakland in 1976, he was a little-used reserve, going 8-for-45 in 29 games. He broke his wrist making a diving catch on May 31 and was not reactivated until mid-August – it took a complaint to Players Association director Marvin Miller to make it happen.[29] On August 25 Finley – in a typical and quite possibly vengeful move – released the veteran.[30]

On September 1 Tovar signed as a free agent with the New York Yankees, becoming their first Venezuelan player. Again Billy Martin – who had landed with New York less than two weeks after Texas canned him – was behind the signing. The

Yankees had been talking to the Rangers about acquiring Billy's old favorite the previous year.[31] He got into 13 games for the Bronx Bombers, going 6-for-39. He joined the club too late to be eligible for the postseason.

In December 1976 the Yankees released Tovar, and his big-league career came to an end. Of greater significance, though, was the development of the players' rights movement in Venezuela. The re-established Caracas Leones had traded both Vic Davalillo and Tovar to Tigres de Aragua before the 1976-77 season. They filed suit for severance pay. A reputable lawyer named Efraín Muñoz took the case to demonstrate to the Caracas front office and in the courts that his clients were workers and consequently deserved their benefits under national law. Muñoz won, setting a precedent.[32]

Tovar was by no means finished playing in the summers, though, as he joined Puebla in the Mexican League in 1977. During his first month, he batted .270, "but he said he was just 'studying the situation.'" He then went on a tear that lifted his average to .337.[33] He finished the year at .345/1/53 in 432 at-bats across 121 games – yet unlike his fellow Venezuelan vet, Davalillo, his performance south of the border didn't write his ticket back to the majors. Pepi returned to Mexico in 1978, playing with Tabasco, but though he hit well again (.336/1/17), it was in just 31 games. From mid-April to mid-June 1979, he also played with the Caracas Metropolitanos of Bobby Maduro's short-lived Inter-American League.

Tovar's winter career at home also continued. After two seasons with Aragua, he spent seven more with Águilas del Zulia. César, who was 39 when he joined Zulia as a player-coach, averaged just 22 games played per winter during his stretch there, the most being 49 in 1981-82. Zulia became league champion in 1983-84, and Tovar got into one game in the playoff finals. It was his eighth title at home, including the two he won as a playoff reinforcement with Tiburones de La Guaira (1965-66) and Navegantes del Magallanes (1969-70).

When Pepito finally decided to retire as a player, he had appeared in 1,116 games in La Liga Venezolana del Béisbol Profesional, tied for fourth in the league's history. He had 1,224 hits (also fourth lifetime) for a .286 average, along with 23 homers and 399 RBIs. As of 2014 he ranked second in runs scored (635) and steals (146), and third in doubles (191).

Tovar maintained his connection with baseball. He had long been known for his support of children in his homeland, for whom he collected uniforms and equipment. He worked as a softball coach for the INH (Instituto Nacional de Hipódromos, or Horse Racing Authority, which sponsored recreation for its workers and their families). He eventually recommended players to the professional teams. He also managed the Venezuelan national team in the 1990 Baseball World Cup, held in Edmonton. His squad won just one game and lost seven.

Mainly, though, Tovar continued to serve Águilas del Zulia as a coach. His special protégé was Carlos Quintana, who played with the Boston Red Sox from 1988 to 1993. Red Sox bullpen coach John McLaren said in 1991, "I remember Cesar Tovar spent hours and hours with Carlos in winter ball." Quintana said, "He's my second father."[34]

Quintana was also worried when Tovar had to spend a month in the hospital with heart problems in 1991. "He smoked too much," said the first baseman. "I told him [to] stop. Maybe he will now."[35] It appears that Tovar traveled to Minnesota in May 1993 for a 1965 Twins reunion featuring more than 20 team members.[36] Not long after, though, Tovar was diagnosed with pancreatic cancer. This swift and deadly form of the disease ended his life on July 14, 1994. When the news reached Minnesota, the Twins called for a moment of silence before that night's game. Such was Tovar's stature in Venezuela that the nation's president, Rafael Caldera, attended the funeral.

César Tovar entered the Venezuelan Sports Hall of Fame in 1996 and the Venezuelan Baseball Hall of Fame as part of its first class in 2003. He is still remembered as one of the greatest players in the history of his nation's winter league. And as Tony Oliva said of their days with the Twins, "If we'd had nine players like him, we wouldn't have needed any others."[37]

This biography originally appeared in *A Pennant for the Twin Cities: The 1965 Minnesota Twins* (SABR, 2015), edited by Gregory H. Wolf.

ACKNOWLEDGMENTS

Grateful acknowledgment to Jhonny Gustavo Tovar Veitia for providing information about his family (via a series of e-mails, August 2011). Continued thanks to SABR member Alfonso Tusa in Venezuela for his assistance.

SOURCES

baseball-reference.com

retrosheet.org

planeta-beisbol.com (Venezuelan statistics)

museodebeisbol.org (Hall of Fame/Museum of Baseball in Venezuela)

Treto Cisneros, Pedro, editor, *Enciclopedia del Béisbol Mexicano* (Mexico City: Revistas Deportivas, S.A. de C.V.: 11th edition, 2011)

Sporting News Baseball Register, 1965

NOTES

1   The others: Bert Campaneris (1965), Scott Sheldon (2000), Shane Halter (2000).

2   Online biographical sketch by Dr. Braulio Arteaga, *César Tovar: Pimienta Caraqueña*. (oocities.org/espanol/elpelotero_online/reportajes/cesar_tovar...). The origins are unclear.

3   The *Sporting News Annual Register* for 1965 showed "TOH-var" – which is how people in the US often pronounced it. One notable exception was Twins P.A. announcer Bob Casey, who put the emphasis on the second syllable, in the Spanish way.

4   Max Nichols, "Dad Delivers a Lecture When Cesar Strikes Out," *The Sporting News*, June 3, 1967: 11; Dick Gordon, "Letter Man at Minnesota," *Baseball Digest*, July 1967: 29.

5   Gordon, "Letter Man at Minnesota," 30.

6   Max Nichols, Sandlot Pals Tovar and Gil Meet Again – In Majors," *The Sporting News*, May 6, 1967: 11.

7   Si Burick, "Blind Man's Buff," *Baseball Digest*, July 1968, 74. Originally published in the *Dayton Daily News*.

8   They were 1961-62, 1963-64, 1966-67, 1967-68, and 1972-73.

9   "Pioneer Names All-Star Team," *The Sporting News*, September 14, 1960: 46.

10   Merle Heryford, "'Little Cesar' Tovar Packing Big Wallop for Texas Rangers," *The Sporting News*, June 22, 1963: 33.

11   Earl Keller, "Champ Padres Praise Bristol – Pilot Instilled Fighting Spirit," *The Sporting News*, October 3, 1964: 29.

12   Max Nichols, "Cal Expects Swifty Tovar To Firm Up Twins' Infield," *The Sporting News*, December 19, 1964: 6.

13   Max Nichols, "Kindall Duels Tovar At Twins' Keystone," *The Sporting News*, April 3, 1965: 8.

14   Max Nichols, "Great Cesar's Ghost, Twins Find Zoilo's Sub in Wraith-Like Tovar," *The Sporting News*, April 16, 1966: 22.

15   Joe Falls, "An Apology to Writer Who's True to Beliefs," *The Sporting News*, December 16, 1967: 2.

16   George Vass, "Ninth Man in the Lineup," *Baseball Digest*, June 1968: 9.

17   Billy Martin and Peter Golenbock, *Number 1* (New York: Dell Publishing, 1981), 268.

18   Nichols, "Great Cesar's Ghost."

19   Mike Lamey, "Little Cesar Tovar Becomes Twins' Mighty Triggerman," *The Sporting News*, May 16, 1970: 6.

20   Alfonso Tusa, "El primer árbitro latinoamericano en ejercer en Grandes Ligas," Beisbol 007 blog, November 10, 2010 (beisbol007.blogia.com/temas/historia.php).

21   Peter C. Bjarkman, *Diamonds Around the Globe* (Westport, Connecticut: Greenwood Press, 2005), 219.

22   Emil Rothe, "The Day Cesar Tovar Played All 9 Positions," *Baseball Digest*, February 1973: 50-51; Bruce Markusen, "When Cesar Tovar Played All Nine Positions in One Game," *Baseball Digest*, December 1998: 86-89.

23   Allen Lewis, "'Now Phillies Can Shoot For 2nd Place'– Ozark," *The Sporting News*, December 23, 1972: 45.

24   "Phils to Put Tovar at 3rd Base," *The Sporting News*, December 16, 1972: 59.

25   Lewis, "Now Phillies Can Shoot."

26   Merle Heryford, "Rangers Get Tovar … Martin Elated," *The Sporting News*, December 22, 1973: 47.

27   Mike Shropshire, *The Last Real Season* (New York: Grand Central Publishing, 2008).

28   Ron Bergman, "Mercury Matt Spurts Into Hearts of A's," *The Sporting News*, September 20, 1975: 7.

29   Ron Bergman, "Catcher Tenace Can Drive a Hard Bargain," *The Sporting News*, September 4, 1976: 7.

30   Ron Bergman, "A's More Flexible With Willie," *The Sporting News*, September 18, 1976: 34.

31   Randy Galloway, "Howell Fires Homer Barrage to Grab Ranger 3rd Base Job," *The Sporting News*, August 30, 1975: 16.

32   Adriana Cortés, *Montesinos: Su Derrota en Venezuela* (Caracas, Venezuela: Los Libros de El Nacional, 2001), 119. According to *The Sporting News* (July 30, 1977: 25), Tovar filed suit for severance pay in 1977 after the trade. The news may simply have been late getting to the United States.

33   "Mexican League," *The Sporting News*, July 9, 1977: 38.

34   Nick Cafardo, "Q. Who's the Red Sox' hit man? A. The Q.⊠" *Boston Globe*, May 29, 1991.

35   Cafardo, "Q. Who's."

36   Original announcement: Charley Walters, "Civic Center Officials Baffled That Green Rejected Their Offer," *St. Paul Pioneer Press*, March 4, 1993. Subsequent ads for the weekend of May 14-16 mentioned that more than 20 members would be at the shows in the Minneapolis suburb of Hopkins, but did not cite Tovar by name.

37   Arteaga, *César Tovar*.

MANNY TRILLO

BY LEONTE LANDINO

Outstanding defense and strong character can be a short description for Manny Trillo's career. He was a slick-fielding second baseman who shined with a legendary Philadelphia Phillies team and played a huge part in the first title in almost 100 years of misery in one of the fieriest sports markets in the world.

Trillo is always remembered by fans for his distinctive fielding. A not untypical description of Trillo after getting the ball: "Seemingly stopping and reading the NL president's signature on the ball before firing it sidearm."[1]

But the path to an All-Star career that started with the power machine of the Oakland Athletics was not an easy one. The story began in the rural town of Caripito in northeastern Venezuela, where Jesus Manuel Trillo was born to Trina Trillo and Ismael Marcano on December 25, 1950.

"My parents were separated since the day I was born and I always lived with my mother," Trillo recalled in 2001. "My mother took care of me and my siblings Ismael, Eneida, and Zunilda. She was the mother and a father figure for us and she took good care of us. I was never too close to my father, we used to see him once in a while but we were never really close."[2]

Trillo's father was a worker in the booming oil industry, which widely promoted little league and other baseball programs. Young Jesús played on the teams and tournaments sponsored by these programs. Jesús grew up in Quiriquire, a small town in the oilfields, and during his middle-school years, his physical education professor, Rómulo Ortiz, took him under his wing, including him on organized teams and taking him to play local tournaments and competitions. Jesús saw Rómulo as a father figure who passed on to the boy his love for the game. Ortiz used to call him Indio (Indian), making fun of the shy character and personality of his pupil. This nickname stuck with Manny for life.

As a youngster Jesús primarily played shortstop, where he developed quick hands and speed. He admired the two All-Star Venezuelan shortstops in the majors, Chico Carrasquel and Luis Aparicio, both local sports heroes. But one day the catcher for his team was injured and he was sent to play behind the plate. Jesús cried the whole game since he was afraid a foul ball was going to hit him. It didn't happen, and the joy and experience of calling and receiving pitches captured his attention. After that game, he became a catcher.

Jesús became passionate for the game, even skipping classes to go practice as a teenager. By the age of 14, he was determined to become a professional baseball player. His parents supported his diamond dreams.

Ortiz contacted Pompeyo Davalillo, who had recently retired as a player after a cup of coffee with the Washington Senators in 1953, and worked as a coach for Leones del Caracas of the Venezuelan League and a scout for the Philadelphia Phillies. In October 1965 Ortiz and his protégé traveled 10 hours Caracas to see him. Davalillo saw something special in him. He agreed to work with the youngster and, with his mother's permission, kept him in Caracas to train.

Trillo spent two years traveling from Caracas to Maturin, where he studied at Escuela Técnica Industrial. He participated in a tryout after an exhibition game in 1967 in Caracas between the Oakland A's and the Minnesota Twins. In January 1968 the Phillies signed him to a contract, and a few days later the 17-year-old flew to Clearwater, Florida, where the Phillies trained.

Facing a new language, a new culture and new challenges and being alone for the first time was ahead for a teenager from a rural oil town in Venezuela. "It was one of the hardest moments of my life," Trillo said. "I cried a lot and for and for many months. Leaving behind my mother was very hard but it was all worthy to try to achieve my dream of becoming a baseball player. And I wanted to play in the major leagues. I was determined."[3]

Jesús Manuel Marcano, his legal name in Venezuela, became Manny Trillo, a common mistake when processing legal paperwork between the US and Latin countries, where last names are usually confused with maiden names. "They started calling me Manny as a short for Manuel and they put my last name as Trillo, instead of Marcano. However that never bothered me since it was my mother's last name and I was proud of carrying her last name on my back. Although in Venezuela they kept using both of my surnames for the records, so it became Manny Trillo for the United States and Jesús Marcano Trillo in my country, even only Marcano Trillo. It was fine in any way for me."[4]

Trillo went to the Phillies camp as a catcher, but Dallas Green, who had just retired as a player and was to manage Huron (South Dakota) in the short-season Northern League, saw him fielding groundballs and realized his potential as an infielder. Trillo was assigned to Huron as a catcher, but after a few games Green decided to try him at shortstop and third base. "There was no way I was going to put this fragile, skinny kid behind the plate," wrote Green in his memoirs. "I found time to give Manny a little extra attention. He was one of the few Latin kids on the team. I could only imagine how difficult was for Manny at that time. In the lower minor leagues you make peanuts. I slipped Manny a few bucks here and there, because I knew he had nothing."[5]

Trillo played only 35 games at Huron, hitting .261 and performing well at shortstop. After the season he returned to

Venezuela to play with Caracas and was already seen as an infielder.

Trillo spent the 1969 season with Spartanburg (South Carolina) of the Western Carolinas League, where he played mostly in the infield but put in some time behind the plate for the last time in his career. He improved with the bat, hitting .280 with 26 RBIs in 83 games, but seemed to attract little attention from the Phillies. But he caught the attention of Oakland owner Charlie Finley, and the Athletics drafted him in the minor-league phase of the 1969 Rule 5 draft. The A's assigned the 19-year-old to Double-A Birmingham (Southern League), where he played shortstop, second base, and third base in 1970 and shortstop and third base in 1971.

Trillo was viewed as a backup infielder, but with more playing time, his offensive performance improved consistently. In 1971 he batted .280 with 5 home runs and 44 RBIs. In the winter league he hit .291 in 35 games for Caracas.

In 1972 Trillo was assigned to Triple-A Iowa, where manager Sherm Lollar played him at shortstop, second, and third, and he batted a strong .301 in 133 games with 9 home runs. After the season, Trillo rejoined Leones of Caracas and played all 61 games of winter baseball as a third baseman, hitting .240 with 5 home runs. He played a huge role in helping his team to the league championship.

Trillo was a four-time Gold Glover and three-time All-Star. He helped the Phillies win the 1980 World Series. (SABR / The Rucker Archive)

It was Trillo's first taste of championship, and he was also in a world championship organization, as the A's beat the Reds in the World Series while he was playing in his home country. After winning the Venezuelan championship, Leones moved to the Caribbean Series (played in Caracas) and lost to Tigres del Licey from the Dominican Republic. For Trillo it was exciting to understand winning in baseball.

The world champion Athletics had Bert Campaneris at shortstop and Sal Bando at third base; so Trillo hoped to make the team as a second baseman. He was assigned to Triple-A Tucson.

"When we were in Triple A in 1973, my good friends Gonzalo Marquez and José Morales told me that the only chance I had to reach the majors with the A's was in second base," Trillo said in 2001. "So every day before each game in Tucson we went early to the park in our own time just to practice. They used to practice a lot of double plays with me and help me a lot with grounders. We did that for one or two hours each day before the team practice. Sherm Lollar saw our hard work and that I was focusing more on becoming a better second baseman and he gave me the chance to play that season every day on my new position."[6]

In 130 games, Trillo made 19 errors but gained confidence on the field and hit .312 with 8 home runs. He led the team with 78 RBIs. With such a solid performance, Charlie Finley saw his promising 22-year-old Triple-A second baseman as part of the team's future. On June 28, Trillo was called up to make his major-league debut, against Kansas City.

"I remember clearly my first at-bat since I hit the ball to right field and I drove in what eventually was our winning run, he recalled."[7] (Two batters later, Trillo was picked off by Kansas City pitcher Steve Busby, but another Oakland run scored in the process.) "Wearing for the first time a major-league uniform was the best sensation I had in my life. I had achieved my goal."[8]

Trillo played 17 games with Oakland and was 3-for-12. The A's advanced to the American League Championship Series, meeting the Baltimore Orioles for the second year in a row. Trillo was supposed to be on the roster but almost didn't. In error, his name was left off the roster submitted to major-league baseball. Fortunately for Trillo, the Orioles allowed him to be added to the roster, along with Allan Lewis, substituting for the injured Billy North. In the end, Trillo didn't see any action in the ALCS, which the A's won in five games.

The story took a turn when the A's advanced to the World Series and had to petition the New York Mets for the roster changes. The Mets allowed Lewis for North but denied the addition of Trillo. (Before Game One an irate Finley had the PA announcer at the Oakland Coliseum tell fans to scratch Trillo from their lineup cards because the Mets had not allowed the roster adjustment, an action for which he was fined by the commissioner's office.)

Trillo started the 1974 season with the A's but was sent to back to Tucson after hitting .100 during the first month. He was recalled in September. He was included on the postseason roster and scored a run as pinch-runner in the ALCS against the Orioles, but did not play in the World Series, which the A's won over the Los Angeles Dodgers, their third title in a row.

Six days after the Series ended, Trillo was traded to the Chicago Cubs along with relievers Darold Knowles and Bob Locker for outfielder and future Hall of Famer Billy Williams.

Trillo was designated the starting second baseman, and never returned to the minors. In his first season with the Cubs, 1975, he hit .248 with 7 homers and 70 RBIs, but his defense was rough (29 errors). "My teammates used to make fun of me in Chicago saying that for me errors were like a vitamin … one a day," he joked. "But I worked hard on the position and little by little the errors were disappearing from my game."⁹ Trillo was third in votes for the National League Rookie of the Year.

Trillo spent four seasons as the Cubs' primary second baseman. In 1977 he made the National League All-Star squad as a backup to Joe Morgan. In February 1979 he was traded to his original club, the Phillies, in an eight-player deal. Philadelphia was seeking to upgrade its infield. It became one of the best trades the Phillies ever made. Under manager Dallas Green, Trillo shone. His improvement with the glove was evident; he made fewer errors, and showed flash and elegance in his defense. He won the first of his three Gold Gloves.

Trillo's trademark style was to catch a groundball and take a brief moment to look at the ball on his hand before making the throw to first base. "Some players used to tell me: Get rid of that ball faster! But I was just taking my time and watched the ball. Some people thought I was cocky, but no, maybe I was too serious on my job. I just like to do things right."¹⁰

After the 1979 season Trillo went back to Venezuela, where he had become a big star with Leones del Caracas. He hit .306 in 30 games and helped Caracas to win its third title in eight seasons. Trillo remained with the team to play the Caribbean Series in Santo Domingo, Dominican Republic, which was won by a Dominican team, Tigres del Licey.

In 1980 the Phillies under Green won 91 games and Trillo was on center stage, batting .292 with 7 home runs and 43 RBIs and winning the NL Silver Slugger award at his position. His momentum rolled over to the NLCS, in which the Phillies defeated the Houston Astros in five games. and Trillo (8-for-21, .381, four RBIs) was declared the NLCS MVP after a key RBI double in Game Four and a two-run triple in the clinching Game Five.

The Phillies advanced to the World Series against the Kansas City Royals. Trillo hit only .217 in the Series, he helped win Game Five with a great relay throw that kept the Royals from scoring a run, and got a ninth-inning infield hit that drove in the game's winning run. Two nights later, in Game Six, the Phillies won their first World Series title.

When Trillo returned to Venezuela, he stepped into controversy, fighting with Leones over its salary offer. A league-appointed arbitrator couldn't settle the dispute and Trillo demanded a trade.¹¹ He was traded to Aguilas del Zulia, probably the biggest and most impactful trade in the history of the Venezuelan Winter League. Trillo became a leader of the team, which reached the playoff finals in 1981 and 1982.

The trade had a big impact on Trillo's career. "It's was painful for me to leave Caracas, but they received me so well in Zulia and they made me feel part of the team so fast that it became my new home," he said. "Also my wife was from Maracaibo and it made perfect sense for the family."¹²

In 1982 with the Phillies Trillo set a major-league record with 479 consecutive errorless fielding chances as a second baseman. When he finally made an error, it was on a high bouncer by Bill Buckner over the pitcher's head. "I thought the ball was going to hit the ground making it routine for me to catch it, but it hit the turf and the bound was higher and hit my elbow. I thought they were going to call it a hit, but my defensive game got people in Philadelphia used to seeing a hard play as an easy one and that tricked me that day." The official scorer took almost three minutes to make a decision and confirmed the error. The game stopped and the crowd gave Manny a standing ovation for over five minutes. "That was very special for me. I said, 'Wow! I made an error and people cheer at you!'"¹³

Trillo won his second consecutive Gold Glove, the third of his career. He was the starting second baseman for the National League in his third All-Star Game.

But happy times in Philadelphia came to an end. Baseball was changing and he understood the business. During his time with the Phillies his agent was David Landfield. In December 1982, while playing with Zulia, Trillo was traded to the Cleveland Indians along with George Vukovich, Jerry Willard, Julio Franco, and Jay Baller for highly-touted prospect Von Hayes. It was one of the worst trades in the Phillies' history, but trading two potential free agents to get a long-term player seemed to make perfect sense.

After the trade Trillo's former wife, Maria Elena, took over as his agent. She became the only female agent in the business, negotiating for her husband. For the Indians he hit .270 in the first half of the 1983 season and made the All-Star Game as the starter at second base.

By August, the Montreal Expos were looking for a solid infielder and they traded minor leaguer Don Carter for Trillo to help in a pennant chase they eventually lost. After the season Trillo became a free agent and signed with the San Francisco Giants. But his offense started to decline and after being used to playing with competitive clubs, he felt less motivation with the last-place Giants, hitting only .238 in 223 games over two seasons and making 18 errors.

In the meantime, Dallas Green had become the general manager of the Chicago Cubs; he needed infield backup, and acquired Trillo in December 1985 for infielder Dave Owen.

"As soon as I came back to Chicago Dallas told me to be ready to play all four infield positions," Trillo said. "It will be hard, but I'm 35. What the heck. The time comes for every ballplayer. I'm happy to be back, and I hope this will be my last stop. I only have one space left on my cap rack back home."¹⁴

Trillo became a mentor for younger Cubs players like Ryne Sandberg and Shawon Dunston. He was also a liaison between the Cubs and Zulia in Venezuela. The organizations had an unofficial agreement to exchange players that helped the Cubs develop prospects in winter ball. Trillo's relationship with the Venezuelan team grew stronger after he was activated for the 1984 Caribbean Series in San Juan, Puerto Rico, in which Zulia won its first international title.

Trillo played three seasons in his second stint with the Cubs. He was a solid backup, hitting .296 in 1986 .294 with a career-high eight homers in 1987 while playing all the positions on the infield. He was a fan favorite and on his at-bats bleacher fans used to chant: "One-O!, Two-O!, Trillo!"[15]

For the 1987-88 winter ball season, Trillo returned to Zulia, this time with double duty as a player-manager. He played his last 33 games as an active player in winter ball, hitting .270 while managing the team to a record of 23-37. "I felt I could play a couple more seasons in Venezuela, but I thought it was time to give back to baseball," Trillo said. "I enjoyed more the coaching side than being a manager and after that experience I asked the team to allow me to continue as a coach." Zulia agreed and in 1988 Trillo became a full-time coach.

Trillo was released by the Cubs after the 1988 season but he got an invitation from the Cincinnati Reds to be a backup infielder. After playing in 17 games during the first two months of the season, he was released. At the age of 38, "I was ready to continue as an instructor," he said.[16]

Trillo's fielding elegance and clutch hitting were his trademarks. He played for seven teams in his 17-year major-league career, with 1,518 games as a second baseman. As of 2014 he had the best fielding percentage of any Phillies second basemen, .994 in 1982, with only five errors in 149 games.

Trillo's passion for teaching baseball and working in the minor leagues took him to work as a minor-league coach for the Cubs, Phillies, Brewers, Yankees, and White Sox. Ozzie Guillén, the White Sox manager, took him to the 2005 World Series as a guest coach.

In Venezuela Trillo continued to work with Aguilas del Zulia as a coach and special adviser. In his 19 seasons in the Venezuelan league he batted .277 with 29 home runs and 325 RBIs. In 2007 he was voted into the Venezuelan Baseball Hall of Fame. In 2012 Trillo was voted into the Latino Baseball Hall of Fame. He attended the induction ceremony in La Romana, Dominican Republic, joining inductees Tony Oliva, Bernie Williams, and Tony Peña among other Latin greats.

In 2014 Trillo had homes in Orlando, Florida, and Maracaibo, Venezuela. He enjoyed spending time with his family and playing golf. In September, Aguilas del Zulia opens its training camp, he was there. "As long as I can and I'm capable, I'll be wearing the baseball uniform on the field," he said. "I enjoy being in the clubhouse, being around the guys and helping them to develop skills. … I am proud of what I did, I was serious about how I handled myself and I always respected the game and that is the biggest legacy of my career."[17]

SOURCES

In addition to the sources cited in the Notes, the author also consulted Baseball-Reference.com, Purapelota.com, Retrosheet.org, YouTube.com, and the following:

Epstein, Dan, *Big Hair and Plastic Grass: A Funky Ride through Baseball and America in the Swinging '70s* (New York: Macmillan, 2012).

Green, Michael G., and Roger D. Launius, *Charlie Finley: The Outrageous Story of Baseball's Super Showman* (New York: Bloomsbury Publishing, 2010).

Westcott, Rich, *Tales From the Phillies Dugout* (Champaign, Illinois: Sports Publishing LLC, 2006).

Westcott, Rich, *Veterans Stadium: Field of Memories* (Philadelphia: Temple University Press, 2005).

Chass, Murray, "Maria Trillo Acts in Family Interest," *New York Times*, November 11, 1983.

Lomartire, Paul, "Trillo Takes Heart Along, Leaves Gloom In S.F.," *Chicago Tribune*, January 12, 1986.

McNesby, Mike, "Hard to Believe!" Lulu.com. 2009.

Mitchell, Fred, "For Dunston, a Season Of Commitment," *Chicago Tribune*, March 2, 1986.

Megdal, Howard, "Jack of All Trades: Manny Trillo," MLBRumors. com, 2010.

Diario Líder, Caracas, Venezuela, archives.

Diario La Verdad, Maracaibo, Venezuela, archives.

Landino, Leonte, personal interviews with Jesús Marcano Trillo in Maracaibo, Venezuela, November 18, 2012, and November 17, 2013; in La Romana, Dominican Republic, February 12, 2012; and in Bristol, Connecticut. March 28, 2014.

NOTES

1   Al Yellon, Kasey Ignarski, and Matthew Silverman, *Cubs by the Numbers: A Complete Team History of the Chicago Cubs by Uniform Number* (New York: Skyhorse Publishing Inc. 2009), 120.

2   Leonte Landino, *¡Aguilas … A la Carga! Episode 79* (Tripleplay Sports Productions, Maracaibo, Venezuela, December 30, 2001.)

3   Augusto Cárdenas, "Un Indio con corazón zuliano," *Diario Panorama*, Maracaibo, Venezuela, December 9, 2009.

4   *Águilas a La Carga!*, 79.

5   Dallas Green and Allan Maimon, *The Mouth That Roared: My Six Outspoken Decades in Baseball* (Chicago: Triumph Books, 2013), 52.

6   *Águilas A La Carga!*, 79.

7   Augusto Cárdenas, *Diario Panorama*.

8   Ignacio Serrano, "Manny Trillo repasa las anécdotas de su carrera," *Diario El Nacional*, Caracas, Venezuela, December 9, 2013.

9   Augusto Cárdenas, *Diario Panorama*.

10 Ignacio Serrano.

11 Ignacio Serrano.

12   *Águilas a La Carga!*, 79.

13   Augusto Cárdenas, *Diario Panorama*.

14   Bob Verdi, "Trillo Happy 2d Time Around," *Chicago Tribune*. March 6, 1986.

15   Yellon, Ignarski, and Silverman, 52.

16   Leonte Landino interview with Manny Trillo, Maracaibo, Venezuela, 2012.

17   *Águilas a La Carga!*, 79.

UGUETH URBINA

BY MARK S. STERNMAN

One of the best closers in the history of the Montreal Expos, a key contributor to the second Florida Marlins team to win the World Series, and a two-time All-Star, Ugueth Urbina had meaningful on-field accomplishments overshadowed by major off-field troubles that resulted in a criminal conviction and a long prison sentence.

The son of Juan Manuel Urbina, an accountant, and Maura Villarreal, Ugueth had two brothers, Ulmer and Ulises. He began his pro career at an early age. On July 2, 1990, Montreal scout Emilio Carrasquel signed Urbina, then just 16.[1] He pitched nearly exclusively as a starter in the minors and won more than 60 percent of his games with an ERA of under 3.00.

In 1994, Urbina's father was killed in a home robbery. "When I remember my dad is when I'm tired, or when I feel like I'm getting lazy," Urbina said. "Then he comes back to me. He pushes me to go on. ... [The gunmen] were caught and dealt with. That's all."[2]

Urbina may have dismissed the impact that the murder of his father had on his life, but the incident understandably seemed to impact him both during and beyond his career. Urbina had a fierce determination to succeed[3] and struggled with anger management. "You have to look at the guy at the plate like you want to cut his throat," Urbina told teammate Miguel Batista.[4] Pedro Martinez, who played with Urbina in both Montreal and Boston, warned, "He's very, very aggressive, like he will do anything. That's why I don't dig too much into his personal life. Because you don't know why, but he's not afraid of anybody."[5] A scout added, "He's tough as nails, a great competitor. But he's a tough character who ... has lived life to the fullest off the field. There's some baggage there. ... That angry approach, that aggressiveness, plays very well on the field, but sometimes it doesn't play as well in society."[6]

Urbina played winter ball in Venezuela for Leones del Caracas and "was part of a Leones bullpen in 1994-95 that recorded 40⅔ consecutive scoreless innings" to set a league record.[7]

Urbina made his big-league debut on May 9, 1995, against the Philadelphia Phillies. He gave up two runs in two innings and struck out two. Urbina pitched three games in May, winning his second appearance in relief, went back to the minors, and returned for four July starts. Making his first start in his first home appearance on July 12, Urbina, 21, had his best game of the year, getting the win after giving up just three hits and one unearned run in seven innings against the Chicago Cubs. "We know he's a can't-miss kid," Expos manager Felipe Alou said of Urbina. "He might not be ready now, but when he is, he's going to be around for a long time."[8]

Alou's analysis proved prescient: While not quite ready, Urbina would have a lengthy career. Montreal sent Urbina back to AAA Ottawa after acquiring Dave Leiper from Oakland. "He didn't have command of his fastball," general manager Kevin Malone explained. "He needs to be developed. You don't develop anybody when they can just go four or five innings every five days. He needs more time, and Triple A is the best place for him."[9]

Prior to the 1996 season, Urbina underwent surgery "to repair a small tear in his right arm"[10] as the Expos wavered about how to handle the promising pitching prospect and contemplated using him as a closer. The idea failed to take hold when Urbina began the season with a 7-3 record as a starter, but after he lost two straight decisions, Montreal moved him to the bullpen, where he once again earned raves from his manager. "I've always said he reminds me of Mariano Rivera," Alou said in September 1996. "I wouldn't hesitate to use him as a closer this month, either, if for some reason Mel Rojas isn't available. He reminds me a bit of what John Wetteland was like when he showed up here, with little command of his fastball."[11] In his second season, Urbina set career highs in wins (10), starts (17), innings (114), and strikeouts (108). He never started a game again.

Again, Urbina had surgery, this time on his elbow.[12] He did not miss any time due to the injury and had 27 saves in 1997, his first season as a closer. Urbina had the best season of his career in 1998. On April 19 against Houston, he became the first Expos reliever to strike out six (all swinging) in two innings.[13] Urbina made his first All-Star Game, where catcher Javy Lopez struggled with the movement on Urbina's pitches.[14] He finished the season with a 1.30 ERA and 34 saves. In 1999 Urbina's ERA rose to 3.69, but thanks to "a 97-mph fastball, a slider consistently over 90 mph and a developing breaking ball,"[15] he led the National League with a career-high 41 saves.

Off the field, Urbina faced allegations of assault stemming from a September 1999 fight at a Montreal bar that also involved his brother Ulmer. In his ruling a year after the incident, a Quebec judge said, "There is a reasonable doubt on the identity of the assailant, so I have to benefit the accused and acquit him."[16] Urbina soon confronted more serious legal problems.

In 2000, Urbina did not replicate his 1997-1999 record of success. He was hit hard early in the season, bottoming out with an ERA of 11.25 after his first five appearances, which featured two blown saves, the second of which resulted in a walk-off win by Pittsburgh. Even his usually optimistic manager Alou said, "Urbina's fastball was slower than usual. Maybe it was the cold weather, I don't know."[17]

Urbina expressed no concerns about his loss of speed. "Sometime if you feel weaker, you have to use your head, try to hit the corners," he said. "I know the league more, so I'm mixing it up more."[18]

Urbina had another injury and required two more elbow surgeries[19] that ended his 2000 season after an unlucky and ineffective 13 games. Younger brother Ulmer's professional career ended after 2000. After signing at the age of 17 on February 10, 1998,[20] he had pitched three minor-league seasons in the Montreal organization, going 5-4 with two saves and a 4.72 ERA.

Urbina's struggles continued in 2001, when he had an ERA of 4.24 with Montreal, his worst figure with the Expos since his 6.17 ERA in 1995. Montreal shopped the struggling closer and nearly traded him to the New York Yankees for two prospects.

Urbina and one of the prospects both flunked their physicals, so the teams did not consummate the trade,[21] a failure that came to haunt the Yankees. In July Montreal traded Urbina to Boston for Tomo Ohka and Rich Rundles. Dan Duquette, the Red Sox' general manager, said he was "not concerned about Urbina's elbow and declared that the reliever was 'death to right-handed hitters.'"[22]

Urbina regained his effectiveness in Boston although he disliked the fact that he served as both a closer and a set-up man due to the presence of Derek Lowe. At the end of the 2001 season, Urbina requested a trade, but then rescinded the request.[23]

Urbina made the All-Star team for the second and last time in his career in 2002. He pitched scoreless ball in 20 straight games over two months, from April 26 through June 26, but then went 0-3 with a 6.75 ERA in July. The Red Sox deemed the valley more indicative of his future than the peak and made no effort to retain Urbina during free agency.[24]

Urbina signed with the Texas Rangers. "Ugueth Urbina has a quality arm and has been very successful in late-inning situations throughout his career," Rangers general manager John Hart said. "A young veteran at the age of 28 … he will be a positive influence on the development of Francisco Cordero and our other young relievers."[25]

Losing baseball squads do not need to pay veteran closers big salaries. Just as Montreal had unloaded Urbina for prospects, Texas followed suit. On July 11 Texas traded Urbina to the Florida Marlins for three Double-A players, first baseman Adrian Gonzalez, the number one overall pick in the 2000 draft, outfielder Will Smith and pitcher Ryan Snare. They also agreed to pay $550,000 of the remaining $2.3 million on Urbina's contract.

The trade could have worked out for both teams. While Smith never made the majors, and Snare appeared in just a single game, Gonzalez hit 317 homers, albeit just seven for the Rangers. Urbina meanwhile made a major impact on the Marlins' second World Series title.

After leading Florida with 28 saves in 2003, Braden Looper had just one playoff save. Setting up Looper at first, Urbina went 3-0 with six saves and a 1.41 ERA for the Marlins during the regular season and then 1-0 with four saves during the postsea-

son. In the NLCS, he pitched three hitless and scoreless innings to close Games Six and Seven in Florida's comeback win over Chicago. Urbina then had two more saves in the World Series as Florida beat the Yankees.[26] He earned a save in Game One, blew a save opportunity in Game Four, then earned another save in Game Five.

In the offseason Urbina had another troubling off-field incident in Caracas but again escaped legal penalty after a judge ruled that he was defending himself against a would-be robber when he fired a gun at him."[27]

Gunplay generally hampers one's free-agent prospects, and Urbina did not land another gig until Detroit signed him on March 29, 2004. Urbina struggled in 2004 with an ERA of 4.50 and only 21 saves. He last appeared on August 31 as Venezuelan kidnappers abducted his mother and demanded a ransom payment of $15 million.[28]

Having already dealt with his father's murder a decade earlier, Urbina must have felt unbearable pressure in trying to rescue his mother "amid concerns that giving in to kidnappers' demands will set a dangerous precedent for other major leaguers and their families … in this baseball-mad country."[29]

Urbina saved 237 games in the majors and helped the Marlins win the 2003 World Series. He was known for his fiery intensity. (Courtesy Boston Red Sox)

Amid news in November that the kidnappers had lowered their demand to $6 million, the Tigers chose to bring Urbina back for 2005 for a $4 million salary.[30] His mother was freed after being held captive for nearly six months.[31]

With a 2.63 ERA, Urbina pitched much more effectively in his second season in Detroit, but a rebuilding team like the Tigers had little need for an aging closer. On June 8, 2005, Detroit sent Urbina and Ramon Martinez to Philadelphia for Placido Polanco. Urbina had just one save for the Phillies, while Polanco played more than four seasons for Detroit, highlighted by being named the MVP of the 2006 ALCS.

After news of the trade broke, a report came out alleging that "Urbina was part of an alcohol fueled altercation" with an unnamed Tiger teammate.[32] Then he was arrested after an incident on October 15, 2005. In March 2007, Urbina was sentenced to 14 years in prison after a dozen witnesses testified that he and others "hit them repeatedly, struck them with machetes, doused them with gasoline and burned them during a torture session to determine who had stolen a pistol from Urbina's farmhouse. ..."[33]

Urbina's son Juan, a left-handed pitcher born in 1993, pitched in the New York Mets farm system for five seasons. New York closer Francisco Rodriguez, a fellow Venezuelan, watched over the younger Urbina at the imprisoned Ugueth's request.

Urbina's son Ugueth, born in 1994, signed with Seattle in 2011 and pitched in the Mariners' farm system for three seasons.[34]

Ugueth Urbina served more than five years of his sentence before winning early release for good behavior. An approving Bobby Abreu, a fellow countryman who had played with Urbina in Philadelphia, said, "I'm very happy because my buddy is ... free. Anyone who knows him well, knows his humanity. ... I love and respect him a lot."[35]

Seeking to make the transition from a prison cell to the pitcher's mound, Urbina, not quite 39, considered a comeback. He had a great deal to prove both on and off the field. "The first order of business is pitching in Venezuela," he said.[36] Urbina pitched in the 2013-2014 Venezuelan winter season with Leones del Caracas, but struggled, ending his playing career by putting on 13 runners in seven innings. Urbina had pitched 10 seasons in Venezuela, finishing with a career mark there of 16-7 with 13 saves and a 2.44 ERA.[37]

At the end of the 2022 season, Urbina remained 10th on the all-time Montreal/Washington franchise leaderboard in games with 296 and third in saves with 125. On the diamond, Urbina shone as a fiery closer who contributed to a championship, but off the field his inability to overcome tragic familial circumstances, which may have caused his own personal demons, and criminal actions forever marred his reputation as an accomplished athlete.

NOTES

1   *Guide 1997* (Montreal Expos media guide), 208.

2   David Beard, "Reliever Urbina's Talent as Rare as His Name," *South Florida Sun-Sentinel* (Fort Lauderdale), March 22, 1998.

3   Urbina "received the news of his father's death from Dave Jauss, his manager at Double-A Harrisburg (Pennsylvania). Several months shy of his 21st birthday, Urbina realized that he was now the head of his family. "It's a tribute to Ugueth how he handled it," Jauss said. "He did not let down his family. He was going to be the breadwinner of his family and take care of his brothers." John Lowe, "Urbina Found Focus after Father's Death," *Detroit Free Press*, April 14, 2004.

4   Brendan Roberts, "Unhittable Urbina," *The Sporting News*, June 15, 1998: 41.

5   Bob Hohler, "Fired-Up Fireman," *Boston Globe*, April 19, 2002: D5.

6   Gordon Edes, "Pirates' Ship Righted by Experienced Hand," *Boston Globe*, April 28, 2002: D11.

7   Jorge Arangure Jr., "Former Pitcher Sentenced for Attempted Murder Is Reportedly Released," *New York Times*, December 28, 2012.

8   "Expos' Rookie Tough Cookie on Cubs," *Titusville* (Pennsylvania) *Herald*, July 13, 1995: 19.

9   Jeff Blair, "Montreal Expos," *The Sporting News*, August 7, 1995: 22.

10   Jeff Blair, "Montreal Expos," *The Sporting News*, February 19, 1996: 28.

11   Jeff Blair, "Montreal Expos," *The Sporting News*, September 9, 1996: 21.

12   Jeff Blair, "Montreal Expos," *The Sporting News*, December 30, 1996: 25.

13   *Guide 1999* (Montreal Expos media guide), 216.

14   Michael Farber, "Underexposed Save Opportunities Are Few and Far Between for Montreal's Ugueth Urbina," *Sports Illustrated*, July 27, 1998.

15   Stephanie Myles, "Montreal," *The Sporting News*, January 24, 2000: 62.

16   Tu Thanh Ha, *Toronto Globe and Mail*, September 6, 2000. Untitled clipping from the National Baseball Hall of Fame and Museum's file on Urbina. Thanks to reference librarian Cassidy Lent of the Hall for scanning the Urbina file.

17   "Aven and Kendall Sink Expos in Ninth," *Tyrone* (Pennsylvania) *Daily Herald*, April 14, 2000: 4.

18   Stephanie Myles, "Decision to Go with Vidro at Second Gets Fast Results," *The Sporting News*, April 17, 2000: 27.

19   Stephanie Myles, "With Urbina Out for Season, Kline Will Get Closer's Role," *The Sporting News*, July 10, 2000: 38.

20   *Guide 2000* (Montreal Expos media guide), 222.

21   Buster Olney, "Urbina Deal Falls Through, So Yanks Still Seek Reliever," *New York Times*, June 20, 2001: D3. More than a month after the failed trade, Urbina did not understand how he had failed to pass the physical, claiming that the New York doctor "said I was fine. I don't know what kind of physical I didn't pass. Maybe their dental physical." Gordon Edes, "Lowe's Direction Altered by U-turn," *Boston Globe*, August 2, 2001: E6.

22   Murray Chass, "Red Sox Pick Up Urbina, And the Expos' $1 Million," *New York Times*, August 1, 2001: D3.

23   Michael Silverman, "Boston Red Sox," *The Sporting News*, January 28, 2002: 57.

24   Michael Silverman, "Boston Red Sox," *The Sporting News*, October 7, 2002: 18.

25   United Press International, "Ugueth Urbina Signs With Rangers," clipping from the National Baseball Hall of Fame and Museum's file on Urbina, December 22, 2002.

26 Urbina "memorably kissed his catcher, Iván Rodríguez, after Game 1 of the World Series" following his save. Sridhar Pappu, "U Want Him, U Got Him: A World Champion Closer Is Stuck on the Market – and in a Pal's Guest Room," *Sports Illustrated*, March 29, 2004.

27 *USA Today*, clipping from the National Baseball Hall of Fame and Museum's file on Urbina, January 26, 2004.

28 "Abductors: $15 Million for Urbina's Mom," *Detroit Free Press*, September 21, 2004.

29 Tom Farrey, "A Matter of Trust," ESPN.com, September 27, 2004.

30 Gene Guidi, "Tigers Pick Up Option for $4 Million on Urbina," *Detroit Free Press*, November 6, 2004.

31 Murray Chass, "Kidnapping Is Frightening Issue for Venezuelan Major Leaguers," *New York Times*, February 22, 2005: D3.

32 "Drunk Punch," The Detroit Tiger Weblog, https://www.detroittigersweblog.com/2005/06/drunk-punchphp/, June 9, 2005 (accessed March 16, 2022).

33 Steven Dudley, "Former Marlin Urbina's Life Takes Dark Turn," *Miami Herald*, March 31, 2007.

34 Larry Stone, "The Ugueth Urbina Name Is Back in Baseball – and the Mariners Have Him," *Seattle Times*, February 27, 2012.

35 Mark Penner, "Ugueth Urbina Pays His Debt to Society," *Philadelphia Daily News*, December 27, 2012.

36 "Ugueth Urbina Returns to Baseball," ESPN.com, December 28, 2012.

37 https://www.pelotabinaria.com.ve/beisbol/mostrar.php?ID=urbiuguo01 (accessed March 18, 2022).

OMAR VIZQUEL

BY AUGUSTO CÁRDENAS

Venezuela has been a cradle of shortstops since 1950, when Alfonso "Chico" Carrasquel made his debut in the majors with the Chicago White Sox.

In his steps followed Luis Aparicio, the only Venezuelan in the Hall of Fame in Cooperstown, David Concepción, Ozzie Guillén, and then another shortstop who played more games at that position than at any other in the majors: Omar Enrique (González) Vizquel.

Vizquel was born in Caracas on April 24, 1967, to Omar Santos Vizquel and Eucaris González, the eldest of three children. He has a younger brother, Carlos Alberto (born 1970), and Gabriela (1980).

"My dad was an electrician in Caracas. My mother was a woman of the household, enterprising, with a very strong character," Vizquel remembered. "We are a very close family, very quiet."

"I grew up in a neighborhood called Bloques de Santa Eduvigis. That is the height of Palos Grandes, in Caracas. There I attended the Santa Gema School for two years, and then we moved to a neighborhood called El Cafetal, where I attended the Josefa Irausquín López School. There I spent most of my school until I graduated and went to Antonio López Méndez School," he recalled. "I ended up graduating in Francisco Espejo College, in El Cafetal. That was the year I received an offer to sign a professional baseball contract. … so I did not attend my graduation party but traveled directly to the United States, after I finished the school year, in 1984."

His love for baseball was instilled by his father, who passed away in 2016.

"My dad played on an amateur team and took me to the games on weekends. That began to motivate me, and I grew to love the game. I was given a Venezuelan brand Tamanaco baseball glove, blue, that was one of my favorites, and with that I started playing baseball to follow the footsteps of my father."

He played baseball in his spare time. "All my friends always invited me to play and I was very happy at Santa Eduvigis blocks with all those friends playing with balls that we (made) with adhesive tape and guava sticks that we used as a bat."

When he was 8, Omar's father took him to the Lyceum Gustavo Herrera to join a children's team, Gran Mariscal, of the Leoncio Martinez League, an affiliate of the Criollitos of Venezuela Corporation, a youth movement similar to the Little League organization.

"The coach put me to play shortstop and I was on that team until I was 16 years old."

With Gran Mariscal Vizquel developed his skills and managed to represent Miranda state in several national and international tournaments, along with another future big leaguer, Carlos Hernández, who caught for the Los Angeles Dodgers.

In 1977, in a Little League Baseball World Series, contested by 12 countries at Universitario Stadium in Caracas, Vizquel's glove work began winning him fans and was instrumental in Venezuela's winning the title. He was only 10 years old.

"At that age you do not feel that you are famous or anything. You are simply playing sports, and not looking to see if you are in newspapers or anything like that," he said. "But the organizers noticed, and when you went to a national or other World Series, your name would stand out. Two years after that World Series, I went to a national tournament, where I won the award for the best infielder. Every two years I was going to a National and I represented Miranda state a couple of times, and I won the best infielder award, and I was invited to numerous competitions."

These tournaments were played in one of the stadiums of the Venezuelan professional baseball league before winter league games, so Vizquel had the opportunity to meet some of his predecessors, Chico Carrasquel, Aparicio, and Concepcion, his main idol and the starting shortstop for the Cincinnati Reds, who also played in Venezuela with Tigres de Aragua.

"We did not go often to the stadium to watch the winter ballgames, just when Dave Concepción was going to play with Tigres de Aragua. My dad, who was a big fan of Dave Concepción, took me to see him play and we sat in the third-base stands to see him play ball," he recalled. "I really liked his style and I followed in his career when he was with the Cincinnati Reds. That's why I wore the famous number 13 in my career, in honor of Dave Concepción."

The shortstop of the Big Red Machine was a big influence and motivation to Vizquel when he decided to pursue the dream of becoming a professional baseball player.

"When I was 14, I knew I had skills to play the sport, and this was actually when I started to get serious with baseball. Back then I worshipped Dave Concepción. I followed his games, was more aware of the details of how he made a double play, how he fielded a grounder, to get the right position when fielding, all these little things that could help me to develop my own game. I also went to a clinic that Alfonso Carrasquel gave and I began attending activities that had to do with baseball to learn a little bit more about it."

One of his teammates on the Gran Mariscal team was Luis Morales, son of Pablo Morales Chirinos, one of the owners of Leones del Caracas, the Venezuelan Winter League team to which he was invited to attend practices at age 16.

"When I went to train with Leones del Caracas, I met Marty Martínez that afternoon, a scout for the Seattle Mariners. In two days I had signed a contract. I was very lucky, because there were players who were training three to four months and had not been offered a contract. But with me it was different. I had just two days' training and Marty had offered me a contract to go play with the Mariners. I was very lucky."

Vizquel signed as a free agent with a nonguaranteed bonus of $4,500, in 1984. He received $2,500 up-front with the rest to come in installments of $500 at each step up the ladder.

He immediately went to America and played Rookie League ball with the Butte Copper Kings; he hit for a .311 average in 15 games.

"The minor-league process was normal. Every year I had the opportunity to move to a different league. I started in rookie league, because I was 16, and then I was promoted to Class-A short-season ball (1985 Bellingham Mariners), then to Class A (1986, Wausau Timbers), and then switched to Class A Advanced (1987, Salinas Spurs). At each level, I was able to develop further."

His participation in winter ball with Leones del Caracas also helped him mature as a player and to better develop his skills.

"When I was in Class A I was added to the roster of Leones del Caracas, playing as a 19-year-old with players from Double A and Triple A. When I got to Double A, I got the chance to play as a starting shortstop in Venezuela and I think that made me a much faster player, because I was already playing with major-league players. I remember that Andrés Galarraga was the first baseman, Baudilio "Bo" Díaz was catching, Antonio "Tony" Armas was one of the outfielders, along with Lloyd McClendon and Donell Nixon; Jesús Alfaro was at third base and Edgar Cáceres at second. I was the youngest guy and I had the nickname 'Chamo Menudo,' because the youth music group Menudo was the band of the moment."

That experience helped Vizquel on his journey through Double A (Vermont Mariners) and Triple A (Calgary Cannons), in 1988, when he became a switch-hitter on the recommendation of Mariners hitting instructor Bobby Tolan.

"In 1988 they took me to the Instructional League to learn to bat left-handed, because they saw that my right-side numbers were a little weak. They thought that batting lefty I could exploit a little more speed and batting skills; it was a change that benefited me a lot and maybe was the key to success for me in the big leagues."

During 1989 spring training the Mariners had Rey Quiñones as first-string shortstop, but he reported late because of a contract dispute, which began to open the doors of the majors to the young Venezuelan shortstop.

"Supposedly that year I had to go to Triple A, but with Quiñones out, Mario Díaz had to play," Vizquel recalled. "He was the shortstop in Triple A and had good numbers, but was injured during spring training and there was nobody else to play shortstop so they threw me into the ring to see what I could do and I surprised the manager, Jim Lefebvre."

Díaz injured his right elbow and Vizquel had the opportunity to display his defensive talents, and he impressed Lefebvre, despite his weaknesses as a batter.

"He liked the way I played, how I defended, and he knew I was learning to bat from the left side that year, but I knew it was going to get difficult to stay in the big leagues, but they made the decision, traded Rey Quiñones to the Pirates, and left Mario Díaz as the utility player, because he continued to suffer arm problems. That left me as the shortstop."

At just 21 years old, a few days shy of 22, Vizquel received the news on the last day of spring training.

"I had to ask one of the coaches, 'What do I do with my bags? Am I going to Triple A? Am I going to be in the big leagues? I need to know, because people are packing,'" he recalled. "I was not told I was going to be the team's shortstop until the last day of spring training. After the final out, they gave me the news. It was a total surprise because the last thing I thought was that I was staying in the majors that year."

Vizquel's debut came on Opening Day, April 3, 1989, at the Oakland Coliseum, facing the reigning American League champions, the Oakland Athletics. Vizquel was not the only rookie debuting in Lefebvre's lineup. So was Ken Griffey Jr., from the start a media sensation.

Vizquel did not make the best of impressions in his debut, with a fielding error on Carney Lansford's roller in the third inning, followed by a Mark McGwire home run, which made all the difference in the A's 3-2 win over the Mariners.

"I felt bad for the error, but I never felt that I was going to be affected by it in the future. They had already given me the confidence to go out and play my game. The manager told me, 'We know you're not ready for this kind of work, but we like the way you play and you will be our regular shortstop.'"

Vizquel's first campaign was not his most productive. He finished with a .220 batting average, the lowest of his career, but he learned how to handle the pressure of playing as a shortstop in major-league baseball.

"I had many things against me. First, I was learning to bat from the left side; it was not going to be easy to learn to bat left-handed against big-league pitchers. The Mariners knew that I wasn't really ready to play in the majors, but I got the job and they gave me the opportunity. By asking questions, and working all day every day with the guys who were there, like Alvin Davis, Harold Reynolds, who were regulars in the organization, learning the little things they were always telling me – how to bat from the left side, it all helped me gradually to become a better player."

Vizquel began the 1990 season on the disabled list after suffering a sprained MCL in the left knee; he played in only 81 games, batting .247 and making seven errors. He played 142 games in 1992; his batting average slipped to .230. Nevertheless, Seattle remained confident in his abilities.

"Obviously the bat was not the reason that I was in the majors. That's for sure. It was the way I played and my glove," he said. "The glove was my best asset, and I could steal some bases, could play the ball, could do hit-and-run. Those are the things that you try to instill in young boys today who expect to reach the majors just hitting all the time. There are other things you have in your repertoire that you can develop, and you can stay in the majors doing small things. That was my case."

By 1992 Vizquel was considered one of the best defensive shortstops in the American League. That season he made only seven errors for a .989 fielding percentage, the best in the majors. For the first time he was a candidate for the Gold Glove Award, though Cal Ripken Jr. got the nod.

"I was very pleased with the work I had done, so was the organization, and that was all that interested me," said Vizquel, who hit a strong .294 that season. "I was improving my game in both batting and fielding."

His reward came the following year, when he turned 108 double plays, tied for the league lead. His fielding percentage of .980 and the growing appreciation of his talent combined to win him his first Gold Glove. One standout moment occurred on April 22, when he preserved Chris Bosio's no-hitter against the Red Sox by making a barehanded grab of an Ernest Riles chopper and firing to first for the last out of the game.

Omar Vizquel was a defensive wizard at shortstop, earning 11 Gold Gloves over a 24-year MLB career. Beloved for his glove, leadership, and longevity, he became a baseball icon in both Venezuela and the majors. (Jerry Coli / Dreamstime)

Vizquel felt settled in Seattle, where he took up residence and married his first wife, Nicole Tonkin, but his plans changed when he was surprised with the news that he had been sent to the Cleveland Indians on December 20, 1993, in a trade for Félix Fermín, Reggie Jefferson, and cash. The Mariners were making room for a talented youngster named Alex Rodríguez.

"When I got the news that they traded me to Cleveland I felt pretty bad. I was down. I wanted to be on a team for 20 years. I did not want to move anywhere else," he said. "I felt good with the Mariners. I had married that year, had bought my house. It was like they gave me a slap in the face, and I had to move to another organization where I knew no one.

"The first time you are traded you think about a lot of things. The first is that the team does not like you, that they trade you because they don't like what you're doing. But I took it otherwise. I took it the positive side. When I got to spring training and met the players and the kind of talent that the team had, I felt much better and I clicked very well on that team. With all the Latin players there, I had a very good time that year with the Cleveland Indians."

Vizquel joined a group of Latinos who helped the Indians change their image from that of a perennial loser, which was satirized in the 1989 movie *Major League*. The Indians had put together a very competitive club in 1994 with Manny Ramírez, Carlos Baerga, Sandy Alomar Jr., Tony Peña, Dennis Martínez, José Mesa, Julián Tavárez, Álvaro Espinoza, Rubén Amaro Jr., and Candy Maldonado.

That group, together with Kenny Lofton, Albert Belle, Jim Thome, Eddie Murray, Charles Nagy, and Jack Morris, helped the Indians to a 66-47 mark, just a game behind the Chicago White Sox for the American League Central lead when the season was suspended because of the players strike.

"You could tell that team was coming together well," said Vizquel. "We had good chemistry and everyone was filled with confidence. The team chemistry was growing and we thought we had a chance to be champions that year; however the strike prevented us finishing the season."

Vizquel, who on April 7 that year got the first stolen base in the history of Jacobs Field, the Indians' new home ballpark, won the second of nine consecutive Gold Gloves in the American League.

There was no strike to stop the 1995 Indians, who were reinforced by veterans like Orel Hershiser and Dave Winfield, and reached their first World Series since 1954.

"In 1995 we felt like we were indestructible," Vizquel said. "We felt that no one could beat us. We had offense, pitching, we ran bases. We had a great team. I was very happy that we finally got to where any player wants to go: the World Series."

The Tribe swept the Red Sox in three games in the Division Series and dispatched the Seattle Mariners in six games in the American League Championship Series, after having 100 victories in a regular season limited to 144 games by the delayed start of the season.

"With this record we looked unbeatable. I never thought we were going to lose, even with the pitching of the Atlanta Braves, but certainly we lacked experience," he said. "I think that was the only thing we lacked; the Braves had a team with more postseason experience."

The Braves, with the future Hall of Famer Bobby Cox as manager, had reached the fall classic in 1991 and 1992, but in 1995 their pitching looked even better with future immortals Greg Maddux, Tom Glavine, and John Smoltz.

"We were like wild horses. What we did was just play ball, score runs, stole bases, and they played a different style of baseball, pitching around," said the Venezuelan, who in his first postseason hit just .138. "They could score two runs and win a game with their relievers. That was what happened. We couldn't hit. Their pitching was dominant. With these three future Hall of Famers (Maddux, Glavine, and Smoltz) it was difficult for us to see the light and we lost that World Series."

In 1997 Vizquel returned to the fall classic with the Indians after playing a key role in eliminating the defending champion New York Yankees in five games in the ALDS.

With the Yankees ahead in the series, two games to one, Vizquel forced a fifth and deciding game at Jacobs Field, hitting a single that drove in Marquis Grissom from second base in a 3-2 walk-off victory. The Tribe won the next day, 4-3. Vizquel ended the series with a .500 (9-for-18) batting average and four stolen bases.

In the ALCS the Indians had their revenge on the Baltimore Orioles, who had eliminated them in 1996, and beat them in six games to advance to the World Series against the Florida Marlins.

"We thought we had more experience than the Marlins. It was a fairly new team, which came almost all from different teams, and we thought we could win."

Vizquel was never closer to winning a World Series ring than that year and again was a key to forcing a decisive contest, Game Six of the Series.

The Marlins led the Series three games to two. In Game Six at Miami's Pro Player Stadium, Cleveland had a 4-1 lead after five innings, due in large part to Vizquel's glove. In the sixth inning, with men on second and third and two outs, the Marlins' Charles Johnson hit a grounder in the hole and Vizquel made a spectacular diving catch to throw him out at first and prevent two runs from scoring.

"Everyone in Cleveland will remember that play, because of the magnitude of the moment. World Series plays are special moments," he said. "It was the biggest play of my career. Logically the moment marked that play. When I talk about the Seattle Mariners, people always remember the play in Chris Bosio's no-hitter. If I had to pick one play, it would be the World Series one, but if you talk about Omar Vizquel the infielder, people always remember the barehanded plays because I made it very often and it's like a brand, the dude grasping a ball without a glove. I'm also recognized by that."

In the deciding Game Seven, with Cleveland two outs away from winning the ultimate prize, the Marlins tied the game in the ninth inning and then won it, 3-2, in 11 innings on Edgar Renteria's walk-off hit.

"We went to Game Seven and couldn't achieve the ultimate victory. It was a game that went to extra innings and in extra innings anything can happen," Vizquel said. "I think that the beauty of this Series was going to Game Seven. It's like a dream that everybody has: Play the seventh game of the World Series. There is no further, everyone is watching the game, and everything is magnified three times. The challenge to be there playing and trying to do your best for your team was one of the things that has filled me as a player. Knowing that I could handle that moment, because not everyone can handle that kind of pressure, made me feel very good about myself."

In 2001, Vizquel won his ninth Gold Glove, matching the American League record held by Hall of Famer Luis Aparicio. He also played in his last postseason.

The golden years of the Tribe were over. Only Vizquel and Jim Thome remained from the winning core that had been formed in the mid-'90s.

Thome left as a free agent after the 2002 season, in which Vizquel set career highs in home runs (14) and RBIs (72), and took part in his third and final All-Star Game, being the sole representative of the Tribe.

The Indians were rebuilding in 2003 and Vizquel, with an injured right knee, played in just 64 games. In 2004, at the age of 37, he returned with a solid .291 average, but the Indians had other plans for 2005 and gave the position to rookie Jhonny Peralta.

"Everybody had already left the team. I was the last that remained of that generation that made the playoffs, the World Series," Vizquel noted. "That's why the people of Cleveland showed me so much affection. But this is a business. I was fortunate that I lasted 11 years in the organization. They treated me great, and I will always take pride in those years."

On November 16, 2004, Vizquel signed a three-year, $12.25 million deal with the San Francisco Giants, moving his magic glove and experience to the National League.

"I knew I still had a lot of baseball ahead. (The Indians) believed that I was going downhill. The knee operation affected me and I think that influenced their decision to let me go. When San Francisco signed me, thank God I made it to a number-one organization, one where I felt good, was offered all possible respect, and could even trust myself. That helped me win two more Gold Gloves at the age of 38 and 39 years."

In 2005 Vizquel had a brilliant debut in the Bay Area, winning his 10th Gold Glove to surpass Luis Aparicio's record for the most Gold Gloves won by a Venezuelan. The following year he repeated the honor and became the oldest shortstop to obtain the distinction.

On May 13, 2007, Vizquel broke the record for most career double plays turned by a shortstop after reaching 1,591, surpassing the 1,590 of Ozzie Smith. His years as a regular shortstop ended the following season, but not until after he established a major-league record for most games for a shortstop with 2,584, surpassing another mark held by Luis Aparicio. When he retired, Vizquel's career total at shortstop was 2,709.

He maintained his physical condition at the highest level, despite his 41 years, but clubs were not very interested in giving him a starting spot. He was seen as a utility player and mentor of young figures, like fellow Venezuelan Elvis Andrus when Vizquel went to the Texas Rangers in 2009.

"I think he was very helpful for me," Andrus said of Vizquel. "And I imagine, putting myself in his shoes, it's hard to play your whole career as a starter and have to change to the role he had here, as a substitute, or as my mentor, actually. He helped me a lot and I feel super blessed. Having him in my first year in the big leagues was like having a bible of how to do things, how to play baseball, how to prepare to play. Mentally I think Omar is one of the best shortstops in the whole story and I think that he helped me very much since day one. He always gave me advice and helped me, especially during the bad times I had that year to keep focused on the positive things and never let the negative consume me. These were tips that I continue to use to this day."[2]

"It was strange to play after turning 40 and hear the comments of people saying I couldn't keep playing baseball. They were wondering if I could be a shortstop, because a 40-year-old shortstop is not the same as a 24-year-old kid in an organization. That boy is going to be as versatile as you, but they never took into account the experience, or anything like that," he said. "It was a stage, in which the mind began to change, to see the game different, with another vision, and I had to make changes, adjustments in every sense of the word, and thank God they were noticing some of the records I was setting and they offered me the opportunity to reach these personal records."

In his one year with Texas he played only 62 games and made no errors, having his only perfect defensive year. On June 25, in Arizona, he surpassed Aparicio as the Venezuelan with the most major-league base hits, with 2,678.

In 2010 Aparicio graciously allowed Vizquel to wear his retired No. 11 jersey with the Chicago White Sox, after the newly-acquired utilityman failed to secure his usual number 13 – that was worn by his new manager Ozzie Guillen, who was also a Dave Concepcion fan.

"That was a truly enjoyable time, because at the time I signed with the White Sox, I was giving a baseball clinic with Luis Aparicio in Venezuela, and the question came up whether I could wear #11 in tribute to him. It was a nice gesture from him to call the owners of the White Sox and let me wear the number not only in his name but on behalf of Venezuela as well."

In 2012 he signed a minor-league contract with the Toronto Blue Jays and managed to make the team in spring training. This time he wore number 17, in honor of Chico Carrasquel, because Brett Lawrie had number 13. He participated in 60 games, his last game at shortstop coming on October 3 in Toronto. In his final game, he went 1-for-3 against the Minnesota Twins, getting his 2,877th hit and passing Mel Ott on the career hits

list. (Two weeks earlier, on September 19, he had collected hit number 2,874, passing Babe Ruth.) He finished his career as the only player with 24 straight seasons at shortstop and, at age 45, the oldest player to play that position.

Just other five major-league shortstops have more career hits than Vizquel: Derek Jeter, Honus Wagner, Cal Ripken Jr., Robin Yount, and Alex Rodríguez, all with over 3,000.

"I think the hits record makes me proud the most,". People believe that is the Gold Gloves one, a record hard to achieve as well. Winning 11 Gold Gloves is not easy at the highest level of baseball, but to connect for 2,800 hits, nearly 3,000, is something especially since I had never been considered a hitter."

Vizquel finished with a career line of .272/.336/.352, with 456 doubles, 77 triples, 80 home runs, 1,445 runs, 951 RBIs, and 404 steals, and he is one of just 11 players to accomplish 2.800 hits and 400 stolen bases. But his trademark was his fielding excellence.

The Venezuelan finished his career with a .9847 fielding percentage, the best in MLB history, just above Troy Tulowitzki (.9846) as of 2018. He the leader in games (2,709) and double plays (1,734) as a shortstop, and ranks third in assists (7,676). His 11 Gold Gloves ranke him second as a shortstop, just behind the 13 that the first-ballot Hall of Famer Ozzie Smith won, another glove wizard with whom he was often compared.

After 24 seasons playing in the majors, Vizquel decided to start a coaching career after spending his last four years mostly on the bench, as a utility player, passing his knowledge to young players while accumulating personal records when he got the chance to go to the field.

"I felt very happy that in each of those organizations in which I played I could break records that meant something beautiful for me on a personal level. I did not play because I wanted to break those records, I just felt really good about myself and my knees were responding fully. I was a gym freak and able to maintain my body in good shape. Even after I retired with the Blue Jays, when I was in Anaheim, I had some regret that I'd retired because I felt I could continue playing, but I was ready to be a coach."

On January 30, 2013, Vizquel was hired as a roving infield coach by the Los Angeles Angels. The next year he returned to the majors with the Detroit Tigers, who made him their first-base coach and infield and baserunning instructor. That association ended after the 2017 season.

"That's something I had to do because I want to be a manager and that was one way of preparation, hearing all the comments from the coaches. Right now I love my job. The fact that I can help a boy to develop his game pleased me very much."

Vizquel, who was a candidate to manage the Tigers in 2018 (Ron Gardenhire was hired), got his first managerial experience with Venezuela in the 2017 World Baseball Classic, but his team couldn't pass the second round.

"The WBC was spectacular. Although we didn't reach the final goal, which was to reach the last playoff, we were able to sneak into the second round. It was a shame we did not score the necessary runs and that the pitching dropped a little bit, because in a short competition anything can happen," Vizquel said. "As a first experience as a manager, I had a great time."

Vizquel came back to the White Sox organization in 2018 as the manager of their Class-A affiliate at Winston-Salem. He still resided in Seattle as of 2018, along with Blanca Garcia, his wife since 2014. They live near his two children, Nicholas, born in 1995, and Kaylee, who was adopted in 2007.

Vizquel was inducted into the Cleveland Indians Hall of Fame on June 21, 2014, and was chosen by the fans as one of the Tribe's Franchise Four in 2015, alongside Bob Feller, Tris Speaker and Thome.

Vizquel had his first shot at election to the Hall of Fame in 2018, when Chipper Jones, Vladimir Guerrero, Jim Thome, and Trevor Hoffman got the call, but he fell short with 37 percent of the votes.

"I'm very happy," he said. "When you are first eligible for the Hall of Fame you do not know what kind of support you will receive from the voters. As time goes by you can increase or you can stay in the same position. I believe that it will continue to increase, although in the sabermetrics there are numbers that do not benefit me, but who saw me playing ball knows the game, knows what I did, knows my skills, what I was able to do and that (is) not numbers. You work for that on the field and the rest is on the part of the voters to discuss it."

Nevertheless, his debut on the ballot was better than that of Aparicio, who finished with 27.8 percent in his first chance and finally made in his sixth opportunity.

"I hope he gets into the Hall of Fame, because he deserves it, but I think the change of position (from shortstop) is going to hurt him," said Aparicio. "It also depends on who else is on the ballots, but I think he's going to make it. I think about the shortstops that I saw and there is none like that little fellow, because he fields grounders like nobody else."[3]

"You flip back and see how time flew," Vizquel said. "Playing 24 seasons in the majors and having all those memories, records, and stats make me feel very humble. I never thought I could go up to the heights of a player like Luis Aparicio and get to have so many good numbers."

SOURCES

baseball-reference.com/.

baseballhall.org/hof/2018-bbwaa-ballot.

cbssports.com/mlb/news/2018-baseball-hall-of-fame-ballot-the-cases-for-and-against-omar-vizquel/.

cleveland.com/tribe/index.ssf/2018/01/path_to_cooperstown_will_not_b.html.

espn.co.uk/mlb/news/story?id=3419650.

mlb.com/es/news/tiene-autenticos-argumentos-omar-vizquel-para-el-salon-de-la-fama/c-262497102.

Vizquel, Omar, and Bob Dyer. *Omar! My Life on and Off the Field* (Cleveland: Gray & Company, Publishers, 2002).

Cárdenas Lares, Carlos Daniel. *Venezolanos en las Grandes Ligas* (Fundación Cárdenas Lares, 1994).

Various Authors. *Todo lo que usted debe saber sobre Omar Vizquel* (Grupo Editorial Macpecri, 2012).

NOTES

1   Author interview with Omar Vizquel on January, 7, 2015. Unless otherwise noted, all comments by Vizquel are from this interview.

2   Author interview with Elvis Andrus on March, 10, 2018. Unless otherwise noted, all comments by Andrus are from this interview.

3   *Luis Aparicio con Augusto Cárdenas, Mi História*; Luis Aparicio (Maracaibo, Venezuela: Cardenas Sports Media, 2011).

CARLOS ZAMBRANO

BY TIM ODZER

During the 2000s, Carlos Zambrano was a mainstay at the top of the Chicago Cubs' rotation. Though lacking the renown of teammates like Kerry Wood, Mark Prior, and Sammy Sosa, the three-time All-Star led the Cubs in wins above replacement during the first decade of the new millennium.

Nicknamed El Toro (Spanish for bull) and Big Z, the 6-foot-4, 275-pound Venezuelan right-hander was a feisty and temperamental competitor. His behavioral antics were infamous, as Zambrano again and again intentionally threw at opposing players, jawed with umpires, and fought with his teammates. But Zambrano's temper tantrums overshadowed his deep faith. He was a devout Christian who credited all his good fortune to God and became a preacher after his playing days ended.

Carlos Alberto Zambrano Motes was born on June 1, 1981, in Puerto Cabello, Venezuela. He was the fifth of seven Zambrano boys born to Saulo and Nora. Zambrano comes from the Cumboto II neighborhood, a small and poor community, where his father worked as a street vendor. The government provided Zambrano's family with a small parcel of land that included a small three-bedroom home.[1] Even without material comforts, Zambrano spoke positively of his childhood, saying: "We were poor but we were happy. We had things more important than money. We had love."[2]

Growing up, Zambrano's life revolved around the neighborhood, the church, and the ballfield. Zambrano received Christian teachings at home and at Sunday school.[3] And he played soccer and baseball. As a teenager, he joined Carisma, his first baseball team. His pitching there caught the eye of a local pitching coach, Julio Figueroa.[4] Figueroa became Zambrano's pitching coach and trainer.

As a teenager, Zambrano joined the Royal Rangers youth group at his church.[5] There, he met his wife, Ismary. At first, Ismary did not like him.[6] But through retreats sponsored by the Royal Rangers, Ismary and Zambrano got to know each other and started dating.

In 1997 Zambrano received an opportunity to throw for scouts from the Chicago Cubs. But the chief scout in the area did not see Zambrano pitch at first, and the underling sent to scout Zambrano was not impressed.[7] Then Zambrano threw for the Blue Jays, Marlins, and Diamondbacks.[8] Around that time, the chief scout set up Zambrano for a second tryout with the Cubs. Impressed, the chief scout invited Zambrano to train for a month at the Cubs academy.[9] While Zambrano was at the academy, the head Latin America scout for the Cubs saw him throw and decided to sign him.[10]

Though Zambrano was heading to the United States, he also wanted to continue his relationship with Ismary. He asked her father if he could marry her. The father approved so long as he respected and visited her.[11]

Zambrano left for the United States in July of 1997. In 1998 he appeared in his first professional games as a member of the Cubs' Rookie ball affiliate in Mesa, Arizona. The next season Zambrano went 13-7 with a 4.17 ERA for the Cubs' Class-A team in Lansing, Michigan. After a strong start to the 2000 campaign with Double-A West Tennessee, Zambrano was promoted to Triple-A Iowa. In Triple A, Zambrano worked as a reliever and posted a 3.97 ERA. Ismary and Zambrano married at the end of the 2000 season. It appears the impetus for the wedding was a leg injury Zambrano suffered during the season. "[The injury] was what we needed to get married," she said. "He needed me."[12]

Newly wed, Zambrano began the 2001 season in the rotation at Iowa. On August 20, 2001, the Cubs summoned him to the majors to pitch the second game of a doubleheader against the Milwaukee Brewers. Only 20 years old, Zambrano arrived in Chicago having gone 9-4 with a 3.98 ERA for Iowa. Through the first three innings, he did not allow a hit. But in the fourth, the floodgates opened. He lost the game 10-2.

After his start Zambrano was sent back to Iowa, but returned to the majors on September 9. During his second stint in the big leagues, Zambrano pitched exclusively out of the bullpen. He made his first relief appearance on September 19 in Cincinnati, working a scoreless frame, and picked up his first win on September 21 in Houston.

Zambrano began the 2002 season in Iowa but was quickly called up to replace the injured Kyle Farnsworth on April 11. For the first part of the season, Zambrano pitched out of the Cubs' bullpen. But he entered the rotation in place of Jason Bere on July 1 against Florida.[13] Zambrano pitched decently, allowing two earned runs in 4⅔ innings. He remained in the rotation the remainder of 2002. Zambrano's best start of the season came on September 4 against the Brewers. He pitched eight shutout innings, striking out six. He also doubled for his first major-league hit. After arriving at second, Zambrano looked to the sky and thanked God. "For giving me the ability to play baseball and for giving me a good life and my arm," he said after the game.[14]

In 2003 Zambrano stayed in the Cubs' rotation for the entire season and emerged as a top-of-the-rotation starter. He particularly excelled in the season's second half as the Cubs battled with St. Louis and Houston for the division title, going 7-3 with three complete games and a 2.51 ERA. On August 12 Zambrano shut out Houston, allowing only five hits and striking out 10 in a 3-0 Cubs victory. On August 22 against Arizona, he flirted with a no-hitter, throwing only 93 pitches in a complete-game effort as the Cubs won 4-1. Zambrano also drew the ire of Barry Bonds in 2003. In a game on July 31, Zambrano retired Bonds with the bases loaded. Ecstatic, Zambrano pumped his fists in exaggerated fashion while staring back at Bonds. "I didn't see it," said Bonds. "But that kid will respect me. He'll learn fast." Zambrano shrugged it off, saying, "It was a big out."[15]

The Cubs won the NL Central Division championship on the final weekend of the season. In the 2003 postseason, the Cubs first squared off against the 101-win Atlanta Braves in the Division Series. After the Cubs won Game One, Zambrano received the start in Game Two. He gave up three runs in 5⅔ innings as the Cubs lost, 5-3. The teams split the next two games, setting up a decisive Game Five in Atlanta. Behind Kerry Wood's eight strong innings, the Cubs won 5-1 and advanced to the National League Championship Series.

Zambrano started Game One against the Florida Marlins. He turned in a shaky performance. The Marlins tagged him for three home runs in a five-run third as the Cubs lost 9-8. After the game, Zambrano promised to adjust for his next start against the Marlins.[16] The Cubs won the next three games and needed one win to advance to the World Series for the first time since 1945. Starting Game Five, Zambrano could be a hero. Facing off against Josh Beckett, he pitched well for five innings, allowing only a fifth-inning two-run home run by Mike Lowell. Beckett was better, pitching a shutout. "Carlos threw the ball well, but it didn't matter – we got shut out," Cubs manager Dusty Baker said.[17] It turned out to be Zambrano's final start of the season. The Cubs dropped the final two games to the Marlins.

Coming into 2004, the Cubs were projected to be among the best teams in baseball. After Greg Maddux was added to the rotation, Zambrano was slotted in as the fourth starter. Zambrano set a goal of winning 15 or 16 games.[18] And he achieved

Three-time All-Star Carlos Zambrano was known for his fiery passion and bat as much as his arm. He threw a no-hitter in 2008. (Jed Jacobsohn / Getty Images Sports)

it, performing the best in a rotation that included Maddux, Wood, and Prior. It started with a strong start to the season, as Zambrano went seven innings and allowed Atlanta only one run. On May 7 Zambrano pitched a two-hitter against the Colorado Rockies, striking out five and inducing 19 groundball outs. "This kid is electric. He overpowered us today," said Colorado manager Clint Hurdle.[19] Zambrano was selected for his first All-Star team after posting a 2.61 ERA in the first half. During the game in Houston, Zambrano pitched one inning, allowing one run via a walk to David Ortiz and a triple by Alex Rodriguez.

Despite the high hopes coming into the season, the Cubs faltered in the second half and missed the playoffs. Zambrano's antics made attention during a game against the St. Louis Cardinals on July 19. He hit St. Louis center fielder Jim Edmonds with a pitch in the first. Edmonds homered in the fourth and admired the flight of the ball, angering Zambrano, who told him to run the bases and stop being cocky.[20] After Zambrano struck out Edmonds in the sixth, he wagged his finger at him. With the game tied, 4-4, in the eighth, Zambrano gave up a tiebreaking home run to Scott Rolen. He then hit Edmonds for the second time and was ejected.

Zambrano's antics against St. Louis aside, it was an impressive season for him: He led the Cubs starters in ERA and wins above replacement and finished fifth in the NL Cy Young Award voting. When Zambrano returned home to Venezuela in the offseason, he was treated like a celebrity. "People were treating me like I was God, and sometimes that made me shy and uncomfortable," he said. "I don't want people to look at me like that. I want them to see me like before, like I'm their friend. But I have to thank God that every dream I had growing up came true."[21]

In 2005 and 2006, Zambrano emerged as the Cubs' ace as the team fell out of contention. He was the Opening Day starter in 2005 after injuries to Kerry Wood and Mark Prior made them unavailable. Facing the Diamondbacks in Phoenix, Zambrano was removed by Dusty Baker in the fifth inning after he allowed three runs. After his removal, Zambrano was ejected for arguing. He was unhappy with home-plate umpire Dale Scott, though Zambrano insisted he merely told Scott he needed glasses.[22] In the early part of the season, Zambrano dealt with some elbow soreness. The Cubs theorized that the problem arose because he spent too much time on the computer. Though Zambrano disagreed, he cut his internet use from five to two hours per day.[23] Zambrano struck out over 200 batters for the first time and was the Cubs' best pitcher in 2005 as the team finished 79-83.

The 2006 Cubs were one of the worst teams in baseball.[24] Even on a bad team, Zambrano's starts became a bright light for Cubs fans in a dire season. Zambrano made his second All-Star team and went 16-7 with a 3.41 ERA. In July he won six starts in a row. His best start during the run came on July 20 against Houston, when he allowed only two hits and one run while striking out 10.

Zambrano was due to qualify for free agency after the 2007 season. After the disappointing 2006 campaign, the Cubs made several changes, hiring Lou Piniella as manager and signing outfielder Alfonso Soriano and starting pitchers Ted Lilly and Jason Marquis. Zambrano struggled during the first two months and came into a start on June 1 (his 26th birthday) with a 5.24 ERA. After a disastrous fifth inning, he argued in the dugout with his catcher, Michael Barrett. After Barrett pointed to the scoreboard, Zambrano punched him in the face. A scuffle ensued that left Barrett with a cut lip and black eye.

Despite the drama, Zambrano improved his performance as the summer heated up, even winning NL Pitcher of the Month in July and becoming the first pitcher to win 14 games. In mid-August, Zambrano and the Cubs agreed on a five-year, $91.5 million contract extension. "Not everything is about money," said Zambrano. "I know if I would go free agent, a lot of things would come to me. I feel good here, my family feels good. I love the town. ... It's my home."[25]

With his future secured, Zambrano and the Cubs finished the season strong. Zambrano went 4-2 in September to finish 18-13 with a 3.95 ERA. And the Cubs used a strong finish to pass the surprising Milwaukee Brewers and win the Central Division title. In the Division Series, Chicago faced Arizona. Piniella tapped Zambrano for the Game One start. Zambrano pitched well, going six innings and allowing one run. But the Cubs lost the game and the next two to end their 2007 campaign.

In 2008 the Cubs were once again expected to contend for the division title. Through the first half of the season, they were tied with the Angels for the best record in baseball. Zambrano also had a stellar first half, going 10-3 with a 2.84 ERA. Zambrano was named to his third All-Star Team and was one of eight Cubs selected for the game at Yankee Stadium.

On September 14, 2008, Zambrano pitched a no-hitter against Houston at Miller Park in Milwaukee.[26] Zambrano, pitching for the first time since September 2, was dominant from the start. He retired the first 14 Astros before hitting Hunter Pence. Pence turned out to be the only baserunner in the game. Working quickly throughout the game, Zambrano entered the ninth having thrown only 99 pitches. He retired the first two batters, Humberto Quintero and Jose Castillo, on routine grounders to shortstop. Zambrano ran the count full on Darin Erstad, then struck out Erstad out on a nasty split-finger pitch to give the Cubs their first no-hitter since one by Milt Pappas in 1972. After finishing the game, Zambrano said, "I guess I'm back."[27]

Zambrano finished the 2008 regular season with two short starts in which he was hit hard. The Cubs won the NL Central Division again, winning 97 games, their most since 1945. Zambrano received the call for Game Two of the Division Series against the Dodgers. After the Cubs lost the opener, their defense betrayed Zambrano in Game Two. The Cubs made four errors and Zambrano allowed seven runs (but only three earned). The Dodgers swept the Cubs.

Zambrano was named the Cubs' Opening Day starter in 2009 for the fifth year in a row. Perhaps his best performance of the season came on April 28 against the Diamondbacks. Zambrano allowed three runs in seven innings pitched, scored three runs himself, and got three hits, including his 17th career home run.[28] In his next start, Zambrano injured his hamstring and required a trip to the disabled list. Once he returned, Zambrano had a major meltdown. Facing Pittsburgh on May 27, he was ejected in the seventh inning after an argument with an umpire. What's more, Zambrano threw a ball to left field, tossed his glove away, and destroyed a water cooler with his bat. His new teammate Milton Bradley, himself known for his temper tantrums, approved: "That was pretty impressive," said Bradley. "It was on [my] level."[29]

It was not Zambrano's final incident of the season. Pitching against the crosstown White Sox on June 28, Zambrano drilled Scott Podsednik and Dewayne Wise while allowing five runs. After throwing a pitchout to the screen on a squeeze, Zambrano hit Wise. White Sox players jumped to the top step of the dugout, although tempers cooled before a brawl ensued.[30] His continued antics aside, Zambrano put together another good season with a 3.77 ERA in 169⅓ innings. But Zambrano was not satisfied with winning only nine games. After pitching a two-hit shutout against the Giants in late September, Zambrano declared he'd retire if he had a second consecutive bad season. "Look, this is the only season I haven't won 16 or 18 or 14 games," he said. "If it happens again next season, two seasons in a row, I'll quit. Believe me, I'll quit. I just have to put this behind me."[31] For the Cubs, it was a disappointing season; They finished 7½ games behind the division-winning St. Louis Cardinals.

Zambrano arrived for spring training in 2010 15 pounds lighter and determined to improve upon what he considered a poor 2009 season. "I'm a proud guy," he told reporters at the start of camp. "Obviously, I wasn't proud of the season I had last year. ... I feel like a new guy. I feel like a rookie again."[32] Regarding offseason rumors that the Yankees tried to acquire him, Zambrano said he told his daughter the family might have to move but was happy no trade materialized.[33] For the sixth year in a row, Zambrano received the Opening Day start. Facing Atlanta, he gave up six runs in the first inning, including a three-run homer by rookie outfielder Jason Heyward.

Zambrano bounced back with three consecutive solid starts. That made the decision to move him to the bullpen to serve as the set-up man for Carlos Marmol particularly shocking. Zambrano said he made the move to help the team: "I told [manager Lou Piniella] I want to help this team until you find somebody."[34] The move was only temporary; Zambrano returned to the rotation at the start of June. Facing the White Sox on June 25, he had another fit. After a four-run first inning, Zambrano blamed his teammates, yelling, "If you're not going to play for me, then I'm not going to play for you!"[35] In the dugout, Zambrano engaged in a shouting match with Derrek Lee and had to be separated from Lee. Piniella sent Zambrano home and the Cubs suspended him indefinitely. After general manager

Jim Hendry called Zambrano a tired act, the media speculated that Zambrano had thrown his last pitch for the Cubs.

But the Cubs kept Zambrano around. He received counseling from anger-management specialists and rehabbed at Triple-A Iowa before returning to the Cubs. He first pitched out of the bullpen then returned to the rotation, starting 11 games and allowing no more than two earned runs in any start. Zambrano put together a solid season when he pitched, posting an 11-6 record with a 3.33 ERA.

For the first time since 2004, Zambrano did not start on Opening Day for the Cubs in 2011.[36] He bashed teammates on June 4 after a loss to St. Louis, calling them Triple-A players.[37] In a mid-August start against Atlanta, Zambrano made his final appearance for the Cubs. It was a rough start: He gave up eight runs on eight hits in 4⅓ innings. After giving up back-to-back homers in the fifth to Freddie Freeman and Dan Uggla, Zambrano threw two inside pitches to Chipper Jones and plate umpire Tim Timmons ejected him. Zambrano cleared out his locker and said he was retiring. It created a lot of confusion for players, sportswriters, and fans. The Cubs suspended Zambrano for 30 days and he remained away from the team the rest of the season.

After the 2011 season, the Cubs hired Theo Epstein to run their baseball operations. Cubs players who met with Epstein told him Zambrano no longer could gain their trust as a teammate.[38] The Cubs dealt Zambrano to the Marlins and paid $15 million of the $18 million he was due in 2012.

Expectations were high for the Marlins in 2012 The team hired Ozzie Guillen as manager and signed Jose Reyes, Mark Buehrle, and Heath Bell. With Buehrle and Josh Johnson anchoring the rotation, the Marlins slotted Zambrano at the back of their rotation. He got off to a rocky start, giving up three runs to Cincinnati in his first inning of the season.[39] At the end of July, the Marlins yanked Zambrano from the rotation. For the rest of the season, he pitched out of the Miami bullpen as the team limped to a 69-93 record. The Marlins decided not to bring Zambrano back.

Zambrano failed to attract much interest in the offseason. As one of the best major-league pitchers to ever come from Venezuela, he had the opportunity to represent Venezuela in the 2013 World Baseball Classic.[40] He started the second game of pool play against Puerto Rico, going 3⅔ innings and allowing two runs. It was his only start of the tournament as Venezuela failed to advance out of the first round.

In mid-May, Zambrano agreed to terms with the Philadelphia Phillies on a minor-league contract. His attempt to return to the big leagues ended when he left his start with Triple-A Lehigh Valley on June 28 with what was described as right-shoulder tightness.[41] He was diagnosed with a Grade 1 (mild) latissimus muscle strain and was released by the Phillies.

Hoping to land a contract for 2014, Zambrano spent his winter pitching in Venezuela's winter league. While there he started a brawl during the winter series final. After a teammate was hit by a pitch in retaliation for the previous batter admiring his home run, Zambrano led the charge from the dugout.[42] He apologized for starting the brawl: "It's something I have to work on. I'm a Christian, but I also believe forgiveness is a part of this. That's why I ask for forgiveness from Venezuela first and [my team] second."[43] Asked whether he believed his on-field antics conflicted with his religious beliefs, Zambrano responded: "If you read the Bible, you'll see that the apostle Paul was like me. The difference is that unlike Paul, I have not learned yet and I'm growing in the process."[44]

No major-league team showed interest in Zambrano, and he announced his retirement in 2014. He appeared on the Hall of Fame ballot in 2018 and received no votes. But he never entirely gave up on playing baseball, and in 2019 attempted a comeback with the Chicago Dogs of the independent American Association at age 38. Zambrano made 35 appearances for the Dogs and posted a 5.16 ERA. Unable to attract any interest from a major-league team, Zambrano retired again with plans to go into coaching.[45]

In the end, Zambrano remained committed to his faith. He has spent his post-playing days preaching in Miami, Argentina, the Dominican Republic, and Venezuela. As for the old Big Z? "God erased that. I've already asked God for forgiveness. It was part of the game and part of my determination to win and to get the Cubs a championship. So when I watched the Cubs win (in 2016), I was so proud."[46]

NOTES

1   Pedro Miranda, *The Big Z: The Carlos Zambrano Story* (Chicago: Triumph Books, 2007), 31.

2   Melissa Isaacson, "Heart on His Sleeve," *Chicago Tribune*, June 22, 2007: 4, 5.

3   Miranda, 32.

4   Miranda, 34.

5   Miranda, 36.

6   Miranda, 50

7   Miranda, 39, 61-63.

8   Miranda, 39, 66.

9   Miranda, 67-68.

10 Miranda, 68.

11 Miranda, 68.

12 Isaacson.

13 Teddy Greenstein, "Poor Hitting, Fielding Sink Cubs to New Low," *Chicago Tribune*, July 2, 2002: 4, 5.

14 Teddy Greenstein, "Zambrano Finally Locates His Zone," *Chicago Tribune*, September 5, 2002: 4, 3.

15 "Top 5 Bonds-Cubs Moments of 2003," *Chicago Tribune*, May 18, 2004: 4, 8.

16 Fred Mitchell, "Fading Starter Carlos Zambrano," *Chicago Tribune*, October 8, 2003: 9, 6.

17 Dan McGrath, "Game 5 Loser Carlos Zambrano," *Chicago Tribune*, October 13, 2003: 8, 6.

18 "Cubs," *Munster* (Indiana) *Times*, April 4, 2004: 25.

19   Nancy Armour, "Zambrano Dazzles in Cubs Romp over Rockies," *De Kalb* (Illinois) *Daily Chronicle* May 8, 2004: 9.

20   Rick Gano (Associated Press), "Red-Hot Cardinals Frustrate Cubs," *Raleigh* (North Carolina) *News & Observer,* July 20, 2004: 26.

21   Paul Sullivan, "Zambrano Truckin' Along," *Chicago Tribune,* February 27, 2005: 3, 10.

22   Paul Sullivan, "Squeeze Play Irks Zambrano," *Chicago Tribune,* April 5, 2005: 4, 5.

23   Paul Sullivan, "Zambrano Says He's Fine," *Chicago Tribune,* May 25, 2005: 4, 6.

24   In fact, Carlos Zambrano hit three more home runs (6) during the season than starting outfielder Juan Pierre (3).

25   Dave van Dyck, "A Big Deal for Big Z," *Chicago Tribune,* August 18, 2007: 3, 1.

26   The game was moved from Houston to Milwaukee because Hurricane Ike hit Houston.

27   Paul Sullivan, "Z for Zeroes," *Chicago Tribune,* September 15, 2008: 4, 1.

28   Zambrano hit 24 home runs during his 12 years in the major leagues.

29   Paul Sullivan, "Big Z's Fireworks Show," *Chicago Tribune,* May 28, 2009: 2, 3.

30   Dave van Dyck, "A Pyrotechnical Knockout," *Chicago Tribune,* June 29, 2009: 2, 3.

31   Paul Sullivan, "Big Z Aims for Big Finish," *Chicago Tribune,* August 10, 2010: 2, 4. While the article is from 2010, it provides a statement Zambrano made in 2009.

32   Paul Sullivan, "Motivation Not a Problem," *Chicago Tribune,* February 19, 2010: 2, 3. Though Zambrano's advanced statistics from 2009 indicated he had a good season, he won only nine games.

33   Sullivan, "Motivation Not a Problem."

34   Paul Sullivan, "Is This A Setup?" *Chicago Tribune,* April 22, 2010: 1, 84.

35   Paul Sullivan, "Lack of Hustle Leads to Tussle," *Chicago Tribune,* June 26, 2010: 2, 3.

36   The Opening Day nod went to Ryan Dempster.

37   Bruce Levine, "Carlos Zambrano: Cubs Embarrassing," ESPN.com, June 5, 2011, available at https://www.espn.com/chicago/mlb/news/story?id=6629129.

38   Paul Sullivan, "Vocal Majority," *Chicago Tribune,* January 6, 2012: 3, 4.

39   Zambrano wound up going six innings and allowing four runs.

40   As of 2022, Zambrano ranked third behind Johan Santana and Felix Hernandez among Venezuelan-born major-league pitchers in wins above replacement as calculated by Baseball Reference.

41   "Zambrano Injured in Pigs sweep," *Allentown* (Pennsylvania) *Morning Call,* June 29, 2013: C1.

42   "There's Plenty of Fight Left in Big Z," *Chicago Tribune,* January 27, 2014: 3, 2.

43   Jesse Sanchez, "Venezuela Embraces Zambrano Despite Erratic Ways," MLB.com, February 4, 2014.

44   Sanchez.

45   Gordon Wittenmeyer, "Ex-Cub Carlos Zambrano," *Chicago Sun-Times,* January 18, 2020, available at https://chicago.suntimes.com/2020/1/18/21072346/cubs-carlos-zambrano-manager.

46   Paul Sullivan, "Zambrano Finds New Life," *Palm Beach Post,* April 7, 2018: C5.

HISTORY OF THE VENEZUELAN PROFESSIONAL BASEBALL LEAGUE

BY J.L. TUCUPIDO C.

To truly appreciate the Venezuelan Professional Baseball League (Liga Venezolana de Béisbol Profesional, or LVBP, in Spanish), one must first grasp the sociopolitical and military events that gripped the country in the late nineteenth and early twentieth centuries.

Baseball's origins are linked to armed conflict. Union Army officer Abner Doubleday was thought to have invented the game in New York in 1839 (though he never made such a claim and subsequent research has proven its falsity). The sport then gripped the island of Cuba in 1865, soon after United States marines visited the port of Matanzas. According to Iglesias Van Pelt, a pair of Cuban generals brought gloves, bats, and baseballs to Puerto Rico in 1896. Colonel Gonzalo Gómez, son of Venezuelan strongman Juan Vicente Gómez, ran his country's baseball leagues, and in the Dominican Republic, dictator Rafael Leónidas Trujillo Molina ruled both country and sport with an iron first for three decades beginning in 1930.

Myths or not, history has proved that these antiheroes played a pivotal role in the spread and development of baseball in the Caribbean. However, the Venezuelan flame was lit in 1895 by members of the upper class returning from their studies in the United States. These *caraqueños*, joined by Cubans fleeing Spanish oppression and American railroad administrators, founded both the Caracas Baseball Club and its amateur opponents.

Venezuela, riddled with a low literacy rate and a high level of disease, idealized baseball as progress. By the end of the 1920s, its amateur sport associations represented both the societal elite (the *Samanes*) and the working class (*Girardot* and the *Independencia de Caracas*). Fans relished their exhibition contests, symbols of modernization.

The 1920s brought the advent of the National Baseball League (*Liga Nacional de Béisbol*), bolstered by "imports" from Puerto Rico, Cuba, and the Dominican Republic. A quartet of teams (the *Royal Criollos*, Maracay, the *Tigres* of Santa Marta, and the *July 29 Military*) played in the San Agustín Stadium, modeled after American ballparks.

Clashes between the *Magallanes* and the *Royal Criollos* soon became the marquee rivalry, highlighted by pitcher Balbino Inojosa and catcher Manuel "Pollo" Malpica. Caribbean-born stars Pelayo Chacón and Manual "Cocaína" García came to play in the nascent league, as did Josh Gibson, Johnny Mize, Martín Dihigo, Silvino Ruiz, and Benito Torres for the newly created *Águilas* de Concordia.

Baseball fever soon spread from the capital to the country's other regions. Leagues soon sprang up in Maracaibo, Barquisimeto, and Coro, where José Antonio Casanova and sibling shortstop virtuosos Luis and Ernesto Aparicio first graced the diamond. *Gavilanes*, *Pastora*, and *Vencedor B.C.C.* de Valencia enthralled fans away from the capital.

Juan Vicente Gómez's passing in 1936 marked the end of the *"béisbol romántico."* The First Division of Venezuelan Baseball (*Primera División*) was officially founded with the *Royal Criollos*, *Magallanes*, Santa Marta, and short-lived squads like the *Concordia*, *Vargas*, *Venezuela*, *Latinos*, *Lucana*, *Caribes*, *Cardenales*, and *Universidad*.

The result? An unbalanced league, a mix of amateur players and those remunerated for their skills. Most, however, had to toil in factories or in the service industry to earn their daily bread. From this formula sprang the first US big leaguer: Alejandro "Patón" Carrasquel.[1]

This evolution reached a significant stage in 1941 as the national team won the fourth Amateur Baseball World Series in Havana. Two more titles (1944 and 1945) would follow. Abelardo Raidi, Jesús Corao, and Herman Ettedgui served as godparents for the sport, scouting talent on the field and handling the business off it. Their economic means and government support, under both General Isaías Medina Angarita and his predecessor López Contreras, nurtured a new generation of stars: Jesús "Chucho" Ramos, Luis Romero Petit, Héctor Benítez, Jesús "Carrao" Bracho, Dalmiro Finol, Daniel Canónico, and José Antonio Casanova, who crossed the threshold from the amateur sphere to the professional ranks.

Entrepreneurs and promoters soon seized the opportunity to develop a booming business. The success of amateur competitions and the expansion of radio (the "social media" of the times) encouraged the creation of a proper professional league. On January 12, 1946, the LVBP was officially born as *Magallanes* and *Venezuela* played the inaugural game in the Cerveza Caracas Stadium (née San Agustín). Under the leadership of Alfredo Scannoney, the circuit's four teams were led by soon-to-be immortals: the *Sabios de Vargas* (winner of the first title with Roy Campanella behind the plate), *Cervecería Caracas* (with Alfonso "Chico" Carrasquel and the bulk of the 1941 national team), *Magallanes* (with Vidal López and Luis Aparicio Ortega), and *Venezuela* (with Juan Antonio Yánez).

SOURCES

Venezuela al Bate. Orígenes de nuestro béisbol 1895 – 1945, Documentary, Cinesa Channel, Bolívar Films Archive, Venezuela.

General José Antero Núñez y Alfredo Méndez, *"Oro y Gloria del Béisbol Venezolano,"* JAN Editor, 1991, Venezuela.

Carlos Figueroa Ruiz and Javier González, *"60 Juegos Memorables en 60 años de la LVBP,"* Grupo Editorial Norma, 2006, Venezuela.

Rafael Ayala Álvarez, *"La Historia del Béisbol,"* Ediciones Reflejos de La Vida, 2005, Colombia.

Jorge Colón Delgado, "Origen del Béisbol en Puerto Rico," https://www.beisbol101.com.

Christopher Díaz, "Rafael Leónidas Trujillo Molina 'Trujillo.'" 2017, https://www.wattpad.com/story/116672978.

NOTES

1　On April 23, 1939, Alex Carrasquel became the first Venezuelan to play in the US major leagues as the Washington Senators hosted the New York Yankees in Griffith Stadium. Carrasquel came out of the bullpen to relieve left-hander Ken Chase with two outs in the top of the fourth inning. With the Senators down 6-3, Carrasquel retired Joe DiMaggio on a fly ball to center fielder George Case. Although the Senators lost the game, the 22,000 Washington fans in attendance witnessed 5⅓ innings of outstanding pitching as Carrasquel demonstrated the caliber of Venezuelan baseball.

Baseball Commissioner Ford Frick, hosting a meeting on August 24, 1953, with Emilio de Aldrey of the Puerto Rican League, Bobby Maduro of the Cuban League, and Luis Alejandro Blanco Chataing of the Venezuelan League. The baseball executive council agreed to permit 48 major-league players to participate in 60 games with Caribbean Confederation-affiliated clubs. (Getty Images)

LUIS APARICIO ORTEGA: THE FATHER OF ALL

BY ELIEXSER PIRELA LEAL

The name Luis Aparicio in the United States is synonymous with one of the best shortstops in history and one of the top base stealers of all time. However, that very name in Venezuela implicates a series of clarifications and cultural ramifications. It's just a question of whom we are making reference to: Either Senior or Junior.

That's why in the South American nation, we differentiate them by using their last and maiden names, respectively: Luis Aparicio Ortega and Luis Aparicio Montiel.

Beyond using both surnames, Aparicio Ortega has been immortalized in Venezuela as El Grande de Maracaibo (The Great One from Maracaibo).

The year 1912 was eventful in several ways. For instance, at the beginning of the year, the United States had 46 states. (The number became 48 when Arizona and New Mexico were admitted to the Union. In that year, most of the streets in the main cities in Germany were the first to be lit by night, with a system called neon gas lighting. 1912 saw the establishment as a republic of what is today the most populous nation and one of the most important economic superpowers on earth; it was January 1 when China was "barely" established as a republic. 1912 might be mostly remembered in popular history because of the most famous maritime tragedy ever remembered: the sinking of the Titanic.

Maracaibo, the city and commercial port in the northwestern part of Venezuela, had electrical lighting since 1888 with the inauguration of the city's public lighting system. Local authorities planned it this way to celebrate the centennial birthdate of the local patriotic figure Rafael Urdaneta, a hero of the Latin American wars for independence.

The year 1912 is also important for Maracaibo because it is the year in which the arrival of baseball is recorded in the city, and it is also the year of the birth of the "first great urban and popular icon": Luis Aparicio Ortega.

The Santa Lucía district of Maracaibo was home to the Aparicio family, headed by Leonidas Aparicio and Adelina Ortega. On August 28, God gave them a special gift: Doña Adelina gave birth to a child who was baptized with the name of Luis Guillermo Aparicio Ortega, who, through his baseball prowess, would become known as "El Grande de Maracaibo."

The Aparicio Ortega family lived on Guayaquil Street, which made a diagonal from the Hospital Central de Maracaibo Doctor Urquinaona, in what is today Avenida El Milagro (The Miracle Avenue).

As a child, Aparicio Ortega shared his studies with his passion for sports. He was initially inclined to soccer, a sport he would start practicing regularly along with his older brother Ernesto. Both were members of First Division teams such as Ayacucho and Guaraní and were teammates of José Encarnación "Pachencho" Romero, a glorious player of Venezuelan soccer, for whom the great Soccer Stadium of the City of Maracaibo, a venue of the 2007 Copa América is named.

The Aparicio brothers learned baseball in the streets of Maracaibo when the sport was becoming popular. And in 1929, they formed a team to compete at the local level: Gavilanes.

Aparicio Ortega was talented in all sports. He was fast in soccer and very skillful in baseball. When he devoted himself to baseball full time at age 14, he caught the eye of local teams, and in December 1930, he went to Caracas to play for the champion of the Venezuelan First Division, the Cincinnati, who hosted the squad from Ponce, Puerto Rico, in a friendly series.

Curiously, his debut in Caracas was with Ponce as a left fielder because an injury left the visitors one man short, and they borrowed Aparicio Ortega to complete their roster. He was hired in 1931 by the Club Lucana of the First Division in Caracas by entrepreneur Alejandro Blanco Chataing, and once he started playing in the capital city, he began to cement his legend, establishing himself as a great shortstop.

Aparicio played for Magallanes and Concordia, the latter owned by the son of General Juan Vicente Gómez, president of Venezuela, a team filled with all-star caliber players that toured the Caribbean. With Concordia, Aparicio Ortega shined in games playing against Puerto Rico and the Dominican Republic, hobnobbing with the best players of the time in the Negro leagues, some who were on the radar of major-league teams.

Aparicio Ortega's performance impressed officials of the Tigres del Licey, of the Dominican Republic, who traveled to Maracaibo to sign him. He became the first Venezuelan ballplayer (or athlete) in history to be exported to a foreign team as a professional. On April 29, 1934, while Aparicio Ortega was playing in the Dominican Republic, his first son was born in Maracaibo: Luis Ernesto. Upon his return to Venezuela, Aparicio Ortega married his fiancée and Luis' Jr. mother, Doña Herminia Montiel.

The game of baseball solidified in the country with the formation of Liga Venezolana de Béisbol (LVBP is the commonly-used Spanish acronym; in English, it's called the Venezuelan Professional Baseball League). The first official game was on

January 12, 1946, when the teams of Venezuela and Magallanes squared off in Estadio Cervecería Caracas, in the San Agustín neighborhood. Luis Aparicio "El Grande," as the leadoff man for Magallanes, wrote his name in golden letters by becoming the first player to get a base hit in the newly formed professional baseball league that still remains as the most solid professional sports league in the country. He also became the first to score a run. That game marked a before-and-after in the history of Venezuelan baseball, being the foundation of the game as it is currently known and revered.

Seven years earlier, in the defunct Estadio del Lago, in Maracaibo, Aparicio Ortega had a starring role in the longest game played in the country, known in history as "El juego de los 20 innings" (The 20-inning game). The game was between Gavilanes and Pastora, the two baseball teams that gave birth to the biggest rivalry in the country during those years. Such rivalry had so much influence that after every game between the two clubs, the streets were filled with the few vehicles circulating back then, with big and noisy caravans as if it was an endless carnival celebrated by Zulian people, made up of followers from both "sides," especially the winning team. In that 20-inning match, Aparicio Ortega was the shortstop for the Gavilanes, who lost 1-0 to the "Pastoreños."

In the Venezuelan domestic leagues in which Aparicio Ortega played: the Primera División (First Division) of Maracaibo and in the LVBP, he coincidentally ended up with a lifetime batting average of .269 in each of them, playing for the G

avilanes de Maracaibo and with Magallanes and Vargas in Caracas.

Perhaps the most relevant episode of his career came upon his retirement. Venezuelan baseball authorities decided to merge its professional leagues for the 1953-54 season, holding a trial tournament with the four best clubs from Caracas (Cervecería Caracas and Magallanes) and Maracaibo (Gavilanes and Pastora).

The special date came on November 18 in Maracaibo, where Aparicio Ortega, already revered by the fans as one of their greatest idols, and at age 41, made a small symbolic act in front of the fans by giving his glove and bat to his son Luis Ernesto, then 17 years old, thus finishing his professional career that started alongside the humble beginnings of baseball in Venezuela.

For fans in attendance to this game, it was an act considered as "magical" in the book of urban legends. The significance of the great idol, opening the doors of baseball to a youngster full of expectations. Father and son starred in a generational switch in the field, all while honoring the Virgin of Chiquinquirá, the holy Saint-mother of this city, to whom the game has been dedicated every November 18th.

As it is well known in history, Aparicio Ortega is the father of the only Venezuelan player who has been inducted into the National Baseball Hall of Fame in Cooperstown; Luis Aparicio Montiel, who was elected in 1984. Quite a significant debut!

There are many things "Luisito" (Little Louie) could say about his father, but what he has emphasized the most has been: "When I decided to become a ballplayer, my mother got really upset because I had to drop out of my studies. But my father said nothing. He just told me, very convinced: "I will only tell you that if you are going to play baseball, you can be second to none… and I think I didn't let him down."

In 1969, Luis Aparicio Ortega was the first manager of the newly professional team Águilas del Zulia, to this date, one of the most prolific baseball franchises in Venezuela and locally, a baseball brand that connects generations as the most followed team in Western Venezuela. One of the three Venezuelan teams to win the Caribbean Series championship twice.

Retired as a player for 16 years, Luis El Grande died of a heart attack on January 1, 1971. That year, because of his impact around the diamonds of Venezuelan baseball, he was inducted into the Venezuelan Sports Hall of Fame, as part of an inaugural class of pioneers that also included Alejandro "El Patón" Carrasquel, the first Venezuelan player in MLB.

He was also inducted into the later-established Venezuelan Baseball Hall of Fame, selected by the Historic Committee, on November 28, 2005.

It is worth considering all cultural aspects to help understand the importance of "El Grande de Maracaibo," whose legacy

Gavilanes shortstop Luis Aparicio Ortega and his son Luis Aparicio Jr on the latter's debut on November 18, 1953 before the game vs Pastora in the Venezuelan Western Baseball League. Aparicio Jr. later signed for the Chicago White Sox and played in the major leagues for 18 seasons. He was elected to the Hall of Fame in 1984. (SABR: The Rucker Archive)

and example at shortstop were followed, years later, by many extraordinary Venezuelan shortstops such as Alfonso "Chico" Carrasquel, his own son Luis Ernesto, Enzo Hernández, David Concepción, Oswaldo Guillén, and Omar Vizquel. Aparicio Ortega and his brother Ernesto left a mark of excellence and integrity on the field. "El Grande" was the first great star of baseball in Maracaibo and the first "franchise player" identified with the Gavilanes, his perennial local team. Ernesto, his sidekick on the field, left Maracaibo after his death and resided in Caracas after his retirement, where he devoted himself to developing players. One of his main pupils became one of the greatest Venezuelan stars in the majors and the first Latino manager to win a World Series: Ozzie Guillen.

Aparicio Ortega is not only the father of a Hall of Famer, but for many players of the developing professional baseball era in Venezuela, he was seen as a father figure. Many of these players dared to take their talent overseas and were the foundation to keep Venezuela as an international superpower in the game and a top exporter for MLB talent.

Information and references in this article come from the book *El Grande: Homenaje en el Centenario del Nacimiento de Luis Aparicio Ortega* by Eliexser Pirela Leal, published in 2012 by Premium Publicidad, Maracaibo, Venezuela.

CARLOS ASCANIO
THE VENEZUELAN LOST EARTHQUAKE IN THE NEGRO LEAGUES

BY JUAN VENÉ AND LEONTE LANDINO

After a life in baseball, becoming famous in his home country as one of the most consistent players of his era, and kind of a "rarity" foreign player in the Negro Leagues, Carlos "Terremoto" ("Earthquake") Ascanio died in poverty, abandoned by his family and with a lost legacy in the dense and deep world of baseball.

Ascanio was the only Venezuelan player who reached the Negro Leagues, playing first base in 1946 with the New York Black Yankees.

He was born in Santa Lucía, a suburb of the capital city, Caracas, in the Miranda state on April 4, 1918.[1]

When Ascanio was enshrined in the Venezuelan Baseball Hall of Fame in 2019, former president J.J. Avila and his team dedicated many weeks searching for anyone who could receive the honor, but were unable to find anyone.

"The Earthquake" passed away at the National Geriatric Institute in his native Caracas on February 27, 1998. Ramón Corro, a longtime Venezuelan sports commentator, led a group of baseball fans who took care of arrangements to bury the revered star at the Cementerio General del Sur in Caracas.

According to Corro. Ascanio's burial site is between that of Lorenzo Mendoza, one of the wealthiest Venezuelan business-men – the owner and founder of the Polar Beer Company – and Carlos "Pantaleon" Espinoza, a longtime shortstop who once was the substitute for Chico Carrasquel for Cervecería Caracas.[2]

After Ascanio's death in February 1998, no family members, relatives, or even acquaintances came forward. It was as though he had been a person who never existed.

Juan Vené had known Ascanio for many years and was shocked to see him in his final year, as the former ballplayer was lying in his hospital bed that year. He interviewed him for *Ultimas Noticias*, a Caracas-based newspaper. Vené was shocked both by the condition he was in and his story.

In a humble bed at the National Geriatric Institute, covered with a dirty bedsheet, the once big, strong, powerful, athletic "mulatto" with a big smile had turned into a sad, depressing face with a dirty, horrible white-hairy beard.

Under his bed sheet, there was a living skeleton. No muscles, just weak bones moving in pain.

Ascanio whispered in pain, "I have been abandoned by the entire world."

In conversations over the years with Vené about his glory days in New York, he constantly said, "There were no feats or greatness. I played only for three months, but I was not able to adapt to that game. So, they fired me."

By 1973, already retired from baseball, Ascanio became a prosperous businessman. He received Vené in his sporting goods store located at the Santa Rosalia neighborhood in downtown Caracas.

Vené remembers his words: "The best of this business is that this is my building. My house. Anything can happen to me, but nobody can kick me out of here. All my savings are in this building and this store."

Carlos and his wife Maria lived in the back of the dwelling. The front was the store, a business that he considered prosperous and invincible. But his future held a tragedy in sight.

Lying on that bed in his final months, Ascanio said, "I don't understand about my son. You know how things are. He got involved with bad people and slowly became addicted to drugs. He asked me for money; he demanded it. I gave him the money to prevent him from robbing it or doing any damage to anyone. One day, they asked me to sell my house because he was in deep debt and they were going to kill him if he didn't pay. It is terrible to think that someone is going to kill your son, so I sold my house and I gave him the money. Sometime later, the new owners kicked me out of the house."

Vené asked, "What is the name of your son?"

"No, please. Do not publish his name! It could do some damage to him, somehow," added Ascanio in physical and emotional pain.

Vené remembers thinking, "What a good soul!"

After Ascanio left his longtime home, his wife disappeared, and he was left on the streets of Caracas. He barely slept, and the food was scarce. On a random afternoon, he collapsed on a downtown sidewalk.

Authorities and emergency personnel picked him up and took him to the Geriatric Hospital. The cause of death was given as respiratory failure.[3] Nobody was waiting for his body or making arrangements for his eternal rest.

That group of fans organized by Corro paid the ultimate homage to a great legend.

Ascanio was one of the most outstanding players of the highly competitive amateur baseball in Venezuela. Several teams from Puerto Rico and Cuba, as well as the Negro League All-Stars toured the country to matchup with local teams, especially after winning the 1941 Amateur Baseball World Series. Some players made such a great impression that they were offered to

Carlos Ascanio, known as 'The Earthquake,' was a consistent player in the Venezuelan Professional Baseball League for 15 seasons. A pure contact hitter with an uncanny ability to spray the ball to all parts of the field, his nickname reflected the havoc he created at the plate. Ascanio played for Vargas, Cervecería Caracas, Venezuela, Valencia, Pampero, Gavilanes, and Industriales de Valencia, between 1946 and 1961, but made history as the only Venezuelan in the Negro Leagues. (Diamante 23 Archive)

play professionally in Cuba and Puerto Rico, where their pro leagues were long established.

He was one of those players who impressed Cuban legend and former major-leaguer Joseito Rodríguez, who managed Cienfuegos. On a visit to Caracas, he offered contracts for the winter of 1940-41 to Alejandro Carrasquel, who had already pitched in the major leagues, and to promising prospects Carlos Ascanio and Vidal Lopez, as well.[4]

The Venezuelan trio became a sensation in Cuba, playing for Cienfuegos. After they returned from Cuba, they were labeled "professional players" and became what was called "First Division Players." Ascanio signed with Magallanes, where he played until 1944.

The 1946 season in Venezuela, the inaugural season of the professional league, started in January, and Ascanio was playing for Sabios del Vargas, managed by Roy Campanella, who won the first league title ever. Ascanio led Vargas with a .378 average. After the Vargas season was over, the New York Black Yankees offer arrived, after a recommendation from Dan Bankhead, who in 1947 became the first African American pitcher in the major leagues. Rights were assigned to the Black Yankees.[5] Ascanio played under manager Marvin Barker,

In New York, just as Ascanio always acknowledged, he was not a solid acquisition. Seamheads shows him with 70 plate appearances, and a .161 batting average – 10 base hits (all singles) in 62 at-bats. He drove in six runs and scored three. Drawing six bases on balls, he had a .235 on-base percentage. For the

three months he played with the Black Yankees, his salary was $1,800.[6] But the experience was one of a lifetime.

The Black Yankees finished in last place in the Negro National League that year. The team had three ballparks as its home parks – Yankee Stadium, the Polo Grounds, and Dexter Park in Queens.

Ascanio returned to Sabios del Vargas, becoming a prominent player for the powerful team that was the champion of the first two seasons of professional baseball in Venezuela. He played alongside Luis Aparicio Ortega, the father of Hall of Famer Luis Aparicio. Vargas, with their championship status, beat the American League's New York Yankees 4-3 in an exhibition game in Caracas on March 1, 1947.[7] The Yankees and Brooklyn Dodgers toured Venezuela as part of their spring training and played the "Caracas Cup."

Carlos Ascanio was a true lefty, a better hitter who hit line drives more than a power hitter. In 15 seasons in the Venezuelan Professional League, he hit for .277 but with only one home run in 1,422 at-bats for Sabios del Vargas, Cerveceria Caracas, Patriotas del Venezuela, Gavilanes de Maracaibo, Pampero, and Valencia Industriales.

Like many Venezuelans, Ascanio was a mix of European white and indigenous. Too light for the Negro Leagues, so that he was considered "white," but too dark-skinned to sign a contract for the major leagues at the time. Lying on his bed, he told the Associated Press a story about playing in the Southern states. Teammates used to send him to buy some food since he was light-skinned, and since he barely spoke English and he tried to communicate with hand signals, store owners thought that he was a white-skinned mute.

Sadly, Carlos Ascanio is the only member of the Venezuelan Baseball Hall of Fame who was without a representative at his induction ceremony.

In the history of Venezuelan baseball, Ascanio has the merit of being part of the first group of players who strengthened baseball as a profession. He was part of the "First Division" or "First Category" players. One of the first ever professional players in Venezuela.

The life and death of Carlos Ascanio is an example of many great Venezuelan players who dedicated their lives to baseball and found only struggles after their playing days. An incipient Professional Baseball League and poor management of the local players' association never created scenarios or mechanisms for players who fell into misfortune and ended up lonely and forgotten. For such players, there was never any public or private aid; many just saw their skill on the field evaporate into depression and impoverishment.

Ascanio was a decent baseball man and a revered player, and will always be remembered as part of that group of players during the years of segregation. He was a man who shared playing time on the field with history greats like Hall of Famers Jackie Robinson, Josh Gibson, Buck Leonard, Roy Campanella, and Ray Dandridge. These Negro leaguers were pioneers of the Venezuelan League after touring the country in the winter of 1945, and some of them returned to join the new professional teams.

During his final days, his wish was for the Negro League Baseball Players Association to provide some help for his long-time achievement. "Who could have though that 50 years after that experience I would be here sick and poor hoping that the Negro Leagues can allow me to die with dignity in my homeland?"[8]

SOURCES

In addition to the sources cited in the Notes, the authors consulted the archives of *El Nacional* in Caracas, the Beisbol 007 blog of Andrés Pascual, Baseball-Reference.com, and Juan Vené, *5000 Años de Béisbol* (Caracas, Venezuela: Ediciones B., 2007).

NOTES

1   According to Seamheads his birthdate was April 4, 1918. Pelota Binaria, a Venezuelan baseball database, has his birthdate as April 4, 1915. According to the report by the Associated Press, he died at age 79.
    https://www.baseball-reference.com/players/a/ascanca01.shtml

2   Personal email from Ramon Corro to Juan Vené referencing the burial and death details of Carlos Ascanio.

3   Jorge Rueda, Associated Press, "Forgotten Negro league great dies," *Daily News* (Bowling Green, Kentucky), March 1, 1998: 10-B. https://news.google.com/newspapers?nid=1696&dat=19980301&id=IfI-aAAAAIBAJ&sjid=3kcEAAAAIBAJ&pg=6830,113943 Accessed May 14, 2021.

4   "Cienfuegos," *Desde Mi Palco de Fanatico* https://desdemipalcodefanatico.wordpress.com/numeros/cienfuegos-li-ga-profesional-cubana-1940-41/

5   "Carlos 'Terremoto' Ascanio," Museo de Beisbol, Salon de la Fama, http://museodebeisbol.com/salon_fama_venezolano/detalles/2019/carlos-terremoto-ascanio. Accessed May 14, 2021.

6   Conversations between Juan Vené and Carlos Ascanio.

7   Bill Nowlin & Walter LeConte, "1947 Yankees Spring Training in Florida," in Lyle Spatz, ed., *Bridging Two Dynasties: 1947 New York Yankees* (Lincoln: University of Nebraska Press and SABR), 2013. https://sabr.org/journal/article/1947-yankees-spring-train-ing-in-florida/.

8   Jorge Rueda, Associated Press, "Forgotten Negro league great dies," *Daily News* (Bowling Green, Kentucky), Marzo 1, 1998: 10-B. https://news.google.com/newspapers?nid=1696&dat=19980301&id=IfI-aAAAAIBAJ&sjid=3kcEAAAAIBAJ&pg=6830,113943 Acceso en Mayo 14, 2021.

WHICH VENEZUELAN BATTER HAS HAD THE BEST SEASON IN THE MAJOR LEAGUES?

BY JOSÉ LUIS LÓPEZ AND OSCAR ANDRÉS LÓPEZ

This research aims to identify the best season by a Venezuelan hitter in the major leagues through the 2023 season. Only hitting parameters are considered. In the first stage, we defined the criteria to select extraordinary offensive seasons. We identified 42 seasons from 19 players. They are arranged chronologically, citing the player in his first extraordinary season: César Tovar, Antonio Armas, Andrés Galarraga, Bob Abreu, Richard Hidalgo, Magglio Ordóñez, Melvin Mora, Carlos González, Miguel Cabrera, Víctor Martínez, David Peralta, César Hernández, José Altuve, Yolmer Sánchez, Eduardo Escobar, Eugenio Suárez, Ronald Acuña, Salvador Pérez, and Luis Arraez.

Then we compared the seasons using two criteria:
1) Traditional offensive parameters.
2) Sabermetric parameters.

Both criteria led to the same result: The best season of a Venezuelan hitter in the big leagues was Miguel Cabrera's in the 2013 season, which was even better than his 2012 season, in which he won the Triple Crown. If stolen bases are included in addition to hitting, Cabrera 2013 would still maintain first place, but second place would be occupied by Acuña 2023, benefiting from his remarkable 73 stolen bases.

Introduction

Since Alejandro Carrasquel got to the major leagues in 1939, there have been almost 500 Venezuelans in major league baseball. In the 80-plus years that followed, there have been excellent players who have led the league in almost every category of hitters, pitchers, and fielders. This research aimed to identify the best single-season offensive performances, compare them, and classify them according to an assessment criterion. The intention is not to determine the best season of a player, which would also require including the pitchers, as well as considering defense and baserunning. We consider only hitting.

The offensive performance of a season will be assessed in two ways: first, using the traditional methods, then using the novel sabermetric parameters, which provide a more objective description, since they allow comparing players of different eras and ballparks. We will use the English acronyms describing offensive parameters, first defined and listed in Annex 1. Additionally, to ease the reader's understanding, we include Annex 2, which brings the definition and way of calculating the sabermetric parameters we used, and some common traditional parameters.

Selection criteria

To determine the best offensive season of a Venezuelan player in the majors, it is necessary to begin by looking at what we will call extraordinary seasons. We define a season as extraordinary if it meets one of the three following criteria:

1. Having led the league in an offensive category during the regular season. We considered: R, H, 2B, 3B, HR, RBI, TB, BB, BA, OBP, SLG, and OPS. (Criterion 1)

2. Having had a global offensive performance equal to or better than 1.5 times the league average, with the required minimum plate appearances. Such performance is measured using Adjusted OPS (OPS+), which should be equal to or better than 150; this is a sabermetric parameter detailed further on. Reaching 150 OPS+ is very good, without question. For instance, in 2018, only seven major leaguers had an OPS+ of 150 or better, which represents just 5% of qualified players (those having the minimum required PA). (Criterion 2)

3. Having reached a single-season record for a Venezuelan player in offensive stats, in some of the categories cited in the first criterion. (Criterion 3)

Considering these three criteria, we list 42 extraordinary seasons of Venezuelan hitters. These 42 seasons belong to just 19 players, given the fact that Tovar, Armas, Galarraga, Abreu, Ordoñez, Cabrera, Hernández, Altuve, and Acuña all repeat with more than one extraordinary season each. Of the 42 seasons, 35 meet Criterion 1, and 19 meet Criterion 2. Two seasons don't meet any of the first two criteria but meet Criterion 3 (Hidalgo and Suárez). Fifteen seasons simultaneously meet the first two criteria.

We must take into account that Criterion 1, which incorporates players leading any of the offensive categories, in some cases includes seasons that, strictly speaking, could not be called extraordinary. This is the case of the good seasons by Tovar (1971), Hernández (2016 and 2020), Sánchez (2018), and

Peralta (2021); although they had some league leads, their OPS+ is not extraordinary, as it was slightly above (Tovar, Hernández) or below (Sánchez, Peralta) the league average, as indicated further on. Even recognizing this limitation, the authors decided to maintain Criterion 1 as a qualifier of an extraordinary season, given the natural importance of leading the league in these offensive categories. We reiterate that the definition of extraordinary season does not include stolen bases; it includes only batting statistics.

Description of Extraordinary Seasons

Table 1 shows the records of each player in the offensive parameters defined by Criteria 1 and 2. Additionally, we list at-bats (AB). All 12 categories were taken from Baseball-Reference. The procedure for calculating the last four parameters (OBP, SLG, OPS, and OPS+) can be seen in Annex 2. The numbers in bold indicate that the player led the league in that category. Seasons with an OPS+ of 150 or higher are highlighted in a gray background.

We hereby summarize the 42 extraordinary seasons, chronologically organized:

César Tovar, 1970 (Minnesota Twins)

The first Venezuelan to lead the league in a category was César Tovar, who led the American League in doubles with 36 (tied with two other players) and triples (13), while being second in runs with 120, third in hits with 195, and sixth in steals (30), making him one of the top hitters in the league.

César Tovar, 1971 (Minnesota Twins)

Tovar continued his good performance, leading the league in hits with 204 while becoming the first Venezuelan to reach 200 hits in a season, ending second in runs with 94 and fourth in batting average (.311), even though his OPS+ was just 104, mainly due to his low number of extra-base hits.

Antonio Armas, 1981 (Oakland Athletics)

In 109 games during a strike-shortened season, Armas led the league in homers with 22 (tied with three other players) while becoming the first Venezuelan to lead a major league in that category.

Antonio Armas, 1984 (Boston Red Sox)

Armas led the American League with 43 homers, 123 runs batted in, and 339 total bases, becoming the first Venezuelan to lead his circuit in RBIs and TB.

Andrés Galarraga, 1988 (Montreal Expos)

This was the Big Cat's first great season, in which he showed his potential as a hitter with a .302 average, 29 homers, and 92 RBIs, leading the league in hits (184), doubles (42), and total bases (329), while becoming the first Venezuelan to reach the 150 OPS+ plateau.

Andrés Galarraga, 1993 (Colorado Rockies)

Galarraga was coming off two bad seasons, with batting averages of .219 in 1991 and .243 in 1992, when in the Rockies franchise's debut in Denver in 1993, he became the first Venezuelan to win the batting title with an impressive .370. He was also the first Venezuelan to close a campaign with a line of .300 BA, .400 OBP, and .600 SLG, by slashing .370/.403/.602.

Andrés Galarraga, 1996 (Colorado Rockies)

This was Galarraga's great season in his power burst when he led the league with 47 homers and 150 RBIs, and was second with 89 extra-base hits, the last two records for a Venezuelan in the majors. More importantly, his 150 RBIs are the National League record for a first baseman.

Andrés Galarraga, 1997 (Colorado Rockies)

Galarraga continued his golden years as one of the Blake Street Bombers, ending with a .318 batting average, 41 homers, and a league-leading 140 RBIs.

Andrés Galarraga, 1998 (Atlanta Braves)

Galarraga hit 44 home runs and drove in 121 runs with a high .991 OPS. He did not lead the league because it was the year of Mark McGwire's 70 homers and Sammy Sosa's 66, but his OPS+ of 157 put him on the list. More importantly, with this season in Atlanta, Galarraga proved that his quality as a slugger was not favored by playing in the hitter-friendly ballpark in Denver.

Bob Abreu, 1999 (Philadelphia Phillies)

This was one of the great years of "El Comedulce" Abreu. He paced the league in triples (tied with Neifi Pérez, Colorado) and was third in batting with .335 and OBP with .446, the latter being the second-best mark by a Venezuelan in the majors, very close to the best, Cabrera's .448 in 2011.

Richard Hidalgo, 2000 (Houston Astros)

Hidalgo had his career year with 44 homers, the third-best mark for a Venezuelan, .636 SLG, 1.028 OPS, and .314 BA. Despite those great numbers, Hidalgo did not lead the league in any category. His OPS+ was 147. His 89 extra-base hits tie Galarraga's best mark for a Venezuelan, and his .636 SLG ties Cabrera's, which makes this season good enough to meet Criterion 3.

Table 1. Offensive parameters of the 42 extraordinary seasons. Bold indicates league leader. OPS+ of 150 or better gets highlighted with a gray background.

Season	AB	R	H	2B	3B	HR	RBI	TB	BB	BA	OBP	SLG	OPS	OPS+
Tovar, 1970	650	120	195	**36**	**13**	10	54	287	52	.300	.356	.442	.798	117
Tovar, 1971	657	94	**204**	29	3	1	45	242	45	.310	.356	.368	.725	104
Armas, 1981	440	51	115	24	3	**22**	76	211	19	.261	.294	.480	.774	126
Armas, 1984	639	107	171	29	5	**43**	**123**	**339**	32	.268	.300	.531	.831	121
Galarraga, 1988	609	99	**184**	**42**	8	29	92	**329**	39	.302	.352	.540	.893	150
Galarraga, 1993	470	71	174	35	4	22	98	283	24	**.370**	.403	.602	1.005	150
Galarraga, 1996	626	119	190	39	3	**47**	**150**	376	40	.304	.357	.601	.958	127
Galarraga, 1997	600	120	191	31	3	41	**140**	351	54	.318	.389	.585	.974	131
Galarraga, 1998	555	103	169	27	1	44	121	330	63	.305	.397	.595	.991	157
Abreu, 1999	546	118	183	35	**11**	20	93	300	109	.335	.446	.549	.995	147
Hidalgo, 2000	558	118	175	42	3	44	122	355	56	.314	.391	.636	1.028	147
Abreu, 2002	572	102	176	**50**	6	20	85	298	104	.308	.413	.521	.934	151
Ordoñez, 2002	590	116	189	47	1	38	135	352	53	.320	.381	.597	.978	154
Mora, 2004	550	111	187	41	0	27	104	309	66	.340	**.419**	.562	.981	155
Ordoñez, 2007	595	117	216	**54**	0	28	139	354	76	**.363**	.434	.595	1.029	166
González, 2010	587	111	**197**	34	9	34	117	**351**	40	**.336**	.376	.598	.974	143
Cabrera, 2010	548	111	180	45	1	38	**126**	341	89	.328	**.420**	.622	1.042	**178**
Cabrera, 2011	572	111	197	**48**	0	30	105	335	108	**.344**	**.448**	.586	1.033	179
Cabrera, 2012	622	109	205	40	0	**44**	**139**	**377**	66	**.330**	.393	**.606**	**.999**	164
Cabrera, 2013	555	103	193	26	1	44	137	353	90	**.348**	**.442**	**.636**	**1.078**	**190**
Cabrera, 2014	611	101	191	**52**	1	25	109	320	60	.313	.371	.524	.895	150
Altuve, 2014	660	85	**225**	47	3	7	59	299	36	**.341**	.377	.453	.830	135
Martínez, 2014	561	87	188	33	0	32	103	317	70	.335	**.409**	.565	**.974**	172
Cabrera, 2015	429	64	145	28	1	18	76	229	77	**.338**	**.440**	.534	.974	169
Peralta, 2015	462	61	144	26	**10**	17	78	241	44	0,312	.371	.522	.893	137
Altuve, 2015	**638**	86	**200**	40	4	15	66	293	33	.313	.353	.459	.812	125
Altuve, 2016	640	108	**216**	42	5	24	96	340	60	**.338**	.396	.531	.928	155
Hernández, 2016	547	67	161	14	**11**	6	39	215	66	.294	.371	.393	.764	106
Cabrera, 2016	595	92	188	31	1	38	108	335	75	.316	.393	.563	.956	155
Altuve, 2017	590	112	**204**	39	4	24	81	323	58	**.346**	.410	.547	.957	160
Sánchez, 2018	600	62	145	34	**10**	8	55	223	49	.242	.306	.372	.678	86
Escobar, 2019	636	94	171	29	**10**	35	118	325	50	.269	.320	511	.831	111
Suárez, 2019	575	87	156	22	2	49	103	329	70	.271	.358	.572	.930	134
Acuña, 2019	626	**127**	175	22	2	41	101	324		.280	.365	.518	.883	122
Acuña, 2020	160	46	40	11	0	14	29	93	38	.250	.406	.581	.987	156
Hernandez, 2020	233	35	66	**20**	0	3	20	95	24	.283	.355	.408	.763	106
Pérez, 2021	620	88	169	24	0	**48**	**121**	337	28	.273	.316	.544	.859	126
Peralta, 2021	487	57	126	30	**8**	8	63	196	46	.259	.325	.402	.728	96
Arráez, 2022	547	88	173	31	1	8	49	230	50	**.316**	.375	.420	.795	128
Altuve, 2022	527	103	158	39	0	28	57	281	66	.300	.387	.533	.920	161
Arráez, 2023	574	71	203	30	3	10	69	269	35	**.354**	.393	.469	.862	133
Acuña, 2023	643	**149**	**217**	35	4	41	106	**383**	80	.337	**.416**	.596	**1.012**	168

Bob Abreu, 2002 (Philadelphia Phillies)

Abreu led the league with 50 doubles (first Venezuelan to reach this mark) and had high percentages in OBP (.413) and OPS (.934).

Magglio Ordóñez, 2002 (Chicago White Sox)

Despite not having led the league in any category, Ordóñez had a great season with 38 HR, 135 RBIs, and a .320 BA. His OPS+ of 154 makes this an extraordinary season (Criterion 2).

Melvin Mora, 2004 (Baltimore Orioles)

This was Mora's best career season. He led the league with a .419 OBP, plus an excellent .340 BA and .981 OPS.

Magglio Ordóñez, 2007 (Detroit Tigers)

Ordóñez had an exceptional season, winning the batting title with a .363 average and a league-leading 54 doubles, apart from 28 home runs and great numbers with 139 RBIs and 1.029 OPS. His 54 doubles top all Venezuelan batters historically.

Carlos González, 2010 (Colorado Rockies)

González had his best season, proving to be one of the best hitters by leading the league with a .336 BA, 197 hits, and 351 total bases. He also drove in 117 runs and had a .974 OPS.

Miguel Cabrera, 2010 (Detroit Tigers)

In what can be considered Cabrera's first super-season, he led the league in three departments, with 126 RBIs, .420 OBP, and 178 OPS+. Additionally, he had a .622 SLG and a .328 BA. For the first time, he had a slash line better than .300/.400/.600.

Miguel Cabrera, 2011 (Detroit Tigers)

Cabrera led the league in three offensive departments: batting (.344), OBP (.448), and doubles (48), and also in games played (161) (tied with Ichiro Suzuki, Seattle), while sporting a 1.033 OPS. His OBP is the highest by a Venezuelan in the majors.

Miguel Cabrera, 2012 (Detroit Tigers)

Cabrera won the Triple Crown – something that had not been accomplished by any major-league player in 45 years – while leading the league in six categories (HR, RBI, BA, TB, SLG, and OPS). His total bases rank first all-time among Venezuelans. He was also awarded the MVP.

Miguel Cabrera, 2013 (Detroit Tigers)

Cabrera led again in six categories (BA, OBP, SLG, OPS, OPS+, and wRC+) with .348, .442, .636, 1.078, 190, and 193 – all of them better than the previous season. For the second time, he had a slash line of .300/.400/.600. His SLG, OPS, OPS+, and wRC+ represent the best single-season performance of anyone from his country. At the end of the season, he won the MVP award again.

Miguel Cabrera, 2014 (Detroit Tigers)

Cabrera led the league with 52 doubles, but his numbers decreased from the previous season. He finished with a .313 BA, 25 HR, and 109 RBIs.

José Altuve, 2014 (Houston Astros)

Altuve had his first extraordinary season, leading the majors with a .341 BA and 225 hits and the American League with 56 stolen bases while ranking second with 47 doubles.

Víctor Martínez, 2014 (Detroit Tigers)

In an extraordinary season, Martínez led the league with a .409 OBP and a .974 OPS, while finishing with 32 homers, 103 RBIs, and a .335 BA.

Miguel Cabrera, 2015 (Detroit Tigers)

Injuries limited him to 119 games, but that didn't keep him from winning his fourth batting title (.338) and leading the league in OBP for the fourth time (.440).

David Peralta, 2015 (Arizona Diamondbacks)

In his first full major league season, David Peralta led the National League with 10 triples and was sixth in slugging percentage with .522 while hitting .312. He was the team's Rookie of the Year in his debut (2014) at age 27, after a surprising transition from pitcher to position player; several injuries that drove him to a temporary retirement; and his emergence as a good independent league hitter.

José Altuve, 2015 (Houston Astros)

Altuve led the league in hits with 200, his second season with 200+ hits, while also leading the league in at-bats with 638.

José Altuve, 2016 (Houston Astros)

Altuve led the league again in hits with 216 and batting average with .338, along with a high OBP (.396) and OPS (.928).

César Hernández, 2016 (Philadelphia Phillies)

This year, César Hernández surprised by leading both circuits with 11 triples (tied with two other players) and a good BA of .294.

Miguel Cabrera, 2016 (Detroit Tigers)

For the first time in the last seven years, Cabrera did not lead any offensive category, finishing with a .316 BA, 38 homers, and 108 RBIs, but his high OPS+ of 155 makes this another extraordinary season.

José Altuve, 2017 (Houston Astros)

In what has been his best year as of 2024, Altuve led the league in hits for the fourth straight time with 204, and in BA for the third time with .346.[1]

Yolmer Sánchez, 2018 (Chicago White Sox)

Sánchez led the American League in triples with 10, tied with Mallex Smith (Tampa Bay), making this an extraordinary season despite having a BA, OPS, and OPS⁺ below the league average.

Eduardo Escobar, 2019 (Arizona Diamondbacks)

In what has been his best season, Escobar led the league in triples, and his 118 RBIs were fourth in the National League. He finished with 29 doubles, 10 triples, and 35 homers, which made him finish close to a select group of players with 30/10/30 in a season.

Eugenio Suárez, 2019 (Cincinnati Reds)

Suárez blasted 49 home runs and at some point led the National League, but he finished second. Despite not having led the league in any category and having an OPS+ below 150, he set the HR record for a Venezuelan in the majors, which meets Criterion 3 and puts him on the list.

Ronald Acuña Jr., 2019 (Atlanta Braves)

At just 21, Acuña led the National League with 127 runs, 37 steals, and 715 PA. An injury in the last week of the season may have kept him from entering the 40-40 club. (Only five other players have hit 40 homers and stolen 40 bases in a season.) He finished with 41 HR and 37 SB.

Ronald Acuña Jr., 2020 (Atlanta Braves)

Injuries slowed Acuña down in a pandemic-shortened season (COVID-19). However, his .406 OBP, .581 SLG, .987 OPS, and 156 OPS+ are the best in his short three-season career. His OPS+ makes this another extraordinary season.

César Hernández, 2020 (Cleveland Indians)

Playing for a new team, Hernández led the league with 20 doubles, plus outstanding fielding, good enough to win the Gold Glove Award at second base.

David Peralta, 2021 (Arizona Diamondbacks)

In his second extraordinary season, at 34 years old, David once again led the National League in triples (3B) with 8.

Salvador Pérez, 2021 (Kansas City Royals)

Pérez surprised many by becoming the home-run (48) and RBI (121) leader in both leagues. After a close competition, he tied for the home run lead with Vladimir Guerrero. His 48 home runs are the second-best for a Venezuelan major leaguer, surpassed only by Eugenio Suárez (49).

Luis Arráez, 2022 (Minnesota Twins)

Arraez won his first batting title (.316) in the American League, which many expected, taking into account his formidable average of .331 in seven years in the minor leagues. Contact was his main virtue; he struck out fewer times (43) than he walked (50).

Jose Altuve, 2022 (Houston Astros)

For the sixth time in his career, Altuve finished with an average of .300 or more. His remarkable 161 OPS+, fourth place in the majors, makes him worthy of being included in this list as an extraordinary season, according to Criterion 3.

Luis Arráez, 2023 (Miami Marlins)

Arráez repeated as the batting champion, but this time in the National League, with an average of .354. Arráez's great season stands out when one notes that only nine major leaguers (among qualified players) reached .300 that season and that the major-league average was a low .248. Additionally, he had 203 hits (third in the majors) and an excellent .393 OBP. More importantly, he became the first player in major league history to win consecutive batting titles in different leagues.

Ronald Acuña Jr. 2023 (Atlanta Braves)

Acuña Jr. had a super season, a legendary one in terms of impact and visibility, leading the league in hits (217), runs (149), OBP (.416), OPS (1.012), and total bases (.383). His 171 OPS+ was also the best in the league. With 41 home runs and 73 stolen bases. Acuña Jr. joined the 40-40 club, which had only four members, and gave rise to a new club (40-70) with a single member.[2]

Note about José Altuve 2023

We must highlight that José Altuve had an excellent season in 2023, with a high OPS+ of 151. However, by not having the minimum number of at-bats (AB), he does not qualify as an extraordinary season according to Criterion 2.

Comparison of extraordinary seasons using the traditional parameters

Which of the 42 seasons in Table 1 can be considered the best offensively? To find the answer, we must establish certain criteria to value each of the offensive categories. It seems reasonable not to give the same value to a single as to a double, a triple, or a home run. On the other hand, we must admit that RBIs and runs, despite being essential to the game, depend on the other players on the team and the opportunities the player has to find men on base (for RBIs) or be driven by other hitters (runs).

Aiming to value quantitatively each one of the extraordinary seasons, we decided to combine the six offensive parameters listed below, using a weight factor of 0.5 for walks (BB), because we considered them less important than a single (1B), which we value as 1. The single can move runners up more than one base, whereas the walk does not. The double, triple, and home run are valued at 2, 3, and 4, respectively, reflecting their increased importance and the number of bases for each. We arbitrarily assigned 2.5 to each RBI, taking into account that they depend not only on the effort of the hitter but also on the contribution of teammates who have been able to get on base. The runs are not included because we don't consider them a direct contribution of the player, but of other players who drive in the run, except for the run they score on their home run, which is already accounted for.

The following formula is proposed to determine a parameter that can be named VOT (Spanish for Season Offensive Value):

$$VOT = \frac{(0.5xBB+1x1B+2x2B+3x3B+4xHR+2.5XRBI)}{AB}$$

VOT is calculated by dividing by the number of at-bats (AB) to incorporate the opportunities the batter had in his offensive production. Noting that equals the total bases, the previous equation can be simplified to:

$$VOT = \frac{(0.5xBB+TB+2x2B+2.5XRBI)}{AB}$$

We can see that the middle term (TB/AB) of the VOT equals the slugging percentage (See Annex 2), but we have added the ability to draw walks (BB/AB) and drive in runs (RBI/AB) with their respective values. VOT is not cumulative; it is simply an index of offensive power. For instance, a batter with two hits in five at-bats will have a .400 VOT, but if he drove a run, it gets to .900, whereas another player with a double, a homer, and two RBIs in the same five at-bats will get to 2.200. Although we can define other criteria different from VOT, the authors consider that it provides a reasonable quantification of the key elements contributing to the offensive performance of a hitter.

Table 2 presents the results obtained by applying the VOT equation to the data included in Table 1. Under those criteria, we conclude that the best season of all was Miguel Cabrera's 2013 with a 1.334 VOT, followed by his own 2010 season with 1.278, Ordóñez with 1.243, Hidalgo's 1.233, and Galarraga's 1996 with 1.232, all at the top five spots. Cabrera's 2012 season, in which he won the Triple Crown, stands sixth with a 1.218 VOT. We must also mention Acuña's 2020 season, in which, despite playing in only 46 games due to the pandemic and injuries, he stands 10th with 1.153. Acuña's 2023 super-season appears in a distant 19th place, due to the fact that, among other reasons, the VOT parameter does not consider stolen bases.

Improving assessment by using sabermetrics

The results obtained with the use of the traditional parameters of hitting (Table 2) have the singularity that they assess equally all players who performed in different times and different ballparks,

when we all know the influence of the latter on performance. For instance, Richard Hidalgo ranks fourth among the best seasons (Table 2), above the sixth place held by Miguel Cabrera in 2012, reflected on a better OPS (1.028 vs .999). Is that a reason to say his 2000 season was better than Cabrera's 2012?

To answer this more objectively, we must take into account that Cabrera's .999 led the majors, whereas Hidalgo's 1.028 ranked 13th in a year better for hitters when 19 players went above 1.000 OPS. Hidalgo indeed had a better OPS than Cabrera in 2012, but Cabrera's performance in OPS was better when analyzing the performance of the other players in the league. This is a weakness of traditional parameters, which can be fixed using sabermetric parameters.

Another aspect to be considered in terms of offense is that some ballparks are more hitter-friendly than others due to their different dimensions and the density of the air in the location. In a place with much less dense air (as in Denver, for instance), the ball travels faster and farther. Looking at 2018, in the Texas Rangers' home, 35 percent more runs were scored than when they played on the road; in Denver, it was 27 percent, whereas the opposite happened in Miami, where teams scored 35 percent fewer runs at home than on the road. So we have a Park Factor PF=1.35 for the Rangers, PF=1.27 for the Rockies, and PF=0.65 for the Marlins. The first two are hitter-friendly ballparks, while the latter is pitcher-friendly. Park Factor is not a constant value; it changes from season to season and might refer to other offensive parameters, apart from runs scored.

For a more objective assessment of offensive performance, we need to take into account individual performance, but compare it to the rest of the players in that season. At the same time, objectivity requires the incorporation of the ballpark effect, whether hitter-friendly or not. It is here that sabermetric parameters have made a significant contribution to baseball, enabling a more objective evaluation of players' performance in general, by incorporating new elements enabling the comparison of performance in different times, different leagues, and different ballparks. For instance, going back to the comparison between Hidalgo's season and Cabrera's 2012 season in which Hidalgo's 1.028 OPS was better than Cabrera's .999, we can see that Adjusted OPS or OPS+, which incorporates the aforementioned correction (see Annex 2) and is defined below, yields a better number for Cabrera (164) than for Hidalgo (147).

Table 2. Best seasons among Venezuelan hitters in Major League Baseball using traditional statistics to calculate VOT (Spanish for Season Offensive Value).

Rank	Season	VOT	Rank	Season	VOT
1	Cabrera, 2013	1.334	22	Armas, 1984	1.037
2	Cabrera, 2010	1.278	23	Cabrera, 2014	1.019
3	Ordoñez, 2007	1.243	24	Escobar, 2019	1.014
4	Hidalgo, 2000	1.233	25	Peralta, 2015	0.991
5	Galarraga, 1996	1.232	26	Abreu, 2002	0.983
6	Cabrera, 2012	1.218	27	Acuña, 2019	0.982
7	Ordoñez, 2002	1.214	28	Altuve, 2016	0.953
8	Galarraga, 1997	1.213	29	Galarraga, 1988	0.950
9	Galarraga, 1998	1.196	30	Altuve, 2017	0.940
10	Acuña, 2020	1.153	31	Armas, 1981	0.933
11	Galarraga, 1993	1.149	32	Altuve, 2022	0.866
12	Cabrera, 2011	1.139	33	Arráez, 2023	0.800
13	González, 2010	1.130	34	Peralta, 2021	0.773
14	Mora, 2004	1.094	35	Altuve, 2015	0.744
15	Martínez, 2014	1.086	36	Altuve, 2014	0.704
16	Suárez, 2019	1.081	37	Arráez, 2022	0.690
17	Cabrera, 2016	1.080	38	Tovar, 1970	0.689
18	Abreu, 1999	1.075	39	Hernandez, 2020	0.674
19	Acuña, 2023	1.070	40	Sánchez, 2018	0.642
20	Cabrera, 2015	1.066	41	Hernández, 2016	0.632
21	Pérez, 2021	1.054	42	Tovar, 1971	0.574

Sabermetric parameters

We selected two sabermetric parameters to qualify offense, both with the same objective but with a difference in the way they are calculated. One is OPS+ from Baseball-Reference and the other is wRC+ from FanGraphs.

Other sabermetric parameters are not considered here, such as WAR (Wins Above Replacement), which considers the global performance of a player (offense, defense, and baserunning), Baseball-Reference's offensive WAR, or Bill James's Runs Created (RC), because they all include baserunning, and this research intends to value hitting alone.

The OPS+ Parameter

The traditional parameter OPS is the sum of the capacity to reach base (OBP) and the slugging or power of the hitter (SLG). The sabermetric parameter OPS+, also known as adjusted OPS, is a correction of OPS taking into account the league average

and ballpark effect. OPS+ has been conveniently designed to make an OPS+ of 100 the league average, and every point above or below the league average is a percentile point above or below the league average. For instance, a 150 OPS+ means that the player produces 50 percent more than the league average, and an OPS+ of 80 means he produces 20 percent below average. OPS+ is a more adequate parameter than OPS because it enables the comparison of players from different times, leagues, and ballparks. For instance, in 2018, only 10 percent of the qualified players had an OPS+ of 136 or better. Qualified players had at least 502 plate appearances. The highest OPS+ in 2018 was Mike Trout with 199. Miguel Cabrera reached 190 in 2013.

Equations to calculate OPS and OPS+ are presented in Annex 2. More details of OPS+ can be found on the Baseball Reference portal.

The wRC+ parameter

The sabermetric parameter wRC+ gets the name of Weighted Runs Created Plus. Runs Created are the number of runs a player contributes to his team during the season. It is a concept that differs from runs (R), which depend on what other players can do. Runs created depend solely on the hitter. In the wRC+ parameter, two adjustments are included: one that takes into account the league average of the rest of the players in the year (enabling the comparison between players from different eras) and another one that incorporates the park factor. Similar to OPS+, the formula is scaled to make 100 the league average. In 2018, only 10 percent of the players had a wRC+ above 137. The best was Mike Trout with 191. Miguel Cabrera had an extraordinary value of 193 in 2013.

The formulae for its calculation are shown in Annex 2. More details can be found in the FanGraphs portal.

Comparison of extraordinary seasons using sabermetric statistics

Table 3 presents the sabermetric parameters OPS+ and wRC+ of the 42 extraordinary seasons of Venezuelan hitters. Note the great similarity between OPS+ and wRC+. Numbers in bold indicate the league leader. Recognizing that both parameters are expressed in the same form based on a median value of 100, we decided to average them out to have a single numeric value that enables us to answer the question as to which was the best offensive season.

Results after averaging can be seen in the last column of Table 3, organized from higher to lower: adding OPS+ and wRC+ and dividing them by two. According to that criterion, the best season turns out to be Miguel Cabrera's 2013 campaign, with 191.5, followed by 2011 Cabrera with 178, 2010 Cabrera with 174.5, 2014 Martínez with 170, 2023 Acuña with 169, 2007 Ordóñez with 167.5, 2015 Cabrera with 166.5, 2012 Cabrera with 165, 2022 Altuve with 162.5, 2017 Altuve with 160 and 2004 Mora with 157. As a curious detail, Cabrera's 2012 Triple Crown season ranks eighth.

Comparing the results of using traditional parameters (Table 2) to sabermetrics (Table 3), we can see the effect of including the influence of year, league, and ballpark in the analysis. Carlos González drops from 13th place (traditional parameters) to 23rd (sabermetric parameters) influenced by having played in Denver, which was the most hitter-friendly ballpark (PF=1.364, as per ESPN). For similar reasons, Galarraga's 1996 season, when he hit 47 homers and batted in 150 runs, plummets from fifth place with traditional to 31th with sabermetrics, while his 1998 season in Atlanta, with fewer homers and RBIs than in 1996, goes up to 13th place (sabermetric parameters) for having played in a pitcher's ballpark (PF=99 according to *FanGraphs*, which uses a normalized scale of 100 for a neutral ballpark, in which better than 100 means hitter-friendly and worse pitcher-friendly).

At the same time, we can notice that Hidalgo drops from fourth place with traditional parameters to 22nd with sabermetrics, because 2000 was a year of great offensive performances, a peak year in the Steroid Era, when there was less control of performance-enhancing drugs (testing began in 2003). Sabermetric parameters correct these statistical anomalies. On the other hand, sabermetrics favored Altuve in 2017 and recognized his extraordinary performance over the rest of the players that year, by incorporating the fact that Houston's ballpark was the most pitcher-friendly (PF=0.826, as per ESPN), climbing from 30th place (traditional parameters) to 10th place (sabermetric parameters). Martínez is a similar case, going up from 15th place (traditional) to 4th (sabermetric); even though the Tigers' ballpark had a park factor of 1.00 (neutral), his performance was way better than the league average.

It should be noted that the evaluation presented in Table 3 only quantifies batting. If you want to include baserunning, in addition to hitting, a better parameter would be Baseball-Reference's Offensive War (oWAR).

Table 4 presents the top 10 seasons according to the oWAR values, ordered from highest to lowest. It can be seen that Cabrera 2013 maintains first place, but Acuña 2023 rises from fifth place (Table 3) to second place (Table 4), influenced by his formidable performance of 73 stolen bases. It is notable that Altuve's 2016 rises from 16th place (Table 3) to third place (Table 4), due to his 30 stolen bases.

Also, Altuve's 2017 rise from position 10 (Table 3) to position 4 (Table 4) benefited from his 32 stolen bases.

Table 3. Best seasons of a Venezuelan hitter in the major leagues using sabermetric parameters, organized by averaging OPS+ and wRC+.

Rank	Season	OPS+	wRC+	Average of (OPS+ and wRC+)
1	Cabrera, 2013	190	193	191.5
2	Cabrera, 2011	179	177	178
3	Cabrera, 2010	178	171	174.5
4	Martinez, 2014	172	168	170
5	Acuña, 2023	168	170	169
6	Ordoñez, 2007	166	169	167.5
7	Cabrera, 2015	169	164	166.5
8	Cabrera, 2012	164	166	165
9	Altuve 2022	161	164	162.5
10	Altuve, 2017	160	160	160
11	Mora, 2004	155	159	157
12	Acuña, 2020	156	158	157
13	Galarraga 1998	157	156	156.5
14	Ordoñez, 2002	154	155	154.5
15	Cabrera, 2016	155	153	154
16	Altuve, 2016	155	152	153.5
17	Galarraga, 1988	150	154	152
18	Galarraga, 1993	150	150	150
19	Abreu, 2002	151	148	149.5
20	Abreu, 1999	147	151	149
21	Cabrera, 2014	150	148	149
22	Hidalgo, 2000	147	149	148
23	González, 2010	143	144	143.5
24	Peralta, 2015	137	137	137
25	Altuve, 2014	135	137	136
26	Suárez, 2019	134	133	133.5
27	Arráez, 2023	133	132	132.5
28	Galarraga, 1997	131	131	131
29	Arráez, 2022	128	131	129.5
30	Pérez, 2021	126	127	126.5
31	Armas, 1981	126	124	125
32	Galarraga, 1996	127	123	125
33	Altuve, 2015	125	124	124.5
34	Acuña, 2019	122	126	124
35	Armas, 1984	121	119	120
36	Tovar, 1970	117	116	116.5
37	Escobar, 2019	111	109	110
38	Hernandez, 2020	106	110	108
39	Hernández, 2016	106	107	106.5
40	Tovar, 1971	104	104	104
41	Peralta, 2021	96	93	94.5
42	Sanchez, 2018	86	87	86.5

Table 4. The top 10 seasons according to the Offensive War (oWAR), which includes hitting and stolen bases, are ordered from highest to lowest.

Rank according to oWAR	Season	Offensive WAR (oWAR)
1	Cabrera, 2013	9.1
2	Acuña, 2023	8.5
3	Cabrera, 2011	7.9
3	Altuve, 2016	7.9
5	Altuve, 2017	7.8
6	Cabrera, 2012	7.7
7	Ordóñez, 2007	7.2
8	Cabrera, 2010	7.0
9	Altuve, 2022	6.8
10	Mora, 2004	6.7

The greatest offensive season ever recorded by a Venezuelan player belongs to Miguel Cabrera, who delivered an extraordinary performance for the Detroit Tigers in 2013, posting an impressive WAR of 7.5. Remarkably, this came just one year after Cabrera achieved baseball immortality by capturing the American League Triple Crown, cementing his status as one of the sport's all-time legends. (Getty Images)

Conclusions

a) The 42 extraordinary seasons for Venezuelan players in major league baseball were compared by using traditional offensive parameters and sabermetric parameters. To integrate the different traditional hitting parameters, we defined the VOT factor or season offensive value, which synthesizes the offensive production of a hitter. To synthesize such production with the sabermetric parameters, we used the criterion of the arithmetic average of OPS+ and wRC+, the former used by Baseball-Reference and the latter by FanGraphs. Sabermetric parameters offer a more objective assessment of performance by incorporating elements that enable comparisons between different eras, leagues, and ballparks.

b) Both procedures – traditional and sabermetric – lead to the same result: the best offensive season of a Venezuelan hitter in the majors has been the one Miguel Cabrera had in 2013. That season was better than the one he had in 2012 when he won the Triple Crown.

c) By incorporating sabermetrics, the top eight spots are Cabrera (2013, 2011, and 2010), Martínez (2014), Acuña 2023, Ordóñez (2007), Cabrera (2015), and Cabrera (2012). The top eight spots with the traditional parameters are Cabrera (2013 and 2010), Ordóñez (2007), Hidalgo (2000), Galarraga (1996), Cabrera (2012), Ordóñez (2002), and Galarraga (1997). The great seasons by Hidalgo and Galarraga are both decreased by sabermetric assessment because they took place in an era of great offensive production, influenced by the use of performance-enhancing drugs (the Steroid Era) and Galarraga's additional for having played in a hitter-friendly ballpark.

d) Cabrera's 2012 season, when he won the Triple Crown, is ranked sixth (traditional) and eighth (sabermetrics). Acuña's 2023 super-season is ranked fifth (sabermetrics), but let's remind ourselves that the analysis presented here does not include stolen bases; it includes only hitting.

f) If stolen bases were included in addition to hitting, performance can be calculated using the offensive war (oWAR)

statistics. Cabrera 2013 would still maintain first place, but second place would be occupied by Acuña 2023, benefiting from his formidable season of 73 stolen bases. Altuve's 2016 and 2017 rise to positions 3 and 5, respectively, thanks to the contribution of his stolen bases.

SOURCES

Baseball Reference, https://www.baseball-reference.com/

ESPN, 2016, http://www.espn.com/mlb/stats/parkfactor

Fangraphs, https://www.fangraphs.com/

MLB, https://www.mlb.com/

ANNEX 1

Abbreviations

This annex describes the meaning of abbreviations used in the article, listed alphabetically.

AB = at-bats

BB = bases on balls

BA = batting average

BPF = ballpark factor for batting

G = games

H = hits

HR = home runs

lg OBP = league On-Base Percentage

lg SLG = league Slugging Percentage

lg wOBA = league wOBA

OBP = On-Base Percentage

OPS = On-Base Percentage plus Slugging

OPS+ = OPS adjusted

oWAR = Offensive War

PA= plate appearances

PF = park factor

R = runs scored

RBI = runs batted in

RC = runs created

SLG = the rate of total bases per at-bat

TB = total bases

VOT = Season Offensive Value

wOBA = Weighted OBP

wRAA = Weighted Runs Above Average

wRC = Weighted Runs Created

wRC+ = Adjusted Weighted Runs Created

2B = Doubles

3B = Triples

ANNEX 2

Sabermetric and traditional formulae used in the research

Aiming to facilitate the reading of this article, we present the definitions of the sabermetric parameters (OPS+ and wRC+) selected to quantify the offensive performance of a batter. We also included definitions and formulae of wOBA and wRC, which are used to calculate wRC+. Despite being more familiar to people, we also included the definition of three classical offensive parameters, OBP, SLG, and OPS. First, we present the traditional or classical parameters, and then we present the sabermetric ones. We also present and discuss the numeric values of these parameters for a better understanding by the reader.

OBP

On-base percentage measures the effectiveness of a hitter at getting on base. It is the resulting division of the times a batter gets on base (without the times he reaches on error) by the total plate appearances. The formula to calculate it is:

$$OBP \;=\; \frac{H \;+\; BB \;+\; HBP}{AB \;+\; BB \;+\; HBP \;+\; SF} \qquad (1)$$

An average player has a .335 OBP (half the qualified batters in 2018 either match or surpass that value), and an excellent one has .378 or higher. (Only 10 percent of the qualified batters had better numbers in 2018.) Qualified batters got at least 502 plate appearances a year.

SLG

Is the rate of total bases per at-bat. Slugging is a measure of the power of the hitter and their capacity to gain bases with their hits. It is the resulting division of his total bases by at-bats. The formula is as follows:

$$SLG \;=\; \frac{TB}{AB} = \frac{1B \;+\; 2x2B \;+\; 3x3B \;+\; 4xHR}{AB} \qquad (2)$$

An average player has an SLG of around .440 (half of the qualified players in the 2018 season have better numbers) while an excellent one has .532 or better; this value was reached or exceeded by only 10 percent of qualified players in 2018, among them Venezuelan Jesús Aguilar.

OPS

It is the sum of OBP and SLG, which measures the capacity to get on base and the power of the hitter. Some analysts interpreted it as the offensive *production* of the hitter. The formula is:

$$OPS \;=\; OBP \;+\; SLG \qquad (3)$$

An average player has an OPS of around .787 (half the qualified hitters in 2018 exceeded that value) while an excellent one has .892 or better, which was what only 10 percent of the hitters in 2018 managed – among them, Venezuelan Eugenio Suárez.

OPS+

This parameter, also known as adjusted OPS, is a sabermetric variable that improves OPS by taking into account the average of all players in the league that season and the ballpark effect of the hitter. It is calculated this way:

$$OPS+ = \left(\frac{OBP}{lgOBP} + \frac{SLG}{lgSLG} - 1\right)x\frac{100}{BPF} \qquad (4)$$

In which lgOBP is the average of the OBP of the players of the league, lgSLG is the corresponding SLG, and BPF is the ballpark factor. The calculation of OPS+ is incorporated in Baseball-Reference. An OPS+ equal to 100 is the league average, and every point above or below 100 is considered a percentile point above or below the league average. In 2018, only 10 percent of the players had an OPS+ above 136.

wOBA

It is a sabermetric parameter used by FanGraphs to measure the general offense of a hitter based on the relative values of each of the offensive categories. The term wOBA means weighted on-base average. It is different from OBP in the fact that it grants a different weight to each time on base, which varies slightly yearly, so that the league wOBA is adjusted to OBP. The 2013 formula goes:

$$wOBA \;=\; \frac{0.69xNIBB+0.722xHBP+0.888x1B+1.271x2B+1.616x3B+2.101xHR}{AB+BB-1BB+SF+HBP} \qquad (5)$$

In which IBB is intentional bases on balls and NIBB nonintentional bases on balls. An average player has a wOBA of around .338 (half the players in 2018 were better than that), and an excellent one goes .376 or better. (Only 10 percent of players were better than that value in 2018, including Venezuelan Eugenio Suárez.)

wRC

Weighted runs created is an improved version of Bill James's runs created (RC). wRC is interpreted as the number of runs a player contributes to the team with his bat during the season. It is a sabermetric statistic used by FanGraphs. The wRC formula goes:

$$wRC = \left(\frac{wOBA - lg\ lgwOBA}{wOBAscale} + lg\frac{R}{PA} \right) x PA \qquad (6)$$

In which lg wOBA is the league wOBA, wOBA scale is a scale factor to compare the wOBA with the league OBP, R is runs scored, PA is plate appearances, and lg R/PA is the league average of R/PA. The values of the wOBA scale and R/PA change every year and can be found on FanGraphs.

wRC is measured in runs, and its numeric values are similar to RC. The main difference is that it does not incorporate stolen bases, something RC does, so wRC only counts for the hitter's production at the plate.

wRC+

The sabermetric parameter wRC+ is named adjusted wRC or adjusted weighted runs created. It is the same variable as wRC but corrected to take into account park factors and the league of play. FanGraphs presents it as the most complete statistic to measure a hitter's performance. The variable is measured in runs created. Just like OPS+, the intention is to compensate for the existence of hitter-friendly ballparks and correct based on league averages. The equation to calculate wRC+ provided in FanGraphs goes

$$wRC+ = \frac{\left(\frac{wRAA}{PA} + lg\frac{R}{PA} \right) + \left(lg\frac{R}{PA} - \left(PF x lg\frac{R}{PA} \right) \right)}{ALor NL\frac{wRC}{PA}} x 100 \quad (7)$$

In which PF is park factor, and the denominator refers to the resulting division by the total league wRC divided by the total PA of the league. AL and NL refer to the American League and National League. In the case of the National League, pitchers were not included prior to 2022, the season when MLB implemented the universal DH.

Changing wRAA of equation 7 for the value provided in *FanGraphs*
$wRAA = \left(\frac{wOBA - lglg\ wOBA}{wOBAscale} \right) * PA$, using formula 6 and consolidating terms, the wRC+ can be rewritten for a better interpretation as

$$SLG = \frac{TB}{AB} = \frac{1B + 2x2B + 3x3B + 4xHR}{AB} \qquad (8)$$

In which the term on the left represents the effect of correcting by year and league, and the term on the right represents the correction of the park effect. Similarly to OPS+, the formula is scaled in such a way that 100 corresponds to the league average, and every percentile point above or below 100 represents a point above or below average. For instance, an average hitter has a wRC+ of around 113 (half of the players in 2018 were better than that number), whereas an excellent one has 137 or better (only 10 percent of the players had better numbers than that in 2018).

NOTES

1   This season, Altuve won every possible award: *The Sporting News* Player of the Year, the Hank Aaron Award to the best hitter in the major leagues, the *Baseball America* Player of the Year, the *Outstanding Player Award* by the MLBPA, which is voted by the players themselves, the Silver Slugger Award, and the American League Most Valuable Player Award.

2   In this – Acuña's super-season – he won the MVP and the Hank Aaron Award in the National League, the *Sporting News* Player of the Year, the National League Outstanding Player Award, and the Silver Slugger Award.

CONTRIBUTORS

Jean Carlos Arias Troisi is a Venezuelan sports journalist with experience covering the Venezuelan Professional Baseball League (LVBP) and major-league baseball since 2005. He worked as assistant in the communications department for Cardenales de Lara (2010–2015), contributed to the newspaper *El Informador*, and appeared on various radio programs, including *Béisbol con Todo* on OK 107.5FM. He has reported on major-league games in Atlanta and Miami, as well as the 2023 World Baseball Classic. Since relocating to Winston-Salem, North Carolina, in 2015, he continues to cover the major leagues and LVBP through social media with stats, videos, and analysis, while also writing for the *El Venezolano* sports section.

Luis A. Blandón, a Washington, DC, native, is a producer, writer and researcher in video and documentary film production and in archival, manuscript, historical, film, and image research. His creative storytelling has garnered numerous awards, including three regional Emmys®, regional and national Edward R. Murrow Awards, two TELLY awards, and a New York Festival World Medal. He was senior researcher and manager of the story development team for two national programs for Retirement Living Television. He served as the principal researcher for several authors including for *The League of Wives* by Heath Hardage Lee and her biography project on First Lady Pat Nixon. He has a master's degree in international affairs from the George Washington University.

Richard Bogovich is the author of *Frank Grant: The Life of a Black Baseball Pioneer*, and his prior book profiled another pre-1920 Hall of Famer, Kid Nichols. He has contributed three dozen biographies to various SABR books. In 2023 he solved the mysterious disappearance of Negro Leagues superstar Dave Brown a century ago. Richard has degrees from Northern Illinois University and is office manager of the Wendland Utz law firm in Rochester, Minnesota.

Augusto Cárdenas lives in Maracaibo, Venezuela, and is the author of *My Story: Luis Aparicio*, the authorized biography of the only Venezuelan inducted into the Hall of Fame. From 2002 to 2017 he was the baseball beat writer of *Diario Panorama*, a local newspaper. He has covered the Venezuelan Winter League since 2000 and has been a special correspondent to cover major-league games, spring training, All-Star Games, the World Baseball Classic, Nippon Professional Baseball, and the Caribbean Series for different outlets, including *Diario Las Américas* and LasMayores.com. Cárdenas is a SABR member who loves to write about the Venezuelan players he saw playing

when he was a kid, such as Tony Armas (*The 1986 Boston Red Sox: There Was More Than Game Six*) and Omar Vizquel (*1995 Cleveland Indians: The Sleeping Giant Awakes*). He is the founder of Cárdenas Sports Media, a Venezuelan media outlet and a PR sports department for Venezuelan athletes, and has been working in the last two winter ball seasons as a special assistant to the general manager of Águilas del Zulia in the Venezuelan Winter League.

Rory Costello has never set foot on the continent of South America but still hopes to do so. Venezuelan baseball is an important part of his coverage of Latin American and Caribbean players for the BioProject. Rory lives in Brooklyn, New York, with his wife, Noriko, and son, Kai.

Reynaldo Cruz Díaz is the founder and head editor of the Cuban-based magazine *Universo Béisbol*, which is hosted in MLBlogs. He is a language graduate of the University of Holguin, in his hometown, and has been leading the aforementioned magazine since March 2010. A SABR member since the summer of 2014, he writes, translates, and photographs baseball and was in the first row of the Barack Obama game in Havana, shooting from the Tampa Bay Rays dugout. In spite of the rich history of Cuban baseball, his favorite player happens to be none other than Ichiro Suzuki, whom he hopes to meet and interview. A retro-ballpark lover, he envisions Fenway Park, Wrigley Field, Koshien Stadium, and Estadio Palmar de Junco as the can't-miss places in baseball. He became a political refugee in Connecticut and works as a high-school Spanish teacher.

Adam Foldes is a lifelong baseball fan, who lives and works in New York City as an archivist for CBS News. He has written a half-dozen pieces for SABR's BioProject and Games Project and is a member of the Casey Stengel Chapter.

Kenneth Fricke has been a member of SABR since 2000 and is a member of the East Tennessee Chapter. He was born in Venezuela and spent his formative years growing up around the oil fields of Venezuela and in Caracas. Baseball was – and still is – a hot topic around his Venezuela relatives. He holds a master's in civil engineering from Case Western Reserve University (Cleveland) and a PhD in civil engineering from the University of Tennessee (Knoxville). He spent 45 years working as a structural engineer in Oak Ridge, Tennessee, retiring at the end of 2021, but resumed part-time in late 2022. He grew up a lifelong Yankees fan, but due to circumstances, he attended many more Cleveland games than Yankees games, so has a warm spot for Cleveland sports teams. He was in the stands for the infamous Ten-Cent Beer night in 1974 but made up for it by being present for Frank Robinson's first managerial game in 1975. He follows the Venezuelan Winter Leagues and always roots for Venezuela in the WBC. His SABR interests include baseball history, statistics, and statistical analysis. He has also spent many years volunteering to improve the playability of Strat-O-Matic's computerized baseball seasons. He lives in Oak Ridge, Tennessee, with his wife, Maureen, and three cats.

Gordon J. Gattie is a lifelong baseball fan and longtime SABR member. He is a civilian US Navy engineer, his baseball research interests include ballparks, minor-league baseball, and statistical analysis. Gordon earned his PhD from SUNY Buffalo, where he used baseball to investigate judgment performance in complex dynamic environments. Ever the optimist, he dreams of a Cleveland Guardians World Series championship. Lisa, his wonderful wife who roots for the New York Yankees, and Morrigan, their beloved Labrador retriever, enjoy traveling across the country visiting ballparks and other baseball-related sites. Gordon has contributed to several SABR publications, including multiple issues of *The National Pastime*, and to the Games Project.

Tom Hawthorn is the author of *Play Ball! The Amazing Stories and Captivating Characters Who Have Made Baseball a Winning Ticket in Vancouver for over 100 Years*, published in 2025. He lives in Victoria, British Columbia.

Lou Hernández is the author of multiple baseball histories and biographies, and two fantasy novels. He resides in South Florida and roots for the Marlins.

Paul Hofmann has been a SABR member since 2002. He has contributed to more than 25 SABR publications and co-edited *The 1883 Philadelphia Athletics: American Association Champions*. Paul is currently the associate vice provost for international affairs at the University of Louisville and teaches in the College of Management at National Changhua University of Education in Taiwan. A native of Detroit, Paul is an avid baseball-card collector and Detroit Tigers fan. He currently resides in Lakeville, Minnesota.

Bill Johnson has contributed over 40 biographies to SABR's BioProject, and presented papers at the 2011 Cooperstown Symposium on Baseball and American Culture, the 2017 Jerry Malloy Negro League Conference, and the inaugural Southern Negro League Conference. He has published a biography of Hal Trosky (McFarland and Co., 2017) and most recently an article about Negro American League All-Star Art "Superman" Pennington in the journal *Black Ball*. Bill and his wife, Chris, currently reside in Florida

Justin Krueger is an assistant professor of social studies education at Delta State University in Cleveland, Mississippi. He enjoys listening to baseball games on the radio.

Bryan Lake is an attorney in Minneapolis. He dislikes the designated hitter, instant replay, and expanded playoffs, but he has learned to tolerate interleague play.

Leonte Landino is a Venezuelan-American journalist. With over 25 years in the baseball industry, he led baseball content production for ESPN International for almost two decades and became the first-ever Venezuelan with an executive position at the Office of the Commissioner. Landino is a member of the Baseball Writers Association of America and chair of SABR's Luis Castro Chapter.

Len Levin is a longtime newspaper editor in New England, now retired. He lives in Providence with his wife, Linda, and an overachieving orange cat. He now (Len, not the cat) is the grammarian for the Rhode Island Supreme Court and copy-edits its opinions. He also copy-edits many SABR books, including this one. He is just down the interstate from Fenway Park, where he has spent many happy – and some not so happy – hours.

Andrea Long is a native and lifelong resident of Charlotte, North Carolina. She fell in love with baseball as a teenager in the 1980s, thanks to her hometown minor-league team, the Charlotte O's. She is devoted to the modern-day incarnation of the O's, the Charlotte Knights, as well as to the Philadelphia Phillies. She joined SABR in 2016 and quickly discovered the BioProject, which gave her the opportunity to write the biography of her hero, Bo Díaz. She also wrote the story of Díaz's ultimate grand slam for the Games Project. She contributed to the first two volumes of *Turnstyle: The SABR Journal of Baseball Arts* and has been the editor of the BioProject newsletter since 2018.

José Luis López Sánchez, is an accomplished hydraulic engineer, specializing in the field of river dynamics and mathematical models. He earned both an M.Sc. and a PhD from the University of Colorado (Colorado State University). He is a professor-researcher at the Institute of Fluid Mechanics (IMF) in the Faculty of Engineering at the Central University of Venezuela (UCV), where his expertise is widely recognized. He boasts an impressive portfolio, including the editorship of four books and authorship or co-authorship of over 100 publications featured in conferences and technical journals pertaining to his area of specialization. Notably, he has also contributed to the *Baseball Research Journal* published by SABR, delving into the physics of baseball. He is notably known as the author of the book *The Physics of Baseball* (2022).In 2023, he received a national In 2023, he received a national accolade from the Ministry of Science and Technology in recognition of his substantial scientific and technological contributions. Further underscoring his prominence in the field, he was honored in 2023 in Vienna by the International Association for Hydro-Environment Engineering and Research (IAHR) for his significant advancements in understanding the physics of hydraulics and engineering. Additionally, he holds the esteemed position of membership in the Academy of Engineering and Habitat of Venezuela (Sillón XXXIII).

Oscar Andrés López Sánchez, a distinguished scholar, holds an M.Sc. and a PhD from the University of California, Berkeley, with a focus on structural dynamics and earthquake engineering. At present he is a professor-researcher at the Institute of Materials and Structural Models (IMME) within the Faculty of Engineering at the Central University of Venezuela, where he has demonstrated his expertise. He has made substantial contributions to the academic world, boasting a portfolio of 70 articles published in both national and international journals, alongside an extensive collection of articles presented at conferences. His advisory role extends to several esteemed national and international institutions in matters of seismic engineering. Particularly noteworthy is his coordination of the team responsible for the development of Venezuela's seismic-resistant construction standard in 2019. He is a four-time recipient of the national award for outstanding scientific contributions in technological research. He is also recognized for his publication in SABR's *Baseball Research Journal,* in which he explored the intricacies of Galarraga's monumental home run. He is the co-author of the book *The Physics of Baseball* (2022). He holds the esteemed position of membership in the Academy of Engineering and Habitat of Venezuela (Sillón XXXV).

Nelson Morales was born in Caracas, Venezuela. He grew up in a popular neighborhood of the city playing with his peers, among other things, a street pastime called "Pelota de Goma" and "Chapita," based on baseball, hence the love they have for this game. As a child he played in an organized neighborhood baseball team, Los Diablitos del Barrio, for children between 13 and 16 years old. All his life he has been involved with baseball and he has participated in his native country in multiple teams and leagues in both baseball and softball. In the local league in Venezuela, he is a fan of the Tiburones de la Guaira. Currently, he works in Venezuela for a company representing North American consortiums in the area of lubricant technology. He is an industrial chemist and industrial engineer.

Katie Murray Neipris graduated Phi Beta Kappa from UCLA, where she studied English and Film, Television, & Digital Media. She spent summer 2012 studying abroad at Oxford and traveling around Europe, a life-changing experience that she credits with inspiring her to fully become a writer. She began work in film and television development and enjoyed writing for multiple formats. *The Inconvenient Process of Falling* (2015) was her first novel. She began a PhD program at UCSD and is an adjunct professor at Orange Coast College.

Bill Nowlin very much enjoyed his one visit to Venezuela, which included both a visit to Angel Falls and a ballgame in Caracas. One of the founders of the Rounder Records label, and more recently Down the Road Records, he lives within a few miles of where he was born, and of Fenway Park. He has written, edited, or co-edited more than 100 books, mostly on baseball and mostly for SABR.

Tim Odzer has a law degree from the University of Chicago and now litigates cases in Miami. In his free time, he enjoys writing articles for SABR and watching baseball. He contributed an article on Rube Foster to Jay Caldwell's *Black Baseball in Living Color.*

Tony S. Oliver is a native of Puerto Rico currently living in Sacramento, California, with his wife and daughter. While he works as a Six Sigma professional, his true love is baseball and he cheers for both the Red Sox and whoever happens to be playing the Yankees. He is fascinated by baseball cards and is researching the evolution of baseball tickets. He believes there is no prettier color than the vibrant green of a freshly mown grass on a baseball field.

Gregg Omoth, a SABR member since 2000, is a lifelong Minnesota Twins fan. He has contributed several bios to SABR books. Gregg and his wife, Dianne, live in Otsego, Minnesota, with their three children, Amelia, Nolan, and Emma.

Eliexer Pirela Leal is a distinguished Venezuelan sports journalist and radio host, renowned for his deep knowledge of baseball and his dedication to preserving the sport's history. He is the author of *El Grande: Homenaje en el Centenario de Luis Aparicio Ortega*, a seminal work that offers profound insights into the life of Luis Aparicio Ortega, the first Venezuelan baseball player to play professionally abroad and the father of Hall of Famer Luis Aparicio. Pirela Leal's commitment to sports journalism has earned him numerous local accolades, including the prestigious Regional Journalism Award for his contributions to digital journalism through his engaging YouTube channel. His work continues to inspire and educate fans, highlighting the rich legacy of Venezuelan athletes in the world of baseball.

Carl Riechers retired from United Parcel Service in 2012 after 35 years of service. With more free time, he became a SABR member that same year. Born and raised in the suburbs of St. Louis, he became a big fan of the Cardinals. He and his wife, Janet, have three children and he is the proud grandpa of two.

Jon Springer is the author of *Once Upon a Team* and *Mets by the Numbers* (with Matthew Silverman) and writes about sports and food marketing for a business publication. He lives in Queens, New York with his family.

A fan of the Expos from 1977 through 2004, **Mark S. Sternman** cheered unreservedly for Ugueth Urbina when he played for Montreal. In addition to this Urbina piece, he has written SABR profiles of four other Expos: Mike Gardiner, Mike Mordecai, Mike Stenhouse, and Jose Vidro.

Andy Sturgill is a college administrator in the Philadelphia area, where he roots for the Phillies and lives with his wife, Carrie, son, Ray, and daughter, Ruth.

J.L. Tucupido C., a Venezuelan journalist, writer, and broadcaster, has been a SABR member since 2021 (Luis Castro/Latin America Chapter), and a member of the International Federation of Journalists (IFJ). A consistent researcher of the national pastime's history, development, and present, he works on research and biographical publications of major-league and Winter League professional baseball players, broadcasts, and announcers. Contributor to Diamante23.com and author of the book *Confabulación* (2025), an exciting novel that describes an unprecedented conspiracy between journalism and baseball.

Rafael D.O. Venancio is a writer, playwright and psychoanalyst who lives in the State of Santa Catarina, Brazil. He holds a PhD and a postdoctoral degree in the area of communication and arts from the University of São Paulo, as well as specific training degrees in the field of psychoanalysis, astrology, Vedic culture and religion. A Brazilian fan of the Chicago Cubs, before the 2020s he used to write sports fiction and historiography in the form of books and scientific articles. Nowadays, he dedicates himself to teaching and writing within the world of spiritual self-knowledge.

Juan Vené is a legendary Venezuelan sports journalist, author, and baseball historian whose career spans more than seven decades of continual coverage. Renowned across Latin America and the United States, Vené has become a revered voice in baseball through his incisive writing, vivid storytelling, and deep knowledge of the game. He is best known for his columns, books, and radio broadcasts that have chronicled generations of Latin American players and major-league history with passion and precision. He is a voting member of the National Baseball Hall of Fame in Cooperstown and an advocate for Latino contributions to the sport. Vené's influence transcends borders, establishing him as one of the most respected chroniclers of béisbol in the Spanish-speaking world.

Joseph Wancho has been a member of SABR since 2005. He lives in Westlake, Ohio.

Darin Watson lives in Hot Springs Village, Arkansas, with his wife, Michelle, and three pets. In 2018 Darin both joined SABR and relocated to Arkansas from the Kansas City area; it was a busy year! This is the fourth time he has contributed to a SABR publication so far and he is excited to add to that list. He grew up in Topeka, Kansas, learning to love the Royals, and still considers himself lucky that he is old enough to remember the 1985 World Series. He works for a media company and explores Royals history at ulstoothpick.com.

Brian Werner has been a SABR member since 1986. Although he grew up a Pittsburgh Pirates fan, he became a full-fledged Rockies fan during their inaugural season in his home state in 1993. He has attended each and every Rockies home opener. Now retired, he currently is living a dream as a tour guide at the Rockies' home ballpark, Coors Field.

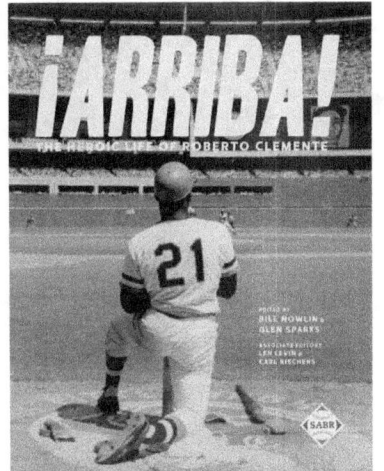

More Books from SABR

Available in paperback and ebook, and in Spanish

Arriba! The Heroic Life of Roberto Clemente
Edited by Bill Nowlin and Glen Sparks

The first Latino inductee into the National Baseball Hall of Fame, Roberto Clemente was the 11th player to reach 3,000 hits, was named to 15 All-Star Game squads, won 12 Gold Gloves, four batting titles, an MVP, and was twice a World Series champion with the Pirates. But off the baseball diamond, Clemente was known for his charitable work. He lost his life while providing relief for earthquake victims in Nicaragua. He was aboard a plane loaded with relief supplies— the fourth such plane he had helped stock—accompanying the flight personally to ensure the supplies would not fall into the hands of profiteers. The plane crashed after takeoff from Puerto Rico, a tragic loss for baseball and the world. This book includes photos from the Clemente Museum and dozens of essays examining Clemente's baseball career, recaps of many of his greatest games, his relationship with the press, his connections to Nicaragua and players such as Monte Irvin, and his continuing effects on players from Latin America as a role model today.

Puerto Rico and Baseball: 60 Biographies
Edited by Bill Nowlin and Edwin Fernandez

Puerto Rico and Baseball: 60 Biographies contains 60 biographies of players — but it also has two "ballpark bios" and articles on major-league games played in Puerto Rico, both spring training exhibition games and several regular-season games from the time when "Los Expos" included San Juan as their home base. Baseball in Puerto Rico has a long history, dating back to the nineteenth century. Over 300 Puerto Rican players have played in the major leagues. This book highlights both the pioneers who played in the Negro Leagues right up through Ivan Rodriguez, elected in 2017 to the National Baseball Hall of Fame. You will get to know Perucho, who was compared with Ty Cobb and called the Babe Ruth of Puerto Rico, Pancho Coimbre, considered one of the best hitters, the great Roberto Clemente, and Ruben Gomez, "el Divino Loco," the first Puerto Rican to pitch in a World Series.

Cuban Baseball Legends
Edited by Peter C. Bjarkman and Bill Nowlin

Minnie Miñoso. Martín Dihigo. Luis Tiant. Orlando "El Duque" and Liván Hernández. Players from the baseball-loving nation of Cuba have made their mark on Major League Baseball for decades. This volume includes biographies of 47 players, a handful of the most memorable and legendary among the many greats to hail from the island. Baseball is truly Cuba's national pastime, perhaps even more than in the United States, and the talent of Cuban players is undeniable.

Dominicans in the Major Leagues
Edited by Bill Nowlin and Julio M. Rodriguez

The Dominican Republic is well-represented by many star players in Major League Baseball. Around 800 Dominicanos have played in the majors—a full 300 more than any country other than the United States. The first was Pedro Alejandro San, who pitched in the Negro Leagues in 1926, later followed by Tetelo Vargas and Horacio "Rabbit" Martinez. Osvaldo "Ozzie" Virgil was the first in the National League in 1956 with the New York Giants. In 1983, Juan Marichal became the first Dominican inducted into the National Baseball Hall of Fame in Cooperstown, since joined by Pedro Martinez, Vladimir Guerrero, and David Ortiz. Also included: Felipe, Jesús, and Matty Alou, Sammy Sosa, Raul Mondesi, and Fernando Tatis, and a recap of the Dominican team's passionate, action-packed sweep of the 2013 World Baseball Classic.

Available on SABR.org and from your favorite bookstore